THE VIRGINIA
LANDMARKS
REGISTER

THE VIRGINIA LANDMARKS REGISTER

THIRD EDITION

Edited by CALDER LOTH

Published for the Virginia Historic Landmarks Board by the University Press of Virginia, Charlottesville

THE UNIVERSITY PRESS OF VIRGINIA
Copyright © 1986 by the Virginia Historic Landmarks Board

Third printing 1987

Library of Congress Cataloging-in-Publication Data
Main entry under title:

The Virginia landmarks register.

Includes index.
1. Historic sites—Virginia. 2. Virginia—History,
Local. I. Loth, Calder, 1943–   . II. Virginia
Historic Landmarks Board.
F227.V864 1986   975.5   85-20374
ISBN 0-8139-1061-7

Printed in the United States of America

CONTENTS

This edition of the *Virginia Landmarks Register* provides eloquent testimony to the broad range of historic and cultural resources that mark the Commonwealth's landscape. From the most ancient of prehistoric archaeological sites to the high-rise office buildings of the early twentieth century, this volume chronicles human habitation in Virginia for thousands of years.

While our landmarks are tangible reminders of a distinguished past, most of the places in this book are ones in which we still live and conduct our businesses. We must, therefore, be keenly aware that we are stewards of an irreplaceable resource that demands and deserves our careful attention.

Publishing this *Register* represents our state government's commitment to the proper management of Virginia's invaluable historic resources. We also invite all Virginians to join us in the task of ensuring continued stewardship of Virginia's historic landmarks.

GERALD L. BALILES
Governor

The Virginia General Assembly has charged the Virginia Historic Landmarks Board with the responsibility for preparing a register of the Commonwealth's significant landmarks and for publishing that register "from time to time . . . setting forth appropriate information concerning the registered buildings and sites." The board is both pleased and proud to present this edition of the *Virginia Landmarks Register*.

This publication, of course, grows out of long hours of research and fieldwork by the board and its staff over a period of eighteen years. While board and staff members have changed over that course of time, an abiding interest in recognizing and promoting an appreciation for Virginia's historic, architectural, and archaeological resources has marked the work of all those who have served here. That work will continue in the years to come. The *Virginia Landmarks Register* has become an effective tool for furthering the interests of historic preservation throughout the Commonwealth.

The ultimate responsibility for preserving Virginia's landmarks rests with those who own them. In publishing a register of significant properties, the board formally recognizes the profound debt all Virginians owe to those people who own and lovingly care for the structures and sites that make up this remarkable legacy.

On behalf of my distinguished predecessors and colleagues I am pleased to present the *Virginia Landmarks Register* to the people of Virginia.

MARY DOUTHAT HIGGINS, Chairman, Virginia Historic Landmarks Board

PREFACE

THE THIRD EDITION

The third edition of *The Virginia Landmarks Register* is an illustrated compilation of all places officially designated as Virginia Historic Landmarks by the Virginia Historic Landmarks Board from its first register meeting on November 5, 1968, through its January 17, 1984, meeting. Places added to the register between January 17, 1984, and June 18, 1985, while this publication was in preparation, are listed in Appendix II.

Each entry in this work is followed by its archives file number, a hyphenated number the first part of which is the numerical designation of the city, town, or county in which the place is located. The second part of the number indicates the numerical order in which the place was added to the statewide inventory within the survey of its respective city, town, or county. The archives file number is followed in parenthesis by the date the place was added to the Virginia Landmarks Register. Those places that have been destroyed since registration, and thus removed from the Virginia Landmarks Register, are illustrated and described in Appendix I.

The information herein on each landmark is taken primarily from the research notes and nomination reports filed in the archives of the Division of Historic Landmarks, Morson's Row, 221 Governor Street, Richmond. Subsequent research by members of the staff or other scholars will inevitably provide information unavailable or unknown during the preparation of this volume.

THE REGISTER PROGRAM

Virginia's many and varied historic resources are inseparably linked with the cultural identity and economic well-being of the Commonwealth. The recognition of this fact prompted the formation in 1965 of a Virginia Advisory Legislative Council study commission to determine what role state government should play in safeguarding this legacy. The study commission recommended that the state take positive steps to identify and protect its historic resources, and in 1966 the General Assembly established the Virginia Historic Landmarks Commission, now known as the Virginia Historic Landmarks Board, charging it with the task of perpetuating "those structures and areas which have a close and immediate relationship to the values upon which the State and the nation were founded."

The enabling legislation charged the board to make a general survey of the state and to designate as historic landmarks the buildings, structures, sites, and historic districts that constitute the principal historical, architectural, and archaeological sites of state-wide or national significance. The criteria that a place must meet in order to be designated a landmark were set forth in the legislation as follows:

> No structure or site shall be deemed to be a historic one unless it has been prominently identified with, or best represents, some major aspect of the cultural, political, economic, military, or social history of the State or nation, or has had a relationship with the life of an historic personage or event representing some major aspect of, or ideals related to, the history of the State or nation. In the case of structures which are to be so designated, they shall embody the principal or unique features of an architectural style or demonstrate the style of a period of our history or method of construction, or serve as an illustration of the work of a master builder, designer or architect whose genius influenced the period in which he worked or has significance in current times. In order for a site to qualify as an archaeological site, it shall be an area from which it is reasonable to expect that artifacts, materials, and other specimens may be found which give insight to an understanding of aboriginal man or the Colonial and early history and architecture of the State or nation.

In an early meeting of the board, it was agreed that the list of designated historic landmarks would be called the Virginia Landmarks Register and that entries made in it would be called Virginia Historic Landmarks. Since the listing of the first property in the Virginia Landmarks Register in 1968, the register has been expanded to more than 1,100 entries. Registration is an ongoing process: the list will lengthen over the next several decades as additional places are found and studied and their significance to state and national history is verified. Because our understanding and interpretation of Virginia history is constantly evolving, the types of places nominated to the register will become more diverse. Buildings and structures that formerly have been thought of as commonplace may, as Virginia grows older and builds anew, eventually appear as important survivals and will require reevaluation. Hence, properties which might not have been regarded as eligible for registration in the early years of the board's work may in time be looked upon more sympathetically.

THE BOARD

The Virginia Historic Landmarks Board is composed of eleven members; nine are appointed by the governor, and two, the state librarian and the director of the Department of Conservation and Historic Resources, serve as ex officio members. In making appointments, the governor is advised by the board's legislation to select representatives from the Association for the Preservation of Virginia Antiquities, the Colonial Williamsburg Foundation, the University of Virginia School of Architecture, the Virginia Historical Society, and the Virginia Society of the American Institute of Architects. Likewise, legislation enacted in 1984 provides that two members of the board shall be professional archaeologists. Members serve terms of four years and may be reappointed. Presiding over the meetings of the board is a chairman, elected by the board from among its members.

The board is an independent body whose primary functions are to make additions to the Virginia Landmarks Register and to accept historic preservation easements on registered landmarks. The board also serves as an advisory board on historic preservation matters. Assisting the board is the professional staff of the Division of Historic Landmarks, a division within the Department of Conservation and Historic Re-

Virginia Historic Landmark Plaque

sources. Prior to a reorganization of state agencies in 1985, the Division of Historic Landmarks was known as the Virginia Historic Landmarks Commission, including both board and staff. On the staff are historians, architectural historians, archaeologists, and various other specialists. The board, in addition, receives valuable assistance and support from various individual groups and organizations having an interest in history and preservation.

THE REGISTER PROCESS

The Virginia Landmarks Register serves both as an honor roll of historic resources and as a planning tool. In order to have sufficient information to justify specific nominations to the register, the board, following its legislative mandate, directed the professional staff to undertake a systematic survey of all places in the Commonwealth having historical, architectural, or archaeological interest. The survey is a continuing cooperative effort between the board and the Commonwealth's citizens in which historical data, photographs, drawings, and maps are assembled for each place surveyed. By 1984 the board's survey files represented approximately 30,000 buildings and structures and more than 14,500 archaeological sites, with nearly 250,000 photographs. All places recorded are mapped on U.S. Geological Survey topographic maps. This extensive data bank on Virginia's historic properties is maintained in the archives of the Division of Historic Landmarks where it serves as an important source of information for historians, architects, and individuals involved in restoration, preservation, or scholarly research. The photographs and maps form an especially valuable planning tool for governmental agencies and private organizations involved in land-use planning or preservation activity.

Like the register, the statewide inventory is an ongoing process. Many counties and municipalities have been surveyed systematically and comprehensively, while others have received only a cursory recording or concentration only on specific types such as pre–Civil War dwellings. Also, many surveys conducted over ten years ago now require updating. Thus, while the statewide inventory of historic properties includes a large number of buildings, structures, and sites, it is by no means the complete record xii The Virginia Landmarks Register

of all places of interest. The board anticipates that the continuing survey will add thousands of properties to the inventory in the coming years.

The statewide inventory serves as a basis for making comparative analyses when evaluating nominations to the Virginia Landmarks Register. Many of the nominations are made by members of the staff, and board members as well suggest places to be studied. Although many nominations originate from within the office, the board increasingly is receiving requests for consideration from property owners, preservation organizations, local governments, and other interested parties. A nomination report, containing detailed descriptions, statements of significance, supporting documentation, and photographs, is prepared for each place to be presented to the board. The report may be prepared either by the staff or by members of the public. Final action on the nominations rests with the full eleven-member board. Approval attests that a property conforms to established criteria and is of significance to the state and nation. The board presents owners or custodians of designated properties with a plaque stating that the property has been registered as a Virginia Historic Landmark.

Listing in the Virginia Landmarks Register does not restrict the owner's use of his property. Architectural controls, such as are imposed through historic district zoning, can be established only by local governing bodies. Registration is primarily an official recognition that a place is an outstanding historic resource and is worthy of preservation. If a private owner wishes to provide legal protection for a registered landmark, he may do so by granting a historic preservation easement on the property to the board. The easement is a legal contract between the state and the grantor stipulating that the historic integrity of the landmark and its setting shall be preserved in perpetuity. Those landmarks which are protected by an easement held by the board, and, in some cases, jointly with the Virginia Outdoors Foundation, are noted throughout this volume.

VIRGINIA AND THE FEDERAL PROGRAM

The program of the Historic Landmarks Board, and consequently that of the Division of Historic Landmarks, is closely aligned with a highly structured federal preservation program. The National Historic Preservation Act of 1966 called for the expansion of the National Register of Historic Places to include properties of state and local as well as of national significance and charged the states with the responsibility of submitting nominations to the National Register. In accordance with the federal act, the director of the Division of the Historic Landmarks is mandated by state legislation to serve as the State Historic Preservation Officer (SHPO), in which capacity he is responsible for maintaining a liaison between the state and federal agencies and carrying out Virginia's functions within the federal preservation program.

The National Register of Historic Places is maintained by the National Park Service within the Department of the Interior. Regulations governing the National Register require each state to establish a State Review Board to examine and make recommendations upon proposed nominations to the National Register. In Virginia, the State Review Board is appointed by the SHPO. The Historic Landmarks Board and the State Review Board act in close cooperation so that proposed nominations generally receive the same treatment from both boards. As the National Park Service ordinarily accepts the nominations made by the states, the Virginia section of the National Register, for the most part, contains the same entries as the Virginia Landmarks Register.

NATIONAL HISTORIC LANDMARKS

Under the authority of the Historic Sites Act of 1935, the secretary of the interior, upon recommendation by the Advisory Board on National Parks, Historic Sites,

Buildings, and Monuments, may declare a property to be a National Historic Land-mark. The owner of such a property is offered a certificate and a bronze plaque stating the designation. In return, the owner agrees to preserve those significant historical values for which the property was so designated. The Virginia Historic Landmarks Board may be consulted on properties under consideration for National Historic Landmark status but does not play an active role in the program. Virginia properties that have been designated National Historic Landmarks are so noted in this volume in the statements of significance and in Appendix III. All National Historic Land-marks are automatically entered into the National Register of Historic Places.

Although it may not have received the specific designation of National Historic Land-mark, any historic property owned by the National Park Service is considered to have National Historic Landmark status.

A CAUTIONARY NOTE

Many privately owned properties included in the Virginia Landmarks Register are not open to the public. Some places are open to visitors on a regular basis; others may be visited by special arrangement or on special occasions. Those properties that are main-tained as museums with regularly scheduled times of visitation have been noted, for the most part, in the statements of significance. The most up-to-date general listing of the various historic properties open to the public is maintained by the Visitor Information Office of the Virginia Division of Tourism, Bell Tower, 101 North Ninth Street, Richmond, VA 23219. More specific inquiries about the public accessibility of privately owned registered landmarks should be addressed to the staff of the Division of Historic Landmarks.

INTRODUCTION: VIRGINIA'S TANGIBLE HISTORY

The history and material culture of Virginia is embodied in the many historic buildings, structures, sites, and districts remaining throughout the Commonwealth. The
tangible evidence of human occupation of the modern political entity that is now
Virginia spans over a hundred centuries, beginning with the remains of the earliest
structure yet discovered in the Western Hemisphere, on a Paleo-Indian site in the
Flint Run Archaeological District in Warren County. The people who occupied Virginia for the first 10,000 years or so treated the land very gently, leaving behind them
little more than bits of broken pottery, stone projectile points, or barely perceptible
deposits of faunal and floral remains at a camp or village site. Such prehistoric sites,
scattered along riverbanks or in fields or woods in all parts of the state, cover all the
periods of Indian habitation from the earliest Paleo-Indian period, to the Archaic and
Woodland periods, to the time of contact with the first European settlers. These elu-
sive prehistoric places constitute the only record of Virginia's longest-term inhabitants. The Historic Landmarks Board has acknowledged the importance of the state's
prehistoric archaeological sites by selecting for landmark designation sites representing various aspects of prehistoric cultures in nearly every region of the state. Some
have been singled out because of the great amount of information they have yielded
through excavation; others have been registered because testing has shown that significant data may be revealed through expert examination and interpretation.

It was not until the early seventeenth century, following the establishment at Jamestown of the first permanent English settlement in America, that the character of the
Virginia landscape began to change noticeably as the result of human habitation.
Braving hardships and hostile elements beyond the imagination of modern Virginians,
a small band of adventurers laid the foundations of a new civilization in Virginia's
Tidewater. As in any frontier society, these first settlers lived simply, and little visible
evidence of their first century of occupation remains. Their original rude wooden
houses, often built on posts driven directly into the ground, have not survived. Only
the few exceptionally well built structures such as Bacon's Castle and St. Luke's
Church stand today; the rest are now only a scattering of archaeological sites. Unearthed with increasing frequency in the path of modern development, the seven-

teenth-century post molds, foundation bricks, pipestems, and pottery sherds are the most tangible material evidence of the formative years of present-day Virginia and indeed of America. Since its inception, the Historic Landmarks Board has taken a particular interest in the state's seventeenth-century heritage and has given special priority to the identification and registration of archaeological sites of the period. Whether the outline of a simple yeoman's cottage perhaps with a related trashpit or a whole village complex of dwellings and commercial structures as at Flowerdew Hundred, the sites hold a valuable store of information on modern Virginia's first century. This archaeological evidence is especially important because of the destruction of written records of the period.

Virginia's ascendancy in the early and mid-eighteenth century, based on its tobacco economy, is illustrated most conspicuously by its great colonial plantations and by the larger number of more modest houses. The large mansions and their associated dependencies, outbuildings, and gardens, situated along the great tidal rivers, represent some of the nation's finest achievements in colonial design and craftsmanship. Westover, Mount Airy, Brandon, Shirley, and many others have few peers on these shores as elegant, refined architectural settings for a society's patrician families. The lesser domestic complexes, while not always architecturally sophisticated, show the development of a building idiom that is uniquely Virginian, one that has provided the basis of a domestic style which has visual appeal and serves to inspire many modern works. Virginia's legacy of colonial houses is rich indeed: characteristic examples of both high-style and vernacular dwellings are given conspicuous representation in the Virginia Landmarks Register. More will be registered in coming years, as additional examples are researched and evaluated.

A particularly important legacy of Virginia's colonial civilization is the collection of some fifty churches and a lesser number of glebe houses remaining from the pre-Revolutionary period. Only a fraction of those which existed in the period, this surviving assemblage of colonial ecclesiastical architecture nevertheless is larger than that in any of the other former colonies. Because the Anglican church was the established church of colonial Virginia, the majority of the surviving houses of worship were built to accommodate that denomination. A handful of colonial meetinghouses built by Quakers and Presbyterians also remains, as well as one colonial Lutheran church. Nearly all of Virginia's extant colonial religious structures and the archaeological sites of several that have disappeared are listed in the register.

Another special category of colonial buildings is courthouses. Virginia, with its eleven colonial courthouses and several clerk's offices and jails, boasts an unusually large number of court structures of the period. A distinctive feature of some of the more noted courthouses is the arcaded front. The use of arches on public buildings in Virginia had its precedent in the first Capitol in Williamsburg, which in turn took its precedent from the arcades of town halls in England dating back to the late Middle Ages.

Colonial Virginia contributed extraordinary talent and dedication to the Revolutionary cause. Many of the nation's founding fathers called Virginia home, including George Washington, Thomas Jefferson, Patrick Henry, the Lees, James Madison, Carter Braxton, and Benjamin Harrison. Fortunately, the homes of nearly all the leading Revolutionary figures remain standing. Many of these houses, most notably Mount Vernon, Monticello, Scotchtown, Stratford, Montpelier, Elsing Green, and Berkeley, are impressive works of architecture in their own right, and they only gain significance as the personal habitations of the men who forged a new nation. The majority of these homes are open to the public and rank among the premier historic landmarks of the country. Perhaps the most momentous of the state's Revolutionary-era places is the Yorktown Historic District containing the Yorktown Battlefield, where American vic-

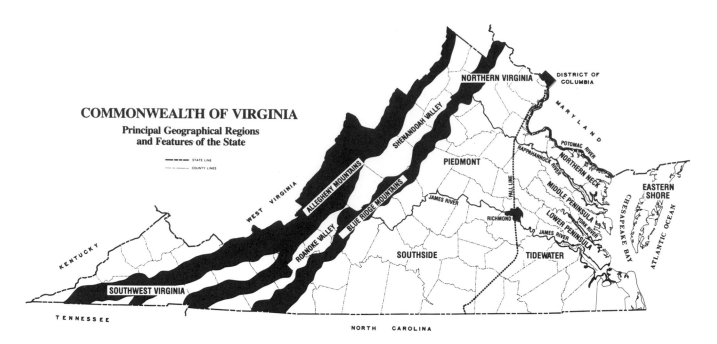

COMMONWEALTH OF VIRGINIA
Principal Geographical Regions
and Features of the State

tory over British rule was achieved. Offshore from the battlefield lies the scuttled fleet of British ships, a unique concentration of maritime archaeological sites.

The end of the eighteenth century saw Virginia changing from a region almost exclusively agrarian, containing counties with only the smallest villages or none, to one gradually beginning to accommodate urban centers. Throughout most of the eighteenth century Williamsburg, the seat of government, was about the only community having much of a semblance of urban life, and even it was hardly more than a large village. Once direct British restraints on trade were removed, river ports, especially those located along the fall line such as Alexandria, Fredericksburg, and Petersburg, became thriving commercial centers and witnessed the development of impressive concentrations of domestic and commercial structures. Historic quarters, some containing scores of Federal-era buildings, survive in each of these cities and are among the most important historic districts listed in the Virginia Landmarks Register.

The late eighteenth century also saw the development of numerous towns and villages in the Piedmont and in western Virginia, particularly along the migration route extending south and west through the Shenandoah Valley. The Piedmont centers of Charlottesville, Warrenton, and Leesburg and principal western Virginia communities such as Winchester, Staunton, Lexington, and Abingdon all began as county seats and over the years acquired a rich diversity of nineteenth- and early twentieth-century buildings in their historic cores. The board has sought to identify these early neighborhoods and officially to acknowledge them as historic resources. Registration of such districts has proved to be a catalyst for much preservation and rehabilitation activity in these communities.

In many of the county seats of the Piedmont and Southside in particular, the county courthouse stands as the central architectural feature. Mostly dating from the first half of the nineteenth century, these often small but stately structures, many in Virginia's distinct Roman Revival style, form a remarkable collection of public buildings. Their simple dignity is a testament to the high regard in which both law and order and justice were held. The board has made a special effort to study these courthouses and to add the foremost examples to the register. The study is an ongoing one; deserving courthouses that have not yet received register recognition will likely be registered at a future time.

For most of Virginia's rural areas, the early Federal era was a period in architecture which some have called the "Great Rebuilding." The once-commonplace one- or two-room colonial dwellings of the small farmers were either replaced or expanded as living standards improved. The new houses, most with a collection of outbuildings, were rendered in a straightforward and dignified style, employing either brick or weatherboarded wood frame. Rural Virginia is rich in domestic architecture of the post-Revolutionary period, and many of the more important or more typical representatives have been included in the register. A large number of them are in what has been termed the I-house form, a symmetrical two-story house, one room deep with a center passage and end chimneys. Having its genesis in the colonial period through a fusion of Georgian and vernacular house-building practices, the I-house became a prevailing domestic type in Piedmont, Southside, and the western regions.

The post-Revolutionary migration of members of Tidewater's leading families to lands they owned farther west resulted in the construction of an outstanding series of plantation houses, especially in Clarke and Loudoun counties. Families such as the Carters, Lees, Burwells, and Pages were responsible for such mansions as Oatlands, Belmont, Carter Hall, Long Branch, and Annefield, all superb works of Federal domestic architecture, scenically sited in the beautiful countryside of the region.

The disestablishment of the Anglican church after the Revolution coincided with the rise of other religious denominations and the construction of ranks of new churches in cities, towns, and the countryside. Many of these churches are architecturally noteworthy and have been emphasized in the register. Baptists, Lutherans, Methodists, Presbyterians, and Roman Catholics erected significant buildings in the late eighteenth and nineteenth centuries, employing the complete range of national and regional architectural idioms. These houses of worship frequently are the most conspicuous landmarks of their respective communities and merit special recognition.

With the designing and building of the Virginia State Capitol, Monticello, and the University of Virginia, Thomas Jefferson brought into being in Virginia what is regarded by many scholars as America's first fully developed native architectural style. Liberally borrowing elements from several traditions, particularly the Palladian, Jefferson synthesized a diversity of influences to create a building style thought appropriate for a young, essentially agrarian republic. His works, combining the native materials of brick, stucco, and whitewashed wood, had a significant influence in the state. Many of the workmen employed on Jefferson's projects carried on his strict adherence to Palladian classicism in their own commissions for nearly two decades after the death of the third president. The buildings of Jefferson and his followers—their courthouses, churches, and residences scattered mainly through the Piedmont and Southside—form one of the most intriguing and valuable parts of Virginia's architectural legacy and are prominently represented in the Virginia Landmarks Register.

Contrasting with the refined classicism of Jeffersonian buildings are the houses and artifacts of the state's early German settlers. Coming mainly from Pennsylvania, the Germans established farms and villages in the Shenandoah Valley beginning in the mid-eighteenth century. Unlike the English and Scotch-Irish settlers, who preferred brick and wood frame for their buildings, the Germans made extensive use of stone and log construction and continued to use room arrangements employed by their forebears on the Continent. Because the German culture was almost completely assimilated into the mainstream of the state's British culture in the nineteenth century, buildings that show an unmistakably Germanic influence are not commonplace in Virginia, with few dating after 1800. Small concentrations remain in the central Shenandoah Valley, particularly in Augusta, Page, Rockingham, and Shenandoah counties, and in the southwest, mainly in Wythe County. The German settlers were also responsible for an interesting series of distinctly carved gravestones located in several rural Lutheran cemeteries, mostly in Southwest Virginia. Decorated with various stylized motifs, these gravestones are exceptional examples of ethnic folk art. A special effort has been made by the board to record such surviving evidences of Virginia's German settlement and to bring long overdue official recognition to this important facet of the state's cultural history.

The board has also worked to acknowledge the importance of other forms of vernacular architecture in the state's cultural landscape. On the Eastern Shore and in Tidewater, the countryside was once dotted with simple domiciles employing regional variations in their room arrangements, timber framing, and brickwork. These traditions spread into the Piedmont and Southside where they persisted well into the nineteenth century. Quaker settlers in Northern Virginia introduced plain but solid forms of brick and stone architecture. Various forms of log construction were spread by several cultures through Northern Virginia and the mountain regions into Southwest Virginia. Most of these vernacular traditions can trace their origins to particular areas of the British Isles, Germany, and Switzerland. Well-preserved examples of these various vernacular traditions, together with their ancillary structures, are fast disappearing through neglect or unsympathetic modernization. It has been an important activity of the board to identify the characteristic representatives of the state's vernacular architecture and to extend register recognition to them.

Virginia architecture began to lose much of its regional character by the mid-nineteenth century; the forms and details of newer buildings increasingly were influenced by the illustrations in pattern books produced by prominent northern architects such as Asher Benjamin and Andrew Jackson Downing. These books, illustrating mainly interpretations of Greek Revival and Gothic Revival styles, were widely used by local builders, who adapted their designs for both rural and urban works of all types. In some buildings, only the details were taken from published sources and were grafted onto traditional forms. In other instances, the whole building was modeled after pattern-book illustrations. Some of the most popular types of pattern-book architecture in Virginia were the temple-form Greek Revival church, the Gothic cottage, and the Italian villa. The state's many buildings in these revivalist styles have great visual appeal and relate Virginia to the broader developments of American architecture. The inclusion of distinctive representatives in the register is intended to establish the value of this type of derivative architecture to the state's built environment.

At the beginning of the nineteenth century, Virginians began to turn to out-of-state architects, particularly from the northern cities of Philadelphia, New York, and Boston, when seeking schemes for major works. As a result, a large number of important mid-nineteenth-century architects are represented by works in the Commonwealth. Thomas U. Walter was commissioned to design buildings for Richmond, Norfolk, Petersburg, and Lexington. Alexander Jackson Davis is known for his impressive design for the Virginia Military Institute and for works commissioned by the Cocke family. Other well-known architects responsible for at least one surviving Virginia building are Minard Lafever, Robert Cary Long, Jr., Robert Mills, Alexander Parris, Calvin Pollard, Samuel Sloan, Thomas S. Stewart, William Strickland, and Ammi B. Young. The practice of commissioning nationally prominent architects extended through the late nineteenth century and into the twentieth century. Thus there are works in the state by Richard Morris Hunt, Elijah E. Myers, Carrère and Hastings, Stanford White, John Russell Pope, and Frank Lloyd Wright, all of which have received register recognition.

While the Virginia Landmarks Register contains important or unusual works of architecture, other, less obvious categories of landmarks forming a significant part of the Virginia scene also are included. A fast-disappearing industrial form that has received special attention in the register program is the rural water-powered gristmill. Throughout the eighteenth and nineteenth centuries, these structures with their dams, races, and large wooden or metal wheels were an essential element of Virginia's grain industry. Hundreds dotted the state's countryside and served to convert vast quantities of grain to flour and meal either for home use or for transportation and sale elsewhere. Strict health regulations adopted in the 1930s forced the abandonment of many of the mills, and the newer urban commercial mills offered competition that the old mills could not withstand. As a result, a vast number of gristmills have disappeared or have decayed beyond the point of repair. Some that have survived reasonably intact have been adapted to other uses. The state's remaining mills, whether in use or not, are historic focal points of the rural landscape and have been given high priority for registration.

An interesting early industrial form which has also received attention from the board is the state's early iron furnaces. Commercial ironmaking began in Virginia in the early eighteenth century. The remains of Tubal Furnace, founded by Alexander Spotswood ca. 1717, is one of the state's most noteworthy iron-related sites. Western Virginia boasted a busy iron industry in the nineteenth century; the mountains were sprinkled with furnaces and forges producing pig iron to be shipped to cities for fashioning into finished products. The only remaining evidences of this industry are the distinctive tapered blast furnaces—massive stone pylons often standing isolated in mountain forests. The board has selected some of the better preserved and better known of these furnaces for registration as representatives of this once-important industry.

Other special categories of landmarks that have become rare as the result of improved technology are canals and old bridges. Virginia's vast network of canals was developed in the antebellum period; canalboats transported grain and tobacco to the large commercial mills and factories of Richmond and other cities. With the coming of the railroads, the canals became obsolete, and many of the rights-of-way were purchased by railroad companies for the laying of tracks. Today, the state has only two operable canals, however, well-preserved sections of other canal systems, many employing beautifully crafted masonry, have been duly recorded and singled out for register recognition as artifacts of our transportation and engineering history.

The other remnants of Virginia's early transportation network, stone, metal truss, and covered bridges, have also become victims of more efficient systems. Most of these early bridges are unable to meet the upgraded standards for highways and bridges; but some have been acknowledged to possess particular scenic value or engineering significance. The State Department of Highways and Transportation through the Virginia Highway Research Council has cooperated with the board in the survey and registration of historic bridges, and where practical, it has set aside representative examples of various bridge types for preservation.

Disappearing building forms of more social interest, such as resort hotels and spa complexes, have also received attention from the board. From the mid-eighteenth century, western Virginia was famous for its many mineral springs and its salubrious climate. Beginning in the nineteenth century, numerous resorts, often employing fanciful architecture, sprang up throughout the mountains and the Shenandoah Valley. People seeking the curative benefits of the waters and an escape from the malodorous summer heat of cities flocked to the mountains. A combination of improved medicine, air-conditioning, and air transportation has put most of these places out of business. Some of the spa complexes such as Craig Healing Springs and Orkney Springs have been adapted to new uses and have survived. However, most of the remaining ones, such as Sweet Chalybeate Springs and Yellow Sulphur Springs, are falling into disrepair. Many have only a building or two where dozens formerly stood. Only two of the Shenandoah Valley's many noted Victorian resort hotels remain standing. Both buildings, one in Waynesboro and one in Buena Vista, survived by being converted to schools. The board has sought to preserve the memory of this important part of Virginia's social and recreational history by singling out the principal survivors. The process of identification has not been completed, and more detailed studies, particularly of spa-related structures, will be made in the future.

Much of the Civil War was fought on Virginia soil, and throughout the Commonwealth are battlefields, fortifications, earthworks, military headquarters, and other places that figured in the events of this bloody war. Richmond, as the former capital of the Confederate States, preserves the official residence of President Jefferson Davis as well as a variety of other buildings and sites identified with the government. The state's main Civil War battlefields—Manassas, Spotsylvania Court House, the Wilderness, Petersburg, Richmond, and Appomattox—along with associated buildings and structures, are preserved by the National Park Service as outstanding, if poignant, historic resources.

The South's defeat in the Civil War brought about changes in Virginia's life-style that affected the built environment, particularly in rural areas. No more elaborate plantation complexes were established; without a slave labor force, plantation agriculture was inefficient. Many of the complexes fell into decay, making those that have survived, even with a reduced number of individual units, the focus of special interest. The board has been diligent in recording and extending recognition to these indigenous and indeed fragile agricultural groupings. Because it remained a productive farming region into the present century, the area of Virginia south of the James River has retained a significant number of plantation complexes with either eighteenth-century or antebellum outbuildings and related farm structures. Less formal than the famous colonial plantations along the Tidewater rivers, the agrestic architecture of southern Tidewater and the Southside is significant in the study of rural vernacular architecture. The surveys of these southern regions of the state have resulted in the identification of several of the most complete complexes and their registration as Virginia Historic Landmarks.

Because of the economic deprivation experienced by Virginia during the Civil War and the Reconstruction period of the 1860s and 1870s, bold works in the Second Empire, High Victorian Italianate, and High Victorian Gothic styles, which are relatively common in the northern states, are the exception here. The board has looked upon the state's architecture of these decades with special interest and has registered representatives of that period which if located elsewhere in the nation might not be held in as high regard. An exception to this building slump was the city of Richmond. With its commerical district leveled in the Evacuation Fire of 1865, the city's businessmen immediately began the task of reconstructing the downtown. Richmond, despite considerable subsequent redevelopment, still retains a large quantity of commercial architecture dating from the years immediately following the war. A distinctive characteristic of these buildings is the extensive use of cast-iron ornamentation, with some of the buildings having entire facades of cast iron. Two of Richmond's historic districts, Shockoe Slip and the Shockoe Valley and Tobacco Row district, have been registered principally for their concentrations of postbellum commercial architecture.

A leading casualty of the social changes following the war was slave quarters. The many "streets" of these elementary domiciles, once dominant features of the larger plantations, have nearly all disappeared. The few authentic quarters that have survived have been singled out for note whenever they are part of a property to be registered. Slave quarters, however, represent only one type of landmark associated with Virginia's blacks. In contrast, a variety of places stand as evidence of the many outstanding contributions to the state's culture and history made by black citizens. Among the foremost landmarks in this category are the schools and colleges established in the post–Civil War years to serve the educational needs of freedmen. Institutions of higher learning such as Hampton Institute, St. Paul's College, Virginia College and Virginia Seminary, Virginia State University, and Virginia Union University illustrate the establishment of black education in the late nineteenth century. Among other landmarks associated with Virginia's largest ethnic minority are two historic districts. Richmond's Jackson Ward, with its streets of late nineteenth-century houses and commercial buildings, represents the growth of black entrepreneurship. The home of Maggie L. Walker, a black business and social leader and the nation's first woman bank president, is a principal landmark of Jackson Ward. Truxtun, a planned neighborhood constructed by the federal government during World War I for black shipbuilders in Portsmouth, is significant in the history of black labor. Churches in particular functioned as institutions significant in black social life, and the board has extended recognition to architecturally or historically important representatives including Lynchburg's Court Street Baptist Church, Norfolk's First Baptist Church, and Richmond's Bethel A.M.E. Church and Fourth Baptist Church. The birthplace of Virginia's most famous black native son, Booker T. Washington, is maintained as a National Monument by the National Park Service.

Virginia's tobacco and textile industries played a large part in returning prosperity to a state devastated by war. Tobacco especially contributed to the maintenance of agricultural productivity and to the growth of cities and towns in the southern part of the state. Cities such as Danville, Lynchburg, Petersburg, and Richmond preserve warehouses and factories connected with the tobacco industry and have fine houses erected by tobacco magnates. The Danville Tobacco Warehouse and Residential District and Richmond's Shockoe Valley and Tobacco Row Historic District give dramatic evidence of the size and importance of the tobacco business to Virginia from the late nineteenth century to the present. Much of the credit for the rebirth of the tobacco trade in the South after the Civil War is due to R. J. Reynolds, founder of the R. J. Reynolds Tobacco Company, whose homeplace in Patrick County has been designated a National Historic Landmark.

Coal mining was another industry which significantly contributed to the growth of Virginia's economy in the late nineteenth century. Southwest Virginia has a variety of places associated with the growth of coal mining. The principal site represented in the register is the town of Pocahontas in Tazewell County, an excellently preserved mining community of the turn of the century. The prosperity that mining brought to Southwest Virginia is particularly evident in several architecturally impressive courthouses in the coalfield counties, among which are those of Buchanan, Dickenson, and Wise counties. Roanoke, a city which grew from the establishment of the Norfolk and Western Railway to transport coal, is rich in landmarks either directly or indirectly associated with the wealth brought about by coal mining.

Virginia, like most other states in the nation, experienced considerable economic growth in the last decade of the nineteenth century and in the years before World War I. The prosperity of the so-called Progressive era is seen in the outstanding quality and impressive scale of much of the period's architecture. Elaborate city halls, post offices, courthouses, schools, churches, and libraries demonstrate a keenly felt sense of confidence and civic pride. Other conspicuous evidence of this prosperity is seen in numerous imposing banks, hotels, apartment blocks, and a variety of fine dwellings. Important works in such turn-of-the-century styles as Romanesque Revival, Queen Anne, Beaux Arts classicism, Renaissance Revival, and Georgian Revival can be found throughout the state, in cities large and small. The larger cities such as Richmond, Norfolk, and Roanoke boast especially fine classical-style bank buildings, while the smaller cities, including Staunton, Lynchburg, and Winchester, preserve many interesting residential structures of the period. Lynchburg and Winchester each contains an unusually elegant turn-of-the-century library: the Jones Memorial in Lynchburg and the extraordinary Beaux Arts–style Handley Library in Winchester.

Several large residential districts, including Ghent in Norfolk, Monument Avenue in Richmond, and Diamond Hill in Lynchburg, hold rich concentrations of turn-of-the-century dwellings in an amazing variety of styles. Individually significant examples of mansions of the period's plutocrats include Mountain View in Roanoke, Swannanoa in Nelson County, Rocklands in Orange County, and Maymont and the Branch house in Richmond.

Since its founding, the board has recognized that the state's more recent landmarks are among its most important resources. The large, oftentimes exuberant buildings serve as principal objects of visual interest in their respective communities. The dome of Richmond's Broad Street Station and the spires of Roanoke's St. Andrew's Roman Catholic Church are enduring landmarks that serve to create a sense of place. While the board in its early years devoted much of its time and energy to extending register recognition to the state's colonial and early nineteenth-century landmarks, in recent years it has given increased emphasis to the survey and registration of structures and districts of the last generation, particularly those in urban areas where threats to preservation are felt most keenly. Only in rare instances, however, has the board given consideration to the registration of places less than fifty years old. The Pope-Leighey house designed by Frank Lloyd Wright, the prototype town-house development of Colonial Village in Arlington, and the Belgian Building, an outstanding example of European modernism erected for the 1939 New York World's Fair and subsequently moved to Richmond, are among the few of Virginia's relatively young registered historic landmarks.

The some 1,100 places contained in this third edition of the *Virginia Landmarks Register* constitute an extensive but not complete record of Virginia's historic resources. The register, a highly structured process of recording and evaluating the places best representing the principal themes of Virginia's history and culture, is an ongoing program. Particular facets have been studied extensively by the board, and their related landmarks have been accorded official recognition. Other themes have thus far received only a cursory examination; the register does not yet reflect the full quantity of their primary associated places. Thus, the board will continue to survey buildings, structures, sites, and districts throughout the state and scrutinize them for eligibility in the register. It is impossible to say when, if ever, the Virginia Landmarks Register will represent the full tangible record of the Commonwealth's civilization, but the process of studying and recognizing the many manifestations of our heritage can only increase our awareness of the value of these historic resources and the importance of their preservation.

THE VIRGINIA
LANDMARKS REGISTER

ACCOMACK COUNTY

*Named for the Indian tribe that occupied the Eastern Shore
at the time of settlement, the present county of Accomack
was formed from Northampton County ca. 1663.
The county seat is Accomac.*

ACCOMAC HISTORIC DISTRICT, *including all but several
fringe areas of the town of Accomac.* The town of Accomac is
noted for its interesting and varied collection of early buildings
and for its continuity as a judicial center for over three hundred
years. The settlement, originally called Matopkin, grew up
around John Cole's tavern at William Freeman's plantation
where court was first held in the 1670s. The county seat was
formally established there by 1690. The town was officially laid
out adjacent to the court square in 1786 and was known as
Drummond or Drummondtown because it was located on
land then owned by Richard Drummond. Renamed Accomac
in 1893, the town has evolved gently so that its quiet, tree-
shaded streets are lined with numerous 18th- and 19th-century
regional building types, both high-style and vernacular. Outstanding Federal houses include the Seymour house with its
distinctive icehouse and the brick St. James's rectory. One of
the smaller 18th-century houses is the Ailworth house (shown),
around the corner from St. James's Episcopal Church of 1838.
The colonial courthouse was replaced in the late 19th century
by the present somewhat plain Victorian structure; however,
the 18th-century debtors' prison survives from the early court
complex. The district contains approximately 150 buildings.
160–20 (12/16/80).

ASSATEAGUE COAST GUARD STATION, *Assateague Island*. Welcome facilities for both seamen and holiday makers, these U.S. Coast Guard stations operated as lifesaving posts. The standard station incorporated living quarters for the lifesaving crews, a lookout tower, a boathouse—usually capable of handling two or more boats—and launchways for the speedy dispatch of crews to those in distress. Established in 1922, the Assateague station was one of a chain of such facilities along the coast, most of which were replaced after World War II by more efficient rescue systems. Although no longer in use, the complex is being preserved by the National Park Service as an interesting facet of nautical history. 01–172 (2/20/73).

ASSATEAGUE LIGHTHOUSE, *Assateague Island*. Few building types more appropriately merit the term *landmark* than lighthouses. These singular structures stand as distinctive and necessary focal points along the nation's coasts. The festively banded Assateague Lighthouse has operated as a nautical guide for the south end of Assateague Island since it was first lighted on October 1, 1867, replacing an earlier but inadequate tower built in 1831. Standing 129 feet from base to light, the lighthouse is built of brick with tapered walls. Its original light mechanism, imported from France, has been replaced by a modern automatic system but remains on display at the site. The lighthouse is maintained by the U.S. Coast Guard. 01–78 (4/17/73).

BOWMAN'S FOLLY, *Accomac vicinity*. This large Federal house was built for John Cropper, Jr., a Revolutionary general and politician. Cropper sited his home on an artificial mound so that it would have a good vantage across the water and marshes. The house was completed ca. 1815 on a tract held by Cropper's wife's family since 1664, replacing an earlier structure destroyed by fire. With its formal main section and trailing service wings and outbuildings, the brick-ended frame house exhibits the combination of sophistication and rusticity so characteristic of Eastern Shore architecture. Two of its outbuildings, a wooden dovecote and wainscoted privy, are unusually fine examples of their types. 01–29 (5/13/69).

CORBIN HALL, *Horntown vicinity.* Commanding a sweeping view from terraced grounds across Chincoteague Bay, this plantation house is perhaps the most refined example of Georgian architecture on Virginia's Eastern Shore. Its Flemish bond brick walls are accented by rubbed-brick belt courses, gauged-brick lintels, and a handsome Palladian window. Inside is a wealth of original woodwork, including a fully paneled parlor and a Georgian stair. The dominant interior feature is a tall stair-hall arch framed by fluted pilasters set on pedestals. The house was built for George Corbin on land purchased by his father in 1745. The construction date of 1787 is assumed from two inscribed bricks. 01–7 (4/18/72).

DEBTOR'S PRISON, *Accomac.* This once-formidable landmark is a rare example for Virginia of 18th-century penal architecture and is Accomack County's oldest public building. The compact structure was built in 1783 as a jailer's residence and was converted to a debtor's prison in 1824. It and the regular jail were originally surrounded by a high brick wall. The jail and wall were demolished by the county in 1909, and custody of the debtor's prison was entrusted to the Drummondtown Branch of the Association for the Preservation of Virginia Antiquities. The building has since undergone renovation and now serves as a local history museum. 160–9 (6/15/76).

THE HERMITAGE, *Craddockville vicinity.* Built on an unpretentious scale, the Hermitage has the architectural quality characteristic of the Eastern Shore's larger residences. With its chevroned-brick gables, dormer windows, and symmetrical facade, the house is an attractive example of Virginia's early rural architecture, exhibiting both quaintness and formality. It is also among the best preserved of its type in the area, retaining a richly decorated parlor chimneypiece and a Georgian stair with molded handrail and turned balusters. The Hermitage was constructed in two stages between 1769 and 1787 by Emmanuel Bayly, a member of an old Eastern Shore family. Bayly conducted a notably successful farming operation on the property, raising corn, oats, flax, cattle, sheep, and hogs. 01–21 (11/18/80).

HOPKINS & BRO. STORE, *Onancock.* Although shifted a short distance to a new location on Onancock Creek, Hopkins & Bro. Store retains the relation to the waterfront it enjoyed when it was a commercial and maritime trading center for the Eastern Shore's bayside. The bracketed and weatherboarded Victorian building housed a business founded in 1842 by Capt. Stephen Hopkins and remaining in the hands of the Hopkins family until 1965. Now owned by the Association for the Preservation of Virginia Antiquities, the store has most of its 19th-century fittings and well illustrates the maritime mercantilism of a small Chesapeake region town. Detailed records of the establishment are preserved in the Virginia Historical Society. In 1983 the store was leased and reopened, operating under the Hopkins name. 273–2 (5/13/69).

KERR PLACE, *Onancock.* This sophisticated Federal mansion in the village of Onancock is regarded as the consummate representative of the Eastern Shore's legacy of fine-quality Federal architecture. Beautifully proportioned and highlighted by a pedimented entrance pavilion, the house was begun in 1799 for John Shepherd Ker (later Kerr), an Onancock merchant, and was completed before his death in 1806. The interior has three reception rooms embellished with applied composition classical ornaments in the style of those manufactured by Robert Wellford of Philadelphia. In 1960 the house and two acres were acquired by the Eastern Shore of Virginia Historical Society, an organization dedicated to the promotion of the cultural heritage of this distinctive area of the state. The gardens have been restored by the Garden Club of Virginia. 273–3 (12/2/69).

MASON HOUSE, *Guilford vicinity.* A compact colonial manor house, the Mason house is an important and rare example of the transition from the Jacobean style to the Georgian as revealed in Virginia vernacular architecture. The treatment of the front and rear walls as paneled bays is a unique survival. Although later painted, the panels not containing openings are set off by diapering formed by glazed header bricks. Although its history has not been precisely documented, the house was probably built after 1722 when the property was acquired by William Andrews. The most striking interior feature is the Jacobean-style closed-string stair with symmetrical turned balusters and pulvinated stringer frieze. 01–29 (9/17/74).

OLD MERCANTILE BUILDING (EASTERN SHORE CHAMBER OF COMMERCE), *Accomac.* A rare and refined example of Federal commercial architecture, the Old Mercantile Building was erected in 1819 by Michael Higgins and Alexander McCollom as a store. It was converted to a bank in 1867 and served in that capacity until the mid-1970s when it was restored with the assistance of a Department of the Interior grant as the headquarters of the Eastern Shore Chamber of Commerce. Despite its changes of function, the building has suffered only minor alterations, including the stuccoing of its facade. It gains interest from its location on the main intersection of the village of Accomac. 160–13 (5/21/74).

PITTS NECK, *New Church vicinity.* The Pitts Neck dwelling house, probably built before 1756 for Robert Pitt IV, is a distinctive example of a mid-18th-century Eastern Shore plantation house. Chief among its interesting features is the scrolled soffit of the molded-brick doorway, a motif common on Georgian buildings in England but exceedingly rare in America. The doorway, along with other brickwork details, the interior paneling, and an earlier wing with a T-shaped chimney combine to make the house a document of colonial building motifs. Now isolated, the plantation was once the scene of bustling activity. A tobacco warehouse was operated by the Pitt family in the 18th century at the plantation's Pocomoke River landing. The landing remained a regular stop for bay steamers as late as 1924. 01–38 (2/17/76).

ST. GEORGE'S EPISCOPAL CHURCH, *Pungoteague.*
Known as Pungoteague Church until 1800 when its name was
changed to St. George's to conform to its parish name, this
much-altered building is the only colonial church remaining in
Accomack County. According to the vestry book, the church
was built by Severn Guttridge in 1763. In its original form the
church had a Latin cross plan with a hipped gambrel roof and
a rounded apse which resulted in the early nickname "Ace of
Clubs Church." Abandoned in 1812 but later restored, the
building was so mutilated in the Civil War by Union troops
that only the north and south walls—the ends of the transepts—could be salvaged in 1880 when it was rehabilitated. The
south wall, now the present facade, survives as one of the most
beautiful examples of colonial Flemish bond brickwork in the
state, its dark red strechers providing a rich contrast to the clear
blue glazed headers. 01–40 (6/2/70).

ST. JAMES'S EPISCOPAL CHURCH, *Accomac.* Built in
1838, this provincial Greek Revival church in the town of Accomac owes its significance to the rare trompe l'oeil fresco decoration of the interior. The apsidal arch, with its false perspec-
tive, and the other architectural embellishments combine to
make an unusually skillful example of a decorative painting
scheme that indeed worked to "fool the eye." The creator of
this interesting work was an itinerant artist named Potts. Another notable feature of the interior is a curious divided stair
to the rear gallery. The bricks used in the church's walls were
salvaged from an 18th-century church which stood nearby.
160–5 (11/5/68).

SCARBOROUGH HOUSE ARCHAEOLOGICAL SITE,
Davis Wharf vicinity. The Scarborough house archaeological
site is believed to be the location of Occohannock House, the
seat of Edmund Scarborough. Scarborough was Speaker of the
Virginia House of Burgesses at the assembly of 1645-46 and
the Eastern Shore's largest 17th-century landholder. Subsurface
features and heavy artifact density indicate that the site remains
essentially intact. Shown is a fragment of Rhenish stoneware
in situ. Scientific archaeological excavation and documentary
research should yield new information about 17th- and 18th-
century Eastern Shore cultural patterns which could be appli-
cable to other areas in eastern Virginia whose official records
have been destroyed. 01–64 (1/18/83).

SHEPHERD'S PLAIN, *Pungoteague vicinity*. Completed in the third quarter of the 18th century, the Shepherd's Plain dwelling house is a formal two-story residence built for Edward Ker, an Accomack County planter and politician. The architectural significance of the house is heightened by the rare rusticated quoins, windows, and gables in its brick ends. Also notable is the large quantity of original interior woodwork, especially the parlor paneling with its pilaster-framed chimneypiece. These skillfully crafted details of brick and wood illustrate the capabilities of the Eastern Shore craftsmen in executing sophisticated designs based on plates in 18th-century English builders' guides. The house is currently undergoing a long-term restoration. 01–32 (10/21/80).

WESSELS ROOT CELLAR, *Hallwood vicinity*. This simple brick structure is possibly a unique example of a decorated outbuilding built solely to serve as a root cellar. It is believed to have been erected sometime after 1768 when William Wessels acquired the property and put up a house for himself. Wessels's home was burned in 1937, but his root cellar remains and continues to serve its original function. Most colonial root cellars were contained within the foundations of other buildings; this example is unusual for being freestanding and for having its gable decorated with a pattern of glazed header bricks. 01–76 (12/2/69).

WHARTON PLACE, *Mappsville vicinity*. John Wharton, a maritime merchant and native of Accomack County, had this stately house built shortly after he purchased the property in 1798. Wharton made his new home the headquarters of his various business interests and maintained a landing for his ships on Assawoman Creek, within sight of the house. With its graceful exterior proportions, its lavish use of marble trimmings, and rich interior plasterwork and woodwork, Wharton Place is an outstanding example for Virginia of the rural application of the Federal style. Of special note are its Federal mantels trimmed with classical ornaments signed by Robert Wellford of Philadelphia. 01–50 (4/18/72).

ALBEMARLE COUNTY

This Piedmont county, home of Thomas Jefferson, was named for William Anne Keppel, second earl of Albemarle and governor of the Virginia colony from 1737 to 1754. It was formed from Goochland County in 1744, with part of Louisa County added later. The county seat is Charlottesville.

ASH LAWN (HIGHLAND), *Simeon vicinity.* James Monroe, minister to France, twice governor of Virginia, and fifth president of the United States, purchased this Albemarle County farm which he called Highland in the 1790s. He completed the simple cottage, the western portion of the present house, in 1799. The house site was selected by Monroe's friend and mentor Thomas Jefferson and was in sight of Jefferson's Monticello on the mountain just to the north. Called by Monroe his "castle cabin," the house was modest by necessity because Monroe was in debt at the time of its construction. Monroe lived there intermittently until he sold the property in 1826. The house was enlarged in 1860 by Parson John E. Massey with the addition of the two-story porticoed section. Saved and exhibited by the late philanthropist Jay Johns, the property is now owned by the College of William and Mary and is a museum commemorating Monroe's Albemarle County residency. 02-99 (1/16/73).

BLENHEIM, *Blenheim vicinity.* Blenheim's low, rambling Gothic Revival dwelling house, built ca. 1846, was the seat of Andrew Stevenson, who served as Speaker of the House of Representatives, ambassador to Great Britain, and rector of the University of Virginia. With its numerous outbuildings, including a colonnaded "book house" or library, and what was perhaps a chapel, Blenheim is a striking if somewhat naive example of the influence of Romantic Revivalism in central Virginia. Except for the addition of modern bay windows, the main house survives without significant alterations. The property was originally the home of Edward Carter, grandson of Robert ("King") Carter, who built a large, H-shaped house there before 1799. Carter's home has disappeared, but its site, just to the north of the present house, may have archaeological significance. 02–5 (12/16/75).

BUCK MOUNTAIN CHURCH, *Earlysville vicinity.* Although moved and altered, this inelaborate house of worship is a rare surviving example of the simple wooden Anglican parish churches scattered through Virginia in the colonial period. Erected to serve Fredericksville Parish, the building was first completed in 1747, a few years after the parish was formed. It was abandoned after the disestablishment, but a rejuvenated parish repurchased the building in the 1860s and had it dismantled and moved to its present site two miles to the west. The church was reduced in size when reerected, but most of its framing along with some of its weatherboards and interior trim was reused. 02–145 (8/15/72).

CARRS-BROOK, *Charlottesville vicinity.* Carrs-Brook is a provincial Piedmont adaptation of the Palladian five-part house, introduced to Tidewater Virginia in the 1760s through Robert Morris's handbook *Select Architecture* (1755). Built in the 1780s for Capt. Thomas Carr, the house served from 1798 until 1815 as the residence and school of Thomas Jefferson's ward and nephew Peter Carr, with whom it is traditionally associated. Because of Jefferson's close relationship with the Carr family and his familiarity with the Morris pattern book, it is thought likely that Jefferson influenced the design of the house. Its proportions, however, veer too far from classical standards for Jefferson to have exercised a direct hand in the final product. The house is interesting from the standpoint of 18th-century building technology for preserving most of its early fabric including siding, sash, flooring, and woodwork. 02–11 (7/21/81); *Virginia Historic Landmarks Board preservation easement.*

CASTLE HILL, *Cismont vicinity.* The earliest portion of this two-part house is a traditional colonial Virginia frame dwelling, built in 1764 by Dr. Thomas Walker, an early explorer of the west. In this house in 1781 Walker's wife delayed the British colonel Banastre Tarleton and his troops to give Jack Jouett time to warn Thomas Jefferson and the Virginia legislators of Tarleton's plan to capture them. The stately brick portion, an example of Jeffersonian classicism by the master builder John M. Perry, was erected in 1823–24 for William Cabell Rives, minister to France, U.S. senator, and Confederate congressman. Rives's granddaughter Amélie, wife of the Russian painter Prince Pierre Troubetzkoy, was a well-known novelist and playwright. She and her husband made Castle Hill their home in the early decades of this century. Castle Hill is noted for its landscaped grounds including its long front lawn lined with tree boxwood. 02–12 (11/16/71).

CHRIST EPISCOPAL CHURCH, GLENDOWER, *Keene vicinity.* The influence of Thomas Jefferson's interpretation of classical architecture is demonstrated in numerous Piedmont buildings erected by master carpenters and masons he had employed at the University of Virginia. No more charming example of the Jeffersonian idiom survives than this small but highly polished rural Episcopal church erected in 1831–32 in southern Albemarle County. Called by Bishop William Meade a "neat and excellent brick church," the building is the product of William B. Phillips, a Jeffersonian workman who designed and built a variety of houses and public buildings in his mentor's mode. A hallmark of Phillips's buildings is exquisite brickwork, especially conspicuous at Christ Church. 02–14 (3/2/71).

CLIFFSIDE, *Scottsville vicinity*. Cliffside, rising from a bluff overlooking the town of Scottsville, is a notable example of Piedmont Virginia Federal architecture. Profiting from Scottsville's rise to prosperity in the antebellum period as a canal and turnpike town, Gilly Lewis, a local doctor and millowner, built Cliffside as his residence in 1835. The house is set apart from the majority of Piedmont village buildings of the period by its large scale, robust exterior detailing, and well-preserved, boldly carved interior woodwork. In March 1865 Cliffside served as Gen. Philip Sheridan's headquarters during the Scottsville raid and also as the quarters of Gen. George A. Custer. 02–16 (10/20/81).

COBHAM PARK, *Cobham vicinity*. Established in the 1850s on land that was once part of Castle Hill, Cobham Park is one of the most beautifully sited and best-preserved antebellum estates in the Commonwealth. The grounds are laid out in the tradition of English romantic landscaping, with sloping lawns and clumps of trees informally arranged to make a pleasing composition. The property originally served as the summer home of William Cabell Rives, Jr., second son of William Cabell Rives of Castle Hill. The house, built ca. 1856, is an unusually early expression of the Georgian Revival, having the form and detailing of an 18th-century mansion. It was executed by an English carpenter named McSparren, initially employed in Albemarle County to fashion the interior of Grace Church in Cismont. 12–153 (1/15/74).

D. S. TAVERN, *Ivy vicinity*. Long a familiar landmark to travelers going west from Charlottesville, the D. S. Tavern is one of Albemarle County's few remaining early ordinaries and the only one in the region to preserve an original tap-bar cage. The tavern marks the site of the D. S. Tree and the zero milepost of the Three Notched Road, a principal artery from Richmond to the Shenandoah Valley in the 18th and 19th centuries. "D. S." probably stands for David Stockton, who blazed a trail from Williamsburg to the west and carved his initials on a tree where he and his partner separated. The log section of the tavern is believed to have been constructed as a claims house. This one-room structure evolved with additions into an ordinary and functioned as such from the late 18th century until 1850. Among its owners was Chief Justice John Marshall, who held title from 1810 to 1813. Although such establishments were once plentiful in Albemarle County, most have disappeared, many because of their vulnerable locations close to expanding highways. 02–231 (8/16/83).

EDGEHILL, *Shadwell vicinity.* Atop one of the rolling hills of eastern Albemarle County, in view of Monticello, Edgehill was the home of Thomas Jefferson Randolph, the favorite grandson of Thomas Jefferson, to whom Jefferson bequeathed his business and personal papers. The stately though conservative brick house was built for Randolph in 1828, his family having outgrown the 1799 frame house on the property built for his father, Thomas Mann Randolph, Jr., husband of Jefferson's daughter Martha. On the basis of its style and workmanship, the house is attributed to the University of Virginia builders William B. Phillips and Malcolm F. Crawford, who continued to employ Jeffersonian qualities in their work into the antebellum period. Such features found on Edgehill include the Tuscan porch with Chinese lattice railing and the Tuscan entablatures on the main part of the house. In 1836 Mrs. Thomas Jefferson Randolph opened a small school at Edgehill for her children and for those of relatives and friends. The school was enlarged by her daughters and continued as the Edgehill School until 1896. Although the house was gutted by fire in 1916, the exterior preserves its original appearance and the interior has been sympathetically rebuilt. The house today is the nucleus of one of Albemarle County's principal country estates. 02–26 (6/15/82).

EDGEMONT, *South Garden vicinity.* Edgemont was built ca. 1796 for James Powell Cocke, a justice of Henrico County who moved to Albemarle County in search of a more healthful climate. The house is an early example of a country residence in the hybrid French and Palladian style advocated by Thomas Jefferson for domestic architecture. Although its design has been credited to Jefferson for some years, precise documentation remains yet to be established. Whoever designed it, the very appealing composition exhibits the strong influence Jefferson's style had on his neighbors. What is otherwise a modest wooden dwelling achieves sophistication through the use of select siting, Tuscan porticoes, rusticated quoins, flush board siding, and carefully calculated proportions. The house stood neglected for many years and almost forgotten by architectural scholars. Charlottesville architect Milton Grigg directed the extensive restoration of Edgemont following its purchase in 1936 by Dr. Graham Clark. 02–87 (9/16/80).

EDNAM, *Charlottesville vicinity.* Designed by Richmond architect D. Wiley Anderson for Edwin O. Meyer, a New York importer, Ednam is an ambitious example of the early Colonial Revival style. With its stately portico, classical detailing, and elaborate interiors, the house, completed ca. 1905, presents a grandiose "Southern" image which was considered appropriate for its location. From the standpoint of social history, Ednam represents turn-of-the-century influx of northerners into Piedmont Virginia. Attracted by the scenic countryside and sociable life style, they purchased old estates or set up new ones, often building pretentious houses in the local idiom. 02–560 (12/16/80).

EMMANUEL EPISCOPAL CHURCH, *Greenwood vicinity.*
Since its founding in the mid-19th century, Emmanuel Episcopal Church has served parishioners living on western Albemarle County estates, among them the Langhorne family at
nearby Mirador. Nancy Langhorne, later Lady Astor, became
involved with the congregation's mission work in the early
20th century. In 1911, along with her brothers and sisters, she
commissioned Washington architect Waddy Wood to remodel
and enlarge the original one-room church. Wood's work at
Emmanuel Church exhibits the refinement and craftsmanship
associated with the best of early Colonial Revival buildings
02–399 (1/20/81).

ESMONT, *Esmont vicinity.* This classic example of a Jeffersonian country house was built between 1816 and 1820 for Dr.
Charles Cocke, nephew of James Powell Cocke of Edgemont
and distant cousin of John Hartwell Cocke of Bremo. Although Cocke corresponded with Jefferson, no documentation
has surfaced to indicate that the statesman-architect had a direct hand in the design. Nonetheless, the wooden Doric entablatures and stuccoed columns, gleaming white against red brick
walls accented with green louvered blinds, present Roman Revivalism as interpreted in local materials for local needs. Except
for the lengthening of the porch and the addition of a side
room, Esmont stands as built. Its interior preserves rich appointments, including a parquet hall floor, ornamental plaster
ceilings, Philadelphia marble mantels, English silver-plated
locks, and cut-glass door knobs. 02–30 (5/17/77).

ESTOUTEVILLE, *Keene vicinity.* Chief among the architectural works designed and built by Thomas Jefferson's workmen
is this grand country house, the creation of James Dinsmore, a
Philadelphia master builder who had worked for Jefferson at
both Monticello and the University of Virginia. The unusually
large dwelling, set off by a monumental Tuscan portico on each
front, was begun in 1827 and completed in 1830 for John Coles
III, member of a family that was building a number of substantial houses in the county. Working from ancient Roman precedent as interpreted in the books of Andrea Palladio, Dinsmore produced a masterpiece in what may be regarded as
America's first native academic style. Few buildings better
meet Jefferson's ideal of an architecturally refined seat suitable
for the young Republic's landed families or so well conform to
the popular image of a patrician southern homestead. 02–32
(4/19/77).

FARMINGTON, *Farmington Country Club, Charlottesville vicinity.* Thomas Jefferson designed the distinctive elongated octagonal wing of this Albemarle County home for his friend George Divers. Accented by a Tuscan portico and bull's-eye windows, the wing was completed in 1802 following Jefferson's drawings, preserved in the Massachusetts Historical Society. The earlier portion of the house, a typical late Georgian side-passage-plan dwelling, was erected before 1780 for Francis Jerdone. In 1927 the house, along with its extensive service buildings and some 350 acres of farmland, was sold to Farmington, Inc., a development company that converted the property into a country club. Although the house has received extensive additions, the original portion maintains its splendid setting and preserves much of its old flavor. 02–35 (7/7/70).

GRACE EPISCOPAL CHURCH, *Cismont.* This fine specimen of the early, more picturesque interpretation of the Gothic Revival is the only known Virginia work of William Strickland, one of the nation's leading architects of the first half of the 19th century. Strickland is better known for his monumental Greek Revival works such as the Tennessee Capitol; Grace Church is a comparatively rare example of his Gothic style. The church was commissioned by Mrs. William Cabell Rives of nearby Castle Hill. Strickland's drawings for the building are preserved in the Rives papers at the University of Virginia. The drawings were made in 1847 and the church was built soon after. The original interior woodwork, executed by an Englishman named McSparren, was destroyed by fire in 1895, but the church was soon rehabilitated with new roof and interior. Its walls and tower remain essentially as designed and continue to house an active congregation. 02–43 (2/17/76)

GUTHRIE HALL, *Esmont vicinity.* Guthrie Hall is perhaps the largest and most architecturally individual country mansion resulting from the influx of plutocrats into Albemarle County around the turn of the century. With its porticoes, loggias, quadrant wings, and curious wide arch framing the entrance, the massive rock-faced house combines Georgian Revival, Palladian, and rustic influences. Guthrie Hall was erected ca. 1901 for Scottish-born John Guthrie Hopkins, a self-made copper magnate who came to Virginia to pursue his hobby of restoring old houses. Hopkins apparently designed Guthrie Hall himself with the aid of a structural engineer. The estate boasted a bowling alley as well as a private railroad station. 02–355 (3/17/81).

MIDWAY, *Millington vicinity.* Nestled in the rolling hills of western Albemarle County with the Blue Ridge Mountains forming a backdrop, this rambling farmhouse is an element of the undulating countryside for which the county is so famous. The dwelling's two-level gallery, stepped parapets, and superb brickwork are all features common to the region's early vernacular architecture. The facade brickwork preserves its red paint and penciled, or white-painted, joints. Although the construction dates of the various sections are uncertain, no part of the house appears older than the early decades of the 19th century. The property was originally part of a large colonial grant to the Rodes family. Hemp, flax, and tobacco in addition to the usual crops were grown on the property by the Rodes. A formal garden to the side of the house was laid out in 1936 by landscape architect Charles Gillette. 02–143 (9/19/78).

MILLER SCHOOL OF ALBEMARLE, *Batesville vicinity.* Miller School's complex of High Victorian Gothic buildings was provided through the 1869 will of Samuel Miller (1792–1869) to house a charitable institution for the children of Albemarle's poor. Miller was born into poverty in Albemarle County and made a fortune in the tobacco and grocery business in Lynchburg. The school, developed on one of Miller's farms, pioneered in industrial education with special emphasis on manual labor. The architectural focal point of the group, Main Building, was begun in 1874. Its designers were Albert Lybrock and D. Wiley Anderson of Richmond, who created a grand statement in the weighty, richly ornamented Gothic style popularized by the English critic John Ruskin. It and most of the other early buildings were erected under the supervision of C. E. Vawter, the school's first superintendent. Still a viable institution, Miller School continues to stress the rewards of the industrial arts and manual labor. 02–174 (4/17/73).

MIRADOR, *Greenwood vicinity.* The Albemarle County estate Mirador was the childhood home of Viscountess Astor, the first woman member of Parliament. Born Nancy Witcher Langhorne, she came with her family to the estate in 1892 at the age of twelve. She lived there intermittently through her first marriage and afterward, until she moved to England upon her marriage to Waldorf Astor in 1906. Throughout her long, eventful life, Lady Astor maintained great pride in her Virginia origins and returned to Mirador for frequent visits. Mirador is also associated with Lady Astor's beautiful sister Irene, wife of illustrator Charles Dana Gibson and prototype of his fashionable "Gibson Girl" of the 1890s. The mansion today is largely the product of an extensive remodeling undertaken for Lady Astor's niece Nancy Perkins and her husband Ronald Tree in the 1920s by New York architect William Adams Delano. Employing many Georgian motifs, Delano transformed the refined Federal plantation house into one of Virginia's more grandly appointed country homes of the period. 02–100 (9/16/82).

MONTICELLO, *Charlottesville vicinity.* There is no more admired or intriguing home in America than Thomas Jefferson's Monticello. Reflecting the genius and versatility of its creator, the estate is a monument to the most scrupulous contemporary thought in the fields of architecture, landscaping, agriculture, and domestic comforts. The house, fortuitously preserved with few significant changes, is filled with ingenious devices and mementos of a man who influenced much of the history of the nation and indeed the world. Jefferson began his complex dwelling on the "Little Mountain" in 1770 and worked on it for over forty years, altering and enlarging it as his taste developed. Before 1793 the house had a tripartite form employing a porticoed two-storied center section flanked by lower wings, a scheme which Jefferson likely derived from Palladian villas as well as illustrations in contemporary pattern books such as Robert Morris's *Select Architecture* (1755). When an extensive revision was finished in 1809, it had become an amalgam of Roman, Palladian, and French architectural ideals, all rendered in native materials and scale to form a unique statement by one of history's great individuals. The Thomas Jefferson Memorial Foundation has maintained Monticello as a place of pilgrimage for hundreds of thousands since 1923. 02–50 (9/9/69); *National Historic Landmark.*

MORVEN, *Simeon vicinity.* Morven was originally part of a large grant made to William Champe Carter. In 1796 it was purchased by William Short, who served as Thomas Jefferson's secretary in France and later as minister to the Netherlands. Short's modest frame house is now the office for the present brick house, built in 1821 by Martin Thacker for the planter David Higginbotham, also a friend of Jefferson. This handsomely detailed five-bay structure, fronted by a dwarf Tuscan portico, combines late Georgian with Roman Revival overtones. It is sited to take advantage of views of the surrounding countryside. To one side is an extensive early formal garden. In 1926 Morven was purchased by Mr. and Mrs. Charles A. Stone, who established a thoroughbred stud farm on the estate. Mrs. Stone directed the restoration of the garden in 1930. 02–54 (2/20/73).

MOUNTAIN GROVE, *Esmont vicinity.* Mountain Grove shares with other Piedmont homes of Palladian tripartite design an architectural tradition which was derived from 18th-century English pattern books. Built on Green Mountain in 1803–4 for Benjamin Harris, an Albemarle County soldier and magistrate, the house is reminiscent of Jefferson's earliest designs for Monticello and reflects the sophistication of its builder in abandoning the usual standard Georgian plan for the more distinctive three-part scheme. The high quality of its brickwork and joinery and the interior decoration by an unknown folk painter demonstrate the availability of skilled craftsmen in the area in the early 19th century. 02–95 (5/20/80).

PLAIN DEALING, *Keene vicinity.* Few of Albemarle County's old estates can match Plain Dealing in architectural interest and pastoral beauty. Similar in plan to Tuckahoe in Goochland County, the main portion of the two-part house was built soon after 1787 for Samuel Dyer, a merchant and planter. Dyer named the estate after a motto affixed to his store located nearby. The interior woodwork, especially that of the parlor with its arched closets, pedimented chimneypiece, and stop-fluted pilasters, ranks with the most elaborate examples of late Georgian trim in the region. The Wilmer family, who owned Plain Dealing from 1855 to the mid 1930s, entertained such visitors as Robert E. Lee and Theodore Roosevelt here. From 1944 to 1949 Plain Dealing was the home of Princess Djordjadze (born Audrey Emery), who was previously married to Grand Duke Dmitri of Russia, one of the assassins of the monk Rasputin. 02–65 (5/17/77).

REDLANDS, *Carters Bridge vicinity.* Of the numerous Piedmont estates owned by the Carter family during the colonial period, only Redlands remains in the possession of descendants bearing the name. The original holding of 9,350 acres was granted to John Carter, secretary of the colony and son of Robert ("King") Carter. The late Georgian mansion at Redlands today was begun ca. 1798 for Robert Carter on a site carefully chosen for its views. The house was erected under the direction of builder Martin Thacker. Its stately but restrained exterior, changed only by the 20th–century addition of dormers, contrasts with the rich interior. The lofty oval-ended drawing room, one of the finest of the period, is ornamented with festive garlanded cornices, overdoors, and mantel. 02–67 (9/9/69).

SCOTTSVILLE HISTORIC DISTRICT, *Scottsville.* Albemarle's river town traces its origins to 1732 when Edward Scott, a Goochland burgess, patented 550 acres on a hill just west of the future town. Nearby, in the great horseshoe bend of the James, a small settlement sprang up and became known as Scott's Landing and, later, Scottsville. The community prospered, reaching its apogee in the early decades of the 19th century with the heavy influx of commerce resulting from construction of the James River and Kanawha Canal. Scottsville soon became one of the state's largest flour markets. The town's decline began in 1865 when Gen. Philip Sheridan and his 10,000 Union troops pillaged the place, wrecking the canal and destroying nearly all the commercial buildings. Scottsville never really recovered, and because of its stymied growth the character of the early river town was preserved. Some 100 old buildings remain, almost half dating to before the Civil War, including several Classical Revival churches and a broad range of vernacular houses. Shown is the former Scottsville Christian Church, built in 1846 and now serving as the Scottsville Museum. Next door is the home of James T. Barclay, the church's first minister. Although further devastated in recent years by fire and floods, Scottsville continues to maintain a historic ambience. 298–24 (4/20/76).

SHACK MOUNTAIN, *Charlottesville vicinity.* Shack Mountain is regarded as the principal architectural work of Sidney Fiske Kimball (1881–1955), the most noted of America's first generation of architectural historians. This gemlike Jeffersonian-style pavilion was built in 1935–36 as Kimball's retirement home. Kimball is credited with nurturing a scholarly interest in American buildings and promoting Thomas Jefferson as a major figure in the nation's early architectural development. He is also remembered as the founder of the University of Virginia School of Architecture and as a pioneer in the restoration of historic landmarks, taking an active role in such projects as Colonial Williamsburg, Monticello, Stratford, Gunston Hall, and numerous National Park Service properties. As an art historian he gained fame from serving as director for many years of the Philadelphia Museum of Art. Kimball wanted Shack Mountain, with its Jeffersonian format, to demonstrate the viability of a regional architectural tradition. 02–200 (6/15/76).

SPRING HILL, *Ivy vicinity.* Spring Hill is a fine example of an early Piedmont farm complex, illustrating the integration of vernacular and academic architectural traditions. The main house began in the late 18th century as a brick cottage of probably no more than two rooms and evolved to its present irregular form through a series of alterations and additions including an early 19th–century frame wing. The hilltop property includes a later 18th–century brick servants' house as well as a dairy and kitchen. Its owners have included Michael Woods, one of the first settlers on the eastern slope of the Blue Ridge; Clifton Rodes, a county magistrate and brother-in-law of Jack Jouett; Thomas Wells, proprietor of the Eagle Tavern of Charlottesville and a trustee appointed in 1814 (with Thomas Jefferson) to oversee the founding of the Albemarle Academy; and Charles Harper, cofounder of Charlottesville's first circulating library. 02–140 (4/19/83).

SUNNY BANK, *South Garden vicinity.* This Albemarle County farm possesses a residence begun ca. 1797 as an imposing if somewhat provincial version of the Palladian tripartite scheme introduced to the region with the first form of Monticello. Its intended outline was obscured when the wings were raised to two stories. The original two-level portico reflects the provincial character by employing posts rather than columns. Like many of the county's old houses, it occupies a carefully selected site commanding panoramic views. On the property are preserved several original outbuildings and a formal garden. The first occupant of Sunny Bank was Andrew Hart, son of a Scottish clergyman, who became an Albemarle County planter and merchant. The property has remained in the ownership of the family to the present. 02–96 (4/20/76).

CITY OF ALEXANDRIA

*Named for John Alexander, an early owner of the tract on which
the town was located, this Potomac River port was established
in 1749. It was incorporated as a town in 1779 and as a
city in 1852. From 1801 until 1846, when it was returned to
Virginia, Alexandria was part of the District of Columbia.*

ALEXANDRIA CANAL TIDE LOCK ARCHAEOLOGI-CAL SITE, *bounded by Potomac River and Lee, Montgomery, and First streets.* The seven-mile-long Alexandria Canal system linking Alexandria to Georgetown was begun in 1834 and completed in 1843. The canal's tide lock no. 4 and adjacent holding basin, the only remaining portions of the city's canal system, are important to Virginia industrial archaeology, as they are part of a waterway that helped to bring on the economic rebirth of Alexandria in the mid-19th century. The canal, which remained in operation until 1886, connected Alexandria with the Chesapeake and Ohio Canal running inland to Cumberland, Md., and was used largely for the transportation of coal. The basin (shown) has since been filled in but is otherwise intact. 100–99 (11/20/79).

ALEXANDRIA CITY HALL, *Cameron Street between North Royal and North Fairfax streets.* One of the state's best examples of the Second Empire style is the dark red brick Alexandria City Hall, designed in 1871 by Washington architect Adolph Cluss. Dominated by its central pavilion with its massive square dome, the elongated composition is inspired by the Louvre in Paris. The building occupies the site of the earlier city hall of 1817, designed by Benjamin Henry Latrobe and destroyed by fire in 1871. On the Royal Street facade, Cluss provided a clock tower with spire based on the clock tower that had graced Latrobe's city hall. As originally built, the present building was U-shaped, with town offices on the upper floors and market stalls on the ground floor. The market stalls have been removed, and the building now functions exclusively as city offices. The interior has undergone numerous remodelings, the last in 1983, but the main facades of the exterior remain without significant alteration. 100–126 (11/15/83).

ALEXANDRIA HISTORIC DISTRICT, *Old Town Alexandria.* Alexandria was established in 1749, and the town was laid off in a uniform grid plan. It quickly became the principal seaport of Northern Virginia, witnessing the construction of numerous mansions, town houses, churches, and commercial buildings. Surviving in the nearly one hundred blocks of the city's historic core is the largest concentration of 18th- and 19th-century urban architecture in the state, constituting one of the finest historic cityscapes in the nation. Especially important are the district's many Federal town houses, including the boyhood home of Robert E. Lee (1785), the Benjamin Dulany house (1780s), the Yeaton-Fairfax house (ca. 1800), and the grand row of 18th-century dwellings in the 200 block of Prince Street. The 100 block of Prince Street, containing a row of Federal town houses known as Captain's Row, (shown) preserves its original cobblestone surface. The numerous early commercial buildings and warehouses along lower King Street are a remarkable survival as well. All this old fabric is still standing because Alexandria suffered a decline following the Civil War. Its excellent condition today has been achieved through a variety of preservation efforts, both public and private, the first ones begun over fifty years ago. 100–121 (11/5/68); *National Historic Landmark.*

BANK OF ALEXANDRIA, *North Fairfax and Cameron streets.* One of the largest surviving early bank buildings in the country, the Bank of Alexandria was built in 1803–7. The bank company was established in 1792 with George Washington among its charter stockholders. After the bank failed in 1834, the building was used first as a post office, then as a hotel wing, later as a Union hospital, and finally as an apartment house. Despite its changes in function, the building has survived with a surprising amount of original fabric. The exterior is embellished with Flemish bond brickwork and stone trim, including a stone-arched entry and a carved stone cornice. The first floor retains the Adam-style window casings, doors, and mantels. The building underwent an extensive restoration in the late 1970s and has been returned to use as a bank with apartments occupying the cashier's quarters on the upper floors. 100–4 (4/17/73).

CARLYLE HOUSE, *121 North Fairfax Street*. Alexandria's prominent mid-Georgian mansion was completed by 1753 for John Carlyle, a Scottish merchant who was one of the original incorporators of the city. Like many Scottish houses of the period, the Carlyle house is built of stone and employs a somewhat austere classicism. In Carlyle's large parlor Gen. Edward Braddock met with the governors of five colonies on April 14, 1755, to plan the early campaigns against the French and the Indians. Located in the heart of the city, the house was long obscured from view by a hotel built across its front. Demolition of the hotel and restoration of the house as a museum were undertaken as a Bicentennial project by the Northern Virginia Regional Park Authority. 100–10 (5/13/69).

CHRIST CHURCH, *North Columbus and Cameron streets*. In the heart of downtown Alexandria, surrounded by its old churchyard, Christ Church was erected in 1767–73 from plans prepared by James Wren, one of colonial Virginia's few identified architects. The Georgian building employs a two-story rectangular format. Aquia Creek stone quoins and keystones, now painted, highlight the exterior. On the inside is much early woodwork, including the tablets and some original pews. The lower story of the four-tier bell tower was added in 1785, and the rest was put on in 1818. George Washington frequently attended services at Christ Church, and Robert E. Lee worshiped here in 1861, just before journeying to Richmond to accept command of the Army of Northern Virginia. 100–12 (9/18/73); *National Historic Landmark*.

FORT WARD, *4301 West Braddock Road.* Fort Ward formed one of the strongest links in a chain of sixty-eight forts and batteries erected between 1861 and 1865 by the U.S. Army Corps of Engineers for the protection of the nation's capital . Guarding the approaches to Alexandria from the west and northwest on an elevated site four miles west of the city, the star-shaped earthwork was the fifth largest fort in the system, with a perimeter of 818 yards, holding thirty-six gun emplacements and as many as 1,200 troops. During the Civil War Centennial, the city of Alexandria restored the northwest bastion and cleared both the perimeter and the outlying gun battery and rifle trench. Fort Ward today serves as a forty-acre historic park and museum. 100—113 (12/15/81).

FRANKLIN AND ARMFIELD OFFICE, *1315 Duke Street.* From this three-story structure on Duke Street, one of the largest slave trades in the South was operated. The Franklin and Armfield partnership was established in 1828 and continued in the slave trade until 1836 when Isaac Franklin withdrew from active involvement. At its peak, the firm had agents in almost every southern city, owned a fleet of sailing ships, and trafficked in thousands of slaves annually. The office was built ca. 1812 as a house for Robert Young, a brigadier general in the District of Columbia militia. While it was occupied by Franklin and Armfield, slave pens were built in the yard. The building continued to serve the slave trade through subsequent owners until 1861 when it was taken over by Union authorities and used as a prison. The slave pens were removed in the 1870s after the house was acquired by Thomas Swann, who added the mansard roof and modified the windows. 100—105 (10/16/79); *National Historic Landmark.*

GADSBY'S TAVERN, *Royal and Cameron streets.* This tavern in its heyday hosted some of the most noted figures of the early Republic. The large three-story section, the ultimate in elegance and comfort for its time, was opened by John Wise in 1792. The earlier two-story dormered section, a finely detailed example of the Georgian style, dates from 1770. The establishment was operated by John Gadsby from 1796 until 1808, during which period the tavern achieved its greatest renown. Although the ballroom woodwork is now in the Metropolitan Museum of Art in New York City, the rest of the two-building complex survives without significant alteration. Handsomely restored in the 1970s, the property is now owned by the city and is operated as a museum and restaurant. 100—29 (9/9/69); *National Historic Landmark.*

JONES POINT LIGHTHOUSE AND DISTRICT OF COLUMBIA SOUTH CORNERSTONE, *Jones Point Park*. The almost cottagelike Jones Point Lighthouse was an expression of federal concern for the improvement of inland navigation in the first half of the 19th century. Built in 1855, the plain weatherboarded structure with its light straddling its gable roof aided Potomac River shipping for seventy years. Next to the lighthouse is the south cornerstone of the District of Columbia. One of the oldest artifacts related to the nation's capital, the stone marks the origin of the 1791 survey that carved the District of Columbia from the states of Virginia and Maryland and originally included the city of Alexandria. The cornerstone marked the district's southernmost point until 1846 when its Virginia portions were returned to the Commonwealth. 100–116 (3/18/80).

LEE-FENDALL HOUSE, *Oronoco and Washington streets*. The Lee-Fendall house is a three-bay, two-and-a-half-story town house erected in 1785 and remodeled in the Greek Revival style in 1850–52. Built as the residence of Philip Richard and Elizabeth Lee Fendall, it is the earliest of several neighboring houses in Old Town Alexandria occupied by members of Lee family. Labor leader John L. Lewis, long head of the United Mine Workers, made his home here from 1937 until his death in 1969. The property is now operated as a historic house museum by the Virginia Trust for Historic Preservation. 100–24 (4/17/79).

LLOYD HOUSE, *220 North Washington Street*. Its formal proportions, Flemish bond brickwork, and refined detailing make this Washington Street house one of Alexandria's most elegant examples of late Georgian architecture. John Wise, a local businessman, built the house ca. 1797 and sold it in 1810 to Jacob Hoffman, one of the city's mayors. Local educator Benjamin Hallowell operated a school in the house from 1826 to 1828. In 1832 it was sold to John Lloyd, whose family owned it until 1918. The house was twice saved from demolition and in 1968 was acquired by the city for preservation. It has since been restored for use by the city library as a repository for special historical collections. 100–90 (2/17/76).

THE LYCEUM, *201 South Washington Street*. The Lyceum was organized under the direction of Benjamin Hallowell as a scholarly society for the citizens of Alexandria. This group and members of the Alexandria Library Company erected this headquarters in 1838 at Washington and Prince streets, one of the city's principal intersections. Alluding to the scholarship of the ancient Greeks, the building appropriately was built in the Greek Revival style, its facade dominated by a Doric portico. The building housed a large lecture hall, a museum, and a library. Attracting such speakers as John Quincy Adams and Caleb Cushing, the Lyceum was a flourishing institution until the Civil War. After the war the Lyceum was dissolved, and the building was converted into a residence. Threatened with demolition in 1969, it was purchased by the city for conversion into a visitor's center and museum. To echo the building's former role, a large lecture hall was provided in the location of the original on the second floor. The restoration was completed in 1974. 100–91 (5/13/69).

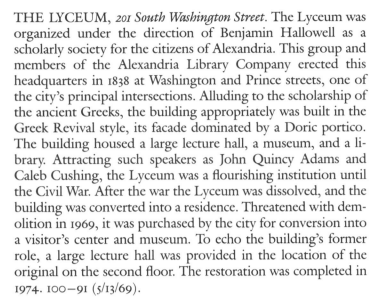

OLD DOMINION BANK BUILDING (THE ATHENAEUM), *201 Prince Street*. The Old Dominion Bank was incorporated in 1851 to serve various businesses connected with Alexandria's port. The bank's temple-form headquarters, conveniently located among the homes of the city's leading merchants, served its original function until 1907. Converted to a warehouse and later a church, the building has been restored as an exhibition gallery for the Northern Virginia Fine Arts Association and has been renamed the Athenaeum. The compact structure is a superlative application of the Greek Revival style to a commercial building. 100–2 (11/20/79).

PROTESTANT EPISCOPAL THEOLOGICAL SEMINARY IN VIRGINIA (VIRGINIA THEOLOGICAL SEMINARY), *3737 Seminary Road*. Virginia's Episcopal theological seminary, established in 1823, acquired its site on a ridge overlooking the Potomac River valley and downtown Alexandria in 1827. Its growth over subsequent decades is represented by several Victorian buildings; chief among them is Aspinwall Hall of 1859, a major example of American mid-19th-century institutional work, designed by Baltimore architect Norris G. Starkweather. For its exterior, Starkweather blended elements of the Italianate and Romanesque styles into a wholly original and imposing composition topped by a fanciful multitiered wooden cupola. Adjacent to Aspinwall Hall is Immanuel Chapel of 1881, an expression of the richly ornamented Ruskinian or High Victorian Gothic mode designed by Charles E. Cassell of Baltimore. The seminary grounds retain elements of a romantically landscaped park designed by Andrew Jackson Downing, his only documented Virginia work. 100–123 (5/16/78).

STABLER-LEADBEATER APOTHECARY, *105–107 South Fairfax Street*. The Stabler-Leadbeater Apothecary is among the oldest preserved apothecaries in the United States and is the only apothecary in Virginia that operated continuously from the 18th into the 20th century. Built ca. 1775 and adapted for use as an apothecary shop by Edward Stabler in 1792, the building's exterior displays the usual straightforward quality of Alexandria's late 18th-century architecture. However, its fanciful Gothic Revival shelves and counters, added in the mid-19th century, are an outstanding example of the use of the style for a shop interior. Among the early patrons of the apothecary was Martha Washington. Robert E. Lee happened to be in the shop when he was presented with orders from the War Department to proceed to Harper's Ferry to quell John Brown's insurrection. The apothecary closed in 1933, and the building along with many artifacts and records was purchased for preservation by the Landmarks Society of Alexandria. 100–106 (3/17/81).

ALLEGHANY COUNTY

Named for the Allegheny Mountains which pass through the county, Alleghany County was formed from Bath, Botetourt, and Monroe (now in West Virginia) counties in 1822, with other parts of Monroe and Bath counties added later. The county seat is Covington.

CLIFTON FURNACE, *Clifton Forge vicinity.* Located in Rainbow Gap, one of the Commonwealth's outstanding natural formations, Clifton Furnace was a major center of ironmaking, a principal industry of mid-19th-century Virginia. The site was in operation as early as 1822, and the present cold-blast charcoal furnace, a stone structure tapering in a gentle curve toward the top, was erected in 1846 by William Lyle Alexander, the forge's owner. The furnace went out of blast in 1854, although iron production continued at the site until it was completely abandoned in 1877. The stone furnace, now owned by the Virginia Department of Highways and Transportation, is the only remaining relic of this once-busy place. The nearby city of Clifton Forge, originally called Williamson's Station, takes its name from this early industrial site. 03–19 (2/15/77).

HUMPBACK BRIDGE, *Callaghan vicinity.* Humpback Bridge is the nation's only surviving curved-span covered bridge and is the oldest covered bridge in Virginia. Constructed in 1835 across Dunlap Creek, it was part of the James River and Kanawha Valley Turnpike, the principal highway of western Virginia. The bridge is the handiwork of a Mr. Venable, a contractor from Lewisburg, W.Va., who built three such bridges. The 100-foot span has no middle support, and the center point of the floor and roof is eight feet higher than the ends, giving the bridge its distinctive hump. The bridge was closed to vehicular traffic in 1953 and is now the focal point of a scenic wayside maintained by the Virginia Department of Highways and Transportation. 03–2 (11/5/68).

MASSIE HOUSE, *Falling Spring vicinity.* In Falling Spring Valley, with a backdrop of wooded mountains, the Massie house is Alleghany County's chief example of the Federal style and is probably the area's oldest formal dwelling. The two-story house with pedimented gables was completed in 1826 for Henry Massie, a planter who served as one of Alleghany's first magistrates. The decorative fanlight entrance incorporates Massie's initials in its tracery. Its interior woodwork consists of a finely executed stair, cupboards, mantels, and wainscoting. Although still owned by the Massie family, the house is unoccupied and deteriorating. 03–11 (12/16/80).

MILTON HALL, *Callaghan vicinity.* Nestled among the mountains in a remote corner of western Virginia, Milton Hall stands as an expression of the renewed British interest in New World real estate, especially in the southern states, in the years just after the Civil War. This distinctly English-looking Gothic villa was erected in 1874 for William Wentworth Fitzwilliam, Viscount Milton, whose wife brought him to Alleghany County for his health. Presenting an exotic contrast to its surroundings, Milton Hall was a late use of the Gothic Revival mode, illustrating the lingering popularity of the style among the British after it passed from fashion for rural residences in this country. 03–8 (1/20/81).

OAKLAND GROVE PRESBYTERIAN CHURCH, *Selma vicinity*. Oakland Grove Presbyterian Church, built ca. 1847, is the oldest known ecclesiastical structure in Alleghany County. The well-crafted but plain brick building is a small, mid-19th-century country church that has survived with few alterations. The church was organized during the religious reawakening that occurred in the 1840s among Scotch-Irish Presbyterian settlers in the mountainous region of the state. It was erected as a mission of the Covington Presbyterian Church and served as a Confederate hospital during the Civil War. 03–4 (12/16/80).

PERSINGER HOUSE, *Covington vicinity*. One of the earliest of Alleghany County's pioneer dwellings, this house was built by Jacob Persinger, member of a settler family. Persinger as a child was captured by the Indians and later adopted an Indian-style life. After he married Mary Kimberlin in 1778, she refused to live in a tepee so he built her the present house, reported to be the finest in the county at the time. The house was enlarged to its present form ca. 1888. The original log section is an interesting vernacular structure retaining numerous original features including a finely joined vertical board partition with beveled joints. It has a hall-parlor plan, a standard one for 18th-century Virginia vernacular dwellings. 03–18 (12/16/80).

SWEET CHALYBEATE SPRINGS, *Sweet Chalybeate*. Sweet Chalybeate is a relic of the 19th-century days when the fasionable world of the North and South came to the spas of western Virginia to "take the waters and play the marriage market." Known since the 18th century, these springs were developed in 1836 into a commercial resort which lasted until 1918. The relatively complete collection of wooden pavilions and cottages, dating from the mid- and late 19th century, attests to the popularity of the resort and provides a remarkably undisturbed picture of a Virginia spa. The springs themselves, claimed to contain the strongest carbonated mineral waters in the nation, still flow freely from the limestone bluff and form pools among the foundations of the bathhouses. Chalybeate is a type of mineral water impregnated with salts of iron. 03–7 (10/16/73).

AMELIA COUNTY

*Formed from Prince George and Brunswick counties in 1734,
this southern Piedmont county was named for Princess
Amelia Sophia Eleanora, daughter of King George II.
The county seat is Amelia.*

EGGLESTETTON, *Chula vicinity.* This medium-size plantation house, dominated by a broad gambrel roof, is an example of colonial domestic architecture in the Virginia idiom and is typical of the type of house occupied by the gentry of the region. The interior boasts unusually fine paneled walls and other ornamental details, all in a good state of preservation. The property was owned by the Eggleston family as early as 1747; the present house was built before the 1770s for Joseph Eggleston, Jr., who served as a major in the Continental army and was later elected to Congress. An inventory taken at his death shows that Eggleston maintained a substantial library at Egglestetton. 04–5 (6/17/75).

FARMER HOUSE, *Deatonville vicinity.* Dating from the early 1820s, the Farmer house is a large wood-frame I-house probably erected for Nelson Farmer. Characterized by a center-passage, single-pile plan, the I-house was a popular form of two-story house design for comfortably situated but not wealthy planters of middle Virginia. The form was derived from the symmetrical 18-century Georgian style and spread through the South and Middle West in the 19th century. The Farmer house stands out from numerous contemporaries because it preserves nearly all of its original fabric, including beaded weatherboards, front porch, stair, Federal mantels, and other trim. The tall chimneys show the high level of workmanship achieved by the region's masons. 04–43 (4/18/78).

HAW BRANCH, *Amelia vicinity.* This outstanding example of Southside Virginia Federal architecture, the finest plantation house in the county, received its present form in the early 19th century under its owner John Tabb, whose family had owned the plantation since 1743. The name was derived from the nearby stream lined with hawthorne trees. The most striking feature of the house is its elaborate interior woodwork carved with provincially interpreted Adamesque motifs, including urns, swags, consoles, and sunbursts. Haw Branch passed by inheritance to Harriet Barksdale Mason, wife of John Young Mason, who served in the cabinet of the Tyler and Polk administrations. The Haw Branch grounds preserve a row of early outbuildings, all with clipped gable roofs. 04–2 (10/17/72).

ST. JOHN'S EPISCOPAL CHURCH, GRUB HILL, *Chula vicinity.* Consecrated in 1852 by Bishop William Meade, this church was part of the reactivation of the Episcopal denomination in rural Virginia during the mid-19th century. It is built on the site of a colonial church known simply as Grub Hill Church, a name derived from the "Grub Hill" slave quarters of the Tabb family, who gave the land for the building. The present church is a simplified expression of the Gothic Revival, which had become widely popular for ecclesiastical architecture by the middle of the century. The church is relatively unaltered and still stands in an unspoiled rural setting. The principal interior furnishings, including an elaborate triptych, are the signed work of a woodcarver, H. Jacob, completed in 1870. Owned by the trustees of Christ Episcopal Church, Amelia, St. John's is used for occasional summer services. 04–7 (4/18/78).

WIGWAM, *Chula vicinity.* Wigwam was the home of William Branch Giles (1762–1830), who served Virginia in both the U.S. House of Representatives and the U.S. Senate and was elected governor in 1827. Giles was also a member of the convention that revised the Virginia constitution in 1830. His Amelia County seat preserves its two-part dwelling, the original portion of which is the 18th-century rear ell. The one-and-a-half-story front section was added in the early 19th century and contains individualized Federal woodwork with no parallels in the region. The house stood derelict for many years but survived without significant alteration. It recently has undergone a careful rehabilitation. 04–3 (5/13/69).

AMHERST COUNTY

Named for Maj. Gen. Sir Jeffrey Amherst, British commander in North America during the latter part of the French and Indian War and governor of the Virginia colony from 1759 to 1768, this central Piedmont county was formed from Albemarle County in 1761. Its county seat is Amherst.

GEDDES, *Clifford vicinity.* The oldest portion of this example of Piedmont vernacular architecture was built ca. 1762 for Hugh Rose, the third son of Anglican clergyman and diarist Robert Rose, with whom the house is traditionally associated. A militia colonel who represented Amherst County both in the field and in the General Assembly during the Revolution, Hugh Rose is best remembered as the friend of Thomas Jefferson who sheltered Jefferson's family after the British raid on Charlottesville. The unusual form of the house, created by the early 19-century addition of the hall and two west rooms, was the work of Rose descendants, who have continued to own the property to the present. 05–7 (10/19/82).

RED HILL, *Pedlar Mills vicinity.* The finest specimen of the Federal style in Amherst County was built from profits amassed by Charles Ellis through various mercantile ventures. Ellis, whose family had owned the property since the 1750s, formed a lucrative partnership with Richmond businessman John Allan, foster father of Edgar Allan Poe. Completed in 1825, Red Hill was the home of Charles Ellis's younger brother, Richard Shelton Ellis, who stayed in Amherst to manage the family properties, although Charles used the place as a summer home. The Adamesque detailing, finely executed spiral stair, and formality of the spacious plan show that the Ellises were familiar with the town houses then being erected in Richmond and adapted those sophisticated forms for their country seat. From 1869 to 1898 Red Hill was owned by the Presbyterian preacher/architect Robert Lewis Dabney. The 20th-century front portico replaced an earlier porch. 05–14 (3/18/80).

SWEET BRIAR, *Sweet Briar College.* Elijah Fletcher, publisher of the Lynchburg *Virginian* and mayor of the city, purchased this early 19th-century Amherst County farmhouse in 1830 to serve as a weekend retreat. His wife changed its name to Sweet Briar for the abundance of wild roses on the property. In 1851 Fletcher began a remodeling which transformed the plain Federal house into a major expression of the Italian Villa style. To the ends of the house were added solid, square towers connected across the facade by a veranda with a two-tiered arcaded portico. The designer of the remodeling is unknown, although it may have been the inspiration of Fletcher's daughter, Indiana, whom Fletcher credited with the project. Indiana Fletcher Williams, who was left the place by her father, directed in her will that her estate, including the house and the plantation, were to provide for the establishment of a school for young women. Sweet Briar College thus received its charter in 1901. The house, still filled with Fletcher possessions, has served since as the home of the president of this well-known women's college. 05–18 (7/7/70).

WINTON, *Clifford.* This late Georgian farmhouse was built in the 1770s for Joseph Cabell, who served with distinction as an officer in the Revolutionary War and was elected to various public offices. Cabell sold Winton in 1779 to Samuel Meredith, who likewise was a distinguished military and civic leader. Meredith was married to Patrick Henry's sister and brought the patriot's mother, Sarah Winston Syme Henry, to live at Winton. Mrs. Henry died at Winton in 1784 and was buried in the cemetery here. The house received its portico and entablature when its exterior was remodeled in the early 20th century. The interior, however, preserves its early robust woodwork, whose outstanding feature is the drawing room chimneypiece decorated with pilasters and pediment. 05–21 (11/20/73).

APPOMATTOX COUNTY

This rural central Virginia county, where Lee surrendered to Grant, was formed in 1845 from parts of Buckingham, Prince Edward, Charlotte, and Campbell counties. It was named for the Appomattox River, which rises in the county. The name is derived from an Indian tribe which lived near the river's mouth. The county seat is Appomattox.

APPOMATTOX COURT HOUSE NATIONAL HISTORIC PARK, *Old Appomattox Court House.* At the remote little settlement of Appomattox Court House, the "drama played in the twilight" ended on Palm Sunday, 1865. After four years of bloodshed, heroism, and extraordinary military ingenuity, Gen. Robert E. Lee, his retreat blocked, surrendered the Army of Northern Virginia to Gen. Ulysses S. Grant. Although other Confederate forces had yet to admit defeat, Lee's capitulation in effect ended the Civil War. The two commanders met in the house of Wilmer McLean where Lee accepted Grant's generous surrender terms. After the surrender and the removal of the county seat to a new location, the village dwindled and almost vanished. The courthouse was destroyed, and the McLean house was taken down for exhibition at a world's fair. Through the efforts of the National Park Service, the village has been restored and the most important lost buildings have been reconstructed. The complex, including some 900 acres of battlefield, is now maintained as a museum and memorial to the moment that reunited the nation. 06–33 (7/6/71).

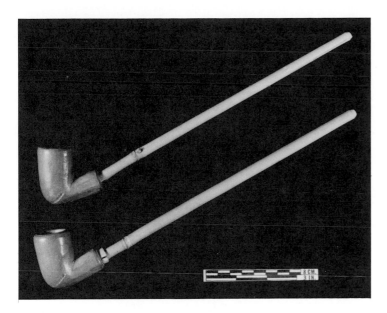

PAMPLIN PIPE FACTORY, *Pamplin*. At one time the largest clay pipe factory in America, supplying a national and international market with one million pipes a month as late as 1935, the Pamplin Pipe Factory preserves not only its kiln and chimney but the archaeological remains of several consecutive periods of clay pipe manufacture. Clay pipes were made here on a regular commercial basis until the factory closed in 1952. Further study and excavation of the facility promises to reveal information on the evolution of pipe-manufacturing technology. It also may determine whether there is truth in the folk tradition that pipe making occurred on the site as early as the European-aboriginal contact period. 277–2 (6/17/80).

ARLINGTON COUNTY

The smallest of Virginia's counties and now almost completely urbanized, Arlington County was first known as Alexandria County and was established in 1847 from that part of the District of Columbia that was ceded back to Virginia in 1846. Before being ceded to the federal government in 1791, the area was part of Fairfax County. The present name, given in 1920, honors Arlington, the Custis-Lee family estate, now the Arlington National Cemetery. The county seat is Arlington.

ARLINGTON HOUSE, THE ROBERT E. LEE MEMORIAL, *Arlington National Cemetery*. This columned mansion overlooking the nation's capital was built to serve a 1,100-acre plantation. Arlington House is best remembered as the home for thirty years of Confederate general Robert E. Lee, from the time of his marriage to Mary Custis until the property was confiscated by the federal government during the Civil War. The house was begun in 1803 for Mary Custis Lee's father, George Washington Parke Custis, step-grandson of George Washington. Only the wings were built at first; the center section was not completed until 1818. The resulting building, designed by George Hadfield, second architect of the U.S. Capitol, is an architectural masterpiece. No other of the nation's domestic works in the Greek Revival style conveys such a feeling of strength and boldness or so effectively dominates its site. In 1874, after the federal occupation, Secretary of War Edwin Stanton ordered that a national cemetery be established on the Arlington property. The house remained the headquarters of the Arlington National Cemetery until 1928 when Congress authorized that it and its immediate grounds be established as the Robert E. Lee Memorial. The parcel was transferred to the National Park Service in 1933 and has since been maintained as a house museum. Directly in front of the mansion is the tomb of Maj. Pierre Charles L'Enfant, overlooking the city he designed in 1791. 00–1 (7/6/71).

BALL-SELLERS HOUSE, *5620 South Third Street.* Most of the simple, often crude dwellings of the average colonial Virginian have disappeared; hence the finer houses that remain tend to give a mistaken notion of the typical life-style of the 18th century. A rare surviving example of such rude housing is the Ball-Sellers house, tucked in an Arlington subdivision. The house, probably built by John Ball before his death in 1766, is now a wing of a later house. However, the simple log construction and rare surviving clapboard roof, one of the most rudimentary of early roof coverings, both hidden under later fabric in this humble one-room house, tell that many Virginians lived far from luxuriously. This singular architectural document is now owned and preserved by the Arlington Historical Society. 00–9 (6/17/75).

COLONIAL VILLAGE, *bounded by Wilson Boulevard, Lee Highway, North Veitch Street, and Queens Lane.* Built in four phases between 1935 and 1940, the Colonial Village garden apartments exemplify the early application of innovative garden-city planning concepts to low-density superblock development for low- and middle-income renters. The complex is also an early illustration of the clustering of apartment units around spacious and well-landscaped courtyards, the separation of pedestrian and automotive traffic routes, the use of an undeveloped interior greenbelt, and the use of staggered setbacks in apartment design to permit increased ventilation and light. The first large-scale Federal Housing Administration–insured rental housing project erected in the United States, Colonial Village was intended as a model for subsequent FHA-backed projects. FHA officials worked with developer Gustave Ring to create an apartment complex displaying exemplary site planning, landscaping, and building orientation. Colonial Village has served since as a prototype for many of the nation's town-house developments. The architect of the first three phases of the development was Harvey Warwick of Washington, D.C. Frances Koenig designed the fourth phase. 00–13 (9/16/80).

CHARLES RICHARD DREW HOUSE, *2505 First Street, S.* Dr. Charles R. Drew (1904–1950) was a surgeon who is specifically remembered for providing leadership in the Plasma for Britain program. Through his research in the use of plasma, thousands of lives were saved during World War II and millions since have benefited from lifesaving transfusions of blood plasma. Drew also was the first black American to receive the Doctor of Science in Medicine degree. The simple wooden dwelling that was Drew's home from 1920 to 1939 expresses his quiet modesty. 00–16 (2/15/77); *National Historic Landmark.*

FORT MYER HISTORIC DISTRICT, *Arlington Boulevard.* Fort Myer, next to the Arlington estate, was erected for the defense of Washington during the Civil War. The signal school started there in 1869 under Gen. Albert J. Myer evolved into a cavalry post in 1887 and eventually became a permanent army post. Because of its proximity to the capital, many of the country's military leaders have been based at the installation. Most important of the post's numerous buildings is the row of large residences erected in the 1890s lining Grant Avenue (shown). Quarters 1 of "Generals' Row" has, since 1908, been the official residence of the army chief of staff. Occupants of the house have included generals Leonard Wood, Douglas McArthur, George Marshall, and Dwight Eisenhower. Gen. George Patton served as post commander between the wars. Fort Myer is also the official residence of the air force chief of staff and the chairman of the Joint Chiefs of Staff. Test flights conducted at Fort Myer by Orville Wright in 1909 led to the army's adoption of the airplane as a military weapon. 00–4 (6/19/73); *National Historic Landmark.*

THE GLEBE, *4527 Seventeenth Street.* The Glebe stands on land included in a farm purchased from Daniel Jennings in 1770 by Fairfax Parish. In 1773 the parish vestry contracted with Benjamin Ray to build a brick glebe house to serve as the parish rectory. One of its occupants was David Griffith, chaplain to George Washington's army at Valley Forge. The house was destroyed by fire in 1808, and in 1815 the land was bought by Wallis Jones, who built the wing of the present house, possibly using bricks salvaged from the ruined glebe house. From 1836 to 1846 the Glebe was owned by John Peter Van Ness, a former mayor of Washington who used the place as a shooting box. The next owner was American sculptor Clark Mills, best known for his equestrian statue of Andrew Jackson in Lafayette Park facing the White House. Mills erected the octagonal section in the 1850s and used it as his studio. This portion of the house is one of Virginia's best examples of the eight-sided buildings promoted by architectural theorist Orson Squire Fowler. From 1870 to 1878 the Glebe was the residence of statesman and diplomat Caleb Cushing, who had negotiated the nation's first treaty of commerce with China in 1844. He served as U.S. minister to Spain from 1874 to 1877. The teakwood eagle atop the house was a gift to Cushing from the people of Spain. The property was subdivided in 1918, and in 1926 the house and two acres were purchased by state senator Frank Ball, who lived there for many years. 00–3 (7/6/71).

HUME SCHOOL, *1805 South Arlington Ridge Road*. This Queen Anne–style building was designed by Washington architect B. Stanley Simmons and built in 1891. Prompted by reforms in education and heightened by municipal support for more sophisticated, often monumental structures, local governments gradually replaced the small schoolhouses of the 19th century with commodious and frequently stylish structures, of which the Hume School is a particularly fine example. The school was named for Frank Hume, an early civic and educational leader in Arlington County. Although it closed in 1956, public regard for the school prompted its being deeded to the Arlington Historical Society for use as a museum of local history. 00–11 (2/26/79).

SW-9 INTERMEDIATE BOUNDARY STONE OF THE DISTRICT OF COLUMBIA, *Eighteenth and Van Buren streets*. One of the original forty boundary stones, this sandstone marker, one foot square and standing fifteen inches high, was set in 1792 to mark the limits of the District of Columbia. The district's boundaries as well as its streets and public building sites were surveyed by Maj. Andrew Ellicott with the assistance of Benjamin Banneker, a black mathematician and scientist. Banneker also became an early advocate of civil rights when he requested Thomas Jefferson to use his influence to end official prejudice against blacks. 00–15 (2/15/77); *National Historic Landmark*.

AUGUSTA COUNTY

Formed from Orange County in 1738 with its government established in 1745, this broad, largely agricultural Shenandoah Valley county was named in honor of Princess Augusta of Saxe-Gotha, wife of Frederick Louis, Prince of Wales, and mother of King George III. The county seat is Staunton.

JAMES ALEXANDER HOUSE, *Spottswood vicinity.* The James Alexander house and adjacent springhouse are early vernacular farm buildings of the region that reveal the flow of central European–inspired architectural traditions from Pennsylvania in the early 19th century. The house, built ca. 1827, integrates the Continental two-level bank form with rationalized Georgian ideals and stylish Federal detailing. The springhouse similarly retains the two-level bank siting and limestone construction typical of German architecture of Pennsylvania. The exterior fireplace on the springhouse, one of the few surviving examples of this utilitarian form, was used in such household and farm chores as butchering, laundering, soap-making, and apple butter cooking. 07–604 (6/16/81).

AUGUSTA MILITARY ACADEMY, *Fort Defiance*. Founded by Confederate veteran and state delegate Charles Summerville Roller in 1879, Augusta Military Academy, until it closed in 1984, was the oldest military preparatory school in the Commonwealth. The dominant architectural feature of the complex is the stuccoed Main Barracks, designed by T. J. Collins and Sons of Staunton in a battlemented Gothic style and completed in 1915. The prototype of Collins's design was Alexander Jackson Davis's Barracks at the Virginia Military Institute. In the wake of World War I and Gen. John J. Pershing's report to Congress in 1920 recommending the early military training of American youth, the academy formed the first Junior Reserve Officers Training Corps in the nation and later achieved an international reputation for excellence in the field of secondary-level military education. 07–241 (9/16/82).

AUGUSTA STONE CHURCH, *Fort Defiance*. Built in 1749 under the supervision of its pastor John Craig, Augusta Stone Church is the oldest Virginia church west of the Blue Ridge Mountains and the oldest Presbyterian church in continuous use in the entire state. Craig was Virginia's first settled Presbyterian pastor and organized the Presbyterian church in Augusta County to serve the Scotch-Irish settlers there. In addition to being pastor of Augusta Stone Church, Craig was instrumental in the founding of many other churches in the area. Craig's building was a very simple rectangular structure with limestone rubble walls and a clipped-gable roof. The building underwent a significant enlargement in 1921–22 when it received transepts, a lengthened sanctuary, and an entrance porch. The original walls and roof remain discernible amid the later additions. 07–4 (2/20/73).

BETHEL GREEN, *Greenville vicinity*. The house built by the contractor Jonathan Brown for James Bumgardner, an Augusta County farmer and distiller, is a rare document of mid-19th-century taste in architecture and interior decoration, essentially undisturbed since its completion in 1857. Although the basic house is conservative with its straightforward double-pile plan, such embellishments as its Gothic-style porches, fancy chimney stacks, and Italianate bracketed cornice make the house a stylish amalgam of contemporary architectural modes. Of exceptional interest is the Victorian interior, especially the parlors, which preserve their original wallpaper, curtains, carpeting, furniture, and other decorations. The property remains in the ownership of Bumgardner's descendants. 07–126 (5/18/82).

BLACKROCK SPRINGS ARCHAEOLOGICAL SITE, *Blackrock Gap, Shenandoah National Park.* A large and functionally complex site near the crest of the Blue Ridge, at the head of Paine Run, the Blackrock Springs site contains datable material from about 5500 to 1000 B.C. The intensive analysis of over 3,000 artifacts from the site has revealed a heretofore unknown aspect of Archaic culture, represented by six separate but contemporary artifact clusters, each indicating a single occupation by a small group. Comparative study of the Blackrock Springs site and two other prehistoric sites lying at the base of the mountain on Paine Run will allow archaeologists to explore problems of altitudinal variation and its effect on intergroup contact and Archaic cultural ecology. 07–1149 (9/16/82).

CHAPEL HILL, *Mint Springs vicinity.* The blending of academic with vernacular architectural traditions lends this brick Valley farmhouse a vibrancy usually lacking in stylistically purer works. In general form the house is the standard vernacular I-house. However, this form is overlaid with such stylish features as a projecting pedimented entrance pavilion, three-part windows with stuccoed arches, and a fanlight doorway, all boldly but naively interpreted. The house was built in 1834 for John Knight Churchman in the farmland of southeast Augusta County. Adding interest is the interior woodwork, with its exaggerated moldings, much of which preserves early graining and marbleizing. The parlor retains a rare set of vividly colored French scenic wallpaper with border and wainscoting papers. 07–12 (7/18/78).

CLOVER MOUNT (STONEHOUSE FARM), *Greenville vicinity.* Clover Mount is one of the earliest and best-preserved examples of a small group of vernacular stone houses built around the turn of the 19th century in southern Augusta County. The recent discovery of early 19th-century stenciled wall designs in seven rooms provides one of the richest records of this appealing form of folk decoration in Virginia. Stenciling is known to have been popular in the area, but few examples survive; Clover Mount's scheme is the most extensive discovered in the central Shenandoah Valley to date. The house was constructed in two sections for Robert Tate, a farmer of Scotch-Irish descent, and was completed in its present form by 1803. Tate acquired the property in 1775 and built the house to replace an earlier one. 07–606 (6/16/81).

COINER HOUSE, *Crimora vicinity.* Colorful graining, marbleizing, and polychromy, as well as elaborate provincial woodwork, were popular decorative treatments of the settlers of German origin in the Shenandoah Valley. The Coiner house, built ca. 1825, contains one of the least altered and most spectacular examples of such decoration yet discovered in Virginia. Installed in a deceptively plain brick I-house, as was often the case, the vibrancy of the colors and the imagination and skill with which the mantels, doors, stair, and other trim are executed serve to make the house a fascinating document of American folk art. The principal mantel is embellished with neoclassical motifs of urns and sunbursts so stylized and elaborated that they bear little resemblance to the pattern-book Federal designs that inspired them. 07–75 (6/21/77).

FOLLY, *Mint Springs vicinity.* This compact Classical Revival house, set off by its outbuildings, old-fashioned gardens, rare serpentine walls, and unspoiled rural setting, is the center of an ensemble uniquely Virginian. The house was begun in 1818 for Joseph Smith, a planter who served in the House of Delegates in 1817–18 and was a member of the Virginia Constitutional Convention of 1850–51. Although the house clearly resembles Thomas Jefferson's interpretation of Palladian forms, there is no documentation to suggest that Jefferson had a hand in its design. Smith, however, most likely would have been acquainted with Jefferson's buildings and probably with some of the individuals for whom they were designed. The house survives little changed except for the removal of one of its three porticoes to make room for a west wing. Folly's serpentine garden wall is the only early 19th-century example of this unusual form in the state. Its prototype, Jefferson's walls at the University of Virginia, have been rebuilt at least twice. Folly remains in the ownership of Smith's descendants. 07–15 (9/18/73).

GLEBE SCHOOLHOUSE, *Swoope vicinity.* This rare mid-19th-century one-room schoolhouse is on the former glebe of the colonial Augusta Parish. The simple gabled structure is in a form that would become standard for rural schoolhouses of the period. It departs from the norm, however, by employing brick rather than wood-frame construction, illustrating the strong masonry tradition that was maintained in areas of the Shenandoah Valley. The school was most likely built as a private schoolhouse by the Thompson family ca. 1850. It was identified as Glebe Schoolhouse no. 19 on the 1884 Hotchkiss map of that section of Augusta County, indicating that it was in use as a public school by that date. The building was converted to a private residence and received a frame wing when the county schools were consolidated in the early 20th century. Now empty, the simple building stands as a picturesque example of a vanishing aspect of rural America. 07–706 (3/16/82).

HARNSBERGER OCTAGONAL BARN, *Mount Meridian.* Built ca. 1867 under the direction of carpenter William Evers, this structure is an unusual example of its type in Virginia and reflects the penetration of popular architectural ideals into the vernacular cultural patterns of rural Augusta County after the Civil War. Although it was inspired by octagonal building styles popularized by Orson Squire Fowler, the Harnsberger barn did not copy Fowler's pattern-book designs directly. The builder rather combined these new ideas with more traditional local barn-building concepts, integrating the novel shape with the older bank barn form. 07–37 (12/16/80).

MIDDLEBROOK HISTORIC DISTRICT, *extending approximately a mile along Route 252.* Nestled in the Augusta County countryside south of Staunton, Middlebrook is one of the oldest rural villages in the region and preserves a grouping of 19th-century vernacular architecture still arranged according to the original town plat. Settlement of the Middlebrook area began in the 1790s by Scotch-Irish immigrants, soon followed by German settlers in the early 19th century. The first lots were divided off and sold by William and Nancy Scott in 1799. The rows of closely spaced dwellings and stores lining the main road maintain the character and scale of the village as it appeared during the height of its prosperity in the 1880s. A variety of archaeological sites complements the architectural record and documents the history of the black settlement at the west end of the village. The town's growth halted in the early 20th century when the Middlebrook Road ceased to be a major traffic artery through the region. 07–236 (7/21/81).

HANNAH MILLER HOUSE, *Mossy Creek vicinity.* This small stone house of 1814 is a rare Virginia example of a Continental bank house, a form employed to take advantage of hilly sites. The type was introduced to America by settlers of German extraction. The house stands on part of the tract owned by Mossy Creek Iron Furnace. Built for Henry Miller's widow Hannah, it is an early example of a *Stöckli,* a Swiss-German term for a small house set aside for retired parents. Such housing for the elderly, although common among the Pennsylvania Germans, was unusual in Virginia. 07–269 (12/19/78).

HENRY MILLER HOUSE, *Mossy Creek vicinity.* On a hillside site next to the county road, this late 18th-century stone farmhouse, one of the earliest large houses in the region, was erected for Henry Miller, a local iron manufacturer. Miller's nearby Mossy Creek furnace produced a wide range of household utensils and supplied cannonballs and arms during the Revolution. His house reflects the amalgamation of British and Germanic building traditions that occurred in the region toward the end of the century. The stonework and floor plan are Germanic in style, while the general outline of the house and the placement of the chimney on the end of the house show a Georgian influence. A brick wing was added to the building's west end in the early 19th century. Most of the original, somewhat heavy woodwork of the older section survives. 07–70 (2/21/78).

MILLER-HEMP HOUSE, *Middlebrook vicinity.* The Miller-Hemp house, built in 1884, contains some of the most extensive and best-preserved works of a rural itinerant painter in the late 19th-century Virginia. The wide variety of painted decoration illustrates the creativity and broad repertoire of local artist G. B. Jones, who signed and dated this work June 17, 1892. Large, brightly painted landscape and hunting scenes and vignettes containing popular figures such as Buffalo Bill line the central hallway, while marbleized mantels with stenciled designs and wood-grained doors highlight the second-floor rooms. An amusing feature is the labeling of each of the rooms above its hall doorway. Although several other examples of Jones's painting have been discovered in Augusta County, the Miller-Hemp house boasts the largest and most varied survival of his work. Like much of the Shenandoah Valley interior painting, Jones's work contrasts with the plain exterior of the house. 07–638 (6/16/81).

HENRY MISH BARN, *Middlebrook vicinity.* Erected ca. 1849 for Henry Mish, a native of York County, Pa. who settled in Virginia in 1839, this brick structure illustrates the diffusion of the forebay bank barn from southeastern Pennsylvania into the Shenandoah Valley. Although the bank barn became standard in Augusta County during the 19th century, this is the only known pre–Civil War example to have survived the Valley barn-burning campaigns by Union forces. Masonry construction had been favored in Pennsylvania, but most of the surviving Virginia bank barns were built of wood frame or log before and after the Civil War. Lending distinction to the Mish barn are the decorative brick lattice ventilators in the gable ends. Most of the interior fittings have been removed or rearranged, but the heavy truss framing system remains intact. The barn has remained in continual use on this family farm, which also includes a mid-19th-century brick farmhouse, log tenant house, and several outbuildings, all in an unspoiled rural setting. 07–122 (12/14/82).

MOUNT TORRY FURNACE, *Sherando vicinity.* Mount Torry, established in 1804, was one of the many iron furnaces in operation in the mountains of western Virginia during the 19th century. Shut down in 1854, it was reopened seven years later in order to supply pig iron to Richmond's Tredegar Iron Works for arms manufacture. The furnace was purchased by Tredegar in 1863 to control its iron supply, but Union troops raided the site in 1864 and put it out of operation. Unlike many of the region's furnaces, Mount Torry was put back into blast after the Civil War and remained in production until 1892 when it was finally abandoned. Now preserved by the U.S. Forest Service as part of the George Washington National Forest, the tapered stone structure is a relic of an important 19th-century Virginia industry. 07–390 (7/17/73).

OLD PROVIDENCE STONE CHURCH, *Spottswood vicinity*. This simple Presbyterian meetinghouse was erected in 1793 to serve a congregation founded a half century earlier. It remained in service until 1859 when its congregation outgrew it and built a larger structure. The building then was used as a school, residence, general store, and finally a social hall. It was gutted by fire in 1959 but was given some semblance of its original appearance with the replacement of its roof and windows. Its exterior now serves to illustrate the plain character of the Shenandoah Valley's early stone meetinghouses. Buried in the church cemetery are the parents of Cyrus McCormick, inventor of the reaper, and the parents of J. A. E. Gibbs, inventor of an early sewing machine. 07–25 (8/15/72).

PAINE RUN ARCHAEOLOGICAL SITE, *near Paine Run Rockshelter, Shenandoah National Park*. A functionally varied site with high artifact density, this area along the bank of Paine Run probably served as a staging ground for seasonal movement into the Blue Ridge in Archaic times. Abundant comparative data from this and other Paine Run sites offer archaeologists an almost unparalleled opportunity to investigate the effects of altitude on prehistoric hunting and domestic patterns on the western face of the mountains. Its high frequency of red jasper artifacts is unique in the Shenandoah National Park and may suggest early Paleo-Indian occupation of the site. 07–1148 (9/16/82).

PAINE RUN ROCKSHELTER ARCHAEOLOGICAL SITE, *beside Paine Run, Shenandoah National Park*. Representing at least 3,000 years of periodic small-scale occupation, the Paine Run rockshelter provides local evidence of stylistic and technological change in the prehistoric lithic industry while permitting examination of the processes of cultural change under controlled conditions. It and the other prehistoric sites in the Shenandoah National Park demonstrate that the area was most heavily populated during the Late Archaic-Early Woodland periods but was little used in Late Woodland times. The site thus helps document that a major change in life-style occurred in the Blue Ridge before the coming of the Europeans. 07–1147 (9/16/82).

LEWIS SHUEY HOUSE, *Swoope vicinity.* The Lewis Shuey house is a rare example of a pure Rhenish-style house in Augusta County. Of log construction sheathed in weatherboards, it possesses one of the two known three-room, central-chimney *Flurküchenhaus* floor plans in the county and has the county's only known German-style common-rafter roof system with heavy underframe. The house was built ca. 1795–1800 for Lewis Shuey, a veteran of the Revolutionary War, whose grandfather had immigrated to Pennsylvania from the Rhineland in 1732, and who himself moved from Pennsylvania to western Augusta County in 1795. 07–700 (3/16/82).

TINKLING SPRING PRESBYTERIAN CHURCH, *Fishersville vicinity.* Founded in the late 1730s, Tinkling Spring Church houses the second oldest Presbyterian congregation in the Shenandoah Valley. The pioneering preacher John Craig was its first pastor. The present building, the third to serve its worshipers, was designed and built under the direction of its incumbent minister, Robert Lewis Dabney, who was the architect of several churches in the state. Dabney described his design, executed in 1850, as "the plainest Doric denuded of all ornaments." The chaste building, similar to the chapel Dabney designed for Hampden-Sydney College, appealed to the austere Calvinist frame of mind and influenced the architecture of a number of Virginia's Presbyterian churches. Among the early congregations of Tinkling Spring were members of the Preston, Breckenridge, and Johnston families. 07–33 (1/16/73).

VALLEY RAILROAD STONE BRIDGE, *Jolivue vicinity.* This example of masonry engineering was part of the now-abandoned Valley Railroad line between Staunton and Lexington. The four-span arched bridge across Folly Mills Creek was erected in 1884 and is maintained as a scenic landmark for travelers along Interstate Highway 81 by the Virginia Department of Highways and Transportation. The bridge is built with rough-faced granite ashlar with smooth-face ashlar employed in the soffits of the arches. The arches are supported on gently tapered stone piers. The Valley Railroad was later absorbed by the Baltimore and Ohio Railroad. This branch was discontinued in 1942. 07–41 (9/17/74).

BATH COUNTY

*Noted for its many mineral springs, Bath County was named for
Bath, England, also famed for its spa. It was formed in 1790
from Augusta, Botetourt, and Greenbrier (now in West
Virginia) counties. The county seat is Warm Springs.*

HIDDEN VALLEY (WARWICKTON), *Bacova vicinity.*
This formal Greek Revival mansion, its facade dominated by
an Ionic portico, takes its name from its matchless setting in a
narrow, remote valley of the Allegheny Mountains through
which the Jackson River flows. The house, originally called
Warwickton, was built ca. 1857 for Judge James Warwick,
grandson of Jacob Warwick, Indian fighter and pioneer settler
of Bath County. Most of the house's detailing was adapted
from designs in Asher Benjamin's *The Practical House Carpenter* (1830), thus illustrating how builders, even in the farther
reaches of the South, made use of this Boston pattern book. In
1965 the house was acquired by the U.S. Forest Service, which
undertook a needed rehabilitation. 08–4 (12/2/69).

THE HOMESTEAD HOTEL, *Hot Springs.* Hot Springs was
first recorded in 1750 by the explorer Dr. Thomas Walker, and
the thermal springs have been accommodating visitors since
1766 when a small hotel, known as the Homestead, was built
there. The place became a popular health spa in the 19th century, and toward the end of the century it developed into a
social gathering place. The large wooden hotel, built in several
stages in the 19th century, was destroyed by fire in 1901. Only
the 1892 bathhouse or spa building, designed by the firm of
Yarnell and Goforth, and several of the cottages survived the
burning. Under its owners, the Ingalls family, the hotel was
replaced by the present Homestead Hotel, a prodigious essay

in the Colonial Revival designed by the firm of Elzner and Anderson of Cincinnati. To this, in 1929, was added the central tower, a tour de force of the Colonial Revival idiom by the architects Warren and Wetmore of New York, known for their luxury hotels. During the early 1920s the Olmstead Brothers of Boston landscaped the Homestead's grounds, creating a park-like setting for the building. Among the resort guests have been Henry Ford, John D. Rockefeller, Andrew Mellon, and numerous U.S. presidents. For nearly nine months, beginning on December 29, 1941, the Homestead was used by the U.S. government for the internment of 363 Japanese diplomats and other citizens after the bombing of Pearl Harbor. In 1943 the hotel was the site of the International Food Conference, a precursor of the United Nations, attended by representatives of forty-four countries. Retaining its early 20th-century character and standard of service, the Homestead continues as an internationally known resort. 08–25 (3/20/84).

OLD STONE HOUSE (ROBERT SITLINGTON HOUSE), *Millboro Springs vicinity*. Erected in the 1790s for Robert Sitlington, a settler who took a leading role in the organization of the county, this fieldstone vernacular farmhouse is one of the oldest dwellings in Bath County. Standing in an area containing few examples of stone architecture, the house shows the influence of the Germanic building practices typical of the Shenandoah Valley. In a conscious effort to imitate the houses of the well-established Valley settlements. Sitlington was attempting to bring a sense of stability and permanence to his far-western home on the Cowpasture River. After several years of neglect, the house has recently undergone a thorough restoration. 08–105 (12/14/82).

WARM SPRINGS BATHHOUSES, *Warm Springs*. One of western Virginia's oldest spas, Warm Springs has been visited by travelers seeking its curative benefits and fresh mountain air since the mid-18th century and was used by Indians before that. The two simple wooden bathhouses, one for men and the other for women, are a rare survival of a bygone era of Virginia's social and medical history and are still used for their original purpose. The octagonal men's bathhouse (shown) traditionally dates from 1761; the twenty-sided women's bathhouse dates to the early 19th century. The houses are owned and operated by the Homestead Hotel in nearby Hot Springs. 08–7 (11/5/68).

CITY OF BEDFORD

Originally known as Liberty, Bedford became the Bedford county seat in 1782 when the court was moved there from New London. It was incorporated as a town in 1839. The name was changed to Bedford City in 1890 and to Bedford in 1912. It was incorporated as a city in 1969.

BEDFORD HISTORIC MEETING HOUSE, *153 West Main Street*. This simple but quite formal Greek Revival structure, built in 1838 as Bedford's first Methodist church, survives as the community's oldest religious edifice. The Methodists outgrew the little church by 1886 and sold it to the Episcopalians for use as a house of worship for former slaves. It was reconsecrated as St. Philip's Episcopal Church, and its parishioners soon opened a day school attached to the building which educated the town's black children until a public school for blacks was established in Bedford. The church was vacated when Bedford's black and white Episcopal congregations merged in 1968, and the building was acquired in 1969 by the Bedford Historical Society to be restored as its headquarters. With its fine brickwork, pedimented roof, and pilastered belfry, the building is architecturally akin to other antebellum churches located in Bedford, Fincastle, Christiansburg, and Floyd. 141–5 (9/20/77).

BEDFORD COUNTY

*Named for John Russell, fourth duke of Bedford, an English
statesman involved with colonial affairs, this Piedmont
county at the base of the Blue Ridge Mountains was formed
from Lunenburg County in 1753, with parts of Albemarle and
Lunenburg counties, added later. The county seat is Bedford.*

ELK HILL, *Forest vicinity.* The fertile soil of Bedford County
spawned the creation of numerous fine farms in the late 18th
century, especially along St. Stephen's Road. One of the oldest
farms, Elk Hill, still possesses its side-passage-plan Federal
dwelling house built ca. 1797 for Waddy Cobb, brother of the
first rector of St. Stephen's Church. Elk Hill's Flemish bond
brickwork, formally spaced openings, and refined interior
woodwork with carved mantels are evidence of the high degree
of architectural sophistication achieved in the early years of the
county. The farm later was owned by three generations of the
Nelson family and was visited by their relative Thomas Nelson
Page, who did some of his writing there. The house was restored in 1928 by Lynchburg architect Preston Craighill, who
added the Federal-style porches on the front and rear entrances. 09–6 (11/21/72); *Virginia Historic Landmarks Board
preservation easement.*

FANCY FARM, *Kelso Mill*. Fancy Farm's brick five-bay dwelling house with its pedimented gable ends ranks with Virginia's best examples of late Georgian domestic architecture. The pilastered parlor with its elaborate chimneypiece and flanking arches is an especially sophisticated room. Completed in the 1780s, the house was the home of Andrew Donald, a Scottish merchant. As suggested by its name, Donald's new residence outshown its more modest neighbors and set a standard for the area. During the Civil War the house was occupied by Union general David Hunter. In 1921 the property was purchased by Sir George Sitwell, Bart., of the English literary family, for his nephew Capt. Herbert FitzRoy Sitwell. Sitwell had been gassed during World War I and used Fancy Farm as a place for convalescence. The house underwent an extensive renovation in the late 1960s. 09—7 (7/6/71).

HOPE DAWN, *Boonesboro vicinity*. This compact early 19th-century farmhouse, in a pastoral location above the James River, is a refined and excellently preserved example of Piedmont Virginia vernacular. Its finely crafted details and balanced proportions illustrate the high standards maintained by builders even for modest houses in relatively remote areas. The property was the country home of Dr. Howell Davies, a Lynchburg druggist who acquired the farm in 1827. Preserved in front of the house is a short section of the old Bethel Road, an early turnpike sometimes used by Thomas Jefferson as a shortcut to his Bedford County retreat, Poplar Forest. 09—43 (9/17/74).

NEW LONDON ACADEMY, *New London vicinity.* Founded in 1795, the New London Academy is the only public secondary school in Virginia to operate under a charter from the General Assembly. A classical school for boys, the school was established at its present location by 1797. By the late 1880s it had become affiliated with the public school system. The academy's oldest building, a simple but formal Greek Revival structure built 1837–39, has continued in use in varying capacities to the present day. Marred by alterations over the years, the building has recently been returned to its original appearance by a careful restoration funded in part by a grant from the General Assembly. 09–47 (12/21/71).

OLD RECTORY, *Forest vicinity.* This old country house is set amid the rolling farmlands of western Bedford County. Dating from 1787, the T-shaped frame dwelling is a typical example of the simple but proud Federal farmhouses erected throughout the Piedmont in the late 18th century. It was the home of Waddy Cobb, who later built the house at Elk Hill nearby. From 1828 to 1904 this house served as the rectory of St. Stephen's Church, thus making it an integral part of the St. Stephen's Road rural community. The Doric portico was added soon after the house was returned to use as a private residence. 09–56 (6/19/73).

POPLAR FOREST, *Forest vicinity.* Thomas Jefferson designed this neat octagonal dwelling to serve as a retreat from his many visitors and busy life at Monticello. Built on a large tract of land inherited by his wife, the house was begun in 1809, with interior work continuing as late as 1823, in Jefferson's eightieth year. Jefferson experimented with octagonal forms in many of his projects and studies before he decided to use the octagon as the dominant theme for a house. From the day that it was complete enough to occupy, the former president regularly visited Poplar Forest three or four times a year, staying there several weeks at a time. The house was gutted by fire in 1845 but was rebuilt within the walls with the floor plan maintained. The roof deck, balustrade, and other original embellishments were not replaced. Remaining on the grounds are original outbuildings including two octagonal privies shielded from view of the house by artificial earth mounds. Much of the surrounding acreage was sold off in the 1970s for a housing development. Poplar Forest and its remaining acreage was purchased by the Corporation for Jefferson's Poplar Forest in 1984 in order to preserve and exhibit this intriguing dwelling. 09–27 (5/13/69); *National Historic Landmark.*

THREE OTTERS, *Bedford vicinity.* One of the most striking examples of Greek Revival domestic architecture in the state, this dwelling illustrates the originality inherent in many of Bedford County's early buildings. Abel Beach Nichols, a Connecticut merchant, settled in Virginia in 1820 and built the house some ten years later. Although its designer/builder has not been identified, much of the detailing was faithfully reproduced from Asher Benjamin's *The Practical House Carpenter* (1830), a popular pattern book of the period. A unique feature of the house is the series of small windows in the metopes that, when opened, form a ventilation system. Other features of interest include the marbleized stair, the Flemish bond brickwork, and the ruins of an original brick chicken house. 09–31 (7/7/70).

WOODBOURNE, *Forest vicinity.* Although built in three stages covering a span of some forty years, this stucco and wood-frame plantation house presents an architecturally unified composition of pleasing proportions and shows Piedmont Federal architecture at its provincial best. The east wing, dating from the 1780s, is the earliest portion. The stuccoed center pavilion with its classical pediment was added ca. 1810 and the west wing in the 1820s. The interior of the center section is marked by richly carved woodwork with designs freely adapted from contemporary pattern books. Woodbourne was erected on land purchased from Thomas Jefferson, who acquired it through his wife, Martha Wayles Skelton Jefferson. The house was built for William Radford and remains occupied by his descendants. 09–33 (4/17/73).

BLAND COUNTY

Probably named for Richard Bland, a Virginia Revolutionary patriot, this sparsely populated mountainous county was formed in 1861 from Giles, Wythe, and Tazewell counties. The county seat is Bland.

SHARON LUTHERAN CHURCH AND CEMETERY, *Ceres vicinity.* This complex descends from the large-scale German settlement of Wythe County and more specifically from a church established here in 1821. The cemetery contains a significant number of boldly carved Germanic gravestones, documenting the artistry and rich folk culture of these settlers. The fifty to sixty surviving Germanic stones relate stylistically to those in early Lutheran cemeteries in both Wythe and Tazewell counties. The present church was built ca. 1883 to replace the 1821 church and retains a little-altered Eastlake-style interior. Both this church and its predecessor were shared by the Lutherans with a Presbyterian congregation until 1911 when the latter group built their own structure. 10−40 (11/21/78).

BOTETOURT COUNTY

Named for Norborne Berkeley, baron de Botetourt, Virginia's
royal governor from 1768 to 1770, this pastoral as well as
mountainous western Virginia county was formed from Augusta
County in 1769, with part of Rockbridge County added later.
The county seat is Fincastle.

BESSEMER ARCHAEOLOGICAL SITE, *Bessemer vicinity.*
On the bottomlands of the James River, the Bessemer archaeological site contains features dating to the Late Woodland period (A.D. 800–1600) of Indian habitation that indicate a
northern expansion of the Dan River culture of the central
Piedmont into western Virginia. Further archaeological work
at the site should yield new data on Late Woodland settlement
patterns, community organization, subsistence, and cultural
interactions in the region. The site contains well-defined remains of a Late Woodland rectangular longhouse, the only evidence of a structure of this type yet identified in western Virginia. 11–188 (9/16/82).

BRECKINRIDGE MILL, *Fincastle vicinity.* Breckinridge Mill is a remnant of the grain and milling industry that figured significantly in the economy of antebellum Virginia. The three-and-a-half-story brick structure was erected in 1822 for James Breckinridge, a leading Federalist politician and landowner of southwestern Virginia, and is one of the oldest mills in the region. The present owner has preserved the formerly abandoned structure through adaptive reuse as apartments. The mill replaced an 1804 mill also erected by Breckinridge. 11–187 (5/20/80).

CALLIE FURNACE, *Glen Wilton vicinity.* Callie Furnace is a late relic of the iron furnaces that dotted the mountains of western Virginia in the 19th century. It was constructed in 1873 by D. S. Cook, who named it after his wife, Caroline Wilton Cook. A high-grade iron ore was mined on the property and the pig iron produced here was transported by rail to waiting mills in Ohio and Pennsylvania. The furnace went out of blast after 1884 but remains in a good state of preservation. The gently tapered stone structure is typical of furnace design and rises thirty-three feet above the firebox. It was fueled first with charcoal but was modified in 1875 to use coke. The structure is now within the George Washington National Forest and is maintained by the U.S. Forest Service. 11–5 (7/17/73).

FINCASTLE HISTORIC DISTRICT, *centered on Main and Church streets and incorporating the historic core of the village.* Named in honor of Lord Fincastle, son of Lord Dunmore, Virginia's last royal governor, this compact, county seat was founded in 1772 as a colonial frontier town and one of the last civilized outposts for pioneers moving through the Valley of Virginia to the west. The town was laid out by William Preston, the county surveyor. Many of the early houses have been lost through devasting fires, although several streets are still lined with weatherboarded log dwellings. The gleaming spires of several antebellum churches as well as of the reconstructed Greek Revival courthouse stand out above the quiet, tree-shaded streets of the tiny community surrounded by rolling farmland and mountains beyond. 218–41 (5/13/69).

LOONEY MILL CREEK ARCHAEOLOGICAL SITE, *Buchanan vicinity.* This tract near the junction of Looney Creek with the James River contains archaeological sites of both prehistoric and historic interest. There is evidence of slight utilization of the area from 6000 to 2000 B.C. More intensive settlement followed during the late Woodland period. Robert Looney established his homestead here in 1742, and his place, known as Looney's Mill or Looney's Ferry, was visited by many settlers traveling on the adjacent Great Road on their way west. 11–184 (4/19/77).

NININGER'S MILL (TINKER MILL), *Daleville vicinity.* When Peter Nininger built this brick mill on Tinker Creek in 1847, he was continuing a milling tradition in Botetourt County that began with the county's first settlers. Beside the Pittsylvania-Franklin-Botetourt turnpike, which connected the farmlands of western Virginia with bustling Southside markets, the mill operated for decades as a quasi-public utility, offering one of the rural economy's most important services. The mill was converted to a restaurant in 1968, but some of the original machinery was preserved. On the exterior is a late 19-century overshot metal wheel. 11–57 (5/20/80).

PHOENIX BRIDGE, *Eagle Rock.* In an unusually scenic setting at Eagle Rock, along Botetourt County's Craig Creek, the Phoenix Bridge is a decorative representative of fast-disappearing metal truss bridge construction. Its manufacturer, the Phoenix Bridge Company of Phoenixville, Pa., was a leading prefabricator of wrought-iron bridges in the late 19th century. The bridge is a pinned flexible structure incorporating a Whipple truss and the special Phoenix post, a compression member composed of four flanged segments riveted together. The whole is decorated with Gothic motifs including finials, quatrefoils, and trefoils. The bridge was built in 1887 and still employs a wooden roadway. 11–95 (2/18/75).

PROSPECT HILL, *Fincastle*. On the summit of a steep grassy hill, this late Federal farmhouse commands panoramic views in all directions, including the Blue Ridge and Allegheny mountains, the town of Fincastle, and Botetourt County farmland. Built ca. 1837–38 for John Gray, the county sheriff, the house preserves an interior with fancy painting and graining. The west parlor's stenciling is a decorative device rarely surviving in Virginia houses of the period. The exterior has a two-level portico, rare flush boarding, and elaborate detailing, all lending the house a lively provinciality. Especially notable are the fanlights and pediment lunette with their intersecting tracery. The one-story wings are later additions. 11–185 (9/18/79); *Virginia Historic Landmarks Board preservation easement.*

ROARING RUN FURNACE, *Eagle Rock vicinity.* Typical of the scores of iron furnaces that were scattered through the hills and mountains of western Virginia is Roaring Run Furnace, a single-stack, hot-blast charcoal furnace built of large squared stones. It was constructed in 1832, rebuilt in 1845, and rebuilt again early in the Civil War. Most of the pig iron produced during its last years was shipped to Richmond for use by the Tredegar Iron Works in the war effort. The furnace was abandoned after Appomattox and was later taken in with lands forming the Jefferson National Forest. The structure is now preserved by the U.S. Forest Service. 11–63 (6/15/76).

SANTILLANE, *Fincastle*. This Botetourt County homestead occupies an elevated site immediately southwest of Fincastle making it one of the architectural focal points in the landscape around the county seat. The property was long owned by the Hancock family; however, the present imposing Greek Revival house was built in the 1830s for Henry Bowyer, formerly an officer in Washington's army and clerk of the court of Botetourt County for forty-three years. The house has beautiful brickwork, spacious rooms, and an unusually wide stair hall. The two-story 20th-century portico replaced an earlier porch. In recent years Santillane was the home of R. D. Stoner, also longtime clerk of the court and author of *A Seed-Bed of the Republic,* a history of Botetourt County and Southwest Virginia. 11–32 (1/15/74).

SPRINGWOOD TRUSS BRIDGE, *Route 630, Springwood.*
This three-span bridge above Buchanan is the state's only major wooden bridge crossing the James River. The structure was
completed in 1884 by the Richmond and Allegheny Railroad
Company and was acquired by the Virginia Department of
Highways when it took over the county roads in 1932. Its superstructure is composed entirely of timbers except for the
wrought-iron bottom chord, hip verticals, and diagonals. The
overall length of the three trusses is 240 feet. The spans are
supported on massive cut-stone piers and abutments. The
bridge is still maintained by the state but is not open to vehicular traffic. 11–103 (11/15/77).

WILOMA, *Fincastle vicinity.* Wiloma is an interesting blending of area vernacular forms with pattern-book detailing. The
main body of the house is a large Valley of Virginia I-house, a
standard vernacular house form of the region in the first half
of the 19th century. Fronting the house is a provincial interpretation of a two-level Greek Revival portico, a device frequently
used in the vicinity to give houses architectural dignity. Many
elements of the interior woodwork, especially the mantels, are
directly adapted from illustrations in the pattern books of Boston architect Asher Benjamin. The house was built in 1848 for
Morgan Utz, a Fincastle merchant who served as a ruling elder
in the Fincastle Presbyterian Church and a trustee of Botetourt
Seminary. Unspoiled rural scenery provides an appropriate setting for the dwelling. 11–39 (10/18/83).

WILSON WAREHOUSE, *Washington and Lower streets, Buchanan.* Buchanan's Wilson Warehouse is a relic of the western
Virginia's antebellum prosperity. The otherwise plain Greek
Revival structure is set off by stepped gables, an architectural
feature often used on commercial buildings of the period to
protect the end of the roof from fire. It was built in 1839 as a
combined dwelling, warehouse, and store for John S. Wilson,
whose business activities prospered with the completion of the
adjacent James River and Kanawha Canal as far as Buchanan
in 1851. Restored by Lynchburg architect Stanhope Johnson in
1928, the building, now known as the Community House, is
owned by the town and is managed by the Town Improvement
Society as a meeting place for local organizations. 180–6
(7/19/77).

CITY OF BRISTOL

*Straddling the Virginia-Tennessee state line, the Virginia
portion of this Southwest Virginia community originally was
called Goodson for Samuel Goodson, its founder. It was
established in 1850 and incorporated as a town in 1856. In
1890 it was incorporated as a city with its name changed to
Bristol to conform to that of its Tennessee neighbor.*

BRISTOL RAILROAD STATION, *State and Washington
streets.* Occupying a commanding position on the edge of Bristol's commercial district, the Bristol Railroad Station, originally known as the Bristol Union Railway Station, was constructed in 1902. The stone-and-brick passenger station is one of the last surviving examples of a series of structures designed and built before World War I by Norfolk and Western Railway employees for the company's rapidly expanding system. Rendered in a knowing blend of Romanesque and European vernacular idioms, the building exhibits a degree of architectural sophistication that is rarely found in the passenger stations of other medium-size cities of the state. The station stood unoccupied for several years after the termination of rail passenger traffic through the city and recently has been converted to a shopping mall. A late 19th-century freight station stands immediately across the tracks and is included in the landmark designation. 102–11 (9/16/80).

BRUNSWICK COUNTY

*Along the state's southern border, this rural county was named
for the duchy of Brunswick-Lüneburg, one of the German
possessions of King George I. It was formed from Prince
George County in 1720, but its government was not organized
until 1732. It was later enlarged with parts of Surry and
Isle of Wight counties. The county seat is Lawrenceville.*

BRUNSWICK COUNTY COURT SQUARE, *Lawrence-
ville*. With its Greek Doric courthouse, Confederate monument, clerk's office, and jail, Brunswick County's court square
has the essential ingredients of a 19th-century Virginia shire
town. The tree-shaded grouping forms a harmonious ensemble which serves as the focus of town and county activity.
Lawrenceville was established as the county seat in 1814. By
1853, a new courthouse was required, and a contract was let to
E. R. Trumbull and Robert Kirkland to provide a building
based on the courthouse in adjacent Mecklenburg County.
Like its model, the new building was temple form, but instead
of a hexastyle Roman Ionic portico, Trumbull and Kirkland
gave their structure a tetrastyle portico in the Greek Doric order, thus creating one of southside Virginia's few Greek Revival court structures. The courthouse was modernized in the
1970s at which time the smooth shafts of the columns were
fluted. The one-story clerk's office was designed by M. J. Dimmock of Richmond and was built in 1893. 251–1 (11/19/74).

FORT CHRISTANNA ARCHAEOLOGICAL SITE, *Lawrenceville vicinity.* This 662-acre tract overlooking the Meherrin River contains the archaeological remains of Fort Christanna, begun in 1714 by Governor Alexander Spotswood to house an Indian school and trading center and to serve as a defense against unfriendly tribes. Within the district are the sites of a Sappony Indian village complex, home of approximately 300 Indians who chose to remain there after the House of Burgesses voted to abandon maintenance of the fort in 1718. The site of a residence of Governor Spotswood, built to encourage growth and settlement of what was then a remote frontier area, exists in the district as well. Other 18th-century sites probably are located on the tract. The worn remains of what are believed to be the fort's earthworks (shown) are now covered with trees and undergrowth. 12–8 (11/20/79).

GHOLSON BRIDGE, *Route 715, Lawrenceville vicinity.* Virginia's many metal truss bridges are fast being replaced by sturdier though less visually engaging spans of concrete. Among the several examples earmarked for preservation because the rarity of their type or their picturesque qualities is Gholson Bridge spanning the Meherrin River in central Brunswick County. The bridge is important from an engineering standpoint as the oldest multispan metal bridge in the state. It was constructed in 1884 by the Wrought Iron Bridge Company of Canton, Ohio, and consists of two through Pratt trusses set on random ashlar sandstone piers. The spans are 86 and 100 feet in length. The wrought-iron trusses consist of top chords and end posts that are two upright channels connected with cover plates and stay plates. Decorative details include cast-metal caps with the construction date. Above each portal is a plaque identifying the builder. 12–80 (11/15/77).

HOBSON'S CHOICE, *Alberta vicinity.* Erected in 1794, this sectioned one-story plantation dwelling is a provincial example of the five-part Palladian scheme popularized by designs illustrated in Robert Morris's *Select Architecture* of 1755, a pattern book that influenced many 18th- and 19-century Virginia houses. Hobson's Choice was the home of Dr. Richard Feild, an Edinburgh-educated physician well known for his expertise in botany and astronomy. Feild also served as editor of the Petersburg *Commercial Advertiser* and the *Intelligencer.* Except for the addition of the 20th-century front porch the house survives without significant alteration. The interior is embellished with paneled mantels and wainscoting. 12–13 (11/20/79).

ST. PAUL'S COLLEGE, *Lawrenceville*. The Saul Building, Fine Arts Building, and Memorial Chapel form the early core of St. Paul's College and embody this institution's growth from a one-room parochial school to a four-year liberal arts college. Serving the educational and spiritual needs of the region's black community, St. Paul's was established in 1883 by an Episcopal deacon, the Reverend James Soloman Russell (1857–1935). Russell was born into slavery in Mecklenburg County and was educated at Hampton Institute. He later trained for the Episcopal clergy at the Bishop Payne Divinity School in Petersburg, a branch of the Virginia Theological Seminary founded specifically for the training of black Episcopal clergy. Assigned to Lawrenceville as a deacon, Russell, as he stated in his autobiography, *Adventures in Faith* (1936), found communicants without a church in a community where "race prejudice seemed rampant and public opinion indifferent if not actually hostile." By February 1883 the first St. Paul's chapel had been constructed, and a parochial school soon was organized in its vestry room. a simple three-room school building was later built with funds contributed by the Reverend James Saul of Philadelphia. In 1888 St. Paul's Normal and Industrial School was founded in the Saul Building and was formally incorporated in 1890. In 1900 the Queen Anne–style residence of the principal was built; it has since been converted to the Fine Arts Building. The Gothic Revival Memorial Chapel (shown), the school's first brick building, was completed in 1904. In 1957 the name of this pioneering institution in black education was officially changed to St. Paul's College. 251–3 (3/20/79).

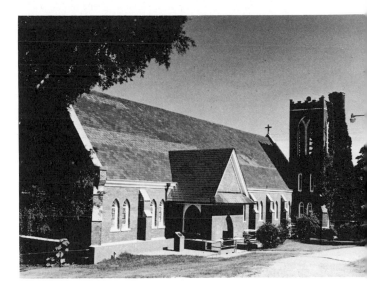

WOODLANDS, *White Plains vicinity*. This Brunswick County plantation dwelling was remodeled from an 1831–33 Federal I-house built by the Brodnax family into a porticoed Romantic Revival residence, a transformation influenced both by regional example and by Philadelphia taste and fashion. The floor plan was adapted from Philadelphia architect Samuel Sloan's *The Model Architect* by Alexander J. Brodnax after his marriage to Ellen A. Mallory of Philadelphia. Brodnax's 1860 edition of Sloan's work, with his penciled notations on Design LVII, plate XC, remains in the house. Family tradition has it that the airy portico, somewhat Italianate in character, was inspired by the Doric portico of Berry Hill in Halifax County. Several features of the 1860 remodeling, especially the Italianate moldings and brackets, show a stylistic similarity to the documented works of Jacob Holt, a Southside builder/architect. Woodlands remains in the ownership of Brodnax descendants. 12–38 (2/16/82).

BUCHANAN COUNTY

Occupying the heart of Southwest Virginia's coalfields,
Buchanan County, was named for President James Buchanan.
It was formed in 1858 from Tazewell and Russell counties.
The county seat is Grundy.

BUCHANAN COUNTY COURTHOUSE, *Grundy.* The Renaissance Revival courthouse at Grundy indicates the importance given to law and order when the area was experiencing its early coal-mining rush. The fourth courthouse to serve Buchanan County since its formation in 1858, the gray sandstone edifice with its tall corner clock tower was designed by Frank P. Milburn and Company of Washington, D.C., and completed in 1906. Milburn's firm was responsible for several other courthouses in Southwest Virginia and also supervised the 1917 reconstructed of the Buchanan courthouse interior after it was gutted by fire in 1915. 229–1 (7/20/82).

BUCKINGHAM COUNTY

*Probably named for the English shire, this rural, largely
wooded upper James River county was formed in 1761 from
Albemarle County. Its county seat is Buckingham Court House.*

BUCKINGHAM COURT HOUSE HISTORIC DIS-
TRICT, *including entire town, stretching for approximately a mile
and a half along U.S. Route 60.* Established in 1818, the county
seat of Buckingham County originally was named Maysville as
it was located on land belonging to Thomas May. A simple
courthouse was built just west of the present village, but within
three years a new courthouse was needed, and a member of the
building committee wrote Thomas Jefferson requesting a set
of plans. Jefferson submitted a design for a temple-form structure with a Roman Doric portico. The building was completed
in 1823, and around it developed a complex of court structures,
law offices, taverns, and dwellings. Several of the buildings followed the Jeffersonian Roman Revival format, most notably
the Presbyterian church, which was based directly on the
courthouse. The courthouse was destroyed by fire in 1869 but
was immediately rebuilt along similar, though somewhat less
refined, lines. After the surrender at Appomattox, General Lee
and his defeated army passed through the village. Lee refused
accommodation in a tavern and pitched his tent with his men
for the last time on the outskirts of the community. Now
known as Buckingham Court House, the village retains a 19th-
century air, little disturbed by modern intrusions. 14–III
(9/9/69).

PETER FRANCISCO HOUSE (LOCUST GROVE), *Sprouses Corner vicinity.* This plain late 18th-century vernacular farmhouse was the home of Peter Francisco from 1794 until the mid 1820s. Francisco appeared in Virginia on the wharf at City Point as a finely dressed abandoned youth speaking only an Iberian dialect. Speculated to be of noble origin, Francisco was brought up in the home of Anthony Winston, uncle of Patrick Henry. He grew to a young man of exceptional physical strength and stature, and in 1776 at the age of sixteen he enlisted in the Revolutionary army. The stories of his wartime feats have become part of Virginia folklore: he is reputed to have carried a 1,100-pound cannon on his shoulders and to have routed an entire squad of Tarleton's cavalry and then captured their horses. Moving to Buckingham County after the war, Francisco worked as a blacksmith and lived in this house, which must have seemed quite small for him. He later served as doorkeeper in the State Capitol. At his death in 1831, the General Assembly passed a joint resolution of regret and held his funeral in the Capitol. Francisco's Buckingham County home stood derelict for many years but is currently undergoing a long-term restoration by the Society of the Descendants of Peter Francisco. 14–97 (1/18/72).

PERRY HILL, *St. Joy vicinity.* Perry Hill is a rare example of Gothic Revival cottage architecture adapted for a country residence in central Virginia. Such building types were popularized in the mid-19th century by the writings of Andrew Jackson Downing and Calvert Vaux. Acceptance of the Gothic style was limited in Virginia partly because of the popularity of the Classical Revival styles that dominated architectural taste until the Civil War. Col. Thomas Moseley Bondurant, a Whig politician and publicist in Buckingham County, built the house for his daughter and son-in-law ca. 1851–52 and is believed to have named it in honor of Oliver Hazard Perry, a naval hero of the War of 1812. Typical of Gothic Revival cottages, Perry Hill has pointed gables decorated with sawn-work bargeboards. 14–19 (7/31/80).

CITY OF BUENA VISTA

*On the Maury River in eastern Rockbridge County, this
community grew up on the site of the Buena Vista iron furnace.
The furnace, in operation as late as 1855, was probably named for
the Mexican War battle won by Gen. Zachary Taylor in 1847.
Buena Vista was established in 1889 and incorporated as a town
in 1890. It became a city in 1892.*

GLEN MAURY (PAXTON PLACE), *Glen Maury Park.*
With its naive use of academic architectural forms and details,
Glen Maury is a provincial though visually appealing attempt
by a local builder to achieve a formal Classical Revival mansion. The local vernacular forms such as the molded-brick cornices and I-plan blend well with academic elements such as the
pedimented portico and round-arch windows. Of particular
interest are the boldly carved mantels in the principal rooms,
which are also provincial interpretations of academic forms.
Built ca. 1830, the house was first owned by William Paxton, a
farmer who named the place for its situation on the banks of
the Maury River. Now owned by the city of Buena Vista,
whose downtown is immediately across the river, Glen Maury
farm serves the community as a city park. 103–4 (5/16/78).

OLD COURTHOUSE, *2110 Magnolia Avenue*. A tremendous land boom took place in 1889–91 in the central part of Virginia's Shenandoah Valley. The boom, a direct result of the construction of the Norfolk and Western Railway, contributed to the establishment of several new towns, including Buena Vista. The land company that developed Buena Vista gave credence to its activity by building in 1890 a simple but dignified Second Empire–style headquarters complete with mansard roof and tower. Two years later, the company sold the building to the town for use as a courthouse and municipal offices. It served Buena Vista in that capacity until 1971 when a new municipal building was built. Local citizens then rescued the old building from threatened demolition and had it converted to the public library. 103–3 (5/16/78).

SOUTHERN SEMINARY MAIN BUILDING, *Ivy and Park avenues*. The several new towns established in the Shenandoah Valley as a result of the land boom of 1889–91 were recognized to be not only prime industrial and commercial sites but choice recreational areas. The scenic mountain landscape and pleasant climate, made accessible by the railroad, were the essential ingredients for large summer resorts. Of the numerous elaborate hotels built in the Valley in this period, the rambling Queen Anne–style structure in Buena Vista is one of only two remaining. Designed by S. W. Foulke of New Castle, Pa. and completed in 1890, the hotel operated for only two years before the panic of 1893 forced its closing. The building was acquired in 1901 by Dr. Edgar H. Rowe, who reopened it as the Southern Seminary. The building remains the nucleus of this girls' preparatory school and junior college. 103–2 (12/21/71).

CAMPBELL COUNTY

Named for Gen. William Campbell, one of the heroes of the
battle of King's Mountain in 1780, this southern Piedmont
county was formed from Bedford County in 1781.
The county seat is Rustburg.

AVOCA, *Altavista.* Avoca, designed in 1901 by Lynchburg architect John Minor Botts Lewis for Thomas and Mary Fauntl-
leroy, is one of Virginia's best examples of a Queen Anne–style
country residence. The style is distinguished by its variety of
surface treatments and window types and its numerous
porches and projections. Associated from colonial times with
the Lynch family, early settlers of Virginia's lower Piedmont,
the Avoca property is the site of two earlier dwellings, including Green Level, the home of Revolutionary War patriot Col.
Charles Lynch. It was at the Lynch homestead that local Tories
were flogged by local citizens for their allegiance to the British
crown, giving rise to the term *Lynch Law.* 15–222 (3/16/82).

BLENHEIM, *Spring Mills vicinity.* This outwardly modest house in the hilly countryside of eastern Campbell County has elaborate, provincially conceived but skillfully executed woodwork. Such decoration is characteristic of the best early houses in the region. Some of the trim shows a general debt to designs illustrated in contemporary pattern books, but it is interpreted in the very free manner of the more skilled provincial craftsmen. The construction date of the house is uncertain, although a sharp increase in tax assessment in 1828 suggests that it was built in that year for William Jones. The place acquired its present name after its purchase in 1869 by John Devereux. The house survives without significant alteration and remains a monument to the rural craftsman's art. 15–66 (2/15/77).

CAMPBELL COUNTY COURTHOUSE, *Rustburg.* This distinguished but unpretentious public building is one of Virginia's collection of Classical Revival courthouses. With its main floor set on a high basement, the porticoed building makes use of the scheme also employed for the Pittsylvania, Patrick, and demolished Bedford County courthouses. It has remained in regular use since completed in 1849 by John Wills. The courtroom with its elaborate plasterwork and woodwork is among the least altered of the period. Especially interesting is the aedicule above the judge's bench framing the Masonic symbol of the all-seeing eye, a unique use of this motif in a Virginia courthouse. The decorative frame is plaster, but the eye itself is realistically executed in glass. 15–1 (6/16/81).

CAT ROCK SLUICE OF THE ROANOKE NAVIGATION, *Brookneal vicinity.* The Cat Rock Sluice is one of the country's best-preserved relics of a rare riverbed navigation system for bateaux. The network of sluices with their associated wing dams and towering walls was constructed by Samuel Pannill in 1827 for the Roanoke Navigation Company to permit passage of poled riverboats, called bateaux, through the falls of the Staunton (Roanoke) River, opening up the river as far as Salem. The company's entire network extended for over 470 miles. The sluices, blasted through rock ledges, are paralleled by substantial stone walls called wing walls, which helped to guide the water into a single channel and provided a platform from which the boatmen could pull the bateaux through the sluice by rope, a primitive but effective system which fed the early economy of southern Virginia. 15–217 (12/20/77).

FEDERAL HILL, *Forest vicinity.* Federal Hill, a provincial tripartite Palladian house built in 1782, was the residence of James Steptoe, the second clerk of Bedford County and a lifelong friend of Thomas Jefferson. Jefferson's Bedford County retreat, Poplar Forest, is only a few miles from Federal Hill, and Jefferson visited Steptoe whenever he was in the area; so it may have been Jefferson's guiding architectural influence that led Steptoe to employ a Palladian-derived plan. Jefferson had used such a plan in his first designs for Monticello and continued to advocate them for the residences of friends and associates. Still standing on the grounds of Federal Hill is the second clerk's office of Bedford County, used by Steptoe throughout his long public service. 15–3 (5/18/82).

GREEN HILL, *Long Island vicinity.* Few plantation complexes in Virginia offer such a wide diversity of outbuildings and farm structures and provide such a complete picture of rural life and agricultural practices in the early Republic. Among the surviving outbuildings are a duck house, icehouse, kitchen, laundry, and servants' house, as well as several farm structures, built of wood, brick, and stone. The nucleus of the complex is a two-story brick dwelling somewhat plain on the exterior but trimmed with provincial Federal woodwork inside. Linking the house and outbuildings is a rare surviving network of stone walkways. Green Hill was established ca. 1800 by Samuel Pannill, who served in the General Assembly as well as on the Board of Public Works and as president of the Roanoke Navigation Company. 15–5 (9/9/69).

MANSION TRUSS BRIDGE, *Altavista vicinity.* The Mansion Truss Bridge, crossing high above the Staunton River into Pittsylvania County, is a unique surviving type among Virginia's collection of metal truss bridges. It consists of two camelback through trusses and two steel-beam approach spans. The bridge was constructed by the Brackett Bridge Company in 1903 and probably replaced a covered bridge. It takes its name from the 18th-century mansion of settler John Smith that stood on a hill nearby. Its stone piers have been replaced by lolly columns, steel cylinders filled with concrete. 15–218 (11/15/77).

MOUNT ATHOS, *Kelly vicinity.* This stone ruin atop a steep ridge overlooking the James River is of a plantation house built ca. 1800 for William J. Lewis. Its elevated site, one-story plan, classical portico, and polygonal projections have led to the speculation that its design was influenced by Thomas Jefferson, who showed partiality to all these elements in his own works. Lewis family tradition holds that Lewis and Jefferson were friends and that Jefferson did advise on the house. Mount Athos was gutted by fire in 1876. The Lynchburg *Daily Virginian* noted the many valuable paintings and fine library it had contained and commented: "It is sad to see an ancient abode of so much refinement, elegance, and hospitality swept away." Archaeological investigation of the ruins and their immediate surroundings could provide additional information on the architecture and artifacts of this structure. 15–19 (2/18/75).

SHADY GROVE, *Gladys vicinity.* Built in 1825 for Paulina Cabell Henry on land inherited from her father, Dr. George Cabell of Point of Honor in Lynchburg, Shady Grove is an example of the interpretation of highly sophisticated and academic architectural embellishments by country craftsmen. It is speculated that Mrs. Henry was attempting at Shady Grove to duplicate the richness of detailing found in her childhood home. The resulting interior work, the product of an unidentified artisan, is naive in its execution, possessing a charm and vitality not found in more academic counterparts. The neat but somewhat plain exterior likewise illustrates a blending of academic and vernacular influences. Paulina Cabell Henry was married to Spotswood Henry, a younger son of Patrick Henry. Henry had no occupation, and ownership of the plantation remained in his wife's name. 15–13 (5/18/82).

CAROLINE COUNTY

Formed in 1727 from Essex, King and Queen, and King William counties, this Middle Peninsula county, bordered by the Rappahannock River, was named for Caroline of Anspach, consort of King George II. The county seat is Bowling Green.

CAMDEN, *Port Royal vicinity.* This wooden mansion, one of the nation's outstanding examples of the Italian Villa style, was designed by Norris G. Starkweather of Baltimore for William Carter Pratt. Construction began in 1857 on the site of the old Pratt house and was completed in 1859. The house was equipped with the latest conveniences, including central heating with cool circulating air for summer, gas lighting, running water in every bedroom, inside toilets, and a shower bath. An elaborate tower above the land entrance was destroyed when the house was shelled by a Union gunboat in 1863. Preserved in the house are the specially ordered furnishings, carpeting, and curtains, as well as Starkweather's architectural renderings. Located on the river's edge, the house served a large plantation still owned by the Pratts. Also on the property is a contact-period Indian archaeological site which yielded two unique silver medals inscribed "The King of the Machotick" and "The King of Patomeck." 16–4 (9/9/69); *National Historic Landmark.*

CAROLINE COUNTY COURTHOUSE, *Main Street, Bowling Green*. The fire that destroyed Caroline County's courthouse ca. 1830 resulted in the construction of this temple-form building with its arcaded ground floor and fine brickwork. Because of the loss of county records, the precise construction date and designer are unknown, but the building's similarity to the Madison and Page County courthouses, both erected by master builders William B. Phillips and Malcolm F. Crawford, has led to the attribution of the Caroline courthouse to them. Phillips and Crawford had been employed by Thomas Jefferson at the University of Virginia where they mastered classical proportioning and detailing. After completing that work, they built numerous public buildings and houses throughout the state. This building is believed to be the sixth courthouse to serve the county. 171–3 (4/17/73).

EDGE HILL, *Woodford vicinity*. On the edge of a bluff overlooking the bottomlands of the Matta River, Edge Hill contains two historic buildings: a brick plantation house and an antebellum academy building. The house, a fine representative of the region's rural Federal architecture, was built for Rice Schooler in 1820–21 and was enlarged ca. 1840 with the addition of the western half. The interior of the first section has highly individualized Federal woodwork. The academy building, located across a pasture, was erected in 1857 by Schooler's son Samuel Schooler, a scholar, writer, and military officer who had previously taught in academies in Hanover and Clarke counties. Known as Edge Hill Academy, the school was founded to meet the growing demand of Virginians seeking preparation for higher education. The academy closed in the late 1860s, and although its building is now used as a barn, it survives as a rare example of rural private school architecture of the antebellum period. The property contains the archaeological sites of the cabins occupied by the academy students. 16–6 (12/14/82); *Virginia Historic Landmarks Board preservation easement*.

GAY MONT, *Port Royal vicinity*. Gay Mont, on the crest of a terraced hill above the Rappahannock River valley, preserves one of the best documented old gardens in the state. The garden was the creation of its owner, John Hipkins Bernard, who during a visit to France in 1818 was much impressed by landscape and garden design there. Upon his return he laid out a formal garden with rectangular beds; its shrubbery-lined gravel paths are still intact. For this garden and the surrounding park, Bernard ordered many plants and seeds from abroad, the records for which survive in the Bernard family papers. The frame house at Gay Mont, built in ca. 1800 for Port Royal merchant John Hipkins by Richard and Yelverton Stern, burned in 1959, but the stuccoed wings and Tuscan colonnade added by Bernard, his grandson, in 1820, survived and were incorporated into the reconstructed house. Gay Mont remained in the possession of Bernard's descendants until 1976 when it was deeded to the Association for the Preservation of Virginia Antiquities with a life tenancy for the donors. 16–32 (1/18/72); *Virginia Historic Landmarks Board preservation easement.*

HAZLEWOOD ARCHAEOLOGICAL SITE, *Port Royal vicinity.* Hazlewood was the home plantation of agrarian political economist John Taylor of Caroline, a champion of Jeffersonian Republicanism. Taylor wrote keenly perceptive political pamphlets. His *Inquiry into the Principles and Policy of the Government of the United States* (1814) is regarded as a significant contribution to American political science. Taylor also wrote essays about his experiments with improved agricultural methods at Hazlewood, published in book form as *The Arator* in 1813. The main house at Hazlewood, erected in the mid-18th century and added to by Taylor, was destroyed by fire when abandoned by the family during the Civil War. The plan of the house is shown on an April 23, 1816, insurance policy. Archaeological excavation of the site could yield new insights on a major plantation complex. 16–58 (6/19/73).

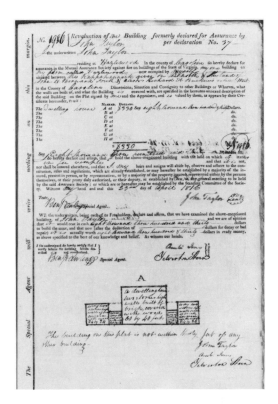

OLD MANSION, *Bowling Green.* The property on which this venerable pre-Georgian manor house is located originally was called Bowling Green after the long green sward before the entrance. The name was changed to Old Mansion when its owner, Maj. John Hoomes, donated property for the courthouse and permitted the newly formed county seat to take the name of his estate. The house, with its fine brickwork, hipped dormers, original sash, jerkinhead roof, and interior paneling, is an excellently preserved example of Virginia's distinctive colonial idiom. A later wood-frame, gambrel-roof rear wing adds to the house's architectural interest. George Washington and his troops camped on the lawn during the Revolutionary War. Old Mansion remains in the ownership of John Hoomes's descendants. 171–4 (11/5/68); *Virginia Historic Landmarks Board preservation easement.*

PORT ROYAL HISTORIC DISTRICT, *bounded by the town limits.* This tiny community on the banks of the Rappahannock was a thriving tobacco port during colonial times. Located near Thomas Roy's tobacco warehouse, the town was officially established in 1744. It prospered through the early 19th century but declined with the advent of the railroads. Thus bypassed by progress, Port Royal remains almost entirely within its original boundaries and preserves the appearance of an early Tidewater river town. Lining its several grid-plan streets are thirty-three 18th- and early 19th-century buildings, including the unusual mid-19th-century Greco-Gothic St. Peter's Episcopal Church and its colonial rectory. The town's former residents include the 18th-century teacher/clergyman Jonathan Boucher; George Fitzhugh, author and prophet of the industrialized South; the Confederate nurse Capt. Sally Tompkins; and architectural historian Thomas T. Waterman. 284–47 (12/2/69).

PROSPECT HILL, *Rappahannock Academy vicinity.* Prospect Hill was built ca. 1842 as the country home of Falmouth merchant Basil Gordon. With its elaborately traceried entrance, precise Flemish bond brickwork, and stone trimmings, the house displays unusually fine craftsmanship. The use of a double-pile Georgian plan and high hipped roof indicates the architectural conservatism of many of the area's wealthier residents and their lack of concern about keeping up with styles in fashion elsewhere in the country. The house is located on a high ridge overlooking the unspoiled rural scenery of the Rappahannock River valley. 16–19 (9/21/76).

SANTEE, *Corbin vicinity.* Adjacent to Prospect Hill on a ridge above the Rappahannock River valley, Santee was created in 1803 by Battaile Fitzhugh from a large family holding. The main house, an example of the rural Federal style, was erected for Fitzhugh in two sections. The two-story frame ell was built ca. 1817, and the brick front section was added ca. 1820. The ell has since had its siding removed to expose its brick nogging. The property passed to Fitzhugh's daughter Patsy, wife of Samuel Gordon of Fredericksburg. During the Gordons' tenure Stonewall Jackson and his troops camped on the grounds. Gordon requested that the soldiers not cut Santee's trees for firewood, and today the huge oaks and other varieties form one of the most impressive rural parks in the state. 16–23 (10/21/75).

SPRING GROVE, *Oak Corner vicinity.* Its stuccoed walls, bracketed cornice, and square cupola make this country mansion an excellent example of the Italian Villa style advocated for the southern states by the architectural theorist Andrew Jackson Downing. The present house, at least the third on the site, was built in 1856 for Daniel Coleman DeJarnette, whose family had owned the property since the 18th century. DeJarnette served in the Virginia House of Delegates, the U.S. Congress, and the Confederate Congress. Spring Grove's interior has heavy molded classical woodwork with its original painted graining. Other interior embellishments include a curved stair, plasterwork ceiling medallions, and marble mantels. The house is still owned by the DeJarnette family and recently has been restored. Its architect remains unknown. 16–25 (9/21/76).

CARROLL COUNTY

Named in honor of Charles Carroll of Carrollton, a Maryland signer of the Declaration of Independence, this mountainous Southwest Virginia county was formed from Grayson County in 1842. Part of Patrick County was added later. The county seat is Hillsville.

SIDNA ALLEN HOUSE, *Fancy Gap vicinity.* This remarkably individual house, a fanciful, if provincial, expression of the Queen Anne style, was briefly the home of the notorious Sidna Allen. Allen was a member of the so-called Allen Clan that was involved in the gory Hillsville massacre of 1912 in which several people, including the judge and court officials, were killed in a barrage of gunfire in the county courtroom during the trial of Allen's brother Floyd. Sidna Allen, although he claimed innocence, was found guilty of participating and sentenced to life in prison but was later pardoned. The house, finished only a year before the shooting, was designed by Allen and his wife and was built by Preston Dickens, a local carpenter. Allen had dreamed of creating and owning the finest house in Carroll County, and this was the result. It was confiscated by the state after his conviction. 17–5 (1/15/74).

CARROLL COUNTY COURTHOUSE, *Hillsville.* The Carroll County Courthouse combines two traditional courthouse forms: the arcaded front and the porticoed temple with flanking wings. Both forms were widely employed by Jeffersonian workmen in Piedmont and Southside Virginia. They had long passed out of fashion when local builder Col. Ira B. Coltrane designed and executed the Carroll County Courthouse in 1870–75, imaginatively placing a Doric portico in front of an arcaded ground floor. Coltrane gave the building additional visual character by using Italianate brackets in the pediment and placing above it an octagonal cupola with a fancy pinnacle. The county's second courthouse, it was the scene of the Hillsville massacre of March 14, 1912, in which five persons, including the presiding judge, were killed in a courtroom battle involving the Allen family. 237–1 (9/15/81).

CHARLES CITY COUNTY

*Named for King Charles I, this largely rural Tidewater county
was one of Virginia's eight original shires, formed in 1634.
Its county seat is Charles City.*

BELLE AIR, *Charles City vicinity*. The original five-bay portion of this modest plantation house illustrates in its form and interior details the transition from 17th-century building methods to 18th-century ones. The rare exposed interior framing and the heavy Jacobean closed-string stair railing are characteristic of the former period. The symmetrical facade, center-passage floor plan, and double-hung sash are all typical of the mid-18th century and later. Because of the destruction of many Charles City County records, the precise date of the house is difficult to document. It is likely, however, that the house was built ca. 1700 by a descendant of David Clarke, who purchased the property in 1662. The three-bay western section appears to have been added after 1800 when the place was bought by Hamlin Willcox. Belle Air is one of the many colonial plantations along Virginia's Route 5 between Richmond and Williamsburg. 18—36 (1/15/74).

BERKELEY, *Charles City vicinity*. Berkeley was originally settled in 1619 as Berkeley Hundred, but the small community was wiped out in the Indian massacre of 1622. In 1691 the property was purchased by the Harrison family, and Benjamin Harrison IV built the present house in 1726. The double-pile, two-story brick dwelling is among the earliest of the great Georgian plantation dwellings that became the foci of colonial Virginia's economic, cultural, and social life. Berkeley was the birthplace of Harrison's son Benjamin Harrison V, signer of the Declaration of Independence. His son William Henry Harrison, ninth president of the United States, also was born at Berkeley. Berkeley was pillaged by Benedict Arnold during his James River campaign in the Revolutionary War, but the Harrisons

repaired the damage and retained ownership until the 1840s. In the summer of 1862 the plantation was occupied by the Army of the Potomac under Union general George McClellan, who regrouped his forces there at the close of the Seven Days Battles. During the occupation the bugle call "Taps" was composed and sounded for the first time. The plantation's present owner, Malcolm Jamieson, inherited Berkeley from his father, who acquired the then run-down place in the late 19th century. Over the past several decades Jamieson has restored the 18th-century character of the house and grounds and has exhibited the property to the public. 18–1 (7/6/71); *National Historic Landmark; Virginia Historic Landmarks Board preservation easement.*

LOTT CARY BIRTH SITE, *Charles City vicinity.* For more than a century and a half, the black community of Charles City County has recognized this late 18th-century vernacular dwelling as the birthplace of Lott Cary (1780–1829), the first black American missionary to Africa and one of the founding fathers of Liberia. The house and its simple rural setting are the only visible remnants of the plantation on which Cary was born a slave and grew up. Cary's owner, John Bowry, hired him out to a Richmond merchant, and Cary eventually purchased his freedom. Through his studies he qualified for ordination as a Baptist minister and became active in the African Missionary Society and the American Colonization Society. With support from the American Baptist Board of Foreign Missions he went to Liberia where he founded the Providence Baptist Church of Monrovia and helped establish native schools. The town of Carysburg in Liberia is named in his honor. 18–16 (5/20/80).

CHARLES CITY COUNTY COURTHOUSE, *Charles City.* Named for Prince Charles, later King Charles I, the Charles City Corporation was established in 1618 and became Charles City County in 1634 when the colony was divided into eight shires. After being located at City Point and then Westover, the county seat was moved to its present, more central site ca. 1730, and this courthouse probably was erected in that same decade. The compact building is one of Virginia's collection of colonial court structures, six of which, including this building, were built with an arcaded facade. The similarity of the carefully executed brickwork details to those of nearby Westover suggest that the two buildings shared common craftsmen. The courthouse was rifled by Union troops during the Civil War, and many of its early records were lost. The arcade was bricked up after the war to provide additional space. The courthouse still serves its rural county after two and a half centuries. 18–5 (9/9/69).

EAGLES LODGE (CLAYBANCKE), *Walker Store vicinity.* On a high bank above the marshy Chickahominy River, Eagles Lodge is a small but carefully crafted colonial dwelling. The house stands on property referred to in a 1729 patent to William Tyree as the "Brick House tract." That the parcel would have been so designated suggests that the present house existed before the patent date. Before 1729 the property was escheat land derived from William Armiger, who died in 1687; since it is unlikely that the house was built before 1700, Armiger may have had an unrecorded heir who built the house sometime between 1700 and 1729. Whatever its precise construction date, Eagles Lodge is a rare surviving example of Virginia's early 18th-century manor houses. Its brickwork is distinctive, being laid in English bond with all glazed headers so that the walls have a striped appearance. Like the Adam Thoroughgood house in Virginia Beach, Eagles Lodge has one interior end chimney and one exterior end chimney. The latter is set off by its tiled haunches and set-back T-shaped stack. The original roof was destroyed when the house was raised to two stories in the early 20th century, but what is likely its original form has been recently restored. Eagles Lodge remained in private ownership until 1973 when it was acquired by the Virginia Commission of Game and Inland Fisheries. The house was conveyed to the Association for the Preservation of Virginia Antiquities in 1979 and was sold in 1981 to the present owners. 18–37 (7/17/73).

EDGEWOOD AND HARRISON'S MILL, *Charles City vicinity.* The storybook Gothic Revival house at Edgewood contrasts with the colonial plantation houses also located along Virginia's Route 5. The house, one of the few Gothic Revival dwellings in the region, was built ca. 1854 for Richard S. Rowland of New Jersey, who moved to Virginia to operate the mill that stands just behind the house. The mill, an 18th-century structure, was originally owned by Benjamin Harrison V of nearby Berkeley and was visited during the Revolution by British troops under Benedict Arnold. The mill was largely rebuilt in the early 19th century to incorporate the automated flour-manufacturing system of American inventor Oliver Evans. During the Peninsula campaign of 1862 Confederate general J. .E. B. Stuart found refreshment at the Rowland house. Two weeks later part of Gen. George McClellan's Army of the Potomac encamped at Edgewood. 18–58 (12/14/82).

EPPES ISLAND, *Charles City vicinity.* Eppes Island has been occupied by successive generations of the Eppes family since 1624, making it the oldest farm in Virginia, and possibly the nation, in continuous ownership by the same family. The rectangular fields into which the island is subdivided reflect some of the earliest extant property lines in America. Each field was originally a separate farm, patented to settlers when private landholding was first introduced in the colony. After the Eppes family acquired the island, the property lines were retained as field boundaries. Before the Eppeses obtained it, the island was part of Shirley Hundred, one of the more prosperous of the Virginia Company settlements. An archaeological investigation of Eppes Island undertaken by the Virginia Division of Historic Landmarks in 1984 revealed at least three early 17th-century sites, two late 17th-century sites, and three 18th-century sites. Also found on the island was a major prehistoric site of the Archaic and Woodland periods. The ca. 1790 Eppes dwelling remains standing on the island's western end. 18–33 (5/13/69).

GLEBE OF WESTOVER PARISH, *Ruthville vicinity.* Built between 1720 and 1757 during the tenure of the Reverend Peter Fontaine, the Westover glebe house served as the residence of the venerable parish's clergymen until 1805 when an act of the General Assembly required the sale of all of Virginia's church lands. Like the other extant buildings of this group, the Westover Parish glebe house exhibits the same fine masonry and careful proportions employed in the churches with which they were associated. Many of the glebe houses were retrimmed inside and out after their sale into private ownership, indicating either that they originally were very simply appointed or that they had fallen into bad condition by the time of their sale. This blending of architectural periods is discernible at Westover glebe house, where the Federal trim in the windows, entrance, and interior contrasts with the mid-18th-century brick walls, neatly laid in Flemish bond with glazed headers. 18–9 (3/18/75).

GREENWAY, *Charles City.* John Tyler, tenth president of the United States, was born at Greenway on March 29, 1790. Standing amid a cluster of outbuildings, the wood-frame, one-and-a-half-story residence is typical of the many lesser plantation houses erected in Virginia during the second half of the 18th century. It was built ca. 1776 for Tyler's father, Judge John Tyler, governor of Virginia 1808–11, who is buried there. The future president lived at Greenway until his marriage to Letitia Christian. He returned in 1821 and made Greenway his home during the period of his own tenure as governor in 1825–27. Tyler sold Greenway in 1829 and eventually purchased nearby Sherwood Forest, where he lived until his death. The unpretentious but formally proportioned dwelling has survived without significant alteration to the present. The interior preserves its original woodwork, including paneled chimneypieces in the principal rooms. The complex is on the flat fields immediately west of Charles City County's tiny county seat. 18–10 (9/9/69).

HARDENS, *Lamtie Hill vicinity.* Hardens, maintained as a distinguishable agricultural unit for nearly three and a half centuries, is a lower James River farm that formerly served as a subsidiary farm, or quarter, of the Shirley plantation. A typical example of mid-19th-century Virginia's rural vernacular architecture, the modest house was erected in 1846 by Hill Carter of Shirley for his son Lewis Warrington Carter. Acquired by David Walker Haxall in 1852 to supply lumber for his family's extensive Richmond milling operations, Hardens served during the Civil War as a Union communications station and as a camp for Gen. Philip Sheridan. 18–45 (12/15/81).

KITTEWAN, *Charles City vicinity.* This weatherboarded dwelling overlooking the marshy Kittewan Creek on the Weyanoke peninsula typifies the medium-size plantation house of the colonial period. Although unpretentious on the exterior, its interior is embellished with paneling that would be noteworthy even in a much larger house. Architectural evidence suggests that the house was built for David Minge before his death in 1779. The Minge family had been established in the region since the 17th century. In 1834 it became the property of Robert C. Harrison. The house was enlarged in the mid-19th century by the addition of an ell, most likely constructed after the purchase of the place by Dr. William A. Selden in 1846. Kittewan was occupied by the Union troops under Gen. Philip Sheridan during the Civil War. Dr. Selden, a surgeon in the Confederate army, appears to have abandoned his home at that time, for he died in Powhatan County in 1865. 18–13 (9/20/77).

THE ROWE, *Rustic vicinity.* The Rowe is one of an architecturally sophisticated group of late 18th-century three- and five-part houses in Virginia adapted from a Palladian model as interpreted in 18th-century English architectural pattern books. The north wing predates the rest of the house and may have been in existence before 1779 when the property was owned by David Minge, who resided at Kittewan. The house apparently was expanded to its present form by Minge's son George Hunt Minge before his death in 1808. Following the precedent of the Semple house in Williamsburg, the Rowe features a three-bay, two-story, pedimented center section flanked by lower wings. The format provides a convincing formality for what is otherwise a small, unpretentious dwelling. 18–20 (11/15/77).

SHERWOOD FOREST, *Charles City vicinity.* John Tyler purchased this farm in his native Charles City County in 1842 while serving as president of the United States, and made it his home from 1845 until his death in 1862. To the original, rather simple, three-bay 18th-century frame house, Tyler added wings, hyphens, and attached dependencies. The western hyphen contained a ballroom and connected to Tyler's office. The additions resulted in a unified facade, 300 feet in length, making it perhaps the longest historic house in the state. Inside, the house was embellished with woodwork based on pattern-book designs by Minard Lafever. Its elaborate parlor wallpaper, ordered from France, was reproduced in a recent restoration. Before becoming president, Tyler had served Virginia as congressman, governor, and U.S. senator, and he was a member of the Confederate Congress at his death in 1862. His home, with its romantically landscaped grounds, remains in the possession of his descendants. 18–21 (9/9/69); *National Historic Landmark.*

SHIRLEY, *Charles City vicinity.* Shirley was patented in 1660 by Edward Hill, ancestor of Charles Hill Carter, the present owner. The name is derived from the early settlement Shirley Hundred, which honored Cessayly Shirley, wife of Governor Thomas West, Lord De La Warr. The dates of the present cluster of buildings—the mansion, dependencies, and farm buildings—are not precisely documented. The forecourt structures may have been built ca. 1723, after the marriage in that year of Elizabeth Hill, heiress of Shirley, to John Carter, son of Robert ("King") Carter. The mansion probably existed before 1740, but its present form is the result of remodeling. The elaborate interior paneling and the unique mansard roof likely were added in the 1770s when Charles Carter made Shirley his principal residence. The two-level porticoes were added in 1831, replacing smaller ones. The gently evolved complex, along with

an accumulation of family furnishings and portraits, presents one of the most memorable pictures of the continuity of Virginia's plantation society. The formally arranged buildings well illustrate the village air of a major colonial establishment and show the more than usual attention given to the architectural treatment of subordinate buildings. Recent archaeological investigation has revealed that the complex was even more extensive, for foundations of two large dependencies were unearthed on either side of the mansion. Charles Carter's daughter Anne Hill Carter, wife of Light-Horse Harry Lee and mother of Robert E. Lee, was born at Shirley in 1773. 18–22 (11/5/68); *National Historic Landmark.*

UPPER SHIRLEY, *Charles City vicinity.* The 1868–70 dwelling at Upper Shirley, on the James River, was a subordinate residence on the Shirley plantation. Built by Hill Carter for his son William Fitzhugh Carter at a time when few houses were erected in the state because of the deprivations of the Civil War, the original portion of the dwelling was constructed by A. H. Marks and Brothers of Petersburg. The walls were laid in bricks taken from a large 18th-century dependency that formed part of the architectural complex at Shirley, seat of the James River branch of the Carter family. Under the ownership of the Edmund Saunders family, the house was enlarged in 1890–91 to nearly twice its original size and became one of the first homes in this rural county to incorporate the most modern turn-of-the-century conveniences. 18–26 (12/15/81).

UPPER WEYANOKE, *Charles City vicinity.* Archaeological excavations at Upper Weyanoke on the James River reveal an almost unbroken succession of settlements from the late 17th to the late 19th century. The present structures on the property include an early 19th-century brick cottage, probably built as a dependency by John Minge, and a large Greek Revival dwelling completed in 1859 for Robert Douthat. With its houses and archaeological remains, Upper Weyanoke should provide much information for the study of three centuries of plantation life on the James. 18–14 (9/16/80).

WESTOVER, *Charles City vicinity.* Westover is the nation's premier example of an 18th-century Georgian domestic complex. Its main house is one of the earliest and most imposing of the surviving Virginia plantation mansions. The grouping was begun in 1709 by William Byrd II, who helped to survey the Virginia–North Carolina border and was the founder of the city of Richmond. His diaries identify him as the epitome of the Virginia gentleman/planter and accord him a significant place in the literary history of colonial America. Byrd's brick mansion, built ca. 1730, is among the most admired houses in the country. Its stately air, graceful proportions, pedimented entrances, and paneled interiors have come to symbolize the high level of architectural quality attained during the colonial era. Complementing the house are original gardens and outbuildings as well as a unique clairvoyée embellished with stone finials and English wrought-iron gates. The plantation remained in the Byrd family until 1817. It then passed through several owners, among whom were John A. Selden and Augustus Drewry, until 1899 when it was purchased by Mrs. Clarise Sears Ramsey, a Byrd descendant. Mrs. Ramsey engaged the New York restoration architect William H. Mesereau to modernize the house and to add the hyphens. Mesereau also designed the library dependency, built on the site of Byrd's library, destroyed during the Union occupation in 1862. The property was acquired in 1921 by Mr. and Mrs. Richard Crane, who left the plantation to their daughter, Ellen Bruce Crane Fisher, the present owner. The name Westover is derived from the first English settler of the land incorporating the later plantation, Francis West, brother of Governor Thomas West, Lord De La Warr, who came to the colony in 1608. 18–27 (9/9/69); *National Historic Landmark; Virginia Historic Landmarks Board preservation easement.*

WESTOVER CHURCH, *Charles City vicinity.* Established as early as 1625, Westover Parish is one of the oldest church units in the country. The first church stood just up river from Westover plantation but was replaced by the present, more centrally located church in 1731. The rectangular form of this church was favored for the colony's smaller ecclesiastical buildings. Westover Church has served the families of the great plantations of Charles City County, including Westover, Shirley, and Berkeley, and presidents William Henry Harrison, Benjamin Harrison, and John Tyler worshiped here. The building stood abandoned for nearly thirty years after 1805 as the result of the disestablishment. It was returned to service but was desecrated by Union troops during the Civil War; the interior remains as it was rebuilt after the war. The molded brick entrance was restored in 1956, and the clipped gable roof was returned to its original form in 1969. The parish owns two outstanding London communion sets, one presented in 1697 by Sarah Braine and one presented in 1727 by Francis Lightfoot. 18–28 (8/15/72).

WEYANOKE, *Charles City vicinity.* Occupying a 1,225-acre peninsula of the James River, Weyanoke has been the site of human occupation for at least 8,000 years and contains numerous prehistoric and colonial sites of potentially significant archaeological value. Surveys undertaken by archaeologists of the Virginia Division of Historic Landmarks indicate that Weyanoke Point first was settled ca. 6500 B.C., during the Middle Archaic period. Pottery fragments also have revealed occupation in the Late Woodland period. In the early 17th century Weyanoke and its environs were inhabited by the Weyanoke Indians, one of the largest groups in the Powhatan chiefdom. English settlement came in 1619, and historical documentation suggests that in the fall of 1619 the first group of blacks brought to Virginia were placed at Weyanoke. The property was nearly abandoned after the Indian massacre of 1622 until the 1650s when Joseph Harwood established a small settlement here. In 1763 Weyanoke was inherited by his grandson, Samuel Harwood, who made his home here and constructed a mill and small shipyard. The present plantation house was erected in 1798 for Fielding Lewis by John Stubbs, a Gloucester County housewright. The two-story, wood-frame dwelling, enlarged in this century with the addition of dormers and wings, is a finely crafted example of Virginia's late Georgian plantation architecture. A notable feature of the otherwise conservative building is the Chinese lattice railing of the main stair. Fielding Lewis, a nephew of Fielding Lewis of Kenmore, was a pioneer in the practice of scientific farming methods, and his advanced agricultural practices at Weyanoke were published by Edmund Ruffin in the *American Farmer.* Gen. Philip Sheridan's troops occupied Weyanoke during the battle of Cold Harbor in 1864. Over a pontoon bridge constructed across the James from Weyanoke Point 15,000 Union soldiers marched toward Petersburg to participate in the final battles of the war. 18–29 (9/21/76).

WOODBURN, *Charles City vicinity.* The house at Woodburn was erected for John Tyler, tenth president of the United States, and occupied by him while he served as a congressman and as governor of Virginia. Tyler purchased the tract in 1813 and had the house built shortly afterwards. He owned it until 1831 when he sold it to his brother Wat H. Tyler. The house, described by Tyler as a "decent and comfortable dwelling," is a provincial version of the tripartite Palladian house, a form popular in the South during the late 18th and early 19th centuries. The form consists of a two-story, gable-fronted center section flanked by one-story wings. Unlike the more formal versions, Woodburn lacks classical proportions and details, but it maintains the form's bold outline. The house preserves its plain but handsome interior woodwork as well as two early outbuildings. After falling into disrepair, Woodburn is undergoing restoration by its present owner, a Tyler descendant. 18–52 (4/19/77).

CHARLOTTE COUNTY

*Formed from Lunenburg County in 1764, this rural county in
the heart of Virginia's southern Piedmont was named for
Charlotte of Mecklenburg-Strelitz, consort of King George III.
Its county seat is Charlotte Court House.*

CHARLOTTE COUNTY COURTHOUSE, *Charlotte Court House*. Charlotte County's temple-form courthouse was built in 1821–23 from plans supplied by Thomas Jefferson. The design was a prototype for numerous stately but unpretentious Roman Revival court structures erected through central Virginia in the second quarter of the 19th century. A local building committee consisting of Clement Carrington, John Morton, Jr., Isaac Read, Harry A. Watkins, William Watkins, and Joseph Wyatt appointed a delegation to visit Monticello to obtain a design from the former president. Jefferson dutifully produced plans, since lost, for a simple but carefully proportioned brick building fronted by a Tuscan portico. The contractor for the project was John Percival, who went on to build other courthouses in the region following the precedent of the Charlotte building. Charlotte's courthouse has survived as one of the least altered of Virginia's courthouses of the period, preserving its two-story courtroom with rear gallery. The building is the dominant element of the tiny village of Charlotte Court House. 185–1 (2/19/80).

GREENFIELD, *Charlotte Court House vicinity.* Greenfield was the plantation of Isaac Read (1739–1777), member of the House of Burgesses and of the Virginia conventions of 1774 and 1775. Read served as an officer in the Revolution and was mortally wounded. The plain but formal dwelling he erected ca. 1771 is the oldest two-story frame house in Charlotte County. Its symmetrical five-bay facade, modillion cornice, and one-story wings, all painted a bold white, give the building a commanding presence amid the rolling green pastures. The Georgian stair, paneled chimneypiece, and paneled wainscoting of the interior combine with the stately exterior to present a picture of 18th-century sophistication and prosperity in this still thinly populated rural area. The property remains in the ownership of Read descendants. 19–8 (10/17/72).

MULBERRY HILL, *Randolph vicinity.* Judge Paul Carrington, a distinguished jurist and a leader in Virginia's movement from colony to commonwealth, made his home at Mulberry Hill in his later years. Carrington in the colonial period was presiding justice of the Charlotte County court and represented the county in the House of Burgesses. In the Revolutionary period he served on the 1776 committee that framed the Virginia Declaration of Rights. From 1789 to 1801 he served as a justice on Virginia's newly created Court of Appeals. His house at Mulberry Hill, overlooking broad stretches of surrounding countryside and the Roanoke River valley to the south, is a blending of two distinct periods of construction. The present facade incorporates the late 18th-century gable end of the original house as its center section. Flanking it are two-story, early 19th-century wings. The place possesses an unusually complete set of early outbuildings including Judge Carrington's office. Also on the grounds are the family graveyard and the remains of a large formal garden. 19–24 (10/17/72).

RED HILL, *Brookneal vicinity.* Patrick Henry, "Orator of the Revolution," assembled this isolated Charlotte County plantation through successive purchases of alluvial bottomlands and undulating countryside and made it his final home. Here he built a modest frame dwelling with a complement of outbuildings including his law office. The house was destroyed by fire in 1919 but has since been accurately reconstructed. The simple law office remains intact. Nearby is the family cemetery containing the graves of the Revolutionary patriot and his second wife, Dorothea Dandridge Henry. The property remained in the ownership of Henry family descendants until 1944 when it was purchased by the Patrick Henry Memorial Foundation, which has since developed the property as a museum. 19–27 (9/18/73).

ROANOKE PLANTATION, *Randolph vicinity.* Few men have been as closely identified with a place as the great but eccentric John Randolph has with his Roanoke plantation and Southside Virginia. So attached was he to this large tract with its hilly pastures and rich bottomlands that he came to be styled John Randolph of Roanoke. A brilliant orator and master of biting invective, Randolph used these talents in becoming a leading member of the House of Representatives and later the U.S. Senate where he opposed any challenge to the vested interests of the South, especially its peculiar institution of slavery. Randolph lived very simply at Roanoke; his house was hardly more than a cottage. With its adjacent outbuildings, the place looked more like a rustic village than the grandiose seats of the South he championed. Although the acreage of his holding has been reduced and the original dwelling house destroyed, the plantation's remaining buildings, along with its fields and woods, still evoke something of the personality, time, and milieu of this colorful planter-statesman. 19–29 (9/19/72).

STAUNTON HILL, *Brookneal vicinity.* Most of antebellum Virginia's plantation houses were rendered in either the Roman or Greek Revival style; only rarely were these stately architectural idioms passed over in favor of more exotic modes. An impressive exception to the norm is the castellated Gothic Revival mansion that architect John E. Johnson designed for Charles Bruce's vast holding in a remote corner of Charlotte County. Johnson based his design on a plate in a London pattern book, *Designs for Cottage and Villa Architecture,* by Thomas Kelly (1829). The house was completed in 1850, and though fashioned with verve, the composition retains the strict symmetry characteristic of classicism. Staunton Hill's romantic qualities are seen primarily in the crenellated parapets, polygonal corner towers, and delicate marble veranda. The dwelling stands as a significant expression of both the exoticism and the historicism that would permeate American architecture for the balance of the century. In recent years Staunton Hill served as the country home of diplomat David K. E. Bruce, a descendant of Charles Bruce who served as the U.S. ambassador to Great Britain and France and as America's first envoy to the Peoples' Republic of China. 19–30 (11/5/68).

CITY OF
CHARLOTTESVILLE

*The county seat of Albemarle County, Charlottesville was named
for Charlotte of Mecklenburg-Strelitz, consort of King
George III. It was established in 1762 and incorporated as
a town in 1801. Charlottesville became a city in 1888.*

ALBEMARLE COUNTY COURTHOUSE HISTORIC DISTRICT, *including Court Square and the properties on Fourth, Jefferson, and Park streets facing onto the square.* This compact quarter in the heart of downtown Charlottesville preserves the atmosphere of a mid-19th-century Piedmont county seat. The principal element of the district is Court Square, which contains the Albemarle County Courthouse of 1803. The courthouse also served originally as a community church, and here, in what he called the "Common temple," Thomas Jefferson sometimes attended Sunday services. The square has been a focus of county activity from the time it was laid out in 1762, and it was not unusual in the early 19th century to see Jefferson conversing here with James Madison and James Monroe. The town hall was built across from the northeast corner of the square in 1851. In 1887 this tall Classical Revival building was purchased by Jefferson M. Levy, then the owner of Monticello, and converted into the Levy Opera House. Around the rest of the square sprang up numerous taverns, law offices, and residences. Among the early tavern buildings remaining are the former Swan Tavern and the former Eagle Tavern, both dating from the second quarter of the 19th century. The most notable law office is No. 0 ("No. Nothing") Court Square, a plain but handsome Federal building of ca. 1823. The courthouse was enlarged in the 1870s with the addition of the south wing with its Ionic portico. Except for the multistoried Monticello Hotel building, the district maintains a consistent scale and architectural harmony, being composed primarily of brick two- and three-story buildings in a Federal or Federal Revival idiom. 104–57 (1/18/72).

BROOKS HALL, *University of Virginia, near University Avenue and Madison Lane*. Providing a lively contrast to the classicism of its neighboring Jeffersonian buildings, Brooks Hall is one of only two examples of late 19th-century eclecticism represented on the University of Virginia grounds. The building was donated in 1875 by Lewis Brooks, a Rochester philanthropist, and was among the earliest natural history museums in the country. Completed in 1877, it was designed by John R. Thomas, also of Rochester, who combined motifs of various historic styles into a wholly original composition. Symbolizing the building's original function is the series of carved animal heads on its keystones. 104–63 (2/15/77).

CHARLOTTESVILLE AND ALBEMARLE COUNTY COURTHOUSE HISTORIC DISTRICT, *Roughly bounded by Park and Seventh streets on the east; by Water Street and the Chesapeake and Ohio Railway tracks on the south; by Saxton and Main streets and McIntire Road on the west; and by an irregular line from the 500 block of McIntire Road behind the properties on the west side of Park Street to the U.S. 250 Bypass.* Charlottesville has served as an important regional political center since its selection as the site of the Albemarle County Courthouse in 1762. In addition to its strong associations with Thomas Jefferson and the University of Virginia, the town is significant for its diversity of 19th-century governmental, commercial, residential, and industrial architecture. Typical of many 19th-century American towns is its courthouse square, containing the courthouse and several 19th-century brick offices set about a small public green. Also in the district is a centrally located late 19th-century main street, with numerous 20th-century modifications including the 1970s pedestrian mall (shown). A turn-of-the-century railroad passenger station with adjacent industrial buildings and several adjoining residential neighborhoods complete the district. While not devoid of intrusions, the district gives Charlottesville's downtown a strong sense of historical continuity and architectural cohesiveness. 104–72 (11/18/80).

OAK LAWN, *Cherry Avenue and Ninth Street.* This unusually appealing example of Jeffersonian Palladianism is one of the many structures scattered through central Virginia whose architecture was influenced by workmen who learned the fundamentals of classicism while in the employ of Thomas Jefferson at the University of Virginia. The three-part house, with its pedimented center section and flat-roof Tuscan portico, was built in 1822 for Nimrod Bramham, a merchant who served in the House of Delegates. The name of no specific builder has yet been associated with the house. After Bramham's death in 1847, Oak Lawn was sold to the Reverend James Fife, an influential Baptist minister who in 1823 helped organize the Baptist General Convention. Born in Scotland, Fife served as the city engineer for Richmond before moving to Charlottesville. Oak Lawn has remained in the ownership of Fife's descendants. 104–31 (4/17/73).

THE ROTUNDA, *University of Virginia, University Avenue at Rugby Road*. The Rotunda represents the single most important architectural achievement of Thomas Jefferson, who, had he pursued no other activity, would be regarded as one of America's leading architects. Designed when he was over seventy and completed in 1826, the year of his death at age eighty-three, the Rotunda was built to be the principal element of the complex Jefferson provided for the University of Virginia. It is modeled after the Pantheon in Rome, which Jefferson considered to be the most perfect example of what he called "spherical" architecture. He reduced the proportions of the Pantheon by half, making the Rotunda seventy-seven feet in diameter and in height. For its interior, Jefferson ingeniously divided the first two floors into suites of oval rooms to serve as classrooms and lecture halls. The domed top floor, with its encircling colonnade of paired columns in the Composite order, was surely one of the most beautiful rooms ever created in America and served as the university's library. The Rotunda was gutted by fire in 1895, leaving only the finely crafted Flemish bond brick walls intact. New York architect Stanford White was commissioned to design the reconstruction. In his rebuilding White eliminated the first-floor oval rooms, creating one large two-story domed space. He also added the north portico and the north esplanades, connecting them to the original south esplanades by handsome colonnades. The Stanford White interior was removed in a mid-1970s remodeling which attempted to recreate, though with numerous modifications, the appearance of the Jeffersonian interior. 104–56 (9/9/69); *National Historic Landmark*.

RUGBY ROAD–UNIVERSITY CORNER HISTORIC DISTRICT, *roughly bounded by University Avenue, Lambeth Field, University Circle, Preston Place, Fourteenth Street, and the Chesapeake and Ohio Railway tracks*. Covering twenty city blocks north of the University of Virginia grounds, the Rugby Road–University Corner Historic District contains the majority of those surviving nonacademic buildings—commercial, residential, and institutional—associated with the university during the period before World War II. Most of the area's physical fabric dates to the boom years between 1890 and 1930 when the student population quadrupled. This era of rapid growth produced the present colorful strip of commercial buildings along University Avenue, long known as the "Corner," directly opposite the university grounds. Noteworthy university structures in the Rugby Road area are Madison Hall, the President's House on Carr's Hill, Fayerweather Gymnasium, the Bayly Museum, and Lambeth Field Stadium, all in various classical idioms following the precedent set by Thomas Jefferson. Scattered among the collegiate structures along the district's leafy streets is a variety of residential buildings including twenty-three fraternity houses and eight sorority houses, a faculty apartment building, and various private apartment houses, many of which also use the classical orders and red brick of the Jeffersonian tradition. Among the more architecturally distinguished fraternity houses are the three grouped around a court along Rugby Road, known as the Quadrangle (shown). The area as a whole forms a well-preserved example of a late 19th- and early 20th-century university neighborhood. 104–133 (11/15/83).

UNIVERSITY OF VIRGINIA HISTORIC DISTRICT, *bounded by University and Jefferson Park avenues and Hospital and McCormick roads*. It was Thomas Jefferson's ambition of many years to found a great university that would serve as "the future bulwark of the human mind in this country." It was not until he was over seventy, after he retired from a long life of public service, that Jefferson found time to devote to the achievement of his dream. As a skilled architect, Jefferson was aware that an institution such as he contemplated must be given appropriate architectural expression. He conceived the idea of an "academical village," a community of scholars living and studying together in an architecturally unified complex of buildings. He selected the site, designed the buildings, and supervised their construction. In his scheme the classrooms and professors' quarters were housed in ten two-story pavilions aligned on either side of a terraced green called the Lawn. Each pavilion was embellished with a different version of an order of Roman architecture, to serve as models of classical taste. To connect the pavilions, Jefferson provided low colonnades fronting the students' cells. Additional student rooms were located in arcaded "ranges" paralleling the Lawn buildings. Each range contained three "hotels," or dining halls. As the focal point of the complex, Jefferson placed at the head of the Lawn the domed Rotunda, a scaled-down version of the Pantheon in Rome, to serve as the library. Construction of the buildings began in 1817, and the General Assembly officially chartered the school as the University of Virginia in 1819. Jefferson also selected the first faculty, drew up the curriculum, and served as the first rector of the Board of Visitors. While the university represents a major achievement in the history of American education, its architectural scheme was revolutionary and provided a prototype for numerous campus designs. Except for the burning of the Rotunda in 1895 and the demolition of the Anatomical Theater in 1938, Jefferson's original buildings have survived without significant alteration. The open south end of the Lawn was closed in the first decade of the 20th century with the construction of three architecturally outstanding academic buildings—Cabell Hall, Cocke Hall, and Rouss Hall—all designed by Stanford White, who was brought to Charlottesville to design the rebuilding of the Rotunda. White also designed the former university commons, now Garrett Hall, which is in the district. Other buildings of significance in the district are Brooks Hall of 1877, the Gothic Revival University Chapel of 1889, and the McIntire Ampitheater of 1921. Acknowledged as one of the most beautiful collegiate groupings in the world, this assemblage of buildings and spaces forms a living monument to Jefferson's genius. 104–42 (10/6/70); *National Historic Landmark*.

CITY OF CHESAPEAKE

*Named for the Chesapeake Bay, this sprawling, largely rural
municipality was formed in 1963 by a merger of
Norfolk County and the city of South Norfolk,
both of which thereby became extinct.*

GREAT BRIDGE BATTLE ARCHAEOLOGICAL SITE, *off Route 168 between Great Bridge and Oak Grove.* The first pitched battle of the Revolution in Virginia was fought on December 9, 1775, at the Great Bridge, a wooden causeway across 360 yards of marsh and open water of the South Branch of the Elizabeth River, south of Norfolk. The bloody engagement proved to be a victory for the patriots, for the British abandoned their fortified position at this strategic point and eventually were forced to evacuate Norfolk because it could not be defended from the south. Artifacts of this engagement likely survive in the marshes adjacent to the bridge site. 131–23 (1/5/71).

CHESTERFIELD COUNTY

*Located immediately south of Richmond and containing many of
the capital's suburbs, Chesterfield County was named for
Philip Dormer Stanhope, fourth earl of Chesterfield,
British statesman and diplomat. It was formed from
Henrico County in 1749. The county seat is
Chesterfield Court House.*

BELLONA ARSENAL, *Midlothian vicinity.* In 1814 Maj. John Clarke started an iron foundry at this site, conveniently adjacent to the James River and the Chesterfield coal mines. Three years later he was instrumental in having the federal government establish an arsenal immediately to the west of the foundry. Named for the Roman goddess of war, Bellona Arsenal soon was used for storing munitions produced in Clarke's foundry. The arsenal was abandoned by the government in 1832, but the foundry remained intact and eventually was leased by the Confederate government for the production of ordnance. Today, four of the eight major buildings of the arsenal remain. Three of these, grouped around a quadrangle, have been converted to residential use. Nearby stands a roofless but otherwise intact 90-foot-long granite powder magazine. Elsewhere on the property are the ruins of two smaller buildings and several archaeological sites. The Bellona complex, together with the site of Clarke's foundry, forms a place significant to 19th-century American industrial archaeology. 20–6 (1/5/71).

BELLWOOD, *Defense General Supply Center, Bellwood*. Originally known as Sheffields and later as Auburn Chase, Bellwood was first settled in 1610 and operated as a working farm from 1634 until 1941. The present dwelling, a large two-story frame structure with pedimented portico, was erected ca. 1800 by Richard Gregory, a planter and entrepreneur. At the beginning of the Civil War the Confederate army erected a fort at Drewry's Bluff, a part of the property. In May 1864 the house served as headquarters for Gen. P. G. T. Beauregard and was visited by President Jefferson Davis. From the 1890s through the 1920s owner James Bellwood and his sons conducted agricultural experiments here that won them international acclaim. The U.S. government acquired the property in 1941, developing it into the Defense General Supply Depot, the main nonordnance supply center for the U.S. armed services. The house is presently used as an officers' club. Nearby is a 21-acre park containing the elk herd established by Bellwood and now maintained by voluntary contributions. 20—7 (6/19/73).

CASTLEWOOD, *Chesterfield Court House*. The neo-Palladian style popular in mid-18th-century England is evident in the complex massing of Castlewood, a five-part house dominating the eastern edge of Chesterfield Court House. The house is an architectural puzzle, erected in several stages of uncertain sequence. The middle section was probably built for Parke Poindexter, the county clerk, shortly after he acquired the property in 1816. The south wing may be part of the initial construction, but its unusually elaborate and highly individualized woodwork, crowned by a paneled plaster ceiling, is in the style of the 1830s. The north wing, with its fancy gouged-work mantel, appears to predate the rest of the house and apparently was moved from elsewhere. Castlewood has had numerous owners in its long life. From 1860 to 1872 it was the property of the Methodist church and was used as a residence for traveling ministers; it is sometimes referred to as the Old Parsonage. The house was carefully remodeled in 1977 to serve as a savings bank. 20—14 (6/15/76).

CHESTER PRESBYTERIAN CHURCH, *Osborne Road, Chester*. This simple Gothic Revival church symbolizes the varied ways northerners and southerners, by individual deeds and personal contact, helped heal the wounds of the nation after the Civil War. The church was built in 1880 by Martin T. Grove, one of a group of northern fortune seekers who came to the Chester area after the war, following up a rumor that Gen. Benjamin Butler had left behind a buried military chest containing $80,000. After two years of fruitless searching, Grove's family returned home, but Grove stayed behind. Out of a sense of guilt over his opportunism in a strife-torn land, he almost singlehandedly built the church to serve the local community. Having performed his act of penitence, Grove moved back north two days after the church was dedicated. 332—3 (6/15/76).

EPPINGTON, *Winterpock vicinity.* Deep in the timber-farm region of western Chesterfield County, Eppington is a dignified colonial homestead built in the 1760s for Francis Eppes, a cousin of Martha Wayles Skelton, who married Thomas Jefferson. Eppes's wife was also Martha Jefferson's half-sister. After Mrs. Jefferson's death, the Eppes family cared for two of the Jefferson daughters at Eppington while their father was serving as minister to France. Jefferson visited Eppington on several occasions, and it was during one of his stays that he received a letter from George Washington inviting him to be secretary of state. The wood-frame house displays a Georgian formality that was usually reserved for brick structures. With its two-story center section and one-story wings, it is an early example of the Palladian massing widely employed by Virginia builders in subsequent decades. The house survives without significant alterations and contains noteworthy interior paneling. 20–25 (9/9/69).

HALLSBOROUGH TAVERN, *Midlothian vicinity.* Travelers on the old Buckingham Road were served by this rambling wooden tavern throughout most of the 19th century. The building was constructed in three stages beginning in the last quarter of the 18th century and ending in 1832, the date the two-story east wing was completed. Much of the original fabric in each section is intact, and traces of a former hipped roof and unusual false-plate construction can be seen in the west wing, the oldest section. The tavern's first owners were the Michaux family, descendants of the Huguenot settlers who came to the region early in the 1700s. From 1826 to 1972 the property was owned by the Spears family. Restoration by subsequent owners has assured the preservation of a landmark familiar to the travelers on today's U.S. Route 60. 20–30 (12/18/79).

MAGNOLIA GRANGE, *Chesterfield Court House.* This wooden plantation house, conspicuously located across the road from the county courthouse, was built for William Winfree in 1823. The dwelling is one of the most sophisticated examples of the Federal style in the region and is noted for its elaborate woodwork and plaster ceiling medallions. The design source for the medallions was Asher Benjamin's *American Builder's Companion* (1806), an architectural pattern book widely used by Virginia builders. The exterior displays the formality characteristic of the Federal mode, having a symmetrical five-bay facade and carefully detailed two-level portico. The house has been restored in recent years, but much of its surrounding land has succumbed to commercial development. 20–74 (11/20/79).

OLIVE HILL, *Matoaca vicinity*. Dominated by a monumental pedimented roof, this three-part plantation house, set on terraces leading down to the Appomattox River, was built in the late 18th century for Roger Atkinson, a public-spirited entrepreneur and letter writer. The house is interesting architecturally for its unusual irregular plan and for the quantity of original fabric it preserves. Still intact are its molded weatherboards, its window sash and their louvered shutters, much hardware, and paneled mantels. A most striking interior feature is the complex Chinese lattice stair rail. Such railings were usually reserved for the finest houses of the period; Olive Hill's may have been inspired by the Chinese stair in Battersea across the Appomattox in Petersburg. The house stood in deteriorated condition for several decades but has been restored by recent owners. 20–49 (12/17/74).

RICHMOND VIEW, *Willis Road, Chimney Corner vicinity*. The small wood-frame plantation house at Richmond View has one of Virginia's few surviving examples of a rare plan incorporating a central chimney rather than end chimneys. This plan was popular in the Chesapeake region in the 17th century but was seldom used in later periods. The house was probably built for William Tazewell, a Richmond physician, shortly after his wife, Mary Page Tanner Tazewell, inherited the property ca. 1805. Tazewell, who farmed over 2,000 acres here, was also president of the Manchester and Petersburg Turnpike Company, which built much of what is now the Richmond-Petersburg segment of U.S. Route 1. Tazewell and his wife maintained their principal residence in Richmond. They may have occupied the Richmond View dwelling, but it could also have been an overseer's house. The house retains most of its exterior and interior detailing but is currently vacant and deteriorating, standing in an area zoned for heavy industry. 20–122 (5/20/75).

SWIFT CREEK MILL, *Colonial Heights vicinity*. Milling operations were conducted at this site from the mid-17th century through the 1950s. The present brick structure dates mostly from the mid-19th century, but its massive stone foundations may incorporate fabric of the original mill erected by Henry Randolph ca. 1660. Civil War action centered around the mill on May 10, 1864, when Gen. Benjamin Butler attempted a crossing of Swift Creek in a move against General Pickett's troops on the north bank. After its milling activity ceased, the building was adapted into a popular restaurant and theater. Preserved adjacent to the mill is a mid-19th-century mill store, a rare surviving example of this type of ancillary structure. 20–31 (9/18/73).

TRABUE'S TAVERN, *Midlothian vicinity.* Trabue's Tavern stands as a relic of Midlothian's busy coal-producing era and is a characteristic example of Southside Virginia's vernacular architecture. The house has had a complex evolution; the oldest part, the west wing, reputedly was built ca. 1730, but the final form of the house was not achieved until an enlargement and remodeling ca. 1815. The property's first owners, the Trabues, were descendants of the area's Huguenot settlers and owned and operated several nearby coalpits. Their home served as an ordinary patronized by travelers and miners alike. The tavern was long known for its collection of frame outbuildings, but several, including an antebellum schoolhouse, have been destroyed in recent years. 20–55 (2/18/75).

VAWTER HALL AND OLD PRESIDENT'S HOUSE, VIRGINIA STATE UNIVERSITY, *College Avenue, Ettrick.* The two oldest buildings at Virginia State University constitute the historic core of the oldest state-supported college for blacks in the United States. The school was chartered in 1882 as the Virginia Normal and Collegiate Institute following up a pledge of the Readjuster party, led by William Mahone, to establish a state institute of higher learning for blacks. The first buildings have disappeared but still standing are the president's house of 1907 and Vawter Hall of 1908. Vawter Hall, a dignified but austere brick structure, is in the plain academic style of the era and originally housed administrative offices, a bookstore, cafeteria, and auditorium. The modified Queen Anne–style former president's home now contains offices. 333–64 (2/19/80).

CLARKE COUNTY

Named for George Rogers Clark, conqueror of the Northwest Territory (who spelled his name without the e), this northern Shenandoah Valley county was formed from Frederick County in 1836. It was later enlarged with parts of Warren County. The county seat is Berryville.

ANNEFIELD, *Boyce vicinity.* Its proportions, detailing, and intricate interior woodwork make Annefield one of Virginia's best examples of Federal architecture. The house's rugged limestone walls set off the ornate Ionic portico and its Chinese lattice railings. Annefield was the home of Matthew Page, who planned the house and gardens and named the place in honor of his wife, Anne Randolph Meade Page, sister of Bishop William Meade. Annefield was later owned by Thomas Carter, whose son William Page Carter was a Virginia poet. Mary Custis, wife of Robert E. Lee, was born at Annefield in 1808 while her mother was visiting here. The house epitomizes the high architectural quality of the numerous plantation houses erected in the northern counties of the state by members of Tidewater families who moved into the fertile region in the latter decades of the 18th century. 21–2 (9/9/69).

BURWELL-MORGAN MILL (MILLWOOD MILL), *Millwood*. Now completely restored and operating as an exhibition mill, this massive gabled structure dominates the center of the village of Millwood. The mill was established in 1785 by Col. Nathaniel Burwell of nearby Carter Hall. Burwell's partner in the enterprise was Gen. Daniel Morgan, the Revolutionary War hero who settled just west of Millwood. The building's original portion is built of native limestone; the wooden third story was added after 1872 when the mill was acquired by T. M. Eddy and A. H. Garvin. Restoration of the mill was undertaken in the 1960s by the Clarke County Historical Association. Its grounds have been landscaped by the Garden Club of Virginia. 21–10 (9/9/69).

CARTER HALL, *Millwood*. With its stately architecture and landscaped park, Carter Hall presents the idealized image of a Virginia plantation. The house was erected in the late 1790s for Col. Nathaniel Burwell, originally of Carter's Grove, James City County. The massive Ionic portico was added in 1814 by Burwell's son George. In 1862 Stonewall Jackson set up headquarters at Carter Hall, using the park as his campground. The plantation was bought in 1930 by the pharmaceutical magnate Gerard Lambert, who commissioned the New York architect H. T. Lindeberg to undertake an extensive remodeling of the house. Lindeberg had the stucco removed from the stone walls and a cupola from the roof. The Georgian-style woodwork and flying spiral stair are also of Lindeberg's design. The property is now the headquarters of the People to People Health Foundation. 21–12 (6/19/73).

FAIRFIELD, *Berryville vicinity*. Fairfield is one of the largest of the several houses erected in the late 18th century by members of the Washington family on their extensive holdings in the lower Shenandoah Valley. Most of these houses are now in West Virginia. Fairfield follows the symmetrical, rectangular format typical of Virginia's Tidewater Georgian houses but is built in the native limestone. It was completed ca. 1770 for Warner Washington, whose first cousin George Washington called on his kinsmen here on numerous occasions. The dormers and terminal wings were added in this century by the Richardson family, who acquired the property from the Washingtons in 1830. The one-story connecting wings are part of the original construction. The house preserves its original Georgian stair and paneled woodwork. 21–29 (12/2/69).

GREENWAY COURT, *White Post vicinity.* Thomas Fairfax, sixth Baron Fairfax of Cameron (1693–1781), was the proprietor of a five-million-acre grant of northern Virginia lands inherited from his mother, daughter of Lord Culpeper. Fairfax set up residence at Greenway Court in 1752 in order to manage this vast holding firsthand. He lived in what was a hunting lodge, replaced in 1828 by the present brick farmhouse. Of the original complex, only the modest stone land office, porter's lodge, and a plank "powder house" remain, all probably dating from the 1760s. George Washington, who began his career as a surveyor for Lord Fairfax, was a frequent visitor at Greenway Court. While the three earliest buildings are significant relics of Fairfax's establishment, the grounds likely hold a rich store of archaeological data relating to what is the region's premier colonial site. 21–28, 60, 61, 81 (9/9/69); *National Historic Landmark.*

HUNTINGDON, *Boyce.* Surrounded by rolling pastures bordered with the region's distinctive stone fences, this commodious, formally proportioned, but architecturally unassertive stone farmhouse was erected in 1830 by John Evelyn Page, third son of John and Maria Horsmanden Byrd Page. Page's parents moved to the area in 1784, during the generation-long migration by members of landed Tidewater families to property held in the state's northern counties. Both the original five-bay house and the single-pile ell added ca. 1850 remain unaltered from the time of their construction. The farm was the scene of considerable Civil War activity. 21–188 (9/19/78).

LONG BRANCH, *Millwood vicinity.* This Classical Revival mansion is one of the few remaining residential works designed—at least in part—by Benjamin Henry Latrobe, America's first professional architect. Latrobe sent plans for the house to Robert Carter Burwell in 1811, several months after Burwell's builder had already begun to work on the foundations. A rendering by Latrobe shows a house without porticoes but with a recessed center section. The porticoes, one Doric and one Ionic, castellated east wing, and interior spiral stair were added after 1842 by Hugh Mortimer Nelson. The Nelson family owned Long Branch into the mid-20th century. Although remodeled, the house remains, as noted by architectural historian Talbot Hamlin, "an important monument in American architecture." 21–95 (11/5/68).

OLD CHAPEL, *Boyce vicinity*. Constructed of limestone rubble, this austere little structure is one of the earliest Episcopal church buildings west of the Blue Ridge Mountains. It was built in 1793 under the patronage of Nathaniel Burwell of Carter Hall, replacing a log church of 1747 which stood nearby. The congregation left Old Chapel in 1834 for a new church in Millwood. It is still maintained by its parish with a special service held there once a year. Most of the original interior wood-wood is intact. Edmund Randolph and Nathaniel Burwell are among those buried in the graveyard. The Episcopal bishop William Meade began his ecclesiastical career as a lay reader at Old Chapel. 21–58 (11/21/72).

OLD CLARKE COUNTY COURTHOUSE, *North Church Street, Berryville*. The Old Clarke County Courthouse belongs to Virginia's collection of Roman Revival courthouses, the prototypes for which were the public building designs of Thomas Jefferson. With its simple tetrastyle Tuscan portico of wood and stucco set against red brick walls, the courthouse follows the Jeffersonian scheme of properly proportioned classical forms and details rendered in native materials. Like most courthouses of the period, it is topped by a classical cupola containing a bell to call the court to session. The building was designed and built by David Meade, younger brother of Bishop William Meade, soon after Clarke County was formed from Frederick County in 1836. Included on the court square are the county jail, sheriff's office, and former clerk's office. The modern courthouse stands nearby. 21–21 (9/16/82).

SARATOGA, *Boyce vicinity*. Revolutionary soldier Daniel Morgan had this limestone Georgian mansion begun for himself in 1779 while on leave from the war. He named it in honor of the battle of Saratoga in which he had recently distinguished himself as a military leader. The house was probably constructed by Hessian soldiers held prisoner in nearby Winchester. Recalled to active service in 1780, Morgan was made a brigadier general and won a brilliant victory against the British at Cowpens in South Carolina. In the antebellum period Saratoga was the home of Philip Pendleton Cooke, Virginia story-writer and poet. It was later occupied by his brother, John Esten Cooke, historical novelist and biographer. The house is a distinguished example of the large stone plantation houses erected in the lower Shenandoah Valley in the late 18th century. 21–70 (12/2/69); *National Historic Landmark*.

THE TULEYRIES, *Boyce vicinity.* This elaborate estate was formed ca. 1833 by Joseph Tuley, Jr., who inherited a fortune amassed by his father in the tanning business. So impressive were the results of Tuley's expenditures that he gave the estate a name alluding to the French royal palace the Tuileries, as well as to his own name. The grounds are dominated by a huge late Federal mansion fronted by a Corinthian portico and crowned by a domed cupola. Included on the property are formal gardens and a complex of elaborate farm buildings. After Tuley's death the Tuleyries was acquired by Upton L. Boyce, an attorney for the Norfolk and Western Railway. In 1903 it was purchased by Graham F. Blandy of New York. In recent years it has served as the country home of Blandy's sister-in-law, Mrs. Orme Wilson. 21–82 (7/6/71).

WHITE POST HISTORIC DISTRICT, *including entire settlement at junction of county roads 628 and 658.* The crossroads village of White Post grew up around the white-painted marker that Thomas, Lord Fairfax, had erected in the 1760s to point the way to Greenway Court, the nearby estate from which he managed his vast proprietary holdings. The post that gives the town its name has been replaced several times, but its form has been maintained as a village landmark and symbol of community identity for over two centuries. Bishop William Meade was born at White Post and later led the remarkable revival of the Episcopal church in Virginia in the decades following the War of 1812. The district is a visually cohesive grouping of some twenty-one residences, two churches, an old post office, and several abandoned commercial structures, all situated along two intersecting roads. The houses generally represent the various vernacular styles characteristic of Valley settlements from the 1790s to the 1920s. The town's most imposing architectural landmark, Bishop Meade Memorial Church (1875), is an example of the rural Gothic Revival style. 21–66 (8/16/83).

CITY OF COLONIAL HEIGHTS

On the heights above the Appomattox River overlooking Petersburg, this city takes its name from the fact that the marquis de Lafayette placed his artillery, known as the Colonials, here to shell British positions in Petersburg in 1781. The community was established in 1910 and incorporated as a town in 1926. It became a city in 1948.

ELLERSLIE, *Ellerslie Road.* The Ellerslie estate was founded in 1839 by David Dunlop, a native of Ayr, Scotland, who became one of the leaders of the Virginia tobacco industry. His castellated Gothic Revival mansion was designed in 1856 by Robert Young, a Belfast architect, and was surrounded by romantically landscaped grounds of unusual elaboration. Gen. P. G. T. Beauregard used the house as his headquarters in 1864, and the grounds were taken over as a rest camp for his troops after action along the Weldon Road. The property passed out of the family but in 1909 was acquired by Dunlop's grandson and namesake, who employed the Richmond firm of Carneal and Johnston to remodel the house in the more fashionable Bungaloid mode. The spreading hipped roof and dormers replaced the original flat roof, but the basic mass of the house and the tower are original. 106–1 (9/18/73).

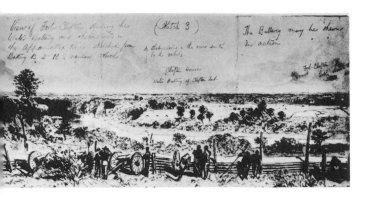

FORT CLIFTON ARCHAEOLOGICAL SITE, *Conduit Road.* The scene of three major confrontations between Union and Confederate forces in 1864 during the Petersburg campaign, the Fort Clifton archaeological site includes the remains of a Confederate fort, as well as those of a 19th-century house traditionally known as Clifton. A Union artist sketched a "View of Fort Clifton" from the Union battery across the Appomattox River in 1864. A representative example of Civil War fortifications, the site is preserved as a historic park by the city of Colonial Heights. 106–5 (10/21/80).

OAK HILL, *151 Carroll Avenue.* Oak Hill, on the heights above the Appomattox River overlooking Petersburg, is a Federal H-shaped plantation house only one story in height. Its front section is an elongated octagon of unusual refinement, with triple-hung sash and rich Federal detailing similar to that found in many Petersburg houses. The shape of this section apparently was inspired by the house at Violet Bank, the plantation immediately to the east. Both plantations have since been developed with 20th-century housing. Oak Hill was originally called Archer's Hill and was used for a gun emplacement by General Lafayette during the Revolution. The house was built for Thomas Dunn in 1825–26. 106–4 (4/16/74).

VIOLET BANK, *Royal Oak Avenue.* This compact and surprisingly sophisticated dwelling is distinguished by its three-part bays, intricate Federal woodwork, and Adamesque plasterwork ceilings. Originally the home of Thomas Shore, the present house dates from 1815 and replaces an earlier structure destroyed by fire. The three-part bays relate the house to a series of Richmond town houses inspired by designs of Benjamin Henry Latrobe. Latrobe visited Shore in 1796 and may have had an influence on the new house. Violet Bank was used as the headquarters of Gen. Robert E. Lee in 1864, and it was here that he learned of the explosion at the Crater. It is now owned by the city of Colonial Heights and is used as a museum. 106–3 (4/16/74).

CRAIG COUNTY

Nestled in the mountains of Southwest Virginia, Craig County
was named for Robert Craig, a 19th-century Virginia
congressman. It was formed from Botetourt, Roanoke,
Giles, and Monroe (now in West Virginia) counties in
1851 and was enlarged through several subsequent
additons. The county seat is New Castle.

CRAIG HEALING SPRINGS, *Craig Springs*. Craig Healing Springs is a collection of nearly thirty well-preserved early 20th-century resort buildings representative of the architecture of Virginia's more modest mountain spas. Developed as a resort between 1909 and 1920 by the Craig Healing Springs Company, the complex flourished with the advent of automobile travel in the years between the two world wars but declined in popularity with changes in travel and vacation patterns in the 1950s. The Christian Church (Disciples of Christ) in Virginia purchased the property in 1960 and has adapted it for use as a conference and retreat center, carefully maintaining the grounds and buildings as well as many of the original furnishings. 22–4 (12/16/80).

NEW CASTLE HISTORIC DISTRICT, *including Court Square and three adjacent buildings.* The secluded mountainous community of New Castle preserves one of the Commonwealth's antebellum court complexes. The principal building of the group is the porticoed courthouse, built in 1851 when New Castle became the county seat. With its tripartite scheme the building was modeled after the Botetourt County Courthouse. Standing to the northwest of the courthouse is the near-contemporary building containing the jail and sheriff's residence, also built in a provincial Greek Revival style. Across the tree-shaded court square is the Greek Revival Central Hotel with its two tiers of galleries, one of the larger surviving county seat taverns of the period. This group of court-related structures attracted enterprise and became the nucleus of a commercial center. Two representatives of late 19th-century commercialism are the First National Bank with its stepped parapet and bracketed cornice and a small, one-story insurance office, both located adjacent to the square. Union troops passed through the settlement during the Civil War and are said to have been responsible for the saber cuts on the courtroom balustrade. 268–13 (9/18/73).

CULPEPER COUNTY

*Formed from Orange County in 1749, Culpeper County was
named either for Thomas Culpeper, second Baron Culpeper of
Thoresway, governor of Virginia from 1677 to 1683, or for his
family, which had long held proprietary rights in the Northern
Neck. The county seat is Culpeper.*

FARLEY, *Brandy Station vicinity.* Farley's large frame house is
one of the least known yet most imposing of the Federal mansions in Piedmont Virginia built to accommodate members of
Tidewater families who moved to up-country estates after the
Revolution. Farley was originally a 3,000-acre tract called Sans
Souci, owned by the Beverley family of Blandfield in Essex
County. In 1801 William Champe Carter of the Albemarle
County branch of the Carters purchased Sans Souci, and renamed it in honor of his wife, Maria Byrd Farley Carter, and
built the present house soon after. With its 96-foot facade
marked by three pedimented pavilions, the house is an impressive, if provincial, interpretation of English neo-classicism. The
formality of the exterior was extended to the interior where the
first floor contains a suite of four reception rooms connected
by a T-plan hall with two staircases. Farley was purchased in
1863 by Franklin P. Stearns, a Vermont-born businessman who
served as director of several railroads, two canal companies,
and several Richmond banks and for a while was Virginia's
largest land proprietor. That same year the house was taken
over by Union general John Sedgwick, who used it as headquarters during the battle of Brandy Station, the largest cavalry
battle fought in the Western Hemisphere. The house stood
empty and neglected for many years but is currently undergoing a long-term restoration. 23–5 (10/21/75).

GREENVILLE, *Raccoon's Ford vicinity.* A massive country residence, Greenville was constructed in 1854 for Philip Pendleton Nalle, a local entrepreneur. The grandiose, if not ostentatious, dwelling is in a freely interpreted Classical Revival idiom, having giant Doric columns, tall bracketed cornices, and windows topped by heavy entablatures. The cornice masks the rare W-roof on all but the rear elevation. Indeed, Greenville is more akin to the antebellum buildings of the Deep South than to the generally more modest and refined structures of Virginia. It was designed by the Culpeper County physician, politician, and architect Jeremiah Morton, who designed several other porticoed plantation houses in the vicinity. Greenville was caught in the middle of considerable Civil War fighting in 1863–64. So heavy was the firing that the adjacent pasture was later called "cannon ball field." Nalle's son, Philip Nalle, Jr., sold Greenville in 1918. The house has been occupied sporadically since then. 23–9 (12/18/79).

GREENWOOD, *1913 Orange Road, Culpeper.* During the early 19th century many rich, influential men of the western Piedmont contented themselves with small yet commodious and carefully built plantation houses. Greenwood, built ca. 1823–24 for John Williams Green, judge of the Virginia Supreme Court, serves to illustrate this dwelling type. With its dormered center section and two-part, one-story wings, the house shows how a standard vernacular type could be enlarged and given a pleasing but unpretentious formality. The interior has been little changed since the 19th century and preserves most of its Federal woodwork. In 1825 Judge Green received at Greenwood the marquis de Lafayette and former president James Monroe during Lafayette's celebrated tour as "guest of the nation." The Civil War touched Greenwood when Federal troops occupied the house and established a gun emplacement on the lawn. 23–10 (1/18/83).

HILL MANSION, *501 East Street, Culpeper.* The Hill mansion is a sophisticated and well-preserved example of the Italianate style, one of the several picturesque architectural modes popular in America in the 1850s. The house was completed in 1857 for Edward Baptist Hill and is still owned by his descendants. It preserves its scored and painted stucco, elaborate cast-iron and wooden porches, and interior appointments, including a broad curving stair. The house served as a Confederate hospital and was visited both by Gen. A. P. Hill, a cousin of the builder, and General Lee, whose wounded son was nursed there. Later in the war it was used as headquarters for Union troops who permitted the Hill family to occupy two rooms. 204–2 (12/18/79).

A. P. HILL BOYHOOD HOME, *102 North Main Street, Culpeper.* Confederate general Ambrose Powell Hill lived in the original portion of this house from age seven until 1842 when he entered the U.S. Military Academy. Hill's parents enlarged the plain Federal town house into the present Italian Villa–style building just before the Civil War, expanding its depth and adding the third story, cupola, and heavy bracketed cornice. Later altered for commercial use, the building remains a dominant architectural element in downtown Culpeper. A. P. Hill was one of General Lee's most valued lieutenants; he assisted him in nearly every major engagement of the Army of Northern Virginia until he was felled in the siege of Petersburg. 204–6 (6/19/73).

LITTLE FORK CHURCH, *Rixeyville vicinity.* Built in 1774–76 as a chapel for St. Mark's Parish, Little Fork Church is one of the few colonial houses of worship surviving in the Piedmont. It replaced an earlier wooden structure destroyed by fire, and it is believed that the simple but dignified Georgian building was designed by John Ariss, to whom the nearly identical Lamb's Creek Church in King George County is also attributed. Although used as a stable by Union troops during the Civil War, the church retains much of its original interior trim, including an elegant paneled reredos. In the churchyard is a large marble monument erected in 1904 to the memory of the Little Fork Rangers, a Confederate company. The building has undergone an extensive restoration in recent years. 23–13 (5/13/69).

MITCHELLS PRESBYTERIAN CHURCH, *Mitchells.* This simple Carpenters' Gothic church contains the most elaborate example of late 19th-century folk-style trompe l'oeil frescoes in the state. Executed in 1892–99 by the Italian immigrant painter Joseph Dominick Phillip Oddenino, born in 1831 in Chieri, Torino, the artwork is a curious transplant in rural Virginia of the ancient art of fresco common throughout Europe. The scheme is architectonic, consisting of a Gothic arcade on the side walls and an apse flanked by pairs of twisted baroque columns. Mitchells Church was built in 1879 under the leadership of the Reverend John P. Strider. Oddenino's frescoes recently have undergone a complete restoration. 23–51 (12/19/80).

SALUBRIA, *Stevensburg.* Among the few representatives of mid-Georgian architecture in Virginia's Piedmont, Salubria was erected for the Reverend John Thompson, probably in the 1760s, around the time of his marriage to his second wife, Elizabeth Rootes. Thompson, a native of Ireland, served as rector of St. Mark's Parish and was first married to the widow of Governor Spotswood. Following the precedent of such better-known contemporaries as the Wythe house and Wilton, Salubria is distinguished by a carefully calculated proportional system and spare exterior ornamentation. Its otherwise plain facades are given an elegant rhythm by the use of segmental brick arches above all the openings. Lending the house special significance as a document of colonial artistry is its outstanding interior paneling, most notably that of the parlor, which is dominated by a paneled corner chimneypiece framed by stop-fluted Doric pilasters and topped by a full Doric entablature. The property was acquired by the Hansbrough family in 1792, who gave it its present name, meaning healthful. In 1853 Salubria was bought by Robert O. Grayson, whose descendants own the property today. Just before the Civil War, Grayson had three sides of his house rendered in scored stucco; the outbreak of the war is said to have prevented completion of the job. The house has been undergoing a careful restoration over the past two decades. 23–20 (12/2/69).

CUMBERLAND COUNTY

*Named for William Augustus, duke of Cumberland, third son of
King George II, this rural upper James River county was
formed from Goochland County in 1749. The county seat is
Cumberland Court House.*

AMPTHILL, *Cartersville vicinity.* The brick section of this
two-part house on a hill above the James River was erected ca.
1835 for Randolph Harrison in the Roman Revival style of
Thomas Jefferson. Jefferson sent Harrison plans and an elevation for a new house in 1815. The drawings do not survive, but
they may well have provided the basis for the house Harrison
built twenty years later, which with its refined classical elements set off by red brick walls is an elegant statement of Jefferson's architectural ideals. Back-to-back with the brick house
is an 18th-century frame house, probably built for Harrison's
father, Carter Henry Harrison of nearby Clifton. The frame
house was enlarged in the same period that the brick section
was added. Its interior has early paneled woodwork, but the
mantels are copied from designs in Asher Benjamin's *Practical
House Carpenter* (1830). Several early outbuildings survive
nearby. 24–32 (1/5/71).

CARTERSVILLE BRIDGE RUIN, *Cartersville*. The late 19th-century composite timber and iron superstructure of this engineering landmark was built on stone piers and abutments constructed in 1822 for a covered bridge. The 843-foot bridge was the last major bridge of such construction across the James River. All but the two end spans were destroyed by tropical storm Agnes in 1972. These spans and the stone piers have been preserved as an interesting eye-catcher from the hilltop village of Cartersville. Title to the ruin has been given by the state to the Cartersville Bridge Association. 24–53 (3/21/72).

CLIFTON, *Cartersville vicinity*. Revolutionary patriot Carter Henry Harrison was the original owner of this large wood-frame Georgian plantation house. As a member of the Cumberland Committee of Safety, Harrison wrote the instructions for a declaration of independence from "any Allegiance to his Britannick Majesty" presented to the Virginia Convention of May 1776. The convention was among the first of such bodies to declare outright for American independence. Clifton originally was included in a grant willed to Thomas Randolph in 1723 by his grandfather Robert ("King") Carter. Dating from the third quarter of the 18th century, the formally arranged house retains its early molded weatherboards and a fine suite of paneled rooms. 24–36 (4/17/73).

GRACE EPISCOPAL CHURCH, *Ca Ira*. Grace Church, Ca Ira, survives as a charming illustration of the stylistic hybridization that occurred with Romantic Revivalism in the antebellum period. Its temple form and finely jointed Flemish bond brickwork are an offspring of Virginia's Classical Revival tradition fostered by Thomas Jefferson, while its Greek and Gothic details were adapted from builders' pattern books. The church was erected in 1840–43 by Valentine Parrish, a local master builder, and is the only remaining building of Ca Ira, a town laid out in 1787 which prospered briefly in the antebellum period as a milling and tobacco warehouse center. The name Ca Ira is probably derived from a French Revolutionary marching song. 24–9 (6/17/80).

MUDDY CREEK MILL, *Tamworth*. Erected in stages, this large merchant mill achieved its present appearance after 1792 when an agreement was reached among its partners to raise the building to its existing height. Combining stone, brick, and wooden construction, the building is the state's only surviving mill with two tiers of dormers. Muddy Creek Mill operated until the 1950s, producing flour, meal, and other products of waterpower for the region as well as for shipment to Richmond. Much of the mill's machinery is intact. Surviving in the complex is the miller's house, a small brick store of ca. 1800, and a late 18th-century farmhouse, now the home of the mill-owners. 24–10 (6/18/74).

CHARLES IRVING THORNTON TOMBSTONE, *Cumberland State Park, Hillcrest vicinity*. The Charles Irving Thornton tombstone in the Thornton family cemetery is the only tangible reminder of Charles Dickens's visit to the Commonwealth during his tour of the United States in 1842. Already regarded as a major literary figure, the author, as a favor for a Thornton family friend, penned the stone's poignant inscription to commemorate the death of the Thornton infant in 1842. The inscription on the simple stone begins: "THIS IS THE GRAVE of a little Child whom God in his goodness called to a Bright Eternity when he was very young." Only one other Dickens epitaph is known, that of his sister-in-law, making the Thornton example unique among his American writings. 24–54 (6/17/80).

CITY OF DANVILLE

Named for the Dan River on which the city is located, this milling center and tobacco market in southern Pittsylvania County was founded in 1793. It was incorporated as a town in 1830 and as a city in 1890.

DAN RIVER INC., *along both sides of the Dan River in downtown Danville.* The Riverside Division buildings of Dan River Inc. represent several stages in the century-long development of one of America's major textile companies, including the firm's first cotton mill at the corner of Main and Bridge streets in downtown Danville. The complex consists of seven cotton mills, a flour mill, two masonry dams, warehouses, a dye house, a machine shop, a research building, the remains of a power canal, and a number of support buildings such as boiler houses and coal bunkers. The major architectural styles range from the relatively small, brick vernacular mills and outbuildings of the "cotton factory fever" of the 1880s and 1890s to the massive concrete modernist structure of the 1920s, with some minor additions from later years. 108–13 (7/20/82).

DANVILLE HISTORIC DISTRICT, *including Main Street south of North Street; Jefferson, Sutherlin, and Holbrook avenues; Pine, Chestnut, and Green streets; and West Main Street to West-moreland Court.* The Danville Historic District boasts perhaps the most splendid and most concentrated collection of Victorian and early 20th-century residential and ecclesiastical architecture in the Commonwealth. Lining Main Street and adjacent side streets is an assemblage of the full range of architectural styles from the antebellum era to World War I. The district is particularly rich in examples of post–Civil War styles such as Italianate, High Victorian Gothic, Eastlake, and Queen Anne. While much of Virginia was slow in recovering from the economic setbacks caused by the Civil War and Reconstruction, Danville's tobacco and textile enterprises brought the city great prosperity. This wealth found tangible expression in the elegant houses built by the local industrialists. The tobacconists were among the first group to erect mansions south of the downtown; the elaborate house built for James G. Penn at 862 Main Street is the most ambitious. The homes of the textile manufacturers soon began to vie with those of the leaders of Danville's tobacco industry. In 1882 the three Schoolfield brothers, along with Thomas Fitzgerald, founded the textile mill known as Dan River Inc. and erected several impressive dwellings in the district. One of them, the Schoolfield-Compson house at 844 Main Street, ranks with the best of the state's Italianate houses. Most of this post–Civil War residential growth, highlighted by several handsome churches, took place on land that was once part of the estate of Maj. William T. Sutherlin, whose Italian Villa–style home in the heart of the district served fleeing Confederate president Jefferson Davis as his last official residence. After suffering several demolitions in the 1960s, the district is now protected by local ordinance. 108–56 (11/9/72).

DANVILLE TOBACCO WAREHOUSE AND RESIDENTIAL HISTORIC DISTRICT, *roughly bounded by the Dan River, the Southern Railway tracks, and Jefferson, Wilson, Newton, Monument, and Patton streets.* Occupying some forty blocks of the heart of the city, this district contains the buildings forming the economic core of 19th-century Danville. The various warehouses, factories, shops, and dwellings represent the commercial development of the city and the rise of its working class. Early industrial activity in Danville grew in conjunction with the development of its transportation systems and with the cultivation of bright-leaf tobacco in the area, which shaped Danville into one of the South's primary tobacco markets. All the elements of a 19th- and early 20th-century tobacco-manufacturing town are present in the district, from working places to rows of workers' houses. Associated with the residential area are three cemeteries reflecting the local social history. One is a typical mid-19th-century municipal cemetery in the romantic landscape tradition; one is a cemetery set aside for blacks after the Emancipation Proclamation; and the third was established for Civil War veterans. The district contains evidence of prehistoric human occupation; however, modern settlement began in 1793 with the establishment of a tobacco inspection warehouse, which coincided with the official establishment of Danville as a town. The construction of a canal in 1818 and the coming of the Richmond and Danville Railroad in 1856 provided the transportation network essential for the area's commercial success. The tobacco industry achieved its greatest growth in the 1870s and 1880s with the emergence of plug and twist manufacture. Textile manufacturing began in the 1890s, although the district remained chiefly associated with tobacco. Today the district is composed of approximately 585 structures related to the development of Danville's tobacco industry, of which thirty-seven are factories, auction warehouses, or storage facilities, all constructed between 1870 and 1910. The residential area contains approximately 450 small single-story workers' cottages erected between 1880 and the 1930s. 108–58 (3/18/80).

PENN-WYATT HOUSE, *862 Main Street*. Indicative of the 19th-century affluence of Danville, the Penn-Wyatt house is the city's most individually exuberant example of Victorian residential architecture. James Gabriel Penn, builder of the house, came to Danville in 1868 and established himself as a tobacco-commission merchant. By 1876 he could afford one of the most extravagant of the many houses then being put up on Main Street. Penn's continued prosperity is reflected in the improvements he made to the house in 1887 and 1894 and in the carriage house be built in 1904. The resulting structure thus exhibits a wide range of stylistic features that characterize late 19th-century eclecticism, among which are the Italianate windows, the mansard roof of the tower, and the Queen Anne porch and belvedere. Consistent with the rich exterior is the ornate interior, which retains many of its fittings including intricately carved woodwork, stained-glass windows, and a variety of light fixtures. Penn's widow sold the house in 1934 to the Wyatt family, who owned it until 1977. The present owners have carefully preserved the Victorian character of the house and grounds. 108–3 (10/17/78).

SUTHERLIN HOUSE (DANVILLE MUSEUM OF FINE ARTS AND HISTORY), *975 Main Street*. This example of mid-19th-century America's Italian Villa style was built in 1857–58 for Maj. William T. Sutherlin, a member of the Virginia Convention of 1861 and later chief quartermaster for Danville. In April 1865 when the Confederate government was forced to evacuate Richmond, Danville was elected to serve as the South's temporary capital. President Jefferson Davis was taken in as a guest of Major Sutherlin. At the Sutherlin house Davis signed his last official proclamation as president of the Confederacy. The Davis occupancy lasted for less than two weeks; he and the remnants of his fugitive government left on April 10 for Greensboro, N.C., and their "flight into oblivion." Typical of the Italian Villa style, the Sutherlin house has a stepped-back facade, heavy bracketed cornice, and a square tower. The house long served as the Danville Public Library but has been restored in recent years as a museum and cultural center. 108–6 (5/13/69).

DICKENSON COUNTY

This mountainous coal-mining Southwest Virginia county was
formed from Russell, Wise, and Buchanan counties in 1880.
It was named for William J. Dickenson, delegate from
Russell County at the time the county was formed.
The county seat is Clintwood.

DICKENSON COUNTY COURTHOUSE, *Clintwood.* The Dickenson County Courthouse is a Colonial Revival landmark in the heart of the Commonwealth's coal-mining region. The straightforward porticoed building was erected during the county's prosperity in the 1910s, which resulted from expanded railroad construction, increased timber production, and coal mining in the area. Completed in 1915 from the design of architect H. M. Miller, the building is the third courthouse to serve the county since its creation in 1880. A modern wing has been added to the rear, but the courtroom located on the second floor behind the three arched windows survives almost unaltered. 196–1 (7/20/82).

DINWIDDIE COUNTY

This rural Southside county was named for Robert Dinwiddie,
lieutenant governor of the Virginia colony from 1751 to 1758.
It was formed from Prince George County in 1752.
The county seat is Dinwiddie.

BURLINGTON, *Petersburg vicinity.* The wood-frame, double-pile plantation dwelling of this Appomattox River property is a classic example of colonial Virginia's domestic architecture. Characteristic elements of the style include the formal proportional system, symmetrical arrangement of bays, weatherboarded walls, pedimented dormers, brick end chimneys, and paneled woodwork. The wainscot paneling is similar to that in several other Dinwiddie houses, suggesting a common craftsman. Unique to the house is an original architectural corner cupboard decorated with Doric pilasters, scrolled keystone, arched doors, and semidomed interior. Other noteworthy features include the paneled chimney piece, and the walnut Georgian stair. Destruction of the Dinwiddie records hinders documentation of the property; however, an 1802 insurance policy shows its owner then was Robert Pleasants. It was later owned by the Friend family for over a hundred years. 26–1 (10/21/75).

BURNT QUARTER, *Five Forks*. The earliest portion of this rambling frame house was built in the mid-18th century for Robert Coleman, ancestor of the present owners. Evolved to its present form by additions and changes, the house has interior woodwork in Georgian, Federal, and Greek Revival styles. The plantation, one of the oldest continuously operated farms in the region, derives its name from British colonel Banastre Tarleton's burning of a grain quarter on one of his marauding expeditions during the Revolution. On April 1, 1865, the property became the scene of fierce fighting during the battle of Five Forks. Union troops used the house as a headquarters and desecrated the interior. A series of family portraits, slashed by the Yankees, hangs unrepaired on the parlor walls. 26–25 (9/9/69).

CONOVER ARCHAEOLOGICAL SITE, *Carson vicinity*. The earliest known Native American occupation in Virginia dates to the Paleo-Indian period (at least ca. 9500 to 9000 B.C.) Archaeological sites dating to this remote era are rare; consequently, knowledge of this cultural period is quite limited. The Conover site located in southern Dinwiddie County represents one of the few identified locations in the state yielding a wide range of Paleo-Indian artifacts. The recovery of various stone tools and manufactured by-products at this prehistoric site indicates that it may have served as a quarry-related base camp or base camp maintenance station. Shown are some chert projectile points found here. 26–121 (6/21/83).

DINWIDDIE COUNTY COURTHOUSE, *Dinwiddie*. Since its completion in 1851, this simple Greek Revival public building has been the architectural focal point for this Southside county. It was described as a "very neat and tasty building" when first opened, doing "great credit to the builder." The courthouse was remodeled in 1858 when its interior was divided into two floors with the courtroom on the upper level. In March 1865 Union general Philip Sheridan, leading his troops in a drive on Petersburg, was checked temporarily at the courthouse. The attack, led by General Pickett, soon led to the battle of Five Forks, which heralded the final defeat of the South. The building received its Doric portico in 1933 through federal government assistance. 26–4 (2/20/73).

FIVE FORKS BATTLEFIELD, *Five Forks.* This decisive battle of April 1, 1865, took its name from the junction of five county roads that became the focus of intense fighting. The defeat of Confederate forces sent here to protect Gen. Robert E. Lee's last supply line forced the southern commander to abandon his defense of Richmond and Petersburg and begin his retreat west. Eight days later, Lee was outflanked by General Grant and surrendered his army at Appomattox. The five forks junction, next to Burnt Quarter plantation, retains the rural, open setting it had during the Civil War. 26–103 (9/9/69); *National Historic Landmark.*

MANSFIELD, *Petersburg vicinity.* This Appomattox River plantation house is one of a group of large houses associated with Roger Atkinson (1725–1784), local planter and Petersburg civic leader. Atkinson purchased the property ca. 1760 and apparently added the two-story section to the early 18th-century story-and-a-half dwelling already standing there. During the 1830s the place was owned by Hugh A. Garland, a biographer of John Randolph of Roanoke, who operated a girls' school here. With its fine interior woodwork and unusual form, Mansfield is one of several neighboring rural plantation dwellings that bear the mark of highly accomplished craftsmen. However, most of its farmland is being developed for modern housing. 26–12 (12/16/75).

MAYFIELD, *Petersburg vicinity.* This example of colonial Virginia architecture is the oldest brick house in Dinwiddie County and is distinguished by its detailing, proportions, and clipped gable roof. Its earliest documented owner was Robert Ruffin, who lived there until 1769. It later belonged to Thomas Tabb Bolling and then to the Goodwyn family. Gen. Robert E. Lee watched the final action at Petersburg from Mayfield before the retreat that led him to Appomattox. In 1882 the property became the site of Central State Mental Hospital. The house, long hidden from public view by surrounding hospital buildings, was spared demolition in 1969 when it was moved intact one mile to its present site on the edge of the property. It has since been restored under private ownership. 26–36 (5/13/69); *Virginia Historic Landmarks Board preservation easement.*

SAPPONY CHURCH, *DeWitt vicinity.* Deep in the timber farms of eastern Dinwiddie County, this simple frame church had as its rector from 1763 to 1801 Devereux Jarrett, a proponent of the Methodist movement within the Episcopal church. Jarrett was one of Virginia's few Anglican clerics to be affected by the Great Awakening and gained a reputation as a vivid and moving orator. He spurred several religious revivals, which he described in his *Brief Narrative of the Revival of Religion in Virginia* (1778). Jarrett's funeral in 1801 at Sappony was conducted by the pioneering Methodist circuit rider Francis Asbury. The church was built in 1725–26 by Edward Colwell as one of the two chapels of Bristol Parish. Tradition has it that the building partially collapsed in 1869 after a service marking the transfer of Jarrett's remains from Amelia County to Sappony. The roof was rebuilt and the body of the church enlarged; however, much colonial fabric, including paneled wainscoting, sections of original pews, and portions of the communion rail, was retained. Although a landmark of American Methodism, Sappony, like Jarrett, maintained its affiliation with Episcopalianism and is used by a local parish on special occasions. 26–19 (10/21/75).

WALES, *Petersburg vicinity*. Built for Howell Briggs (1709–1775), a militia captain, magistrate, and vestryman, Wales is a well-preserved, architecturally distinctive Southside plantation house. Howell Briggs's son Gray Briggs (ca. 1731–1807), born and raised at Wales, was a planter and an attorney and served in the House of Burgesses. He made Wales his home after completing his term in the assembly. The original ca. 1730 portion of the house is a simple hall-parlor dwelling in Virginia's traditional vernacular. This core was expanded ca. 1752 into a five-part Palladian-inspired structure with an overall facade 104 feet in length. The half-hip roofs covering the terminal wings are very unusual. The house has undergone remarkably few changes since the enlargement; the exterior preserves its early weatherboarding, window sash, shutters, hardware, and doors. Inside, nearly all of the original woodwork of each section remains. The most elaborate room, the west-wing parlor, is elegantly treated with a projecting paneled chimneypiece framed by massive Doric pilasters. In contrast to the many more elementary domiciles inhabited by Virginia colonists, Wales stands as an indication of the refined taste maintained by some of the leading families of outlying areas. 26–24 (11/19/74).

WILLIAMSON ARCHAEOLOGICAL SITE, *Dinwiddie vicinity*. This prehistoric archaeological site consists of a quarry workshop of Paleo-Indians dating back to about 9000 B.C. The twenty-acre site has yielded a full assemblage of fluted points, scrapers, knives, burins, hammers, and workshop debris. Most of the points and tools are made of chert, taken from a local outcrop. One of these chert projectile points is shown here. The site is one of the largest of its type and age located thus far in the county. Occupying a plateau overlooking Little Cattail Run, the site currently consists of cultivated farmland with some adjacent woodland. 26–35 (5/13/69).

1 IN.
4 CM.

CITY OF EMPORIA

Formed in 1887 from a merger of Hicksford and Belfield, the Greensville county seat was named for Emporia, Kans., hometown of a business associate of the local delegate. The charter was revoked in 1888, but the town was reincorporated in 1892.

GREENSVILLE COUNTY COURTHOUSE COMPLEX, *South Main Street*. Greensville County's courthouse square, which has served as the location of the county's seat of government since 1787, contains three buildings of architectural interest. The main element, the courthouse, was built in 1831 by Daniel Lynch as a three-part Palladian structure and was later embellished with a portico. The excellently documented clerk's office was built in 1894 by the Southern Fireproof Company after the plans of Reuben Sherriff. The former Greensville Bank building of 1900, now the county administrator's office, contains an extraordinary locally produced interior of decorative stamped sheet metal. The square was the scene of military action in the Civil War when Gen. Wade Hampton undertook to defend the railroad bridge across the Meherrin, General Lee's link to southern supply sources. 109–2 (9/16/82).

H. T. KLUGEL ARCHITECTURAL SHEET METAL BUILDING, *135 Atlantic Street*. The facade of the H. T. Klugel building is a highly original example of the use of galvanized architectural sheet metal. This singular work was fabricated in 1914 to ornament the newly built headquarters of Harry T. Klugel's metalworks firm, founded in 1902. The ornaments served as an advertisement of the rich decorative elements manufac-

tured by the company. Unlike most firms, Klugel did not produce a catalog but designed each piece to order with emphasis on style and craftsmanship. Other examples of his work in Emporia include the cornice of the Old Merchants and Farmers Bank and the interior paneling of the county office building. 109–5 (11/21/72); *Virginia Historic Landmarks Board preservation easement.*

OLD MERCHANTS AND FARMERS BANK BUILDING, *South Main Street.* The Old Merchants and Farmers Bank Building, completed in 1902, is a miniature version of the commercial structures that gave turn-of-the-century America's main streets imposing ostentation. Even such a small structure could project a sense of monumentality through the use of a mansard roof and a richly ornamented sheet-metal cornice manufactured locally by H. T. Klugel. The building was later used as the public library but was deeded by the city to the Greensville County Historical Society in 1977. It has since been restored and is now a law office. 109–8 (11/21/78).

VILLAGE VIEW, *221 Briggs Street.* Located amid spacious, parklike grounds, Village View is Emporia's outstanding example of Federal domestic architecture. A provincial expression of the Adamesque mode, the house features a refined main stair, highly ornamental mantels on the first and second floors, and scrollwork decoration in the fanlight and sidelights on the main entry. The construction date of the original portion of the house is uncertain. It probably was built ca. 1811 for William Parham and his wife, Elizabeth Wall Parham, who acquired the property from her first husband's estate in 1810. It was enlarged in 1819, and further improvements had been made by 1826 when the property was owned by Nathaniel Land, a planter. The house served as Confederate headquarters during the Civil War. It was later operated by the Briggs family as a boys' academy. 109–4 (11/18/80).

ESSEX COUNTY

On the Rappahannock River side of the Middle Peninsula, Essex County was probably named for the English shire. It was formed from the extinct Rappahannock County in 1692. The county seat is Tappahannock.

BLANDFIELD, *Caret vicinity.* Robert Beverley II, member of one of Virginia's great landed families and grandson of Robert Beverley, Virginia's first native-born historian, began planning this brick mansion for the family plantation on the Rappahannock in the late 1760s. He commenced ordering building materials from London in 1769 and started construction about the same time. Although the house probably was ready for occupancy by 1774, Beverley continued to order furnishings and other items for it over the next twenty years. The east dependency likely was not completed until after the Revolutionary War. The resulting five-part structure is an outstanding illustration of the influence of English Palladianism on Virginia architecture and represents colonial American house building at its grandest and most formal. The massive center section is highlighted by central pedimented pavilions and flanked by two-story dependencies connected by one-story hyphens. The dependencies frame a wide forecourt on the land side. The entire composition is constructed with exceptionally fine brickwork. The symmetrical floor plan of the center section follows illustrations in James Gibbs's *Book of Architecture* (1728), employing two lateral stair halls. During a remodeling of 1844 the original woodwork was removed and replaced with plain Greek Revival trim. Blandfield was sold by the Beverley family in 1983. The current owners have undertaken an extensive restoration of the house to its 18th-century appearance based on Beverley family papers and a scientific investigation of the building's fabric. 28–5 (5/13/69).

BROOKE'S BANK, *Loretto vicinity*. The charm of this small colonial plantation house may result from the fact that it was built for a woman, Sarah Taliaferro Brooke, who personally supervised its construction. Completed in 1751, the rectangular house, with its formal lines, fine brickwork, spare exterior ornamentation, and spreading hipped roof, is a good example of Virginia's early Georgian architecture. An odd note is the conspicuous diamond patterns formed by glazed headers in the two massive chimneys. The most important architectural feature of the interior is the broad paneled arch separating the center passage and the stair hall. Some of the woodwork in the principal first-floor rooms may have been installed by Mrs. Brooke's son. Because of its location on the edge of Rappahannock River, the house was an easy target when shelled by the Union gunboat *Pawnee* in the Civil War; but the damage was not irremediable. The house was restored in the 1930s after standing empty for many years. 28–7 (6/1/71); *Virginia Historic Landmarks Board preservation easement.*

CHERRY WALK, *Dunbrooke vicinity*. The outbuildings, farm buildings, and residence at Cherry Walk form an unusually complete eastern Virginia plantation complex of modest size, providing a rare, essentially undisturbed picture of a vanished life-style. The dwelling house, with its steep gambrel roof, plain interior, and unadorned brick walls, is a characteristic example of late 18th-century Tidewater architecture, built ca. 1795 for Carter Croxton, whose family had owned the property since 1739. The supporting outbuildings comprise two dairies, a smokehouse, privy, and kitchen. The farm buildings consist of a much-enlarged early barn, a plank corncrib, and a late 19th-century blacksmith shop. The buildings, erected over a long span of time, illustrate various rural construction techniques. Set along a country road with surrounding fields and a woodland backdrop, the grouping maintains its agrarian context. 28–8 (12/14/82).

ELMWOOD, *Loretto vicinity*. The wealth and influence of the Garnett family in the 18th century is illustrated by Elmwood, one of the most ambitious of Virginia's colonial mansions. Muscoe Garnett, whose family had been large landowners and public officeholders in Essex County since the 17th century, had the house built ca. 1774. The austere formality of the 100-foot facade contrasts with the highly ornamented woodwork of the interior, some of the finest of the late colonial period in the state. The drawing room, occupying the east end of the house, is especially grand in scale and elaboration, having broken-scroll pediments supported by Ionic pilasters decorating the doorways and chimneypiece. The house underwent a partial remodeling in the Italianate style in 1852 during the ownership

of Muscoe R. H. Garnett, a Confederate statesman. After standing empty for many years, Elmwood was carefully renovated in the 1950s by a descendant of the builder. The house is set off by a largely intact formal garden and a park, all situated on a ridge overlooking the Rappahannock River valley. 28–11 (6/2/70); *Virginia Historic Landmarks Board and Virginia Outdoors Foundation joint preservation easement.*

GLEBE HOUSE OF ST. ANNE'S PARISH, *Champlain vicinity.* Less than a dozen colonial glebe houses survive in Virginia, making these specialized dwellings a rare architectural group. The St. Anne's Parish glebe house is one of the finest and probably the oldest of this nearly extinct building type. Glebe houses were built on church lands rented or owned for the support of the parish. Although the houses themselves were sometimes rented, more often they were used as rectories. Because they frequently were built by craftsmen employed on the churches, it is not unusual for glebe houses to display a similar refined quality, especially in the brickwork. The construction date of the St. Anne's glebe house is uncertain. It probably was begun around the same time as the 1719 section of nearby Vauter's Church, for the brickwork is very similar. Its first occupant was the diarist the Reverend Robert Rose, who came to the parish in 1725. The property was sold by its parish as the result of the disestablishment and became a private residence known as Cloverfield. It has stood unoccupied since the 1960s. 28–14 (11/19/74).

GLENCAIRN, *Chance vicinity.* This informal old manor house has an unusual plan and was put up with rare framing techniques, which offer important clues to early building technology in Virginia. The oldest portion of the house began ca. 1730 as a one-room dwelling with exposed ceiling joists and exposed framing for an exterior cornice. This elementary dwelling was expanded to its present form with its long rear porch in the fourth quarter of the 18th century, during the ownership of the Waring family. The shed dormers likely date from a mid-19th-century renovation. An oddity of the plan of the later section is the exceptionally wide center passage. Glencairn has recently undergone a careful restoration after a period of neglect. It remains a conspicuous point of interest along U.S. Route 17. 28–15 (2/21/78).

TAPPAHANNOCK HISTORIC DISTRICT, *roughly bounded by Queen Street, Church Lane, Cross Street, and the Rappahannock River and including the grounds of St. Margaret's School.* The approximately eight-block core of this colonial port town on the Rappahannock preserves an assemblage of 18th- and 19th-century architecture. The district's principal building is the 1848 Roman Revival courthouse dominated by a Tuscan

portico in antis. On the same block is the 1728 courthouse partially burned by the British in 1814 and since remodeled as a Methodist church. The 18th-century debtors' prison and ca. 1808 clerk's office stand nearby. Houses in the district include the mid-18th-century Ritchie house on Prince Street, the late 18th-century Brockenborough house on Water Street, now part of St. Margaret's School, and the Roane-Wright house of 1850 of Duke Street. These houses respectively were the residences of three cousins, editor Thomas Ritchie, banker John Brockenborough, and Spencer Roane, members of a political circle known as the Essex Junto or Richmond Junto. The three men helped the Jeffersonian Democratic-Republican party maintain its national dominance in the early 19th century. Ritchie was the founder of the Richmond *Enquirer,* mouthpiece for the Virginia Democrats. Tappahannock began as a village known as Hobb's Hole in the mid-17th century. The town was formally chartered in 1682. 310–24 (8/15/72).

VAUTER'S (VAWTER'S) CHURCH, *Loretto vicinity.* The ability of the colonial mason to give articulation and dignity to an otherwise elementary structure is no better illustrated than in the brickwork of Vauter's Church. With glazed-header Flemish bond set off by rubbed-brick corners, gauged-brick arches, and molded-and-gauged pedimented doorways, the well-preserved masonry is a textbook of early 18th-century craftsmanship. The T-shaped building was erected in two stages: the rectangular section was completed ca. 1719 to serve as the upper church of St. Anne's Parish; and the south wing was added in 1731, as noted by an inscribed brick. The church underwent an interior remodeling in conjunction with the resumption of regular services in 1827, but much colonial fabric was reused. Unlike many other Virginia colonial churches, Vauter's escaped damage during the Civil War. 28–42 (8/15/72).

WOODLAWN, *Millers Tavern vicinity.* Woodlawn, also known as the Trible house, is an example of the fast-disappearing single-cell domiciles built in great numbers beginning in the late 18th century. These small but well-crafted dwellings demonstrate the newly acquired ability of modest Virginia farmers to create shelters more substantial and more refined than the rude cottages of the colonial period. The first portion of the tiny gambrel-roofed structure was constructed ca. 1816 for John Haile. The house was expanded with a lean-to addition ca. 1840 when it was acquired by George Trible. Recently restored after standing empty for several years, Woodlawn is a point of interest on U.S. Route 360, the old highway connecting Richmond and Tappahannock. 28–47 (2/21/78).

CITY OF FAIRFAX

*Originally named Providence, this former crossroads became
the site of the Fairfax County Courthouse in 1805. Its
name was changed to Fairfax in 1859. The community was
incorporated as a town in 1874 and became a city in 1961.*

FAIRFAX COUNTY COURTHOUSE, *400 Chain Bridge
Road*. The Fairfax county seat first was located at Colchester
but soon was moved to a site near present-day Tyson's Corner
where it remained until 1799. When Alexandria and what is
now Arlington County were made part of the District of Columbia in that year, the county seat was relocated to the town
of Providence, now the city of Fairfax. The design for the new
courthouse was obtained from James Wren, who also designed
Falls Church and Christ Church, Alexandria. In his design
Wren combined an arcade, a distinguishing feature of Virginia
colonial courthouses, with the temple form, a building shape
favored for many Classical Revival buildings. This combination was refined in subsequent decades for a number of courthouses designed and built by master builders who had worked
for Thomas Jefferson. During the Civil War the courthouse
was used as a military outpost by both Union and Confederate
soldiers. At various times in the war, the courthouse was visited
by Confederate generals P. G. T. Beauregard and J. J. Johnston,
as well as by President Jefferson Davis. The building continues
to house court functions and serves as a reminder of the largely
suburbanized county's link with the past. Its 1885 jail stands
nearby. 151–3 (10/20/73).

RATCLIFFE-LOGAN-ALLISON HOUSE, *200 East Main Street*. This early 19th-century residence is representative of the simple, vernacular architecture once common in Northern Virginia's towns and villages. It remains one of the few early structures in this rapidly urbanizing county seat community. Long known erroneously as Earp's Ordinary, the house was built between 1803 and 1813 for Richard Ratcliffe, a landowner who donated the lot for the county courthouse. Between 1820 and 1837 the building was operated by Gordon and Robert Allison as a postal station and stagecoach stop. The house was rescued from demolition in 1920 by Dr. Kate Waller Barrett, a Virginia social worker, and was restored soon after by her son-in-law and daughter, Mr. and Mrs. Charles Pozer. 151–2 (1/16/73).

FAIRFAX COUNTY

*This Northern Virginia county, accommodating many
surburban communities of metropolitan Washington, D.C., was
named for Thomas Fairfax, sixth Baron Fairfax of Cameron,
proprietor of the Northern Neck. It was formed from Prince
William County in 1742. The county seat is Fairfax.*

BELVOIR MANSION ARCHAEOLOGICAL SITE AND
FAIRFAX GRAVE, *Fort Belvoir.* Belvoir, built 1736–41, was
one of the great mansions of colonial Virginia. On a bluff overlooking the Potomac between Mount Vernon and Gunston
Hall, the house was the seat of Col. William Fairfax, cousin
and land agent to Thomas, Lord Fairfax. Belvoir was inherited
in 1757 by Fairfax's son George William Fairfax, who accompanied George Washington during a 1748 expedition to the
frontier to survey the Fairfax holdings. The house was gutted
by fire in 1783, and its ruins were demolished by mortar and
cannon shots fired from British ships in August 1814. The site
was eventually incorporated into Fort Belvoir, a large installation of the U.S. Army. Archaeological excavations have revealed the original configuration of the house, from which the
conjectural drawing shown here was made. The foundations
and associated sites are now protected by the army. Nearby are
the graves of Colonel Fairfax and his wife. 29–41 (7/17/73).

COLVIN RUN MILL, *Colvin Run.* Constructed between
1810 and 1820, this gable-roofed brick structure is a survivor of
the hundreds of early gristmills that once dotted Virginia's
countryside and were long essential to the economy of the
state. Its first owner and miller was most likely Philip Carper,
who held the property from 1811 until 1842. The mill remained
in operation through the 1930s; however, the realignment of
the adjacent highway disrupted the water supply, and the mill
fell into disuse and disrepair. By the time it was purchased in
1965 by the Fairfax County Park Authority, the mill was ap-

proaching a ruinous condition. Painstakingly restored, with its machinery patterned after the principles of Oliver Evans, Colvin Run Mill now is museum of 19th-century milling practices and design. 29–86 (9/21/76).

CORNWELL FARM, *Great Falls vicinity.* One of the landmarks along the Georgetown Pike, the Cornwell Farm residence is a well-preserved example of Northern Virginia's antebellum plantation architecture. Built in 1831 for John Jackson, the house, with its Georgian outline, displays the architectural conservatism that was prevalent among many of the landowners of the region. The Flemish bond brickwork of the facade is exceptionally well crafted and is comparable in quality to that found on the finest town houses of Alexandria or Georgetown. Union soldiers bivouacked on the grounds during the Civil War, and before the restoration of the house in 1936, the names of soldiers from several northern states could be seen inscribed on the interior walls. Despite the heavy suburban development of Fairfax County, Cornwell Farm retains a pleasant rural setting. The property takes its present name from B. F. Cornwell, who purchased the place after the Civil War. 29–9 (9/21/76).

DRANESVILLE TAVERN, *Dranesville vicinity.* This vernacular hostelry is a relic of the days when teamsters and settlers traveled the busy Leesburg Turnpike, one of the lines of trade and migration between the eastern cities and the newly settled lands of the west. The tavern was built in three stages; the earliest portion dates from ca. 1830, when its proprietor was Sanford Cockerille. Turnpike taverns of the period served various specialized functions: the Dranesville Tavern originally catered almost exclusively to teamsters and thus was known as a wagon stand. The tavern functioned through the Civil War although its period of prosperity had ended with the coming of the railroads. In 1968 Dranesville Tavern was acquired for preservation by the Fairfax County Park Authority and was moved about a hundred feet to accommodate the widening of Route 7. The building has since been restored. 29–11 (4/18/72).

FAIRFAX ARMS, *Colchester.* During the 18th century the Potomac River creeks were dotted with small port towns settled by Scottish merchants who acted as middlemen for trade between the planters and the mother country. When the harbors silted up, several of these towns became dormant. A typical case is Colchester on the Occoquan River at the southeastern tip of Fairfax County, a town which did not survive the 18th century. A relic of this once-prosperous community is the Fairfax Arms tavern, one of only two surviving 18th-century buildings of the settlement. The building was standing as early as 1763 when William Linton was cited for operating an ordinary on the parcel. William Thompson kept a tavern there from 1779 until his death in 1800, after which it became a private residence. The modest structure, with its frame construction, brick-and-stone chimneys, and hipped dormers, is representative of the simple vernacular style that characterized the buildings in these early ports. 29–43 (12/19/78).

FORT HUNT, *Alexandria vicinity.* Fort Hunt was part of the Endicott system of seacoast defenses erected between 1889 and 1901 to guard twenty-six of the nation's major ports. Located at Sheridan Point overlooking the Potomac, the complex was equipped with four concrete batteries and some thirty support structures, of which four remain. Battery Mount Vernon is shown. The fort was garrisoned until World War I; during World War II it served as an interrogation area for captured enemy officers. It was made part of the National Park Service system in 1948. 29–103 (12/18/79).

GUNSTON HALL, *Lorton vicinity.* Gunston Hall was the home of planter and Revolutionary patriot George Mason, the author of the Virginia Declaration of Rights as well as much of the Constitution of Virginia. The Declaration of Rights (1776) was the inspiration for the Bill of Rights of the U.S. Constitution. Mason's home overlooking the Potomac is one of the nation's more remarkable examples of colonial architecture. The compact but refined exterior was constructed ca. 1755. The extraordinarily rich architectural detailing of the interior was designed by William Buckland, a skilled English architect and joiner indentured to Mason. Employing both Chinese and Palladian elements, the masterful woodwork was crafted by William Bernard Sears, one of a team assembled by Buckland to execute his designs. The house and its extensive formal gardens, following the outline of the original landscaping, present one of the most elegant expressions of colonial taste. The property was given to the Commonwealth by Louis Hertle in 1932. Since his death in 1949, Gunston Hall has undergone a continuing restoration and is now exhibited and administered by the National Society of the Colonial Dames. 29–50 (9/9/69); *National Historic Landmark.*

HERNDON DEPOT, *Elden Street, Herndon*. This small board-and-batten rail depot in the center of Herndon is one of the many simple railroad stations that served modest rural and suburban communities in the last century. Twenty-one miles from Washington, D.C., Herndon was a busy commuter stop and a shipping point for dairy products going to the national capital around the turn of the century. The depot was in existence as early as 1857, serving what was then the Alexandria, Loudoun, and Hampshire Railroad. When the town was founded in 1879, the first town council meetings were held in the depot. Rail service through the community was discontinued in the 1960s, but the building later was restored to house town offices. Since that time, the depot has been made an architectural highlight of a redesigned town square. 29–212 (4/17/79).

HOPE PARK MILL AND MILLER'S HOUSE (ROBEY'S MILL), *Pope's Head Road*. This plain wooden mill and miller's house began as an adjunct to a large plantation, Hope Park. It later gained importance as a neighborhood mill, serving the needs of a few nearby plantations, as opposed to the larger merchant mills that served a greater area on a more commercial basis. The two buildings probably were erected ca. 1800 during the ownership of David Stuart. The property was caught in the crossfire of the Civil War, and during the winter of 1861–62 the mill was Post No. 3 for many Confederate units. The mill prospered once again around the turn of the century under the ownership of Frank Robey, whose death in 1906 brought an end to its commercial life. The complex includes several early outbuildings and presents an excellent picture of a neighborhood mill establishment. 29–18, 64 (11/16/76).

HUNTLEY, *Groveton vicinity*. An intriguing Federal dwelling, Huntley was built ca. 1818 as a secondary home for Thomson Francis Mason, a grandson of George Mason of Gunston Hall. Although compact and unpretentious, the house has singular architectural sophistication and exhibits the refined imagination inherent in the buildings of the English Regency period. Convincing arguments have been made for both Benjamin Henry Latrobe and George Hadfield as the author of its design. Both were English-born practitioners of their trade and were familiar with the latest architectural fashions of the mother country. Other than the change of roof form from a clipped gable to a full gable in the 20th century, the house has suffered few alterations. Preserved on the grounds are several original outbuildings including an icehouse and an unusually large brick privy. Huntley was sited on a steep ridge to take advantage of a distant view of the Potomac River. 29–117 (3/21/72).

LANGLEY FORK HISTORIC DISTRICT, *Langley.* The intersection commonly known as Langley Fork retains its historic identity and appearance in a region that is undergoing intense modern development. It includes an assemblage of local vernacular buildings scattered among large leafy lots. Six structures form the nucleus of the district: the Langley Ordinary, built ca. 1850; the mid-19th-century Langley Toll House; Gunnell's Chapel (shown), built after 1865 for a black Methodist congregation; the Friends Meeting House, erected in 1853; the Mackall house, now the site of Happy Hill Country Day School; and Hickory Hill, once the residence of Robert F. Kennedy. In the 19th century it was a junction on a major turnpike in Northern Virginia; and during the Civil War, Union general McCall of the Pennsylvania Reserves made Langley Ordinary his headquarters. 29–214 (09/16/80).

MOOREFIELD, *Nutley Road, Vienna.* Moorefield was the home of Jeremiah Moore (1746–1815), a pioneer Baptist preacher and reformer who was an early advocate of religious freedom and of the separation of church and state in Virginia. Moore was known to Thomas Jefferson, George Washington, George Mason, and Patrick Henry, and he encouraged their active support of his principles. His home, now surrounded by modern suburban housing in the town of Vienna, was a simple wood-frame vernacular farmhouse, typical of the area, until it was significantly modified in the 1950s when it was veneered with brick and had its dormers altered. Much of the original fabric remains intact beneath the later work, and it is hoped that it will be restored by its owner, the town of Vienna, to its original appearance. Moore lies buried in a family cemetery near the house. 153–4 (9/20/77).

MOUNT VERNON, *Mount Vernon, Alexandria vicinity.* Completed in its present familiar form by 1787, this was the home of George Washington, throughout his military and political careers. Washington became the proprietor of Mount Vernon in 1754 and through a series of alterations and remodelings transformed a simple farmhouse built by his father into the mansion that it is today, set off by its portico, cupola, and rusticated wooden siding. Every aspect of the estate—the architecture of the mansion, the decoration of its interior, the planning of the outbuildings, the layout of the gardens, and the operation of the plantation—received Washington's most careful attention, making the place a remarkable expression of his tastes and interests. After Washington's death at Mount Vernon in 1799, the property gradually fell into disrepair. In 1858 some 200 acres of the original 8,000-acre plantation were acquired for preservation by the Mount Vernon Ladies' Association organized by Ann Pamela Cunningham. The Ladies' Association continues to maintain the meticulously restored complex in its matchless setting on the Potomac as a reminder of the life and times of the nation's first president. 29–54 (9/9/69); *National Historic Landmark.*

MOUNT VERNON MEMORIAL HIGHWAY, *Alexandria, Arlington County, and Fairfax County.* First opened to traffic in 1932, the Mount Vernon Memorial Highway was the first parkway constructed and maintained by the U.S. government and the first such road with a commemorative function explicit in its name and alignment. The design consultants were Jay Downer, engineer; Gilmore D. Clarke, landscape architect; and Henry Nye, arborist. All three were employees of the Westchester County Park Authority where they gained experience in parkway design. The highway, with its stone-faced arch bridges, concrete slab base, beveled curbing, and lush landscaping affords fine views of both the Potomac River and an axial vista of the Washington Monument. Approximately fifteen miles long, the route begins at the western end of the Arlington Memorial Bridge and extends south along the Potomac through Alexandria and on through riverside woodlands and meadows to Mount Vernon. 29–218 (3/17/81).

PATOWMACK CANAL AT GREAT FALLS HISTORIC DISTRICT, *Great Falls.* The Patowmack Company was organized in 1785 to make the Potomac River navigable for trade from Georgetown to Harper's Ferry, as part of an effort by Maryland and Virginia to bring western trade to the Chesapeake region. The canal, one of the earliest in the country to have locks, was innovative from an engineering standpoint. George Washington, a prime mover in Potomac River improvements projects, served as the company's first president. The Patowmack Canal Corporation went bankrupt and dissolved its charter in 1826. The canal was abandoned in 1830. Now preserved by the National Park Service, the district contains numerous archaeological sites relating to the canal and the town of Matildaville, which was planned to serve the canal at Great Falls but failed to prosper and eventually disappeared. A remarkable engineering feat is the deep cut through the rock cliffs for the canal trace. 29–211 (9/19/78); *National Historic Landmark.*

POHICK CHURCH, *Fort Belvoir vicinity.* A sophisticated essay in the Georgian style, the exterior of Pohick Church, with its domestic aspect, recalls the more refined dissenter chapels of 18th-century England. The design of the building, erected 1769–74, is attributed to James Wren as it is very similar to Falls Church, a documented Wren work. George Washington and George Mason served on the vestry at the time of construction and may have had a hand in the design as well. The exterior is highlighted by carved pedimented doorways of Aquia Creek stone, which are likely the work of William Copein, the church's mason. The interior woodwork, executed by William Bernard Sears, was destroyed in the Civil War when the church was desecrated by Union troops who used it as a stable. The present Georgian-style woodwork is the result of a restoration of 1901–16. Pohick remains an active Episcopal church. 29–46 (11/5/68).

POPE-LEIGHEY HOUSE, *Fort Belvoir vicinity.* A monument in domestic architecture to the egalitarian faith of architect Frank Lloyd Wright, the Pope-Leighey house is the third and perhaps the most representative of Wright's Usonian houses. Wright developed the Usonian, or U.S.-onian, concept as a means of providing practical, economic housing that contained the quality and clarity of design he believed essential for making modern American life livable. The house was designed in 1939 for Loren Pope, who lived in it until 1946 when it was sold to Mr. and Mrs. Robert A. Leighey. Threatened by highway construction, the house was moved from its original site in 1965 and rebuilt not far away under the sponsorship of the National Trust for Historic Preservation in a wooded setting on the grounds of Woodlawn plantation. The house, preserving most of its Wright-designed furniture, is exhibited by the National Trust as a landmark of Wrightian design and American modernity. 29–58 (10/6/70).

ST. MARY'S ROMAN CATHOLIC CHURCH, *Fairfax Station.* Clara Barton, first president of the American Red Cross, established a field hospital at St. Mary's Church in 1862 during the second battle of Manassas. It was here that she first achieved note for her humanitarianism, heroism, and organizational ability. From St. Mary's as many as 1,000 wounded Union soldiers at a time were moved by train back to Washington. The simple rural Gothic building was erected 1858 to serve the Irish immigrants recruited to work on the construction of the Orange and Alexandria Railroad. Although its interior suffered as a result of its wartime use, the exterior remains little altered since its construction. The churchyard contains the graves of many soldiers who died during their hospitalization. 29–169 (2/17/76).

SALONA, *McLean vicinity.* With its extensive grounds, early outbuildings, and plain Federal architecture, Salona recalls an earlier era of Fairfax County when such country seats were common in the fine farmlands of the region. Built in 1812, the house first served as the home of the Reverend William Maffit and his wife, Henrietta Lee Maffit. President James Madison spent the night at Salona after he escaped from Washington during the British sack of the city in 1814. War touched Salona again in the winter of 1861–62 when the house was occupied as the headquarters of Union general George B. McClellan. Soldiers removed much of the interior trim, but the house later was restored and received its Italianate brackets and a two-story wing. Today the property is surrounded by the busy community of McLean, but the tree-dotted lawn preserves a rural setting for the house. 29–34 (6/19/73).

SULLY, *Chantilly vicinity.* Richard Bland Lee, younger brother of Light-Horse Harry Lee and uncle of Robert E. Lee, had this rambling farmhouse built in 1794. Lee was one of the founders of Phi Beta Kappa and served as a U.S. congressman. At Sully, Lee entertained such notables as George Washington and James Madison. Although it is not a formal mansion, the fine quality of the woodwork demonstrates the care and attention that was often given to less pretentious Virginia houses. Adding to its visual interest is the inviting piazza across the rear first floor, decorated with scalloped eaves. Among the several early outbuildings is a stone dairy/servant's quarters displaying a rare use of galleting (small stones inserted in the mortar joints for decoration) in Virginia. Sully was threatened with destruction when Dulles International Airport was built nearby. However, through a special act of Congress, it was spared and is now exhibited as a museum by the Fairfax County Park Authority. 29–37 (10/6/70).

WOODLAWN, *Fort Belvoir vicinity.* This five-part mansion was completed in 1806 on a site overlooking lands that formerly were part of Mount Vernon. The plantation was the wedding gift of George Washington to Eleanor Parke ("Nelly") Custis and her husband, Lawrence Lewis, respectively Washington's ward and nephew, who were married at Mount Vernon on Washington's last birthday. The crisply detailed, beautifully crafted mansion displays the refinement that has made the Federal style so admired. Woodlawn eventually fell into disrepair and was acquired by a group of Quakers in 1846. The house was restored in the early part of the present century for Elizabeth Sharpe, who had the wings and hyphens enlarged. Senator and Mrs. Oscar Underwood of Alabama made their home here before its acquisition in 1948 by the Woodlawn Public Foundation. The property has since been restored and furnished by the National Trust for Historic Preservation, which maintains it as a museum and a center for historical studies. 29–56. (12/2/69).

CITY OF FALLS CHURCH

Located in Fairfax County, Falls Church was named for the colonial church erected there in 1767–69. The church was so named because of its proximity to Little Falls on the Potomac River. The community was established in 1850 and was incorporated as a town in 1875. It became a city in 1948.

BIRCH HOUSE, *312 East Broad Street*. The Birch house stands out as one of the few surviving relics of Falls Church's mid-19th-century heritage. Conspicuously located on Route 7, the former Alexandria-Leesburg Turnpike, the original portion of the house was erected as a farmhouse before 1845 and evolved to its present form by the 1870s when it received its tall gable with Gothic-style bargeboards. The house was long the home of Joseph E. Birch, who assisted in the incorporation of Falls Church as a town in 1875 and served on the first town council. In 1968 his grandson deeded the house to Historic Falls Church, Inc. for preservation. The house has since been restored and sold with protective covenants. 110–10 (6/21/77).

CHERRY HILL, *312 Park Avenue*. The former rural character of the heavily developed city of Falls Church is embodied in the farmstead that now forms part of a six-acre park in the heart of the community. The grouping consists of a wooden Greek Revival house and a plain wooden barn, both built ca. 1840. The proximity of the farm to major roads made it a strategic point during the Civil War. Several skirmishes took place here, including the battle of the Peach Orchard, which was fought immediately behind the house. Cherry Hill also is said to have been a hiding place for Confederate soldiers. From 1870 to 1956 Cherry Hill was owned by the Riley family, cousins of the poet James Whitcomb Riley. The poet visited Cherry Hill many times, and some of his poems include descriptions of the farm and its residents. Judge Joseph Riley of Cherry Hill took a leading role in the incorporation of Falls Church in 1875 and served the town as an alderman. Court sessions for some time were held in the house. Judge Riley's son, J. Harvey Riley, was an ornithologist associated with the Smithsonian Institution. The house, barn, and old-fashioned yard are now maintained by the city as a civic amenity. 110–4 (6/19/73).

FALLS CHURCH, *115 East Fairfax Street*. Lending its name to the modern city of Falls Church, this colonial house of worship was preceded by a wooden church built in 1733. When it was determined unfit to repair after thirty years of service, the church wardens George Washington and William Fairfax advertised for persons willing to construct a new building. A design by James Wren was accepted, and the new church was completed under Wren's supervision in 1769. With its rectangular, two-story mass topped by a broad hipped roof, Wren's scheme has the plain, almost domestic aspect favored in the 18th century by low-church Anglicans on both sides of the Atlantic. During the Revolution, Falls Church was used as a recruiting station for the American forces. The church was abandoned after the disestablishment but was returned to service in 1839. As with many of Virginia's colonial churches, Union troops caused considerable damage, using the building first as a hospital and then as a stable. After the war the federal government awarded the parish $1,300 for damages. The church suffered a serious compromise to its architectural integrity in 1959 when the east wall was demolished in order to add a new chancel. Originally in an isolated setting next to a rural crossroads, the church is now in a vortex of suburban Washington traffic arteries. 110–1 (12/2/69).

FAUQUIER COUNTY

Named for Francis Fauquier, lieutenant governor of Virginia from 1758 to 1768, this Northern Virginia county, known for its scenic countryside and numerous estates, was formed in 1759 from Prince William County. Its county seat is Warrenton.

ASHLEIGH, *Delaplane vicinity.* Exceptionally handsome and well sited, this unusual Greek Revival villa was the home of Margaret Marshall, granddaughter of Chief Justice John Marshall. She received a portion of the family's Oak Hill estate and had the house built ca. 1840. Tradition has it that she designed the house herself after obtaining ideas on a trip through the Deep South. The tradition is plausible as the house is not typical of Virginia and resembles the raised one-story antebellum dwellings of Alabama and Mississippi. However, Ashleigh's graceful proportions and imaginative massing lend it a superior sophistication and make it one of Virginia's most appealing examples of the Greek Revival style. The house was constructed by master builder William S. Sutton, who erected many houses in the area. The property remained the home of Margaret Marshall and her husband John Thomas, whom she married in 1845, until 1860 when it was sold to a relative. It has since passed through several owners but has always been maintained as a prestigious estate. 30–85 (2/20/73).

BOXWOOD (GENERAL WILLIAM ["BILLY"] MITCHELL HOUSE), *Middleburg vicinity.* Gen. Billy Mitchell (1879–1936) made his home at this Northern Virginia estate from 1926 until his death ten years later. During his military career, Mitchell became the foremost advocate of air power as an essential element in the nation's defense. He foresaw that the airplane would replace the battleship as the military's most effective weapon. Frustrated by the official indifference to his ideas, he accused the military establishment of "almost treasonable administration of national defense." His resulting court-martial received nationwide attention and won him considerable public sympathy. The Fauquier County estate to which Mitchell and his wife moved after his court-martial consists of an 1826 stone house built for William Swart which the Mitchells enlarged by adding a wing. The property remains essentially as it was when the Mitchells lived here. 30–91 (2/15/77); *National Historic Landmark.*

BRENTMOOR (SPILMAN-MOSBY HOUSE), *173 Main Street, Warrenton*. This commodious example of the Italian Villa style in the heart of the community of Warrenton was built in 1859–61 for Edward M. Spilman, a judge of the Fauquier County circuit court. The Spilman family sold the place in the 1870s to James Keith, who served as president of the Virginia Court of Appeals. In 1875 the property was purchased by John Singleton Mosby, the Confederate ranger who was then Northern Virginia's best-known citizen. During the Civil War, Colonel Mosby and his small band of partisans outwitted and outfought the Union army to the extent that the region from the Potomac to the Shenandoah Valley became known as "Mosby's Confederacy." Mosby sold the house in 1877 to former Confederate general Eppa Hunton, who then represented the district in Congress. The house was the childhood home of Eppa Hunton III, a founder of the Richmond law firm now known as Hunton and Williams, one of the largest in the South. In his pattern book *The Architecture of Country Houses* (1850), Andrew Jackson Downing illustrated a design for a house resembling Brentmoor which he described as a "simple, rational, convenient, and economic dwelling for the southern part of the Union." 156–14 (2/15/77).

GERMANTOWN ARCHAEOLOGICAL SITES, *Midland vicinity*. In 1714 Governor Alexander Spotswood brought a group of German immigrants to Germanna in Orange County to mine and refine ore from his iron mines. The first party of colonists included mechanics from the Nassau-Siegen district of Westphalia. In 1718 twelve families dissatisfied with conditions at Germanna acquired a warrant for lands twelve miles north near the Fauquier County village of Midland. The site of the 1721 Tilman Weaver house and the adjacent Germantown Tavern site are the only identified archaeological remains of the settlement. The stones of the Weaver house chimney (shown) remain scattered amid the undergrowth. The ca. 1721 house site, together with the remains of the ca. 1780 tavern, should yield information about the home life of this early immigrant ethnic group. 30–239 (6/15/82).

MELROSE, *Casanova vicinity.* This rugged country house is rated among Virginia's most important expressions of the castellated mode of the mid-19th-century Gothic Revival. Constructed between 1856 and 1860 by George Washington Holtzclaw, a Fauquier County builder, Melrose was the home of Dr. James H. Murray and his brother, Edward Murray. With its battlemented stone walls, central tower, and dramatic siting, Melrose well illustrates the impact on southern landed families of the 19th-century romantic movement, especially the medievalism popularized by Sir Walter Scott. Melrose was the site of Federal troop occupation during the Civil War. More recently it served as the inspiration for Mary Roberts Rinehart's mystery *The Circular Staircase.* 30–70 (9/15/81).

THE MILL HOUSE (CHINN'S MILL), *Atoka vicinity.* The Mill House is an extraordinarily complete and well-preserved group of structures associated with a Federal-period rural Virginia gristmill operation and a 20th-century hunt country estate. A mill was operated on the site by Charles Chinn as early as 1768. Leven Powell, the founder of Middleburg, was responsible for many of the buildings of the complex, which includes, in addition to the present mill, the miller's house, the cooper's house and shop, the millowner's house (now the centerpiece of the complex), and what was likely a dairy-smokehouse. After the mill ceased operation, the property took on an entirely new aspect with its purchase by John S. Phipps, son of Henry Phipps, a partner of Andrew Carnegie and founder of the United States Steel Corporation. From 1924 to 1929 Phipps enlarged the millowner's house, renovated several of the outbuildings for use as guest quarters, added a stable and swimming pool, and undertook landscaping to tie the various elements together. That the complex harmoniously integrates both phases of its history speaks well for the soundness of the original configuration and for the sensitivity demonstrated in the 20th-century alterations. 30–650 (6/21/83).

OAK HILL, *Marshall vicinity.* John Marshall, chief justice of the Supreme Court, lived at Oak Hill from 1773, when his father, Thomas Marshall, acquired the property, until 1783. The seven-room wood-frame dwelling his father built is a typical example of Virginia's colonial vernacular. John Marshall became sole owner of the farm in 1785 when his father moved to Kentucky. Although Marshall lived mostly in Richmond and Washington after his marriage, he maintained an interest in his Fauquier County property, enlarging and improving the estate and using the house as a country home. In 1819 he built a Classical Revival temple-form house attached to the older dwelling to serve as a residence for his son Thomas. After the deaths of both John Marshall and his son in 1835, Oak Hill became the home of Thomas Marshall's son John Marshall II, whose overindulgence in hospitality forced him to sell the place to his brother Thomas. The property passed out of the Marshall family after Thomas Marshall, Jr.'s mortal wounding in the Civil War. 30–44 (4/17/73).

OAKLEY, *Upperville vicinity*. Oakley's residence, which sits grandly amid the undulating pastures of Northern Virginia'a countryside, is a sophisticated and well-preserved country house in the Italian Villa style, which was infrequently employed in the region. Completed in 1857, the house retains a romanticism symbolic of the life-style of its first owner, Richard Henry Dulany. Dulany was the founder of the Upperville Colt and Horse Show, the oldest in the country and a focal point of equestrian activity in Virginia's hunt country. Cavalry skirmishes took place on the Oakley property in the Civil War, and the house was occupied successively by Confederate and Union troops. The architecturally conspicuous rear veranda was given its intermediate balcony in recent years by its present owner, Mrs. Archibald Cary Randolph, who continues to maintain the estate as a leading horse farm. 30–46 (6/15/82).

OLD FAUQUIER COUNTY JAIL, *Courthouse Square, Warrenton*. Warrenton's former jail is one of the more complex representatives of the state's early county penal architecture. Included in the grouping is the 1808 brick jail, converted in 1822 with the addition of a stone kitchen to the jailer's residence, and the parallel 1822 stone jail with its high-walled jailyard. Located next to the courthouse, the group provides a telling picture of conditions endured by inmates of such county facilities over the past century and a half. A jail was built for the county in 1779, but it proved to be inadequate within a number of years. The more substantial brick structure was finished in 1808, and on October 24 the keys to the new jail were turned over by the court to the sheriff. With the completion of the stone jail of 1822, the resulting two-part building served the county until 1964. Since that time the ensemble has been given over to the Fauquier County Historical Society to serve as a county history museum. The 1822 stone jail preserves its original plank-lined cells. 156–4 (2/15/77).

UPPERVILLE HISTORIC DISTRICT, *including the entire village extending approximately a mile along U.S. Route 50*. The small hamlet of Upperville is one of Northern Virginia's best-preserved linear villages. Surrounded by the region's well-tended farmland, Upperville is a principal geographic reference point for Virginia's hunt country. The town was laid out in 1797 by Joseph Carr along the Alexandria-Winchester Turnpike and was established officially as a town in 1818. Carr planned for the lower or western end to be devoted to commerce and the upper or eastern end to be residential, a scheme generally preserved to the present, with the town taking its name from the residential portion. Surviving along the entire length of the community is a range of detached provincial versions of the various 19th-century styles in brick, wood, and log, all shaded by masses of trees. A striking, albeit modern, accent in the middle of the community is Trinity Episcopal Church, crafted in the style of a French medieval parish church. The church

was donated in the 1950s by philanthropist Paul Mellon in memory of his first wife. Upperville is the home of the nation's oldest horse show, founded in 1853 by Richard Henry Dulany. The rules of the American-English Foxhound Trials were signed on the gallery of an Upperville inn in 1905 by sportsmen Harry Worchester Smith and A. Henry Higginson. 400–64 (1/18/72).

WARRENTON HISTORIC DISTRICT, *including the early part of the town occupying the ridge above U.S. Route 29 and extending down Culpeper Street.* From its beginnings as a late colonial crossroads village, this prosperous courthouse town has known such lawyers and politicians as John Marshall, who practiced law here; William Smith, governor of Virginia in 1846–49 and 1864–65; and Eppa Hunton, a Confederate general and U.S. congressman. The town, known as Fauquier Court House until its incorporation in 1810, takes its present name from Warren Academy, the first of the private academies and seminaries that flourished here from the late 18th century to the early 20th century. As a Northern Virginia county seat since 1759 and a community long noted for its beautiful setting, healthful climate, and cultivated society, Warrenton boasts an exceptional collection of governmental, residential, and commercial buildings reflecting a wide range of 19th-century styles and tastes, as well as a general prosperity. The district also preserves a number of structures associated with the Civil War, when Warrenton served as headquarters and camp for armies of both sides. The architectural focal point of the district is the county courthouse, a Classical Revival building erected in 1890 on the site of an earlier one destroyed by fire. The most prestigious residences line Culpeper Street, which leads down the hill from the courthouse. 156–19 (8/16/83).

WAVERLEY, *Middleburg vicinity.* This ochre-colored mansion with its Greek Revival portico and Gothic Revival rear wing is an architectural highlight on the scenic Halfway Road connecting Middleburg and The Plains. The core of the house is an 18th-century stone cottage which was significantly enlarged and embellished during antebellum times, so that it reflects the changing architectural modes of the region as well as the changing tastes and life-styles of its occupants. Signaling the era when the region became popular for country estates, the house was restored in the 1940s by Mr. and Mrs. Thomas Furness, who employed Chicago architect David Adler to direct the work. The property now serves as the home of the Piedmont Vineyards. 30–226 (9/19/78); *Virginia Historic Landmarks Board preservation easement.*

FLOYD COUNTY

This mountainous Southwest Virginia county was named for
John Floyd, governor of Virginia from 1830 to 1834. It was
formed from Montgomery in 1831, and part of
Franklin County was added later. The county seat is Floyd.

FLOYD PRESBYTERIAN CHURCH *Floyd*. This simple Greek Revival church in the county-seat community of Floyd was a result of the Second Great Awakening of the 1840s, which brought about the expansion of Presbyterianism into southern and western Virginia. The Floyd congregation flourished and in 1850 erected a new brick building in the popular Grecian taste. It was built by Henry Dillon, an Irish immigrant who grew up and trained in Charleston, S.C. After moving to Floyd County, Dillon built several buildings in the area including a now-demolished courthouse. As was the practice among country builders of the day, Dillon relied on a pattern book for many of the church's details, in this case *The Practical House Carpenter* (1830) by Asher Benjamin. The church, the oldest public building in the county, remained in continuous use by the Presbyterians until 1974. It is currently used as a Baptist church and art gallery. 219–3 (12/16/75).

ZION LUTHERAN CHURCH AND CEMETERY, *Floyd vicinity*. Zion Lutheran Church in Floyd County is a landmark to the religious history of Southwest Virginia and to the enduring cultural traditions of German pioneers who moved into the region at the end of the 18th century. Formed in 1813 to serve the spiritual needs of settlers north of the town of Floyd, the Zion congregation occupied three successive buildings before the present structure was erected in 1898. A large cemetery to the rear of the building holds a rich collection of 19th-century funerary art, including a number of distinctive German-style markers carved by local artisans. The oldest inscribed stone in the group is dated 1817. 31–24 (6/16/81).

FLUVANNA COUNTY

*Fluvanna County takes its name from the 18th-century term for
the upper James River, meaning "river of Anne," in honor
of Queen Anne. It was formed from Albemarle County in
1777. The county seat is Palmyra.*

A

BREMO HISTORIC DISTRICT, *Bremo Bluff vicinity*. The Bremo Historic District includes three separate but related estates, all created by the planter, soldier, and reformer Gen. John Hartwell Cocke (1780–1866) out of his family's 1714 land grant, now in Fluvanna County. Still owned by Cocke's descendants, the three properties—Upper Bremo (*A*), Lower Bremo (*B*), and Recess (*C*)—preserve three architecturally singular dwellings and numerous associated buildings, all erected under Cocke's close supervision. The principal architectural piece is the Palladian mansion at Upper Bremo, completed in 1820, for which Cocke sought advice from Thomas Jefferson and other builders. While the house contains much of the architectural character as well as many forms and devices found in Jefferson's works, the residence is actually the creation of Cocke himself, in collaboration with the architect and master builder John Neilson, who had worked for Jefferson at Monticello and the University of Virginia. Contrasting markedly with the classical Upper Bremo are the houses at Lower Bremo and Recess, both in a neo-Jacobean style, the inspiration for which Cocke took from Bacon's Castle in his native Surry County and the Custis house (since destroyed) in Williamsburg. Lower Bremo incorporates a ca. 1723 stone hunting lodge which had been expanded into a farmhouse by the time Cocke and his family began seasonal visits from 1803 until 1809 when Recess was completed. The family moved from Recess to Upper Bremo in 1820; in the 1830s Cocke remodeled the two earlier houses for two of his sons. Recess was completed for his son John in 1836, and a new Jacobean wing was added to Lower Bremo for his son Charles in 1839. Lower Bremo was further remodeled by Baltimore architect Robert E. Lee Taylor in 1917 when the old-

B

C

est portions were encased in the Jacobean style to match the section built by Cocke. In addition to the three houses, the estates contain an amazing variety of outbuildings, farm dwellings, and farm buildings, including the extraordinary porticoed stone barn at Upper Bremo and an elaborate stable at Recess. Also in the district is an elegant little Doric temple designed by Alexander Jackson Davis to shelter Cocke's Temperance Spring. The temple originally stood on the lower edge of the property next to the James River and Kanawha Canal but was later moved to its present location up on the grounds of Upper Bremo. The many and varied structures and landscape features represent General Cocke's wide range of interests—from agricultural reform to temperance. Cocke also was an outspoken opponent of slavery, serving as senior vice-president of the American Colonization Society. He was a strong believer in public education, supporting Jefferson in the creation of the University of Virginia and serving on its board for thirty-three years. 32–2 (9/9/69); *National Historic Landmark; Virginia Historic Landmarks Board preservation easement (Lower Bremo)*.

BREMO SLAVE CHAPEL, *Bremo Bluff*. The simple Gothic Revival structure now serving as the parish hall of Grace Episcopal Church in Bremo Bluff was constructed in 1835 as a slave chapel for Bremo, the adjacent plantation of John Hartwell Cocke. It is the state's only known slave chapel and represents Cocke's deep concern for the religious and moral edification of slaves. Although Cocke felt that immediate emancipation was impractical, he believed that the South should be preparing for the future when freeing the slaves would become a reality. As part of the emancipation process, Cocke illegally taught his slaves to read and decided that it was his Christian duty to provide them with religious instruction. General Cocke frequently conducted services for his slaves in the chapel and demonstrated his conviction in this regard by taking communion in Richmond's African Baptist Church in 1852. The chapel fell into disuse after the Civil War, and ca. 1883 it was moved from the chapel field of Lower Bremo to the village of Bremo Bluff to serve the local Episcopal parish. Consecrated in 1884, it was used as a house of worship until 1924 when the present church was built. 32–30 (12/18/79).

FLUVANNA COUNTY COURTHOUSE HISTORIC DISTRICT. *including the whole of the village of Palmyra.* Termed by architectural historian Talbot Hamlin the "Acropolis of Palmyra" this tiny cluster of court structures, dominated by a temple-form courthouse, stands grandly overlooking the surrounding buildings and rural setting of the county-seat settlement. Gen. John Hartwell Cocke of nearby Bremo served as one of the five commissioners who drafted plans for both the courthouse and jail, and tradition attributes to Cocke the primary responsibility for their final appearance. The 1829 stone jail was built by John G. Hughes and is markedly similar in style to the distinctive outbuildings at Bremo. Construction of the courthouse, completed in 1831, was supervised by Walker Timberlake, a Methodist preacher who undertook various architectural and engineering works in the county. The courthouse is one of the few antebellum courthouses in the state to remain without additions and to retain both its original interior arrangement and many of its original fittings. While it lacks the bookish, academic quality of many later Greek Revival buildings, it conveys the bold, no-nonsense character and feeling of personal attention evident in all buildings associated with General Cocke. Conspicuously inscribed on the stone lintel above the entrance is "THE MAXIM HELD SACRED BY EVERY FREE PEOPLE / OBEY THE LAWS." 32–40 (1/5/71).

GLEN ARVON, *Bremo Bluff vicinity.* William Galt, a native of Scotland who became a leading Richmond merchant, left at his death ca. 1825 his vast Fluvanna County holdings to his great-nephews William and James Galt. Out of concern for his poorer relatives, the elder Galt had sent for his great-nephews from Scotland and raised them to assist with his business ventures. They divided the property evenly, James Galt taking Point of Fork, the lower tract, and William Galt II taking Glen Arvon, the upper tract. In 1836 they built identical Classical Revival mansions on their tracts. Among the most impressive dwellings of the upper James River region, the houses have graceful proportions and fine detailing. With their large Greek Doric porticoes, they illustrate the stylistic transition from the delicate Adam style of the Federal period to the more monumental Greek Revival idiom. An inventory of Glen Arvon's contents made at the second William Galt's death in 1851 lists a $300 piano, $462 worth of silverware, 800 books, and 212 bottles of Madeira wine, indications of the elegant life-style he maintained here. 32–15 (12/16/75).

POINT OF FORK ARSENAL ARCHAEOLOGICAL SITE, *Columbia vicinity.* An arsenal serving the Commonwealth forces was established at this strategic point during the Revolution and was raided on June 5, 1781, by Col. John Graves Simcoe, commander of the Queen's Rangers, in a move coinciding with Tarleton's raid on the Virginia legislature at Charlottesville. Simcoe's men destroyed the buildings and burned the supplies, leaving only the stone foundations. New buildings were erected near the site after the war, and Point of Fork was operated as a state arsenal until 1801 when it was abandoned in favor of the more centrally located arms manufactory in Richmond. During its brief period of service, Point of Fork was used for the manufacture and repair of arms and equipment and supplied material to combat the Whiskey Rebellion and to aid the Fallen Timbers campaign. Study of the foundation remnants and excavation of the site could provide a more complete understanding of the nature of one of the nation's few 18th-century arsenals. 32–36 (11/5/68).

POINT OF FORK PLANTATION, *Columbia vicinity.* Named for its situation at the junction of the James and Rivanna rivers, Point of Fork plantation is marked by a Classical Revival mansion, one of two identical houses built in 1836 as residences for the two great-nephews of William Galt, a Richmond merchant. The Galts' houses are major examples of the plantation architecture of the upper James River region, illustrating the transition from the Adam influence of the Federal period to the Greek Revival style. The interior of each house has large, airy rooms on either side of a center hall dominated by a spiral stair. Union general Philip Sheridan set up headquarters at Point of Fork in March 1865. His troops robbed Galt's slaves of their personal possessions and destroyed the croplands and fencing. Point of Fork is also believed to be the site of Rausawek, capital of the Monocan Indian nation, which Capt. John Smith noted on his map of 1607. 32–24 (4/16/74).

CITY OF FRANKLIN

The city of Franklin started in the 1830s as a stop in
Southampton County along the Portsmouth and Roanoke
Railroad line. The origin of the name is uncertain;
it may have been named for Benjamin Franklin or for
an individual named Franklin who kept a store in
the vicinity. It became a post village in 1855
and was incorporated as a town in 1876.
Franklin became a city in 1961.

THE ELMS, *Clay Street.* Built by Paul D. Camp, founder of the Camp Manufacturing Company, today's Union Camp Corporation, the Elms stands as a tangible indication of the success of a large industrial enterprise. The lumber industry that Camp and his brothers developed in Southampton County after the Civil War revived the economy of southeastern Tidewater Virginia and also enabled the Camp family to create new cultural resources for the Franklin area in the form of schools and libraries. The rambling late Victorian house, built in 1898, is characteristic of the residences built by small-town businessmen and community leaders in the late 19th century. Typical of such houses, it has numerous gables, a corner tower, long front porch, and fancy interior woodwork. 145–5 (9/15/81).

FRANKLIN COUNTY

Formed from Bedford and Henry counties in 1785, this largely rural county at the base of the Blue Ridge Mountains south of the Roanoke River was named in honor of Benjamin Franklin. Its county seat is Rocky Mount.

BOOKER T. WASHINGTON NATIONAL MONU-MENT. *Hardy vicinity.* Negro educator Booker T. Washington was born a slave on the Burroughs plantation in Franklin County on April 5, 1856. With his freedom gained following the Civil War, Washington attended Hampton Institute and later taught there. Because of his achievements as an educator, he was selected to establish a normal school for blacks in Alabama which became the Tuskegee Institute. As stated on a monument erected in his honor at Tuskegee, Washington "lifted the veil of ignorance from his people and pointed the way to progress through education and industry." Washington's career as the preeminent black leader of his generation is documented in his autobiography *Up from Slavery.* He exerted his great influence both in the Republican party and as a humanitarian for the benefit of his fellow blacks. The Burroughs plantation has been acquired by the National Park Service and is maintained as a living historical farm. Washington's humble origins are memorialized with a replica of the slave cabin in which he was born. 33–15 (1/16/73).

WASHINGTON IRON FURNACE, *Old Furnace Road, Rocky Mount*. Ironmaking was taking place at this site as early as 1770 under the direction of John Donelson, the father of Rachel Donelson Jackson, wife of President Andrew Jackson. The industry was sold in 1779 to Jeremiah Early and James Calloway, who patriotically changed its name from the Bloomery to Washington Iron Works. The Saunders brothers bought it ca. 1820, and Peter Saunders, Jr. became the manager. The industry flourished and by 1836 employed as many as a hundred workers to operate the furnace and forge. All that remains of this once-busy place is the furnace itself, a tapered granite structure with its hearth and bellows opening at the base of its front. Standing thirty feet high, the furnace is one of the earliest and best preserved of its type and is an impressive reminder of Virginia's former leading role in the iron industry. 157–29 (10/17/72).

WOODS-MEADE HOUSE (GREER HOUSE), *118 Maple Street, Rocky Mount*. One of the landmarks of Rocky Mount, a community which retains only a few antebellum structures, the Woods-Meade house is a vernacular dwelling with sophisticated overtones and a complex evolution. The front section was built ca. 1830 for Robert T. Woods, who served in both the Virginia House of Delegates and Virginia senate. It has distinctive masonry details including a molded-brick cornice, gauged-brick jack arches, and curious half-round brick pilasters and rounded brick porch supports. Morrison Meade acquired the property in 1834 and enlarged the house by adding a frame section on the rear wall, connecting the house to a kitchen outbuilding. The two-story addition, with side porches, made a small house into a relatively commodious one. The difference in the trim of the two sections illustrates the changing tastes in regional domestic architecture. 157–3 (10/20/81).

FREDERICK COUNTY

Formed from Orange County is 1738, with parts of Augusta added later, this northernmost Shenandoah Valley county was named in honor of Frederick Louis, Prince of Wales, son of King George II. Its county seat is Winchester.

BELLE GROVE, *Middletown vicinity.* Belle Grove's dwelling house was erected in 1794–96 for Maj. Isaac Hite, Jr., a Revolutionary officer and grandson of Jost Hite, pioneer settler of the Shenandoah Valley. Isaac Hite, Jr., was married to Nelly Conway Madison, sister of James Madison. When planning for the house began, Madison wrote to his friend Thomas Jefferson asking for suggestions on the plans, requesting him specifically to comment on the portico. Although Jefferson apparently suggested refinements, the house, despite its stone construction, is more in the spirit of the Adam-inspired Federal architecture of the day than the monumental Classical Revivalism espoused by Jefferson. The delicacy of the Federal style is seen particularly in the interior woodwork, which is some of the most beautiful and finely crafted in the state. Belle Grove remained in the Hite family until 1860. Considerable activity took place in and around the plantation during the Civil War, culminating in the battle of Cedar Creek on October 19, 1864, when the successful Union counterattack led by Gen. Philip Sheridan effectively ended the Valley campaign in favor of the North. The house served as Union headquarters during the battle. Exactly a century later, Francis Welles Hunnewell bequeathed the property to the National Trust for Historic Preservation. Belle Grove has since served as a museum interpreting the history of the lower Shenandoah Valley. 34–2 (11/5/68); *National Historic Landmark.*

WILLA CATHER BIRTHPLACE, *Gore*. The American novelist and short-story writer Willa Cather (1873–1947) was born in this plain weatherboarded house with a log core set alongside the road in the tiny community of Gore in the Back Creek valley north of Winchester. In 1883 the young Willa and her parents moved to Red Cloud, Nebr., where she spent her formative years. In her writings Cather concentrated on the pioneer traditions of the Nebraska prairie and the deserts of the Southwest, emphasizing the themes of courage, struggle, and respect for the land. She received the Pulitzer Prize for her novel *One of Ours* (1922). Cather's simple Virginia birthplace was built in the early 19th century for her great-grandfather Jacob Seibert. It was enlarged and remodeled ca. 1850. The house was owned and occupied by her maternal grandmother, Rachel E. Boak, when her parents were married there in 1872. 34–161 (9/21/76).

HOPEWELL FRIENDS MEETING HOUSE, *Clear Brook vicinity*. Quakers began to lose their predominance in eastern Pennsylvania by the second quarter of the 18th century, and large numbers of them moved into unsettled lands of the Shenandoah Valley in hopes of establishing communities that would be largely of their denomination. The Hopewell Society of Friends was established in Frederick County in 1734, and in 1759 the congregation replaced its first simple meetinghouse with the earliest portion of the present building, erected by Thomas McClun, who completed it in 1761. In 1788–94 the two-story limestone structure was doubled in size by the addition of its western half. A schism developed within the society in 1827, and a partition was erected through the interior so that each group could have its respective meeting place. The factions reunited in 1910, and the partition was removed. Echoing the quiet sobriety of the Quakers themselves, the plain building, one of the oldest religious structures in the region, remains in use. 34–6 (11/15/77).

ST. THOMAS'S CHAPEL, *Middletown*. An awesome starkness lends this Gothic Revival country church a visual strength lacking in most of its more elementary contemporaries. The verticality of the Gothic style is given full play in the tall pointed windows and the three arches of the facade. St. Thomas's was built ca. 1835 to serve the Episcopal congregation of the village of Middletown and was completed by 1837 when Bishop Meade officiated at confirmation there. The Episcopalian denomination traditionally has been attentive to the architectural quality of its churches; hence it is not surprising that St. Thomas's is a quite early and indeed quite successful use of the Gothic style. The church was used as a Confederate hospital during the Civil War, and Northern troops later used it as a stable. The building was closed in 1930, and in 1966 it was given over by its parish to the town of Middletown. It has since been restored for use as an interdenominational chapel. 260–1 (1/16/73).

SPRINGDALE, *Bartonville vicinity*. Springdale was originally the home of Jost Hite, the earliest European settler in the lower Shenandoah Valley. The ruins of what was probably Hite's home and tavern, built in the 1730s next to the Indian trail that became the Valley Turnpike, still stand in the yard of the Springdale property. The present dwelling, a large stone house in the German vernacular tradition, was built in 1753 by mason Simon Taylor for Hite's son John. John Hite held numerous public positions in Frederick County including trustee for the town of Winchester. He was a friend of George Washington, who is recorded to have been a visitor at Springdale. Although the limestone walls survive without significant alteration, the interior and exterior trim, including the portico and dormers, date from mid-19th- and early 20th-century remodelings. 34–127 (4/21/81).

SPRINGDALE MILL COMPLEX, *Bartonville*. Springdale Mill was erected ca. 1788 by David Brown and replaced an earlier mill established by Jost Hite. A well-preserved example of an early industrial form that is fast disappearing, the stone structure with the characteristic corner chimney served the later community of Bartonville as a merchant mill for the buying, selling, and milling of local grain. Although currently not in operation, the mill's machinery, most of which dates from the late 19th century, is maintained in working order. Included in the complex is an early stone dwelling and a log and frame house, both of which probably housed early millers. 34–128 (3/17/81).

CITY OF FREDERICKSBURG

At the falls of the Rappahannock River, this river port
between Spotsylvania and Stafford Counties was named for
Frederick Louis, Prince of Wales, eldest son of King
George II. Fredericksburg was established in 1728 and
was incorporated as a town in 1782.
It became a city in 1879.

BROMPTON, *Sunken Road and Hanover Street*. Brompton, so named by Fredericksburg businessman John Lawrence Marye, who purchased the property in 1824, figured prominently in the two Civil War battles of Fredericksburg. The original simple house was enlarged and remodeled into an imposing Roman Revival dwelling fronted by a flat-roofed Ionic portico during Marye's long tenure. The steep hill known as Marye's Heights, which the house dominates, was the scene of fierce combat during the battles of 1862 and 1863. The pedimented roof was added in the course of repairing war damage. Now owned by the Commonwealth, the house is the official residence of the president of Mary Washington College. III–8 (5/15/79).

THE CHIMNEYS, *623 Caroline Street*. Distinguished by its massive exterior chimneys, this large Georgian town house is one of Fredericksburg's most important colonial dwellings. Significant among its architectural features is the unusually elaborate woodwork in the southwest parlor, which includes carved swags and garlands on the chimneypiece and latticework friezes on the window and door frames. Remnants of a terraced garden leading toward the river survive in the rear.

The house was built ca. 1771 for John Glassell, a Scottish merchant who returned to his native land after the outbreak of the Revolution. Owned in recent years by the Historic Fredericksburg Foundation, the Chimneys has since been sold and restored as a restaurant. 111–15 (12/17/74); *Virginia Historic Landmarks Board preservation easement.*

FALL HILL, *Fall Hill Avenue*. This hilltop plantation next to the falls of the Rappahannock River originally was included in the 8,000 acres of Spotsylvania County patented by Francis Thornton I ca. 1720. Francis Thornton III (1711–1749) maintained a summer residence at Fall Hill although his main home was the now-vanished house the Falls located on the lowlands closer to Fredericksburg. The present house at Fall Hill probably was built for Francis Thornton V (1760–1835) around the time of his marriage to Sally Innes in 1790. Francis Thornton V served as Spotsylvania County justice of the peace and is noted in county records as being of Fall Hill. The house was extensively remodeled in the 1840s by Francis Thornton V's granddaughter and her husband, John Roberts Taylor, who closed up several windows and replaced most of the woodwork. During the Fredericksburg campaign Robert E. Lee established a breastworks at the foot of the hill to guard the river crossing. The house was spared destruction by a shift in action. The property, with its ancient trees, scattering of outbuildings, and panoramic view of downtown Fredericksburg, is today owned by descendants of the builder. 111–149 (4/17/73); *Virginia Historic Landmarks Board preservation easement.*

FEDERAL HILL, *Hanover Street between Jackson and Prince Edward streets*. Federal Hill is a late 18th-century architecturally formal dwelling which illustrates the dignity that could be achieved with wood-frame construction. It was built ca. 1795 for Robert Brooke, governor of Virginia 1794–96. Complementing its exterior is an elegant interior. The ballroom, occupying the entire north end of the first floor, has woodwork similar to that from the ballroom of Alexandria's Gadsby's Tavern now displayed in the Metropolitan Museum of Art. The most conspicuous elements are the scrolled pediments above the openings. The dining room opposite features a chimney-piece ornamented with foliated consoles and unusual intertwining rope carving. A rare early summerhouse with louvered sides and ogee-domed roof stands in the garden. 111–30 (11/19/74).

FREDERICKSBURG AND SPOTSYLVANIA COUNTY BATTLEFIELDS MEMORIAL NATIONAL MILITARY PARK, *Fredericksburg and nearby areas in Spotsylvania, Caroline, Orange, and Stafford counties*. Gen. Robert E. Lee's Army of Northern Virginia achieved significant victories at Fredericksburg in 1862 and Chancellorsville in 1863 but suffered an

irreparable blow with the death of Gen. Stonewall Jackson, and defeat at Gettysburg followed soon after. In 1864 the armies returned to the Fredericksburg area and met at the sanguinary battles at the Wilderness and Spotsylvania Court House. Preserved by National Park Service in a 6,100-acre network of battlefield sites are some thirty miles of earthworks, approximately forty monuments, and several buildings including Salem Church in Spotsylvania County and the colonial mansion Chatham in Stafford County. In Fredericksburg, the Park Service has preserved much of the property lining the Sunken Road (shown), scene of some of the fiercest fighting of the battles. 111–147 (1/16/73).

FREDERICKSBURG GUN MANUFACTORY ARCHAEOLOGICAL SITE, *Dunmore and Gunnery streets.* The Fredericksburg Gun Manufactory was established by the Virginia Convention in 1777 for the purpose of repairing and manufacturing small arms for the Revolution. The gun manufactory functioned in this strategic role until 1783, supplying arms to the regiments of numerous Virginia counties. The enterprise was run by Fielding Lewis and Charles Dick. Its stone magazine was ordered to be built with the same plan and dimensions as Williamsburg's powder magazine. Other structures in the complex included a coal house, storage house, and millhouse. In 1783 the property became the site of the Fredericksburg Academy, which remained here until 1801. Located at the southern edge of the city's historic district, only fragments of foundations remain above ground today. The site, however, should hold significant archaeological information on late 18th-century American arms technology. 111–145 (4/19/77).

FREDERICKSBURG HISTORIC DISTRICT, *roughly bounded by the Rappahannock River, Hazel Run, Canal Street, and Prince Edward Street.* Fredericksburg's historic district is a forty-block area including the fifty acres designated as a town site in 1728 and the land that was added to the town in 1759. Fredericksburg was created to serve as a frontier river port at the falls of the Rappahannock River for the settlers of Spotsylvania County and lands to the west. It was an active trading center and also the county seat for Spotsylvania during the colonial period. The town enjoyed a period of optimism and prosperity during the decades after the Revolutionary War, and over two hundred Federal buildings remain in the district. The town was laid out on a symmetrical grid which today contains Fredericksburg's central business district and composes one of the more important historic townscapes in the South. While the basic character of the architecture is Federal, the district is also rich in fine examples of colonial, Victorian, and early 20th-century buildings. Especially notable structures are the 18th-century Hugh Mercer Apothecary Shop, the 1814 City Hall (shown), the 1851 Gothic Revival courthouse designed by James Renwick, and several distinctive churches, among which is the Romanesque-style St. George's Episcopal Church of 1849. Two of the more noted individually registered buildings in the district are the Mary Washington house and the Rising

Sun Tavern. Fierce fighting took place around Fredericksburg during the Civil War, but the downtown was spared significant devastation. Considerable rehabilitation has taken place in the district in recent years, all of which has enhanced the historic character of the community. 111–132 (3/2/71).

KENMORE, *1201 Washington Street*. Kenmore was begun in 1752 and completed ca. 1756 by Fielding Lewis for his bride Betty, sister of George Washington. Contrasting with its plain but dignified exterior is an exceptionally elaborate interior containing the finest 18th-century plasterwork ceilings and chimneypieces in the country. The ceiling designs are based on a plate in Batty Langley's *City and Country Builder's Treasury* (1740), an English pattern book widely used in the colonies. Fielding Lewis later became a Revolutionary patriot, serving as commissioner of the Fredericksburg Gun Manufactory, in which he invested much of his personal fortune. Threats to Kenmore's preservation were overcome in 1922 with the purchase of the property by the Kenmore Association. The association has since restored the house and now maintains it as a museum. 111–47 (11/15/68); *National Historic Landmark*.

JAMES MONROE LAW OFFICE *908 Charles Street*. James Monroe moved to Fredericksburg in 1789 and began his law practice in an office on Charles Steet, launching a career in public service that would carry him on to be a U.S. senator; American minister to France, England, and Spain; governor of Virginia; secretary of state; and fifth president of the United States. This building, erected in several stages, the last being perhaps as late as the 1840s, is a well-preserved example of a Federal-period attorney's office. It is owned by the Commonwealth and is maintained as a museum. Exhibited here are many possessions of Monroe and his wife, Elizabeth Kortright Monroe. 111–66 (9/9/69); *National Historic Landmark*.

NATIONAL BANK OF FREDERICKSBURG (FARMERS' BANK OF VIRGINIA, *900 Princess Anne Street*. Erected in 1819–20 by Robert and George Ellis, as the Farmers' Bank of Virginia, this Federal commercial building has served continuously as a bank except for intervals during the Civil War when the town was occupied by Federal troops. The residential part of the building, originally occupied by the bank's cashier, was the boyhood home of the 19th-century naval captain William Lewis Herndon. During the Union occupation of Fredericksburg, the bank was used as headquarters by the Union command. President Lincoln addressed troops and citizens from its steps on April 22, 1862. The bank failed at the end of the war, and the building became the home of the National Bank of Fredericksburg, chartered in 1865. The bank is distinguished by its pedimented temple form and fine detailing, including stone lintels and keystones, precise Flemish bond brickwork, and handsome entrance. Some interesting original woodwork remains within. 111–21 (1/18/83).

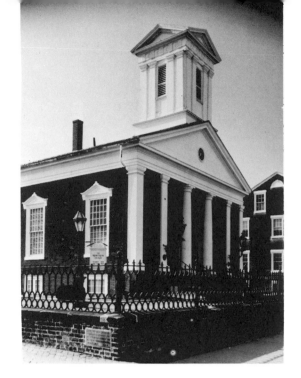

PRESBYTERIAN CHURCH OF FREDERICKSBURG, *Princess Anne and George streets.* The Presbyterian Church of Fredericksburg ranks among the finest surviving examples of Jeffersonian Roman Revival in the Commonwealth. Dominated by a Tuscan portico in antis and a handsomely detailed belfry with the entablature employing the Doric order of the Baths of Diocletian, this 1833 church was Fredericksburg's first temple-form public building. Although its architect is unknown, the striking similarity of the design details to the work of master builders Malcolm B. Crawford and William B. Phillips, two of the most talented promoters of Jefferson's style, raises the possibility of their involvement in its construction. The building survives little changed from its original appearance. During the Civil War the church served as a hospital for both Union and Confederate soldiers, and it was in this building that Clara Barton came to nurse the wounded after the battle of Fredericksburg in 1862. 111–34 (5/17/83).

RISING SUN TAVERN, *1306 Caroline Street.* This building was built in the 1760s for Charles Washington, younger brother of George Washington, and served as his residence while he lived in Fredericksburg. In 1792 John Frazer converted the house into a tavern known as the Golden Eagle. The building was maintained for that purpose until just before the Civil War. It was struck several times by Union artillery shells in the 1862 battle of Fredericksburg. Acquired by the Association for the Preservation of Virginia Antiquities in 1907, the building has been restored as an 18th-century hostelry and is now exhibited as a museum. Examination of the structure during the 1970s restoration revealed that the building was fronted by a long porch in the 18th century. The long-missing feature has since been reconstructed. The name Rising Sun comes from an early Fredericksburg tavern sign which was thought to have been made for this building. Recent research indicates that the original Rising Sun Tavern was probably elsewhere in the city. 111–88 (9/9/69); *National Historic Landmark.*

MARY WASHINGTON HOUSE, *1200 Charles Street.* George Washington bought this property in 1772 for his mother, Mary Ball Washington, so that she would be close to her daughter Betty Lewis and her son Charles. She lived here seventeen years until her death in 1789. The present structure consists of the building purchased by Washington and an addition he had built, as well as later 19th-century additions. This house was acquired by the Association for the Preservation of Virginia Antiquities in 1890 to prevent it from being dismantled and moved to the Chicago Exposition. It was subsequently restored and furnished with period furniture, including several Washington pieces. The garden was restored in 1968 by the Garden Club of Virginia. 111–110 (3/18/75).

GILES COUNTY

Named for William Branch Giles, U.S. senator from Virginia
at the time of its formation in 1806, this mountainous
county was made up of sections of Montgomery, Monroe
(now in West Virginia), and Tazewell counties.
Its county seat is Pearisburg.

GILES COUNTY COURTHOUSE, *Pearisburg*. The earliest and most prominent landmark of Pearisburg, this Federal building is the third courthouse to stand on the town's central public square since the county was established in 1806. The two-story central block with its delicately ornamented octagonal cupola was constructed in 1836 by Thomas Mercer and bears a stylistic similarity to several area residences traditionally attributed to one unidentified Bedford County builder. In May 1862 the courthouse square became the scene of an encounter between Union and Confederate troops that is graphically recorded in the diary of Lt. Col. Rutherford B. Hayes, the commanding Union officer present and later 19th president of the United States. The courthouse has undergone various alterations; the portico was added in 1900. 279–3 (7/20/82).

GLOUCESTER COUNTY

*Between the York and the Piankatank rivers, on Virginia's
Middle Peninsula, this Tidewater county was probably named
for the English shire, although the name may have honored
Henry, duke of Gloucester, third son of King Charles I. It was
formed from York County in 1651. The county seat is Gloucester.*

ABINGDON CHURCH, *White Marsh vicinity.* Abingdon Parish was formed in 1655 to serve lower Gloucester County. The present church, the parish's second, was built ca. 1755 and is one of Virginia's most refined colonial structures. The church is distinguished by its cross-shaped plan and its superb brickwork, especially the molded-brick doorways. Although the building's interior was damaged by Federal troops during the Civil War and was remodeled during the course of repairs, much of the fabric is original, including the galleries, some wainscoting, sash, portions of the altarpiece, and part of the pulpit. The church was inactive in the early 1800s as the result of the disestablishment. Episcopalians reoccupied the building in 1826, and the parish has remained active to the present. A restoration of the interior to its colonial appearance is in progress. 36–1 (7/7/70).

ABINGDON GLEBE HOUSE, *White Marsh vicinity.* This colonial dwelling belongs to Virginia's collection of 18th-century glebe houses, structures built to serve their parishes either as rental property or as rectories. The house was standing as early as 1724 when it was mentioned in a report by Thomas Hughes, rector of Abingdon Parish, to the bishop of London. The T-shaped house with its original low wings illustrates the transition from the informal vernacular structures of the 17th century to the symmetrical houses of the Georgian period. The hipped roofs on the wings may be one of Virginia's oldest uses of that roof form. The house and its glebe were confiscated from the parish and sold during the disestablishment. The property has remained a private farm ever since. 36–2 (7/7/70).

BURGH WESTRA, *Ware Neck.* An illustration in *Cottage Residences* (1842), the influential pattern book by Andrew Jackson Downing, provided the inspiration for this Tudor-style cottage. The dwelling was completed in 1851 for Dr. Philip Alexander Taliaferro, who owned a copy of Downing's book. Design III in *Cottage Residences*, the plate after which the house was modeled, was recommended by Downing for a site on a body of water. Taliaferro's house conforms to the recommendation; Burgh Westra is sited on the banks of Gloucester's North River. The property has remained in the ownership of the builder's family to the present. The house was gutted by fire in 1983, but the walls survived and the interior has been reconstructed. 36–10 (4/20/76).

FAIRFIELD ARCHAEOLOGICAL SITE, *White Marsh vicinity.* An unusually large and elaborate 17th-century mansion, probably built by Lewis Burwell ca. 1692, stood here for two centuries until it was destroyed by fire in 1897. Its external appearance, distinguished by Jacobean diagonally set chimney stacks, is well known through several early photographs, including the ca. 1892 one shown here. Archaeological investigation of the site could reveal much information about the plan, sequence of development, and architectural details of one of Virginia's oldest formal plantation houses. Near the house site are the sites of several outbuildings as well as the site of what may be an earlier 17th-century residence. 36–61 (2/20/73).

GLOUCESTER COUNTY COURTHOUSE SQUARE HISTORIC DISTRICT, *including the court square and adjacent buildings.* Set off by its T-shaped courthouse of ca. 1766, this cluster of public buildings and law offices in the heart of the community of Gloucester is a classic example of a Tidewater county-seat complex. The governmental buildings are within a grassy walled area, more of an oval than a square, bordered by U.S. Route 17. The courthouse, although having undergone later alterations including the substitution of the present 1895 portico for an earlier porch, remains among the more sophisticated of Virginia's colonial court structures. Other county buildings on the square are the early 19th-century clerk's office and the late 19th-century sheriff's office. A small early 19th-century brick debtors' prison stands just to the west of the courthouse. Across the road from the square, to the east, stands the former Botetourt Hotel, originally John New's ordinary, of ca. 1770. This two-story brick building is a rare example of a large colonial hostelry with architectural refinement. It was restored in the early 1970s to serve as the county office building. On the north and south sides of the square are groupings of simple frame structures of the mid-19th and early 20th centuries, housing law offices and commercial offices. 36–21 (2/20/73).

GLOUCESTER WOMAN'S CLUB, *Gloucester.* At the junction of two colonial roads, this building began in the 18th century as a one-room, side-passage structure, one of the more common early regional forms. Significant original interior features include the closed-string stair, wide-muntin sashes, and deep molded cornices. The building received its porches and other additions in the early 19th century. A local tradition holds that the building initially served as an ordinary. The organization of the interior spaces and certain documentary evidence points instead to the likelihood that it served as a mercantile establishment. Throughout much of the 19th century, the property was known as the Hill or Edge Hill. The building was occupied by a dressmaker and the Gloucester Agricultural Society before its purchase in 1923 by the Gloucester Woman's Club. It continues to serve as the club's headquarters. 36–21 (11/20/73); *Virginia Historic Landmarks Board preservation easement.*

HOLLY KNOLL, *Cappahosic.* Holly Knoll was the retirement home of black educator Robert R. Moton (1867–1940), successor to Booker T. Washington at Hampton Institute and Tuskegee Institute. Moton was one of the founders of the National Urban League and developed Tuskegee Institute from a vocational and agricultural training school to a fully accredited collegiate and professional institution. An adviser to five U.S. presidents, from Woodrow Wilson to Franklin D. Roosevelt, Moton sponsored the early Tuskegee communicable disease studies and programs that contributed to the enactment of the Communicable Disease Act of 1938 and the establishment of national communicable disease centers. Built in 1935, his house, a porticoed Georgian Revival structure on the banks of the York River, is now the core building of the Robert R. Moton Memorial Institute, Inc., which operates a college endowment funding program and uses the property as an executive conference center. 36–134 (3/16/82); *National Historic Landmark.*

KEMPSVILLE, *Glenns vicinity.* Built in the third quarter of the 18th century, this manor house takes its name from the Kemp family, early settlers of northwestern Gloucester County. By 1805 the property was owned by William Broaddus, in whose family it remained until the Civil War. The location of the house on the edge of Dragon Swamp has led to the modern mistaken identification of the place as Dragon Ordinary, a building which actually stood over a mile away. Characteristic of the region's early vernacular architecture, the house combines sophisticated detailing with an asymmetrical facade. The walls are laid in Flemish bond, and the chimneys have distinctive T-shaped stacks. Inside is a Georgian stair and a paneled chimney wall. The clapboard roof preserved under the present roof is a rare surviving example of the crude, inefficient roofing employed on some colonial buildings. Another feature of interest is the fragment of 18th-century wallpaper lining the semidome of the parlor cupboard. 36–15 (9/20/77).

LANDS END, *Naxera vicinity.* At the tip of Robins Neck overlooking the Severn River, this brick dwelling was the home of sea captain John Sinclair, who began his career as a privateer. At the outbreak of the Revolutionary War, he contributed both his ships and services to the war effort. With his small, maneuverable vessels, he was among the first to take British ships as prizes. A native of Hampton, Sinclair acquired his Gloucester County property in 1796 and built his house here soon after, maintaining it as his home until his death in 1820. Unusually tall because of its above-grade basement, the structure is a characteristic example of late 18th-century Tidewater architecture, making use of a gambrel roof, a form employed by many Gloucester County houses of the period. The house was restored in the 1970s by historian Claude O. Lanciano, Jr. 36–28 (9/17/74).

LITTLE ENGLAND, *Gloucester Point vicinity.* This symmetrical two-and-a-half-story plantation house, in a commanding position at the mouth of Sara's Creek opposite Yorktown, is a classic example of mid-18th-century Tidewater Virginia architecture. Typical of the colony's finest dwellings, the house is very plain on the exterior, relying on its regular fenestration, geometrical proportions, and fine brickwork for aesthetic effect. In contrast to the exterior, the original interior woodwork is richly paneled and highlighted by architectural chimneypieces and a notably fine stair. The property was granted to John Perrin in 1651; the present house was built by his descendant, also named John Perrin, some 100 years later. One of the frame wings is an 18th-century addition that originally was attached to the center of the land front. It was moved to the north end in the 1930s when the house was restored and a matching south wing was added. 36–30 (10/6/70).

LOWLAND COTTAGE, *Ware Neck.* Lowland Cottage stands on land that was included in a 1642 grant to Thomas Curtis. Robert Bristow, Curtis's son-in-law, became the owner of the property shortly after his marriage in 1665 and made it his home plantation. Bristow, a prosperous merchant, maintained a wharf and storehouse here, both despoiled by Nathaniel Bacon's rebels in 1676. Bristow moved to England after the rebellion, and for the next 112 years his Virginia lands were managed for him and his heirs by a series of resident agents. When the existing cottage was erected is not known. In its original form, with its center chimney, rear staircase, and exposed ceiling joists, it was a variant of the vernacular architecture of the period, more akin to the early center-chimney houses of New England. The chimney was removed in the 19th century and replaced with end chimneys. A new center stack was later added. Despite these and other modifications, the original appearance is discernible. The property may well contain archaeological sites that will provide information on 17-century Tidewater history and architecture. 36–32 (4/6/71); *Virginia Historic Landmarks Board preservation easement.*

WALTER REED BIRTHPLACE, *Belroi*. Dr. Walter Reed, medical researcher and conqueror of yellow fever, was born in 1851 in this cottage at the Gloucester County crossroad of Belroi. The tiny house, a rural Virginia one-room vernacular dwelling, is typical of a house type once prevalent throughout Virginia's Tidewater and Piedmont. The Reeds were using it as a temporary home until a parsonage could be completed for Reed's father, the local methodist minister. In the aftermath of the Spanish-American War, Dr. Reed was appointed to head a commission to Cuba in 1900 to investigate the cause of yellow fever. His discovery that the disease was transmitted by mosquitoes led to its eradication. Dr. Reed's birthplace was acquired for preservation in 1926 and restored by the Medical Society of Virginia. In 1968 the property was transferred to the Association for the Preservation of Virginia Antiquities. 36–80 (4/17/73).

ROARING SPRINGS, *Gloucester vicinity*. Deriving its name from a large spring on the property, Roaring Springs is an old Virginia homestead developed to its present form through enlargements and remodelings by its various owners. The western end began as a one-room with side passage pre-Revolutionary cottage, possibly an overseer's house, on a corner of Church Hill, a Throckmorton family plantation. In 1794 it was sold to Francis Thornton, who enlarged the house to its present form before 1802. Notable features of the enlargement are the stair with its beaded, diagonally set balusters and the parlor fireplace wall with its fine paneling and arched openings. Both the stair and the parlor woodwork have strong similarities to the woodwork in nearby Toddsbury, suggesting a common craftsman. The house was further remodeled in the mid-19th century when Greek Revival doors and window trim were installed. In 1978 the property was donated by its owners, Samuel A. and Emily R. Janney, to the Association for the Preservation of Virginia Antiquities. 36–40 (8/15/72); *Virginia Historic Landmarks Board preservation easement.*

ROSEWELL, *White Marsh vicinity*. The ruins of Rosewell excite the imagination to a romantic vision of the milieu of Virginia's plantation aristocracy. The most imposing and probably the largest of all colonial mansions, Rosewell was begun in 1726 for the wealthy planter Mann Page I. Its architect is not recorded, but he obviously was acquainted with contemporary fashions in the mother country, for Rosewell lacks the regional character of most Virginia houses, comparing in quality, form, and detailing with fine early Georgian English manor houses and merchants' dwellings. The house stood uncompleted at Page's death four years later but eventually was finished by his son Mann Page II. It stood three stories high with stair pavilions on either end and was crowned by a brick parapet above which projected twin octagonal cupolas. Its masonry walls, considered to have the finest brickwork of any colonial house, sparkled with scattered glazed headers and featured gauged-brick belt courses and elegantly carved brick entrances. The

windows were ornamented with stone sills and keystones and had panels of gauged brick below each sill. Little is known of the interior other than it was elaborately paneled and had marble mantels. Most of the interior trim was removed when the house was extensively altered after its sale by the Page family in 1838. The richly carved staircases, recorded by photographs, survived the alteration but were destroyed when the house was gutted by fire in 1916. The brick walls survived the fire remarkably unscathed but defied numerous plans to secure them and restore the house. The walls gradually but steadily crumbled from want of maintenance so that only the south wall, the chimneys, and sections of the north and west walls remain. These surviving sections were finally stabilized by the Gloucester Historical Society after it gained title to the ruins in 1979. 36–41 (11/5/68).

TIMBERNECK, *White Marsh vicinity.* Timberneck, on a broad peninsula bordered by creeks flowing into the York River, was a Mann family homestead in the 17th and 18th centuries. The property was purchased ca. 1793 by John Catlett from John Page of Rosewell. The present house on Timberneck is a rambling post-Revolutionary farmhouse built for the Catletts. The two-story weatherboarded structure has well-preserved appointments including a fine stair and much original hardware. With its rural setting, early smokehouse, rare 19th-century picket fence, old trees, and commanding view of the York, Timberneck is a substantially undisturbed Tidewater plantation in an area of Gloucester County undergoing suburban development. 36–74 (6/19/79).

TODDSBURY, *Nuttall vicinity.* Toddsbury is a sophisticated example of a medium-size Tidewater plantation house containing outstanding paneled woodwork. The property was owned by the Todd family from the third quarter of the 17th century, but the original portion of the present dwelling, probably a simple side-passage structure, most likely was erected for Christopher Todd before his death in 1743. By 1782 Toddsbury was in the ownership of Philip Tabb, a grandson of Christopher Todd. Tabb enlarged the house in 1784 by adding the library wing. He also remodeled the original section by changing the gable roof to a gambrel roof and by adding the present paneling and other interior trim. The paneling and stair were likely executed by the same craftsman who installed similar woodwork in nearby Roaring Springs. The porch and porch chamber were probably added after 1800. The house underwent an extensive renovation after 1946 when it was acquired by Mrs. Alice Bolitho, at which time the kitchen wing was added and the porch modified. In 1957 Toddsbury became the home of Virginia preservationist Gay Montague Moore. The house is surrounded by landscaped grounds and formal gardens on the banks of the North River, a tributary of Mobjack Bay. 36–45 (9/9/69); *Virginia Historic Landmarks Board preservation easement.*

WARE CHURCH, *Gloucester vicinity.* The unusually large scale of this beautifully crafted colonial church indicates the importance of its parish, which served many of Gloucester County's leading plantations. The precise construction date is unknown; however, the building most likely was put up in the second quarter of the 18th century during the rectorship of the Reverend James Clack. Few of Virginia's colonial churches can boast more handsome or better-preserved brickwork. Its clear blue glazed headers provide a sparkling contrast to the rich red of the stretches and gauged work, all showing 18th-century masonry at its best. Ware is also Virginia's only rectangular colonial church served by three entrances, each with gauged-work architectural surrounds. Although abandoned following the disestablishment, the church was later reoccupied by the Episcopalians and continues to serve as a parish church of that denomination today. 36–48 (10/17/72).

WARNER HALL, *Naxera vicinity.* At the head of the northwest branch of the Severn River, Warner Hall is one of Gloucester county's major colonial plantations. Here lived councillors Augustine Warner I, Augustine Warner II, John Lewis I, and John Lewis II. Remaining from the colonial period are two brick dependencies, probably built by John Lewis II along with a center dwelling house to replace the Warners' late 17th-century house which burned ca. 1740. The later house was itself destroyed by fire ca. 1845. On its site was constructed ca. 1905 the present wood-frame Colonial Revival mansion for the Cheney family. This house is connected to the colonial dependencies by one-story hyphens. Among the early outbuildings on the property is a rare colonial stable of brick construction. Sites of various vanished 17th- and 18th-century supporting structures at Warner Hall are likely to be of considerable archaeological interest. The walled colonial cemetery of the Warner and Lewis families, in a field to the south of the house, has been owned and maintained by the Association for the Preservation of Virginia Antiquities since 1903. 36–49 (6/17/80).

GOOCHLAND COUNTY

*This pastoral Piedmont county bordering the James River
was named in honor of William Gooch, lieutenant governor of
Virginia from 1727 to 1749. It was formed from Henrico
County in 1727. The county seat is
Goochland Court House.*

BOLLING HALL, *Goochland Court House vicinity.* Organized education for the deaf in America had its origins in the second decade of the 19th century at this Bolling family plantation when William Bolling (1777–1845) brought the Scottish teacher John Braidwood here to educate his two deaf children. His success led Bolling to establish the nation's first formal school for deaf children at Cobbs, a family house in Chesterfield County (burned 1829). Bolling Hall was built either for William Bolling or his father before 1799 on land that had been in the family since the early 18th century. It apparently began as a side-passage dwelling and was later enlarged. The plain but architecturally formal frame house, with its paneled fireplace walls, is one of the early plantation residences of the upper James River region. 37–2 (4/6/71).

ELK HILL, *George's Tavern vicinity.* The solid and imposing mansion at Elk Hill is a Greek Revival country house which illustrates a degree of sophistication in its proportions, plan, and interior woodwork comparable to that of Richmond town houses of the period. The house was built for Randolph Harrison, Jr., between 1835 and 1839 on a portion of land formerly owned by Thomas Jefferson, acquired from his wife. Like the finer urban dwellings of Richmond, Elk Hill has a spacious rear veranda rather than the monumental front portico more typical of the Greek Revival houses of the Deep South. The first-floor interior is enriched by elaborate doorways with Greek fret friezes. In 1943 Elk Hill became the country home of Buford Scott, a Richmond stockbroker. The house is used today as the administrative headquarters of Elk Hill Farm, a private school for young men requiring remedial tutoring established by Scott in 1970. 37–91 (10/17/78).

GOOCHLAND COUNTY COURT SQUARE, *Goochland Court House.* Like several Piedmont counties, Goochland is graced by a dignified Roman Revival courthouse designed and built by a master builder who worked under Thomas Jefferson during the construction of the University of Virginia. The Tuscan order, temple-form building, completed in 1826, is the work of Dabney Cosby, Sr., who is credited with courthouses, churches, houses, and educational buildings throughout central Virginia. Cosby was assisted at this courthouse by Valentine Parrish. The courthouse is one of the few to retain its apsidal end. Other significant early structures on the grassy square are the stone jail, a brick clerk's office, and the surrounding brick wall, erected to keep out wandering cattle. 37–136 (7/7/70).

HOWARD'S NECK, *Pemberton.* The centerpiece of this upper James River plantation is the unusually refined Federal residence built ca. 1825 for Edward Cunningham, a leader in the Richmond milling industry. Cunningham's Richmond town house, the Cunningham-Archer house (demolished), was designed by Robert Mills, and it is believed that Mills also was engaged to design the house at Howard's Neck. With its sophisticated proportions and rich interior appointments, the house shows the hand of a talented architect. Adding interest to the place is a full complement of outbuildings including an 18th-century "old dwelling," a kitchen, smokehouse, toolhouse, and orangery, as well as several old farm buildings. Of special significance is a street of three log slave houses, an exceptionally rare survival. The plantation takes its name from Allen Howard, who acquired it in 1741. 37–100 (11/16/71).

THE LOCK-KEEPER'S HOUSE, *Cedar Point*. This relic of Virginia's bygone canal era was built shortly after 1836, following the opening of the Maidens-to-Lynchburg portion of the James River and Kanawha Canal. Serving lock no. 7, the stone and frame structure, with its typical center chimney, was the scene of much activity during its some thirty years of service. Horses were changed there, invoices checked, and tolls collected. The house also served as a tavern and furnished accommodations for passengers and canalboat crews. It is believed to be one of only two remaining lockkeeper's houses along the James. 37–105 (9/17/74).

POWELL'S TAVERN, *River Road, West Richmond vicinity*. A landmark along River Road, this old tavern consists of two distinct parts. The earliest, a traditional two-story frame dwelling, was built after 1768 for William Powell. His son, William, Jr., added shed wings to the house when he acquired a license to operate it as an ordinary in 1808. The brick, two-story Federal front section was erected in 1820 to serve Powell's growing business, River Road then being the main road to the Upper James region. General Lafayette stopped at Powell's tavern in 1824 during the course of his American tour, and Joseph Martin wrote in his *Gazetteer of Virginia* (1836) that Powell's Tavern offered "good order and excellent accommodations." Although now a private residence, this singular structure remains an important artifact of Virginia's transportation history. 37–23 (4/18/72).

ROCK CASTLE, *Rock Castle*. Named for a high rock bluff overlooking the James River, this property, patented in 1718 by Charles Fleming, contains a small but sophisticated manor house erected in the third decade of the 18th century for the patentee's son Tarleton Fleming. The house was raided in 1781 by the Fleming family's distant cousin, Col. Banastre Tarleton, who was attempting to capture Governor Thomas Jefferson and members of the Virginia General Assembly then meeting in Albemarle County. Later encased in Victorian additions, the house was restored to its original appearance in 1935 when it was moved a few hundred feet so that its site could be used for the construction of a Normandy manor–style house. Even on its new site, the Rock Castle house is one of the purest examples of traditional 18th-century Virginia architecture in the Piedmont. The first floor is fully paneled. 37–54 (7/7/70); *Virginia Historic Landmarks Board preservation easement.*

TUCKAHOE, *River Road, Richmond vicinity.* The contrasting qualities of elegance, domesticity, and remoteness, all characteristic of Virginia's colonial plantation life, are keenly felt at Tuckahoe. Standing on a bluff above the upper James, the H-shaped house, which retains its early masonry, woodwork, siding, and sash, is perhaps the most complete and least altered of the state's early plantation dwellings. The property was one of several large plantations established by William Randolph of Turkey Island for each of his sons. By 1723 his second son, Thomas, was living at Tuckahoe, and it was for him that the earliest part of the house, the north wing, is presumed to have been built. The brick-ended south wing, connecting saloon, and handsome woodwork were most likely added by Thomas's son William Randolph, following his marriage in 1734 to Maria Judith Page, daughter of Mann Page I of Rosewell. The woodwork, most notably the north stair with its richly carved balusters, brackets, and facia, ranks with the finest of the period in the nation. Stretching to the north of the house is a row of early outbuildings making up the plantation "street," the best remaining example of the typical grouping of domestic support structures necessary for the household operation. The tiny schoolhouse to the east of the main house is where Thomas Jefferson is said to have attended classes while he and his parents lived at Tuckahoe. Tuckahoe remained in the ownership of the Randolph family until 1830. The property was acquired in 1935 by Mr. and Mrs. N. Addison Baker, whose descendants have preserved and maintained the place with special sensitivity to its historic importance. 37–33 (11/5/68); *National Historic Landmark.*

WOODLAWN, *Oilville vicinity.* Elisha Leake, a Goochland miller, built this Federal house near the end of the 18th century, after his service in the Revolutionary War. In 1806 the property was leased to John Trevillian, who, because of its convenient location on Three Chopt Road between Richmond and Charlottesville, opened a tavern here. Woodlawn was sold in 1834 to Thomas Taylor, later a Mexican War hero who is remembered for placing the American flag on Chapultepec Castle. The boldly proportioned house has Flemish bond brickwork with stuccoed jack arches, delicate dentil cornices, and completely surviving original interior trim. Lending special distinction are the unusual two-story pent closets between the chimneys, one of which contains a secret stair. 37–35 (7/6/71).

GRAYSON COUNTY

In the mountains along the state's southern border, Grayson County was named for Col. William Grayson, one of the first two U.S. senators from Virginia. It was formed from Wythe County in 1792, with part of Patrick County added later. Its county seat is Independence.

OLD GRAYSON COUNTY COURTHOUSE, *Independence*. The center of the county-seat town of Independence is dominated by the exotic former courthouse, an eclectic structure highlighted by octagonal corner towers and curvilinear gables. Its architect was Frank P. Milburn of Washington, D.C., who designed some half-dozen courthouses in Southwest Virginia as well as courthouses for neighboring counties in West Virginia and Kentucky. The building was completed in 1908 during the brief boom that allowed many mountain counties to erect impressive new courthouses. The courthouse was the third to serve the county; its function has recently been taken over by a fourth court structure. 240–1 (6/21/77).

RIPSHIN, *Troutdale vicinity*. Author Sherwood Anderson (1876–1941) had this rustic but comfortable log and stone dwelling built after visiting Grayson county in 1925 and falling in love with its breathtaking, unspoiled landscape. The house, completed in 1927, was designed by Anderson's architect-friend James Spratling of New Orleans. The property was named for a nearby creek. A native of Ohio, Anderson regarded Ripshin as his home and lived here until his death. Anderson's most memorable writings include *Winesburg, Ohio; Poor White; Many Marriages;* and *Memories*. These and other of his books and short stories were part of the American school of realism in this century. While he lived at Ripshin he served as publisher, editor, and reporter for two Marion, Va., newspapers he purchased in 1925. The house is preserved as Anderson left it. 38–8 (3/2/71); *National Historic Landmark*.

GREENE COUNTY

This rural Piedmont county was named for Gen. Nathanael Greene, Revolutionary War military hero. It was formed from Orange County in 1838. The county seat is Stanardsville.

GREENE COUNTY COURTHOUSE, *Stanardsville.* The Greene County Courthouse is one of the simplest of the Roman Revival courthouses scattered through the Virginia Piedmont that were designed and built by the various master builders who had learned the classical vocabulary from Thomas Jefferson while building the University of Virginia. This courthouse, built in 1838 by William Donoho and William B. Phillips, follows the standard temple-form format and is topped by a properly executed Doric entablature. As originally finished, the facade had only the four pilasters; the present portico was added in 1927–28. The elaborate octagonal cupola is presumably original. The courthouse was gutted by fire in 1979, but the exterior survived without significant destruction, and the interior has since been rebuilt. 302–1 (12/2/69).

OCTONIA STONE, *Stanardsville vicinity.* This rounded outcropping in the Greene County countryside marked the terminus of the westernmost boundary line of the 24,000-acre Octonia Grant. The grant was made in 1722 by Lieutenant Governor Alexander Spotswood to eight Virginians: Bartholomew Yates, Lewis Latane, John Robinson, Jeremiah Clowder, Harry Beverley, Christopher Robinson, William Stanard, and Edwin Thacker. The grant, some two miles wide and twenty miles long, began in the east on the Rapidan River near Spicer's Mill in Orange County. The stone is identified by its mark, a figure eight composed of two nearly perfect circles topped by a cross. 39–3 (6/2/70).

GREENSVILLE COUNTY

Greensville County was named either for Gen. Nathanael Greene or for Sir Richard Grenville, leader of the Roanoke Island settlement of 1585. Located along the North Carolina border, it was formed from Brunswick County in 1780. It was enlarged later with parts of Brunswick and Sussex counties. The county seat is Emporia.

JOHN GREEN ARCHAEOLOGICAL SITES, *Emporia vicinity.* The John Green sites, named for a recent owner of the property, are two adjacent and related Indian sites that are among the few in southeastern Virginia containing postcontact elements that have been tested archaeologically. Limited excavation at one of the sites has revealed well-preserved house patterns, human burials, and refuse-filled pits. The mixture of typical aboriginal artifacts with colonial trade items, floral and faunal remains, and unique organics preserved by copper salts provide a rare opportunity for studying Indian settlement patterns and subsistence practices as well as the acculturation of the interior Coastal Plain Indians during the period 1680 to 1730. In addition to what has already been salvaged, a wide variety of pre-and postcontact period artifacts probably remain on the sites and should aid the study of interaction and trade between Indians of Virginia's Piedmont and Coastal Plain. A copper spoon and copper kettle are among the colonial trade items found in one of the burial sites. 40–18 (5/17/83).

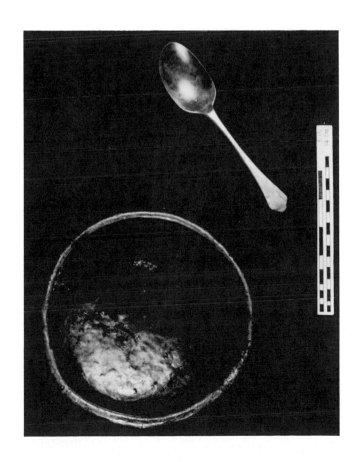

WEAVER HOUSE, *Cowie Corner vicinity*. The Weaver house is one of the earliest houses in Greensville County, a county in which early 19th-century houses are scarce. The house was built on land formerly owned by the Waller family of Williamsburg for Jarrad Weaver between 1838 and 1840. It has a number of features typically associated with vernacular Southside farmhouses, including what was originally a hall-parlor plan, painted wood graining, and the rather late use of Federal woodwork. Weaver developed a successful plantation on this estate while holding a proprietary interest in one of the county's more prosperous antebellum mills. The house is presently covered with modern asbestos shingles; otherwise it has suffered few alterations. 40–6 (6/16/81).

HALIFAX COUNTY

*This Southside county was named for George Montagu Dunk,
second earl of Halifax, president of the Board of Trade
from 1748 to 1761. It was formed from Lunenburg County
in 1752. Its county seat is Halifax.*

BERRY HILL, *South Boston vicinity.* This monumental Greek Revival mansion was erected in 1842–44 for tobacco planter James Coles Bruce, son of James Bruce, a Halifax County planter and entrepreneur. The recently discovered building contract confirms that the house was designed by John E. Johnson, a West Point graduate who also designed the Gothic Revival mansion Staunton Hill for James Coles Bruce's half-brother Charles. Construction of the work was undertaken by Josiah Dabbs, a talented local contractor. Bruce family tradition holds that James Coles Bruce was inspired to build a temple-form house after a stay in Philadelphia where he saw Nicholas Biddle's home Andalusia. Fronted by a heroic octastyle Doric portico reminiscent of the Parthenon, the house is flanked by small porticoed dependencies, creating an exceptionally dramatic as well as romantic composition. No less impressive is the spacious interior with its grand divided stair that curves to meet in a single flight. Richly decorated plaster ceilings and carved marble mantels adorn the reception rooms. A colonnaded service wing projects from the rear of the house. Architectural historian Fiske Kimball said of Berry Hill: "Nowhere else, perhaps, is the ante-bellum plantation to be found in equal architectural magnificence." 41–4 (11/5/68); *National Historic Landmark.*

CARTER'S TAVERN, *Pace's vicinity.* Carter's Tavern on Halifax County's River Road, is a handsomely restored example of an early southern Virginia ordinary. The River Road was a lap on the main stage road between New York and New Orleans. With mostly all of its original interior fabric intact, the capacious frame building provides a rare picture of the character and arrangement of a once-common Virginia institution. Among its most interesting features is the great quantity of original graining and marbleizing on the woodwork, most of it well preserved and unusually ornate. Licenses issued in 1802 and 1804 indicate that Joseph Dodson, Jr., operated an ordinary here in what was also his residence. The place was acquired in 1807 by Samuel Carter, who enlarged the building to its present size by adding the two-story main section. Carter managed the tavern until his death in 1836 when his widow Betsy continued as proprietress until her own death in 1843. The building stood derelict and decaying until 1972 when Mr. and Mrs. Robert H. Edmunds acquired it and began a thorough restoration, making the building available for tours and special events. 41–8 (9/17/74).

GLENNMARY, *Riverdale vicinity.* Glennmary is a documented work of Dabney Cosby, Sr., an enterprising builder-architect who is first recorded as being employed by Thomas Jefferson at the University of Virginia. Cosby went on from Charlottesville to design and build houses, public buildings, churches, and schools throughout southern Virginia. As noted in Cosby's account book, Glennmary was begun in 1837 for Archibald Glenn, son of a Halifax merchant. Although located on a Dan River plantation, the house is a three-bay, side-hall-plan dwelling, a house type more common in urban rather than rural areas. The purity of the form is compromised, however, by the original one-room wing. Typical of Cosby's works, Glennmary employs excellent Flemish bond brickwork, and its detailing carefully follows classical precedent. By the time Glennmary was built, Cosby had veered from the purely Roman Classicism favored by Jefferson and was making use of Greek Revival elements. Several of the mantels are based on designs for Greek-style mantels published by Asher Benjamin

in *The Practical House Carpenter* (1830). An interesting quality of the house is its large scale and correspondingly large windows. Glennmary stood neglected in recent years but without significant alterations or deterioration. Now stabilized, the house is undergoing long-term rehabilitation. 41–104 (11/21/78).

HALIFAX COUNTY COURTHOUSE, *Halifax.* Occupying a site that has been used for court purposes since the Revolution, the Halifax County Courthouse of 1838–39 is one of the Classical Revival court buildings erected by master builders influenced by Thomas Jefferson while constructing the University of Virginia. Its designer and builder was Dabney Cosby, who with his son, Dabney Cosby, Jr., provided Southside Virginia with a variety of houses, churches, and public buildings. Before building the Halifax courthouse, where he abandoned the strict temple form in favor of a T-plan and a Greek Ionic order, the elder Cosby also built the Goochland, Lunenburg, and Sussex courthouses. The courthouse has been enlarged by an extension of the rear wing. 230–77 (12/15/81).

INDIAN JIM'S CAVE ARCHAEOLOGICAL SITE, *Brookneal vicinity.* A natural formation on the banks of the Staunton River, Indian Jim's Cave was a place of prehistoric occupation dating to 2000–1000 B.C. and possibly earlier. The floor of the cave preserves intact cultural layers of its various periods of occupancy. The shelter takes its name from the tradition that during the 18th century Indian Jim, Halifax County's last surviving aboriginal inhabitant, lived in the cave with his black wife. The archaeological remains here are likely to reveal data on subsistence patterns and adaptations to seasonal changes over time by prehistoric Indians, as well as their local cultural chronologies and social interaction patterns. 41–106 (3/17/81).

THE LITTLE PLANTATION (FOURQUREAN HOUSE), *South Boston vicinity.* In the early 19th century numerous small plantations growing tobacco as the principal cash crop were established in south central Virginia. Each plantation was served by an unpretentious frame dwelling house surrounded by a cluster of outbuildings. The design and layout of these complexes was completely utilitarian. Such modest regional units are exemplified by the Little Plantation, established in 1830 by Daniel Fourqurean and consisting of a compact vernacular dwelling where the only elegance is a marbleized stair. Its original outbuildings include a stone kitchen and a log office. The present owner has added early outbuildings salvaged from nearby farms to replace missing ones and exhibits the grouping as a museum of the area's early rural life. 41–73 (9/21/76).

MOUNTAIN ROAD HISTORIC DISTRICT, *Halifax, including properties along Mountain Road between Edmunds Boulevard and Mimosa Drive.* Mountain Road, in the courthouse town of Halifax, has been noted for its handsome houses and churches and lush landscaping for the past century. Named for its location near White Oak Mountain, the tree-shaded road stretches west from the courthouse square into the countryside. The road was built up slowly so that it now presents a range of buildings from the early 19th century to the present. The principal churches are St. Mark's Episcopal Church (1831), now Halifax Methodist Church (shown with neighboring Masonic Hall), and St. John's Episcopal Church (1846). Architectural styles seen in the residences include late Federal, Greek Revival, Italianate, Queen Anne, and Colonial Revival, all in a generally restrained idiom. Several of the earlier houses were designed by Dabney Cosby, Jr., son of the Jeffersonian workman Dabney Cosby, Sr. Cosby worked with his father on the courthouse, and he also built St. John's Church. From the mid-1840s generations of residents on Mountain Road have labored to provide attractive settings for their homes. Many of the older plantings have survived and serve to maintain the 19th-century ambience of the district. 230–78 (8/16/83).

REDFIELD, *Oak Level vicinity.* Although antebellum Halifax County was dotted with small farm complexes, the area also saw the establishment of large plantations with architecturally sophisticated houses. John R. Edmunds, owner of 1,110 acres on Birch Creek, was able to build an Italian Villa–style house with money he earned from the sale of his grain to Russia in the Crimean War. The house, with its formal facade and bracketed cornice, was completed in 1857 and follows the prescription for a "small Villa in the Classical manner" promoted by Andrew Jackson Downing in *The Architecture of Country Houses* (1850). Emphasizing the formality is a monumental single-run central stair in the entrance hall. Edmunds, in addition to being a successful planter, was an advocate of reconciliation during Reconstruction. His handsomely restored house is owned by his descendants. 41–47 (7/18/78).

SEATON, *Halifax vicinity.* This Gothic Revival cottage, set off by its bargeboard-ornamented dormers and the crenellated parapet of its small front porch, was the creation of the Halifax master builder Josiah Dabbs, who built numerous houses throughout the region. Completed in 1857, Seaton was the home of William M. Howerton, son of tobacco entrepreneur Philip Howerton. The house illustrates the popularity of the Gothic style among educated people in the years just before the Civil War. Seaton was enlarged by the addition of a two-story wing in 1887. At the same time the parlor of the original section was remodeled with the installation of an early Jardine pipe organ salvaged from a local church and framed by an ornate openwork wooden screen in the Moorish taste. Preserved on the grounds are remnants of 19th-century romantic land-scaping as well as several early outbuildings, including a kitchen and a large 1887 carriage house. Seaton remains in the ownership of Howerton descendants and contains an assemblage of early decorations, among which are carpeting, curtains, and furnishings. 41–50 (3/18/80).

TAROVER, *South Boston vicinity.* On Halifax County's River Road, Tarover is one of the distinguished architectural works commissioned by the Bruce family. A mid-19th-century Gothic Revival villa, this stone house was built in 1855–56 for Thomas Bruce, son of James Coles Bruce for whom the nearby Greek Revival mansion Berry Hill was built. Both Berry Hill and the Gothic-style Staunton Hill, home of James Coles Bruce's half-brother Charles, were designed by architect John E. Johnson; thus it is presumed that this third Bruce house, equally sophisticated in its own right, was commissioned of Johnson as well. Typical of Gothic Revival villas, the house is fronted by a projecting porch with chamber above, lighted by a delicate oriel. The locally quarried stone is said to have been cut and laid by Richmond masons. The house lost some of its original picturesque character around the turn of the century when the icicle-like bargeboards were removed from its gables. Tarover remained in the Bruce family until 1891 and has been restored in recent years by its present owners. 41–53 (7/18/78).

WILEY'S TAVERN ARCHAEOLOGICAL SITE, *Danripple vicinity.* The 18th-century Wiley's Tavern served alternately as the headquarters of British general Lord Cornwallis and his American counterpart, Gen. Nathanael Greene, during the decisive military stratagem known as the retreat to the Dan River. The tavern was built ca. 1771 for William Wiley. Constructed of log, the small, rude structure was typical of the establishments that dotted the farther reaches of Virginia in the late colonial period. The photograph shows it ca. 1924; the building eventually collapsed in the 1950s. Archaeological excavation of the tavern site should reveal architectural and artifactural data helpful to understanding rural life in Halifax County during the Revolutionary period. It may also yield data on the construction and operation of a backcountry tavern, as well as information on intercolonial trade on a major north-south thoroughfare. 41–39 (7/31/80).

CITY OF HAMPTON

*Named for Hampton Creek, earlier called the Southampton
River in honor of the earl of Southampton, this community
began as an English settlement in 1610. It was established by an
act of the Assembly in 1680 and was designated as a port in 1708.
It was incorporated as a town in 1849 and became a city in 1908.
Its size was greatly expanded in 1952 by a merger with Elizabeth
City County and the town of Phoebus, both of which thereby
became extinct.*

CHESTERVILLE ARCHAEOLOGICAL SITE, *Langley
Air Force Base.* Chesterville was part of a tract patented in 1619
by John Leyden. It was purchased in 1692 by Thomas Wythe,
a burgess for Elizabeth City County. Wythe's great-grandson
George Wythe, a signer of the Declaration of Independence
and first professor of law at the College of William and Mary,
is believed to have been born here. George Wythe inherited
the plantation in 1755 and made it his country residence. His
main residence was in Williamsburg, in the house built by his
father-in-law, Richard Taliaferro, now known as the Wythe
house. In 1771 Wythe began construction of a new house on
the Chesterville property that stood until destroyed by fire in
1911. A photograph of the house shows that it had a gable-end
front with an arcaded first floor. Chesterville was sold by
Wythe in 1802. It was acquired by the National Aeronautics
and Space Administration in 1950. Excavation of the house site
and sites of 17th-century occupation could reveal information
on the architecture and life of the Wythe family and its predecessors. 114–98 (6/20/72).

FORT MONROE, *Old Point Comfort.* Constructed between 1819 and 1834 to guard Hampton Roads, this vast moated fortification is one of the nation's most ambitious examples of early military architecture. It was designed by Gen. Simon Bernard, who had served as a military engineer under Napoleon before he became head of the U.S. Board of Engineers, charged with constructing coastal defenses. During the Civil War, Fort Monroe was a staging area for Union military and naval expeditions, and the fort witnessed the epic fight between the ironclads *Monitor* and *Virginia.* Former Confederate president Jefferson Davis was kept prisoner in one of the fort casemates from 1865 to 1867. Still an active military post, Fort Monroe is now the headquarters of the Continental Army Command. The landmark designation applies not only to the fortifications but to the numerous buildings erected by the army both within the fort and just outside through World War II, all representing a wide variety of styles and types. 114–2 (9/9/69); *National Historic Landmark.*

FORT WOOL, *island between Willoughby Spit and Old Point Comfort.* Originally known as Fort Calhoun, this island defense work was begun in 1819, along with Fort Monroe opposite, to protect the entrance to Hampton Roads harbor. Robert E. Lee, then an army engineer, supervised its completion in the 1830s. Its name was changed to Fort Wool in 1862 in honor of Maj. Gen. John Wool, commandant of fortifications at Hampton Roads. From Fort Wool, President Lincoln watched the embarkation of Union troops to seize Norfolk. Abandoned in 1886, the fort was reactivated and expanded during both world wars so that it now possesses a variety of military architecture. The fort was abandoned once again in 1953, with ownership reverting to the Commonwealth. In 1985, the fort was deeded by the state to the city of Hampton, which has opened it to visitation. 114–41 (11/5/68).

HAMPTON INSTITUTE, *East Queen and Tyler streets.* This school was founded in 1868 through the efforts of Samuel Chapman Armstrong, local agent of the Freedmen's Bureau, to train the many former slaves who had gathered in the area. Though begun with only fifteen students, the institute prospered and was chartered as the Hampton Normal and Industrial Institute in 1870. By 1874 the school was embellished with its modified Châteauesque main building, Virginia Hall, designed by New York architect Richard Morris Hunt and built by the students. Hunt also designed the plainer Academic Hall, completed in 1882. The Romanesque Revival chapel with its bell tower, designed by J. C. Cady, was completed in 1882. Also on the grounds is the Mansion House, an early 19th-century plantation dwelling now used as the residence of the president. Booker T. Washington was an alumnus of Hampton. 114–6 (9/9/69); *National Historic Landmark.*

HERBERT HOUSE, *Marina Road.* Erected ca. 1753 at the tip of Armstrong Point facing on Hampton's harbor, the Herbert house is the oldest dwelling in the city of Hampton. It remained in the Herbert family for whom it was built until 1808. One of its owners, Capt. Thomas Herbert, held a commission in the Virginia navy during the Revolution. The home was spared the burning that destroyed most of Hampton during the Civil War because it was a plantation house outside the community proper. It is a sophisticated example of colonial Georgian style, exhibiting the careful proportions and fine brickwork typical of Virginia's more substantial mid-18th-century houses. Insensitive additions made during the last century detracted from its appearance; most, however, have been removed, and the house awaits restoration. Recently constructed housing has hidden the harbor from view of the house. 114–4 (11/16/71).

LITTLE ENGLAND CHAPEL, *4100 Kecoughtan Street.* Little England Chapel is a landmark to the achievements of Hampton's first generation of freedmen. Erected between 1878 and 1880 under the sponsorship of the American Missionary Association, it was used as a church and Sunday school in the heavily populated black area known as Cock's Newtown. It was one of several missions established in the Hampton area to minister directly to the spiritual and educational needs of freed slaves. The modest weatherboarded structure was built by students of Hampton Institute, the black normal and industrial college. Hampton Institute students continued to teach Sunday school here into the 1930s. The building is currently used for church services by the Church of Jesus. The only known surviving black missionary chapel of its type in the Commonwealth, Little England Chapel is one of the first of many community institutions established in Hampton by blacks in the postbellum era. 114–40 (6/16/81).

OLD POINT COMFORT LIGHTHOUSE, *Fenwick Road, Fort Monroe.* A temporary light to guide ships into Hampton Roads existed at Old Point Comfort as early as 1774. Recognizing the importance of a navigation guide at this site, the Virginia General Assembly in 1798 conveyed the point to the federal government for the purpose of building a permanent light. The present tapered polygonal structure was completed in 1802, seventeen years before the construction of Fort Monroe began. Built of sandstone ashlar painted white, the tiny structure has been in regular use since its completion, functioning as a round-the-clock navigation aid. The lighthouse, along with Fort Monroe, was maintained under Federal authority for most of the Civil War. It was just offshore from the light that the clash between the world's first two ironclad ships, the *Virginia* and the *Monitor,* took place on March 9, 1862. 114–21 (6/20/72).

ST. JOHN'S CHURCH, *West Queen and Court streets*. Completed ca. 1728 by builder Henry Cary, Jr., St. John's is the fourth building to serve Elizabeth City Parish, believed to be the oldest active parish of the Anglican communion in America. Its Latin-cross plan indicates its status, as the form was usually reserved for the larger, more important churches such as Bruton Parish Church in Williamsburg. Like most of Virginia's colonial churches, St. John's has suffered considerably from the wars that have plagued the Tidewater area. The building was damaged during the bombardment of Hampton in 1775. In the War of 1812 British troops ransacked the building and used it for a barracks. It was renovated in 1830 and reconsecrated as St. John's Church. Retreating Confederate forces burned the church along with the town in 1861, leaving only the brick walls standing. Save for the collapsed tower added in 1761, it was rebuilt within its walls following the war and given a handsome Victorian interior with finely crafted appointments. The church is the oldest building in its community and possesses a 1619 communion service, in use longer than any other in the country. 114–1 (12/2/69).

WILLIAM H. TRUSTY HOUSE, *76 West County Street*. One of the black leaders who arose after Emancipation, William H. Trusty (1862–1902) overcame his humble origins through thrift and diligence and became an entrepreneur and property owner in what was then the town of Phoebus. Trusty's effectiveness as a community leader was demonstrated in 1900 when he was elected city councilman from Phoebus's fifth ward. Three years before his election, Trusty erected this stylish residence decorated with the fancy porches and projections fashionable in the 1890s. Its builder was P. A. Fuller. Recently restored after many years of neglect, the dwelling remains a symbol of that generation of blacks directly inspired by Booker T. Washington and his doctrine of self-help. 114–108 (2/26/79).

HANOVER COUNTY

Situated in both the Tidewater and the Piedmont, Hanover County was named for King George I, who at the time of his accession was elector of Hanover in Germany. It was formed from New Kent County in 1720. Its county seat is Hanover Court House.

ASHLAND HISTORIC DISTRICT, *approximate center of the community extending along the RF&P Railroad and along Route 54.* With its large collection of late Victorian and Edwardian frame dwellings and its brick commercial core, all set among hundreds of trees, the Ashland Historic District survives as a fine example of a turn-of-the-century railroad and streetcar suburb. The spine of the district is Center Street paralleling the railroad tracks, which displays a full range of Victorian styles from the Italianate and Second Empire to the Eastlake, Queen Anne, and Colonial Revival. Also along the tracks is the small but sophisticated Ashland depot. Of interest as well is the early 20th-century downtown area between Henry Clay Road and Myrtle Street, an assemblage of brick structures exemplifying the commercial ethos of the 1920s. With the addition of three of the academic buildings of Randolph-Macon College, the district illustrates the vital role that both the railroad and the college have played in Ashland's development. 42–105 (3/16/82).

CLOVER LEA, *Old Church vicinity.* Clover Lea's broad lawns and old trees combine with the porticoed house to present an idealized picture of an antebellum plantation residence. Although the residence is not large compared to the Greek Revival houses of the Deep South, its tall square pillars, high-ceilinged rooms, and handsome woodwork give it the stately air inherent in the Grecian mode. The house was built in 1845–46 for George Washington Bassett, in whose family it remained until the end of the century. The use of the portico on the facade is a departure from the Richmond-vicinity practice of placing the portico on the rear or garden elevation. 42–47 (10/17/78).

FORK CHURCH, *Ashland vicinity.* Fork Church was erected ca. 1736 as the second Lower Church of St. Martin's Parish. It is a typical rectangular colonial Anglican church, with a front and side entrance, no transepts, and a simple gable roof. One of Virginia's few colonial churches not to have been vandalized by Northern troops during the Civil War, Fork Church retains many of its early fittings, including its rear gallery, portions of the original pews, and an early altar table. Also surviving is a fine 1834 pipe organ. Patrick Henry, Dolley Madison, and Thomas Nelson Page were all regular worshipers at Fork Church. 42–12 (12/2/69).

HANOVER COUNTY COURTHOUSE, *Hanover Court House.* Hanover County's courthouse survives as the archetypal example of colonial Virginia's arcaded court structures, of which only six remain. Each of these buildings has refined brickwork and an arcade or arcades topped by a tall hipped roof. The Hanover courthouse was erected ca. 1735 and has been in continuous use ever since. In 1763 its courtroom was the scene of Patrick Henry's first well-known case, the Parson's Cause, in which he attacked the misrule of the king and the greed of the Anglican clergy. The courthouse has undergone several renovations, leaving little of the original interior fabric. The exterior, however, continues to convey the simple dignity inherent in colonial Virginia's public architecture. 42–16 (11/5/68); *National Historic Landmark.*

HANOVER COURT HOUSE HISTORIC DISTRICT, *includes the core of the settlement of Hanover Court House.* The remarkably well preserved administrative seat of Hanover County retains all of the essential ingredients as well as the atmosphere of a rural Virginia courthouse settlement. Included in the complex is the arcaded courthouse of ca. 1735, a major monument of Virginia's colonial public architecture. Its surrounding green contains an 1835 stone jail and a brick clerk's office of approximately the same date. Across the road is the rambling wood-frame Hanover Tavern (shown), an unusually large 18th-century hostelry of which Patrick Henry's father-in-law John Shelton served as proprietor. Patrons of the tavern included Lord Cornwallis and the marquis de Chastellux. It is now the Barksdale Theatre. A later addition to the assemblage is the 1942 Pamunkey Regional Library, a carefully designed Colonial Revival structure given along with many similar buildings to rural Virginia county seats by diplomat David K. E. Bruce. Hanover Court House was caught in the crossfire of much Civil War activity, and J. E. B. Stuart was commissioned a major general in the Confederate cavalry here. 42–86 (7/6/71).

HANOVER TOWN ARCHAEOLOGICAL SITE, *Studley vicinity.* The 18th-century port village of Hanover Town grew up beside tobacco warehouses on the uppermost part of the Pamunkey River, which was navigable for cargo ships of the period. The village site was patented in 1672 by Col. John Page, and the first warehouse began operation in 1730. The community was formally established in 1762 by the House of Burgesses through the efforts of Mann Page II of Rosewell, who had inherited much of John Page's property. Hanover Town was raided by Lord Cornwallis's army during the Revolution and declined after the war when the silting of the river inhibited commerce. By the mid-19th century it had almost completely disappeared; shown are the foundations of Page's warehouse. The absence of modern intrusions has left this village site an area of special archaeological interest where information could be obtained about the streets, dwellings, shops, warehouses, and artifacts of a colonial port town. 42–97 (6/18/74).

PATRICK HENRY'S BIRTHPLACE ARCHAEOLOGICAL SITE, *Studley vicinity.* Documentary research has confirmed the oral tradition that this site in southeastern Hanover County contains the remains of the 18th-century Studley farmhouse in which Patrick Henry was born in 1736. Scientific excavation of the site could yield new insights into the early life of the Revolutionary patriot, who lived here until he was fourteen. The plantation dwelling house also was occupied by burgess and magistrate John Syme, cartographer John Henry (Patrick Henry's father), and by Judge Peter Lyon, a member of Virginia's first court of appeals. 42–114 (3/17/81).

HICKORY HILL, *Hanover Court House vicinity.* This extensive Hanover County plantation has been the property of the Wickham family since 1820 when Robert Carter of Shirley left 1,717 acres to his daughter and son-in-law Anne Butler Carter and William Fanning Wickham of Richmond. The Wickhams' son, Williams Carter Wickham of Hickory Hill, was a Confederate general and legislator and later served as president of the Chesapeake and Ohio Railway. The original house, completed by 1827, burned in 1875 and was replaced by the present brick house. An 1857 brick wing survived, however, as well as numerous early outbuildings. The grounds around the house are a remarkable example of antebellum landscaping, containing an informal park with outstanding specimen trees, a geometric boxwood garden, and a tree-box walk with boxwood averaging forty feet in height. A later series of gardens is highlighted by a collection of old varieties of roses. 42–100 (9/17/74).

MARLBOURNE, *Old Church vicinity.* Edmund Ruffin, the pioneering agronomist and ardent secessionist, made this Hanover County plantation a laboratory for his agricultural theories. By showing that exhausted soils could be revitalized with the application of marl, scientific crop rotation, and other advanced farming methods, he contributed to a renaissance of agriculture in the South. Violently opposed to any political interference from the North, he symbolized his dedication to the Confederate cause by firing the first shot on Fort Sumter. Although sacked by Union troops, Ruffin's substantial frame house at Marlbourne, built ca. 1845, still overlooks the broad, fertile bottomlands of his splendid farm, owned and operated by his descendants. Ruffin, who committed suicide over grief at the Confederate defeat, lies buried in the family cemetery. 42–20 (9/9/69); *National Historic Landmark.*

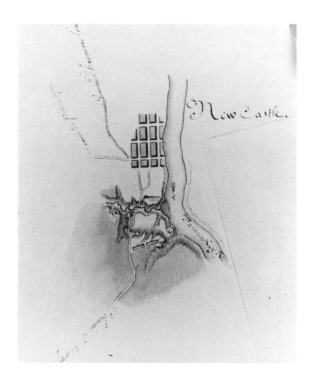

NEWCASTLE TOWN ARCHAEOLOGICAL SITE, *Old Church vicinity.* Newcastle was a colonial port town established by act of the Assembly on a forty-acre tract on the Pamunkey River owned by William Meriwether. In 1739 its fifty-two lots, along with six lots reserved for warehouses, were surveyed by John Henry, father of Patrick Henry. On May 2, 1775, at the summons of Patrick Henry, the Hanover volunteers met at Newcastle to protest Governor Dunmore's removal of the colony's gunpowder from Williamsburg. Considerable military activity took place in the vicinity in 1781. Baron von Closen, aide-de-camp to Rochambeau, visited the town at that time and described its location as "situated rather pleasantly on the banks of the Pamunkey." A French army cartographer drew the map shown. The silting of the river in the early 19th century, however, led to Newcastle's decline and eventual disappearance, making the site valuable today for archaeological investigation of the remains of a pre-Revolutionary port town undisturbed by modern development. 42–101 (12/16/75).

OAKLAND, *Montpelier vicinity.* Oakland was the birthplace and childhood home of Virginia author Thomas Nelson Page (1853–1922). Here Page absorbed the atmosphere and legends of Virginia that gave realism to his somewhat idealistic novels and short stories about the Old South. Among his most popular works is the children's book *Two Little Confederates.* His major novel, *Red Rock,* depicts the southern view of Reconstruction. The original house burned in 1898, but Page had it immediately rebuilt in similar form on the original foundations. In addition to his literary activities, Page served with distinction as U.S. ambassador to Italy. Oakland is still owned by the Page family. 42–24 (2/19/74).

RANDOLPH-MACON COLLEGE COMPLEX, *College Avenue, Ashland.* Randolph-Macon College, chartered in 1830, is the oldest Methodist-related college in the United States still in operation. On the southwest corner of the present 85-acre tree-studded campus are Washington-Franklin Hall, Pace Lecture Hall, and Duncan Memorial Chapel, the first brick buildings constructed after the institution's move from Mecklenburg County to Ashland in 1868. Erected in the Italianate and Gothic Revival styles, the buildings were designed by B. F. Price of Alexandria and William W. West of Richmond. Together they form a nostalgic image of a small late Victorian collegiate complex. 42–103 (4/17/79).

RURAL PLAINS, *Rural Point vicinity.* The gambrel-roofed house at Rural Plains in central Hanover County is a substantial, nonacademic rural Virginia farmhouse of the mid-18th century. Interesting features of the building are its large scale, its Flemish bond brickwork, and the curious porch chamber above the entrance, a structure apparently original to the house. The property has been the home of the Shelton family since 1670. An 18th-century owner, John Shelton, also proprietor of Hanover Tavern, was the father of Patrick Henry's first wife. The patriot and his bride made their first home on 300 acres of Rural Plains presented by Shelton as a wedding present. Most of the house's original woodwork was removed in the course of 19th-century remodelings. 42–29 (3/18/75).

SCOTCHTOWN, *Negro Foot vicinity.* Patrick Henry, the Revolutionary orator, made his home at this Hanover County plantation from 1771 to 1778, when he was a leader in shaping the course of events leading to Independence. Henry was living at Scotchtown when he was elected Virginia's first non-royal governor in 1776. The barnlike house was built as the country residence of Charles Chiswell of Williamsburg soon after he acquired the property in 1717. Dolley Payne, later the wife of James Madison, lived here as a child. Scotchtown is probably the largest one-story colonial house in Virginia, with eight rooms and a center passage on the same floor. The otherwise plain exterior is given visual interest by the use of a clipped-gable roof. Scotchtown was rescued from deterioration in 1958 when it was acquired by the Hanover Branch of the Association for the Preservation of Virginia Antiquities, which undertook a careful restoration and now exhibits the place. 42–30 (9/9/69); *National Historic Landmark.*

SLASH CHURCH, *Ashcake vicinity.* This white weather-boarded structure was erected in 1729–32 by Thomas Pinchback and Edward Chambers, Jr., as the Upper Church of St. Paul's Parish, Hanover County. The building survives as the best preserved wooden colonial church in the state, the only one to avoid enlargement. Its roof framing employs a very early king-post truss system. Next to the swampy woods whence it derives its present name, the church claims among its early worshipers Patrick Henry, Dolley Madison, and Henry Clay, all once residents of the area. The church fell into disuse after the disestablishment and was eventually taken over by the Methodists and the Disciples of Christ. The latter denomination has used the church exclusively since 1842. 42–33 (8/15/72).

SYCAMORE TAVERN, *Montpelier.* Virginia's vernacular architecture is well illustrated by this simple tavern with its dormers and front porch, a feature characteristic of early taverns. Its construction date is unknown, but it was first recorded as a tavern in 1804 when it was serving as the fourth stagecoach stop between Richmond and Charlottesville. In the mid-19th century it was known as Shelburn's Tavern after its preacher-innkeeper the Reverend Silas Shelburn. In this century, author Thomas Nelson Page, a Hanover County native, founded a library here in memory of his wife. Although owned by the county, the Florence L. Page Memorial Library continues to be funded by a trust established by Page. 42–85 (2/19/74).

TOTOMOI, *Rural Point vicinity.* Named for Totopotomoy, husband of the queen of the Pamunkey Indians, who was slain in 1656 in a battle nearby, Totomoi is an undisturbed plantation complex in the midst of rapidly developing Hanover County. The centerpiece is a ca. 1795 frame dwelling house which preserves its original side porches with their scalloped eaves, as well as a curious two-level entrance porch. The rear is dominated by a pair of chimney stacks connected by pent closets. Nearly all of the house's original fabric, inside and out, survives. Complementing it are numerous early outbuildings, an informal park with a copse of ancient trees, a family cemetery, and a formal garden. The complex as a whole evokes a memorable picture of rural life in old Virginia. The property was granted to Thomas Tinsley in 1689 and is still owned by his descendants. 42–39 (2/17/76).

CITY OF HARRISONBURG

Harrisonburg, the county seat of Rockingham County, was named for Thomas Harrison, who donated land for the town site. It was established in 1780 and incorporated as a town in 1849. Harrisonburg became a city in 1916.

THOMAS HARRISON HOUSE, *30 West Bruce Street*. The modern city of Harrisonburg grew up around this stone house erected for Thomas Harrison ca. 1750. Harrison laid out the town that was to bear his name on fifty acres of his holdings and was also instrumental in having Harrisonburg established as the Rockingham county seat in 1780. The first courts were held in his home. Bishop Francis Asbury, pioneer leader of the Methodist Episcopal church, often visited Harrison and conducted some of the county's first Methodist services in the house. The first annual Methodist conference west of the Blue Ridge Mountains was held here in 1794. The Harrison house is an example of the very earliest stone vernacular construction in the Shenandoah Valley. It remained in the Harrison family until 1870 and is now used as an office. 115–8 (6/19/73).

ANTHONY HOCKMAN HOUSE, *Market and Broad streets*. Anthony Hockman, one of Harrisonburg's local builders, designed and built this elaborately ornamented Italianate residence for himself in 1871. An excellent example of the domestic architecture built during that decade, the frame dwelling retains the traditional symmetrical plan characteristic of early country and town houses while incorporating elaborate stylish ornament both inside and out. Its fanciful sawn trim is typical of Harrisonburg houses in the last decades of the century, reflecting the town's growing awareness of architectural styles. The house is set apart from more standard dwellings by its multiwindowed cupola with an odd concave curved pyramidal roof. 115–23 (1/20/81).

ROCKINGHAM COUNTY COURTHOUSE, *Court Square*. One of nearly 200 buildings designed by Staunton architect T. J. Collins, the Rockingham County Courthouse reveals his mastery of the fashionable Richardsonian Romanesque and Renaissance Revival styles of the late 19th century. The building was constructed by the Washington, D.C., firm of W. E. Spiers between 1896 and 1897 and is the fifth courthouse to stand on the site since the county was formed from Augusta in 1778. With its lively and contrasting elevations and lofty clock tower, all faced with rough-hewn sandstone ashlar, the courthouse remains Harrisonburg's most prominent architectural landmark. 115–2 (7/20/82).

JOSHUA WILTON HOUSE, *421 South Main Street*. The Joshua Wilton house on Harrisonburg's South Main Street is one of the Shenandoah Valley's more interesting examples of Victorian domestic architecture. The house also represents the practice of late 19th-century businessmen of erecting proud, self-assertive, often extravagantly embellished dwellings along principal streets to serve as statements of their wealth and position in the community. Joshua Wilton came to Harrisonburg from Canada in 1865 and quickly became one of the town's mercantile and civic leaders. His fanciful house, showing Gothic, Italianate, and Queen Anne influences, was completed in 1890 and clearly illustrates how such residences lent prestige to their owners while giving embellishment to the town. 115–20 (10/17/78).

HENRICO COUNTY

Located at the fall line of the James River, Henrico County was named for Henry, Prince of Wales, son of King James I. The county was one of the colony's eight original shires established in 1634. The courthouse was originally located in downtown Richmond. The county seat is now a modern government complex in the suburbs west of the city.

FLOOD MARKER, *Curles Neck*. The disastrous flood of May 27, 1771, when "all the great Rivers of this county were swept by Innundations Never before experienced, Which changed the face of nature," is commemorated on this stone obelisk deep in the woods of eastern Henrico County. The flood was 18th-century Virginia's worst natural disaster. The monument, erected that same year by Ryland Randolph on a bank above the James River bottomlands, was intended as a memorial to his parents, Richard and Jane Bolling Randolph. The flood so impressed Randolph that he had the monument inscribed with a description of the disaster, partially quoted above. The obelisk is an unusually large and impressive example of a colonial memorial piece. Its capstone was lost through Civil War damage. 43–23 (7/7/70).

HENRICO SITE, *Farrar's Island*. Because of the low, unhealthy siting of the Jamestown settlement, the Virginia Company of London early on planned to relocate the colony's chief town to a more salubrious, easily defended place farther up the James River. In 1611 Sir Thomas Dale selected a site on Farrar's Island, some fifty miles upstream, naming it Henrico in honor of Prince Henry, eldest son of James I. Under Dale's direction

340 workmen labored to build a palisaded village. Meanwhile, across the river to the south, Dale's men began construction of a "guest house for sick people," often cited as the first hospital in English America. Dale's ambitious plan to build a "cittie" at Henrico failed, and the seat of government remained at Jamestown. Henrico continued as a fortified outpost for several years, but by 1619 it had degenerated into "three old houses and a ruinated church." Although Henrico never became what the colony's early leaders had envisioned, it did serve as a wilderness foothold from which settlers set out to establish private tobacco farms. Settlement of the area progressed so well that by 1618 a "university and college"—designed primarily to educate and Christianize the Indians—was chartered at Henrico. Tenant farmers were soon settled on the college lands, but the enterprise was cut short by the great Indian uprising of 1622. Today, the only archaeological remains that have been identified on the isolated, wooded island are the ruins of a turn-of-the-century lightkeeper's house. Two monuments mark the island: a stone obelisk erected in 1910 by the Colonial Dames to commemorate the college and the church and a stone cross placed nearby in 1911 by the Episcopal Diocese of Virginia. The site of the original Henrico settlement was probably destroyed in 1864 by massive earthmoving operations undertaken by the Union army in an effort to shorten the course of the James River and thus make the Confederate capital more vulnerable to Federal gunboat attack. While some archaeological evidence of Dale's settlement may still remain at Farrar's Island, it has yet to be discovered. 43–36 (12/21/71).

MALVERN HILL, *Varina vicinity.* Malvern Hill is marked by the foundations of a late 17th-century brick manor house built for Thomas Cocke (died 1697), sheriff of Henrico County and a member of the House of Burgesses, who was the son of Richard Cocke, progenitor of the Cocke family in Virginia. The property remained in the Cocke family until the late 18th century, and the house was destroyed by fire in 1905. Its exterior appearance, however, is well known through photographs. It apparently began as a two-room-plan brick-ended frame house. In the early 18th century the house was extended at front and rear, creating a cruciform plan, a configuration favored for finer houses in the 17th and early 18th century. Malvern Hill figured in three wars. Lafayette encamped there in July and August 1781, and the Virginia militia made camp there in the War of 1812. The bloody battle of Malvern Hill took place nearby during the Peninsula campaign of the Civil War. Some 5,500 Confederates fell on the slopes of the ridge on July 1, 1862. The house served as a Union headquarters. 43–8 (5/13/69).

MEADOW FARM, *Glen Allen vicinity.* Meadow Farm figured in the 1800 insurrection led by the slave Gabriel, who was owned by Thomas Prosser of a neighboring farm. Gabriel's goal was to have an army of slaves capture Richmond. Warned of the revolt by his own slaves, Mosby Sheppard of Meadow Farm notified Governor James Monroe, who was able to halt

the revolt before it began. News of the would-be insurrection spread fear and demand for repression through the South, resulting in the execution of Gabriel, his confederate Jack Bowler, and some thirty-five other slaves associated with the plot. The two slaves who had warned Sheppard were purchased by the Commonwealth and given their freedom. Sheppard's late-18th-century farmhouse, a well-preserved medium-size vernacular dwelling of the period, was given to Henrico County by a descendant and is now exhibited as a museum of early rural life of the region. 43–31 (5/21/74).

VIRGINIA RANDOLPH COTTAGE, *2200 Mountain Road.* This brick cottage on the grounds of the Virginia Randolph Educational Center was the office of a black woman who gained national repute for promoting innovative teaching methods among her race. In 1908 the Henrico County training school instructor Virginia Randolph (1874–1958), daughter of parents born slaves, was appointed the nation's first Jeanes supervising industrial teacher. The Jeanes supervisor was the outgrowth of an idea of a wealthy Philadelphian, Anna T. Jeanes, to establish a fund to employ black supervisors to upgrade vocational training in the public schools for blacks in the South. The program became institutionalized under sponsorship of the Negro Rural School Fund, and the idea spread throughout the southern states and eventually to countries in Africa, Asia, and Latin America. Virginia Randolph thus became a model for thousands of teacher supervisors who followed. Throughout her career, she maintained an interest in Mountain Road School where she first worked in the 1890s. Preserved here is the 1937 brick cottage where she taught home economics and later kept an office. When the school was closed and reestablished as the Virginia Randolph Education Center in 1969, the cottage was converted into a museum honoring the distinguished educator, who is buried on the grounds nearby. 43–43 (3/18/75); *National Historic Landmark.*

RICHMOND NATIONAL BATTLEFIELD PARK, *eastern Henrico County, also in Hanover County and Richmond.* In order to protect their capital from Union invasion, Confederate forces constructed an extensive system of earthen fortifications around Richmond. These were put to the test during the Peninsula campaign of 1862 when Union general George McClellan pushed to the outskirts of the city but ultimately was outfought by Gen. Robert E. Lee during the Seven Days Battles. Heavy action again took place on the eastern edges of Richmond in May 1864, when Gen. Ulysses Grant moved south from Spotsylvania and confronted General Lee at Cold Harbor where the Union army was beaten back with heavy losses. Today, the network of battlefields, fortifications, and associated buildings extending from north of the city around its eastern outskirts to the James River, and including the site of Chimborazo Hospital in the city, is preserved and exhibited as a 746-acre historical park by the National Park Service. 43–33 (1/16/73).

TREE HILL, *Osborne Turnpike*. On a commanding bluff overlooking the bottomlands of the James River and the Richmond skyline in the distance, this frame house with its surrounding outbuildings was the home of two Henrico County families, the Seldens and the Roanes. The original portion of the much-evolved and enlarged structure was erected in the late 18th century by Miles Selden, the county clerk and a local politician. The property passed to Selden's son-in-law William Roane, a U.S. congressman and senator. At Tree Hill in April 1865 Richmond mayor Joseph Mayo surrendered the Confederate capital to the local Union commander. The plantation survives as a tract of open space on the eastern edge of the city. 43–32 (5/21/74).

VARINA PLANTATION, *Varina vicinity*. Varina plantation is part of the ancient Varina Neck, just east of Henrico Island. Settled during the second decade of the 17th century, Varina Neck was the site of the glebe of Henrico Parish, established before 1640. The first Henrico County Courthouse was built next to the glebe before 1666. In 1680 Varina was one of twenty sites in the colony selected for development as a port town. A tavern was built there during the 1680s, and a ferry traversed the river on Sundays, court days, and other public holidays. The Reverend James Blair, who later became the first rector of the College of William and Mary, made his home at the Henrico or Varina Glebe between 1685 and 1694 when he was rector of Varina Parish. During the 1720s Thomas Randolph of Tuckahoe purchased land at Varina, and his son and successor, Thomas Mann Randolph, developed Varina into a prosperous working plantation. In 1828 Thomas Mann Randolph, Jr., sold Varina plantation to Pleasant Aiken of Petersburg, whose son and heir, Albert M. Aiken, built the present Varina plantation house, a relatively late expression of the Classical Revival, just before the Civil War. Aiken's Landing became one of two major points in the South where Union and Confederate prisoners of war could be exchanged. In the mid-19th century a romantic legend arose linking Varina Neck with John Rolfe and Pocahontas, a tale which lingers to this day. 43–20 (9/21/76).

WOODSIDE, *South Gaskins Road*. Just off River Road in the western end of Henrico County, Woodside was a farm tract of John Wickham, builder of the Wickham-Valentine house in Richmond. Wickham's son Littleton Waller Tazewell Wickham, built the present Greek Revival villa at Woodside in 1858. On the basis of an original paint contract, the design of the house is attributed to Albert L. West, the most noted of Richmond's mid-19th-century architects. The unaltered dwelling is significant for its unusual massing and floor plan, as well as its sophisticated interior and exterior detailing. Much of the building's original color scheme and decorative graining is intact, including rare fragments of exterior stuccoing painted to resemble cut stone. The house and surrounding park remain in the ownership of John Wickham's descendants. 43–12 (2/20/73); *Virginia Historic Landmarks Board preservation easement*.

HENRY COUNTY

Named in honor of Patrick Henry, this southern Piedmont
county was formed from Pittsylvania County in 1776.
Its county seat is Martinsville.

BELLEVIEW, *Ridgeway vicinity.* This forthright wooden plantation house, a provincial interpretation of the Georgian style, was built in the late 18th century for John Redd, a pioneer settler in the region who served as a member of the county court and participated during the Revolution in several actions on the frontier directed against the crown's Tory and Indian supporters. The property descended in the family to Justice Kennon C. Whittle (died 1967), member of the Virginia Supreme Court of Appeals. In the hilly reaches of the county, the dwelling enjoys a splendid view across the undulating countryside with few intrusions on its setting. The interior is noted for its robust woodwork, which includes carved mantels, paneled wainscoting, and dentil cornices, all somewhat freely based on pattern-book illustrations. Sheltering the center bay of the house is a naive though graceful two-level Ionic portico original to the house. 44–2 (5/21/74).

MARTINSVILLE FISH DAM, *Smith River, Martinsville vicinity.* The Martinsville fish dam is one of the few aboriginal fish traps of its type remaining in the state. The structure consists of stones piled in the bed of the river to form a low, V-shaped wall extending from bank to bank with the apex of the V pointing downstream. The wall originally was probably a foot or more higher. The apex of the V was left open, and baskets were held there to catch fish forced through by the current. The dam is partially exposed when the river is low and is in a good state of preservation. It likely was associated with a prehistoric Indian village site nearby on the south bank of the river. The dam is now owned by the Patrick-Henry Chapter of the Archeological Society of Virginia. 44–86 (9/18/73).

STONELEIGH, *Stanleytown.* Built 1929–31 after the plans of Leland McBroom of the firm of Tinsley and McBroom of Des Moines, Iowa, Stoneleigh, a handsome example of the Tudor Revival style, was the home of Thomas B. Stanley, later governor of Virginia. The Tudor Revival, an outgrowth of the English Arts and Crafts movement, enjoyed popularity in America in the 1920s and 1930s. The construction of this beautifully crafted house coincided with the end of Stanley's active career as a furniture manufacturer and the beginning of his long political association with the state Democratic party that led to the governorship in 1954. The extensive gardens at Stoneleigh, designed by E. S. Draper of North Carolina and later reworked by Charles Gillette of Richmond, were the inspiration of Mrs. Stanley, neé Anne Pocahontas Bassett. In 1980 the house, gardens, and surrounding land were donated to Ferrum College by the Stanleys' three children for use as an educational and cultural center. 44–87 (3/16/82).

HIGHLAND COUNTY

Named for its mountainous terrain, this western Virginia county was formed from Pendleton County (now in West Virginia) and Bath County in 1847. Its county seat is Monterey.

MONTEREY HOTEL (HIGHLAND INN), *Main Street, Monterey.* Built in 1904, this three-story wooden hotel is the town of Monterey's principal architectural landmark. From the mid-19th century through the early decades of the 20th century western Virginia was dotted with numerous resorts and spas offering a salubrious climate and healthful waters for visitors seeking to escape the summer heat and unwholesome airs of the seaboard cities. A more hurried life-style, easier long-distance travel, and air-conditioning resulted in the demise of nearly all of Virginia's mountain hostelries, making the Monterey Hotel a rare survival. The hotel's first owner was S. W. Crummett of Staunton, who commissioned the Eustler brothers of Grottoes to construct the building for $6,000. The outstanding feature of their effort is the elaborate two-level Eastlake gallery with its delicate spindle friezes. Early guests of the establishment included Harvey Firestone and Henry Ford. After falling into decline, the hotel has been renovated and reopened under the name Highland Inn. 262–4 (10/16/73).

CITY OF HOPEWELL

At the junction of the Appomattox and James rivers, Hopewell
was established in 1613 as Bermuda City. The settlement
became known as City Point. In 1913 E. I. du Pont de Nemours
and Company established a factory and residential area for
munitions workers on the adjacent Hopewell Farm, named for
the ship Hopewell *on which Francis Eppes arrived in Virginia*
in the early 17th century. Eppes had received a 1635 land
grant that encompassed much of the City Point lands. The
Hopewell industrial community was incorporated as a city
in 1916 and enlarged by the annexation of City Point in 1923.

APPOMATTOX MANOR *Cedar Lane and Pecan Avenue.*
Occupying the tip of City Point, the strategically located peninsula at the confluence of the James and Appomattox rivers,
Appomattox Manor is one of the oldest extant estates in America. In 1607 Capt. Christopher Newport briefly considered the
site for a town before settling on Jamestown Island. The property was patented by Francis Eppes in 1635 and remained in the
ownership of the Eppes family until 1979. The main part of the
present house was built ca. 1763. The several outbuildings were
erected in the 19th century. An east wing was added in 1840,
and further modifications were made in the early 20th century.
British soldiers under Gen. Benedict Arnold marched through
the property during the Revolution. From June 1864 until
April 1865 the east lawn contained the headquarters of Gen.
U. S. Grant. From his tent and later a cabin, Grant directed
the efforts of the far-flung Union armies during the final ten
months of the Civil War. President Abraham Lincoln visited
Appomattox Manor in 1864 and 1865, using the drawing room
as his office. The National Park Service purchased Appomattox
Manor for inclusion in the City Point unit of the Petersburg
National Military Park. 116–1 (11/5/68).

CITY POINT HISTORIC DISTRICT, *bounded by the James River, the Appomatox River, and an irregular line between Cedar Lane and Water Street.* A settlement was established at City Point as early as 1613, giving rise to the claim that the port is the oldest continuously occupied settlement of British origin in America. First called Bermuda City, the village was later renamed Charles City Point, and eventually City Point. It was incorporated as a town in 1826 and annexed to Hopewell in 1923. The community remained small throughout the 18th and 19th centuries, having less than 100 people in 1836; hence, only a scattering of pre–Civil War buildings remains in the district. Most notable among them is Appomattox Manor, the home of the Eppes family. The weight of history descended on City Point in 1864 when Gen. U. S. Grant established his headquarters here and made it his base of operations for the eventual conquest of Richmond. Thousands of soldiers disembarked at City Point, and numerous wharves, warehouses, depots, tents, and temporary one-room log shelters were quickly erected. President Abraham Lincoln visited City Point and observed the progress of the war. The community once again became a sleepy port village following the conflict and remained thus until World War I when the E. I. du Pont de Nemours and Company munitions plant was established nearby in 1913. Today, City Point is one of the more attractive residential neighborhoods of Hopewell, with 18th- and 19th-century buildings scattered among architecturally harmonious later ones. 116–6 (9/19/78).

WESTON MANOR, *off Twenty-first Avenue.* This Georgian plantation house stood almost unknown until the mid-1970s when it was donated by Raymond Broyhill to the Historic Hopewell Foundation and restored with the assistance of grants from the Department of the Interior. The house is on land acquired by William and Christine Eppes Gilliam in the latter part of the 18th century and probably was erected for them in the 1780s. The frame structure follows the formal rectangular plan of mid-18th-century Virginia plantation dwellings and is notable for preserving nearly all of its original fabric, including molded weatherboards, window sash, and interior woodwork. The house was shelled by a Northern gunboat in the Civil War and photographed by Mathew Brady during its occupation by Northern troops. In the course of restoration, an unexploded bomb was found lodged in the framing. The surrounding farmlands were sold off after their incorporation into the city of Hopewell, but the house preserves a pleasant setting on terraced banks overlooking the Appomattox River. Weston Manor now serves as a museum and cultural center for the city. 116–2 (11/16/71).

ISLE OF WIGHT COUNTY

Named for the Isle of Wight off the southern coast of England, this Tidewater county on the south shore of the James River was first called Warrosquoyoake and was one of Virginia's eight original shires formed in 1634. Its present name was given in 1637. The county seat is Isle of Wight Court House.

BASSES CHOICE ARCHAEOLOGICAL DISTRICT, *Mogarts Beach vicinity.* At the confluence of the James and Pagan rivers, the Basses Choice Archaeological District reflects a nearly continuous span of human occupation from ca. 4000 B.C. through the 19th century. Prehistoric site types range from small, temporary Archaic and Woodland camps to larger, more sedentary Woodland communities. Historic period occupation includes portions of three Virginia Company settlements, two of which suffered heavily in the 1622 Indian massacre. Archaeological excavation of the sites should yield new information on the material culture and architecture of Virginia's earliest English settlers. The site takes its name from Nathaniel Basse, who patented land here in 1622. The property was occupied by the Wilson family in the early 19th century and by the Blackwell family during the Civil War. 46–94 (4/19/83).

BOYKIN'S TAVERN, *Isle of Wight Court House.* Standing next to Isle of Wight's county buildings, Boykin's Tavern illustrates the functional relationship these hostelries had with the rural courthouse complexes in the days before more efficient travel rendered them redundant. The original core of the tavern was constructed ca. 1780 as a residence for Francis Boykin, who was a Revolutionary officer, county clerk, and justice of the county court. In 1800 Boykin gave land for the relocation of the county seat from Smithfield to a more central spot in return for permission to erect the new county buildings. After Boykin's death in 1804, his son Francis Marshall Boykin enlarged the building by raising it to two full stories and adding the gambrel-roof rear wing. The portico was probably added at this time as well. When the building was first used as a tavern is uncertain, but it was referred to as the "old hotel" by 1882. Despite further changes made ca. 1900, the tavern retains exceptionally fine 18th-century paneling in two of its rooms. 46–28 (5/21/74).

FOUR SQUARE, *Smithfield vicinity.* This Isle of Wight farmstead boasts one of southeastern Virginia's best collections of domestic outbuildings and early farm buildings. The two-story, L-shaped plantation house was built in 1807 for the Woodley family on land they had owned since the late 17th century. Its generous proportions and robust interior woodwork make the house representative of the more prosperous homes of the area and period. The associated outbuildings consist of an office, dairy, three smokehouses, shed, and slave house. The farm buildings include two granaries and several modern structures. One of the granaries is unusual in its use of triple-pen construction. The sites of a number of other subsidiary buildings have been identified, giving the complex archaeological interest. A family member once described Four Square in its heyday, when all of its early buildings were standing, as being "like a busy village." The surviving structures still project a villagelike image. 46–26 (4/17/79).

JOSEPH JORDAN HOUSE, *Raynor vicinity.* Built for the planter Joseph Jordan, this small brick-and-frame farmhouse with distinctive architectural detailing is a well-preserved moderate-sized southeastern Virginia plantation house of the late 18th century. It belongs to a group of architecturally related houses in the Blackwater River area representing the first flush of prosperity for the small planters who settled there. These houses are characterized by a long shed dormer lighting the top floor rather than the usual separate dormers. The later additions on the house, the outbuildings, and the 150-acre tract complete the picture of a typical 19th-century farmstead of the region. The property has been known variously as Jordan's or Boykin's Quarter and the Hattie Barlow Moody farm. 46–82 (2/26/79).

OLD ISLE OF WIGHT COURTHOUSE, *Main and Mason streets, Smithfield.* Restored in 1959–61 to its mid-18th-century appearance by the Association for the Preservation of Virginia Antiquities, the former Isle of Wight courthouse is one of Virginia's six remaining arcaded colonial court structures. After Smithfield's incorporation in 1752 and the removal of the county seat from Glebe Farm, three brick buildings were erected to serve the county government at its new location: the courthouse, clerk's office, and jail, all of which survive. The courthouse was built by William Rand and is notable among its contemporaries for having a distinctive curved apse, following the precedent of the curved apses on the first Capitol in Williamsburg. After the transfer of the county seat from Smithfield in 1800, the courthouse was converted to a residence. Its arcade was blocked up and its roof changed from a hip to a gable. The building was acquired by the Isle of Wight Branch of the APVA in 1938 and has been used since its restoration as a museum and for special events. 300–2 (6/2/70).

ST. LUKE'S CHURCH, *Benns Church.* This house of worship, known originally as Newport Parish Church, is the purest expression of Gothic architecture standing in the United States. Although the church is simple in design, its buttressed walls, lancet side windows, and traceried east window have for more than three centuries formed the New World's most direct link with the architectural glories of the Middle Ages. Except for its Flemish bond brickwork, which was not used by English masons before the 17th century, the church is hardly distinguishable from its small ancient counterparts dotting the British countryside. The exact construction date is controversial; estimates range from 1632 to 1682. More likely it was built with its tower in the last quarter of the 17th century when the colonists began to indulge in more substantial architectural endeavors. St. Luke's fell into disrepair after the disestablishment and stood more or less ruinous throughout most of the 19th century. A series of repairs was begun in 1894, culminating in the thorough and meticulous restoration completed in 1957. No longer a parish church, St. Luke's is an officially designated historic shrine of the Episcopal Diocese of Southern Virginia and is maintained by Historic St. Luke's Incorporated. 46–24 (9/9/69); *National Historic Landmark.*

SMITHFIELD HISTORIC DISTRICT, *roughly bounded by the Pagan River, Little Creek, the north town line, and the western edge of the historic area.* The compact community of Smithfield on the banks of the Pagan survives as perhaps the best preserved of Virginia's colonial seaports. World-famous for the Smithfield hams produced here commercially for over two centuries, the quiet little town has escaped most of the modernizations that have marred many of the state's oldest communities. Smithfield was founded in 1749 on part of the plantation of Arthur Smith and was incorporated in 1752. Excellently preserved examples from nearly every period of American architecture intermingle throughout the district. With a population of little over 1,000, the district has approximately fifty buildings of exceptional architectural interest. A rich sampling includes the 1752 courthouse; the late 18th-century Todd house, home of the town's earliest meat-packers; the Grove, a formal Federal house similar in form to the Moses Myers house in Norfolk; the lavish Queen Anne–style Gwaltney house, home of a modern meat-packing family; and the Georgian Revival Boykin house, the largest of the many fine residences lining the tree-arched Church Street. Numerous lesser buildings of various types contribute to the overall ambience of the place. 300–87 (2/20/73).

WOLFTRAP FARM, *Smithfield vicinity.* An architectural curiosity, this Isle of Wight Federal vernacular farmhouse survives as Virginia's only known example of an early dwelling with a double tier of dormer windows. Another such house, Bewdley in Lancaster County, was destroyed by fire in 1917. Unlike Bewdley, Wolftrap has its two rows of dormers on only one slope of its gable roof, giving the house an unusual asymmetrical profile. Multiple tiers of dormers are common in central Europe but rare in Britain; hence, this roof treatment was not widely used in America. In Virginia, rows of dormers were sometimes employed for the roofs of large industrial buildings, especially urban mills, but almost never for houses. Wolftrap was erected for the Jones family in the second decade of the 19th century and is still in the possession of descendants of the original owners. Although in need of repair, the house has had few significant alterations. 46–70 (9/17/74).

JAMES CITY COUNTY

*Bordered by the James and York rivers, James City County
was named for King James I and was the site of the first
permanent English settlement in America. Established in 1634,
the county was one of the colony's eight original shires.
Parts of New Kent and York counties were added later.
Its county seat is Williamsburg.*

CARTER'S GROVE, *Williamsburg vicinity*. Among the nation's richest expressions of colonial architecture is this James River plantation house built 1750–55 for Carter Burwell, grandson of Robert ("King") Carter of Corotoman. The excellently documented mansion was constructed by David Minitree, a Williamsburg brickmason, and the magnificent interior woodwork, regarded by many authorities as the most beautiful and most sophisticated of the colonial period, was executed by Richard Baylis, an English joiner brought over by Burwell for the task. The focal point of the inside is the broad segmental arch of the hall framing a Georgian stair. Carter's Grove stood essentially unaltered until 1928 when the owners, Mr. and Mrs. Archibald McCrea, engaged architect W. Duncan Lee to restore and enlarge the house. Between 1928 and 1931 the hipped roof was heightened to accommodate an extra story and the dependencies were enlarged and connected to the main house by brick hyphens. The property was acquired by the Colonial Williamsburg Foundation in the 1960s and is exhibited as a museum of high-style plantation life and architecture. The extensive original garden at the base of the riverfront terraces was reconstructed in the 1970s after a detailed archaeological investigation which also uncovered the site of an early 17th-century village near the river's edge. 47–1 (9/9/69); *National Historic Landmark*.

CHICKAHOMINY SHIPYARD ARCHAEOLOGICAL SITE, *Lanexa vicinity*. In 1776 the Virginia Committee of Safety decided to establish a small navy for the protection of the colony during the Revolutionary War. Master shipbuilder John Herbert was employed to examine the James River and its tributaries for sites suitable for a shipyard. The site selected was on the Chickahominy, sixteen miles west of Williamsburg. The ships *Thetis* and *Jefferson* were constructed here, as were numerous other vessels. Many Virginia naval craft were also repaired and outfitted at the shipyard. Activity lasted from 1777 until 1781 when the British seized and burned the shipyard. The site consists of both submerged and dry land components and is the only known essentially intact archaeological site of its type in the state. A modern fish house stands near the site of the colonial ships' ways, and foundations of associated buildings are in nearby fields. Scientific archaeological investigation could uncover important information about this Revolutionary-period industry. 47–78 (2/26/79).

GOVERNOR'S LAND ARCHAEOLOGICAL DISTRICT, *Jamestown vicinity*. The 1618 instructions of the Virginia Company of London to Sir George Yeardley specified that 3,000 acres immediately northwest of Jamestown Island be set aside for the use of the colonial governor and his successors. The tenants of the property were to give over half of their profits from farm produce for the support of the Governor's Office. This land was among the first areas outside Jamestown to be settled, and hence was one of the nation's first suburbs. The Governor's Land included Argall's Town, a small settlement established in 1617. By 1619 eighty tenants had been assigned to live on the property. These homesteads survived through most of the 17th century but eventually disappeared. Some twenty 17th-century homesites have been identified through an extensive survey of the area conducted by the Virginia Division of Historic Landmarks. Excavations undertaken with grant assistance from the National Endowment for the Humanities have revealed many significant artifacts, shedding new light on Virginia life-styles during the first decades of European settlement. Some of the most significant artifacts include pieces of English armor as well as an unusual 17th-century Portugese majolica plate from the Joseph Petitt site. 47–82 (7/17/73).

HICKORY NECK CHURCH, *Toano vicinity*. This tiny brick building is the remaining part of the Lower Church of Blisland Parish and is a relic of one of the Virginia colony's more important rural churches. The original portion of the building, a large nave, was completed in 1736. Its builders were John Moore and Lewis Deloney, both of whom worked on Williamsburg's Bruton Parish Church. To this was added a north transept in 1773–74 by builder Daniel Lyon. Following the disestablishment, the nave of the then abandoned church was taken down and a bay was added to the north transept, creating the present structure, which was put into service as a local academy. The name Hickory Neck, used for the church by the late 18th century, was preserved for the school. The academy lasted until 1907 when the building was reconsecrated as an Episcopal parish church. Today, this fragment stands as tangible evidence of the difficulties suffered by Anglican churches in the early 19th century. 47–8 (11/9/72).

JAMESTOWN NATIONAL HISTORIC SITE, *Jamestown Island.* Jamestown is the site of the first permanent English settlement in America, founded in 1607. The village that grew up on the island served as Virginia's capital for nearly a century. In 1619 the first meeting of the Virginia House of Burgesses was held here, signaling the beginning of representative legislative government in the New World. The same year, the first blacks arrived in America, brought to Jamestown and sold as indentured servants. After the seat of government was moved to Williamsburg in 1699, Jamestown declined, and much of the island became part of the plantation of the Ambler family. By the late 19th century, the only remaining structures on the island were the 1640s brick tower of the Jamestown church, a Confederate earthwork fort, and the ruins of the 18th-century Ambler house. To halt the extensive erosion of the fort site, the Association for the Preservation of Virginia Antiquities acquired 22½ acres of the island in 1893 and constructed a seawall along the southwest point. In 1907 the National Society of the Colonial Dames in America erected the memorial church on the foundations of the first brick church. In 1940 Jamestown was designated a National Historic Site and a joint agreement was made between the APVA and the Department of the Interior to provide unified development of the whole of Jamestown Island. Extensive archaeological excavation undertaken by the APVA and the National Park Service has uncovered what are believed to be the foundations of Virginia's first statehouse, as well as the foundations of the third and fourth statehouses. These and numerous other archaeological sites have provided important documentation of the material culture of 17th-century Virginia. Jamestown Island is today preserved and exhibited by both the APVA and the National Park Service. 47–9 (10/18/83).

KINGSMILL PLANTATION ARCHAEOLOGICAL DISTRICT, *Williamsburg vicinity.* This large tract of land along the James River immediately east of Williamsburg boasts a series of colonial archaeological sites excavated by Virginia Division of Historic Landmarks archaeologists between 1972 and 1976 under the sponsorship of Anheuser Busch, Inc. The principal site (shown), marked by a pair of matching brick dependencies, is of the ca. 1736 plantation mansion of Lewis Burwell. Excavations showed the house to have had a formal plan, elaborate paved forecourt, extensive terraced gardens, and numerous outbuildings. Burwell's Landing nearby, a center of commercial activity in the second half of the 18th century, contains a warehouse and tavern site, as well as Revolutionary War and Civil War fortifications. Excavation of three 17th-century sites—Kingsmill tenement, ca. 1625–60; the Thomas Pettus plantation site, ca. 1641–1700; and the Utopia site, ca. 1660–1710—provided information on Virginia architecture and material culture in the first century of colonial settlement. Kingsmill tenement and the Pettus site revealed the configurations of large post-constructed dwellings. Other excavations on the tract include the James Bray plantation, ca. 1700–90, North Quarter, ca. 1770–1800; and Hampton Key, ca. 1770–90. The sites have been preserved and incorporated into the landscaping scheme of Kingsmill on the James, a residential community developed by Busch Properties, Inc. 47–10 (3/21/72).

PINEWOODS, *Norge vicinity.* Pinewoods, also known as the Warburton house, is a modest plantation dwelling of the pre-Georgian period, one of the few remaining in the Williamsburg area. The house was set apart from most of its vanished contemporaries by its brick construction, which was employed only rarely for rural houses in the early colonial period. The architectural forms and details of the house suggest that it was erected in the first decade of the 18th century. The house was gutted by fire in the early part of this century, but the Flemish bond brick walls and the decorative T-shaped interior end chimneys survived. Owned by the Warburton family throughout its history, Pinewoods has been rebuilt within its walls for use as a hunting lodge. 47–14 (10/6/70).

POWHATAN, *Williamsburg vicinity.* Richard Taliaferro, referred to as a "most skillful architect" by Thomas Lee in 1749, lived at Powhatan from 1755, when he turned his Williamsburg house over to his daughter and son-in-law Elizabeth and George Wythe, until his death in 1775. Some scholars have stated that Taliaferro designed the house for himself; however, it is also claimed that Taliaferro did not purchase the Powhatan property until 1752 at which time the house was likely already standing. The house, therefore, may have been designed by Taliaferro for a previous owner. Marked by beautiful brick walls laid in Flemish bond with glazed headers and by massive T-shaped interior end chimneys, Powhatan is a classic essay in early Georgian design. The interior was destroyed by fire during the Civil War but was rebuilt shortly afterward. The house was restored closer to its original appearance in 1948 when the later gable roof was replaced with the present dormered hipped roof, and the interior was fitted with Georgian-style woodwork. 47–16 (7/7/70).

STONE HOUSE ARCHAEOLOGICAL SITE, *Toano vicinity*. The Stone House, called by James Galt Williamson in 1838 "one of the most antique buildings in the country," has been the subject of speculation and legend for over two centuries. Built of stone in an isolated location, in difficult topography above twisting Ware Creek, the structure has been claimed to be everything from a stronghold for Nathaniel Bacon's rebels to the storage house for Blackbeard's plunder. The structure had fallen into ruin by the time it was visited by Edmund Ruffin in 1841. The print of the ruins shown here appeared in Henry Howe's *Historical Collections of Virginia* (Charleston, S.C., 1845). Parts of the walls survived into this century. A survey of the site in 1972 by the Virginia Division of Historic Landmarks identified the foundations, which were of uncut sandstone, two feet thick. More extensive investigation of the site could likely solve the mystery of this intriguing structure. 47–36 (2/20/73).

TUTTER'S NECK ARCHAEOLOGICAL SITE, *Williamsburg vicinity*. Frederick Jones, later chief justice of North Carolina, bought this property between Kingsmill and Jamestown Island ca. 1701 and later sold it to Elizabeth Bray. A simple colonial manor house built either by Jones or a previous owner marked the property until it was destroyed in the last quarter of the 18th century. Archaeological test excavations of the site conducted by Ivor Noël Hume in 1960 and 1961 revealed evidence of a frame house measuring 42 by 19 feet (see conjectural rendering). Complete excavation of the Tutter's Neck homesite likely will increase knowledge of the life, possessions, and architecture of colonial Virginians in the rural area immediately adjacent to the colony's capital. 47–33 (12/2/69).

KING AND QUEEN COUNTY

formed from New Kent County in 1691, King and Queen County was named for William III and Mary II, who were called to the English throne in 1688. The county seat is King and Queen Court House.

BEWDLEY, *St. Stephen's Church vicinity.* On a high bank overlooking a wide bend in the Mattaponi River, this L-shaped brick house, a notable representative of Tidewater colonial architecture, was begun before 1760 as a plantation dwelling for lawyer Obadiah Marriott. The interior of the house stood unfinished at Marriott's death in 1767, apparently because he had been caught up in the Speaker John Robinson scandal. At Robinson's death, it was revealed that he had made numerous illegal loans from the colonial treasury to his political cronies and allies, among whom was Marriott. Marriott's association with the scandal and the debts owed by him to the Robinson estate, it is believed, caused work on the conspicuously fine house to be stopped. In the settlement of Marriott's estate, Bewdley was described in the Virginia *Gazette* as "a new brick house . . . which may be finished at small expense." The present, relatively simple woodwork mostly dates from the early 19th century when Bewdley was owned by the Roy and Mason families. 49–4 (7/18/78).

218 *The Virginia Landmarks Register*

HILLSBOROUGH, *Walkerton vicinity.* Hillsborough is King and Queen County's largest colonial plantation house. On the edge of the Mattaponi River, in the midst of cultivated fields and orchards, the massive frame house, with its generous proportions and weatherboarded walls, has a stately provinciality. It is distinguished by its brick ends, being the only known house of the period to combine masonry side walls with a hipped roof. Brick-ended houses are common in the Chesapeake Bay region but are rarely found west of the York River. The interior preserves much of its original paneled woodwork. A rare survival at Hillsborough is the colonial store building constructed of thin, Dutch-type bricks. The main house was most likely built for Col. Humphrey Hill, who is recorded as owning the property in 1752. The plantation remains the home of Hill family descendants. 49–31 (3/2/71).

HOLLY HILL, *Aylett vicinity.* This Mattaponi River plantation was established in 1784 by Moore Fauntleroy from land that was formerly part of Ring's Neck, a property owned in the late 17th century by Joseph Ring, clerk of York County. The present house was built in the second decade of the 19th century for Fauntleroy's son, Samuel Griffin Fauntleroy. In form and detail the house varies little on the exterior from the dwellings erected in the region over a half century earlier and thus illustrates the architectural conservatism in eastern Virginia. Like its predecessors, Holly Hill has a symmetrical facade, relatively unadorned brick walls, and a hipped roof with modillion cornice. The interior preserves restrained Federal woodwork. The place remained in the Fauntleroy family until 1946 when it was purchased by Gen. and Mrs. Edwin Cox. 49–33 (6/19/73).

MATTAPONI CHURCH, *Cumnor vicinity.* Mattaponi Church is an impressive example of a cruciform church, a plan reserved for colonial Virginia's larger, more important Anglican parish churches. Typical of such buildings, the walls are laid in Flemish bond with glazed headers, and the entrances are framed with pedimented frontispieces of gauged and molded brick. The church was originally designated Lower Church, St. Stephen's Parish, which was formed from Stratton Major Parish ca. 1674. The present church is the second on its site, and although its construction date has not been documented, it probably was erected in the second quarter of the 18th century. Abandoned by its congregation after the Revolution, it was taken over in 1803 by the Baptists, who have occupied it to the present. Fire destroyed the original interior in 1922, but the building was immediately repaired and returned to use. Mattaponi Church retains its isolated rural setting. 49–43 (9/19/72).

NEWTOWN HISTORIC DISTRICT, *Newtown and imme-diate vicinity.* Newtown originated in the late colonial period as a crossroads settlement on the Great Post Road that ran from Williamsburg to Philadelphia. Supporting a long succession of private academies and schools, Newtown prospered in the antebellum period as the largest post village in King and Queen County and was later the scene of several important maneuvers by both Northern and Southern troops during the Civil War. Today Newtown, with its cluster of two-story frame houses, survives in a rural setting as an example of a 19th-century Tidewater crossroads. 49–145 (3/17/81).

UPPER CHURCH, STRATTON MAJOR PARISH, *Shanghai vicinity.* The artistry of the colonial brick mason is demonstrated in this compact, finely crafted former Anglican church. The otherwise simple rectangular building is accented by walls of Flemish bond with glazed headers, deep red gauged-brick round arches above each window, rubbed-brick corners and water table, and beautiful molded-brick doorways. A molded-brick triangular pediment is employed on the south doorway; the west entrance, disfigured by a modern addition, is set off by a segmental pediment, also of molded brick. Upper Church was built between 1724 and 1729 and is the only one of the parish's several colonial churches to survive. The church was abandoned by the Anglicans as early as 1768 and was used by the Baptists until about 1842. It was gutted by fire several years later but was rebuilt within the undamaged walls. Methodists shared the building with the Baptists and eventually gained full control. The building is identified by its Methodist congregation as Old Church. 49–50 (10/17/72).

KING GEORGE COUNTY

*Named in honor of King George I, this Northern Neck county
was formed from Richmond County in 1720. Part of
Westmoreland County was added later.
The county seat is King George.*

BELLE GROVE, *Port Conway.* The lower Rappahannock River valley, the most unspoiled of Virginia's Tidewater river basins, is studded with noteworthy 18th-century plantation houses. Belle Grove, directly across the river from the village of Port Royal, exemplifies the quality of the wooden houses of the region. It belongs to a group of late 18th-century dwellings that feature wide elliptical arches on the interior and curious projecting entrance halls. It was built between 1790 and 1796 by John Hipkins for his only child, Fannie, who had married William Bernard in 1789. Its design is attributed to the master housewrights Richard and Yelverton Stern, who built a similar house for Hipkins at Gay Mont in Caroline County. After Belle Grove's purchase in 1839 by Carolinus Turner, the house underwent interior first-floor remodeling and received its wings and porticoes. The riverfront portico conceals the original engaged Ionic portico. During the mid-18th century the property was owned by the Conway family, and in 1751 in a long-vanished house that stood to the east of the present mansion, Eleanor Rose Conway Madison gave birth to James Madison, fourth president of the United States. 48–27 (9/19/72).

LAMB'S CREEK CHURCH, *Graves Corner vicinity.* The refinement of Virginia's colonial architecture is best seen in the numerous Anglican churches scattered about the Tidewater region. The elegant proportions, precise brickwork, and restrained classical gauged-brick doorways of Lamb's Creek Church, built in 1769–77 to serve Brunswick Parish, show a sophistication achieved with minimal ornamentation. Because of its similarity to Payne's Church (destroyed), the design of Lamb's Creek Church is attributed to the colonial architect John Ariss, or "Ayres" as noted in church records, the documented designer of Payne's. Union troops used the church as a stable during the Civil War. It was restored to use by the Episcopalians in 1908 but at present is inactive, being used only for an annual memorial service. 48–10 (8/15/72).

MARMION, *Osso vicinity.* Marmion was the seat of the Fitzhughs, one of colonial Virginia's landed families, who acquired the property in the 17th century. The present plantation house probably was built in the second quarter of the 18th century for John Fitzhugh or his son Philip. Although it appears plain and unrefined in contrast to the brick mansions of the James River, its paneled drawing room, now exhibited in the Metropolitan Museum of Art, is one of the most elegant of the surviving colonial interiors. The house's remaining interiors are simpler and more typical of the period. The stack of the south chimney, an early panel chimney, boasts Virginia's only known example of all glazed-header brickwork. The outbuildings, grouped as a formal quadrangle around the main house, include a kitchen, office, dairy, and smokehouse, all comparatively large. To the east of the house are remnants of an early formal garden. Marmion was sold by the Fitzhughs ca. 1785 to George Lewis, son of Fielding Lewis of Kenmore. It was owned by Lewis descendants until 1977 and has since undergone a careful restoration by its current owners. 48–12 (12/2/69).

NANZATICO, *Index vicinity.* The architectural formality and indeed monumentality that could be achieved in a relatively small wooden house is no better illustrated than in Nanzatico, a plantation dwelling at the head of a small bay on the Rappahannock River. The house is traditionally dated ca. 1770 and said to have been built for Charles Carter, Jr. However, its architectural style and detailing point more to a date after 1780, the year in which the property was purchased by Thomas Turner. Nanzatico was built as a twin to Belle Grove upstream (before the latter's alterations of ca. 1839), which also was given an engaged Ionic portico, projecting entrance hall, interior elliptical arch, and enclosed stair. Richard and Yelverton Stern, who are documented as the builders of the also similar first house at Gay Mont in Caroline County, may have constructed both Belle Grove and Nanzatico. Unlike the other two, Nanzatico survives almost without alteration, both inside and out, retaining remarkably lively Federal woodwork in the principal rooms. 48–15 (5/13/69); *Virginia Historic Landmarks Board preservation easement.*

NANZATTICO INDIAN TOWN ARCHAEOLOGICAL SITE, *Index vicinity.* In a field to the east of the Nanzatico plantation house is the site of a village occupied by the Nanzattico Indians. The village, which was established in prehistoric times, was the largest and most important Indian settlement on the Rappahannock from 1650 to ca. 1702. It was similar to the village shown in Theodor de Bry's engraving in Thomas Harriot, *A Briefe and True Report of the New Found Land of Virginia* (1590). The name is a corruption of Nantaughtacund, a tribal name originally identified by Capt. John Smith. Although partial examination of the site has already uncovered significant artifacts, complete archaeological investigation could provide important information on Indian life during the contact period. 48–84 (9/19/72).

ST. PAUL'S CHURCH, *Berthaville.* One of two remaining of Virginia's colonial churches with a true Greek Cross plan and two tiers of windows, St. Paul's was constructed in 1766 and is the third church to serve its parish. The simplicity of its exterior, relieved only by its fine brickwork and modillioned cornice, make the building more akin architecturally to English dissenter chapels of the period than to the richer Church of England buildings. Although the church fell derelict after the disestablishment, it was renovated as a school by 1813 and by 1830 was returned to the Episcopalians. As a result of this unsettled period, the present woodwork, both inside and out, is mostly 19th century. The church retains its colonial communion service of 1721 and its Bible of 1762. 48–21 (1/16/73).

KING WILLIAM COUNTY

Formed from King and Queen County in 1701, this rural Tidewater county between the Pamunkey and Mattaponi rivers was named for King William III. Its county seat is King William Court House.

BURLINGTON, *Aylett vicinity.* The Gwathmey family has made this upper King William County plantation their home since the third quarter of the 18th century. The scenic 700-acre tract is dominated by a small plateau on which stands a two-part residence overlooking the Mattaponi River valley. The earliest section of the house, a rear wing, is part of a mid-18th-century frame dwelling built by the Burwell family. The main portion is an architecturally conservative Classical Revival stuccoed house erected in 1842 for William Gwathmey, grandson of Owen Gwathmey II who settled in King William County as early as 1767 and was described in an 1831 letter as being "of Burlington." The property has descended through five generations of the Gwathmey family and is now preserved under the administration of the Burlington-Gwathmey Memorial Foundation. Evidence of prehistoric occupation, probably by the Mattaponi Indians, has been found on Burlington over the years. The most important artifact is a rare log canoe now owned by the Valentine Museum. 50–10 (3/15/77); *Virginia Historic Landmarks Board preservation easement.*

CHELSEA, *West Point vicinity.* Chelsea is an example of Virginia's mid-Georgian plantation architecture. The five-bay, two-story front section illustrates how colonial builders were able to instill formality into a relatively compact dwelling. The gambrel-roofed rear wing is more typical of the Virginia's colonial vernacular. Excellently preserved, the house has outstanding brickwork. Within is fine paneling and a notable Georgian stair. Chelsea was originally the property of the Moore family. The present house probably was built for Bernard Moore after his father's death in 1742. The wing was likely added by Moore before 1766. From this plantation Governor Alexander Spotswood and his "Knights of the Golden Horseshoe" embarked on their expedition across the Blue Ridge in 1716. Lafayette camped at Chelsea before the battle of Yorktown. 50—12 (9/9/69).

CHERICOKE, *King William Court House vicinity.* On a rise above the Pamunkey River, this King William County plantation has been the property of the Braxton family and their descendants since the mid-18th century. The property was first owned by George Braxton (died 1757), who left it to his son Carter Braxton, a signer of the Declaration of Independence. Carter Braxton built a large house at Chericoke in 1770, reputedly because he wanted a home even bigger than his substantial dwelling at nearby Elsing Green. The Chericoke house was destroyed by fire only five years later, but its undisturbed site remains of potential archaeological significance. Braxton is thought to lie buried nearby in an unmarked grave. The present plantation dwelling, erected in 1828 for Charles Hill Carter Braxton, grandson of the signer, is characteristic of homes of prosperous Virginia planters of the Federal period and has many architectural parallels to Richmond houses of the era, including a formal but restrained entrance front and a porticoed garden or river front. Its setting is dramatized by a long axial approach. 50—13 (4/18/78).

ELSING GREEN, *Lanesville vicinity.* One of the most impressive of the Tidewater plantations, Elsing Green is marked by a prodigious U-shaped house that ranks among the purest expressions of colonial Virginia's formal architectural idiom. The broad, level tract, stretched along the Pamunkey River, was owned in the 17th century by Col. William Dandridge, who is said to have named it after his native village in Norfolk, England. The property was purchased ca. 1753 by Carter Braxton, a signer of the Declaration of Independence, who probably built the main house. The house burned in the early 19th century, but its brick walls, regarded as a superb example of Virginia's colonial masonry, survived unmarred. Rebuilt within the walls, the house served as the home of the Gregory family for much of the 19th and early 20th centuries. In the 1930s, during the ownership of Mr. and Mrs. Beverley D. Causey, the roof was restored to its original pitch and 18th-century-style woodwork was installed both inside and out. Edgar Rivers Lafferty, Jr., who purchased Elsing Green in 1949, developed the plantation into a model farm and has set aside the extensive woodlands and marshes as a wildlife preserve. 50–22 (5/13/69); *National Historic Landmark; Virginia Historic Landmarks Board and Virginia Outdoors Foundation joint preservation easement.*

HORN QUARTER, *Hanover Court House vicinity.* Both richly ornamented and exquisitely crafted, Horn Quarter has few peers among the Commonwealth's Federal-period residences. Its pedimented portico and generous scale combine with the refined Adamesque detailing to produce a composition endowed with both strength and delicacy. The house was built in 1829–30 for George Taylor, son of the agrarian reformer and pamphleteer John Taylor of Caroline County, on land owned in the early 18th century by Frederick Jones of North Carolina and later by the Nelson family of Yorktown. The house belongs to an architecturally related group of Federal mansions that includes Hampstead in New Kent County and Magnolia Grange in Chesterfield County, all probably sharing a yet unidentified common designer and common craftsmen. A triumph of Horn Quarter's interior is a spiral stair that ascends from basement to attic. Notable as well are the plasterwork ceilings and cornices and the Adamesque door and window cases. The house has a formally arranged complement of outbuildings and remnants of elaborate terraced gardens. 50–32 (3/18/80).

KING WILLIAM COUNTY COURTHOUSE, *King William Court House.* King William County's courthouse is the best preserved of Virginia's eleven colonial court buildings. Erected in the second quarter of the 18th century, it is one of the nation's oldest public buildings in continuous use. Its arcaded front took its precedent from the arcade connecting the wings of the first Capitol in Williamsburg. Its fine brickwork is in generally good condition for an old public building. Most of Virginia's early colonial courthouses were located near the geographic center of their counties, unrelated to any town. King William's courthouse followed this pattern and still preserves its isolated rural setting. 50–38 (11/5/68).

MANGOHICK CHURCH, *Mangohick.* This simple but dignified colonial church was built ca. 1730–32 as a chapel of ease for St. Margaret's Parish but soon became the upper church of St. David's Parish. Although no less well crafted, such chapels were nearly always considerably plainer than their parent churches. William Byrd II of Westover passed by Mangohick in 1732 and noted it as the "New Brick Church" in his journal of the "Progress to the Mines." The church was abandoned after the disestablishment and later became a free church, available for use by any denomination. Since the late 19th century it has been the home of a black Baptist congregation. The colonial-style window sash were installed in 1980. 50–41 (8/15/72).

PAMUNKEY INDIAN RESERVATION ARCHAEO-LOGICAL DISTRICT, *Lanesville vicinity.* Over 7,000 years of aboriginal occupation on this 1,700-acre, marsh-rimmed peninsula on the Pamunkey River give this tract unique archaeological interest. A survey of the area undertaken by archaeologists from the Virginia Division of Historic Landmarks and Virginia Commonwealth University in 1979 identified fifteen sites ranging from the Middle Archaic period (5000–3000 B.C.) to the postsettlement era. The Pamunkey tribe was first identified by Europeans when Capt. John Smith explored the upper reaches of the York River in 1607 and observed the tribe occupying the region between the Pamunkey and the Mattaponi rivers. Today, the reservation, one of two in the state, maintains about seventy inhabitants, representing a remarkable continuity. Scientific excavation of the sites could reveal much information about the early antecedents of the Native Americans in Tidewater Virginia. Archaeological research could also trace the cultural evolution and adaptation of the Pamunkey tribe from the time of their initial contact with European civilization through subsequent phases of Virginia history. The reservation's Tribal Cultural Center, its design inspired by the round-roofed Indian huts shown in early engravings, displays Pamunkey Indian artifacts and native crafts. 50–34 (10/21/80).

ST. JOHN'S CHURCH, *Rose Garden vicinity.* An outstanding example of the colonial mason's craft, St. John's Church was completed ca. 1734 and enlarged to its present T-shape before 1765. During the 1770s the church's eloquent and popular rector, the Reverend Henry Skyren, drew large crowds to his services. Among the church's regular worshipers was Carter Braxton, a signer of the Declaration of Independence. St. John's fell into disuse after the disestablishment, but the building is once again being used by Episcopalians and is in the process of a long-term restoration. The church is noted for its sparkling Flemish bond brickwork and its pedimented molded-brick doorways. 50–61 (10/17/72).

SEVEN SPRINGS, *Enfield.* This brick colonial manor house boasts a unique square plan with a center chimney. Despite its small size and architectural informality, the house is comparable in quality to many of the more pretentious plantation dwellings. The construction date of Seven Springs is undocumented, but the house likely was built for Capt. George Dabney shortly before his death in 1729. Although it was remodeled in the early 19th century, some important original features, such as the walnut stair, several paneled doors, and rare foliated hinges, remain intact. Distinguishing exterior features are the jerkinhead roof, the glazed-brick raking courses, and the gauged-brick jack arches. 50–64 (12/21/76).

SWEET HALL, *Sweet Hall vicinity.* Sweet Hall is the only known surviving Virginia house employing an upper-cruck structural system for its roof framing and is one of only two known cruck-roof houses in the country. Crucks—massive curved timbers providing roof and wall support—were used for rude cottages in medieval England. The form continued to be used for roofs of more substantial, though still modest, English masonry houses of the 17th century. The use of crucks was rare in Virginia and apparently was abandoned altogether by the mid-18th century. Aside from its unusual roof framing, Sweet Hall, with its T-plan, formal facade, elaborate T-shaped chimney stacks, and hall-parlor plan is one of the state's most impressive pre-Georgian manor houses. Although the destruction of county records has prevented precise dating, the house most likely was erected in the first or second decade of the 18th century for Thomas Claiborne (1680–1723), grandson of Secretary of the Colony William Claiborne. The house received some modification in the early 19th century when Federal sash were installed and dormers were added to the roof. Sweet Hall preserves a quiet remoteness on the banks of the Pamunkey, overlooking broad reaches of marshland. 50–67 (2/15/77).

WINDSOR SHADES, *Sweet Hall vicinity* Windsor Shades, sometimes known as Waterville, is a little-altered Tidewater planter's house of the mid-18th century. Although built of wood and employing a gambrel roof, the house has much of the refinement found in the larger brick houses of the period. Setting it apart from its contemporaries is the massive east chimney structure, incorporating two stacks and five fireplaces, one of which is a large basement kitchen fireplace. The chimney structure also contains two closets, each lighted by its own window. On the interior, the center passage has a Georgian stair with vase-and-column balusters. The parlor is embellished with a Georgian chimneypiece and paneled wainscoting. The early history of Windsor Shades has not been verified because of the destruction of the county records; however, it is reasonable to assume that the house was built in the third quarter of the 18th century when the property was owned by Thomas Chamberlayne and his wife, neé Wilhemina Byrd of Westover. 50–70 (12/21/76).

WYOMING, *Etna Mills vicinity.* This two-story, five-bay frame house was built ca. 1800 for the Hoomes family. While maintaining the Georgian flavor of earlier decades traditional for Virginia's finer houses, Wyoming is considerably larger both in exterior dimensions and room sizes than other Tidewater houses of the same style, and it may be the largest hall-parlor/center-passage house in eastern Virginia. The house was part of a wave of construction of residential architecture that took place in the Virginia countryside following the Revolution, a building boom that resulted in the remodeling or replacement of the majority of the small, often rude colonial farmhouses of the Tidewater region. Like many of these post-Revolutionary structures, Wyoming is embellished on the interior with paneled chimneypieces and wainscoting. Its name may allude to the Revolutionary battle of Wyoming Valley, Pa., or to the Indian word for plain. 50–75 (9/18/79).

LANCASTER COUNTY

*Probably named for the English shire, Lancaster County was
formed from Northumberland and York counties in 1651.
Bordered by the Chesapeake Bay and Rappahannock River, the
county occupies the southern tip of the Northern Neck.
Its county seat is Lancaster Court House.*

BELLE ISLE, *Litwalton vicinity.* The formal, symmetrical arrangement of buildings and grounds of the great Tidewater Virginia seats is present in a much reduced scale at Belle Isle, a plantation which takes its name from a marshy island on the north shore of the Rappahannock. The complex, approached by a mile-long axial avenue, consists of a compact Georgian manor house flanked by two perpendicularly sited dependencies forming a forecourt. On the river side are formal gardens laid out on the original terraces. The earliest portions of the grouping probably were built for William Bertrand before his death in 1759. The house received its one-story wings around 1790 during the ownership of Rawleigh Downman. Sections of the interior paneling were removed in the 1920s and later were acquired by the Henry Francis du Pont Winterthur Museum. The complex has since been carefully restored under the direction of architectural historian Thomas T. Waterman. 51–1 (3/2/71).

CHRIST CHURCH, *Irvington vicinity.* Enhanced by its quiet rural setting, Christ Church is without peer among Virginia's colonial churches in the quality of its architecture and state of preservation. The elegant Latin-cross structure owes its fine quality to the fact that it was commissioned by Robert ("King") Carter, the most prosperous and influential of Virginia's colonial planters. Completed by 1735, the exterior is set off by its beautiful brickwork, especially the exquisitely crafted molded-brick doorways, the finest of their type in the nation. The full entablature, complete with cushion frieze, is a feature rarely used on colonial buildings. The windows, which preserve their original sash, are accented by stone keystones and sills, as well as by gauged-brick arches. Inside, the church retains its original pews and stone pavers. The architectural highlights of the interior are the handsomely trimmed pulpit and the walnut altarpiece. Behind the church are the imported tombs of Carter and his two wives. The ensemble is the epitome of colonial Virginia design and craftsmanship. 51–4 (9/9/69); *National Historic Landmark.*

COROTOMAN ARCHAEOLOGICAL SITE, *Weems vicinity.* An extensive archaeological excavation conducted by the Virginia Division of Historic Landmarks in 1978 revealed the form and size of the mansion of Robert ("King") Carter, colonial Virginia's richest and most powerful planter. Carter began construction of the house in 1720 and lived there until it was destroyed by fire in 1729, three years before his death. The excavation uncovered the foundations of what must have been the most prodigious and richly appointed house of the period: a 40-by-90-foot two-story structure with towers at each corner of the river side. Between the towers was a long veranda with a paved area beneath. The archaeological excavations showed that the hall was paved with marble and that the fireplaces had marble trim and were lined with delft tiles. The thousands of artifacts unearthed in the rubble, including pieces of ceramic tankards and storage vessels, porcelain teacups, wine bottles, buckles, clasps, and hardware, help to reconstruct the life-style of one of the great figures of America's colonial era. 51–34 (12/2/69); *Virginia Historic Landmarks Board preservation easement.*

FOX HILL, *Lively vicinity.* Named for the 17th-century owner of the property, planter David Fox, this Northern Neck plantation contains an L-shaped Federal dwelling conspicuously situated amid broad flat fields. The severely formal house echoes the Georgian style of the preceding generation and is set off by its even Flemish bond brickwork and molded-brick cornices and its restrained but well-crafted Federal interior woodwork. Complementing the house is a two-story kitchen of the same formal character. It and a brick smokehouse are the remnants of an original complex of five outbuildings. Although no survey has been conducted, the property may also contain the archaeological site of David Fox's manor house. The plantation was acquired in 1793 by Richard Selden II, who apparently built the present house before his death in 1823. 51–9 (4/18/78).

LANCASTER COURT HOUSE HISTORIC DISTRICT, *extending for a quarter mile along State Route 3, taking in the historic core of the community.* The tiny community of Lancaster Court House is one of the best preserved of Virginia's rural courthouse villages. The principal element of the district is the late antebellum courthouse with its 1937 portico. The courthouse complex includes the former jail and old clerk's office, both dating from the 18th-century. Immediately to the east is an 1872 Confederate memorial, believed to be the first such monument erected in Virginia. A ca. 1800 tavern, mid-19th-century post office, Carpenters' Gothic church, turn-of-the-century store, and several detached 19th- and early 20th-century dwellings complete the linear village. Shown are the old clerk's office and, across the street, the tavern. Nearly free of modern intrusions, the district maintains a harmony of scale, color, texture, and materials, all within a larger agrarian setting. The county seat was established at this location in 1740. 51–81 (1/18/83).

MILLENBECK ARCHAEOLOGICAL SITES, *Millenbeck.* The area around the present settlement of Millenbeck on the Corotoman River, a tributary of the Rappahannock, contains several colonial archaeological sites. A fort, known as the fort at Ball's Point, was established there around the time of Bacon's Rebellion, and traces of it are believed to remain. The site of the late 17th-century family home of Hannah Ball, great-grandmother of George Washington, probably remains intact near the fort site. The site of a later Ball mansion, as well as that of another colonial-era house, remains undisturbed. The early date of the fortification and the residences of Washington's ancestors give this complex particularly important archaeological potential. 51–29 (12/2/69).

ST. MARY'S WHITECHAPEL, *Lively vicinity.* The vicissitudes suffered by Virginia's Anglican church are expressed in the fabric of this tenacious Northern Neck parish church named for the London suburb that was home for some of its first communicants. The oldest portion of the church may have been built as early as 1669. This rectangular structure was made cruciform in 1740–41 with the construction of the existing transepts. The building was abandoned after the disestablishment but was reoccupied in 1832. To accommodate a much-diminished congregation, the deteriorated nave and chancel were removed, and their bricks were used to fill the voids between the transepts. Though severely altered from its 18th-century form, the building's remaining portions are reminders of its importance in the past. St. Mary's was the parish church of the family of Mary Ball, mother of George Washington. 51–22 (9/9/69).

LEE COUNTY

Lee County was named for Henry ("Light-Horse Harry") Lee, governor of Virginia from 1791 to 1794. Occupying the extreme southwestern tip of the state, Lee County was formed from Russell County in 1792, with part of Scott County added later. Its county seat is Jonesville.

CUMBERLAND GAP HISTORIC DISTRICT, *Cumberland Gap, Tennessee vicinity.* Cumberland Gap, at the extreme western tip of the state, for centuries was the only easily accessible route through the Allegheny Mountains to the west. Witnessing the movement of peoples from aboriginal Indians to modern man, the gap played an important role in the western expansion of the nation. After Dr. Thomas Walker discovered the gap in 1750, pioneers began to venture through it in search of fertile lands and good hunting in Kentucky, Tennessee, and beyond. Trailblazers such as Daniel Boone finally established a safe route known as the Wilderness Road. During the 1790s as many as a hundred settlers a day journeyed through the gap to a new life. Cumberland Gap was strongly fortified by both sides during the Civil War but was never the scene of a major battle. Many remains of the fortifications survive along the scenic trace. The district includes property within the Cumberland Gap National Historical Park, owned and maintained by the National Park Service. 52–17 (10/18/83); *National Historic Landmark.*

ELY MOUND ARCHAEOLOGICAL SITE, *Rose Hill vicinity*. Dating to the Late Woodland/Mississippian period (ca. A.D. 800–1750), the Ely Mound archaeological site is the only clearly identified substructure or town-house mound in Virginia. As such, the mound and associated occupation areas should supply much information on the development of increasingly complex societies in southwestern Virginia during the Late Woodland/Mississippian period and the interactions of those societies with the more complex societal groups in what are now North Carolina and Tennessee. The Ely Mound is also significant in the history of American archaeological studies, for his excavations here in the 1870s led Lucien Carr to reject emphatically the "lost race" hypothesis for Mound Builders in eastern North America, a popular theory among 19th-century American archaeologists. 52–18 (4/19/83).

JONESVILLE METHODIST CAMPGROUND, *Jonesville vicinity*. A surge of evangelical fervor in the early 19th century resulted in the establishment throughout the country of campgrounds to hold religious revival meetings. Spacious, shedlike auditoriums were built to shelter the large numbers attending the services. A particularly early example is this building at Jonesville in the southwestern tip of the state. Surrounded by a wide lawn used for campsites, the 1827–28 structure was built on land established by the Methodist-Episcopal Church of Lee County as a religious campground in 1810. The building has a long gable roof supported on massive oak timbers and side panels that can be raised for ventilation. It has been in continuous use since its completion. 52–7 (7/17/73).

CITY OF LEXINGTON

*This collegiate community and county seat of Rockbridge County
was probably named for Lexington, Mass., where the first
battle of the Revolution was fought. The town was
established in 1778 and incorporated in 1874.
It became a city in 1965.*

ALEXANDER-WITHROW HOUSE, *Main and West Washington streets*. A curious but impressive landmark in the heart of Lexington's downtown, the Alexander-Withrow house is distinguished by its corner chimneys and diaper-pattern brickwork decoration. Corner chimneys are a peculiarity of several early Rockbridge County houses, and diapering is seen in only a few isolated dwellings in the Shenandoah Valley. The house was completed by 1790 for William Alexander to serve as his store and residence. Originally the house was covered by a gable roof, which must have looked odd with corner chimneys. It received its present stone-lined shopfronts and low roof with heavy Italianate cornice when Main Street was lowered in the 1850s. After years of neglect, the restoration of the exterior was undertaken by the Historic Lexington Foundation in 1969. The building now serves as a guest house and shop. 117–1 (1/5/71).

STONEWALL JACKSON HOUSE, *8 East Washington Street*. This unassuming early 19th-century town house, located around the corner from the county courthouse, was the home of Confederate general Thomas J. ("Stonewall") Jackson from 1858 until he was mortally wounded at Chancellorsville in 1864. Its first owner was Cornelius Dorman, who built this typical Valley I-house in 1801. The facade was altered and a stone wing was added before Jackson bought it. After Jackson's widow died in 1901, the house was sold to the United Daughters of the Confederacy and remodeled into the Stonewall Jackson Memorial Hospital, with the front being completely restyled. In the 1970s the Historic Lexington Foundation directed the restoration of the house to its appearance during Jackson's tenure, even reproducing the facade showing its shifted openings. The house now serves as a museum dedicated to one of the most brilliant military tacticians in history. 117–9 (9/19/72).

LEE CHAPEL, *Washington and Lee University*. Robert E. Lee, the president of what was then Washington College, was instrumental in having the school chapel constructed in 1867. Although the design of the simple, modified Romanesque-style building has long been attributed to Lee, documentation now proves that the building is the work of Col. Thomas Hoomes Williamson, professor of civil and military engineering at the Virginia Military Institute. Williamson, however, apparently worked closely with Lee in formulating the design. The body of the former Confederate commander lay in state in the chapel in 1869 and was later interred in a family crypt in the basement. In 1883 a rear extension designed by J. Crawford Neilson was completed to house Virginia sculptor Edward V. Valentine's recumbent statue of Lee. General Lee's office in the chapel basement has been carefully preserved as he left it. 117–19 (9/9/69); *National Historic Landmark*.

LEXINGTON HISTORIC DISTRICT, *incorporating the town's major historic areas, including the campuses of Washington and Lee University and the Virginia Military Institute, the commercial area, and the residential areas between Main Street and Jackson Avenue and southeast of Main Street and northeast of Nelson Street*. Set amid the beautiful mountains and farmland of Rockbridge County, the city of Lexington boasts an outstanding variety of architecture. Building types range from the early Shenandoah Valley vernacular forms through sophisticated examples of Romantic Revivalism. Lending luster to the district are buildings designed by the nationally prominent architects Thomas U. Walter, Alexander Jackson Davis, and Bertram Grosvenor Goodhue. The town was authorized in 1778, and by the 1790s it was a prospering county seat. A fire in 1796 resulted in the replacement of many of the wood and log buildings with brick ones. Outstanding among these early Federal brick struc-

tures are the Central Hotel (1809), the Jacob Ruff house (ca. 1829), and the Dodd Building (1820 and 1826). Growth was stimulated not only by the fact that Lexington was the county seat and a regional trading center but by the establishment of Washington College (later renamed Washington and Lee University) and the Virginia Military Institute. The adjoining campuses of the two institutions, the former embellished with Classical Revival structures and the latter with Gothic Revival ones, constitute one of Virginia's great architectural assemblages. Scattered through the well-maintained, tree-shaded residential areas of the district is a mixture of Federal, Greek Revival, Gothic Revival, Italianate, Queen Anne, and Georgian Revival styles. Among the prominent representatives are the Federal Reid-White house, designed in 1821 by Samuel McDowell Reid; the Gothic Revival Presbyterian Manse in the mode popularized by Andrew Jackson Downing; the Italian Villa–style dwelling Silverwood; and the Queen Anne–style Corse house, designed by T. J. Collins of Staunton with W. G. McDowell. The district is now protected by a historic zoning ordinance, and the commercial area has undergone extensive rehabilitation spearheaded by the Historic Lexington Foundation. 117–27 (3/2/71).

LEXINGTON PRESBYTERIAN CHURCH, *Main and Nelson streets*. The 19th-century Philadelphia architect Thomas U. Walter provided the design for this chaste but noble Greek Revival church, the best representative of its style in this community. Samuel McDowell Reid, clerk of the county court and an amateur architect, was instrumental in having Walter commissioned for the job. The church was completed in 1845. Although Walter worked in a number of historic styles, his proficiency in the Grecian mode is evident both here and in several other Greek Revival churches designed by him for Virginia congregations. His Doric temple in Lexington, capped by a belfry and spire, demonstrates how the simplest classical forms could be adapted for Christian purposes and were especially suited for the lean liturgy of the Presbyterians. 117–12 (5/16/78).

MULBERRY HILL, *U.S. Route 60 West*. With its complicated evolution from a one-story, double-pile core to a two-story, gable-roof dwelling, and finally to a hipped-roofed mansion, Mulberry Hill illustrates changes in architectural taste in Lexington spanning a hundred-year period. Adding to its interest is the unusually elaborate, regionally stylized Georgian woodwork and plasterwork in the principal rooms, some of the finest of its period in the region. Begun ca. 1790 for Andrew Reid, first clerk of the court for Rockbridge County, the house was enlarged in the mid-19th century for his son Samuel McDowell Reid, and given its present appearance ca. 1903 by the local architect William C. McDowell. Complementing the house is a handsome early 20th-century garden. 117–10 (6/15/82); *Virginia Historic Landmarks Board preservation easement.*

STONO, *Institute Hill*. Erected in 1818 by builder John Jordan as his own residence, Stono is noteworthy for its use of the three-part Palladian scheme favored for a number of early 19th-century Virginia houses. Though its proportions and details are somewhat exaggerated, the layout and the use of a columned portico reflect Jordan's exposure to the architecture of Thomas Jefferson, who was especially fond of these elements. Jordan was briefly associated with construction work at Monticello in 1805. He also designed and built the porticoed Washington Hall at nearby Washington and Lee University, as well as other buildings in the Lexington area, several with the same exaggerated verticality as Stono. He sited Stono commandingly high on a bluff above the Maury River, immediately east of the property where Virginia Military Institute was later established. 117–16 (12/17/74).

VIRGINIA MILITARY INSTITUTE HISTORIC DISTRICT, *Institute Hill, north of North Main Street*. Organized in 1839, the Virginia Military Institute is the earliest of the nation's state-supported military schools and has supplied the country with many outstanding military leaders, including General of the Army George C. Marshall, U.S. Army chief of staff during World War II. The school's physical plant consists of some twenty-five major buildings by prominent architects, all united by a castellated Gothic Revival style. The heart of the school, the backdrop of the Parade Ground, is the Barracks, a much evolved complex, whose initial concept was the work of the mid-19th-century New York architect Alexander Jackson Davis. The Barracks was burned by Union troops under Gen. David Hunter, but Davis was called back after the war to supervise its reconstruction. Davis also designed the Gothic Revival faculty houses lining the Parade Ground, of which the Gilham house (1852) and the Superintendent's Quarters (1860) survive. Early in the 20th century, another New York architect, Bertram Grosvenor Goodhue, was commissioned to enlarge the Barracks and to design additional faculty houses and the Jackson Memorial Hall. The complex has received numerous buildings since that time, but the original Gothic character established by Davis has been carefully maintained and has served as a prototype for the design of military schools throughout the country. 117–17 (9/9/69); *National Historic Landmark*.

WASHINGTON AND LEE UNIVERSITY HISTORIC
DISTRICT, *northwest of Washington and Jefferson streets*. The
historic core of Washington and Lee University is composed
of an architecturally harmonious and spatially related collection of buildings that is one of the most dignified and beautiful
college campuses in the nation. The central and most significant element of the complex, the Colonnade, along with flanking paired faculty residences, gives the impression of being a
single architectural concept. It is, in reality, the end product of
a building program extending over nearly 150 years. As the
school grew, its administrators and builders enhanced the visual quality of the institution without falling into monotony
or sacrificing unity. The first buildings on College Hill, erected
in 1803 for what was then Washington College, have long since
disappeared. It was, however, the oldest existing building,
Washington Hall, erected in 1824, that established the architectural theme of the campus. Its builder-architects, John Jordan
and Samuel Darst, were able to transform the prevailing style
of the time, the Roman Revival, into a sturdy regional idiom.
This central columned building was flanked by Payne Hall in
1831 and by Robinson Hall in 1843. The four faculty houses,
each with a Tuscan portico, were also erected in 1843. The principal departures from this simple classicism, the President's
House of 1868 and the chapel of 1866–67, serve as architectural
foils. Architectural historian Talbot Hamlin has written: "No
more impressive expression of the educational ideals of the
time could be imagined than this Classic group, its pediment
and orders seen through embowering trees, over swelling
American lawns, its cupola crowned with the image of the Pa-
ter Patriae." 117–22 (10/6/70); *National Historic Landmark*.

LOUDOUN COUNTY

*This scenic Northern Virginia county, formed from Fairfax
County in 1757, was named for John Campbell,
fourth earl of Loudoun, who was commander of British forces
in North America during the early part of the French and
Indian War and governor of Virginia in 1756–59.
Its county seat is Leesburg.*

ALDIE MILL HISTORIC DISTRICT, *Aldie*. Charles Fenton Mercer, military officer, legislator, and advocate of the colonization of blacks, settled here in 1804. He named his property Aldie for Aldie Castle, his ancestral home in Scotland. In 1807 he began the construction of a large merchant mill where the Little River Turnpike crossed Little River. The mill, built by Mercer's partner William Cooke, survives as one of the best-outfitted early mills in the state. With the gristmill in the center, the three-part complex includes what was a plaster mill at one end and a store at the other. Its twin overshot Fitz wheels, installed in 1900 to replace the original wooden wheels, are a unique survivor in Virginia mill construction. On a hill overlooking the mill is a fine Federal house, built by Mercer in 1810 as his residence. Behind the mill is a brick miller's house. Completing the grouping is a stone bridge across Little River which marked the western end of the Little River Turnpike leading to Alexandria. Aldie Mill remained in operation into the 1970s and has since been donated by a descendant of Mercer's miller to the Virginia Outdoors Foundation. The mill is currently undergoing restoration for public exhibition. 53–114 (6/2/70).

BELMONT, *Leesburg vicinity.* This superlative five-part Federal plantation house, erected 1799–1802, was the home of Ludwell Lee, son of Richard Henry Lee, signer of the Declaration of Independence. The house ranks in quality with the five-part mansions of Washington, Baltimore and Annapolis; no name, however, has been associated with its design. Ludwell Lee served as aide-de-camp to General Lafayette in the campaign of 1781. His political career faltered, and he spent the rest of his days as a planter at Belmont. Later owners of the estate include Mr. and Mrs. Edward B. McLean, Washington socialites, and Patrick J. Hurley, secretary of war in the Hoover administration. Belmont is now owned by the IBM Corporation. 53–106 (9/21/76).

BENTON, *Leithtown vicinity.* Benton's dwelling house and outbuildings were the center of a prosperous Northern Virginia plantation of the antebellum period. The complex includes a formal brick residence built 1831–33, complete with dependencies and a rare early brick barn. Although the house is architecturally conservative, the high quality of the construction reflects the skill of its builder and first owner, William Benton. Benton was an expert brickmaker and mason who served as the foreman for the building of Oak Hill, James Monroe's Loudoun County home. He is credited with making bricks for most of the early brick houses in the Middleburg area and with supervising their construction. Except for a remodeling of the north front and some of the interior after 1908 when it was purchased by Daniel Sands, the house has changed little since it was completed. 53–107 (5/17/83).

BLUEMONT HISTORIC DISTRICT, *including entire village, extending along county road 734 between Butchers Branch and State Route 7.* Bluemont is a small settlement on the eastern slope of the Blue Ridge Mountains at Snickers Gap. Known originally as the town of Snickers Gap and by 1824 incorporated as the town of Snickersville, the village arose along a primary 18th- and 19th-century trade route between the Shenandoah Valley to the west and the Tidewater ports on the Potomac. The community took its name from the Snickers family, who pioneered settlement in the area in 1769. Snickersville was the scene of several skirmishes during the Civil War as both armies vied for control of the fertile Shenandoah Valley grainshed. After the war Snickersville declined as a business center until the arrival of the railroad in 1900. In order to promote the town as a small mountain resort, managers of the Washington and Old Dominion Railroad persuaded residents to change the town's name to Bluemont. Prosperity returned to the village during the first quarter of the 20th century when Bluemont served as a resort for city dwellers in Washington. Bluemont today retains much of its turn-of-the-century character. Although the majority of the structures date from that era, a number of earlier stone and log structures survive along the main road, serving as reminders of the town's importance as a 19th-century trade center. 404–12 (1/17/84).

BROAD RUN BRIDGE AND TOLLHOUSE, *Sterling Park vicinity.* Although the bridge was destroyed by tropical storm Agnes in 1972, its ruins and its accompanying stone tollhouse form the only such combination extant in Virginia. The bridge and tollhouse were part of the Leesburg Turnpike system incorporated in 1809 to connect Leesburg with Alexandria. Construction of the project went slowly; the bridge was not completed until 1820. Tolls ceased to be collected by the Civil War, and the bridge was abandoned in 1949 for a larger one close by. At the west end of the ruined bridge, the tollhouse now serves as a private residence. 53–110 (12/2/69).

CARLHEIM (PAXTON HOUSE), *Leesburg vicinity.* Carlheim, on the outskirts of Leesburg, is a large Victorian country house dating from the 1870s, a period when few important dwellings were erected in Virginia because of the economic deprivation following the Civil War. The thirty-two-room stone house, combining the Italian Villa style with the Second Empire taste, was designed by Henry C. Dudley of New York for Charles R. Paxton, a Pennsylvania industrialist. The interior is well appointed with polychrome stone mantels, rich ceiling medallions, and a grand staircase. To assure comfort, the house was equipped with central heating, hot and cold running water, and carbide gas lighting. The original concave mansard roof atop the tower was destroyed in recent years when struck by lightning. Among the surviving outbuildings is a peacock house. Now known as the Paxton Memorial Home, the estate is a children's boarding school. 53–380 (10/16/79).

CATOCTIN CREEK BRIDGE, *Waterford vicinity.* A typical example of Pratt-truss construction, this 150-foot, single-span bridge was once numbered among scores of similar structures but is now one of the last overhead metal truss bridges in the northern part of the state. It was manufactured in 1900 by the Variety Iron Works of Cleveland, Ohio, and was originally located on Route 7 spanning Goose Creek in Loudoun County. It was dismantled and moved to its present location ca. 1932 where it now serves a tree-shaded, unpaved country lane bordered by well-tended estates. 53–131 (1/15/74).

FARMER'S DELIGHT, *Leithtown.* Surrounded by Loudoun County's lush countryside, this estate boasts an architecturally sophisticated dwelling patterned after the Georgian plantation houses of the Tidewater region. One of the oldest brick houses in the county, it was built ca. 1791 for Joseph Lane, son of Maj. James Lane, an agent for Robert Carter of Nomini Hall. Joseph Lane served in the Virginia General Assembly and was a lieutenant colonel in the army during the Whiskey Rebellion of 1793. The property was acquired from Lane's descendants in 1856 by the Leith family, who held it until 1919 when it was purchased by the horseman Henry J. Frost, Jr., who added the wings. The original portion of the house is constructed with Flemish bond brickwork highlighted by a belt course and gauged-brick jack arches. The interior preserves restrained Federal woodwork typical of the region. The house is set in a landscaped park dotted with specimen trees. Since 1948 Farmer's Delight has been the home of George C. McGhee, former ambassador to Germany, who commissioned the formal garden, laid out in a series of terraces by the Washington landscape architect Boris Timchenko. One of the features of the garden is a pergola composed of columns from the 13th-century Benedictine Abbey at Samaron, France. 53–121 (4/17/73); *Virginia Historic Landmarks Board and Virginia Outdoors Foundation joint preservation easement.*

GLEBE OF SHELBURNE PARISH, *Lincoln vicinity.* On a hill above Goose Creek valley, the former glebe house of Shelburne Parish is one of only a handful of colonial glebe houses remaining in the state and perhaps the only one for which the original specifications survive. It is also the only surviving glebe house in Northern Virginia. Unlike most other glebes, Shelburne Glebe was not relinquished immediately after the disestablishment of the Anglican church but was held tenaciously for thirty-eight years by its parish following the act ordering the sale of such properties. The present house was begun on the 465-acre glebe in 1773 by the builder Appolis Cooper. Although extensively remodeled and enlarged after its sale to private owners in 1840, its colonial brick walls attest to the house's early origins. 53–186 (11/19/74).

GOOSE CREEK HISTORIC DISTRICT, *roughly bounded by North Fork Creek, routes 611, 662, and 704, and the towns of Hamilton and Purcellville.* The Goose Creek Historic District is a scenically cohesive rural area of some 10,000 acres in central Loudoun County that sustained Virginia's largest concentration of Quaker settlers. The English Friends who came into the area from Pennsylvania, Maryland, and New Jersey beginning in the 1730s gave their community a distinctive cast that is still reflected in the region's small farms, many of which are yet defined by the boundaries of the original 18th-century land patents. Worked without slave labor, the Quaker farms were limited in size to what could be run by a family unit. The district, which centers on the village of Lincoln, has a rich collection of 18th-, 19th-, and 20th-century rural vernacular architecture, much of it incorporating the superb stone masonry peculiar to Quaker settlers and their descendants. No other area of Northern Virginia contains more examples of stone architecture, and few other areas of the Commonwealth possess such a high degree of unspoiled pastoral beauty. Shown is Janney's Mill Farm, a typical Quaker farmstead. 53–02 (7/21/81).

GOOSE CREEK MEETING HOUSE COMPLEX, *Lincoln*. This simple complex of three buildings on the edge of the hamlet of Lincoln illustrates the continuity of the Quaker tradition in Northern Virginia. The 1765 stone meetinghouse (shown), now used as a residence, is the second oldest Friends' meetinghouse in the state. Its successor, a brick structure across the road, was erected in 1817 and has remained in regular use. This latter building originally had two stories, but a windstorm in 1944 so damaged it that it was reduced to its present height. On the meetinghouse grounds is the Oak Dale School, a one-room brick structure dating from 1815, now used for Sunday school. Also in the complex is the Quaker burying ground. The Goose Creek meeting was organized ca. 1750 under the leadership of Jacob Janney of Bucks County, Pa. The group first met in a log building erected at the place in the woods where Janney's wife, Hannah, held regular private devotions. 53–176 (1/15/74).

GOOSE CREEK STONE BRIDGE, *Atoka vicinity*. The Goose Creek Stone Bridge is the longest of the remaining early stone turnpike bridges in Northern Virginia. The exact construction date of the massive four-span, 200-foot structure has not been determined, but it may date as early as 1810, the year the General Assembly authorized the Ashby's Gap Turnpike to be extended from the then western end of the Little River Turnpike at Aldie through Ashby's Gap to the Shenandoah River. The earliest documented reference to the bridge appears in the 1820 report of the Board of Public Works, which mentions the collecting of tolls on the Goose Creek Bridge. The bridge has been bypassed with the realignment of U.S. Route 50 but has since become a point of interest for motorists traveling through the area. 53–156 (5/21/74).

HILLSBORO HISTORIC DISTRICT, *lining State Route 9, Purcellville vicinity*. A typical 19th-century linear community, Hillsboro grew along a minor trade artery connecting Leesburg with Charles Town (now West Virginia) during the early 19th century. Its residents provided economic and social services to farmers of the vicinity, and the town retains a rural character. Hillsboro has many two-story, gable-roof stone residences, illustrating the influence of Pennsylvania vernacular building types on Northern Virginia. Victorian porch and bay window additions indicate that residents remained current with architectural styles popular in urban areas. 236–40 (9/19/78).

INSTITUTE FARM, *Aldie vicinity.* The Loudoun County Agricultural Institute and Chemical Academy erected this large but plain building ca. 1854 for its Institute Farm, the first agricultural school in the Commonwealth and one of the first schools of scientific agronomy in the United States. From the late 18th century, Loudoun's citizens had pioneered in agricultural experimentation, and the school's founders included a number of larger landholders and agriculturalists. Once part of the Oak Hill estate of President James Monroe, the property since 1916 has been the headquarters of the National Beagle Club of America. 53–139 (3/17/81).

LEESBURG HISTORIC DISTRICT, *coinciding with original boundaries of the town centered at the junction of U.S. Route 15 and State Route 9.* Established in 1758, the original sixty-acre portion of Leesburg, laid off around Nicholas Minor's tavern, is a well-preserved Piedmont county seat with a varied assemblage of domestic, commercial, and governmental buildings dating from the late 18th through the 19th centuries. The town is centered around a parklike court square containing the 1895 classical courthouse with a domed belfry and a porticoed Greek Revival academy building, now used for county offices. The district has an interesting collection of regional vernacular architecture, including shops, modest town houses, and three early taverns. A scattering of Victorian structures contrasts with the plainer buildings. Leesburg was first known as Georgetown in honor of George II, but its name was changed in recognition of Francis Lightfoot Lee, signer of the Declaration of Independence, who owned property nearby. The district's thirty-six blocks are intersected by a rough grid of largely tree-lined streets, many of which are bordered by brick sidewalks and well-tended yards. 253–35 (12/2/69).

MIDDLEBURG HISTORIC DISTRICT, *incorporating the blocks that line Marshall, Washington, and Federal streets.* The focal point of Northern Virginia's hunt country, Middleburg is a compact and fastidious village retaining the qualities of its early years. Founded in 1787 by Leven Powell, a Revolutionary officer and regional Federalist leader, the town developed as a coach stop and relay station on Ashby's Gap Turnpike, becoming by mid-century a commercial and institutional center for lower Loudoun and upper Fauquier counties. The town saw frequent cavalry action and won a reputation for fierce Confederate loyalty in the Civil War but then declined in wealth and population until the second decade of the 20th century, when it assumed a new role as a social and sporting capital of international reputation. With its tree-lined streets, brick sidewalks, and harmonious scale, the town has a diverse collection of late 18th- to early 20th-century architectural styles highlighted by early stone and brick structures. 259–162 (12/15/81).

MORVEN PARK, *Leesburg vicinity.* Morven Park is best known as the home of Westmoreland Davis, governor of Virginia from 1918 to 1922. From the time he acquired the property in 1903, Davis set a standard for hospitality and grand-scale living that has had few equals in Virginia. Davis, an advocate of progressive farming methods, made Morven Park a model dairy farm. The sprawling mansion, dramatically set against the Catoctin Mountain range, has had a complicated architectural history. Buried within the existing fabric is a 1780s farmhouse, first owned by Wilson Cary Selden. Judge Thomas Swann enlarged the house after he bought it in 1808. In the 1840s Swann's son, Thomas Swann, Jr., later governor of Maryland, engaged the Baltimore firm of Lind and Murdock to remodel the house into a grandiose combination of the Greek Revival and Italianate styles. Except for the omission of four Italianate towers, the scheme, which included a stately Doric portico, was carried out as planned, converting the house into a Romantic Revival villa of almost English scale. In 1955 Governor Davis's widow, who had created the extensive formal gardens, established the Westmoreland Davis Foundation, and Morven Park was opened to the public as a museum, cultural center, and equestrian institute. 53–87 (11/19/74).

OAK HILL, *Aldie vicinity.* James Monroe began construction of his home on his Loudoun County estate between 1820 and 1823 and lived there after his retirement from the presidency in 1825 until 1830, the year before he died. Oak Hill was the scene of the reunion of Monroe and Lafayette in 1825 during the latter's triumphal tour of America. The source of the design of the distinctive Classical Revival mansion has been the subject of much speculation. Strong cases have been made for both Thomas Jefferson and James Hoban influencing its appearance. Both men were well known to Monroe and could easily have provided him with ideas. The house was constructed by the local builder William Benton. The dominant feature of the composition is the unusual pentastyle portico overlooking the extensive formal gardens. The estate passed out of the family after Monroe's death. From 1850 to 1920 it was the home of the Fairfax family. The house was increased in size in 1922 by the enlargement of its wings and the addition of their terminal porticoes during the ownership of Frank C. Littleton. Still maintained as a private residence, this historic seat is a fitting monument to the last of the "Virginia Dynasty" of presidents. 53–90 (9/9/69); *National Historic Landmark.*

OATLANDS, *Leesburg vicinity.* Begun in 1804 and embellished over the next two decades, this monumental mansion, along with its numerous outbuildings and extensive formal gardens, forms one of the nation's most elaborate Federal estates. The complex was developed by the son of Robert Carter of Nomini, George Carter, one of the scions of the great Tidewater families who migrated after the Revolution to the state's northern and western counties. Carter derived his ideas for its design from illustrations in William Chambers's *A Treatise on Civil Architecture* (1786). With its stuccoed walls, demioctagonal wings, parapeted roof, and a portico of slender Corinthian columns added by Carter in 1827, the house has a lightness and elegance matched by few other dwellings of the period. The airy rooms with their intricate Federal ornamentation complement the exterior. Oatlands remained in the Carter family until 1897. In 1903 the property was acquired by William Corcoran Eustis, grandson of banker and philanthropist William Wilson Corcoran. The house and part of the farm were donated to the National Trust for Historic Preservation in 1965. 53–93 (9/9/69); *National Historic Landmark.*

OATLANDS HISTORIC DISTRICT, *extending along U.S. Route 15 between Oatlands and Mountain Gap.* The Oatlands Historic District incorporates the Oatlands estate and several associated structures in the immediate vicinity. At the southern end, along Goose Creek, is the archaeological site of Oatlands Mills, an area milling complex established by George Carter of Oatlands in the early 19th century. The large mill stood until 1905 when it was destroyed, leaving today only a small section of ruin and extensive archaeological remains. Surviving from the village of Oatlands nearby are several houses and the Episcopal Church of Our Savior, a simple brick structure erected in 1878. A later parish hall stands next to it. At the northern end of the district is the Mountain Gap School, a red-painted, one-room rural schoolhouse. Dating from the last quarter of the 19th century, the school was the last operating one-room school in the county when it closed in 1953. It is now maintained as a museum. Most of the property in the historic district is protected by preservation easements or is owned by the National Trust for Historic Preservation, all being part of an effort by the National Trust to maintain the rural setting of the plantation. 53–446 (2/19/74).

ROKEBY, *Leesburg vicinity.* Built in the 1760s for Charles Binns, Sr., first clerk of the circuit court of Loudoun County, Rokeby is reputedly the place where the Declaration of Independence and other important documents were stored in 1814 during the British occupation of Washington. At that time the property was owned by Binns's son Charles, who did not live there. A large vaulted room remains in the cellar of the house where the papers are believed to have been kept. Rokeby is the largest and most formal colonial house in the region. Much of its original Georgian character was changed in 1836 when, in the course of an extensive renovation by its owner, Benjamin Shreve, Jr., the clipped gables were removed, the windows were remodeled, and the interior trim was replaced. The house was enlarged in 1886 with an extensive rear addition and was returned somewhat to its early appearance during a 1958 restoration. 53–97 (5/20/75).

TAYLORSTOWN HISTORIC DISTRICT, *around the junction of routes 633 and 688 at Catoctin Creek.* A steady supply of waterpower and the surrounding fertile farms of the Quaker settlers made Taylorstown an ideal site for milling operations. The first mill was established here in the 1730s by Richard Brown, whose stone house, Hunting Hill, survives in the middle of the tiny hamlet. The present stone mill (shown) was erected by Thomas Taylor soon after he acquired the Brown property in 1784. Also included in the district is an 18th-century stone cottage known as Foxton, an example of Loudoun County's early vernacular; an early 19th-century store building; a rusticated concrete store of 1904; and two late Victorian dwellings. Free from modern intrusions save for a new concrete bridge across Catoctin Creek, Taylorstown has been reduced to a sleepy crossroads since milling operations ceased in 1958. The mill, one of the few remaining in a county once noted for its many mills, has been converted to a private residence. 53–603 (12/21/76).

WATERFORD HISTORIC DISTRICT, *incorporating the entire village and several hundred acres of surrounding open space.* Nestled in the countryside of Loudoun County's northern tip, the village of Waterford was a 19th-century Quaker milling community. The settlement traces its origins to ca. 1733 when Amos Janney and other Quakers arrived from Pennsylvania and established a mill complex within what became the town limits. By the 1830s the town was a flourishing community of some seventy houses and a tannery, gristmill, chairmaker, and boot manufacturer, along with the usual shops and a tavern. The industrial and mercantile establishments declined by the early 20th century, leaving Waterford an excellently preserved hamlet free of modern intrusions. Its shady streets remain lined with pleasant examples of the region's vernacular styles built in brick, stone, log, and wood. Some of the houses are freestanding; others are town houses closely spaced on narrow lots. A mid-19th-century mill remains at the north edge of town. Through a variety of preservation efforts carried out over the past two decades, the maintenance of the historic character of the village and its setting is being secured. 401–123 (5/13/69); *National Historic Landmark; preservation easements held by the Virginia Historic Landmarks Board, the Virginia Outdoors Foundation, and the National Trust for Historic Preservation.*

WAVERLY, *212 South King Street, Leesburg.* Built ca. 1890 as the retirement home of Robert T. Hempstone, a Baltimore businessman, Waverly is a symbol of personal prosperity rarely expressed with such ostentation in the Victorian architecture of Northern Virginia. At a time when the economy of Loudoun County still suffered from the devastating effects of the Civil War, large dwellings such as Waverly were built only by individuals who had acquired their wealth elsewhere. A finely appointed example of a late Victorian residence displaying features of both the Colonial Revival and Queen Anne styles, the house was built by the Leesburg firm of John Norris and Sons. The house has recently been restored and is the centerpiece of a town-house development. 253–48 (5/18/82).

WELBOURNE, *Upperville vicinity.* Set in the heart of Loudoun County's hunt country, Welbourne is an old homestead enlarged over a century and a half to meet the tastes and needs of five generations of the same family. John Peyton Dulaney purchased the nucleus of the present house, an 18th-century stone farm dwelling, in 1819 and enlarged it into a five-bay Federal-style structure. The house was further enlarged in the 1830s with the addition of one-story wings with demioctagonal ends. Further embellishment came in the 1850s with the erection of the Italianate porticoes on the facade and rear ell. A two-story south wing rounded out the house in the 1870s. Each part of the house retains its own distinctive character. Located on the parklike grounds is an early formal garden and an extensive collection of old outbuildings. Filled with an accumulation of family possessions, Welbourne offers a continuity with the past which is rarely so keenly felt in a historic house. 53–120 (7/6/71).

WOODBURN, *Leesburg vicinity.* This Loudoun County estate contains a large Federal farmhouse and collection of outbuildings and farm structures illustrating the century-long evolution of a Northern Virginia farm from the earliest period of settlement. The property was patented in the middle of the 18th century by George Nixon, who put up the oldest buildings, including the 1777 log patent house, a stone-and-frame gristmill, and the miller's house. Nixon's son or grandson, also named George Nixon, undertook major improvements in the second quarter of the 19th century when he built the brick house, known locally as "Nixon's Folly," the springhouse, and the large brick bank barn. This elaborate barn has an arcaded ground level, fine brickwork, and brick lattice vents. 53–105 (9/21/76).

LOUISA COUNTY

Located in the heart of the Virginia Piedmont, this rural
county was named in honor of Princess Louisa, a daughter of
King George II. It was formed from Hanover County in 1742.
Its county seat is Louisa.

ANDERSON-FOSTER HOUSE, *Holly Grove vicinity.* This simple side-hall-plan rural cottage documents the continuity of Virginia's vernacular style over more than a century. Appearing little different from a house dating at least seventy-five years earlier, the Anderson-Foster house was actually built in 1856, long after more stylish locales and clients had abandoned the regional idiom. The first owner of the dwelling was Dr. James B. Anderson, a country physician who bowed somewhat to contemporary taste by installing interior trim with a more Greek Revival aspect. The house has been restored recently after standing empty for a number of years. 54–181 (7/18/78).

BOSWELL'S TAVERN, *Boswell's Tavern.* A landmark for travelers since its construction in the mid-18th century, this wood-frame structure on the edge of the Green Springs Historic District is one of the state's best-preserved rural taverns. Its original proprietor is not documented; however, it probably was John Boswell, who operated the establishment throughout the most significant part of its history. The tavern was used on one occasion during the Revolution as headquarters of the marquis de Lafayette. The marquis de Chastellux made reference to the hospitality of Mr. and Mrs. Boswell in his *Travels in North America in the Years 1780, 1781, and 1782.* The tavern is divided into two sections: a public area containing two large public rooms, a warming room, stair hall, and bar area and the innkeeper's wing containing one large room with a corner stair leading to sleeping quarters. 54–7 (11/5/68).

GRASSDALE, *Boswell's Tavern vicinity*. This brick dwelling, embellished with a festive bracketed cornice and veranda, is one of Virginia's very few fully developed Italianate country houses built before the Civil War. Such houses are relatively common in northern states, but the economic and political uncertainty in Virginia inhibited the construction of plantation houses in the period's prevailing taste. Grassdale was completed in 1861 for James Maury Morris, Jr., and is an important architectural component of the Green Springs Historic District. The house is situated to take advantage of a view across broad, gently sloping pastures. Immediately around the house is a park of large old oak trees. 54–32 (2/20/73).

GREEN SPRINGS, *Poindexter vicinity*. Overlooking the verdant farmland of the Green Springs area, near the springs whence its name is derived, the Green Springs house is the area's best example of the formal vernacular of the late 18th century. The tall, two-story frame house, accented by its slender exterior end chimneys, shows the influence of Virginia's academic Georgian style. Its double-pile floor plan is interesting for combining a hall-parlor with a center-passage scheme. The two front entrances reflect the former plan type, and the stair chamber between the two rear rooms reflects the latter plan type. The surviving outbuildings add to the picture of a rural domestic group of the period. The house was built for Col. Richard O. Morris, whose family settled and developed this section of Louisa County. 54–57 (5/16/72).

GREEN SPRINGS HISTORIC DISTRICT, *centered along U.S. Route 15 between Boswell's Tavern and Zion Crossroads*. From the earliest days of the settlement of Piedmont Virginia, the Green Springs area of Louisa County has been known as a region of exceptional fertility, prosperity, and beauty. Its farms, buildings, and families represent many generations of agricultural, architectural, and social history. Contrasted with Louisa's surrounding hilly land with its thin soil grown up in scrub pine and oak, this 11,000-acre bowl, a geological formation that defines Green Springs, is composed of lush, rolling pastures and high-yield fields. First settled in the 1720s by families from Tidewater Virginia, the area takes its name from a mineral spring located near its center which served as a local spa during the late 18th century. Two families in particular built a number of plantation houses here. Members of the Morris family built or extended Green Springs (late 18th century), Sylvania (1738–50 with later alterations), Hawkwood (1851–54), and Grassdale (1861). The Watson places include Ionia (1770s), Bracketts (1800 and 1860), and Westend (1849). These and numerous other buildings, including the colonial Boswell's Tavern and the Carpenters' Gothic St. John's Chapel, form an assemblage of rural architecture of extraordinary variety and outstanding quality in a countryside gently civilized over a period of two and a half centuries. 54–111 (2/20/73); *National Historic Landmark*.

HAWKWOOD, *Zion Crossroads vicinity.* Until it was gutted by fire in 1982, Hawkwood was the best remaining example of the Italian Villa–style houses designed by New York architect Alexander Jackson Davis. Begun in 1851 and completed by 1855, the house was built for Richard O. Morris, a local planter interested in the promotion of scientific agricultural methods to restore Virginia's depressed economy. While much of Davis's architecture was inspired by Greek and Gothic forms, he was a leader in the popularization of the Italian Villa style fostered in America by his collaborator Andrew Jackson Downing. Downing wrote that with its shading eaves, verandas, and picturesque massing, the villa style was most appropriate for country houses in the South. A hallmark of the style, demonstrated in Hawkwood, is the square tower. Hawkwood's walls and tower were spared in the fire and have since been stabilized. Complete restoration of the house is contemplated. 54–36 (9/1/70).

IONIA, *Poindexter vicinity.* Ionia's dwelling house, with its symmetrical facade, hall-parlor plan, shed-roof porch, weatherboarded walls, and narrow dormers, illustrates the rational simplicity of the colonial Virginia farmhouse. Despite its small size and simple materials, the house has the architectural dignity inherent in many of the vernacular buildings of the period. Built in the early 1770s for Maj. James Watson, it is one of the oldest homes in the Green Springs area of Louisa County. Added onto at least four times by different generations of the family, the house retains its self-effacing aspect. Several early domestic outbuildings, including a large early barn, add to the rural flavor of the place. 54–43 (5/16/72).

PROVIDENCE PRESBYTERIAN CHURCH, *Gum Spring vicinity.* Providence Church is one of Virginia's few remaining wood-frame colonial churches and is among the first churches to be built in the central part of the state by the Presbyterian denomination. The congregation was organized ca. 1747 under the aegis of Samuel Morris, an early dissenter; the church was put up that same year. The first minister was the Reverend Samuel Davies, the pulpit orator and founder of the Hanover Presbytery. Davies remained at Providence until 1759 when he left to assume the presidency of the College of New Jersey (later Princeton University). The severely plain weatherboarded building, in a clearing at the end of a wooded lane, has a typical early meetinghouse arrangement with side and end entrances and an original gallery extending around three sides of the interior. The English evangelist George Whitefield preached here ca. 1755. 54–61 (1/16/73).

WESTEND, *Boswell's Tavern vicinity.* Thomas Jefferson's vision of a prosperous agrarian republic with landowners occupying modest but sophisticated classical villas is given tangible expression at Westend, one of the principal homesteads of the Green Springs Historic District. Employing the Palladian format of a two-story, temple-form center section flanked by one-story wings, a design greatly admired by Jefferson, the house was completed in 1849 for Mrs. James Morris on land inherited from her husband. The contractor for the house was James Magruder. The Roman details of its woodwork were rendered accurately by Malcolm F. Crawford, a master carpenter trained in the classical idiom while employed in the construction of the University of Virginia. The dominant element of the composition is the pedimented Tuscan portico. Both of the flanking wings were originally used as orangeries. The house and its formally positioned outbuildings are the nucleus of a nearly 600-acre farm in the center of this rural historic district. 54–73 (9/1/70); *Virginia Historic Landmarks Board preservation easement.*

LUNENBURG COUNTY

*Named for Lüneburg, one of the German possessions of Great
Britain's Hanoverian kings, this Southside county was formed
from Brunswick County in 1746. Its county seat
is Lunenburg Court House.*

FLAT ROCK, *Kenbridge vicinity.* Flat Rock's interestingly evolved plantation house is significant to the study of Southside Virginia's vernacular building tradition. The oldest part of the dwelling, one of the earliest houses in the county, was erected in the late 18th century for James Hooper in a two-story, side-hall format. It was later purchased by the Chambers family, who added an east room just before 1820. Around 1856 a second story was put on the east room and one-story wings were added, making a relatively large, formal house out of what was originally a very unpretentious one. A stylish note of this later enlargement is the unusual hexagonal chimney stacks added to the older chimneys. The interior woodwork is almost completely intact and reflects the changes made to the house. On the grounds are an early smokehouse, unusual for employing plank construction, and a large, granite-lined ice pit. 55–3 (12/19/78).

LUNENBURG COURT HOUSE HISTORIC DISTRICT, *at the junction of state routes 40 and 49 and county road 675.* This rural Southside county seat is dominated by its dignified Roman Revival courthouse, one of the unique group of Virginia public buildings reflecting the influence of Thomas Jefferson's strictly interpreted classicism. The commission appointed to supervise its construction directed that the building should be modeled after the newly completed courthouse in Charlotte County, designed by Jefferson himself. Master builders William A. Howard and Dabney Cosby, Sr., admirably carried out their charge, completing Lunenburg's finely detailed temple-form building in 1827. The exterior stairs were added later in the century when the courtroom was divided into two levels. On an elevated site surrounded by fields, the tiny settlement presents a picturesque scene, especially from the south where the courthouse and its gleaming white portico stand above the village's sprinkling of 19th-century structures. 55–105 (3/2/71).

CITY OF LYNCHBURG

*Named for John Lynch, owner of the town site, this industrial
and business center, located along the James River between
Bedford and Campbell counties, was established in 1786
and was incorporated as a town in 1805.
It became a city in 1852.*

ACADEMY OF MUSIC, *522–526 Main Street.* Lynchburg's elegant Academy of Music is a turn-of-the-century vaudeville theater and opera house, one of the few surviving in Virginia. Completed in 1905, it was designed by the local architectural firm of Frye and Chesterman, which embellished Lynchburg with many of the city's best buildings. The theater was gutted by fire in 1911 but was rebuilt within its walls, presumably by the same architects. The present facade is a very sophisticated essay in the neoclassical style recalling 18th-century English Palladianism. The rich interior has strikingly handsome plaster decoration and a richly painted ceiling of clouds, muses, and cherubs. Performers at the Academy in its heyday included Sarah Bernhardt, Pavlova, Otis Skinner, and Paderewski. Following many years of neglect, the building is currently undergoing long-term restoration. 118–1 (11/5/68).

THE AVIARY, *Miller Park, 402 Grove Street*. An adaptation of the Queen Anne style, this pagodalike building is the state's earliest known municipal aviary. Designed by the local firm of Frye and Chesterman and opened in Miller Park in 1902, the building was the gift of Randolph Guggenheimer, a Lynchburg native who became a New York businessman. The aviary is an expression of the nationwide interest in the development of zoological parks and gardens in metropolitan areas that prevailed in the late 19th and early 20th centuries. It originally housed cages containing monkeys, alligators, cockatoos, doves, parrots, and canaries. The interior was remodeled in 1931 when the building was converted to a library. Since 1975 the building has been leased by the city to the Lynchburg Council of Garden Clubs for use as a garden center. 118–155 (4/15/80).

COURT STREET BAPTIST CHURCH, *Court and Sixth streets*. Court Street Baptist Church is Lynchburg's chief architectural landmark associated with its black population. Begun in 1879 and completed in 1880, it was then the largest church edifice in the city, with its slender spire the tallest object on the downtown skyline. The building was designed by a local white architect, Robert C. Burkholder, but black labor was used exclusively in its construction, and black artisans in large part were responsible for the decorations and furnishings of the auditorium. The tall brick structure survives without significant alteration, even preserving its original pipe organ, and remains one of downtown Lynchburg's most conspicious historic buildings. 118–156 (6/16/81).

DANIEL'S HILL HISTORIC DISTRICT, *Cabell, Norwood, Hancock, and Stonewall streets from A through H streets*. This downtown residential neighborhood, on the prow of a steep hill adjacent to Lynchburg's central business district and overlooking the James River, has a rich variety of architectural styles and house types dating from the early 19th century through the early 20th century. Concentrated building activity began in the 1840s after the subdivision of the plantation established in the early 19th century by Dr. George Cabell, whose mansion, Point of Honor, forms the focal point of the district. The district's only thoroughfare, Cabell Street, is lined with a progression of mid- and late 19th-century mansions, all excellent examples of their respective styles. One of the most interesting is the Y-shaped dwelling at Cabell and B streets, built in 1875 as his own home by local architect Robert C. Burkholder. More typical is the Greek Revival Dabney-Scott-Adams house at 405 Cabell Street (shown), erected in 1852–53 for Albert G. Dabney, proprietor of the Phoenix Foundry, and later remodeled with Georgian Revival accents. Contrasting with these architecturally sophisticated buildings are the vernacular workers' houses scattered along the streets adjacent to Cabell Street. Although many of the houses, especially the larger ones, stand neglected, the neighborhood is protected by historic zoning and is experiencing steady rehabilitation. 118–198 (12/14/82).

DIAMOND HILL HISTORIC DISTRICT, *roughly bounded by Dunbar Drive and Main, Jackson, and Arch streets*. Diamond Hill, once one of Lynchburg's most fashionable residential neighborhoods, was first built on in the 1820s, but it enjoyed its greatest prosperity at the turn of the present century. This period was marked by the construction of numerous residences, ranging from speculative rental units to stately architect-designed houses usually in either the Georgian or the Colonial Revival style. The family homes of businessmen and civic and political leaders were clustered in this area along Washington, Clay, Pearl, and Madison streets. Representatives of the fine quality of the architecture found on Washington Street are the Beaux Arts Ernest Williams house (1911) and the ca. 1901 Queen Anne–style house next door (both shown). Other houses of note include the Queen Anne–style John Kinnier house (1897) and the Richard A. Carrington house (1909), one of the neighborhood's best Georgian Revival examples. The neighborhood has been the focus of considerable rehabilitation activity after several decades of decline. 118–60 (5/15/79).

FEDERAL HILL HISTORIC DISTRICT, *roughly bounded by Eighth, Twelfth, Harrison and Polk streets*. One of the earliest and most distinctive of several neighborhoods situated on the hills surrounding the commercial area of Lynchburg, Federal Hill has served primarily as the residential area for merchants and civic leaders. Contained within the district's dozen blocks is an assemblage of freestanding dwellings in the architectural styles popular from the early 19th century through the early 20th century. Most significant are the neighborhood's early Federal houses, which include some of the oldest and finest dwellings in the city, among which are the ca. 1816 Roane-Rodes house and the 1817 Norvell-Otey house (shown), built at 1020 Federal Street for banker William Norvell. The area was incorporated into the city through annexations in 1814 and 1819. 118–56 (5/20/80).

FIRST BAPTIST CHURCH, *Court and Eleventh streets*. This lively composition with its many gables highlighted by a needle spire stands with Virginia's best representatives of the High Victorian Gothic, a richly ornamented interpretation of the Gothic style inspired by the writings of John Ruskin. The spire, seen from many points in the city, serves as a landmark for downtown Lynchburg. The church's architect was John R. Thomas, who first practiced in Rochester and later in New York City. Thomas's other well-known Virginia work is Brooks Hall at the University of Virginia. Construction of the church began in 1884, and although several additions have since been made, the building appears essentially as it was completed in 1886. One of the highlights of the building is its richly colored Victorian stained glass displayed in large rose windows. The church houses an old and influential congregation and was the product of an era of growth and prosperity in Lynchburg. 118–25 (4/21/81).

GARLAND HILL HISTORIC DISTRICT, *roughly bounded by Fifth and Federal streets and the Norfolk and Western Railway tracks.* Named for Samuel Garland, Sr., a Lynchburg lawyer who was among the first residents of the hill, Garland Hill is perhaps the best preserved of the prosperous neighborhoods that sprang up on Lynchburg's various hills during the 19th century. The hill was subdivided into approximately ten blocks in 1845 and developed slowly, so that it now has a rich mixture of fine freestanding houses representing most of the styles that were in vogue from the 1840s to World War I. The grandest of the houses line Madison Street and date ca. 1900. At the western end of the street are two large Queen Anne residences: the 1897 Frank P. Christian house and the 1898 George P. Watkins house (both shown), both designed by the able local architect Edward G. Frye. The most singular structure in the district is the huge Ambrose H. Burroughs house, a castlelike dwelling designed by J. M. B. Lewis and completed in 1900. Because none of the streets are through ones, an air of quiet dignity still pervades the district. 118–26 (8/15/72).

CARTER GLASS HOUSE, *605 Clay Street.* This elegantly crafted Federal house was the home of the statesman Carter Glass from 1907 to 1923, the period in which he exerted great influence on national political and economic life. In addition to serving as Woodrow Wilson's secretary of the treasury, Glass was for many years a U.S. senator and is best remembered for drafting the legislation establishing the Federal Reserve System. Glass's home, one of Lynchburg's larger dwellings of the early 19th century, was built in 1827 for John Wills, who may have been its architect. The house survives in its original condition except for the present roof, cornice, and dormers, all added by Glass. It now houses parish offices for St. Paul's Episcopal Church next door. 118–6 (2/15/77); *National Historic Landmark.*

HAYES HALL, *DeWitt Street and Garfield Avenue.* The black school now known as Virginia College and Virginia Seminary was authorized in 1886 at the 19th session of the Virginia Baptist State Convention held in the First Baptist Church in Lexington. The oldest institution of higher learning in the Lynchburg area, the school espoused the self-help educational principles for blacks advocated by Booker T. Washington. In its early years the school was a pioneer in the field of black education, placing its primary emphasis on the training of teachers and ministers for work within the black community. This large mansard-roof structure erected in 1888 to hold classrooms and student housing was the school's first brick building. It was later named in honor of Gregory Willis Hayes, the institution's second president. The building is now vacant and awaiting restoration. 118–59 (2/26/79).

JONES MEMORIAL LIBRARY, *434 Rivermont Avenue*. The Jones Memorial Library is Lynchburg's finest example of the Neoclassical Revival style that dominated the architecture of American public and institutional buildings during the first decades of the 20th century. Designed by the local firm of Frye and Chesterman, the library was given by Mary Frances Watt Jones as a memorial to her husband, George Morgan Jones, a Lynchburg industrialist, merchant, and financier. Opened in 1908, the Jones Memorial Library is an expression of the philanthropy and cultural development that followed Lynchburg's growth at the end of the 19th century. The series of steps and terraces was designed by Boston landscape architect Bremer Pond and was added in 1924. 118–53 (7/31/80).

MILLER-CLAYTOR HOUSE, *Riverside Park at Miller-Claytor Lane*. The Miller-Claytor house, erected in 1791 for John Miller, a local tavern keeper, is Lynchburg's only remaining 18th-century town house. It originally stood at the corner of Eighth and Church streets downtown but was moved to its present location at the entrance to Riverside Park in 1936 to protect it from demolition. The two-story frame structure is an intriguing example of urban vernacular architecture. The numerous exterior doors of its two-room plan suggest that part of the house may have been intended for commercial use. The house's orientation and garden size at the present location were carefully selected to approximate its original siting. 118–12 (10/21/75).

JOSEPH NICHOLS'S TAVERN (WESTERN HOTEL), *Fifth and Madison streets*. Joseph Nichols built this Federal tavern on Lynchburg's busy Fifth Street in 1815 to replace his previous establishment, which had been destroyed by fire. The simple but dignified structure has long been a familiar landmark on what was for many years the western entrance to the city. This location was the inspiration for a later designation, the Western Hotel, by which the building was known for over a century. The tavern, one of Lynchburg's earliest surviving commercial structures, stood derelict for many years but was rehabilitated sensitively in 1975 by the Restoration and Housing Corporation, a local nonprofit organization. 118–20 (6/18/74).

OLD CITY CEMETERY, *Fourth and Monroe streets*. This public burying ground in the heart of the city was opened in 1806 on land donated by John Lynch, founder of Lynchburg. First known as the Methodist Cemetery, it is perhaps best remembered for its Civil War associations. During the battle of Lynchburg its 1827 brick wall was breached and trenches were dug in an effort to incorporate the cemetery into the city's inner defenses. Cadets from the Virginia Military Institute used the cemetery as a campground. After the war the cemetery became the final resting place of over 2,000 Confederate and 187 Union soldiers. Located among their grave markers is an 1868 obelisk to the Confederate dead and a domed speaker's stand. The arched entryway, erected in 1926, leads to the Confederate section. 118–27 (9/19/72).

OLD LYNCHBURG COURTHOUSE, *Ninth and Court Streets*. Described as "Lynchburg's Parthenon," this temple-form Doric building has been a dominant element of the city's skyline since its completion in 1855. One of the state's most successful Greek Revival public buildings, the courthouse was designed by William S. Ellison, who came to Lynchburg as a division engineer with the Virginia and Tennessee Railroad. It originally housed the hustings and the district courts. Although many of its details are derived from architectural pattern books of the period, Ellison's design, employing engaged side porticoes and a dome topped by a belfry, is a strikingly original composition. The courthouse is located at the top of the hill overlooking the central business district. Its setting has been dramatized by the construction in 1925 of Monument Terrace, a great flight of terraced stone steps leading up to the building, to serve as the city's war memorial. The courthouse was restored in the 1970s and now houses Lynchburg's local history museum. 118–2 (4/18/72).

POINT OF HONOR, *112 Cabell Street*. On the prow of Daniel's Hill overlooking the James River and downtown, Point of Honor is an outstanding example of Virginia's Federal style. Originally the focal point of a 900-acre plantation, the house was built ca. 1815 for Dr. George Cabell. Distinguished by its polygonal projections and beautifully executed interior woodwork, the house is one of several fine houses in the Piedmont erected for the Cabell family. Its designer is not known, but many of its details are adapted from illustrations in Owen Biddle's *The Young Carpenter's Assistant* (1810). Point of Honor was remodeled in the Italianate style in the mid-19th century but most of its original embellishments, save for the front porch, survived under the later modifications. It was acquired by the city in 1928 and received hard use as a neighborhood center until 1968 when the Historic Lynchburg Foundation undertook the restoration of the house to its original appearance for use as a museum of early Lynchburg life and craftsmanship. 118–14 (12/2/69).

QUAKER MEETING HOUSE, *5810 Fort Avenue*. Quakers settled in the area of present-day Lynchburg in the mid-18th century and built their first meetinghouse in 1757. The present meetinghouse, completed in 1798, is the third on the site. Originally known as the South River Friends' Meeting House, it lost most of its congregation to migration in the 1830s. The building stood as an abandoned ruin from the 1850s until 1904 when its stone walls were restored and it was reroofed for use by the Presbyterians. Buried in the adjacent Quaker cemetery are John Lynch, Lynchburg's founder, and his mother, Sarah Clark Lynch, one of the original Quaker settlers. The building is currently maintained by the Quaker Memorial Presbyterian Church. 118–15 (5/20/75).

RANDOLPH-MACON WOMAN'S COLLEGE MAIN HALL, *2500 Rivermont Avenue*. Randolph-Macon Woman's College was founded in 1890 under the original Randolph-Macon College charter of 1830 and was the first college for women admitted to membership in the Southern Association of Colleges and Secondary Schools. Main Hall, erected in stages over a nine-year period beginning in 1891, remains the principal architectural landmark of the school. The huge structure appears as a large range of connecting buildings stretched along a ridge at the head of a tree-dotted campus. It was designed by Washington architect William M. Poindexter and is the state's most ambitious and probably most successful example of the Queen Anne style of the late 19th century. Poindexter's use of red brick, white trim, towers, turrets, classical detailing, and a multiplicity of window types closely relates the building to contemporary Queen Anne–style academic buildings of Great Britain. 118–149 (2/26/79).

ROSEDALE, *Old Graves Mill Road*. Rosedale encompasses several related structures of significance in the development of the Bedford/Campbell County section of Piedmont Virginia. The oldest structure, the Christopher Johnson cottage, was built ca. 1767 and is one of the area's few remaining houses associated with the Quaker migration from eastern Virginia to what was then the colony's frontier. The adjacent mansion, built ca. 1836 for Gen. Odin Clay, the first president of the Virginia and Tennessee Railroad, is one of the earliest houses in the area to display Greek Revival details obviously copied from mid-19th-century architectural pattern books. It was enlarged with a rear wing in 1902 and a side wing in the 1920s. With the nearby remains of an 18th-century mill, numerous subsidiary farm buildings, and its hilly, forested terrain, the Rosedale property is a rural ensemble on the fringe of the city's urban development. 118–201 (10/19/82).

ST. PAUL'S EPISCOPAL CHURCH, *Seventh and Clay streets*. This robust architectural composition is Virginia's finest ecclesiastical example of the Romanesque Revival, an individualized interpretation of the medieval style fostered by Boston architect H. H. Richardson. Typical of the style, St. Paul's features a solid outline and richly patterned and textured stonework. The church, built in 1889–95, was designed by Frank Miles Day of Philadelphia, who is best remembered for his partnership with Charles Z. Klauder and their neo-Gothic collegiate buildings at Princeton and other universities. The belfry was added in 1912 and departs slightly from Day's design. St. Paul's is the third church of Lynchburg's oldest Episcopal congregation. It is one of several architecturally imposing churches in the neighborhood, each having a distinctive tower forming an important element in the Lynchburg skyline. 118–196 (4/21/81).

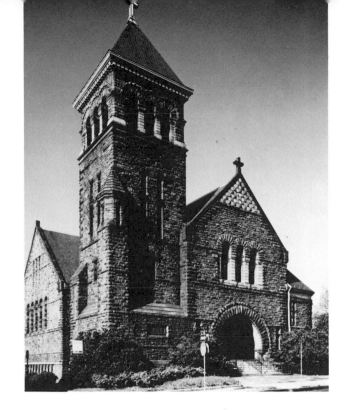

SANDUSKY, *Sandusky Drive*. This brick farmhouse, formerly on the outskirts of the city but now within a suburban neighborhood, was built ca. 1808 for Charles Johnston, who named it after the Ohio Indian camp where he was once held prisoner. The two-story structure, with its Doric cornice and arched recesses on the interior, was one of the first houses in the Lynchburg area to display the details and refinement of Federal-era architecture. The front porch is a later addition but may be similar in form to an original one. In 1864 during the battle of Lynchburg, Sandusky served as headquarters of Union general David Hunter. Two of Hunter's staff at Sandusky were the future presidents Rutherford B. Hayes and William McKinley. Hunter had been a West Point classmate of Confederate major George C. Hutter, who owned Sandusky at the time of the Civil War occupation. 118–17 (2/16/82).

ANNE SPENCER HOUSE, *1313 Pierce Street*. During her long and active life, Anne Spencer (1881–1975) was recognized by her friends and associates as a lyric poet of considerable talent. For a black woman, to win recognition from her intellectual peers was a remarkable feat. Through quiet determination and dedication to her craft and causes, she gained respect not only as a gifted writer but as a cultural leader and humanitarian. Among the many visitors to her Lynchburg home were W. E. B. Du Bois, Martin Luther King, Jr., Thurgood Marshall, and Adam Clayton Powell, Jr. Mrs. Spencer's commodious, comfortable, but unpretentious modified Queen Anne–style house of 1903 remains unchanged since her death. Also preserved as she knew it is Edankraal, a small, one-room cottage in her garden where she wrote and thought. Her desk is shown. The property is now owned and exhibited by the Friends of Anne Spencer Memorial Foundation, Inc. 118–61 (9/21/76).

J. W. WOOD BUILDING, *23–27 Ninth Street*. Dating from ca. 1853, the J. W. Wood Building is the largest and best preserved of the few pre–Civil War commercial structures remaining in Lynchburg. Its cast-iron shopfront is the sole survivor of its type in the city. Located in a now-underused section of downtown, the Italianate structure is one of the few visual reminders of the city's tremendous commercial activity of the 1850s, the decade in which Lynchburg was declared by the U.S. Census to be the second richest city in the country on a per capita basis. 118–132 (5/18/82).

MADISON COUNTY

In the hills of the Piedmont, against the Blue Ridge Mountains, Madison County was formed from Culpeper County in 1792 and was named for James Madison, who then represented the area in Congress. The county seat is Madison.

BIG MEADOWS ARCHAEOLOGICAL SITE, *Big Meadows, Shenandoah National Park.* The Big Meadows site, one of the most carefully explored sites in the Shenandoah National Park and the entire Blue Ridge province, has revealed a formerly unknown florescence of Indian habitation in the Big Meadows area between ca. 2500 B.C. and A.D. 800. Yielding the park's oldest example of prehistoric art and the oldest evidence of a possible dwelling in the Blue Ridge, the site also has produced large quantities of locally and regionally imported raw materials, indicating the extent to which its prehistoric occupants exploited a large and varied territory on a seasonal basis through local exchange networks. The population peak of the site was reached in Late Archaic–Early Woodland times and contrasts with subsequent sparse use of the mountains by Late Woodland peoples (ca. A.D. 800–1600). 56–56 (9/16/82).

CLIFF KILL ARCHAEOLOGICAL SITE, *Big Meadows vicinity, Shenandoah National Park.* This site in the Shenandoah National Park on the crest of the Blue Ridge is the only known example of a cliff kill site in Virginia. Despite the absence of faunal remains due to unfavorable soil conditions, analysis of the lithic assemblage supports the interpretation of the site as a kill site of mainly Middle to Late Archaic date (ca. 4000–1500 B.C.) with a Late Woodland component. The prehistoric tribes killed game by driving it over the edge of the cliff, a sheer drop on the eastern edge of Big Meadows. The probable interrelationship between the Cliff Kill site and identified sites on top of Big Meadows renders it essential to an understanding of the full range of activities of the Archaic peoples in the Blue Ridge Mountain region. 56–59 (9/16/82).

GENTLE ARCHAEOLOGICAL SITE, *Fishers Gap vicinity, Shenandoah National Park.* One of the largest Woodland period archaeological sites in the Shenandoah National Park, the Gentle site near the crest of the Blue Ridge, poses several tantalizing questions concerning its relationship to well-known Late Woodland sites in the Piedmont and its place in the life of the Late Woodland peoples of the Blue Ridge Mountains. Sites such as this one may well have been connected with large-scale fire hunts, trading, and raiding expeditions regularly conducted by the Piedmont horticultural village peoples along this cultural frontier. By raising the question of the identity of the Blue Ridge as a frontier zone in Late Woodland times, the site might also provide evidence of a link with early European settlement of the mountains by various ethnic groups. 56–58 (9/16/82).

HEBRON LUTHERAN CHURCH, *Madison vicinity.* Dating from 1740, this simple cruciform church in the countryside of Madison County is the oldest house of worship in continuous use by Lutherans in America. The congregation was formed in 1725 by sixty German families, some of whom came to Virginia in 1715 to work at Governor Spotswood's frontier mining community at Germanna. The building was enlarged ca. 1800, at which time Hebron's pipe organ crafted by David Tannenburg of Lititz, Pa., was installed. The interior has been remodeled several times. An interesting Victorian adornment is the elaborate frescoed ceilings painted by the Italian-born artist Joseph Oddenino. 56–6 (3/2/71).

MADISON COUNTY COURTHOUSE, *Madison.* Master builders William B. Phillips and Malcolm F. Crawford embellished central Virginia with a series of dignified courthouses in Thomas Jefferson's Roman Revival idiom, which they learned while working at the University of Virginia. The Madison courthouse, completed in 1830, survives as perhaps the best-preserved example of the builders' architectural skills. The most prominent Jeffersonian devices employed in the courthouse are the monumental Tuscan entablature and pediment. The arcaded ground floor, a holdover from colonial courthouses, is given a more classical, hence Jeffersonian, quality with the use of keystones and impost courses. The beautiful brickwork, with its even-color Flemish bond and precise jointing, is characteristic of the fine craftsmanship found in Phillips's buildings. Virginia lawyer William Wirt began his legal career in the Madison courthouse. 256–2 (5/13/69).

THE RESIDENCE, *Woodberry Forest School, Madison Mills vicinity.* This one-and-a-half-story, wood-frame house was built ca. 1793 for William Madison, representative of Madison County in the House of Delegates for seven consecutive terms and brother of President James Madison. In 1793 Thomas Jefferson, at the request of James Madison, supplied plans for a house for William Madison. James Madison later wrote to Jefferson saying that his brother had adopted the plans. No Jefferson drawings have been positively identified as being those for Madison's house, but the correspondence authenticates William Madison's home as a work by Jefferson. The house passed from the Madison family in 1870 to Robert Walker, who enlarged and remodeled it in 1884, disguising much of its Jeffersonian character. Walker here founded a male preparatory school named Woodberry Forest School after the Madison plantation. The Madison home was renamed the Residence and served for many years as the headmaster's house. It is now used as the guest house of the school, whose many brick buildings now dominate the property. 56–55 (2/26/79).

ROBERTSON MOUNTAIN ARCHAEOLOGICAL SITE, *Robertson Mountain, Shenandoah National Park.* One of only two sites in the Shenandoah National Park to provide clear evidence of vertical stratification, Robertson Mountain was occupied by Native Americans for the entire span of the Archaic period (8000–1000 B.C.), making it a valuable record of major cultural and environmental changes in the Blue Ridge. Scientific excavation of the elevated site may illuminate the impact of rainfall/snowfall and temperature variation on the timing of seasonal food-gathering activities in the highland zone. In one of the most botanically unaltered sections of the park, the site is a reminder of the habitat in which the first inhabitants of the mountains flourished for thousands of years. 56–57 (9/16/82).

CITY OF MANASSAS

The county seat of Prince William County began in 1852 as the Manassas junction of the Manassas Gap Railroad and the Orange and Alexandria Railroad. It was incorporated as the town of Manassas in 1874 and became a city in 1975.

LIBERIA, *8700 Centerville Road*. This two-story Federal plantation house on the edge of Manassas was used as a headquarters by both Confederate and Union forces in the Civil War. Gen. P. G. T. Beauregard occupied it in 1861 during the first battle of Manassas, and President Jefferson Davis visited it July 21, 1861, to confer with his generals. A year later, Union general Irving McDowell set up headquarters at Liberia, and President Lincoln along with Secretary of War Edwin Stanton held council with McDowell on June 19, 1862. The house was built in 1825 for William Weir, whose wife, Harriet Bladen Carter Weir, inherited the property from her Carter ancestors. During the late 19th century, Liberia was owned by Robert Portner, an inventor and businessman. The house preserves most of its handsome original woodwork; the front portico is a modern addition. Standing in a rapidly urbanizing area, Liberia remains a conspicious reminder of Manassas's role in the Civil War. 155–1 (12/18/79).

MATHEWS COUNTY

*At the eastern tip of Virginia's Middle Peninsula, Mathews
County was named for Thomas Mathews, Speaker of the
Virginia House of Delegates. It was formed from Gloucester
County in 1790. The county seat is Mathews.*

FORT CRICKET HILL, *Cricket Hill.* This simple, worn
earthwork, now overgrown by forest, witnessed the end of
British rule in the Virginia colony. In July 1776 Virginia troops
commanded by Gen. Andrew Lewis took up position here to
keep in check the camp set up by Lord Dunmore, Virginia's
last royal governor, across Milford Haven inlet on Gwynn's
Island. Lewis's batteries opened fire on the British on July 8,
forcing Dunmore to abandon his position and sail with his
fleet for England. 57–14 (12/2/79).

HESSE, *Blakes vicinity.* Named for the German landgraviate,
Hesse was the seat of the Armisteads, a colonial family whose
members, by virtue of marriage, were progenitors or relatives
of nearly every great landed family in Virginia. Archaeological
investigation in recent years has revealed the foundations of
the original colonial house, burned in 1798 and replaced soon
afterwards by the present brick structure, a few feet away. The
siting was likely kept because of the impressive view of God-
frey Bay at the mouth of the Piankatank River. This house,
with its formal, five-bay Georgian facades and paneled woodwork, illustrates the architectural conservatism of Virginia's
eastern counties in the Federal period. The house received its
wings during a restoration in the late 1970s. 57–7 (11/20/73).

MATHEWS COUNTY COURTHOUSE SQUARE, *Mathews*. Mathews County's modest but decorous collection of brick government buildings forms a well-integrated complex begun when the county was formed from Gloucester in 1790. Completed by 1795, the compact, T-shaped courthouse, the county's first and only courthouse, is the best-known work of Richard Billups, a Mathews County master builder in the Federal period. Included on the grassy square are the sheriff's office, built about the same time as the courthouse, and the 1827 clerk's office. The small old jail, now used as a furnace building, was constructed in the mid-19th century. Also on the square are the public library building of the 1930s and a colonial-style county office building of the 1950s. A monument to the county's Confederate dead stands next to the courthouse. The whole grouping remains remarkably functional as it approaches its second century of service. 57–5,11,22,31 (12/21/76).

METHODIST TABERNACLE, *Mathews vicinity*. The Methodists were among the first and most enthusiastic supporters of revivals—special religious events, frequently held outdoors, designed to renew and intensify faith. All through the 19th century revivals grew less spontaneous and more routine and institutionalized. Erected in 1922, Mathews County's tabernacle is one of the state's few remaining examples of the permanent shelters required as revivals became regularly scheduled occasions. The airy structure is essentially a pavilion and preserves most of its original accoutrements, including speaker's platform, choir tiers, and "mourners" bench. 57–30 (4/15/75).

MILFORD, *Moon*. At the head of Billups Creek amid the marshy flats of Mathews County, Milford is typical of dwellings erected by Tidewater Virginia's gentry in the late 18th century. Characteristically, the wood-frame house has a plain but pleasantly proportioned exterior and comparatively elaborate interior woodwork, including a grandly paneled parlor chimney wall and a fine Georgian stair. The house stands on property that has remained in the ownership of the Billups family since the 17th century. It is likely that the present house was erected for John Billups or his son John Billups, Jr., between 1774 and 1784. Except for the modern shingle siding and a 20th-century wing, the house survives without significant alteration. 57–75 (5/17/77).

NEW POINT COMFORT LIGHTHOUSE, *Bavon vicinity.*
The New Point Comfort peninsula has served as a point of
reference for navigators entering the Mobjack Bay since the
17th century and has been known by its present name since
before 1690. Because of the continuous threat to navigation
caused by the point and its adjacent shoals, Congress appro-
priated funds in 1801 for the erection of a permanent lighthouse. Constructed by the Mathews County resident Elzy Burroughs, the lighthouse was completed in 1805 and put into use
the following year. Similar to the lighthouse at Old Point
Comfort, the gently tapering structure of whitewashed sandstone ashlar continued in regular use until 1963 when a new
light was constructed on piers in the water to the south. The
original lighthouse has been turned over by the Coast Guard
to Mathews County to be preserved as a historic landmark
and as a day reference for passing boats. With changes in currents,
the lighthouse is no longer at the tip of the peninsula but
stands on an island. 57–64 (6/20/72).

POPLAR GROVE MILL AND HOUSE, *Mathews vicinity.*
Poplar Grove Mill is the only surviving tide mill in Virginia.
Tidal power, along with wind power, was harnessed by necessity in the low-lying coastal regions where ordinary waterpower did not exist. A mill has existed at Poplar Grove since
colonial times; the present structure replaced the first mill,
which burned during the Civil War. The mill continued in operation until 1912 and has since been restored. Across the mill's
lagoon is the several-sectioned Poplar Grove house, the earliest
portion of which was probably built for John Patterson before
the Revolutionary War. The central portion of the house was
constructed in the Federal period and has the distinct styling
and details of the local builder Richard Billups. Patterson's
granddaughter, the nurse Capt. Sally Tompkins, the only
woman to be commissioned an officer in the Confederate
army, was born at Poplar Grove in 1833. Among the modern
owners of the property were John Lennon, member of the Bea-
tles, and his wife Yoko Ono. 57–8,9 (5/13/69).

MECKLENBURG COUNTY

*Formed from Lunenburg County in 1764, this Southside county
was named in honor of Charlotte of Mecklenburg-Strelitz,
consort of King George III. The county seat is Boydton.*

BOYD'S TAVERN, *Washington Street, Boydton*. The original
core of this tavern was erected in the early 19th century, probably by Alexander Boyd, Jr., an area businessman and founder
of the village of Boydton. While he was proprietor, Boyd
boasted that the tavern had a "Table amply supplied with all
the meats raised in this part of the Country and a cellar furnished with the Liquors of Europe." The county seat's popular
hostelry evolved with alterations and additions over the next
decades into a rambling frame structure highlighted with fancy
sawn-work detailing. The festive ornamentation was designed
by the imaginative builder-architect Jacob W. Holt, who made
such enrichments a hallmark of his work. The tavern operation
ceased in this century, and the building was divided into apartments. It fell into neglected condition but has since excited
local preservation interest. The Boyd Family Memorial Association is in the process of rescuing the tavern and having its
architectural and social vibrancy restored. 173–1 (2/17/76).

ELM HILL, *Elm Hill State Game Management Area, Castle Heights vicinity.* Elm Hill is an early plantation house in the Roanoke River basin. Although unoccupied and in deteriorated condition, the house has suffered few alterations and preserves nearly all of its original fabric including its boldly provincial Federal woodwork. It has a T-shaped plan, with its center section framed by two massive chimneys made of blocks of local sandstone. It was built ca. 1800 as the residence of Peyton Skipwith, although title to the property was held by his father, Sir Peyton Skipwith, Bart., of Prestwould. Elm Hill was held by the Skipwith family into the late 19th century and is now owned by the Virginia Commission of Game and Inland Fisheries. It is currently the subject of preservation efforts by the Association for the Preservation of Virginia Antiquities. It stands in a commanding position overlooking Lake Gaston and the John H. Kerr Dam. 58–66 (5/15/79).

ELM HILL ARCHAEOLOGICAL SITE, *Elm Hill State Game Management Area, Castle Heights vicinity.* In a bottomland field of the Elm Hill plantation, the Elm Hill archaeological site preserves stratified deposits dating from the Late Archaic through Late Woodland periods that would contribute significantly to the limited data currently available about this portion of the Roanoke River. Late Archaic projectile points and flakage have been documented in a stratified context from the lowest test level of the site. Multiple Woodland period occupation is denoted by the presence of preserved strata, pit features, hearths, and human burials. These features have both dense concentrations of ceramic artifacts and well-preserved animal bones and shellfish remains. The Elm Hill site is one of the last, if not the last, intact stratified bottomland sites between Roanoke Rapids, N.C., and South Boston, Va., for other potential sites have been inundated by Buggs Island Lake and Lake Gaston. 58–84 (11/15/83).

EUREKA, *Baskerville vicinity.* Jacob W. Holt (1811–1880), a regional architect and builder, erected this Italian Villa–style house for the Baskervill family in 1854–59. Born in Prince Edward County, Holt began his career in Warren County, N.C., and moved to Mecklenburg County in the mid-1850s. Typical of Holt's work, Eureka is lavishly ornamented with scrollwork brackets, heavy moldings, and other fancy wooden ornaments. The house is exceptionally well built and spacious in scale and has a provincial originality not found in the more academic works of the period. Eureka was first owned and occupied by Dr. Robert D. Baskervill and remained the property of his descendants until 1974 when the house and surrounding acreage were purchased by Mr. and Mrs. William Blaylock, who have since restored the place. Preserved on the interior is much original woodwork retaining its painted graining. In the parlor are still hanging the original draperies with their mid-Victorian lambrequins. The whole place conveys the gregarious, self-confident optimism more typical of the Deep South than of Virginia on the eve of the Civil War. 58–10 (7/19/77).

MECKLENBURG COUNTY COURTHOUSE, *Washington Street, Boydton*. Of Virginia's numerous Roman Revival courthouses influenced by the public buildings of Thomas Jefferson, none has a more elegant formality than Mecklenburg's courthouse of 1838–42. It is the only temple-form building of the group with a hexastyle portico and the only one to use the Roman Ionic order. With its brick walls now whitewashed, the building has a striking resemblance to Jefferson's Virginia State Capitol, for both employ angled volutes in their Ionic capitals. The courthouse was built by the area master builder William A. Howard, who also built the Cumberland courthouse and helped build the Lunenburg courthouse. As was the custom of the day, Howard likely exerted a strong influence on the proportions and detailing of all three buildings. Boydton was established as the county seat in 1811. The county quickly outgrew its first structure and in 1838 voted the construction of this new one. The present courthouse is on a tree-shaded square which also contains the clerk's office and a monument to the county's Confederate dead. 173–6 (6/17/75).

PRESTWOULD, *Clarksville vicinity*. Sir Peyton Skipwith, the only baronet born in Virginia, moved from the Petersburg area to his Roanoke River lands following marriage to his second wife, Jean Miller, in 1788. In 1795 he completed his large Georgian mansion, the nucleus of a plantation of some 10,000 acres acquired thirty years earlier in a gambling game with Col. William Byrd III. Built of local dressed sandstone, Sir Peyton's house is an imposing expression of the elegant life-style maintained by Virginia's gentry in the remote countryside, with its French scenic wallpapers in the parlor and dining room, many fine furnishings, and an extensive library. The formal garden, partially restored by the Garden Club of Virginia, was laid out by Lady Jean Skipwith and is among the best documented gardens of the period in the state. In it is an octagonal pavilion, one of Virginia's few such garden follies. There is also an unusually complete collection of 18th-century plantation outbuildings. Prestwould remained in the possession of Skipwith descendants until 1914. In 1956 the house and forty-six acres were acquired by the Prestwould Foundation, which has since opened the place to the public and has undertaken the restoration of various elements of the property. 58–45,46,47 (11/5/68).

SHADOW LAWN, *27 North Main Street, Chase City*. Shadow Lawn is a white-painted Italianate dwelling providing a festive note for its Southside community. The house evolved in tandem with the town's transformation from a crossroads village known as Christiansville into a thriving colony of northern immigrants after the Civil War. Begun ca. 1834 as the home of Richard Puryear, it was enlarged to its present form in 1869–70 by Jacob W. Holt for George Endly, the cofounder of Chase City, who moved to the area from Pennsylvania in 1868. Holt, a Virginia-born architect/builder who lived and worked in North Carolina before returning to his native state, erected an interesting group of wooden structures employing an assertive and delightfully ornamented Italianate style. 58–130 (12/15/81).

MIDDLESEX COUNTY

*Formed from Lancaster County ca. 1669, Middlesex County,
on the Rappahannock River side of Virginia's Middle
Peninsula, was named for the extinct English shire which
bordered London. Its county seat is Saluda.*

CHRIST CHURCH, *Christchurch*. The second church of the
Christ Church Parish was ordered in 1712 and worked on into
the 1720s. Alexander Graves served as its mason, and John Hipkins, Sr., as its carpenter. Among its principal patrons was the
Wormeley family of Rosegill. Although it is modest in proportion, there is evidence that the interior was richly appointed
and had a chancel screen. Like many of Virginia's Anglican
churches, Christ Church was abandoned after the disestablishment and fell into ruin; only its handsome Flemish bond walls
survived. The parish was revived in 1840, and the church was
restored to use in 1843. In 1921 Christchurch School, a boys'
preparatory school, was established nearby, and the church
since has served as both the school chapel and the local parish
church. Further renovations took place in 1931. The churchyard
contains one of the finest collections of colonial tombstones in
the state, the most elegant ones marking the graves of the Wormeleys. 59–2 (3/21/72).

DEER CHASE, *Healys vicinity*. Deer Chase, with its brick
construction, jerkinhead roof, and center-passage plan typifies
the better-quality, medium-size colonial plantation house of
Virginia's Tidewater region. Although modest in appearance,
the house is generously proportioned compared to the rude
wooden cottages of the average farmers of the period. The
original occupant is not known, but the property was owned
by the Cary family in the late 18th century. The house was gutted by fire in the early 19th century; hence, the present interior
woodwork dates from that time. The repair to the fire damage
also resulted in the number of bays on the facade being
changed from five to three. An 1885 plat of the property shows

that the plantation at that time had as many as seventeen out-buildings and farm buildings as well as a formal garden. Of these, a frame schoolhouse and the foundations of an office remain. Deer Chase has a remote rural location near the banks of the Piankatank River. 59—17 (6/19/73).

HEWICK, *Urbanna vicinity.* Hewick was the seat of the Robinson family for most of the 18th century. Although popularly believed to have been constructed in two sections, with the ell dating from the 17th century, the house is more likely to have been built all at once in the mid-18th century for the planter Christopher Robinson III (1705–1768), grandson of Christopher Robinson I, councillor and secretary of state for the colony, who probably had an earlier house on the property. In its original form the house was only one story high and had a clipped gable roof. The roof was changed to a gambrel roof in the early 19th century, and ca. 1849 the front section was raised to two full stories and given its present low gable. These various changes illustrate the changing tastes in house forms in the region. The property, with its broad, level yard and surrounding fields, is approached by a long, tree-lined lane. It remained the home of Robinson family descendants until 1875. 59—6 (7/18/78).

LANSDOWNE, *Virginia Street, Urbanna.* This mid-18th-century T-shaped brick mansion in the village of Urbanna was built as a secondary residence for Ralph Wormeley IV of nearby Rosegill. Although not generally known to architectural scholars, the house is rated among Virginia's finest representatives of the Georgian style. The front portion of the house is the earliest; the brick rear wing was added probably within five years. The interior was altered in the early part of the 20th century with the relocation of the stair and other changes, but the large quantity of surviving original paneling is outstanding. In 1791 Lansdowne became the home of Arthur Lee, diplomat and governmental figure during and after the Revolution. At Lee's death the next year, Lansdowne was inherited by his brother Richard Henry Lee. It later was owned by Francis Lightfoot Lee, another brother, who sold it in 1803. 316—3 (9/17/74).

LOWER CHAPEL, *Hartfield vicinity.* Lower Chapel is one of two chapels ordered in 1710, along with the main parish church, to serve Middlesex County's Christ Church Parish. The other chapel does not survive. Lower Chapel, begun in 1714, was so named because it was located in the lower part of the parish. As might be expected of a secondary structure, the building is relatively simple, having plain English bond walls with no rubbed or otherwise decorated brickwork. It achieves visual distinction, however, through the use of a steep clipped gable roof. Completed in 1717, the chapel served the parish until it was abandoned following the disestablishment. The building was acquired by the Methodists in 1857 and has been used by that denomination, with the designation Lower Church, ever since. 59—7 (10/17/72).

MIDDLESEX COUNTY COURTHOUSE, *Saluda*. Conspicuously located at an intersection in the county seat village of Saluda, the 1852 courthouse is a late example of the temple-form, arcaded-front court structures erected by many Virginia counties in the early decades of the 19th century. Beginning with the 1701–4 Capitol in Williamsburg, the arcade has been a traditional architectural feature of Virginia public buildings. The county seat was moved from Urbanna to Saluda in 1849, and John P. Hill was commissioned to erect this new courthouse. The building has since been enlarged, but its original section, still serving its intended function, is clearly evident. 59–8 (4/18/78).

OLD MIDDLESEX COUNTY COURTHOUSE (MIDDLESEX COUNTY WOMAN'S CLUB), *Virginia Street, Urbanna*. Although much altered from its original, probably very simple, appearance, the former courthouse of Middlesex County is one of Virginia's pre-Revolutionary court structures and is the principal historic element in the old port of Urbanna. Construction of a courthouse in the community was ordered in 1685, but because of local arguments over ferry access to the county seat, the building was not begun until 1745. The routine business of the county was conducted in the courthouse for the next century; and, during the Revolution, the local Committee of Safety met in the building to try some members of the county's gentry for suspected loyalty to the crown. In 1847 the Middlesex justices moved the county seat to the more accessible settlement of Saluda. The former courthouse was sold for conversion into an interdenominational chapel and was remodeled in the Gothic taste. During the Civil War the building served as a barracks for Confederate troops. From 1920 to 1948 it housed an Episcopal congregation, after which it was deconsecrated and deeded to the Middlesex County Woman's Club, which it continues to serve. 316–2 (6/15/76).

OLD TOBACCO WAREHOUSE, *Virginia Street, Urbanna*. Dating from the 1760s, this simple porch-fronted storehouse, built for the factor James Mills, is a rare example of a commercial structure run by a resident factor of a British company. At such an establishment, tobacco, instead of being consigned directly to England, was sold to the factor, who sent it to England in trade for English goods to be bought by the local planters. Mills and his employers were Scottish, as were many of the merchants active in Virginia's early tobacco trade. The building passed through various owners during the 19th century and was purchased by the Association for the Preservation of Virginia Antiquities in 1938. It has since been adapted to serve as the local library. 316–4 (4/18/72).

ROSEGILL, *Urbanna vicinity*. Established in 1649, Rosegill was the colonial seat of the Wormeley family. Ralph Wormeley I patented the original tract of 3,200 acres. Sir Henry Chicheley, deputy governor of the colony, married Wormeley's widow and made his home at Rosegill, giving it a status above other Virginia seats of the period. Ralph Wormeley II (1650–1700), holder of several public positions including that of president of the Council, made the plantation an elaborate estate consisting of some twenty buildings. Lord Howard of Effingham, a colonial governor in the late 17th century, used Rosegill as a summer home. The present complex, consisting of a range of four brick buildings, most likely was erected during the tenure of Ralph Wormeley IV (1715–1790). The main house evolved from a small brick dwelling to a large U-shaped structure covered by a gambrel roof. In the 1850s the later extending wings were removed and the weatherboarded second story was added. The existing buildings give Rosegill considerable architectural interest, but the probable concentration of many 17th-century building sites also make the plantation of paramount archaeological significance. 59–9 (2/10/73).

WILTON, *Stampers vicinity*. Built in 1763 for William Churchill, Wilton is one of the more sophisticated and least-altered of the late colonial plantation houses of Tidewater Virginia. Churchill was clerk of the county court for nearly three decades. Notable features of his house include its T-plan, brickwork, Georgian stair, and fully paneled parlor. Like many of the medium-size plantation houses of the Middle Peninsula, Wilton has one story and a dormered gambrel roof. The rear wing is interesting for having its gambrel hipped rather than terminated in a gable. Local tradition has it that the house was built in several stages; however, an examination of the structure does not support this notion. 59–10 (10/17/78).

WORMELEY COTTAGE, *Virginia Street, Urbanna*. The Wormeley cottage is the simplest of the handful of early houses remaining in the once-bustling colonial port town of Urbanna. The lot on which the house stands was the property of the Wormeleys of Rosegill, and it is assumed that they erected the building as rental property in the second half of the 18th century. The small house, with its side-hall plan, dormer windows, and large end chimney, is a typical example of Tidewater Virginia vernacular. The house was rescued from threat of demolition and restored in 1976 by Robert L. Montague III. 316–6 (12/20/77).

MONTGOMERY COUNTY

Named for Gen. Richard Montgomery, who was killed in the American assault on Quebec in 1775, this Southwest Virginia county was formed from the extinct Fincastle County in 1776. Parts of Botetourt and Pulaski counties were added later. The county seat is Christiansburg.

CHRISTIANSBURG PRESBYTERIAN CHURCH, *107 West Main Street, Christiansburg*. The Christiansburg Presbyterian Church is the most refined of a group of Greek Revival churches concentrated in and around the Roanoke Valley. Common features of these buildings are the temple form, usually with a portico in antis; precisely laid brickwork; and a square belfry framed by paired pilasters and topped by a steeple. The architectural details mostly are adapted from builders' pattern books of the period, particularly those of Asher Benjamin. The Christiansburg church was built in 1853 by James E. Crush of Fincastle, who was assisted by the brothers Samuel M. and James W. Hicock. In contrast to the many simple small-town churches of the period, Christiansburg Presbyterian displays remarkable inventiveness rendered in a bold simplicity. Presbyterians came to Montgomery County in the late 18th century, and the Christiansburg congregation was organized in 1827 by the Reverend John McElhenney of Lewisburg. 154–3 (6/21/77).

FORT VAUSE ARCHAEOLOGICAL SITE, *Shawsville*. A simple palisaded fort was established here in the mid-18th century. The fort was attacked by Indians in June 1756, and a relief party led by Maj. Andrew Lewis arrived too late to save most of its occupants. The fort was quickly rebuilt by Capt. Peter Hogg and probably was a composite earth and palisade structure. George Washington inspected Fort Vause in October 1756. Archaeological test excavations undertaken in 1968 identified the location and general size of the second fort as well as evidence of its predecessor. More extensive examination may provide data on living conditions along Virginia's frontier during the mid- to late 18th century. 60–17 (12/2/69).

FOTHERINGAY, *Shawsville vicinity*. Fotheringay was the home of George Hancock (1754–1820), who served as a colonel in the Virginia Line during the Revolution and was aide-de-camp to Count Casimir Pulaski. He also represented the region in both the Virginia House of Delegates and in the U.S. Congress. Sited dramatically against the Blue Ridge Mountains overlooking the bottomlands of the South Fork of the Roanoke River, Hancock's house, built soon after he acquired the land in 1796, is an elegant provincial interpretation of the Federal style. The unusually ornate interior woodwork, highlighted by delicately carved chimneypieces and doorways, exhibits the high quality of the area's post-Revolutionary craftsmanship. As originally built for Hancock, the house lacked the two bays south of the portico, giving the front an unfinished look. A wing in the style of the original fabric was added in the 1950s so that the house now has a symmetrical facade. 60–5 (5/13/69).

INGLES BOTTOM ARCHAEOLOGICAL SITES, *Radford vicinity*. The tract of floodplain along the banks of the New River just south of Radford incorporates a variety of human occupation sites documenting man's utilization of the region from 8000 B.C. to the present. Prehistoric sites range from the Archaic through the Woodland periods. The area takes its name from the Ingles family, its first white settlers. Test excavations have revealed the site of a log house, probably the home of Mary Ingles, widow of the pioneer William Ingles. The family operated a ferry here which served the many settlers traveling up the Valley of Virginia to western lands. Other sites on the property associated with the Ingleses include those of a stable, a tannery, and the family cemetery. A large late 19th-century house here, Ingleside, remains the home of the Ingles family. 60–80 (6/15/76).

OLD CHRISTIANSBURG INDUSTRIAL INSTITUTE AND SCHAEFFER MEMORIAL BAPTIST CHURCH, *570 High Street, Christiansburg.* The Old Christiansburg Institute (Hill School) and the Schaeffer Memorial Baptist Church, both built in 1885, are monuments in the social, educational, and religious history of the black community of Montgomery County. Through the early efforts of Capt. Charles S. Schaeffer, an agent of the Freedmen's Bureau and later an ordained Baptist pastor, formal instruction was begun for the area's blacks in 1866, several years before the public school system served the county at large. Technical, academic, and religious training were emphasized during Schaeffer's thirty-year affiliation. In 1895 the program was revamped in line with those pioneered at Tuskegee and Hampton Institute. The church, with its 1888 frame annex, remains in use by black Baptists, but the institute has long been closed. Both of the buildings are solid but unprepossessing representatives of late Victorian institutional architecture. 60–85 (5/16/78).

SMITHFIELD, *Blacksburg.* Smithfield was the home of William Preston (1729–1783), Revolutionary officer, Indian fighter, and member of the House of Burgesses, who was instrumental in opening up much of the region to settlement. His L-shaped frame residence, completed in 1774, is remarkable as an expression of architectural sophistication in what was then the edge of frontier wilderness. Indistinguishable from a prosperous Tidewater Virginia plantation house, Smithfield has the generous scale, refined proportions, and careful detailing typical of the colonial Virginia architectural idiom, even boasting a stylish Chinese lattice railing on the main stair. Preston's son James Patton Preston and a grandson, John Buchanan Floyd, both of whom served as governors of Virginia, were born at Smithfield. The house was acquired by the Association for the Preservation of Virginia Antiquities in the 1960s and subsequently restored. It is now exhibited as a museum of the Preston family and of life in early Southwest Virginia. 60–18 (11/5/68).

YELLOW SULPHUR SPRINGS, *Blacksburg vicinity.* Developed in the early 19th century, the Yellow Sulphur Springs complex afforded its patrons the usual middle-class leisure-time and therapeutic pursuits of the mid-Victorian era. Despite the loss of a later main hotel building and several cottages, the original mid-19th-century hotel structure with its galleried facade survives. Also remaining are the cottage row, the proprietor's house, and an early bowling alley, making the group one of the most complete spa complexes in the state. The focal point of the group is the polygonal gazebo covering the spring. Most of the cottages are now rented as apartments, and the old hotel building is abandoned and in poor condition. 60–13 (9/20/77).

NELSON COUNTY

In the foothills of Virginia's Piedmont, Nelson County, formed in 1807 from Amherst County, was named in honor of Thomas Nelson, Jr., governor of Virginia from June to November 1781. The county seat is Lovingston.

BON AIRE, *Warminster vicinity.* Bon Aire, built ca. 1812 for Dr. George Cabell, Jr., is a three-part Federal country house inspired by Palladian forms published in mid-18th-century English pattern books such as Robert Morris's *Select Architecture* of 1755. The designer of Bon Aire has not been identified, but the tripartite organization of the plan and many details relate the house to Point of Honor in Lynchburg, built for Dr. Cabell's cousin, Dr. George Cabell. Constructed in native materials of red brick and whitewashed wood trim, Bon Aire exemplifies the process by which Virginia builders manipulated the scale, plan, details, and materials of Morris's designs to conform to local vernacular traditions. The present portico and dormers are modern additions. 62–89 (4/15/80).

MIDWAY MILL, *Midway Mills.* So named because of its situation on the James River midway between Richmond and Lynchburg, this prodigious stone structure was built in 1787 for William H. Cabell, governor of Virginia from 1805 to 1808. According to tradition, the mill was constructed by Italian shipbuilders who were stranded in Virginia after the cancellation of a ship construction project for which they had been brought over from Europe. During the mid-19th century the mill became a familiar landmark for travelers passing close by on the James River and Kanawha Canal. The canal traffic prompted the establishment of a small settlement here to serve the passengers and boatmen. Midway Mill remained in operation until ca. 1925 when outdated machinery rendered it unprofitable and forced its closing. Although in a decayed state, the structure is one of Virginia's few remaining 18th-century mills and is evidence of the high standards maintained in the building arts in that century. 62–23 (1/16/73).

MONTEZUMA, *Norwood vicinity.* Erected ca. 1790, Montezuma is a singular example of Piedmont Federal architecture. Its impressive scale, distinctive floor plan, fine woodwork, and Roman Revival dwarf portico set it apart from the more standard farmhouses of the period and region. Montezuma was built for William Cabell, Jr., a son of the immigrant William Cabell who settled in the region in the second quarter of the 18th century. The Cabells built nearly a dozen architecturally distinguished houses in what became Nelson County; Montezuma, Bon Aire, and Soldier's Joy are among the few that remain. Thomas Jefferson was a friend of the Cabells and may have had an influence on the design of Montezuma. The combination of a Chinese lattice railing with a classical portico is a distinctly Jeffersonian touch. 62–10 (4/15/80).

NELSON COUNTY COURTHOUSE, *Lovingston.* The tradition of applying arcades to public buildings can be traced from the loggias of Italian town squares and the ground floors of English Renaissance town halls. This tradition was maintained with the arcades of the first Williamsburg Capitol and the facades of several colonial courthouses. Nelson County's court structure of 1810 exemplifies the persistence of this motif, in this case grafted onto a provincially interpreted temple-form building. The temple form was widely used for Virginia courthouses in the first half of the 19th century. The Nelson courthouse was constructed under the supervision of George Varnum according to plans submitted by Shelton Crostwait, one of the justices. It has been in continuous use since completion, and though enlarged and modified over the years, it survives with less damage to its integrity than most of its contemporaries. 62–9 (4/17/73).

OAK RIDGE RAILROAD OVERPASS, *Route 653, Shipman vicinity.* Spanning the tracks of the Southern Railway System, this metal truss bridge is an excellently preserved representative of the many graceful structures that have efficiently guided vehicular traffic across obstacles since their development in the late 19th century. The bridge employs the popular single-span through Pratt truss, 100 feet in length, with two wooden-beam approach spans, each 19 feet long. It was manufactured by the Keystone Bridge Company in 1882 and has remained in continuous service since its installation. The Highway Research Council's 1977 survey of Virginia metal truss bridges rated the Oak Ridge Overpass the state's best example of its type. 62–85 (11/15/77).

RIVER BLUFF, *Wintergreen vicinity.* On a steep bank of the South Fork of the Rockfish River, in the shadow of the Blue Ridge Mountains, this brick farmhouse began as a side-passage, one-room house in 1785 for Nathaniel Clarke. It was made into a three-part dwelling by the addition of wings ca. 1810, during the ownership of Thomas Goodwin. Through its transformation from a small rectangular structure to a stylish, if simplified, Palladian type, River Bluff illustrates how dwellers of Virginia's remoter regions traded their rustic image for one more socially acceptable. River Bluff and its scenic setting have changed little since the 19th century. 62–88 (5/20/80).

SOLDIER'S JOY, *Wingina vicinity.* One of the surviving Cabell family houses in the Piedmont region, Soldier's Joy was built in 1783–85 and enlarged in 1806. Samuel Jordan Cabell, for whom the house was built, was an officer during the Revolutionary War and served as the Republican congressman of the district from 1795 to 1803. Although its early 19th-century wings were reduced in size in this century, Soldier's Joy remains one of the most ambitious of the Cabells' building efforts. The late Georgian dwelling has fine proportions and interior detailing, much of which was added when the house was enlarged. Giving additional interest is extensive documentation, including the detailed contract of the builder, James Robards. The woodwork of the dismantled ballroom wing, executed by James Oldham, is now displayed in the Cincinnati Art Museum. 62–15 (4/15/80).

SWANNANOA, *Afton vicinity.* Richmond railroad magnate and philanthropist Maj. James H. Dooley built this palatial mountaintop villa as a summer home for himself and his wife, Sallie May. The designer of the monumental undertaking, completed in 1913, was the Richmond firm of Noland and Baskervill, who took as inspiration the Villa Medici in Rome. The exterior of the house is faced entirely in Georgia marble, while the interior is richly appointed with costly materials. The outstanding interior feature is the huge Tiffany stained-glass window at the landing of the grand stair, depicting Mrs. Dooley in the gardens. Typical of the period, each of the principal rooms has its own architectural character, ranging from the Louis XVI music room to the Turkish office. Completing the image of a Gilded Age estate is an Italian-style terraced garden highlighted by a pergola at the top level. Also on the grounds are a campanilelike water tower and a huge stable. Since 1949 Swannanoa has housed the University of Science and Philosophy, a cultural and religious institution founded by American sculptor Walter Russell and his wife Lao. 62–22 (11/5/68).

NEW KENT COUNTY

Most likely named for the English shire of Kent, this largely
wooded Tidewater county east of Richmond was formed from
York County in 1654. Its county seat is
New Kent Court House.

CEDAR GROVE, *Providence Forge vicinity.* This inland New Kent farm was acquired in 1789 by Robert Christian, who represented the county in the General Assembly. The present house, erected for Christian ca. 1810 as an addition to the original 18th-century house, is a provincial adaptation of the Richmond town house of the period. Like its urban counterparts, the house has a side-passage plan and its facade is embellished with Flemish bond brickwork and a modillion cornice. Also like many Richmond town houses, Cedar Grove had stuccoed lintels and keystones, but they have been filled in with modern brickwork. Christian's daughter Letitia, born at Cedar Grove in the earlier house, was the first wife of President John Tyler and died in the White House in 1842. She is buried in the Christian family cemetery at Cedar Grove. The original section of the house was replaced by the present wing in 1916. 63–36 (10/16/79).

CRISS CROSS, *New Kent Court House vicinity.* The few Stuart-period houses surviving in Virginia mostly follow traditional English vernacular forms of earlier decades and show little of the classical influence that characterized the mother country's more sophisticated contemporary works by such architects as Sir Christopher Wren. Criss Cross, an engaging little manor house hidden in the woods of New Kent County, reveals this phenomenon most clearly. Named for its cross-shaped plan, the one-and-a-half-story house, erected ca. 1690 for George Poindexter, is dominated by a two-story projection containing the entrance and chamber above. The house re-

ceived a rear wing in 1790 which may have replaced an original stair tower that would have made the house cross shaped originally. Irregularities in the brickwork tell of other alterations to the exterior. Inside are rare exposed framing members and decorative details. The paneled doors between the entrance room and the hall and the scroll-carved post supporting a large summer beam have a decidedly postmedieval quality, illustrating the persistence of traditional forms in remote areas. 63–6 (1/16/73).

FOSTER'S CASTLE, *Tunstall vicinity.* Joseph Foster, a native of Newport, England, was the first owner of this T-shaped manor house overlooking the Pamunkey River and its marshes. Although the loss of New Kent's early records complicates precise dating, the house probably was constructed between 1685 and 1690 when Foster represented New Kent in the House of Burgesses. Foster's Castle shares with nearby Criss Cross and Bacon's Castle in Surry County the distinction of being Virginia's only remaining Stuart-period manor houses fronted by enclosed porches with chambers above, a vernacular architectural feature typical of postmedieval English houses. The house has undergone significant alterations. Most of its interior was replaced in the early 19th century, and the walls in the main body of the house were raised to two stories in 1873. Despite these changes, the surviving original walls constitute a significant document of Virginia architecture in the first century of settlement. 63–3 (1/16/73).

HAMPSTEAD, *Tunstall vicinity.* The full drama of the Federal style is played in this strongly architectural plantation house, one of the most ambitious and successful works of its era in the state. All features of the house—the delicate classical detailing, the monumental proportions, and the beautiful masonry and joinery—exude fine quality. Dominating the interior is a flying circular stair winding from basement to attic and separated from the hall by an arched screen of columns. The designer of Hampstead has not been identified, but many of the architectural parallels of the house to the works of John Holden Greene of Providence, R.I., have suggested an attribution. As in several of Greene's documented works, much of Hampstead's detailing follows illustrations published in Asher Benjamin's *American Builder's Companion* (1806). Hampstead was built ca. 1825 for the planter Conrade Webb. Webb was educated at Brown University and could well have sought assistance from his university city's leading architect to carry out such a singular undertaking. The house is sited on the edge of a steep ridge with one of its twin porticoes framing a view of the Pamunkey River bottomlands. 63–13 (10/6/70).

MOYSONEC ARCHAEOLOGICAL SITE, *Lanexa vicinity.* During his exploration of the Chickahominy River in 1607, Capt. John Smith observed the Indian village of Moysonec, sited, as he noted, "where a better seat for a town cannot be

desired." The exact site of this Late Woodland period village was identified in the course of a 1967–71 survey of the region conducted by the Department of Anthropology of the College of William and Mary. Artifacts revealed evidence of Indian occupancy from as early as the Archiac period, or 7000–6000 B.C. Shown are fragments of knotted net-impressed ceramics of the Middle Woodland period (500 B.C.–A.D. 900) found on the site. The 1644 massacre led by the Pamunkey leader Opechancanough prompted the establishment of Fort James in the immediate vicinity of the village, which the Indians by then had abandoned. The undisturbed village site provides a valuable opportunity for the study of aboriginal Virginians at the time of contact with European civilization and could furnish information on house forms, tools, diets, and physical conditions of the village inhabitants. 63–77 (12/17/74).

OLIVET PRESBYTERIAN CHURCH, *Providence Forge vicinity.* The formality of the Greek Revival style lent dignity not just to urban public buildings and great houses but to simple, rural structures, especially churches. Tucked deep in the New Kent woods, Olivet Church shows the effectiveness of the Grecian mode in its most elementary and provincial form. The otherwise austere wooden church is in a temple form and is fronted by a simple Doric portico. Of no less interest is the interior, essentially unchanged over the past century. The doors and pews remain decorated with their original mahogany and bird's-eye maple graining. The pulpit is set off by marbleized steps. Presbyterians came to this area of New Kent County as early as the mid-18th century. By 1800 a congregation was meeting in the colonial St. Peter's Church, which by then had been abandoned by the Episcopalians. In 1857 they decided to erect their own church nearby, calling it Mount Olivet and later merely Olivet. The congregation relocated in Providence Forge in 1934, retaining Olivet Church for annual memorial services. 63–105 (7/19/77).

ST. PETER'S CHURCH, *Talleysville vicinity.* This small colonial church, with all of its quaint provinciality, represents the closest Virginia architecture ever approached the baroque style. The main body of the building, erected 1701–3 by William Hughes, carpenter, and Cornelius Hall, bricklayer, shows the influence of the style in its restored curvilinear gables. The tower, added in 1739–41 by William Walker of Stafford, has baroque vestiges in the molded cornices, massive corner pilasters, recessed panels, and pyramidal roof with its four pedestals topped by crude stuccoed urns, one of which serves as a chimney. The building is structurally interesting for the use of English bond with oversize bricks in the walls of the oldest part and fine glazed-header Flemish bond with gauged and molded work in the tower. The church's interior suffered the loss of almost all of its original fabric in the course of its nearly three-century history but was carefully restored to its original form in 1964–65. St. Peter's was the parish church of Martha Dandridge Custis Washington during her youth. 63–27 (11/5/68).

CITY OF NEWPORT NEWS

The name of this Hampton Roads port city probably commemorates Capt. Christopher Newport, who made five voyages to Virginia between 1607 and 1619. The community was but a small village until the late 19th century when it became the eastern terminus of the Chesapeake and Ohio Railway. The town was established in 1880 and incorporated as a city in 1896. The city's size was greatly expanded in 1958 when it was consolidated with Warwick County, which thereby became extinct.

BOLDRUP PLANTATION ARCHAEOLOGICAL SITE, *Moyer Road.* Boldrup plantation's archaeological remains, located on a remnant of Newport News farmland currently being developed, date to the first part of the 17th century. Patented by William Claiborne in 1626, Boldrup was later the home of Elizabeth Piercy Stephens, who in 1638 married Virginia governor Sir John Harvey. The property then reverted to Samuel Stephens, second governor of Albemarle (North Carolina). At Stephens's death in 1669, Boldrup passed to his widow, Frances Culpeper Stephens, who in 1670 married Sir William Berkeley, then governor of Virginia. Sir William and his wife did not live at Boldrup but rather made their home at Green Spring near Jamestown. In 1671 they sold Boldrup to Lt. Col. William Cole, who served as the colony's secretary of state. Cole's 1691 grave marker remains on the site. The property was later owned by the Cary family. Salvage excavation of the plantation's complex of sites is being undertaken by the Virginia Division of Historic Landmarks and is providing data on living conditions in Virginia's earliest century of settlement. One of the sites is that of a pit house, a rude dwelling made from a pit lined with boards and covered by a gable roof. 121–5 (9/15/81).

FIRST DENBIGH PARISH CHURCH ARCHAEOLOG-ICAL SITE, *Walters Drive*. The site of the first Denbigh Parish Church is the earliest dated identifiable ecclesiastical site within the former Warwick County, now incorporated into the city of Newport News. Constructed before 1635 and taking its name from the nearby Denbigh plantation, the parish church served the inhabitants of what was the upper portion of Elizabeth City Corporation, later Warwick County, in the earliest days of the colony. The church foundations, located and identified in a test square by archaeologists of the Virginia Division of Historic Landmarks, make up one of the few surviving 17th-century archaeological sites within a rapidly urbanizing area. Complete excavation could shed new light on the nation's earliest church architecture. 121–37 (9/15/81).

FORT CRAFFORD ARCHAEOLOGICAL SITE, *Fort Eustis*. Located on Mulberry Island Point, this site takes its name from Carter Crafford, who obtained title to the land in 1749 and built his home here. Crafford operated a ferry between Mulberry Island Point and Isle of Wight County on the south side of the James River. A fortification was built on the point during the Revolution to defend the river against British ships attempting landings to reinforce Yorktown. Fort Crafford dates from the summer of 1861 when it was constructed on order of Gen. Robert E. Lee to guard against a Union landing. During the Peninsula campaign of 1862, the fort played a role in Gen. J. E. Magruder's defense and delayed the Northern advance long enough to give the Confederates time to assemble a force capable of defending Richmond. The well-preserved pentagonal earthwork consists of an inner wall twenty feet high and covers approximately seven and a half acres. Within the fort area are the foundations of the Crafford house, as well as the Crafford family graveyard and a slave graveyard. There are also the sites of three magazines and two bombproof shelters of Civil War vintage. The house was demolished in 1925 in order to obtain bricks to repair the Wren Building in Williamsburg. 121–17 (10/16/73).

HILTON VILLAGE HISTORIC DISTRICT, *bounded by the James River, the Chesapeake and Ohio Railway tracks, Hopkins Street, and Post Street*. Hilton Village, an area of some eighteen blocks containing houses, play areas, a city square, a commercial street, and land for schools, parks, and churches, was one of the first planned communities in the nation financed with U.S. government funds. The village was conceived and built to offset the critical shortage of good housing for the employees of the Newport News Shipbuilding and Dry Dock Company in World War I. The company, along with the U.S. Shipping Board, chose a tract along the James River that was easily accessible to the shipyard by trolley. The architect of the buildings was Francis Y. Joannes, and the landscape architect was Vincent Hubbard. A modified English cottage style with steeply pitched roofs, stuccoed or clapboarded walls, and ample lawns was chosen as the principal theme. The houses

varied in size and were intended for different income levels; included were detached houses, double houses, and row houses. Over sixty years later, Hilton Village remains in excellent condition and is one of the most popular addresses in Newport News. It is protected by local ordinance against inappropriate change. 121–9 (11/5/68).

MATTHEW JONES HOUSE, *Fort Eustis.* The main body of this T-shaped colonial dwelling probably was built for Matthew Jones in 1727, whose name and date are found on inscribed bricks. The projecting entrance with chamber above is a holdover from 17th-century house types and is one of the state's four remaining examples of this architectural form. The exterior end chimneys, with their great sloping haunches and divided stacks, seem to have been built to serve an earlier dwelling, probably frame, for the chimney bricks are smaller in size than those on the rest of the house and are not bonded to its walls. In 1893 all of the original interior trim was removed and the wings were raised to two full stories. Despite these changes, the house, with its glazed-header Flemish bond brickwork, is a key landmark of Virginia architecture, illustrating the transition of the colonial plantation house from the post-medieval vernacular to the Georgian style. Now located in the U.S. Army installation at Fort Eustis, the house is sealed against deterioration, but its exterior is accessible to the public. 121–6 (11/5/68).

LEE HALL, *Route 238, Lee Hall.* The Italianate plantation house at Lee Hall was built ca. 1850 for Richard Decatur Lee. Lee's fashionable new house is said to have been financed by a $10,000 sale of a bumper crop of tobacco. With the coming of the Civil War, Lee was placed in charge of the area's civil defense. The mansion was used as headquarters of Confederate general J. B. Magruder during the Peninsula campaign of April and May 1862. A small earthen fort on the front lawn remains the only evidence of the property's military occupation. Lee's conscientious support of the Confederate cause brought about his financial ruin and the forced sale of the plantation in 1866. The village that developed in the 1880s at the rail crossing to the southeast of the place took its name from the house. Still a well-maintained dwelling for a working farm and the only major antebellum house remaining on Virginia's Lower Peninsula, Lee Hall is a landmark on the former turnpike connecting Williamsburg and Hampton. 121–16 (8/15/72).

MATHEWS MANOR (DENBIGH PLANTATION ARCHAEOLOGICAL SITE), *Lukas Creek Road.* Much has been learned of domestic life in the first decades of settlement in Virginia from the excavations undertaken by archaeologist Ivor Noël Hume. Among the sites he has excavated is that of the first Mathews Manor house, apparently a Tudor-type,

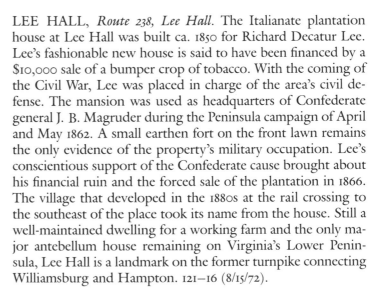

brick-nogged, half-timber structure with a center chimney and projecting porch, built ca. 1626 for Capt. Samuel Mathews (foundations shown). The house burned and was replaced by a simpler post house in the 1650s. Mathews returned to England in 1653, so the latter house was probably constructed by his son Samuel Mathews, Jr., who managed his father's property. Samuel Mathews, Jr., served as governor of the colony under the English Commonwealth from 1656 to 1660. Also within the registered area is the site of an 18th-century plantation house erected by the Digges family. The property further contains several 17th-century industrial sites, one of which has been preserved and incorporated into the layout and landscaping of a modern housing development. A valuable collection of artifacts from Mathews Manor is now part of the Colonial Williamsburg Foundation collection. 121–8 (12/2/69).

QUEEN HITH ARCHAEOLOGICAL SITES (OAKLAND FARM), *U.S. Route 60 at Enterprise Drive.* The Queen Hith sites include three significant and distinct archaeological sites within a tract of land proposed for development as the Oakland Industrial Park. Surviving intact are the archaeological remains of prehistoric occupation dating to the Early to Middle Woodland periods; the Queen Hith plantation complex, occupied by the Harwood family from the 1630s until after the Revolutionary War; and one Confederate earthwork (shown), the southern terminus of a band of fortifications constructed by Gen. J. B. Magruder in 1862 during the Peninsula campaign. Thomas Harwood, who patented the property in 1632, named it Queen Hith; *hith* is an Old English word for river landing. The sites are preserved by the Hampton and Newport News Regional Redevelopment and Housing Authority and are expected to yield significant research data on prehistoric Early to Middle Woodland periods, as well as on the settlement and cultural development of the James River basin through the 18th century. 121–41 (9/16/82).

RICHNECK PLANTATION ARCHAEOLOGICAL SITE, *Richneck Drive.* Richneck was one of two principal colonial seats of the Cary family. Archaeological and documentary evidence suggest that the dwelling, an unusual cruciform brick house with projecting porch and stair tower, was built in the last quarter of the 17th century for Miles Cary, Jr. (1655–1709), son of the immigrant. The property was inherited by the younger Cary at his father's death in 1667. Miles Cary, Jr., held several important colonial offices including the rectorship of the College of William and Mary. His son Wilson Cary and grandson Wilson Miles Cary were also prominent in colonial affairs. The grandson was among those Revolutionaries who met in the Raleigh Tavern in Williamsburg to sign the "Association of 1774." Richneck passed out of the Cary family in the early 19th century, and the house was destroyed by fire in 1865. A descendant came to the site in 1868 and reported: "the man-

sion was a pile of ruins, though from the remains of the walls still standing, I could estimate its former extent. It was a long-fronted, two-storied brick building with the usual outhouses and must have been very commodious." The immediate area of the house remains undisturbed and should reveal important information on the 17th- and 18th-century life-style of a Lower Peninsula family. The graves of Miles Cary, Jr., and his first wife, Mary Milner Cary, remain on the property. 121–28 (2/17/76).

RIVERSIDE APARTMENTS, *4500–4600 Washington Avenue.* Among the few government-initiated apartment buildings of the World War I era to survive without significant alteration, the Riverside Apartments were begun in 1918 by the Emergency Fleet Corporation, an agency of the U.S. Shipping Board, to alleviate the housing shortage created by the great increase of workers at the Newport News Shipbuilding and Dry Dock Company during the war. The architect of the project was Francis Y. Joannes, who also designed the houses for Hilton Village nearby. Consisting originally of four buildings of the New York City open-stair tenement type, the apartments incorporated the very latest in construction techniques and fittings for fire safety, light, ventilation, health, and convenience. The complex, with its easy accessibility to the shipyard and to the city center, filled an important need in America's war production effort. Two of the original four apartment blocks have been demolished. The remaining two were allowed to deteriorate in recent years but since have been extensively renovated by private developers for upgraded urban housing. 121–39 (1/18/83).

USS *CUMBERLAND* MARITIME ARCHAEOLOGICAL SITE, *James River off downtown Newport News.* The mid-19th-century shipwreck situated 200 yards offshore from Newport News is believed to be that of the USS *Cumberland,* sunk March 8, 1864, as the result of extensive damage sustained during an engagement with the Confederate ironclad *Virginia.* The *Cumberland,* a full-rigged sailing sloop built in the Boston Navy Yard, was launched in May 1842. The ship was serving as part of the Union blockade of the James River when the ironclad *Virginia* entered Hampton Roads. The *Cumberland* was the first of the several ships taken on by the *Virginia,* which first fired on it at close range and then rammed it. Helpless against the ironclad, the *Cumberland* sunk within an hour. Military artifacts salvaged by archaeologists confirm that the wreck is a naval one, and documentary evidence points to the fact that the wreck's location corresponds to that where the *Cumberland* went down. More extensive scientific archaeological investigation should identify the wreck positively and yield new research data on Civil War naval architecture and artifacts. Shown is a print of the *Cumberland* being rammed by the *Virginia* published in *Battles and Leaders of the Civil War* (1887–88). 121–42 (10/19/82).

CITY OF NORFOLK

The name of Virginia's principal port is derived from the extinct New Norfolk County, formed in 1636, which in turn was named for the English shire. The community was established in 1680 and was created a borough by royal charter in 1736. It became a city in 1845.

ALLMAND-ARCHER HOUSE, *327 Duke Street.* The streets of antebellum Norfolk were lined with elegantly proportioned two-story, side-passage town houses. Almost all have disappeared through commercial expansion and subsequent demolitions by the local redevelopment and housing authority. A rare survival is the unassuming but dignified dwelling erected on Duke Street in the 1790s by Matthew Hervey, a local merchant. The house became the property of Harrison Allmand in 1802 and passed through marriage to the Archer family, who owned it until the 1970s when it was acquired for preservation by the Historic Norfolk Foundation. The foundation later sold the house to serve as a private residence. The facade was remodeled in the mid-19th century when it received its Greek Revival entry and heavy window lintels. 122–1 (11/3/70); *Virginia Historic Landmarks Board preservation easement.*

ATTUCKS THEATRE, *1010 Church Street.* The Attucks Theatre is an early motion picture theater financed, designed, and built exclusively by blacks. A landmark in the Huntersville area of Norfolk, the theater was erected in 1919 after the designs of black architect Harvey N. Johnson. The theater is named for Crispus Attucks, a black resident of Boston who is traditionally regarded as the first colonial to be mortally wounded in the American Revolution, during the Boston Massacre. The theater retains its original fire curtain, painted with a scene of Attucks's death by Lee Lash Studios of New York. 122–74 (7/21/81).

AUSLEW GALLERY (VIRGINIA BANK AND TRUST COMPANY BUILDING), *101 Granby Street.* Erected in 1909 as the headquarters of the Virginia Bank and Trust Company, this building is one of the "Temples of Finance" that banks of the period constructed. The classical architectural themes of the solid and often huge edifices displayed their commercial strength and reassured clients of their soundness. The building was designed by two firms: Wyatt and Nolting of Baltimore, serving as the principals, and Taylor and Hepburn, Norfolk's leading architects of the period. With its grandiose scale and giant order, the building's general form follows the design provided by McKim, Mead and White for the Knickerbocker Trust and Safe Deposit Company in New York, a bank that inspired many institutions in northern cities but few others in the South. The building now houses the Auslew Gallery, an art gallery established by Donald S. Lewis in 1977. This adaptive reuse has preserved the character of an elegant reminder of Norfolk's commercial importance at the beginning of the century. 122–78 (1/17/84).

BOUSH-TAZEWELL HOUSE, *6225 Powhatan Avenue.* This little-known late Georgian town mansion dates from 1784 when it was completed for John Boush, grandson of Norfolk's first mayor and himself a mayor of the city. In 1810 the house became the home of Littleton Waller Tazewell, a statesman who served as U.S. senator and Virginia governor. Among his visitors here were Lafayette, John Tyler, and John Randolph of Roanoke. The house was enlarged in the mid-19th century with two-story Greek Revival wings. In 1894 it was acquired by Arthur Clarico Freeman, who later had it dismantled and removed from its commercializing location on the Elizabeth River and reerected three miles north on a waterfront site near the mouth of the Lafayette River. Recently restored, the exterior is set off by its graceful two-tier portico; the interior possesses much of its original Federal woodwork. 122–2 (2/19/74).

CHRIST AND ST. LUKE'S EPISCOPAL CHURCH, *560 West Olney Road*. Its traceried windows, elaborate detailing, pinnacled tower, and interior carvings all set apart Christ and St. Luke's Church, one of the state's purest expressions of the Late Gothic Revival. As are many churches of the movement, this example is a skillful adaptation of the English Perpendicular style. A notable interior feature is the carved reredos containing statues of dignitaries of the Episcopal church. The congregation traces its ancestry to the Elizabeth River Parish, whose first church was put up in 1637. Erected as Christ Church in 1909–10, the present edifice is effectively sited at the head of Smith's Creek in Norfolk's Ghent neighborhood. Its architects were Watson and Huckle of Philadelphia, experts in the scholarly interpretation of medieval English styles so popular with affluent early 20th-century congregations. 122–75 (3/20/79).

FIRST BAPTIST CHURCH, *418 East Bute Street*. Norfolk Baptists organized in 1800 and included both blacks and whites. The free blacks had largely split off by 1830 when they built a church on Bute Street. The present church was built in 1906 on the site of the 1830 church after the designs of the early 20th-century Tennessee architect Reuben H. Hunt. The Romanesque Revival structure is among the best representatives of its style in the state and is a major landmark in downtown Norfolk. Hunt's practice centered on southern ecclesiastical buildings, most notably in Birmingham, Chattanooga, and Dallas, and included Court Street Baptist Church in nearby Portsmouth. The building, with its unusually large scale and imposing quality, reflects the growing economic strength of Norfolk's black community by the end of the 19th century, as well as the position of black religious institutions in the urban life of the South in more recent times. 122–40 (4/19/83).

FORT NORFOLK, *803 Front Street*. A fortification guarding Norfolk's port was established by local citizens at this spot during the Revolutionary War. Recognizing the strategic importance of the location, the federal government purchased the site in 1795. In 1809 the government erected the fort's most dramatic feature, the massive walls with their great rounded bastion. Within these walls is a complex of military structures ranging in date from the early 19th to the 20th century. In 1862 the fort fell along with the city to Federal forces, but it was not the scene of any significant engagements. Today, the complex is a headquarters of the U.S. Army Corps of Engineers and remains an important example of early military architecture. 122–7 (12/16/75).

FREEMASON STREET BAPTIST CHURCH, *Freemason and Bank streets*. Philadelphia architect Thomas U. Walter designed this church and the nearby Norfolk Academy and collaborated on the City Hall (now the MacArthur Memorial). Contrasting vividly with the austere Grecian academy building, the lofty church is a noble representative of Walter's essays in the Gothic mode. Completed in 1850, the church, with its mixture of wood, stucco, stone, and metal, all painted to resemble masonry, typifies the Early Gothic Revival's emphasis on dramatic effect at the expense of truth in materials. The church's steeple was somewhat modified in design after it was blown down in 1879. Although its neighborhood has been obliterated through urban renewal demolitions, the church continues to serve an active congregation. 122–8 (4/6/71).

GHENT HISTORIC DISTRICT, *roughly bounded by Olney Road, Virginia Beach Boulevard, Smith's Creek, and Brambleton Avenue*. The decades between 1890 and 1930 were a time of intensive land speculation across the nation with one of the results being a large number of planned residential suburban neighborhoods. Providing airy, attractive alternatives to dense older neighborhoods, these suburbs usually combined one or more of the popular planning theories of the day. Norfolk's Ghent neighborhood, built along the Y-shaped Smith's Creek, with its concentric, semicircular, tree-lined streets and landscaped open spaces, combines elements of the City Beautiful landscaping school with Beaux Arts planning concepts. The neighborhood was laid out by John Graham, a Philadelphia civil engineer, and was developed with a splendid range of middle- and upper-class houses between 1890 and 1905. Queen Anne, Colonial Revival, and Shingle styles predominate, with most of the houses observing a common setback line. Except for the loss of houses along Olney Road, the historic district has suffered few alterations and remains free from visual intrusions. Ghent was Norfolk's first planned suburb to offer such modern amenities as sewer, water, and gas lines. The district remains one of the most prestigious residential areas in the city. 122–38 (6/19/79).

JAMESTOWN EXPOSITION BUILDINGS, *U.S. Naval Base, Sewell's Point*. The seventeen remaining buildings of the 1907 Jamestown Exposition form a unique collection of early exposition pavilions. Erected as part of the celebration of the tricentennial of the founding of the first permanent English settlement in the New World, the complex originally contained twenty state pavilions, a history pavilion, an auditorium, and other structures. Among the remaining buildings are the Pennsylvania pavilion, a copy of Independence Hall (shown); the Maryland pavilion, a copy of Homewood; and the Ohio pavilion, a copy of Adena. Unable to agree on what to copy for Virginia, the state built a typical Georgian Revival mansion. The complex was purchased by the federal government in 1917, and the site was made into a naval base and naval air station. Most of the pavilions have since been converted to officers' quarters, and today they are known collectively as Admiral's Row. 122–54 (2/18/75).

LAFAYETTE GRAMMAR AND HIGH SCHOOL, *3109 Tidewater Drive*. The Lafayette School exhibits the architectural quality that characterized the buildings of Virginia's public school system at the beginning of the 20th century. The state constitution of 1902 provided for increased funding for public education and associated facilities, and handsome public school buildings became focal points of civic pride throughout the state. Completed in 1906, the original portion of this school was designed by Vance Hebard and was the largest school in the Norfolk County system at the time. The architect rendered the exterior in a very robust Georgian Revival style, possibly influenced by the Virginia colonial mansions. The building was enlarged in 1910 by the addition of a high school wing designed by the firm of Leigh and Deihl. The school became part of the Norfolk city system when the area was annexed in 1923. Phased out of use in the 1970s, the building is scheduled for conversion into housing. 122–43 (12/14/82).

GENERAL DOUGLAS MacARTHUR MEMORIAL, *421 City Hall Avenue*. This imposing Classical Revival public building, dominated by its Doric portico and lofty dome, was erected in 1846–50 as a city hall shortly after Norfolk became an independent city. Its architect was Portsmouth native William B. Singleton, with Thomas U. Walter of Philadelphia as consultant. It served as the city hall until 1913 when the city offices were relocated and the building became exclusively a courthouse. In 1960 the city offered the structure as a memorial and tomb for General of the Army Douglas MacArthur, whose mother was born in Norfolk. The body of World War II's allied supreme commander in the Southwest Pacific was interred under the dome in 1964. The rest of the remodeled interior now serves as a museum containing MacArthur's papers and memorabilia. 122–19 (11/16/71).

MONTICELLO ARCADE, *south end of Monticello Avenue between City Hall Avenue and Plume Street*. Although the form evolved earlier, shopping arcades became de rigueur for major cities both in Europe and the United States in the last half of the 19th century. Nearly always highly ornamented and employing large amounts of glass, these arcades provided handsome settings for fashionable shops. Designed by the firm of Neff and Thompson and opened in 1908, Norfolk's Monticello Arcade is one of only two such arcades remaining in the state. Its developer was Percy S. Stephenson, an attorney and real estate agent. Providing grand entrances to the arcade are the heroic colonnades of the two facades with their Beaux Arts ornamentation made of polychromed terra-cotta. The lofty interior has two tiers of shops above the ground floor, all flooded in daylight through a glass ceiling. Much of the arcade's original character was hidden for many years behind tawdry later shopfronts, but a recent careful restoration had brought out the building's former suave elegance. 122–66 (4/15/75).

MOSES MYERS HOUSE, *Freemason and Bank streets.* One of the finest examples of Federal architecture in the state, this town house was completed ca. 1792 for Moses Myers, a New York merchant who settled in Norfolk after the Revolution. Myers held several important mercantile and public offices including president of the Common Council and collector of customs. He entertained in his home such dignitaries as James Monroe, Lafayette, Daniel Webster, and Stephen Decatur. Along with the Taylor-Whittle house, the Myers house illustrates the sophistication of life-style achieved in this port city in the early 19th century. Contrasting with its restrained exterior are the rich Adam-style interior decorations including elaborate plasterwork ceilings, fine mantels, and other trim. Members of the Myers family occupied the house until the 1930s; hence many of the original furnishings are preserved. The house and its contents are now owned and exhibited by the Chrysler Museum. 122–17 (12/2/69).

OLD NORFOLK ACADEMY BUILDING (NORFOLK CHAMBER OF COMMERCE), *420 Bank Street.* This Greek Revival Doric temple was built to house the Norfolk Academy, a boys' school whose origins are traced to 1728 when the local authorities set aside land for the construction of a school. The school received its present name in 1787 and was chartered by the General Assembly in 1804. The cornerstone of the present building was laid in 1840; its designer was Philadelphia architect Thomas U. Walter, who also designed the dome of the U.S. Capitol. The academy vacated the building in 1915, and in 1919 it was converted to serve the juvenile and domestic relations court. In 1971 this leading example of the state's Greek Revival architecture was restored to house the Norfolk Chamber of Commerce. 122–18 (9/9/69).

OLD NORFOLK CITY HALL, *235 Plume Street.* Old Norfolk City Hall, with its fine stonework, classical decoration, and grand formality, is a beautiful example of the Neo-Palladian Revival that was popular at the end of the 19th century, especially in Great Britain. Designed in 1898 as the U.S. Post Office and Courts Building by the Baltimore firm of Wyatt and Nolting, the building illustrates the quality of works commissioned by the federal government in this period. Converted into a city hall in 1937 but abandoned with the construction of a modern city hall, the building has been carefully restored for private offices. A remarkable feature of the building is the large interior court surrounded by richly ornamented arcades. 122–82 (7/21/81).

ST. MARY'S ROMAN CATHOLIC CHURCH, *232 Chapel Street*. Dominated by its richly decorated spire, this gleaming stuccoed church is the most elaborate expression of the Early Gothic Revival mode in the state. It was erected in 1858–59 to replace an earlier building destroyed by fire and serves the Tidewater region's founding Catholic parish. The architect has not been documented, but the scholarly use of French Gothic forms has led to the attribution of the design to James Renwick, one of the few American architects of the day to rely on Gallic-Gothic precedents. No less rich than the exterior is the lofty vaulted interior containing a profusion of Victorian furnishings, stained glass, and ornamentation paralleled by no other Virginia church of the period. Noteworthy also is its 1858 pipe organ built by Richard M. Ferris and Levi U. Stuart of New York. 122–24 (2/21/78).

ST. PAUL'S EPISCOPAL CHURCH, *201 St. Paul's Boulevard*. This cruciform church, constructed in 1739, is the third to serve the Elizabeth River Parish and is the oldest building in the city of Norfolk. Originally known as Elizabeth River Parish Church, it is believed to stand on the site of a 1641 chapel, for its burying ground has been in use since that time. The building was gutted by fire during the Revolutionary War when the entire city was destroyed. It was restored within its Flemish bond brick walls and returned to active use in 1786. Congregational divisiveness caused its abandonment to the Baptists in 1805. In 1832 it received both a new Episcopal congregation and its present name, and it has remained in active use ever since. The bell tower was added in 1901; the present Georgian-style interior is the product of a very thorough renovation of 1913. 122–25 (3/2/71).

TAYLOR-WHITTLE HOUSE, *225 West Freemason Street*. The prosperity enjoyed by the Atlantic Coast port cities from Maine to Georgia in the post-Revolutionary period is reflected in the Federal town houses erected by merchants and civic leaders. Many of these cities, such as Charleston or Salem, retain quantities of these dwellings; others, New York and Norfolk among them, have only a handful remaining to show the sophisticated architecture enjoyed by leading citizens. The architectural quality of Norfolk's Taylor-Whittle house is comparable to the finest Federal houses in any of the ports, displaying the style's refined proportions and detailing on its exterior and handsome ornamentation on the interior. Located on once-fashionable West Freemason Street, the house was built ca. 1791 for either the merchant George Purdie or Norfolk mayor John Cowper. It was purchased in 1802 by Richard Taylor, an importer and recent immigrant from England. A later occupant, Taylor's son-in-law, Richard Lucien Page, accompanied Commodore Perry to Japan and later organized the state navy for Virginia's Confederate government. In 1972 the house was left to the Historic Norfolk Foundation. It is now owned by the city of Norfolk and leased for an association headquarters. 122–21 (11/3/70).

U.S. CUSTOMS HOUSE, *101 East Main Street.* Ammi B. Young (1798–1874), supervising architect of the Treasury Department, provided designs for some seventy customs houses and other government buildings throughout the country. All were solid, sophisticated schemes and established a high standard for federal government architecture. Befitting Norfolk's status as a major port, Young's customs house here ranks among his most ambitious works. For it he departed from his usual Tuscan Palazzo schemes in favor of a richly classical design with overtones of 18th-century English Palladianism. Remaining free from significant alteration since its completion in 1859, the granite structure is an early essay in fireproof construction and still serves its original function. 122–32 (12/2/69).

U.S. POST OFFICE AND COURTHOUSE (WALTER E. HOFFMAN COURTHOUSE), *600 Granby Street.* Designed by Norfolk architect Benjamin F. Mitchell and completed in 1934, the U.S. Post Office and Courthouse is Virginia's outstanding federal building in the monumental Art Deco style. The design follows the trend of the 1930s for federal architecture to serve as bold symbols expressive of democratic ideals and the strength of government. Like many federal projects of the Depression era, the building blends stylized classical forms with the Art Deco format to enhance the monumental character inside and out. Consistent with its dignified exterior is the main lobby, a grand hall ornamented with colorful stone veneers, metalwork details, and a richly decorated ceiling. The building has recently been renovated to accommodate the U.S. district court. 122–58 (10/18/83).

WELLS THEATRE, *Tazewell Street and Monticello Avenue.* Designed by the New York firm of E. C. Horne and Sons and opened in 1913, the Wells Theatre is both an expression of early 20th-century popular culture and an outstanding example of Beaux Arts theater architecture. Part of the southern vaudeville chain operated by Jacob and Otto Wells, it was described at its opening as the "most pretentious playhouse of the chain." The building displays all the lavishness associated with theaters of the period: sculptures, ornate light fixtures, stained glass, murals, and heavily encrusted plasterwork, all of which survive in a good state of preservation. Converted to a motion picture theater in the 1920s, the Wells eventually degenerated to showing X-rated films. In 1980 it was acquired and restored by the Virginia Stage Company for use as a playhouse. 122–67 (3/18/80).

WEST FREEMASON STREET HISTORIC DISTRICT, *roughly bounded by Brambleton Avenue, Boush Street, College Place, and the Elizabeth River.* The compact section near the Elizabeth River that includes West Freemason, Bute, Duke, Botetourt, Dunmore, and Yarmouth streets was one of the first neighborhoods to be established beyond the original colonial limits of Norfolk. From the 18th century through the early 20th century it was the city's leading residential area and thus contains examples of nearly all the architectural styles popular during those 120 years. Conspicuous examples are the Federal Taylor-Whittle house, the Greek Revival Lamb and Camp-Hubard houses, and the Georgian Revival Roper house. The district was spared the leveling that destroyed most of the other early downtown residential neighborhoods during the massive urban renewal programs of the 1960s. However, considerable demolition has taken place within the district since that time. While the district's cohesiveness has been weakened, it retains a sufficient quantity and variety of historic structures that an integrity of the whole yet exists. On the tree-shaded, block-paved western end of West Freemason Street the quiet dignity of old Norfolk is still keenly felt. 122–60 (12/21/71).

WILLOUGHBY-BAYLOR HOUSE, *601 East Freemason Street.* This conservative town house is a good representative of the middle-class housing erected when the city was rebuilt after its destruction during the Revolution. The lot was purchased in 1794 by William Willoughby, a local merchant and contractor, and the house was completed soon after. It was acquired in 1845 by Dr. Bayrham Baylor, who probably added the present porch and other Greek Revival touches. In 1964 the house was spared the destruction that befell many of its contemporaries through purchase by the Historic Norfolk Foundation. The foundation restored the Willoughby-Baylor house as a museum illustrating the taste of Norfolk's middle-income families of the period, in contrast to the more elegant Moses Myers house. It is now owned and exhibited by the Chrysler Museum. 122–33 (4/6/71).

NORTHAMPTON COUNTY

Probably named for the English shire, Northampton County
originally included the entire peninsula of Virginia's
Eastern Shore. The area was one of Virginia's eight original
shires established in 1634 and was first called Accomack.
The name was changed to Northampton in 1643, with the
present Accomack County separating from it ca. 1663.
Its county seat is Eastville.

BROWNSVILLE, *Nassawadox vicinity.* Sitting lonely on the edge of the Eastern Shore's oceanside marshes is this elegant and urbane Federal residence of 1806, the home of John Upshur. Upshur's ancestor John Browne, from whom the property derives its name, patented the land there in 1652. With its beautiful woodwork, the side-passage house is one of several Eastern Shore Federal houses boasting design, construction, and detailing of highest quality and perhaps sharing common craftsmen. Upshur added a long wooden wing in 1809 to accommodate his numerous relatives. The property remained in the hands of Upshur's descendants until 1978 when it was acquired and restored by the Nature Conservancy as an operations center for its program to protect the Eastern Shore's barrier islands. 65–3 (12/2/69).

CUSTIS TOMBS, *Capeville vicinity.* The monument of ca. 1750 marking the grave of John Custis IV is one of Virginia's most singular examples of colonial funerary art. The elaborately carved, pyramidal-topped marble block is decorated with the Custis family coat-of-arms, a drapery-framed inscription, and a human skull motif, all of which is the signed work of William Colley of Fenn Church Street, London. Also in the cemetery is the limestone slab of John Custis (1630–1696). The tombs are located near the site of Arlington, the Custis family seat. John Custis IV's great-grandson George Washington Parke Custis named his Fairfax County plantation, now Arlington National Cemetery, after his Eastern Shore ancestral home. The Custis tombs are maintained by the Association for the Preservation of Virginia Antiquities. 65–66 (11/5/68).

EYRE HALL, *Cheriton vicinity.* Of the Eastern Shore's many early seats, perhaps none provides a more complete picture of its upper-class plantation life than Eyre Hall. The rambling gambrel-roof house was completed in 1796, though its wing is said to incorporate a ca. 1750 dwelling. The interior of the main section is embellished with superb woodwork consisting of paneled walls and pilaster-framed chimney breasts. Adding interest is a set of ca. 1816 French scenic wallpaper by Dufour, "Les Rives de Bosphore." On the grounds are original outbuildings, formal gardens, and a family cemetery with a fine series of table tombs. The main house was built for John Eyre, grandson of Littleton Eyre who acquired the plantation from the Lee family in 1754. The property remains in the ownership of Eyre's descendants. 65–8 (9/9/69).

GLEBE OF HUNGARS PARISH, *Bridgetown vicinity.* Virginia's colonial glebe houses normally served as residences for the parish parsons and usually exhibited the same care in design, execution, and detailing found in the churches themselves. The Hungars Parish glebe house, with its glazed-header Flemish bond and interior paneling, well illustrates this consistency of quality and survives as one of the best preserved of the state's colonial glebe houses. It probably dates soon after 1745, the year in which the General Assembly authorized the building of glebe houses. The house was ordered to be sold by the Commonwealth as the result of the disestablishment. The vestry protested, and the case dragged on for years. When it was finally settled by the state Supreme Court, the parish lost possession in 1859. The property was sold by the state to a private owner in 1870. The house was restored in the 1970s after standing empty for several years. 65–33 (12/2/69).

GRAPELAND, *Wardtown*. Grapeland belongs to the Eastern Shore's group of architecturally sophisticated Federal houses that includes Brownsville, Kerr Place, Wharton Place, and others. Among the distinguishing features of these houses are precise brickwork, excellent proportions, and rich Federal detailing, both inside and out. The house, set at the head of terraces leading down to Occohannock Creek, was erected for Edward W. Addison between 1825 and 1830. Its interior contains outstanding examples of original painted wood graining and marbleizing. Grapeland stood derelict and decaying for many years but has been carefully restored by its present owner. 65–35 (6/21/77); *Virginia Historic Landmarks Board preservation easement*.

HUNGARS CHURCH, *Bridgetown*. This third church of Hungars Parish was begun in 1742 and completed by 1751 and is one of two remaining colonial churches on Virginia's Eastern Shore. As originally built, it was over 90 feet in length, making it the longest Anglican parish church in the colony. It was abandoned after the disestablishment but was restored to use in 1819. Declared unsafe in 1850, its west wall and first bay were taken down, shortening the building's length to 74 feet. The church nevertheless remains an outstanding example of colonial ecclesiastical architecture. Very precise gauged-brick arches with the rare addition of keystones highlight the windows. The intersecting window tracery dates from 19th-century repairs. The church has a beautiful isolated setting in a clearing of pines. 65–12 (7/7/70).

KENDALL GROVE, *Eastville vicinity*. Kendall Grove was erected ca. 1813 for George Parker, a member of the Virginia Convention of 1788 and later judge of the Virginia General Court. The house is one of the elegant Federal plantation houses on Virginia's Eastern Shore, most of which are of brick construction. On the interior are fine plaster cornices, reeded doorframes, paneled wainscoting, and Federal mantels, all illustrating how the Eastern Shore gentry adapted styles and fashions of urban centers to make architecturally sophisticated country residences. A long, low passage, or "colonnade," connecting the dwelling house to the kitchen is a feature indigenous to the region. 65–60 (10/21/80).

NORTHAMPTON COUNTY COURTHOUSE SQUARE HISTORIC DISTRICT, *Eastville*. The assemblage of buildings on and around the court square in Eastville includes the present (and fifth) courthouse of 1899, the 1731 courthouse and clerk's office (shown), and a ca. 1814 debtors' prison. The latter three buildings, maintained as museums by the Association for the Preservation of Virginia Antiquities, create a very interesting early court complex. The 1731 courthouse was moved to its present location in 1913 from elsewhere on the square in order to preserve it; the front wall was rebuilt in the process. Also included in the district is the ca. 1780 Eastville Inn, a rambling frame structure south of the courthouse which has had many additions. Eastville has served as Northampton's county seat since 1690. 214–7 (11/16/71).

PEAR VALLEY, *Machipungo vicinity*. This one-room yeoman's cottage is a textbook of vernacular design and displays the refinement that the colonial housebuilder could give even to the most elementary dwelling. Few other such small houses survive in Virginia; and of those that do, none is so architecturally interesting or in such a good state of preservation as Pear Valley. The interior retains its chamfered plate and chamfered ceiling joists, and the roof framing has the rare treatment of exposed rafter ends pegged into the plate. Lending the house dignity and stability is the brick end with its glazed headers forming decorative chevrons. The massive pyramidal chimney with its long tiled weatherings is typical of the Eastern Shore's earliest vernacular buildings. Historians variously date Pear Valley from the mid-17th century through the mid-18th century, but the precise date is unimportant. The significance of the structure rests with its value as a rare and indeed beautiful example of a one-room yeoman's cottage. 65–52 (5/13/69).

SOMERS HOUSE, *Jamesville vicinity*. Eastern Shore house builders gave architectural quality and fine detailing not only to their larger works but to the smaller ones as well. An excellent illustration of this phenomenon is the tiny Somers house, now standing abandoned and deteriorating in a field on Northampton County's Occohannock Neck. The glazed-header Flemish bond brickwork, careful proportions, and a refined interior paneled wall give this otherwise simple house all the dignity of a grand colonial mansion. Unlike mainland Virginia with its great plantations, the Eastern Shore was divided early into many small but prosperous independent farms whose owners took pride in their homes and made them anything but rude. The house dates after 1727, the year in which Thomas Smith gave the land to his grandson Leaven Smith, for whom the house was built. The Somers family owned it in the late 19th century. 65–23 (12/2/69).

STRATTON MANOR, *Cape Charles vicinity.* This house was erected in the third quarter of the 18th century by Benjamin Stratton, member of a Northampton County family that had owned the land since 1636. The dwelling is an example of the 18th-century vernacular architecture distinctive of Virginia's Eastern Shore. Features associated with the region are frame construction with Flemish bond brick ends, chevron patterns in the gables (obscured by paint), exterior chimneys with steep sloping haunches, and finely paneled interior chimney walls. Stratton was a chairmaker, making the house interesting as an artisan's dwelling of the Revolutionary era. 65–24 (9/16/80).

VAUCLUSE, *Bridgetown vicinity.* Named for a region of southern France, Vaucluse was long the seat of the Eastern Shore's Upshur family. It is believed that the brick-ended section of the present house was built for Littleton Upshur ca. 1784. His son Abel Parker Upshur expanded the house to approximately its present size in 1829, making it into one of the region's grandest plantation dwellings. The detailing of the newer section repeats that of the original. An annex connecting the house to the kitchen outbuilding was added ca. 1889. Abel Parker Upshur (1791–1844), who was born at Vaucluse, served President Tyler as secretary of the navy. In 1843 he was appointed secretary of state and was responsible for negotiating the treaty annexing Texas. His promising career ended abruptly in 1844 when he and other officials were killed aboard the USS *Princeton* when a cannon accidentally exploded. The plantation was subdivided for a housing development in the 1970s, but the waterfront setting of the house has been preserved. 65–28 (12/2/69).

WESTERHOUSE HOUSE, *Bridgetown vicinity.* This home of the Westerhouse family, a compact brick dwelling of ca. 1700, is a notable and rare example of the Eastern Shore's early vernacular architecture. The prototype of this small housing type is the two-unit medieval cottage of the West Country and Highland zone of England. Characteristic features of the type are the one-story elevation, steep gable roof, hall-parlor plan, and uneven arrangement of the openings. The massive pyramidal chimney is also a distinguishing feature of these houses. No influence of the bookish classicism that was to mark the Georgian style is evident. The house stood in a state of advanced deterioration until recent years when it underwent a renovation and received a new rear wing. 65–30 (9/17/74).

WESTOVER, *Eastville vicinity.* An example of 18th-century Eastern Shore colonial vernacular architecture, Westover features handsome interior paneling and a Flemish bond brick end incorporating an exterior English bond chimney with steep sloping haunches. Westover's original section, covered by a gambrel roof, probably dates to ca. 1750, the period when this roof form gained widespread popularity in both the Delmarva peninsula and Tidewater Virginia. It probably was erected for Michael Christian, Jr., who is also believed to have added the western parlor. The house has been unoccupied for many years but is protected from deterioration. 65–38 (11/18/80).

WINONA, *Bridgetown vicinity.* Winona is one of only two pre-Georgian houses in America to preserve true Jacobean diagonally set chimney stacks. Like the other example, Bacon's Castle in Surry County, Winona has a group of three stacks above a massive, exterior end chimney breast. Such chimneys were a popular form on both vernacular and sophisticated buildings in Jacobean England but were used only infrequently in the New World, probably because they were difficult to construct. Remnants of foundations projecting from the west end of the house and the wooden construction of its west end wall indicate that the house was originally a symmetrical building with a second set of stacks. The construction date has not been precisely determined, but it probably was built after 1681, the year Mathew Patrick acquired a reversionary interest in the property. 65–32 (11/5/68).

NORTHUMBERLAND COUNTY

At the tip of the Northern Neck, Northumberland County was named for the English shire. It was formed ca. 1645 from the district of Chickacoan, the name given during the 17th century to the area between the Potomac and the Rappahannock rivers. The county seat is Heathsville.

ST. STEPHEN'S EPISCOPAL CHURCH, *Heathsville.* One of the architectural highlights of the county seat community of Heathsville, St. Stephen's is an unusually pure example of the wooden Carpenters' Gothic style popular throughout America in the mid-19th century. Parish records list the church's architect as T. Buckler Chequiere, a Baltimore architect who probably was inspired by illustrations in Richard Upjohn's *Rural Architecture* (1852). Many of the building's fittings were shipped to the county by boat from Baltimore. Consecrated in 1881, a full generation after the Gothic style had reached its zenith in other parts of the country, the building is evidence of rural Virginia's slowly evolving architectural taste. St. Stephen's Parish was originally formed in 1698 and was reactivated in 1824 as part of the reawakening of the Episcopal church in Virginia after a long period of dormancy. 66–27 (9/18/79).

SPRINGFIELD, *Heathsville*. Springfield is a Federal house dominating an extensive tract of land on the edge of the village of Heathsville. Erected in 1828 by merchant William Harding, the house was enlarged in 1850, so that it now presents a blend of two different styles and is one of the more imposing 19th-century houses on the Northern Neck. The stylistic contrast can be seen particularly on the interior where rich Greek Revival ceiling medallions add interest to the otherwise restrained Federal mantels and wainscoting. The main block of the house is framed by unusual stepped parapets on the wings. Preserved on the grounds are an early office, a dairy, and a servant's house. The gardens originally were embellished with a box-wood maze. 66–11 (9/18/79).

NOTTOWAY COUNTY

*Nottoway County, in the heart of Southside Virginia, was
formed from Amelia County in 1788 and most probably was
named for the Nottoway River, which in turn was named for an
Indian tribe living along it during the early 17th century.
The county seat is Nottoway Court House.*

BURKE'S TAVERN, *Burkeville vicinity*. This simple vernacular hostelry is a reminder of a flourishing period in the area, when taverns were the scene of much local socializing and political activity. Located at a rural crossroads on the Nottoway/Prince Edward County line, the tavern fostered a tiny settlement which took the name Burke's Tavern. Although a tavern had existed at the site since the mid-18th century, the present structure was erected ca. 1827 for Samuel Burke, a militia colonel, Whig politician, and local entrepreneur. Thomas A. Smythe, the last Union general mortally wounded in the Civil War, died in the tavern on April 9, 1865. 67–47 (6/17/75).

NOTTOWAY COUNTY COURTHOUSE, *Nottoway Court House*. Nottoway's sophisticated Roman Revival courthouse is the focal point of its tiny county-seat village. Like many of Virginia's antebellum courthouses, this example shows the influence of Thomas Jefferson's architecture on the state's public buildings. It was completed in 1843 by master builder Branch H. Ellington and features such devices favored by Jefferson as the three-part Palladian scheme, Tuscan portico, triple-hung sash, and carefully crafted brickwork. 67–4 (7/17/73).

OAKRIDGE, *Blackstone vicinity.* This weatherboarded modified Georgian structure is a typical example of a residence of a prosperous planter of Virginia's southern Piedmont. It was built ca. 1800 for Burwell Smith, a Southside landowner who, in contrast to his surroundings, was described by one writer as "a particularly parsimonious and illiterate man." Although the generously proportioned house appears to have been built in two sections, the one-story wing is part of the original construction. The main rooms are ornamented with paneled wainscoting and paneled chimneypieces framed by fluted pilasters. A notable interior feature is the Chinese lattice stair railing, a stylish device for a remote rural dwelling. 67–14 (3/15/77).

SCHWARTZ TAVERN, *111 Tavern Street, Blackstone.* With much of its original fabric intact, this rambling 99-foot-long former tavern is Blackstone's oldest building. The property on which it stands was deeded to John Schwartz in 1790, and in 1798 he was granted a license to operate an ordinary. Tradition has it that the town derives its name from his last name, German for "black." In recent years the building has undergone a thorough restoration under the sponsorship of the Schwartz Tavern Authority. 142–1 (6/18/74).

ORANGE COUNTY

*Formed from Spotsylvania County in 1734, this pastoral
Piedmont county was named for William IV, Prince of Orange-
Nassau, who married Princess Anne, eldest daughter of
King George II, that same year.
Its county seat is Orange.*

BARBOURSVILLE, *Barboursville*. Until it burned on Christmas Day, 1884, James Barbour's home at Barboursville stood essentially as completed ca. 1822 from the designs supplied by Barbour's friend Thomas Jefferson. The drawings, preserved in the Massachusetts Historical Society, called for a dwelling with a recessed portico on the north front and a polygonal bay fronted by a portico on the south front, with dome above—a scheme resembling Jefferson's own home Monticello. The dome, however, was not built. Even in its ruinous state, the house presents a romantic image of the Jeffersonian ideal, a compact but architecturally sophisticated country villa in a carefully contrived landscape setting. James Barbour (1775–1842), a statesman and diplomat, held many public offices, including governor of Virginia, secretary of war, and minister to England. The ruins have recently been stabilized, and the estate has become one of Virginia's first large-scale wineries. 68–2 (9/9/69).

BERRY HILL, *Orange*. On a hill overlooking the town of Orange, Berry Hill is a Jeffersonian-style house attributed to William B. Phillips and Malcolm F. Crawford, master builders employed by Thomas Jefferson during the construction of the University of Virginia. In its original form, with its arcaded ground floor supporting an open portico above (later walled in), the house closely resembled Pavilion VII at the university. The house was constructed in 1824 for Reynolds Chapman, the county clerk, and remains, even in its altered form, one of the most successful adaptations of the Jeffersonian idiom for a private residence. Although Phillips and Crawford cannot be documented as having worked on Berry Hill, they were known to Chapman and were building Jeffersonian structures in the area at the time. 68–4 (2/19/80).

EXCHANGE HOTEL, *South Main Street, Gordonsville.* This familiar Gordonsville landmark is a forerunner of the large railroad hotels that played such an important role in the transportation history of late 19th- and early 20th-century America. The galleried structure was built in 1860 for Richard F. Omohundro next to an important railroad junction. It served as a popular stopping place for travelers until the outbreak of hostilities when, because of its strategic location, it became part of the Gordonsville Receiving Hospital, admitting more than 23,000 Confederate wounded in less than a year. It again became a hotel after the war and enjoyed a fine reputation for several decades. The building has been acquired by Historic Gordonsville, Inc. and has recently been restored. 225–8 (7/17/73).

FRASCATI, *Somerset vicinity.* Frascati, built 1821–23 for Supreme Court justice and statesman Philip Pendleton Barbour, is one the outstanding architectural monuments of the Piedmont. With its complete specifications surviving, the house is also among the best documented 19th-century dwellings of the region. It was designed and built by John M. Perry, an Albemarle County contractor who was one of the master builders employed by Thomas Jefferson for the building of the University of Virginia. With its Tuscan portico and correctly proportioned classical detailing, the house shows a strong Jeffersonian influence. The plan and general outline, however, follow the more conventional Federal schemes of that day. Remnants of the extensive original gardens survive. 68–14 (9/16/80).

GERMANNA ARCHAEOLOGICAL SITE ("ENCHANTED CASTLE" SITE), *Germanna Bridge vicinity.* After completing his term as lieutenant governor, Alexander Spotswood took up permanent residence on his extensive Orange County holdings where he erected ca. 1724 a brick mansion with numerous outbuildings and terraced gardens overlooking the Rapidan River. This country seat was near a settlement of German families called Germanna established by Spotswood a decade earlier to house workers of his iron mines and furnace. The house was destroyed by fire in the 1750s after Spotswood's death. The site remained undisturbed until the spring of 1984 when excavation was begun by the Virginia Division of Historic Landmarks. The excavation has revealed numerous pieces of stone moldings, suggesting that the house was elaborately trimmed. This conforms to William Byrd's impression of the place; after a visit in 1732, he called the house an "enchanted castle" and described it as being opulently furnished. Shown is an iron fireback produced in Spotswood's furnace and found in the rubble of the house. The excavation should provide important information on what was undoubtedly one of the foremost examples of early 18th-century domestic architecture in the colony and give new insight into the domestic life and taste of a colonial leader. The site is now owned by Historic Gordonsville, Inc. 68–43 (6/21/77).

GORDONSVILLE HISTORIC DISTRICT, *including properties along North and South Main streets and West Baker Street.* The assemblage of 19th- and early 20th-century residential, commercial, and institutional buildings composing the Piedmont community of Gordonsville reflects the vicissitudes of a Virginia railroad town. Named for Nathaniel Gordon, who kept a crossroads tavern here in the late 18th century, the hamlet exploded into a thriving transportation hub with the arrival in the 1840s and early 1850s of two railroads and two major western turnpikes. Gordonsville's growth, which reached its peak in the two decades after the Civil War, ended suddenly with completion in the early 1880s of a rival north-south railroad bypassing the town to the west. The district centers on a three-quarter-mile stretch of Main Street leading south past tree-shaded 19th-century residences and churches to the Chesapeake and Ohio Railway overpass, where the streetscape suddenly changes to a solid row of World War I–era brick commercial structures forming the town's main retail and business district. 225–30 (8/16/83).

MAYHURST, *Orange vicinity.* The vibrancy that American architects gave to the Italian Villa style is no better shown than in Mayhurst, described by William B. O'Neal as "a delicious Victorian fantasy." The architect has not been recorded; however, the stylistic similarity of Mayhurst to Camden in Caroline County has led to the attribution of the design to Norris G. Starkweather of Baltimore. The tall structure, decked out with a bracketed cornice, rusticated wood siding, and a cupola terminating in a scroll-ornamented finial, illustrates the mid-19th-century taste for the exotic, a clear break with the restraint of the previous century. Begun in 1859, the house was commissioned by Col. John Willis, a great-nephew of James Madison. Mayhurst retains its parklike setting, a rolling lawn dotted with large trees of various species. 68–25 (9/9/69).

MONTPELIER, *Montpelier Station.* James Madison, "Father of the Constitution" and fourth president of the United States, made this Orange County plantation his home for seventy-six years. Born in King George County, Madison moved with his parents to Montpelier as a young child. The core of the present mansion was built by Madison's father in 1755. Through his close friendship with Thomas Jefferson, Madison acquired a taste for classical architecture and remodeled and enlarged the house, adding a Tuscan portico in 1797–1800. He commissioned James Dinsmore and John Neilson, master builders who were working for Jefferson at Monticello, to carry out additional changes between 1809 and 1812. Among the additions they made was a neoclassical domed garden temple, a handsome example of garden architecture. The house was further enlarged ca. 1900 after it was purchased by William du Pont. Today it remains the nucleus of an estate containing farmlands, park, formal gardens, and a racetrack. Madison and his beloved wife Dolley lie buried in the family cemetery. In 1984 Montpelier became the property of the National Trust for Historic Preservation. 68–30 (9/9/69); *National Historic Landmark.*

ORANGE COUNTY COURTHOUSE, *North Main Street and Madison Road, Orange.* The Orange County Courthouse marks a radical departure from the traditional Virginia courthouse, illustrating public acceptance of exotic styles in late antebellum times. Designed by the Washington firm of Haskins and Alexander and erected in 1858–59, the building has all of the major characteristics of the Italian Villa style: deep-bracketed cornices, shallow-hipped roofs, and square tower. The building is the fourth courthouse built for Orange County. It is complemented by its clerk's office, jail, and Confederate monument. 275–3 (9/18/79).

ROCKLANDS, *Gordonsville vicinity.* Occupying a long, narrow valley between the town of Gordonsville and the estates of Montpelier and Frascati, Rocklands boasts a porticoed Georgian Revival mansion set in landscaped grounds that were once the scene of considerable Civil War activity. The mansion was erected in 1905–7 for Thomas Atkinson of Richmond on the site of a mid-19th-century residence of Richard Burton Haxall of the Richmond milling family. Its architect has not been determined, but William Lawrence Bottomley was responsible for an extensive remodeling undertaken in the 1930s at which time the high basement was removed and the whole house lowered in order to give it a more direct relationship with the surrounding parklike landscape. Bottomley also designed service buildings based on those at Upper Bremo in Fluvanna County. The work was undertaken by Mrs. Doris Neale, who also commissioned landscape architect Umberto Innocenti to design the formal gardens. 68–181 (7/20/82); *Virginia Historic Landmarks Board and Virginia Outdoors Foundation joint preservation easement.*

ST. THOMAS'S EPISCOPAL CHURCH, *119 Caroline Street, Orange.* This expression of Classical Revivalism is the successor to the original church of St. Thomas's Parish, demolished after the disestablishment. Erected 1833–34, its design, with its Tuscan portico in antis, was based on Christ Church in Charlottesville (now demolished), Thomas Jefferson's only ecclesiastical work. The designer and builder of St. Thomas's was most likely William B. Phillips, who worked for Jefferson at the University of Virginia and later built numerous Jefferson-style buildings throughout the Piedmont. The church was remodeled and enlarged in 1853 when it probably received its Gothic windows. During the Civil War, St. Thomas's served as a Confederate hospital after the battles of Cedar Mountain, Chancellorsville, the Wilderness, and Spotsylvania Court House. 275–8 (2/17/76).

SOMERSET CHRISTIAN CHURCH, *Somerset*. An unaltered example of a mid-19th-century country church, this diminutive building was erected ca. 1857 to serve a small but active Christian community in the rural neighborhood of Somerset. With its bracketed cornice and porch echoing the Italianate mode, the church departs stylistically from the Greek Revival and Gothic architecture of most country churches of the period. The interior retains its original furnishings, including its pews, still decorated with painted wood graining. The church is maintained by a diminished but dedicated congregation with services being held a minimum of once a year. 68–80 (9/19/78).

WADDELL MEMORIAL PRESBYTERIAN CHURCH, *Rapidan vicinity*. Named in honor of James Waddell, Orange County's blind preacher, this country church is Virginia's finest specimen of Carpenters' Gothic architecture. A forest of spires sprouts from the nave, transepts, and vestry of the board-and-batten structure. All of the details are formed from milled boards reduced by sawing to the desired shapes and nailed together. Built in 1874, the church was designed by J. B. Danforth, an amateur architect on the faculty of Richmond's Union Theological Seminary. His drawings are in the possession of the church. The church is on a hill overlooking the Rapidan River and broad stretches of countryside. 68–54 (6/17/75).

WILLOW GROVE, *Madison Mills vicinity*. Built in the late 18th century for Joseph Clark, the original frame residence at Willow Grove was substantially enlarged in 1848 by the addition of a brick wing and a unifying Tuscan portico. The remodeling was done for Clark's son William, who inherited Willow Grove in 1839. The resulting structure stands as an example of the influence of Thomas Jefferson's Classical Revival style on the country homes of Piedmont Virginia. The portico is accented by the distinctly Jeffersonian touch of Chinese lattice railings. The house is enhanced by its pastoral setting and collection of outbuildings. 68–49 (11/21/78).

PAGE COUNTY

Between the Blue Ridge and Massanutten mountain ranges,
Page County was most likely named for John Page,
Revolutionary patriot, congressman, and governor of Virginia
from 1802 to 1805. It was formed from Rockingham and
Shenandoah counties in 1831. Its county seat is Luray.

AVENTINE HALL, *143 South Court Street, Luray.* This Greek Revival house, with all of its ornaments and surfaces skillfully executed in wood, was built in 1852 for Peter Bock Borst, Commonwealth's attorney and a founder of the Shenandoah Valley Railroad. The house is one of the state's outstanding examples of its style, but with its slender proportions and large windows it is more akin to the Greek Revival of the North than that of the South. Lending it distinction are its columns in the Tower of the Winds order, elaborate Doric entablature, pilastered cupola, and rich interior detailing. Borst, originally from New York State, selected the various designs for the house and had them executed by his carpenter, a Mr. O'Neal. The house formerly stood west of the town and was moved to its present location in 1937. 159–1 (12/2/69).

JOHN BEAVER HOUSE, *Salem vicinity.* A decorative design formed of glazed headers in the facade brickwork distinguishes this Valley farmhouse. Such decoration is a rarity, and unfortunately it has been disfigured by a later window. Built 1825–26 for John Beaver, the two-story dwelling combines architectural elements from both Continental and Anglo-American vernacular building traditions. The decorative brickwork, double entry, and four-bay facade are related to German house forms. The hall-parlor plan and Federal woodwork are more standard eastern Virginia features. John Beaver's wife, Nancy Strickler Beaver, was a descendant of Abraham Strickler, one of the Shenandoah Valley's first settlers. 69–120 (3/20/79).

CATHERINE FURNACE, *Newport vicinity.* A relic of western Virginia's once-important iron industry, Catherine Furnace was constructed in 1836 in the tapered square shape typical of iron furnaces of the period. The furnace produced high-quality pig iron used for shells in both the Mexican and Civil wars. It went out of blast in 1887 and stood abandoned until its purchase in this century by the federal government as part of the George Washington National Forest. The structure is maintained today by the U.S. Forest Service as one of Virginia's best examples of a formerly prevalent industrial form. 69–130 (7/17/73).

FORT EGYPT, *Hamburg vicinity.* Fort Egypt, a large, full-dovetailed log house near the Shenandoah River, is one of the earliest and most complete of a small group of Germanic farmhouses. These houses recall the settlement of the Massanutten region by Germans and Swiss from Pennsylvania in the second quarter of the 18th century. Owned through most of its early existence by the Strickler and Stover families and still in the hands of Strickler descendants, the house is a voluminous building whose interior spaces were organized for work, storage, and family life throughout the agricultural year. Typical of such dwellings, it has a vaulted cooling cellar, or *Gewölbekeller.* The plan of the first floor, arranged around a massive center chimney, follows a standard Continental vernacular form. The first floor also preserves a large quantity of original woodwork and hardware, including vertical board partitions and a variety of door types. The house was built with a gable roof, but this was replaced in the 19th century by the present low hipped roof. 69–1 (2/26/79).

FORT PHILIP LONG, *Alma vicinity*. This little house is one of the early Shenandoah Valley stone houses erected by Virginia's German settlers. On the edge of a bank, the simple structure is dominated on its uphill side by a massive exterior end chimney. The house is unusual in having two cellar levels, one below the other. The lower level has a tunnel leading to a well located 100 yards away beneath a frame outbuilding. The date of this early complex is not known, but it likely was constructed in the late 18th century for Philip Long II, grandson of Philip Long who settled on this tract in 1737. Also on the property is a Greek Revival brick farmhouse built in 1856 for Isaac Long, Jr. The parlor has its original Victorian decorations, with walls painted to imitate molded plaster panels and ceilings painted to resemble intricate foliated plasterwork. 69–2 (11/21/72).

FORT RODES, *Luray vicinity*. Probably built by John Rodes II in the fourth quarter of the 18th century, this center-chimney log *Flurküchenhaus* (three-room-plan house) was, like many Rhenish style houses in Page County, anglicized in the mid-19th century by the removal of the central stack and the construction of end chimneys. The *Flurküchenhaus* plan consists of a narrow *Küche* (kitchen), a *Stube* (parlor), and a *Kammer* (chamber). Like most German-type houses, Fort Rodes has a vaulted cellar space used as a food storage room. It is believed to stand on the site of the first Rodes house, scene of the last recorded Indian attack in Page County, in 1764. 69–18 (11/15/77).

FORT STOVER, *Luray vicinity*. This two-story stone house, built in the late 18th century for the Stover family, is one of Page County's early German dwellings. Remarkably well preserved, Fort Stover retains early woodwork still covered with what appears to be original paint. As in a number of these houses, the architecture shows the influence of Anglo-American models, particularly in the use of end chimneys instead of the more purely German center chimney. Despite this, the house employs the traditional German three-room floor plan, known as the *Flurküchenhaus* plan because of the location of the kitchen, or *Küche*, in the main part of the house. Another Germanic feature is the vaulted cellar room associated with vernacular houses of the Rhineland and used as a cool area for the storage of perishable foods. The defensive appearance of these cellar vaults has led to the mistaken notion that houses having such rooms were built as forts. 69–5 (11/15/77).

HEISTON-STRICKLER HOUSE, *Luray vicinity*. On a bank above the South Fork of the Shenandoah River, the Heiston-Strickler house, also known as the Old Stone House, is among the best preserved of Page County's Germanic dwellings. The house was built ca. 1790 either for Jacob Heiston or his son Abraham and has remained in the ownership of their descendants. The three-room floor plan, vaulted cellar, two-bay facade, and hillside siting are all architectural features inherited from central European prototypes and introduced into the region by settlers of Germanic origin moving from Pennsylvania. Evidence of English ideas influencing the ethnic tradition is shown in the use of common-rafter framing and end chimneys rather than principal-purlin framing and a center chimney, features more characteristic of German houses. The house underwent alterations in the early 19th century, but the original plan is evident, and much of its original plain woodwork survives. 69–17 (4/18/78).

JEREMEY'S RUN ARCHAEOLOGICAL SITE, *Shenandoah National Park*. The location of Jeremey's Run to the south of a complex of springs and marsh yet within several rich ecological zones probably drew prehistoric peoples to this spot for millennia. The relatively confined habitable area contains a concentration of lithic debris from the Middle Archaic through the Late Woodland periods (ca. 5000 B.C.–A.D. 1600), making the site important for understanding prehistoric life in the Shenandoah Valley. 69–202 (9/16/82).

MASSANUTTON HEIGHTS, *Salem vicinity*. Massanutton Heights is an undisturbed early 19th-century Valley farmstead, providing an informative picture of the material culture of German-American families in the region. The plain exterior of the main dwelling masks gaily painted interior wall decorations executed soon after the house was built. Provincial in character, the parlor work includes stenciled floral borders imitating the printed border papers popular in the Federal period. In place of a cornice are painted swags of drapery with fringe and tassels. Below the chair rail the plaster is painted to resemble paneled wainscoting. Woodwork in other parts of the house is painted in imitation of tiger maple. The artist has not been identified, but it may have been Johannes Spitler, a relative of the owner who was known for his fancy painted furniture. The property derives its name from its site above Massanutton Old Fields, one of the earliest settled areas of Page County. The house, dating from ca. 1820, was built for John R. and Elizabeth Strickler Burner, whose descendants own it today. Several early farm buildings are preserved on the property. 69–123 (2/17/76).

MAUCK'S MEETING HOUSE (MILL CREEK MEET-ING HOUSE), *Hamburg.* The congregation that built Mauck's Meeting House was organized ca. 1772 by John Koontz and consisted of both Mennonites and Baptists, dissenters who played an influential role in the early society of the Shenandoah Valley. The earliest mention of the building was recorded in 1798. The plain log structure was erected on land owned by Daniel Mauck. In 1807 Mauck's son Joseph deeded the property to the "Sundry persons . . . friends of religion and good order" who had been using it. The Mennonites eventually left the area, leaving the Baptists in control. The congregation also consisted of black slaves and "free men of color." Although dominated by Baptists, the church was maintained for use by all Christians and attracted preachers of various denominations. The building is maintained today as a historic shrine by the Page County Heritage Association. 69–6 (12/16/75).

PAGE COUNTY COURTHOUSE, *116 South Court Street, Luray.* Page County's Roman Revival courthouse, atop one of the highest points of the town of Luray, is one of Virginia's antebellum public buildings erected by master builders formerly employed by Thomas Jefferson for the construction of the University of Virginia. Completed in 1833, the building was designed and constructed by William B. Phillips, mason, and Malcolm F. Crawford, carpenter, both of whom adopted the third president's distinctive style. This talented pair incorporated into their design a temple-form building with a Tuscan pediment containing a large lunette window, characteristics associated particularly with Jeffersonian buildings. The brick arcade is a feature favored by Jefferson but was also a form traditional for Virginia courthouses since the colonial period. The arcaded one-story wings are original. The general design and detailing of the courthouse are very similar to that provided by Phillips and Crawford for the Madison County Courthouse. 159–4 (1/16/73).

STEVENS COTTAGE, *210 Maryland Avenue, Shenandoah.* This sophisticated little structure was completed in 1891 to serve as the office of the newly organized Shenandoah Land and Improvement Company. Like numerous Valley communities, the town of Shenandoah experienced the land boom of the 1890s that accompanied the construction of the Norfolk and Western Railway. Anticipating growth from industrial and resource development, land companies were formed to attract residents and investors. To design its office, the Shenandoah Land and Improvement Company selected Washington architect William M. Poindexter, who designed numerous other buildings in the state, including Randolph-Macon Woman's College and the Virginia State Library building in Richmond. Poindexter provided a compact, imaginative composition in the Queen Anne style. Shenandoah's boom was short-lived. In 1902 the office was sold to Mary and Edna Stevens. After the latter died in 1968, the building was acquired by the Page County Heritage Association and has been developed into a museum of local history. 69–94 (12/16/75).

THE WHITE HOUSE, *Hamburg vicinity*. Taking its name from its whitewashed stucco covering, the White House was erected ca. 1760 by the Reverend Martin Kauffman II. Kauffman founded the Mennonite Baptist Church and held meetings in his house. He later removed himself from the Baptists in a disagreement over their promilitary stand and in 1793 formed the Separatist Independent Baptist Church. Kauffman's house began as a two-story, center-chimney *Flurküchenhaus,* or three-room-plan house with interior kitchen. Other features of the house type are a vaulted cooling cellar and a two-level storage loft. The interior finish of the White House was remodeled in the Federal style, and it retains striking woodwork and much early paint from that alteration. Currently unoccupied but maintained, the house preserves its rural setting in the shadow of Massanutten Mountain. 69–12 (11/15/77).

PATRICK COUNTY

Named for the Revolutionary patriot Patrick Henry, this county at the southern end of Virginia's section of the Blue Ridge Mountains was formed in 1790 from Henry County. Its county seat is Stuart.

BOB WHITE COVERED BRIDGE, *Woolwine vicinity.* Covered bridges are a distinctly American building form. Hundreds of these structures formerly adorned rural byways across the country. Most have disappeared, but those that remain excite an intensity of affection given few other types of structures. In Virginia covered bridges are a rarity, and the Bob White Bridge is one of only two still in use as part of the state's highway system. Later than most, the bridge was constructed in 1920–21 under the direction of Walter Weaver, whose family assisted in the endeavor. The bridge is an eighty-foot span of heavy oak timber framing. The exterior is covered in board and batten, while the interior has diagonal sheathing. Today, the bridge is used mainly by churchgoers heading to the nearby South River Church of the Brethren. 70–27 (4/17/73).

JACK'S CREEK COVERED BRIDGE, *Woolwine vicinity.* Probably the most elementary of the state's few remaining covered bridges, the Jack's Creek Bridge presents a nostalgic image of rural America. Like the nearby Bob White Covered Bridge, the Jack's Creek Bridge was designed by the local carpenter Walter Weaver. Charlie Vaughan served as the builder. The 48-foot span was completed in 1914 and employs heavy oak framing covered with board-and-batten sheathing. A space just below the eaves was left open for light and ventilation. The bridge is preserved as a landmark but is no longer in use, being paralleled by a later bridge. 70–2 (4/17/73).

PATRICK COUNTY COURTHOUSE, *Main and Blue Ridge streets, Stuart.* The courthouse in the village of Stuart has served as the focal point of its southern Piedmont county for over 150 years. The dignified albeit provincial edifice is an example of the tripartite Roman Revival public buildings whose designs were inspired by the works of Thomas Jefferson and the master builders who worked under him. The building was commissioned in 1819 but not put up until 1822. It was designed and built by Abram Staples, a local contractor who had served on the building committee. 307–1 (9/17/74).

REYNOLDS HOMESTEAD, *Critz vicinity.* Richard Joshua Reynolds (1850–1918), who founded the R. J. Reynolds Tobacco Company in 1875, was born one of sixteen children at this Patrick County homestead. The plain Greek Revival plantation house was begun in 1843 for Reynolds's father, Hardin William Reynolds, and was later enlarged to its present form. R. J. Reynolds is credited with the founding of the modern tobacco industry, which helped bring about the economic rehabilitation of the South after the Civil War and has contributed to the economic stability enjoyed by many Virginia and North Carolina cities today. Originally called Rock Spring, the 700-acre plantation is now maintained as a research center by the Virginia Polytechnic Institute Educational Foundation. Seven acres of the property, including the house, outbuildings, and family cemetery, were retained by the Reynolds family and have been developed as a museum and learning center for mid-19th-century plantation life. 70–5 (11/3/70); *National Historic Landmark.*

CITY OF PETERSBURG

The origins of Petersburg are traced to 1645 with the founding of a garrison and fur-trading post known as Fort Henry on the site of an Indian village called Appamattuck. The present name, dating from 1733, honors Peter Jones, who accompanied William Byrd II on expeditions to the Virginia backcountry. Petersburg was officially established in 1748 and incorporated as a town in 1784. It was incorporated as a city in 1850.

APPOMATTOX IRON WORKS, *20–28 Old Street*. This complex of some nine functionally related structures forms one of the most complete physical records of an early iron foundry in the country. The buildings are part of a block of Federal-period commercial/residential structures lining Old Street in the heart of the city's historic district. Although the principal buildings were not originally intended for industrial use, iron was made here as early as 1850. The Appomattox Foundry Company, as it was first called in 1876, began at 33 Old Street but moved to its present location after 1899. The foundry remained in business until 1946. The machine shop operated until 1952, and the mill and supply store finally closed down in 1972, leaving an undisturbed collection of patterns, molds tools, machines, and other associated objects. The property has been developed for retail and museum use, preserving the artifacts and flavor of a segment of Virginia's industrial history. 123–87 (4/20/76).

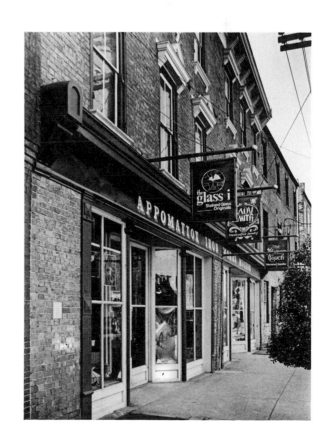

BATTERSEA, *793 Appomattox Street*. Battersea displays, perhaps best, the Palladian influence on Virginia's finer colonial plantation houses. With its five-part format, Battersea has the broken massing strongly advocated by Palladio for villa and farmhouse design. The elegant but unpretentious house was built ca. 1770 for John Banister, a Revolutionary delegate, congressman, and signer of the Articles of Confederation. Battersea's design may have been influenced by Thomas Jefferson, a close friend of Banister and an advocate of Palladian forms. The house has been remodeled more than once. The three-part windows and much trim, both inside and out, date from the early 19th century, although the elaborate Chinese lattice stair, the finest of its type in the state, is original. The center block at one time was fronted by a two-level portico, of which only the lower tier remains. Whether the stucco is an original feature is debatable. Despite the development of much of the plantation's former acreage for industrial and residential use, the house preserves a well-protected rural setting above the Appomattox River. 123–59 (5/13/69).

BLANDFORD CHURCH, *319 South Crater Road*. This structure, Petersburg's oldest building, was built by Thomas Ravenscroft in 1737 as the third church of Bristol Parish. Its north wing and the brick wall surrounding the church's original burying ground, were added between 1752 and 1770. The church was abandoned after the disestablishment and fell into ruins, but its brick walls survived relatively unharmed. Around the ruins was developed Blandford Cemetery, a large municipal graveyard. In 1901 the city council authorized the Petersburg Ladies' Memorial Association to restore the building as a monument to the Confederate dead. As part of the restoration, the Ladies' Association commissioned Louis Comfort Tiffany to design stained-glass windows for each state of the Confederacy. This collection of Tiffany glass, including a special window donated by Tiffany, is one of Virginia's artistic treasures. 123–39 (4/18/72).

CENTRE HILL, *Centre Hill Lane*. Few of Virginia's antebellum houses were given the scale and elegance of Centre Hill, a town mansion which illustrates the prosperity and sophistication enjoyed by Petersburg in the first half of the 19th century. The house was built in 1823 for Robert Bolling, who amassed a fortune in Petersburg real estate and industrial development. It was made more architecturally elaborate through a remodeling of the 1850s when the present veranda was added and much of the interior trim was replaced by fancier work. After the siege of Petersburg, the house was taken for Union headquarters by Gen. G. L. Hartsuff, who was visited here by President Abraham Lincoln on April 7, 1865. Centre Hill remained the home of the Bollings until 1900 when it was purchased by Charles Hall Davis, who further embellished the interior. President William Howard Taft was a guest at Centre Hill when he visited Petersburg in 1901. Recently restored by the city, the house is now a museum. 123–57 (11/21/72).

CITY MARKET, *bounded by Old Street, River Street, Rock Street, and Cockade Alley*. Orson Squire Fowler's treatise *A Home for All, or the Gravel Wall and Octagon Mode of Building* (1848) extolling the advantages of octagonal buildings resulted not only in the construction of numerous octagonal houses but in the erection of other eight-sided structures, including Petersburg's City Market of 1879. The focus of the city's commercial area, the unusual market building is the fourth to be located on the site, the first one having been erected in 1787. The building is notable both for its shape and for its decorative cast-iron brackets supporting the canopy and projecting market shed. Although the exterior still provides stalls for area farmers, the interior has been converted into a restaurant. 123–50 (11/5/68).

EXCHANGE BUILDING, *15–19 West Bank Street*. In Petersburg this splendid Doric temple-form Greek Revival building was erected in 1841 to house the Exchange, the city's cotton and tobacco auction house. The design for the building was supplied by a Mr. Berrien of New York. As originally constructed, the Exchange stood on an open arcade where the products were displayed and traded. Public meetings took place in the domed hall above. The building was converted into a police court in this century, and the arcades were closed in. The building was restored by the city in the mid-1970s and is now a museum commemorating Petersburg's Civil War years. The arcades, however, have remained closed. 123–51 (11/5/68); *National Historic Landmark*.

FARMERS' BANK, *19 Bollingbrook Street*. The Farmers' Bank of Virginia, incorporated in 1812, opened its Petersburg branch in 1817 with the completion of this three-story Federal structure on Bollingbrook Street. As was customary, well-appointed living quarters were provided on the upper floors for the bank's executive officer. The branch continued in operation through the Civil War but was forced to liquidate its assets in 1866 by an act of the General Assembly affecting all state banks. The building then passed through numerous owners and served various functions until the 1960s when it was conveyed to the Association for the Preservation of Virginia Antiquities, which restored it as a banking museum. Still preserved is the fine woodwork of the residential stories and the vault in the banking area. 123–67 (1/18/72).

FOLLY CASTLE HISTORIC DISTRICT, *on West Washington and Perry streets*. This one-block residential neighborhood containing fourteen late 18th- and 19th-century houses and one 19th-century church was once one of Petersburg's leading residential neighborhoods. Folly Castle (center), a wood-frame Georgian mansion with later modification, was erected in 1763 for Peter Jones V., whose progenitor and namesake was the source for the name of Petersburg, and is the best known individual structure within the district. The Rambout-Donnan and McIlwaine-Friend houses, the Jonathan Smith residence and schoolhouse, and the Gothic Revival Second Presbyterian Church are also architecturally noteworthy structures. The church contains outstanding Gothic-style plasterwork on its interior. 123–96 (2/26/79).

NATHANIEL FRIEND HOUSE, *27–29 Bollingbrook Street*. Nathaniel Friend, Jr., an import-export merchant and former mayor of the city, had this component of Petersburg's urban Federal architecture built in 1815–16. Standing across Cockade Alley from the Farmers' Bank building, the Friend house is in the heart of the downtown. Although the house has been abandoned for many years and has had its first floor altered, the excellent Federal woodwork of the upper floors remains largely intact. Several recent attempts to have this structure restored have failed, leaving it in jeopardy. It remains, however, a significant historic and architectural resource in an area of the city which has seen much of its early fabric disappear. 123–66 (4/20/76).

McILWAINE HOUSE, *Market Square at Pellam and Cockade alleys*. No finer expression of the quality of Petersburg's Federal wooden architecture remains in the city than the McIlwaine house. Relatively conventional on the exterior, its interior, most notably the parlor, is enriched with woodwork displaying the intricate elaboration characteristic of the city's older buildings. The delicate parlor chimneypiece flanked by arched recesses is a testament to the talent and sophistication that existed in the city by 1815 when the house was built. Its first occupant was George Jones, one of the city's mayors. From 1831 to 1878 it was the home of Archibald Graham McIlwaine, an industrialist and financier. The house was threatened with demolition in the early 1970s when a road was planned through its lot on South Market Street. The building was donated to the Association for the Preservation of Virginia Antiquities and was moved to its present site near the City Market where it has undergone restoration. 123–18 (6/19/73).

PETERSBURG CITY HALL, *129–141 North Union Street*. In the 1850s Ammi B. Young, supervising architect of the U.S. Treasury Department, was commissioned to design a series of customs houses in cities across the country. Although each design differed, each was a superb statement in the then popular Renaissance Revival mode. With this effort, the Treasury Department was attempting to establish consistency and to set a high standard for federal buildings. Young's Petersburg Customs House, now the City Hall, was erected in 1856–59 and followed his formula of fireproof construction, dignified proportions, lean ornamentation, and granite masonry. The building served as the city's Confederate headquarters in the Civil War, and the raising of the American flag from the rooftop on April 3, 1865, signaled the end of the siege of Petersburg, one of the longest battles of the war. The building was expanded three bays ca. 1900 and in 1938 was acquired by the city to serve as the City Hall. 123–35 (4/18/78).

PETERSBURG COURTHOUSE, *Court House Square*. One of the Commonwealth's most beautiful public buildings, the Petersburg Courthouse is a testament to the talents of its architect, Calvin Pollard of New York. Completed in 1840, the Greek Revival structure employs the Tower of the Winds order in both its slender portico and its elaborate octagonal clock tower. The tower, topped by a statue of Justice, was used as a sighting mark by Union artillery during the Civil War siege of the city. The courthouse's exterior survives unchanged; the interior has undergone considerable remodeling but preserves an outstanding coffered domed ceiling in the courtroom. The building still houses the city's courts and remains a dominant architectural element of Petersburg's skyline. 123–45 (4/17/73).

PETERSBURG NATIONAL MILITARY PARK, *extending from the western side of Fort Lee, through south Petersburg into Dinwiddie County.* The Petersburg National Military Park consists of a vast network of fortifications and entrenchments constructed by both Union and Confederate armies during the siege of Petersburg from June 1864 to April 1865. The earthworks meander for twenty-seven miles along the eastern, southern, and western outskirts of the city. Perhaps most prominent among these scars of war is the Crater, a large depression resulting from a Union army effort to tunnel under Confederate lines and breech them by setting off a huge charge of explosives in the tunnel. The charge went off on July 30, 1864, but the effort failed because of the quick response by Confederate general William Mahone. Abundantly supplied by convoys docking at City Point, the Union forces gradually wore down the starving remnants of Lee's army, forcing the Confederate commander to abandon his lines and retreat west, giving up defense of the capital in Richmond in the process. The siege of Petersburg, the first instance of modern trench warfare, was the final great effort of the Civil War. Outmaneuvered by Grant's army during his retreat, Lee was forced to surrender within a week at Appomattox. 123–71 (10/18/83).

PETERSBURG OLD TOWN HISTORIC DISTRICT, *including the lower part of the central business district as well as the High Street and Grove Avenue neighborhoods.* This large district incorporates approximately 250 buildings on 190 acres of downtown Petersburg. One of Virginia's oldest cities, Petersburg began as a fur-trading post in the mid-17th century. The district possesses a diversity of residential, commercial, and industrial architecture, mostly of the 19th and early 20th centuries. Of special interest are the 19th-century houses in a variety of styles lining High Street (shown), as well as a group of early workers' cottages clustered in the southwest portion of the area. Railroad buildings, factories, tobacco warehouses, an ironworks, and a variety of automotive buildings are spread along the Appomattox River. Although it has suffered fires, Civil War destruction, and commercial redevelopment, the district preserves a notable assemblage of historic buildings. 123–97 (11/20/79).

POPLAR LAWN HISTORIC DISTRICT, *roughly bounded by Surrey Lane and South Jefferson, Mars, and Harrison streets.* The Poplar Lawn Historic District is a 19th-century residential neighborhood centered on a two-block public park originally known as Poplar Lawn and now designated Central Park. The park was set aside as a place of recreation as early as 1800. In 1846 it was acquired by the city and developed into a romantically landscaped common in the style of Andrew Jackson Downing. The park has been the scene of many public gatherings and military exercises. Through the mid- and late 19th century, many houses were erected in the adjacent eleven blocks, most of them detached and set in tree-dotted yards. Although the park itself has lost much of its early character, it has seen some recent restoration. The neighborhood has retained its genteel air, and many of its houses have been rehabilitated. Architectural highlights of the district are the Federal-period Zimmer house and the Georgian Revival Trinity United Methodist Church. 123–94 (2/26/79).

STRAWBERRY HILL, *235 Hinton Street*. When it was built for William Barksdale in the 1790s, Strawberry Hill followed the tripartite Palladian form, consisting of a two-story center section flanked by one-story wings. The house was sold in 1800 to William Haxall, who in 1815–16 enlarged it by raising the wings to two stories. Despite this change, the house retains its rich early appointments, including a delicately carved pedimented doorway approached by marble steps with scrolled wrought-iron railings. The interior woodwork is highlighted by shell-carved cupboards flanking a paneled dining room chimneypiece. The house underwent significant alterations in the 1880s when it was partitioned into three separate residences, and the entrance was placed off center. The disfiguring changes are being removed in an effort to restore the house as one of Petersburg's finest late Georgian residences. 123–86 (11/19/74).

TABB STREET PRESBYTERIAN CHURCH, *21 West Tabb Street*. Philadelphia architect Thomas U. Walter gave Virginia a powerful interpretation of the Grecian mode with his 1843 Tabb Street Presbyterian Church. Walter, who is remembered chiefly for his work on the U.S. Capitol, was perhaps most adept with the Greek orders, as shown in the church's Doric portico and its interior apse. The apse is fronted by a colonnade in a freely adapted Tower of the Winds order, creating one of the more dramatic spaces of its type in the country. The church originally had a square belfry topped by a tapered spire, but this was removed in 1938. The present building is the third to serve the congregation since its organization in 1813. 123–43 (2/21/78).

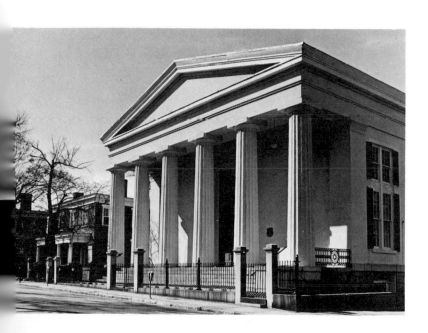

THOMAS WALLACE HOUSE, *South Market and Brown streets*. Thomas Wallace, a merchant and lawyer, had this Italianate residence erected in 1855 on Market Street, then the main street of the city's most fashionable quarter. The finely built structure features a deep bracketed cornice, pressed-brick veneer, and cast-iron window cornices. The house served briefly as the headquarters of Gen. Ulysses S. Grant. On April 3, 1865, Grant met with President Abraham Lincoln in Wallace's library to discuss the final strategy of the Civil War, a meeting which was Lincoln's last with his commanding general. Today, the house is among the few remaining of Market Street's grand dwellings. The classical veranda with its curved projection is a later embellishment. 123–31 (4/15/75).

WASHINGTON STREET METHODIST CHURCH, *14–24 East Washington Street*. Erected in 1842, the Washington Street Methodist Church was for many years the leading church of its denomination in the state. Here was held the first General Conference of the Methodist Church South in 1846, an outgrowth of the schism that developed among Methodists over abolition. It was also the scene of the first consecration of bishops of the Methodist Church South. The building was converted into a Confederate hospital in the Civil War. The church has undergone two major alterations since its completion, resulting in an impressive composition. A full Doric portico was applied to the original portico in antis in 1890. The steeple was removed in 1906, and in 1923, under architect Fred A. Bishop, the flanking wings were added, each with its own Doric portico. 123–44 (6/17/80).

PITTSYLVANIA COUNTY

The largest of Virginia's counties, Pittsylvania, near the center of the state's southern border, was named for the English statesman William Pitt. It was formed from Halifax County in 1766. The county seat is Chatham, which honors Pitt's earldom.

BERRY HILL, *Berry Hill vicinity.* Located hard along the North Carolina border, Berry Hill is a remarkably complete Southside Virginia plantation complex with a sprawling, much-evolved dwelling house and twenty outbuildings, an unusually high number. Most of the farm structures are of log construction, while the outbuildings directly serving the house, including the kitchen/laundry, dairy, and smokehouse are wood frame, illustrating an architectural hierarchy sometimes employed in secondary structures. The present form of the main house is the result of accommodating the nine generations of the Perkins-Wilson-Hairston-Sims family who have owned the property since the 1760s. Begun ca. 1812 as a plain three-bay, two-story structure, it is now a jumble of wings, chimneys, porches, and roofs, the latest section of which was built ca. 1910. 71–6 (2/15/77).

DAN'S HILL, *Danville vicinity*. The main house of this Dan River plantation is one of the large brick dwellings erected during the region's period of ascendancy in the early 19th century. The formal five-bay structure was built ca. 1833 for Robert Wilson, a Pittsylvania County planter. Its close similarity to another Pittsylvania County house, Oak Hill, designed and built by James Dejarnett, an area builder, has led to the attribution of Dan's Hill to Dejarnett. In contrast to its relatively plain exterior, the interior of Dan's Hill is finely trimmed with Federal woodwork, early marble mantels, and ornamental plasterwork ceilings. The several contemporary outbuildings include an octagonal summerhouse and a brick greenhouse, both relatively scarce examples of their respective types. The formal gardens, maintaining a 19th-century layout of walks and beds, are a significant element of the complex. 71–11 (10/17/78).

LITTLE CHERRYSTONE, *Chatham vicinity*. This Pittsylvania County farmhouse has two distinct and contrasting sections. Its one-story frame wing, a rural 18th-century Virginia vernacular dwelling, was probably standing before Thomas Hill Wooding acquired the property in 1790. The otherwise simple house has a handsome exterior end chimney with glazed-header Flemish bond and two sets of weatherings. To this small house Wooding added in the early 19th century a two-story brick section, a finely detailed provincial interpretation of the Federal style. The interior woodwork of the later section is some of the most interesting in the region, consisting of elaborately carved mantels, wainscoting, and cornices. Some of the woodwork retains early marbleizing. Although one of the county's best examples of regional architecture, Little Cherrystone has stood in run-down condition for many years. 71–36 (9/9/69).

MOUNTAIN VIEW, *Tight Squeeze vicinity*. Virginia's southern Piedmont experienced great agricultural prosperity between 1800 and the Civil War. Evidence of this can be seen in a group of large brick houses scattered through Pittsylvania and Halifax counties that formed the cores of vast plantations. While a few were in the more stylish Greek and Gothic modes, most were executed in a relatively restrained Federal style, employing fine brickwork, symmetrical facades, and refined interior trim. Mountain View, built between 1840 and 1842 for Thomas Smith Jones, is typical of these dwellings. It may have been designed and built by James Dejarnett, a regional builder. The house's double parlors are noteworthy for their plasterwork ceilings, glazed cupboards, and Greek Revival mantels. The place has remnants of an extensive formal garden and landscaped park, features found at many of the region's estates. Completing the picture of a flourishing plantation seat are several formally placed outbuildings, including an office, a schoolhouse, and a kitchen. 71–25 (6/19/79).

OAK HILL, *Oak Ridge vicinity.* Oak Hill's Federal plantation house is probably the most ambitious of a group of dwellings erected in the first half of the 19th century along the Dan River in Pittsylvania County. It was built in 1823–25 as the home of Samuel Hairston, one of the state's largest landholders and slave owners. Hairston engaged local builder James Dejarnett to erect the house, which, according to the original contract, was "to be fully built of brick fifty fore feet wide, to contain three seller rooms, fore rooms a passage and pass way first floure above the seller, & appropriate rooms the second floure." Although large, the house is conservative for its date. The woodwork, however, was decorated with fancy graining and marbleizing, much of which survives. Complementing the house was an extensive terraced garden, of which a writer for the *Richmond Whig and Public Advertiser* stated in 1851: "I have traveled over fifteen states of this union and have never seen anything comparable to his yard and garden." The house has been unoccupied for many years, and only the skeleton of the garden remains. The place, however, is being preserved against further deterioration by Hairston descendants. 71–26 (9/18/79).

OLD CLERK'S OFFICE, *Chatham.* Built in 1812 to serve the 1783 Pittsylvania courthouse, the clerk's office is the oldest public building in Chatham. Formerly the chief repository of the county's official records, it served from 1813 to 1852 as the office of William Tunstall, Jr., and his son William H. Tunstall, who succeeded him as clerk in 1836. The simple brick structure lost its intended function in 1853 with the construction of the present courthouse, which accommodated a new clerk's office. A one-room addition of 1833 has been destroyed, leaving the building its original size and form. 187–2 (10/20/81).

PITTSYLVANIA COUNTY COURTHOUSE, *Chatham.* The Pittsylvania County Courthouse is Chatham's principal architectural landmark. Typical of Virginia's mid-19th-century court structures, the building has a quiet, understated dignity. L. A. Shumaker, a regional master builder, was paid $10,000 to design and erect the building to replace an earlier wooden structure which had become inadequate for the tobacco-rich county. Completed in 1853, the new courthouse was modeled after that of Campbell County, a one-story T-shaped structure on a high basement. The courthouse facade is fronted by a Doric portico above which is an Italianate clocktower. Of particular interest is the well-preserved courtroom embellished with rich plasterwork, some of the best of its type in the state. The ceiling has an elaborate medallion with Gothic-style ornamentation and is framed by a heavily ornamented plaster cornice. The courthouse is the third to serve the county and remains in regular use. 187–7 (6/16/81).

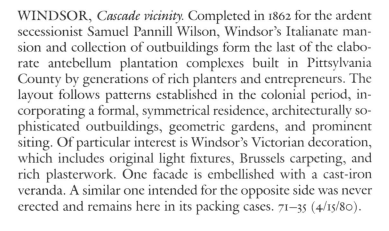

WINDSOR, *Cascade vicinity.* Completed in 1862 for the ardent secessionist Samuel Pannill Wilson, Windsor's Italianate mansion and collection of outbuildings form the last of the elaborate antebellum plantation complexes built in Pittsylvania County by generations of rich planters and entrepreneurs. The layout follows patterns established in the colonial period, incorporating a formal, symmetrical residence, architecturally sophisticated outbuildings, geometric gardens, and prominent siting. Of particular interest is Windsor's Victorian decoration, which includes original light fixtures, Brussels carpeting, and rich plasterwork. One facade is embellished with a cast-iron veranda. A similar one intended for the opposite side was never erected and remains here in its packing cases. 71–35 (4/15/80).

YATES TAVERN, *Gretna vicinity.* Yates Tavern is a key landmark in Virginia's vernacular architecture, representing an intermediary state in the transition and translation of the 17th-century Tidewater hall-parlor house form into the mountain region building forms prevalent in the 19th century. Its two-room plan, exterior end chimney, and corner stair are features common to simple houses in both regions and both centuries. A strikingly curious element of Yates Tavern is the eight-inch jetty, or overhang, at the second-floor level on each long side, a detail common in early New England houses but unique in Virginia. The jetty is probably not original but rather the result of an early remodeling which placed a full second story upon the existing framing of a box cornice. The tavern's construction date is uncertain but a court order of 1788 mentioning "Yates's Old House" may refer to the present building. Samuel Yates, who is buried near the building, bought a license in 1818 "to keep a house of public entertainment where he now resides." The tavern stood unmaintained for many years but was restored by Pittsylvania County as a Bicentennial project. 71–60 (11/19/74).

CITY OF PORTSMOUTH

One of several port cities lining Hampton Roads, Portsmouth was established in 1752 and named by its founder, William Crawford, for the English naval port. It was incorporated as a town in 1836 and as a city in 1858.

CRADOCK HISTORIC DISTRICT, *bounded by George Washington Highway, Victory Boulevard, and Paradise Creek.* A model community developed by the federal government, Cradock was laid out in 1918 to accommodate the rapid influx of workers to the Norfolk Naval Shipyard during World War I. The planning of the community was sponsored by the U.S. Housing Corporation with architectural work provided by the New York firm of George B. Post and Sons. Named in honor of British rear admiral Sir Christopher Cradock, whose fleet was sunk by the German navy in 1914, the street layout followed the form of an anchor, with the focal point being Afton Park, the central town square highlighted by a bandstand. Some 759 single-family frame dwellings were built in several styles to prevent monotony, and schools, recreational areas, churches, and commercial areas were provided. Cradock was originally segregated; black shipyard workers were accommodated in federally sponsored housing in Truxtun nearby. Cradock remains largely a working-class neighborhood; a strong sense of community pride has helped to maintain its identity for more than half a century. 124–37 (5/21/74).

DRYDOCK NUMBER ONE, *Norfolk Naval Shipyard.* Constructed of large blocks of Massachusetts granite, with its sides built up in a series of stepped tiers, this structure is one of the first two drydocks erected by the U.S. government. Begun in 1827 and completed in 1834, it remains in daily use at the Norfolk Naval Shipyard, the nation's oldest shipyard. Here the Confederate navy rebuilt the frigate *Merrimac*, which was renamed the *Virginia* and became the world's first battle-tested ironclad ship. The overall length of the drydock is 319½ feet; it remains as built except for the replacement of its caisson. 124–29 (12/2/69); *National Historic Landmark.*

OLD PORTSMOUTH COURTHOUSE, *Court and High streets*. Portsmouth's former courthouse, the pivotal landmark of the city's Four Corners, dates from 1846 when it was constructed as the Norfolk County Courthouse. It continued to function in that capacity until 1960 when the county was incorporated as the city of Chesapeake and the seat of government was moved to Great Bridge. The building served as the Portsmouth Courthouse until the next decade when its judicial functions were transferred to more modern facilities. The Greek Revival building, designed by Portsmouth native William B. Singleton, was described after its completion as "a beautiful structure, highly ornamental to the town." The courthouse has been restored as a cultural center with the exterior returned to its original appearance, including the reconstruction of its long-vanished cupola. 124–6 (4/7/70).

PORT NORFOLK HISTORIC DISTRICT, *roughly bounded by Bay View Boulevard, Douglas Avenue, Hartford Street, and Chautauqua Avenue.* Port Norfolk is a turn-of-the-century planned suburb of Portsmouth. On the banks of the Elizabeth River, the neighborhood has suffered few changes and consists mostly of freestanding wooden houses typical of the period. Styles range from elaborate Queen Anne examples to the popular bungalows of the first quarter of the 20th century. The site of Port Norfolk served successively as the glebe holdings of Portsmouth Parish and Trinity Church, as a strategic landing point in the British capture of Portsmouth and Norfolk in the Revolution, and finally as a 19th-century farm. Beginning in 1890, with the formation of the Port Norfolk Land Company, and continuing to ca. 1920, the planned community grew to its present form, providing a healthful and attractive housing for employees of the expanding railroad and shipping facilities that adjoin it. Port Norfolk exemplifies the widespread efforts in the late 19th and early 20th centuries to accommodate the growing demand for uncrowded neighborhoods conveniently located near shops, recreational areas, and churches, as well as places of employment. 124–51 (8/16/83).

PORTSMOUTH NAVAL HOSPITAL, *Naval Regional Medical Center, Hospital Point.* The Portsmouth Naval Hospital, originally known as the Norfolk Naval Hospital, was an outgrowth of the 1798 act of Congress creating the Marine Hospital Service. Its site was chosen in 1826 at Fort Nelson, a Revolutionary defense work guarding the harbors of Norfolk and Portsmouth. Selected to design the facility was John Haviland, a Philadelphia architect who produced a preeminent work of Greek Revival institutional architecture. The decastyle Doric portico, finished in what Haviland described as "chisel-dressed Virginia freestone," is a masterpiece of monumentality which ranks among the period's largest expressions of this classical form. The shallow dome was added during a 1907 enlargement and modernization. The hospital has had a distinguished record of service, treating naval casualties of every American conflict since its opening. 124–36 (11/16/71).

PORTSMOUTH OLDE TOWNE HISTORIC DISTRICT, *bounded by Crawford Parkway, London Street, Washington Street, and the Elizabeth River.* The historic core of Portsmouth occupies over twenty blocks in the northeastern corner of the city overlooking the harbor. Preserved in the grid-plan area is an assemblage of late 18th- and 19th-century urban buildings, composing the only early townscape remaining in the Hampton Roads area. Most distinctive among the district's housing are the tall, narrow Federal and Greek Revival town houses, most with side-hall plans, basements fully aboveground, and principal entrances reached by long flights of wooden steps. There are also a number of Victorian dwellings with fancy exterior woodwork and porches. Portsmouth was founded in 1752 when Col. William Crawford laid off the corner of his plantation for a new town named in honor of the great English naval city. Unlike Norfolk, Portsmouth was spared the torch during the Revolution. The preservation of the district was facilitated by the 1968 Olde Towne Conservation Project, Virginia's first federally assisted urban conservation effort. 124–34 (6/2/70).

PYTHIAN CASTLE, *610–612 Court Street.* This three-story brick-and-stone building is one of the best surviving examples of Romanesque Revival architecture in Portsmouth. Designed by local architect and builder Edward Overman, Pythian Castle was built between 1897 and 1898. Typical of late 19th-century fraternal lodges, the exotic castle housed the meetings of the Knights of Pythias, a secret organization. It and similar fraternal societies were the chief patrons of stylistically heavy buildings in the period, usually the most elaborate structures in their communities. 124–46 (7/31/80).

QUARTERS A, B, AND C, NORFOLK NAVAL SHIPYARD, *Lincoln and Third streets.* These three houses, located behind a high brick wall on the edge of the Norfolk Naval Shipyard, were erected between 1837 and 1842 to serve as residences of the shipyard's commanding officers. Many of their details, mostly in a Greek Revival idiom, follow designs illustrated in the architectural pattern books of Asher Benjamin. The three houses survived the 1861 burning of the shipyard by evacuating Union forces and a burning the next year by departing Confederates. Well maintained, they continue to house the yard's ranking officers, with Quarters A (shown), the largest of the three, traditionally serving as the commandant's house. 124–16 (11/19/74).

TRINITY EPISCOPAL CHURCH, *"High and Court streets.* Trinity Church was built between 1828 and 1830 on the site of the parish's original colonial church dating from 1762. The congregation of the first church dwindled after the disestablishment but was revived in 1820 under the leadership of the Reverend John H. Wingfield. When the time came to enlarge the church in 1828, its fabric was found to be so decayed that it was pulled down and replaced by the present building. The church was used as a Confederate hospital in the Civil War but was restored to ecclesiastical service soon after. The somewhat conservative Federal building has been altered and redecorated many times in its long history. The most conspicuous addition, the tower, was added in 1893. Its churchyard, a quiet corner of the busy downtown, contains gravestones dating as early as 1763. 124–28 (4/17/73).

TRUXTUN HISTORIC DISTRICT, *Portsmouth Boulevard, including Hobson, Manly, and Dewey streets.* Truxtun was the first wartime government housing project in the United States constructed exclusively for blacks. Named for Thomas Truxtun, an early naval hero, the forty-two-acre neighborhood of 250 houses was developed in 1918 to accommodate the growing work force at the Norfolk Naval Shipyard in Portsmouth. Truxtun exhibits the high planning standards of the U.S. Housing Corporation, the federal agency that financed and built the community as a model village for black workers. The residential portion of the district is characterized by closely spaced five-room structures with gabled and jerkinhead roofs, so arranged that a repeated pattern is almost indiscernible. The principal architect for the project was R. E. Mitchell, with H. P. Kelsey serving as the chief planner. Though it has undergone moderate alterations beginning in the 1920s, Truxtun retains much of its original character and is still a black neighborhood. 124–47 (4/15/80).

POWHATAN COUNTY

*Named for the Indian chieftain, this upper James River county
was formed from Cumberland County in 1777, with part of
Chesterfield County added later. The county
seat is Powhatan Court House.*

BELMEAD, *Powhatan Court House vicinity.* New York architect Alexander Jackson Davis designed this upper James River plantation house for Philip St. George Cocke in 1845. Although many of its decorative elements have been lost through later alterations, the house remains one of the country's preeminent examples of a Gothic Revival villa, the epitome of mid-19th-century rural romanticism. Philip St. George Cocke served as a president of the Virginia Agricultural Society and was a board member of Virginia Military Institute where he was instrumental in having Davis commissioned as architect of its new complex in 1850. In the 1890s Belmead was purchased by Mr. and Mrs. Edward de Vaux Morrell of Philadelphia, who in 1897 conveyed the estate to the Roman Catholic church in order to establish a training school for blacks. Known as St. Emma's Industrial and Agricultural School, it was in operation until the early 1970s. The plantation remains in the ownership of the Sisters of the Blessed Sacrament, a Philadelphia-based order. 72–49 (5/13/69).

BELNEMUS, *Powhatan Court House vicinity*. The three-part Palladian scheme used throughout Virginia in the Federal period gave to rural houses a formality and architectural sophistication which is well illustrated in Belnemus. In *The Mansions of Virginia*, architectural historian Thomas T. Waterman stated that its design has "an appealing rural quality heightened by its frame construction." The house was erected between 1783 and 1799 for James Clarke, a Powhatan County landowner and politician, on land purchased from Col. William Mayo. It received its present porch, siding, and rear addition at the turn of the century when it was owned by the Valentine family. Adding interest to the scheme is the curious finial at the apex of the pyramidal roof and the well-executed Georgian chimneypiece and matching cupboard in the hall. On the property is a variety of early outbuildings including a mid-19th-century tobacco barn. 72–2 (9/19/78).

KESWICK, *Midlothian vicinity*. Inspired by the nearly a century earlier Tuckahoe directly across the river in Goochland County, this wood-frame, H-shaped house was built for Maj. John Clarke, founder of the Bellona Arsenal, sometime after 1800. The house survives with few modifications; its interior preserves Federal woodwork including a broad, finely crafted arch in the parlor. On the grounds is a collection of brick outbuildings including an enigmatic circular structure with a conical roof and central chimney whose original function has not been determined. With its varied forms and apparently single building period, the complex has much to teach about the physical layout and social organization of an early 19th-century Virginia plantation. 72–45 (11/19/74).

NORWOOD, *Fine Creek Mills vicinity*. In contrast with the many colonial plantation houses of the lower James River, the upper James boasts a collection of planters' homes dating from the early national and antebellum periods. One of these is Norwood, a Federal manor house in an informally landscaped park overlooking the river's broad bottomlands. The center portion of the two-story brick house was built in the late 18th century for John Harris, Jr., who in 1775–76 had served as a member of the Cumberland Committee of Safety. The Harris family sold Norwood in 1812 to Harry Heth, who, with his son-in-law Beverley Randolph, operated the Midlothian coal mines nearby in Chesterfield County. In 1835 the two-story wings and Ionic front porch were added, and elaborate but provincial Adam-style woodwork was installed in the principal first-floor rooms, so that the house now exhibits harmonious blending of 18th- and 19th-century architectural modes. Preserved on the property is a complex of mid-19th-century brick farm buildings. Norwood remains in the ownership of Heth and Randolph descendants. 72–48 (3/18/75).

POWHATAN COURT HOUSE HISTORIC DISTRICT, *Powhatan Court House*. The compact historic district in the county seat village of Powhatan Court House focuses on the sophisticated but unusually small courthouse of 1849, a masterpiece of Greek Revival design by Alexander Jackson Davis. Davis's association with this rural Virginia county resulted from the patronage of Philip St. George Cocke, who commissioned Davis to design his Gothic Revival villa, Belmead, a few miles to the north. Cocke served as a commissioner for the building of the new courthouse and supplied a design by Davis. The original drawings have not survived, but a small sketch plan and elevation are in Davis's account book, entered on May 29, 1848, under the heading: "Court-House . . . Powhatan, Va. for Philip St. Geo. Cocke, Esq, Virginia $30.00." The builder of the courthouse was K. Lewis Johnson of Hanover County. Other early buildings on the court square are the former clerk's office, a brick, T-shaped structure built in 1796–97, and the ca. 1826 jail. Also on the square are the town pump and a particularly handsome monument to the county's Confederate dead. A small ca. 1870 Italianate law office, formerly on the west side of the courthouse, recently was moved to a lot just across the street on the western side of the square. Dominating the western side of the square is the rambling Courthouse Tavern, a well-preserved example of a county-seat hostelry. The tavern was begun in the late 18th century and evolved to its present form through various alterations and additions. Known also as Grove Tavern and Atkinson's Hotel, the galleried building has housed a post office, school, and Masonic hall and was renovated in the early 1970s for a residence and offices. The village was laid out soon after Powhatan County was founded in 1777 and originally was called Scottsville after Gen. Charles Scott of the Continental army. 72–79 (12/2/69).

PRINCE EDWARD COUNTY

Formed from Amelia County in 1753, this rural south-central Virginia county was named in honor of Prince Edward Augustus, a son of Frederick Louis, Prince of Wales, and a younger brother of King George III. Its county seat is Farmville.

BRIERY CHURCH, *Briery vicinity.* In an isolated woodland setting in southern Prince Edward County, this multigabled wooden church is among the more singular expressions of the mid-19th-century Gothic Revival style in the state. With its verticality emphasized by its board-and-batten siding, the sharp angles of its gables, and its narrow lancet windows, the building displays the individualism inherent in many of the architectural endeavors of rural America. The congregation of this Presbyterian church was organized in 1755; the present building, erected in 1856, is the third on the site. Its design is attributed to the Reverend Robert Lewis Dabney, a theologian and amateur architect who served as a supply minister to the Briery congregation from 1856 to 1858. Dabney at the time was a professor at the nearby Union Theological Seminary, then part of Hampden-Sydney College. He also designed the Hampden-Sydney chapel, a plain but dignified Greek Revival building. Briery Church survives without alteration, preserving all of its original interior appointments including pews, pulpit, and "vaulted" pine ceiling. 73–38 (5/13/69).

DEBTORS' PRISON, *Worsham*. The present-day settlement of Worsham was founded in 1745 as Prince Edward Court House and served as the county seat until 1872 when the court was moved to Farmville. The 1855 former clerk's office and the solid little structure authorized in 1786 to serve as the "Gaol for Debtors" are the only remaining public buildings in the tiny community. The last courthouse (built 1832) was demolished ca. 1900 after standing abandoned for several years. Constructed by Richard Bigg using square-hewn, half-dovetailed logs for its walls and with closely set squared logs for both floor and ceiling, the jail was built with security in mind. Debtors' terms of imprisonment were usually comparatively short in the 18th century, and their places of incarceration generally were kept separate from those of criminals. The practice of jailing debtors was abandoned in the early 19th century, and by 1820 the jail had been converted to a private residence. The building was acquired in 1950 by the Association for the Preservation of Virginia Antiquities, which restored and deeded it to Prince Edward County in 1976. 73–7 (8/15/72).

FALKLAND, *Redd Shop vicinity*. One of the earliest remaining houses in Prince Edward County, Falkland was built ca. 1800 for the Watkins family. The four-bay, two-story, hall-parlor dwelling is a little-altered vernacular house of the type found throughout the upper South from the Virginia Piedmont westward. Falkland is an unusually large example, with generous scale and flanking one-story wings of unequal lengths. The house also possesses an interesting store of original woodwork, most of which is a provincial interpretation of late colonial trim. The house's first occupant was Francis Watkins, Jr., son of a longtime county clerk and trustee of Hampden-Sydney and himself a county magistrate and captain of the local militia. Upon his move to Alabama in 1820, Watkins sold Falkland to his brother-in-law James Wood, a tobacco manufacturer who also was a Hampden-Sydney trustee. 73–39 (3/20/79).

HAMPDEN-SYDNEY COLLEGE HISTORIC DISTRICT, *Hampden-Sydney*. The origins of Hampden-Sydney College extend back to 1774 when the ministers of the Hanover Presbytery suggested to their Prince Edward and Cumberland County congregations that money be raised for "a public school for the liberal education of youth . . . on the southside of the Blue Ridge." The effort was successful, and the school was founded in 1776. Incorporated by the General Assembly in 1783, it was named in honor of John Hampden and Algernon Sydney (or Sidney), two 17th-century champions of English liberty. From 1823 to 1898 Union Theological Seminary was operated as part of the college. Hampden-Sydney also sponsored a medical school in Richmond from 1837 to 1854 when the school was chartered as the Medical College of Virginia. Today, the rural college community, surrounded by the woods and farmland of Prince Edward County, has a collection of collegiate structures dating from the first half of the 19th century. The early buildings, several of which are by the builder Dabney

Cosby, Sr., are scattered across leafy grounds, interspersed with architecturally harmonious newer structures. Two of the earliest buildings are the Alamo, a faculty residence dating from 1817, and Cushing Hall, a four-story residence hall begun in 1822 and later expanded. Cushing Hall was the main college building for many years and at one time held a chapel, lecture rooms, and society halls. Across a vale are the buildings originally erected to serve the Union Theological Seminary. Included among them are two brick residences: Penshurst (1830) and Middlecourt (ca. 1829), currently used as the home of the college's president. Between them is what was the main seminary building, Venable Hall of 1825 and 1831, a large brick structure with a central pavilion and cupola. The most architecturally noteworthy of the early buildings is College Church, a Greek Revival chapel built ca. 1860 to the design of preacher/architect Robert Lewis Dabney, who also designed the similar Tinkling Springs Church in Augusta County. Cushing Hall and College Church are shown. 73–50 (12/2/69).

LONGWOOD HOUSE, *Longwood Avenue, Farmville*. Longwood House, one of the Farmville area's architectural landmarks, illustrates the evolution of a simple Federal farmhouse into one of Prince Edward County's finest antebellum mansions. The massive wood-frame structure began as a one-and-a-half-story dwelling built for Nathaniel E. Venable in 1815 soon after a fire destroyed an earlier house. After his rise to prominence as a state delegate and senator, Venable had his residence enlarged and refashioned in the Greek Revival style. The house has survived without significant alterations to the present, retaining its early porches, siding, and interior woodwork. Since 1929, when the property was acquired by the State Teachers College at Farmville as a rural student retreat, Longwood House has become the identifying symbol of the college community, giving its name to the institution in 1949 and serving more recently as the official home of its president. 144–25 (10/18/83).

OLD PRINCE EDWARD COUNTY CLERK'S OFFICE, *Worsham*. The former clerk's office of Prince Edward County, the third to serve the county, is a reminder of the years from 1754 to 1872 when the tiny settlement of Worsham was the county seat, known then as Prince Edward Court House. The last courthouse to stand here was built in 1832, and it is presumed to have been a Classical Revival structure similar to the several antebellum courthouses in the neighboring counties. It was demolished after the county seat was moved to Farmville. The clerk's office, erected in 1855 by the builders Guthrey and Thaxton, is a relatively late expression of the Classical Revival idiom and illustrates the style's persistence in rural areas. After the removal of the county seat, the clerk's office was used as a dormitory for Prince Edward Academy. The building later housed a public school and eventually was converted to a residence. In 1977 it was reacquired by the county with the intention of converting it to a museum of county history. 73–3 (6/19/79).

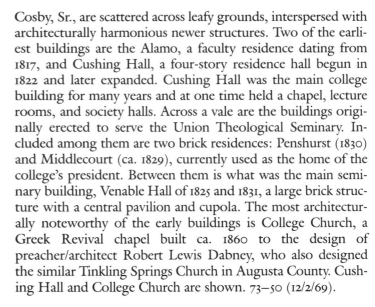

PRINCE GEORGE COUNTY

In the Tidewater region on the south side of the James River, Prince George County was formed from Charles City County in 1702. It was named for Prince George of Denmark, husband of Queen Anne of England. Its county seat is Prince George.

BRANDON, *Burrowsville vicinity.* The influence of the villa designs of the 16th-century Italian architect Andrea Palladio is well documented in several late colonial Virginia houses, chief among which is Brandon. One of the more popular pattern books of Palladian-style designs used in Virginia was Robert Morris's *Select Architecture* (1755); plate III, a design for a seven-part farmhouse, provided the inspiration for Brandon. The house was built ca. 1765 by Nathaniel Harrison II as a wedding present for his son Benjamin. Benjamin Harrison was a friend of Thomas Jefferson, and Harrison family tradition holds that Jefferson designed the house as a favor. His authorship cannot be documented, but Jefferson was familiar with Morris's book and adapted designs from it for some of his later schemes. The first stories of Brandon's terminal wings are earlier than the main part of the house and presumably were built as detached dependencies with the expectation that they would flank a conventional Georgian dwelling. Although occupied by Union troops and riddled with gunfire during the Civil War, the house escaped significant alteration except for the remodeling of the stair hall in the early 19th century and the rebuilding of its porches later in the century. Brandon remained in the Harrison family until 1926, when it was purchased by Mr. and Mrs. Robert W. Daniel, who undertook a careful restoration of the house and its extensive formal gardens. The place takes its name from the fact that it is on part of the early 17th-century patent known as Martin's Brandon. 74–2 (9/9/69); *National Historic Landmark.*

EVERGREEN, *Hopewell vicinity.* Evergreen is a James River plantation established by the Ruffin family in the mid-18th century. The present late Georgian dwelling was erected ca. 1807–8 for George Ruffin (1765–1810), probably on the site of the original Ruffin home. With its symmetrical five-bay facade articulated by pilaster strips, the stuccoed house has an elegant formality. Insurance records note that the house was originally roofed with slate rather than the usual wood shingles, an indication of the building's superior quality. One of George Ruffin's sons was Edmund Ruffin III, the southern agriculturalist and ardent secessionist. Another son, George H. Ruffin, conveyed the house in 1832 to his half-sister's husband, Harrison H. Cocke, a Confederate naval captain who served as commanding officer of James River defenses. The house fell into decay in the early 20th century and was used as a barn. The interior was extensively rebuilt when the house was reclaimed for residential use in the 1930s. Its rural setting above the tidal flats of the James remains unspoiled. 74–5 (5/15/79).

FLOWERDEW HUNDRED ARCHAEOLOGICAL DISTRICT, *Hopewell vicinity.* Flowerdew Hundred was one of the earliest English settlements in the New World. The tract, located twenty miles up river from Jamestown, was granted in 1618 to Governor George Yeardley, who named it in honor of his wife, neé Temperance Flowerdew. It was here, on Windmill Point, that America's first windmill was erected ca. 1621, signaling one of the nation's earliest industrial efforts. This fact was commemorated by the construction of a 17th-century-style windmill in the 1970s. The settlement survived the Indian massacre of 1622 and was occupied through the 18th century. It disappeared ca. 1800, and in 1804 the property was purchased by the Willcox family. It continued as a plantation through the 20th century. Owned today by the Flowerdew Hundred Foundation, the property has been the scene of extensive archaeological investigation since 1971. Over sixty-five sites have been investigated, including a complex of early 17th-century structures at the river's edge that contained a T-shaped house with a stone foundation. Archaeological evidence of Indian occupation dating from 9000 B.C. also has been found. The plantation is now exhibited to the public. 74–6 (5/20/75).

MARTIN'S BRANDON CHURCH, *Burrowsville.* The fourth church of one of the oldest parishes in Virginia, Martin's Brandon Church exemplifies ecclesiastical architectural taste at the time of the revival of the Episcopal church in Virginia. Attributed to the Baltimore architectural firm of Niernsee and Neilson, the Tuscan-style church was consecrated in 1857. It stands across the road from the site of the parish's 18th-century frame church. A chalice and paten left to the congregation by a parishioner in 1656 are believed to be the nation's oldest Communion service in continuous possession of the original parish. The parish was established in 1655 and was named for Martin's Brandon, land patented by John Martin in 1618. 74–3 (7/31/80).

MERCHANT'S HOPE CHURCH, *Hopewell vicinity.* Expressing the plainness of low-church Anglican worship, Merchant's Hope lacks architectural adornment, except for its modillion cornice, but achieves dignity from its Flemish bond brickwork, careful proportions, and the graceful splaying of its gable roof. Although nearly all of its original interior features were lost during the Civil War, its early sash windows and roof framing have survived. Claims have been made that the church dates as early as 1657. Although a building of that date may have served the parish, nothing of the style or fabric of the present building has a mid-17th-century character; its form and details parallel those of several churches dating from the first half of the 18th century. Merchant's Hope suffered the usual vicissitudes of a Virginia colonial church, undergoing a period of abandonment and neglect in the 19th century. The Episcopal Diocese of Southern Virginia has recently restored Merchant's Hope to parish church status. 74–9 (11/5/68).

PRINCE WILLIAM COUNTY

Named for William Augustus, duke of Cumberland and third son of King George II, this Northern Virginia county was formed from Stafford and King George counties in 1730. Its county seat is Manassas.

BEL AIR, *Minnieville vicinity*. This brick farmhouse of ca. 1740 was originally the home of the Ewell family. Mason Locke Weems (1759–1825), clergyman, first biographer of George Washington, and inventor of the popular Washington story of the hatchet and cherry tree, married into the Ewell family and lived at Bel Air from 1809 until his death. Parson Weems lies buried in the family cemetery here. With its robust but somewhat casual proportions, the house is a backwoods interpretation of the Georgian style. Its interior retains ambitious and unusual woodwork, including a removable paneled partition between the hall and drawing room. In the partition are original casement windows for lighting the hall. Like a number of colonial houses in Northern Virginia, Bel Air has a fieldstone foundation. 76–1 (12/2/69).

BEN LOMOND, *10914 Studley Manor Drive, Manassas vicinity*. Built in 1837 by Benjamin Tasker Chinn, a grandson of Robert ("Councillor") Carter, Ben Lomond is one of the only remaining plantation houses in an area which once exhibited such fine country residences as Portisi, Pittsylvania, Hazel Plain, Mountain View, Elmwood, Sudley, and Woodland. Constructed of native fieldstone, the house follows the single-pile, five-bay-facade format typical of its time and place. Its interior retains rather bold original woodwork. Ben Lomond was used as a hospital during the Civil War battles of First and Second Manassas, which were fought nearby. Because its once-rural surroundings are succumbing to intense development, Ben Lomond remains an important reminder of the region's agricultural and Civil War history. 76–4 (5/20/80).

BEVERLEY MILL, *Broad Run*. In Thoroughfare Gap, in full view of motorists traveling on nearby Interstate Highway 66, Beverley Mill is a landmark of both the stone construction of the region and Virginia's milling industry. The bottom three stories belonged to a mill operated by John Chapman built before 1759, the year the mill was cited as a boundary marker between Prince William and Fauquier counties. The upper two stories were added in the 1850s, making the building one of the tallest gristmills remaining in the state. It is claimed that the mill supplied meal to troops in five wars, from the French and Indian War through the Civil War. With improved machinery, Beverley Mill was grinding approximately 100,000 bushels of grain annually as late as the 1940s. The mill is no longer in use, but most of its equipment, including its 1900 metal waterwheel, remains intact. 76–2 (11/16/71).

CONNER HOUSE, *Conner Drive, Manassas Park vicinity*. The Conner house achieved significance in the Civil War first as the headquarters of Confederate general Joseph E. Johnston from July to November 1861 and then as a hospital for the wounded of the second battle of Manassas. One of the few remaining antebellum residences in the growing Manassas region, the plain stone house was built ca. 1820, probably as an overseer's house, and survives as an example of a dwelling type indigenous to the area. During the first half of the 20th century the property was owned by the Conner family, proprietors of one of Prince William County's major dairy farms. The house stands stabilized but unrestored. 76–13 (1/20/81).

MANASSAS NATIONAL BATTLEFIELD PARK, *Groveton*. The 300-acre tract north of the town of Manassas and bordered by Bull Run was the scene of two important Confederate victories. The first battle of Manassas, fought July 21, 1861, was the opening engagement of the Civil War and pitted Union general Irvin McDowell's unseasoned troops against ill-trained but spirited Confederates under Gen. P. G. T. Beauregard. The Union attack was repulsed by Confederates inspired by Gen. Thomas J. Jackson and his Virginians, who stood against the enemy like a "stone wall," earning Jackson his famous epithet. Second Manassas, fought the next year on August 28–30, cleared the way for Gen. Robert E. Lee's first invasion of the North. Landmarks surviving on the battlefield include the Dogan house, used by Union troops in Second Manassas as a snipers' nest; the Stone House, used as a field hospital by Union troops in both battles; and the stone bridge, blown up after the Union retreat in First Manassas but reconstructed in the 1880s. The battlefield is owned and exhibited by the National Park Service. 76–271 (1/16/73).

MOOR GREEN, *Brentsville vicinity*. Moor Green was erected shortly before 1820 by the Hooe family. In addition to its handsome brickwork and sophisticated but simple interior woodwork, the house is distinguished by its banded American bond side and rear walls and its flounder-roofed rear ell. These features and the floor plan with its separate stair for the second-floor ell room relate the house more closely to the architecture of the Middle Atlantic states than with Tidewater Virginia. The house has stood empty for a number of years and has been seriously vandalized. 76–14 (7/18/78).

NOKESVILLE TRUSS BRIDGE, *Aden Road, Nokesville*. The mass-produced metal truss bridges of the late 19th century were a remarkable technical innovation which made rural travel safer and led to the replacement of the majority of the earlier wooden covered bridges. Although sturdy and easily maintained, most of these graceful structures are too narrow to meet today's safety standards and are in turn being supplanted by wider concrete bridges. Certain especially significant metal truss bridges, however, have been cited by the Virginia Department of Highways and Transportation as worthy of preservation. Among these is the Nokesville Bridge, manufactured in 1882 by the Keystone Bridge Company of Pittsburgh, a pioneer in metal truss technology. The Nokesville Bridge consists of a single-span through Pratt truss employing wrought-iron members. It was erected to cross a line of the Southern Railway and is still owned by the Southern Railway System. 76–81 (11/15/77).

OCCOQUAN HISTORIC DISTRICT, *roughly bounded by the Occoquan River, Center Lane, Washington Street, and the western end of Mill Street*. The site of a tobacco warehouse as early as 1736, the present town of Occoquan arose as the focus of the commercial and manufacturing activities of John Ballendine, who erected an iron furnace, forge, and two sawmills at the falls of the Occoquan River before 1759. After the Revolution the settlement emerged as a flour-manufacturing center which boasted one of the first gristmills in the nation to employ the laborsaving inventions of Oliver Evans. Although the silting of the river gradually reduced Occoquan's stature as a major Northern Virginia shipping point, the town continued to thrive as a center of commerce and industry into the 1920s. The district contains a collection of mostly vernacular residential and commercial structures dating from the late 19th and early 20th centuries. Most of the older buildings have succumbed to the ravages of fire and flood; however, surviving from the antebellum period or before are Rockledge, a stone Georgian house erected ca. 1760 for John Ballendine; the Mill House, a ca. 1800 structure thought to have served as an office for the Occoquan Flour Mill; and the Hammil Hotel, built in the early 19th century and enlarged ca. 1900. 272–12 (8/16/83).

RIPPON LODGE, *Woodbridge vicinity.* Richard Blackburn, colonial entrepreneur and public servant, built the core of this small plantation dwelling in the second quarter of the 18th century on a tract which he named after his native Rippon (Ripon), England. Among his many pursuits, Blackburn was a building contractor and is said to have designed and built Rippon Lodge himself. Carefully sited on a hill with a view down Neabsco Creek to the Potomac, the house has acquired a picturesque aspect with its numerous later additions, such as the columned veranda, but preserves much original fabric, including two fully paneled rooms. Blackburn's son Thomas was active in the Revolutionary effort and entertained George Washington at Rippon Lodge on several occasions. The architect Benjamin Henry Latrobe also visited here in 1796 and made a sketch of the house showing a now-vanished companion structure. 76–23 (1/5/71); *Virginia Historic Landmarks Board preservation easement.*

ROCKLEDGE, *Telegraph Road, Occoquan.* Built of stone taken from a nearby quarry, this ca. 1760 Georgian house was the home of John Ballendine, who established a foundry and milling operation immediately down the hill in the village of Occoquan. Ballendine sited his house on a ledge to overlook the falls of the Occoquan River as well as his enterprises. Although undocumented, the house is said to have been designed by William Buckland. Later owners of Rockledge include Ballendine's business partner, James Semple, and Nathaniel Ellicott, member of one of the nation's foremost Quaker milling families. Ellicott was also the founder of the Maryland milling town Ellicott City. The house stood abandoned for many years but was restored in the 1970s. Subsequently burned by arsonists, the house has since been re-restored. 272–1 (6/19/73).

ST. PAUL'S EPISCOPAL CHURCH, *Haymarket.* This structure, now serving the village of Haymarket as an Episcopal church, was built in 1801 as a district courthouse for the counties of Fairfax, Fauquier, Loudoun, and Prince William. It is one of the early 19th-century Virginia courthouses that employ a two-story temple form and arcaded entrance. The building housed the district court until 1807 when changes in the court system resulted in its eventual sale and conversion to an academy. It was first used as an Episcopal church in 1822 and was consecrated by Bishop William Meade in 1834. Close to both the first and second battles of Manassas, it was taken over as a hospital by both sides. Union troops desecrated the building in November 1862 by converting it to a stable and then burning it. The congregation rebuilt the church within the original walls in 1867, at which time the belfry and bracketed cornice were added and the arcade was closed up for the narthex. 233–2 (12/17/74).

WEEMS-BOTTS HOUSE, *Duke and Cameron streets, Dumfries.* Parson Mason Locke Weems built the earliest portion of this commercial structure in the village of Dumfries ca. 1798 to serve as a bookshop and temporary lodging after he retired from the Episcopal ministry. Weems, author of numerous moral tracts and lives of prominent Americans, was convinced that small, cheap books with uplifting messages would be an effective tool for enlightening the public and used the simple building as the center of his successful writing and bookselling business. Here he wrote his pamphlet *The Life and Memorable Actions of George Washington* . . . , the first biography of the father of the country. Weems sold the building in 1802 to Benjamin Botts, an attorney who served on the team of lawyers who defended Aaron Burr in his trial for treason. Botts used the building as his office until his death in the Richmond Theatre fire of 1811. The building received its two-story wing in the mid-19th century when it was converted to a residence. In recent years it has been restored by Historic Dumfries, Virginia, Inc. for use as a museum. 212–10 (4/15/75).

WILLIAMS'S ORDINARY, *U.S. Route 1, Dumfries.* This Georgian structure is Virginia's only surviving colonial building employing all-header-bond brickwork. Header bond was popular for finer-quality 18th-century buildings in England and is found on several mansions in Annapolis, Md., but it was used practically nowhere else in the colonies. It is likely that the ordinary is the work of Maryland masons from across the Potomac River. The building is on the old King's Highway (now U.S. 1) connecting northern and southern Virginia and has been a familiar landmark for travelers on this busy way since its completion in the third quarter of the 18th century. The formality of the ordinary is emphasized by its regularly proportioned five-bay facade, hipped roof, stone quoins, keystone lintels, and rusticated doorway. Abandoned for a number of years, the building is currently undergoing a long-term restoration. The early history of the building is obscure. It may have been built as a merchant's house, but George Williams was the proprietor of an ordinary here as early as 1788. It has also been known as Love's Tavern, Stagecoach Inn, and the Old Hotel. 212–1 (5/13/69).

PULASKI COUNTY

Formed in 1839 from Montgomery and Wythe counties, this Southwest Virginia county was named for Count Casimir Pulaski, the Polish patriot who served in the American army during the Revolution. The county seat is Pulaski.

BACK CREEK FARM, *Dublin vicinity*. Back Creek Farm's house and outbuildings are products of the second generation of settlement in Southwest Virginia, after the Revolution. Nestled at the foot of Cloyd's Mountain, Back Creek Farm was established by Joseph Cloyd, whose pioneer parents had been killed in an Indian skirmish. In the 1780s, on what Cloyd described as "the sun shiny ridge," he built his brick mansion, fronted by a dwarf portico and trimmed on the interior with elegantly carved provincial Georgian woodwork. The outbuildings, including a brick dairy and a two-story kitchen, are unusually large and finely crafted. There is also a splendid late 18th-century stone barn, a Pennsylvania type with a supported fore-bay, one of the few early western Virginia barns to survive the Civil War. The war touched Back Creek Farm in May 1864 when the battle of Cloyd's Mountain was fought on the property. The house served as both a hospital and headquarters for Union general George Crook under whose command at the time were captains Rutherford B. Hayes and William McKinley. 77–2 (2/18/75).

INGLES FERRY, *Radford vicinity*. Ingles Ferry was started by William Ingles in 1762 when he obtained a license to operate a ferryboat across the New River. Ingles was assisted in his enterprise by his brother-in-law John Draper. Over the ferry moved a major portion of the settlers taking up land in Kentucky and Tennessee; the boat ran day and night with tolls amounting to over a thousand dollars a month. The Ingles Ferry Tavern, erected in 1772 on the Pulaski side of the river, became a popular social center for the travelers. Andrew Jack-

son and George Rogers Clark were among its more noted patrons. The ferry was eventually replaced by a bridge which was burned in the Civil War. The ferry was again put into operation and continued until 1948. The 1840 ferry-house, which held the winch to pull the boats, burned in 1967, leaving only its chimneys. Today the tavern stands in a state of disrepair, but the crossing, looking from the ridge on the Pulaski side over to the broad bottomlands of the Ingles plantation, remains undisturbed by modern intrusions. 77–13 (5/13/69).

NEWBERN HISTORIC DISTRICT, *immediately east of Interstate 81 and including the entire village, Dublin vicinity.* The linear village of Newbern, stretched along a sharp ridge for approximately one mile, is an exceptionally well-preserved 19th-century turnpike town. Newbern was laid out in 1809 by Adam Hance with twenty-nine lots along the Wilderness Road. Purchasers were required to put up a house within two years "at least 16 feet square, 1½ stories high of hewn logs with a stone or brick chimney." The dominating house types—the two-story rectangular log house and the long, compounded two-story log or frame house, both sheathed in weatherboards—conform to these standards, which were based on a strong log house tradition in the area. These finished log buildings with their masonry chimneys make the district representative not of a frontier settlement but of a second-generation provincial southwest Virginia village. Most of the houses were complemented with a scattering of outbuildings, some of which remain. Newbern became the county seat of the newly formed Pulaski County in 1837. The town prospered and acquired several businesses and small industries; but when the courthouse burned in 1893, the county seat was moved to the town of Pulaski, a more promising site on the railroad. Newbern then declined in population and activity, becoming a quiet residential community unmarred by modern development. 77–43 (2/18/75).

PULASKI COUNTY COURTHOUSE, *Main Street, Pulaski.* The massive Pulaski County Courthouse, the dominant landmark in the town of Pulaski, is one of the state's few large public buildings illustrating the influence of the Romanesque style of H. H. Richardson. The firm of W. Chamberlin and Co. of Knoxville, Tenn., designed the building, employing stone quarried from nearby Pear Creek. In contrast to the earlier and much smaller courthouses of eastern and central Virginia, the Pulaski courthouse is typical of the showy structures built in county seats of midwestern states at the end of the century, serving as symbols of local pride and prosperity. Such large structures housed all the county offices rather than having them contained in a cluster of small buildings as in many Virginia county seats. A controversy concerning the location of the county seat at Dublin or Pulaski was permanently settled when the town of Pulaski took the initiative to have the courthouse built. The county took formal possession of the courthouse in 1896. 125–1 (9/15/81).

CITY OF RADFORD

*This Montgomery County community has had many names,
including Lovely Mount, English Ferry, Ingles's Ferry, and
Central Depot. It was established as a town with the name of
Central City in 1885 and incorporated in 1887. In 1890 the name
was changed to Radford in honor of local citizen John Blair
Radford. Radford was incorporated as a city in 1892.*

HARVEY HOUSE, *706 Harvey Street.* This demonstration of shingled walls binding curved and angled volumes is an expression of the Queen Anne style in the usual loose American interpretation. Radford, like many western Virginia towns, was founded in the industrial boom of the 1890s. Developers drawn to the area by iron deposits and an abundant water supply formed the Radford Land Improvement Company, which laid out the town. The company's general manager, J. K. Dimmick, had this Queen Anne dwelling built as his own residence in 1891–92. Although its architect has not been identified, the able Philadelphia architect Frank Miles Day was credited with the design of a new house in Radford in the *Builder's, Decorator's, and Woodworker's Guide of August 1890.* As Day's early works were in the Queen Anne style, it may be speculated that his Radford commission was for this house. The panic of 1893 brought the collapse of the Radford land boom; Dimmick left town, and the house stood empty for several years. In 1906 it was purchased by Lewis Harvey, in whose family it remained until 1974. The present owner has undertaken an extensive preservation program in an effort to retain the early character of the house. 126–1 (4/20/76).

RAPPAHANNOCK COUNTY

*Scenically situated against the east side of the Blue Ridge
Mountains, this sparsely populated county was named for the
Rappahannock River, which forms its northern border.
It was formed from Culpeper County in 1833.
The county seat is Washington.*

BEN VENUE, *Ben Venue*. Occupying a hilltop with broad views of the Blue Ridge Mountains, Ben Venue is one of the more elaborate farmsteads established in Rappahannock County in the first half of the 19th century. The two-story brick house was constructed between 1844 and 1846 for William V. Fletcher and is attributed to James Leake Powers, a local builder. Its parapet gables, corbeled shoulders, and chimneys oddly placed against the front wall give the house architectural distinction. Among its several stylistically related outbuildings are three brick slave houses lining a ridge in a field to the south. Like the main house, the slave houses have parapet gables and corbeled shoulders. Slave quarters rarely are found in the Piedmont uplands, and no others in the state possess such relative architectural pretension. 78–3 (10/16/79).

MONTPELIER, *Sperryville vicinity*. The core of this sprawling porticoed mansion was built in the late 18th century by Francis Thornton as a residence for his son William. Francis Thornton, a member of a Spotsylvania County family, settled in present-day Rappahannock County ca. 1740, obtaining a grant for thousands of acres, including the F.T. (Francis Thornton) Valley. On a hill with views toward the Blue Ridge Mountains and down the F.T. Valley, the late Georgian farmhouse was enlarged in the mid-19th century with end wings, and the whole was united by a huge unacademic colonnade crowned by a bracketed cornice and pediment. The resulting edifice makes for an arresting, if provincial, composition with a wonderful backdrop of pastoral and mountainous scenery. Montpelier was inherited by William Thornton's son Dr. Philip Thornton, who lived there with his French wife, Caroline Homassel Thornton. The property passed out of the Thornton family after her death in 1876. The house stood unoccupied in recent years but has since been renovated by its present owner, James W. Fletcher, whose wife is a descendant of Francis Thornton. 78–28 (1/16/73).

MOUNT SALEM BAPTIST MEETING HOUSE, *Washington vicinity*. Although the Mount Salem Baptist congregation was organized in 1824, the present meetinghouse was not begun until March 1850. The congregation, which included both whites and blacks on its first membership list, flourished for many years, remaining active until World War II. The remotely located house of worship survives unaltered from its original state, exhibiting rural Virginia's conservative taste in church architecture in the mid-19th century. The exterior is in a simplified Federal style, and the few details of the interior show the influence of Greek Revival pattern books. Its construction was supervised by Henry Miller, a local builder. The meetinghouse closed in 1942 but was restored in 1977 and returned to monthly service. 78–33 (12/19/78).

SPERRYVILLE HISTORIC DISTRICT, *coinciding approximately with town boundaries*. Sperryville is an upper Piedmont crossroads town that has remained little changed since the 1920s. Laid out in 1820 by Francis Thornton, Jr., on a small plain between the Thornton River and the hills of the northern Blue Ridge, the village grew slowly until 1867 when the Smoot family of Alexandria established a tannery here. The resulting influx of workers led to the construction of many of the simple wooden residences that are still standing in Sperryville. Intermingled arc postbellum houses influenced by the 19th-century Romantic Revival and a scattering of late 19th-century workers' houses. In the center of the community is an early brick-and-frame tavern. Most of the district's buildings line U.S. Route 522 and local route 1001, which form Sperryville's main street. 78–93 (12/14/82).

WASHINGTON HISTORIC DISTRICT, *including the entire village of Washington.* At the base of the Blue Ridge Mountains, the village of Washington is perhaps the best preserved of the several county seat communities of the Virginia Piedmont. The name honors George Washington, who as a young surveyor platted the present grid plan in 1749. As originally laid out, the town had two main north-south streets and five cross streets. The community was incorporated in 1796 at which time it received its present name. It became a county seat thirty-seven years later when Rappahannock County was set off from Culpeper County. Although most of its buildings, both commercial and residential ones, are in the regional vernacular styles, the district has several more sophisticated structures, among which is the 1833 Roman Revival courthouse built by Malcolm F. Crawford, who had worked for Thomas Jefferson at the University of Virginia. Next to the courthouse is a cluster of mid-19th-century governmental structures including the clerk's office, treasurer's office, and jail. Chief among the vernacular structures is the Washington House Tavern, originally known as Coxes Hotel, a rambling early 19th-century building with numerous wings and additions. Washington has remained within its 19th-century limits and has few modern intrusions. In recent years many of its neglected buildings have been rescued from deterioration and renovated in an effort to preserve the community's early character. 322–11 (4/15/75).

WASHINGTON MILL, *Washington.* A landmark on the eastern edge of the county seat village of Washington, Washington Mill served as the town mill for most of the 19th century. Built ca. 1800 with subsequent additions in 1840 and 1860, the mill retains much early machinery and is a well-preserved artifact of the grain and milling economy. The structure is believed also to have served as a neutral bartering place between Union and Confederate lines during the Civil War. No longer in operation, the mill is planned for preservation through adaptive use. 78–89 (11/18/80).

CITY OF RICHMOND

*Virginia's capital was named by William Byrd II after the
Thameside borough of Richmond, England. Byrd, along with
William Mayo, laid out the town in 1737. It was established in
1742 and was designated the capital of the state in 1779.
Richmond was incorporated as a town in 1782 and was
incorporated as a city in 1842. From 1861 to 1865 Richmond was
the capital of the Confederate States of America. The city has
been enlarged through several annexations of portions of Henrico
and Chesterfield counties.*

AGECROFT, *4395 Sulgrave Road.* Set in a tree-dotted park
with broad lawns and formal gardens, this half-timber Tudor
mansion is a product of the antiquarianism and Anglophilia
that permeated Virginia's upper classes in the 1920s. Agecroft
was originally a postmedieval manor house built by John Langley near Manchester, England. By 1925 it had fallen into decay
and was surrounded by coal mines and railroad tracks. Against
protests voiced in the House of Commons, Richmond businessman Thomas C. Williams, Jr., purchased the house and
had it carefully dismantled and shipped to Richmond where it
was reconstructed in modified form under the direction of
New York architect Homer G. Morse. Outstanding original
features of the house include the elaborately patterned half-
timbering in the entrance court and a magnificent mullioned
bay window with original leaded glass lighting the great hall.
Agecroft's formal gardens were designed by Charles Gillette.
The property is now owned by the Agecroft Association and
is exhibited as a museum. It is located overlooking the James
River on the southern edge of Windsor Farms, a garden suburb developed by Williams in the 1920s. 127–23 (7/18/78).

ALMSHOUSE, *210 Hospital Street*. Built in 1860–61 as a place of refuge for the city's white poor, the Richmond Almshouse is an impressive monument to the reform ferment of the antebellum period. Designed by Richmond city engineer Washington Gill, the Italianate structure replaced an older poorhouse built before 1810. Gill gave the new building a striking outline by using three pedimented pavilions. The Almshouse served during the Civil War as the first major hospital of the Confederacy and as a home and school for the Virginia Military Institute cadets in 1864–65, after the V.M.I. barracks in Lexington had been gutted during the Valley campaign. The institutional use of the Almshouse ceased in recent years, and the building was sold by the city for private development. It was renovated in 1984–85 to house apartments for low-income old people. 127–353 (7/21/81); *Virginia Historic Landmarks Board preservation easement*.

BARRET HOUSE, *15 South Fifth Street*. This Greek Revival mansion is perhaps the finest and best-preserved survivor of the many dwellings that once dotted the hills of downtown Richmond. The house was built in 1844 for William Barret, son of John Barret who served as the city's mayor for three terms. William Barret was a tobacconist and was regarded as the city's richest citizen at his death in 1870. In 1876 the house was rented to the vicomte de Sibour, the French consul. It was spared a threatened demolition in 1936 when Richmond architectural historian Mary Wingfield Scott and her cousin Mrs. John Bocock purchased it for preservation. Scott donated the property in 1978 to the Virginia Foundation for Architectural Education. The building now serves as the headquarters of the foundation as well as of the Virginia Society of the American Institute of Architects. Typical of Richmond's finer antebellum houses, the entrance of the Barret house is sheltered by a dwarf portico and its garden front is covered by a monumental portico. The garden portico supports two tiers of galleries that afforded panoramic views of the city and the James River. The interior preserves Greek Revival woodwork and a curved stair. A carriage house with servants' quarters survives on the lot. 127–29 (11/16/71); *Virginia Historic Landmarks Board preservation easement*.

BEERS HOUSE, *1228 East Broad Street*. Sheltered by magnolia trees, this town house is a lone reminder of the former residential character of downtown East Broad Street. It also serves as an architectural link between its two nationally significant neighbors: Monumental Church and the Egyptian Building. Dating from 1839, the house was built for William Beers, a merchant tailor. The house's gable roof was removed in 1860 and replaced with a full story topped by an Italianate cornice. Preserved without significant alteration since that date, the structure is now owned by the Medical College of Virginia Foundation. 127–356 (11/5/68).

BELGIAN BUILDING, VIRGINIA UNION UNIVERSITY, *North Lombardy Street and Brook Road.* This singular work of architecture was originally the Belgian Pavilion for the 1939 New York World's Fair. It was designed by Victor Bourgois and Leo Stynen under the direction of the Belgian architect Henri van de Velde, a leader of the International style. It was to be dismantled and rebuilt in Belgium after the fair, but the outbreak of World War II led to its presentation to Virginia Union University where it was reerected in 1941. The choice of Richmond stemmed from the availability of a good site and the need of the school for additional facilities. Dominated by what was originally a clock tower containing a carillon, the sprawling building with its clean geometry is a monument to the modernism of the 1930s. 127–173 (12/2/69).

BELL TOWER, *Capitol Square.* Long a familiar landmark in the southwest corner of Capitol Square and terminating Franklin Street, this brick edifice was built in 1824 as a guardhouse and signal tower for the Public Guard. Levi Swain, its contractor and presumably its designer, gave the otherwise solid structure a liveliness by using blind archs on the facades and a fanciful cupola topped by a fish weathervane. The tower's bell sounded in 1861 to warn of the approach of the Federal gunboat *Pawnee* and again in 1864 to sound the alarm for Dahlgren's raid. During the administration of Governor John N. Dalton, the tower served as the office of the lieutenant governor. In 1982 it was converted to the visitor's center for the Virginia State Travel Service. Its bell still rings to call members of the General Assembly to session. 127–121 (11/5/68).

BLUES ARMORY, *Sixth and East Marshall streets.* The castellated Blues Armory in the heart of Richmond's commercial area is a fine example of the massive armories erected in the country's larger cities from the 1870s to the 1920s. The building was designed by the Washington, D.C., firm of Averill and Hall and was completed in 1910. Actually built to withstand seige, it was until the early 1960s the headquarters of the Richmond Light Infantry Blues and had a market on its ground floor. Formed in 1789, the Blues served with distinction in every major conflict from the War of 1812 to World War II. Now disbanded, the unit is remembered for its dress uniforms patterned after the uniforms of the Swiss Guard of Marie Antionette. The building has recently been restored as a market and exhibition hall with the west facade incorporated in a glass-enclosed courtyard. The project is part of Richmond's Sixth Street Marketplace. 127–278 (12/16/75).

BRANCH BUILDING, *1015 East Main Street*. After its destruction during the Evacuation Fire of 1865, most of Richmond's commercial area was rebuilt with structures employing cast-iron trim or completely cast-iron facades, nearly all in a rich Italianate style. Of the three iron fronts remaining in the area, the Branch Building of 1866 stands as a distinguished representative of this American architectural type. Built as the headquarters of the Virginia Fire and Marine Insurance Company, the building is set off by its ground-floor arcade. It has recently undergone a complete rehabilitation. 127–196 (12/2/69).

BRANCH HOUSE, *2501 Monument Avenue*. This Monument Avenue mansion commissioned in 1916 for John Kerr Branch, Jr., is the work of New York architect John Russell Pope, who had just designed Richmond's Broad Street Station. Constructed in 1917–19, this house is an excellent example of an urban residence planned in the Tudor-Jacobean style. It is the only house of its type by Pope in which the interiors have survived intact and is one of the earliest examples of this style of architecture in Virginia. The house was designed as a setting for the collection of Renaissance tapestries, furniture, and paintings amassed by Branch, a Richmond stockbroker and bank president. Pope and his partner Otto R. Eggers blended their own interior detailing with woodwork salvaged from several 16th-century English country houses. The house design is a manifestation of the admiration for English styles and their upper-class associations that swept the country during the first three decades of this century. The United Way of Richmond used the house as offices from 1954 until 1982. It has since been sympathetically restored for offices of an insurance company. 127–246 (1/17/84); *Virginia Historical Landmarks Board preservation easement*.

BROAD STREET STATION (UNION STATION OF RICHMOND), *West Broad Street at Robinson Street*. Richmond's Broad Street Station is one of the nation's last great terminals built during the Golden Age of railroads. It was the result of a competition won by the New York architect John Russell Pope in 1913. Working in the tradition of McKim, Mead and White, Pope employed a noble and serene classicism that he later used on the Jefferson Memorial and the National Gallery of Art. Faced with Indiana limestone and dominated by a Tuscan colonnade and a Roman dome, the first use of a dome for a major railroad station, the building was completed in 1919 for the Richmond, Fredericksburg and Potomac Railroad Company. The property has since been acquired by the state, and the interior has been remodeled sympathetically to house the Science Museum of Virginia. 127–226 (11/16/71).

BYRD THEATRE, *2908 West Cary Street*. Opened in 1938, the Byrd Theatre is one of the movie palaces that sprang up around the country in the 1920s. Built when lavish architectural decoration was still relatively inexpensive, these glittering confections vied with one another to attract and dazzle cinemagoers. Dazzling still, the theater was designed and built by Fred A. Bishop of Richmond with the decoration and artwork of the baroque interior executed by the Brounet Studios of New York. It was one of the first theaters outfitted for sound motion pictures, being equipped with Vitaphone, a sound synchronization system pioneered by Bell Telephone Laboratories. Many recordings have been made on its outstanding Wurlitzer organ. A recent change of ownership brought with it a refurbishing of the interior to its original brilliant state. 127–287 (6/21/77).

HENRY COALTER CABELL HOUSE, *116 South Third Street*. This antebellum residence is the sole survivor of the many large houses that once formed Gamble's Hill, a fashionable 19th-century neighborhood. It was build in 1847 for William O. George but was rented for three decades beginning in the 1850s to Richmond lawyer Henry Coalter Cabell. The portico uses an order invented for American buildings by the Brooklyn architect Minard Lafever and popularized throughout the country through his architectural design books. Although sometimes described as Egyptian, the order is actually composed of Grecian motifs. The house has served as the headquarters of the Virginia Education Association since 1951. 127–225 (11/16/71).

CATHEDRAL OF THE SACRED HEART, *Laurel Street and Floyd Avenue*. Framed by Richmond's Monroe Park and forming the visual pivot between the city's commercial area and the residential Fan District, the Cathedral of the Sacred Heart is Virginia's best ecclesiastical representation of the Italian Renaissance Revival style. The domed and porticoed limestone structure, along with its cloisters, diocesan gardens, and episcopal residence, is the work of Joseph H. McGuire, a New York architect whose practice centered on Roman Catholic churches and institutional buildings. It was begun in 1903 and completed in 1906 with funds given by financier, promoter, and philanthropist Thomas Fortune Ryan, a Nelson County native who made his fortune in New York. The cathedral has a lofty interior with elaborate, richly colored architectural decoration. 127–137 (12/15/81).

CENTENARY CHURCH, *411 East Grace Street*. A landmark in the heart of Richmond's Grace Street shopping district, Centenary Church is the city's oldest Methodist church and is one of its chief examples of the Gothic Revival style. In its original form it was a Greek Revival building, erected in 1841–43 by the local builder/architects John and Samuel Freeman to replace the congregation's first building, which was in Shockoe Valley. The simple temple-form building was completely remodeled in the Gothic style in 1874–76 by Richmond architect Albert L. West, complete with traceried windows and a tall, square bell tower. Methodists were in Richmond in the late 18th century but were not organized. In 1799 Bishop Francis Asbury sent the Reverend Thomas Lyell to Richmond to take charge of the group. He formed a congregation and had the parent church of the Centenary congregation built by the end of the year. 127–321 (10/16/79).

CENTRAL FIDELITY BANK, *West Broad and North Third streets*. Originally named the Central National Bank, this office tower is Virginia's outstanding example of the Art Deco skyscraper. New York architect John Eberson was commissioned to design it; the local firm of Carneal, Johnston and Wright served as consultants. Ground was broken in 1929, and the building was completed the next year. In addition to its soaring exterior, the bank has a great vaulted banking hall containing Art Deco ornamentation executed in rich colors and fine materials. The Central National Bank was founded in 1911 when the retail merchants of the western end of Broad Street decided to start a bank that would be conveniently located and would serve them directly. 127–309 (4/18/78).

COLUMBIA, *West Grace and Lombardy streets*. One of a small number of upper-class Richmond houses surviving from the Federal period, Columbia was built in 1817–18 as a suburban residence for Philip Haxall, a Petersburg native who moved to Richmond in 1810 to manage the Columbia Flour Mills, from which the house derives its name. In 1834 the Virginia Baptist Educational Society purchased the residence and converted it to the main academic building of Richmond College, which grew to become the University of Richmond. Except for the Civil War years when the house was used as a Confederate hospital and later as a barracks for Union troops, Columbia functioned over a century and a half as an educational facility. From 1917 to 1954 the house was the University of Richmond's T. C. Williams School of Law. A wing was added in 1924 to accommodate the expanded law school. In 1984 the property was purchased by the American Historical Foundation to serve as its headquarters. The original portion of the house, although altered over the years, retains much early fabric. Of note is the richly carved Federal woodwork in the entrance hall and stair hall. The entrance hall is further decorated with a plasterwork ceiling. 127–45 (3/16/82); *Virginia Historic Landmarks Board preservation easement.*

COMMONWEALTH CLUB HISTORIC DISTRICT, *400 block West Franklin Street and adjacent properties*. The area around West Franklin Street's 400 block retains one of Richmond's best-preserved clusters of turn-of-the-century upper-class town houses. Its focal point is the architecturally robust Commonwealth Club, a gentlemen's club designed in the 1890s by Carrère and Hastings of New York. Although the block was once part of an unbroken progression of fine residences extending from Capitol Square to Monument Avenue, it is now a detached enclave in the midst of high-rise development. The stylistic diversity of the turn of the century is well illustrated here with houses in the Italianate, Romanesque, Gothic Revival, and classical styles, all executed with harmonious scale and materials. This consistency of quality is evident in the row of town houses (shown) directly opposite the Commonwealth Club. The Commonwealth Club remains an influential social institution for the city; most of the houses in the district have recently been rehabilitated for offices. 127–373 (10/19/82).

CONFEDERATE MEMORIAL CHAPEL, *2900 Grove Avenue*. The modest white-painted Gothic-style chapel on the grounds of the Virginia Museum was built in 1887 to serve the veterans of the Confederate Soldiers' Home that then stood on the block. Designed by local architect M. J. Dimmock and built by Joseph Wingfield, the building was paid for by the veterans themselves and was dedicated to their dead comrades. It served the former "Rebs" until the last one died in 1941 and has been in sporadic use ever since. It is now maintained by the state. The windows contain a colorful variety of Victorian stained glass. 127–224 (11/16/71).

CROZET HOUSE, *100 East Main Street*. This well-proportioned Federal town house on Richmond's Main Street was built ca. 1815 by Curtis Carter, a local brickmason and contractor, as his own home. From 1828 to 1832 it served as the home of French engineer Col. Claudius Crozet. Appointed engineer of the state of Virginia in 1823, Crozet mapped watercourses and planned highways, railroads, canals, and tunnels. He is perhaps best remembered as engineer of the first tunnel through the Blue Ridge Mountains and as one of the founders of the Virginia Military Institute. The house was restored in 1940 when it received its present colonial-style brick doorway. Much of the original interior woodwork survives. 127–47 (11/16/71).

DONNAN-ASHER IRON-FRONT BUILDING, *1207–1211 East Main Street.* Built in 1866 as part of the reconstruction of Richmond's commercial area after the Evacuation Fire of 1865, this ornate building has one of only three completely cast-iron facades remaining in the city. The iron front was popular at the time because it could provide maximum elaboration with minimal expense and construction time; most of the iron facades were rendered in an Italianate style inspired by the Renaissance palaces of Venice. The ironwork on this facade was designed by George H. Johnson, an Englishman who came to this country in 1851. The iron was produced by Hayward and Bartlett of Baltimore, by whom Johnson was employed at the time. A 1960s shopfront mars the otherwise unaltered facade. 127–163 (12/2/69).

EGYPTIAN BUILDING, *College and East Marshall streets.* No purer expression of the Egyptian Revival of the mid-19th century survives in the nation than this temple-form structure, a masterpiece by Philadelphia architect Thomas S. Stewart. Completed in 1846, the Egyptian Building housed the medical department of Hampden-Sydney College, established in Richmond in 1837. The department became an independent institution in 1854 and came under state control in 1860. In 1893 it combined with the University College of Medicine to form the present Medical College of Virginia. The college has since been expanded into a vast complex of surrounding buildings, but the Egyptian Building, the oldest medical education building in the South, remains the architectural symbol of the institution. The choice of style alluded to Egypt's ancient medical tradition. Emphasizing the Egyptian theme is the cast-iron fence with its posts in the form of stylized mummies and its granite piers in the shape of obelisks. 127–87 (11/5/68); *National Historic Landmark.*

ENGLISH VILLAGE, *3418–3450 Grove Avenue.* English Village was one of the earliest ventures in cooperative planned communities in Richmond, a precursor of today's condominiums. Notable for its Tudor-style architecture and innovative planning and design, the U-shaped multifamily complex was designed by Richmond architect Bascom J. Rowlett and built in 1927 by Davis Brothers, a large local contracting firm. Although most of the cooperative housing in America at that time was built for workers and owned collectively, English Village was built for upper-middle-class families with each owner holding title to his own unit. All but one of the first owners lost their titles through mortgage foreclosures in the Depression. Home ownership gradually resumed, however, allowing the complex to survive as a successful cooperative to the present. One of its bylaws included a restriction on exterior changes, a factor critical to the maintenance of English Village's architectural integrity. 127–374 (8/16/83).

EXECUTIVE MANSION, *Capitol Square*. Authorized in 1810 and first occupied in 1813 by Governor James Barbour, the Executive Mansion continues to serve as the residence of the governor of Virginia. It is the oldest governor's mansion built as such in continuous use in the nation. Its architect was Alexander Parris, a native of Maine who lived for a brief while in Richmond before settling permanently in Boston where he became one of the city's leading architects. Executed by the builder Christopher Tompkins, the mansion is a pleasingly proportioned essay in the Federal style endowed with a strong domesticity rather than the monumentality normally expected in an official residence. During its many years of service, the mansion has accommodated such guests as Lafayette, the Prince of Wales (later King Edward VII), Marshal Foch, Winston Churchill, and Queen Mother Elizabeth. The body of Stonewall Jackson was brought to lie in state here. Except for architect Duncan Lee's 1908 addition of an oval dining room to the rear and various later minor modifications, the exterior remains as completed. The rear principal rooms were rebuilt after a fire in 1926; much of the woodwork in the front rooms, including the two stairs, is original. 127–57 (11/5/68).

FIRST NATIONAL BANK BUILDING, *Ninth and East Main streets*. The First National Bank Building, with its terracotta ornaments, carefully proportioned Corinthian columns, and elegant banking room, is an excellent example of turn-of-the-century Neoclassical Revival architecture. Designed by Alfred Charles Bossom, an associate with the New York architectural firm of Clinton and Russell, the building was completed in 1913 as the city's first high-rise building, combining monumental scale and fine detailing with the technological daring inherent in early steel-frame skyscraper construction. In the heart of Richmond's financial district, the structure served for more than half a century as headquarters for the state's oldest banking institution, now known as Sovran Bank. The exterior appearance was changed some twenty years ago when its deep projecting cornice was removed. The building has recently been restored for office condominiums. 127–381 (12/16/82).

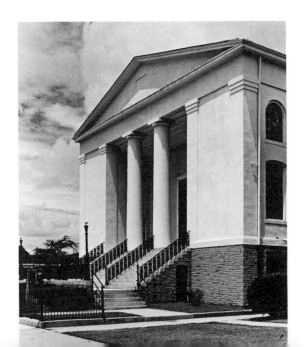

FOURTH BAPTIST CHURCH, *2800 P Street*. Fourth Baptist Church is a symbol of black religious strength in the Confederacy's former capital in the decades following emancipation. It is also an expression of Richmond's conservative architectural taste in the late 19th century. Its congregation began as a regular assembly of prayer by slaves in their quarters and transferred to the basement of Leigh Street Baptist Church in 1861. In 1865, under the leadership of the Reverend Scott Gwathmey, the blacks took control of their own group and built their own church with lumber salvaged from a Union hospital. This was replaced in 1875 by a frame church near what was to be the site of the present building. The 1875 structure burned in 1884, a month before the completion of the present church. Situated on the northern side of Church Hill, the present building boasts a stylish Victorian interior behind a plain but dignified Greek Revival exterior inspired by Richmond's Old First Baptist Church by Thomas U. Walter. The church continues to house one of the city's oldest black congregations. 127–318 (5/15/79).

o–100 BLOCK EAST FRANKLIN STREET HISTORIC DISTRICT, *including the first block of East Franklin Street and portions of the first blocks of East Grace and East Main streets*. This small urban neighborhood is a cohesive grouping of 19th-century residential architecture surrounded by commercial buildings and parking lots. The district is on lands once part of Rutherfoord's Addition, property owned by cotton and tobacco manufacturer Thomas Rutherfoord, who started selling tracts there in 1795 to friends and business associates. Although some of the lots were developed immediately after their sale, the existing fabric of the neighborhood dates from the 1840s through the 1920s. Including sophisticated examples of Greek Revival, Italianate, Queen Anne, and Georgian Revival styles, most of the houses were built as side-hall-plan town houses, two and three stories in height. An outstanding exception is the 1845–46 Kent-Valentine house, a freestanding mansion designed by Isaiah Rogers and enlarged to its present form in 1904. Most of the houses have been sympathetically converted to offices, shops, or apartments. 127–317 (10/16/79).

WEST FRANKLIN STREET HISTORIC DISTRICT, *including three blocks of West Franklin Street from Monroe Park to Ryland Street*. An 1867 annexation brought the area of West Franklin Street as far west as Lombardy Street into the city limits, and sophisticated town houses soon went up. From Monroe Park west is a colorful progression of architectural styles, including French Renaissance, Second Empire, Italianate, Romanesque, Queen Anne, and Georgian Revival, with an underlying harmony derived from the uniformity of scale and repetition of materials. Individually outstanding houses are the 1888 Queen Anne–style Ginter mansion (901 West Franklin), home of tobacco magnate Maj. Lewis Ginter, and next to it the opulent 1906 Scott-Bocock house (909 West Franklin), an adaptation of the Petit Trianon by the Richmond firm of Noland and Baskervill, which also designed the French Renaissance Eppa Hunton house (810 West Franklin), completed in 1916. The oldest house in the district is the Ritter-Hickock house (821 West Franklin), built in the 1850s as a suburban villa and modernized in the Georgian Revival taste in 1910. The most architecturally individual of the dwellings is the eclectic Millhiser house (916 West Franklin), a Romanesque–Queen Anne confection designed by William M. Poindexter (shown at extreme right). Most of the buildings in the easternmost blocks of the district have been acquired by Virginia Commonwealth University and now serve as the core of the academic division of this urban state university. 127–228 (3/21/72).

200 BLOCK WEST FRANKLIN STREET HISTORIC DISTRICT, *200–212 West Franklin Street.* Located in this one block of Richmond's Franklin Street are eight houses forming perhaps the most diverse concentration of 19th-century domestic architecture in the city. Except for the demolition of two houses, the block has been little changed since before World War I when it was one of Richmond's best addresses. Shown in the center here is the earliest house in the group, the ca. 1800 Cole Diggs house (204 West Franklin), which has a galleried facade and ornamental Federal woodwork. The Price house (208–212 West Franklin) was begun ca. 1805 and was subsequently enlarged and remodeled in the Second Empire style, finally becoming a hospital building. The Classical Revival is represented by the Palmer house (211 West Franklin) with its dwarf Doric portico. Typical Richmond Italianate is seen in the A. S. Smith house (209 West Franklin), a side-hall dwelling with a heavy modillioned cornice. Of the two Eastlake houses, the ca. 1886 T. Seddon Bruce house (207 West Franklin), designed by M. J. Dimmock, is especially well appointed. The Second Empire style is best represented by the mansard roof and woodwork of the Ida Schoolcraft house (200 West Franklin Street). Finally, a beautiful example of the French Renaissance is the Carter-Mayo house (205 West Franklin), designed by the New York firm of Carrère and Hastings and completed in 1896. The buildings were owned for a number of years by a psychiatric hospital and were rescued from possible redevelopment in 1977 by the Historic Richmond Foundation. Since that time all the buildings have been sold to individual owners and have been rehabilitated for alternative uses. Shown are 200–204 West Franklin Street. 127–281 (5/17/77); *Virginia Historic Landmarks Board preservation easements on all houses.*

ELLEN GLASGOW HOUSE, *1 West Main Street.* Virginia author Ellen Glasgow made her home in this Greek Revival mansion from 1887, when it was purchased by her father, until her death in 1945. She inherited it from her father in 1916. Glasgow's many novels depicted life in the South with a realism devoid of the nostalgic sentimentality that characterized much southern writing of the period. For her literary accomplishments she was elected to the American Academy of Arts and Letters in 1938. Her last novel, *In This Our Life,* won her the Pulitzer Prize in 1942. Her home, typical of the large Greek Revival houses that once lined the streets of downtown Richmond, was built in 1841 for David M. Branch, a tobacco manufacturer. From 1846 until 1887, 1 West Main Street was the home of the Davenport family, developers of Richmond's paper industry. Glasgow's "square gray house" was purchased by the Association for the Preservation of Virginia Antiquities in 1947. It recently has been sold by the APVA and sympathetically renovated for use as an attorney's office. 127–56 (1/18/72); *National Historic Landmark.*

WILLIAM A. GRANT HOUSE, *1008 East Clay Street*. This residence opposite the Valentine Museum is an early example of the Italianate style in Richmond. The style's massive scale and square proportions were inspired by the palaces of Florence. Notable features of the house include the thin-jointed brick veneer, marble entrance steps, elaborately detailed entrance porch, and cast-iron hood moldings over the windows. Dating from 1853, the house was the home of William A. Grant, a tobacco manufacturer whose tobacco factory still survives in Shockoe Valley. It was sold to the Sheltering Arms Hospital in 1882, which has since moved, and the mansion is now used for offices of the Medical College of Virginia. Along with a few remaining neighboring houses, the Grant house was once part of a series of dwellings that formed a leading residential street. 127–17 (11/5/68).

2900 BLOCK GROVE AVENUE HISTORIC DISTRICT, *2901, 2905, 2911, 2915 Grove Avenue*. Departing from the tight town-house development of most of Richmond's west end is this tree-shaded block of four freestanding houses across Grove Avenue from the Virginia Museum. Although the easternmost house is a fairly conventional turn-of-the-century square dwelling with Craftsman overtones, the remaining three form a trio of highly individualized interpretations of the Queen Anne style with the flavor of suburban villas. Faced with gray granite, each house has a lively outline with angled projections and a corner tower. Although their architect has not been identified, they are among Richmond's more interesting examples of late Victorian architecture. Adding to the fanciful quality of the district are the ornamented wooden carriage houses behind the main dwellings. Both 2911 and 2915 Grove Avenue have been sympathetically converted to doctors' offices. 127–238 (10/17/72).

HANCOCK-WIRT-CASKIE HOUSE, *Fifth and East Main streets*. Benjamin Henry Latrobe's design for a Richmond house with demioctagonal bays provided the prototype for this Fifth Street house erected for Michael Hancock in 1808–9. One of the few examples of Richmond's outstanding Federal architecture still standing, the dwelling displays the refinement achieved by the capital's builders in the early 19th century. The arcaded gallery, Flemish bond brickwork, marble trim, and interior woodwork are all of the highest quality and unite to form an elegant composition. The house was purchased in 1816 by William Wirt, a year before he published his biography of Patrick Henry and became U.S. attorney general. The house next served as the home of two mayors of the city, Benjamin Tate and later his son Joseph. It was long the residence of Mrs. Benjamin Caskie and became the headquarters of the Richmond Chapter of the American Red Cross after her death in 1941. The William Byrd Branch of the Association for the Preservation of Virginia Antiquities purchased the house in the 1970s and has since sold it for use as an attorney's office. 127–42 (12/2/69).

HASKER AND MARCUSE FACTORY (CHURCH HILL HOUSE), *2300 and 2400 blocks of Venable and Burton streets*. Constructed between 1893 and 1895, the Hasker and Marcuse Factory developed the process of manufacturing polychromatic printed tobacco tins. Shipped nationwide, the firm's tobacco tins were the primary means of advertising and marketing the products of the newly consolidated tobacco companies formed in Richmond during the 1890s. Integral to this manufacturing process was the development and application of the technology of tin-printing processes, which resulted in the invention and widespread use of offset lithography and had a profound effect on the development of the modern packaging industry. The four-story brick building with its unadorned walls and large window areas is typical of the industrial architecture of the period. It is being preserved through adaptation as housing for low-income people and has been renamed Church Hill House. 127–299 (4/19/83).

HOLLY LAWN, *4012 Hermitage Road*. Amid clusters of mature oaks and holly trees in what was a turn-of-the-century streetcar suburb of Richmond, Holly Lawn is an ambitious Queen Anne–style residence. Typical of its mode, it has a complex roofline, irregular plan, and one-story porch wrapping around the facade. Built in 1901 for Andrew Bierne Blair, a Richmond insurance agent, the house was the home of Dr. Ennion G. Williams from 1913 until his death in 1931. Under Dr. Williams's leadership as the Commonwealth's first commissioner of public health, a post to which he was appointed in 1908, Virginia's health board became one of the first such departments in the country to apply scientific knowledge to the improvement of public hygiene by a system of prevention as well as cure. The house now serves as the headquarters of the Richmond Council of Garden Clubs. 127–55 (5/18/82).

HOLLYWOOD CEMETERY, *412 South Cherry Street*. This cemetery was laid out in 1848 according to plans by John Notman, a Scottish architect and landscaper who settled in Philadelphia where he pioneered in romantically landscaped parks and cemeteries. The cemetery follows Notman's usual format, being spread across hills and ravines along a river, in this case the James, with winding roadways and paths shaded by a variety of trees. Such hilly riverside sites were ideal for cemeteries as the land was good for little else. The cemetery takes its name from its fine stand of hollies, which Notman incorporated into the design. Large landscaped cemeteries were both popular and practical in their day, for the older churchyards and municipal burying grounds were reaching capacity, and the parklike settings of the new cemeteries made them attractive places to visit as well as objects of civic pride. Over the next century, Hollywood became an outdoor pantheon of well-known Virginians and was embellished with an outstanding collection of monuments and ornamental ironwork. Interred here are U.S. presidents James Monroe and John Tyler and Confederate president Jefferson Davis, as well as John Randolph of Roa-

noke, J. E. B. Stuart, Matthew Fontaine Maury, and Fitzhugh Lee. A dry-laid stone pyramid at the cemetery's northwestern corner marks the graves of 18,000 Confederate soldiers. The entrance to Hollywood is marked by a Gothic Revival mortuary chapel designed by M. J. Dimmock of Richmond. 127–221 (9/9/69).

JACKSON WARD HISTORIC DISTRICT, *roughly bounded by Belvidere, Marshall, and Fourth streets and the Richmond-Petersburg Turnpike.* Around the turn of the century, Richmond had one of the most thriving black business communities in the nation. The hub of this professional and entrepreneurial activity was the Jackson Ward neighborhood with its fraternal organizations, cooperative banks, insurance companies, and other commercial and social institutions, all founded and run by blacks, including bankers Maggie L. Walker and John Mitchell, ministers W. W. Browne and John Jasper, Common Council members John H. Adams and S. W. Robinson, and attorney Giles B. Jackson, the first black admitted for practice before the Supreme Court of Virginia. Perhaps the neighborhood's most popularly known son was the motion-picture dancer and actor Bill ("Bojangles") Robinson. Jackson Ward developed as a neighborhood in the decades before the Civil War when the area was largely populated by citizens of German and Jewish extraction but had a growing number of free blacks. After the war Jackson Ward became the predominantly black neighborhood it is today. Urban redevelopment and expressway construction reduced its size, but the some forty blocks or fractions of blocks remaining make Jackson Ward Richmond's only residential neighborhood in the city center and the nation's largest historic district associated primarily with black culture. The neighborhood is dominated by three-bay, side-passage town houses in Greek Revival, Italianate, Eastlake, and Queen Anne styles. Many of the Italianate houses have locally manufactured cast-iron porches, the state's richest display of ornamental ironwork. Despite commercial expansion, poverty, and neglect, the surviving portions of Jackson Ward form a remarkably cohesive urban area which recently has become the focus of increasing rehabilitation activity. 127–237 (4/20/76); *National Historic Landmark.*

JAMES RIVER AND KANAWHA CANAL HISTORIC DISTRICT, *extending from the ship lock in downtown for several miles into western Henrico County to Bosher's Dam.* George Washington strongly advocated developing the navigation of the James River west of Richmond and bypassing the city's rapids. The James River Company was founded in 1785 to construct a 200-mile canal system from the capital to Botetourt County, and Washington served as the company's honorary president. The company first removed obstructions from long stretches of the river and constructed a "Tidewater Connection," a series of locks through downtown Richmond linking the regions along the upper portion of the river with the sea.

In 1835 the James River and Kanawha Canal Company was formed from the original company to connect the James to the Kanawha River and thus provide a navigation system between the Atlantic Ocean and the Ohio and Mississippi rivers. A canal with ninety locks and many aqueducts was completed as far as Buchanan by the early 1850s, and a system of basins, locks, and docks was built through downtown Richmond, beginning with the Great Ship Lock. The canal remained in operation until 1880 when the system was purchased by the Richmond and Alleghany Railway Company, which laid its tracks on the towpath. Although much of the system has since fallen into ruin or has been built on, its course can yet be traced through the city. Much of the canal remains intact from the west of downtown into Henrico County. Several of the Tidewater Connection locks have been destroyed by expressway construction, and the headquarters of the CSX Corporation was built over the Great Basin. However, the lower locks of the Tidewater Connection have been restored by the Reynolds Metals Company, so that the craftsmanship of the canal's stonework can still be admired. 127–171 (9/9/69).

HOTEL JEFFERSON, *bounded by West Franklin, Jefferson, West Main, and Adams streets*. The opulence of America's Gilded Age was given full play in the hotel commissioned in the 1890s by Richmond tobacconist Maj. Lewis Ginter. For its design, Ginter engaged the New York firm of Carrère and Hastings, a leading practitioner of the Beaux Arts style, and charged the architects to provide the city with the finest hostelry in the South. Completed in 1895, the hotel exhibits an architectural exuberance seldom seen in commercial buildings with its towers, pavilions, and loggia all ornamented with white terra-cotta classical decorations. The magnificent interior, with its regal progression of public rooms, was complemented by such advanced technological devices as service telephones, electric lighting, central heating, and hot and cold running water for each of its 342 guest rooms. A fire destroyed the south half of the building, but it was sympathetically rebuilt in 1901 by architect J. Kevan Peebles of Norfolk, who replaced the original glass-and-iron court with the present Edwardian Baroque lobby and its grand stair. After enjoying a long reputation for unmatched service and surroundings, the hotel declined in popularity and eventually closed; but a comprehensive rehabilitation has returned this architectural and social landmark to its former magnificence. 127–1 (11/5/68).

KENT-VALENTINE HOUSE, *12 East Franklin Street*. In 1844 merchant Horace L. Kent commissioned Boston architect Isaiah Rogers to design this Franklin Street mansion in order to accommodate his large family. Most of Rogers's buildings, including Richmond's Exchange Hotel, have been destroyed; his house for Kent is his only remaining residential work. In its original form 12 East Franklin Street was a three-bay Italianate dwelling skirted by a cast-iron veranda, an early use of this

motif. In 1904 Granville G. Valentine, owner of a meat extract company, bought the house, and in 1910 he engaged the local firm of Noland and Baskervill to expand it into a five-bay composition and to replace the veranda with the present Ionic portico. The resulting structure is a successful amalgam of antebellum and early 20th-century styles. In the interior Noland and Baskervill's richly carved Georgian Revival drawing room provides an interesting contrast to Rogers's pair of Gothic Revival reception rooms opposite. The house was restored in the early 1970s to serve as the headquarters of the Garden Club of Virginia. 127–112 (10/6/70); *Virginia Historic Landmarks Board preservation easement.*

BENJAMIN WATKINS LEIGH HOUSE, *1000 East Clay Street*. John Wickham, owner of the town house across the street that later became the Valentine Museum, had this house built for his daughter Julia between 1812 and 1816. Julia Wickham Leigh and her husband, Benjamin Watkins Leigh, a Richmond lawyer who served as a U.S. senator during the Jackson administration, were living there by 1826. The house was originally a typical Federal town house but was remodeled in the Italianate mode with a bracketed porch and cornice after 1851 when it was sold to Lieutenant Governor John M. Gregory. In 1932 the house was incorporated into the Sheltering Arms Hospital complex. It is now used for offices of the Medical College of Virginia. 127–65 (11/5/68).

LEIGH STREET BAPTIST CHURCH, *East Leigh and Twenty-Fifth streets*. This Greek Revival church was designed by Philadelphia architect Samuel Sloan and was completed in 1857. Sloan, in addition to his numerous commissions, was the author of *The Model Architect* (1852), a design book which had a great influence on the architecture of mid-19th-century America. The congregation was organized in the early 1850s by Baptist missionary Reuben Ford, and under its auspices seven other Richmond Baptist churches were started. It is the oldest white Baptist church in the city still occupied by its congregation. Although the interior has been remodeled and the south wall hidden by a later wing, Sloan's strong, clean design, dominated by a hexastyle Greek Doric portico, remains discernible. 127–11 (11/16/71).

LINDEN ROW, *100–114 East Franklin Street*. The British idea of a row of connected town houses, or terrace, is effectively interpreted in American red brick and crisp, white-painted wooden trim on Linden Row, a block of architecturally unified three-story dwellings highlighting Richmond's Franklin Street. Named for the linden trees that once shaded a garden on the site, the eastern five houses of the original row were erected as a business venture by Fleming James in 1847. The block was completed in James's formula by Samuel and Alexander Rutherfoord in 1853. The simple, straightforward design of the facades serves to set off the beautifully executed Greek

Doric dwarf porticoes sheltering the entrances. Linden Row has been a sought-after address since its completion, housing families, schools, businesses, and administrative offices to the present. The two easternmost houses were demolished in 1922. Between 1950 and 1957 the remaining houses were purchased by Richmond architectural historian and preservationist Mary Wingfield Scott, who in 1980 gave Linden Row to the Historic Richmond Foundation. 127–22 (7/6/71).

LOEW'S THEATER (THE CARPENTER CENTER), *East Grace and Sixth streets.* Designed by theater architect John Eberson, Loew's Theater is in the front rank of the movie palace architecture of the 1920s. It was part of the national chain of theaters built by the Loew's Theater Corporation. With its mixture of Moorish and Spanish baroque influences, Loew's was considered the most up-to-date theater in the South when it opened to a capacity audience on April 9, 1928. The auditorium, with churrigueresque facades and a smooth ceiling on which special lights created the illusion of a starry night sky with moving clouds, gave the effect of an open Spanish plaza. Such architectural theatricality was essential to the so-called atmospheric motion-picture house, where the viewer, seated in the proper atmosphere, would achieve the greatest satisfaction from the film. Few designers approached Eberson's ability to create such exoticism. Although Loew's suffered some insensitive alterations in the 1960s, the theater has since been acquired and restored by the Virginia Center for the Performing Arts as the home of the Richmond Symphony and a performance hall for major music and stage events. It has been renamed the Carpenter Center. 127–324 (9/18/79).

MAIN STREET STATION, *East Main Street between Fifteenth and Seventeenth streets.* Completed in 1901, the Renaissance-style Main Street Station was designed by the Philadelphia firm of Wilson, Harris, and Richards. While not as large as many urban railroad terminals of the period, the station is an impressive composition, dominated by its steep hipped roof with its tiers of dormers and by its ornamental corner clock tower. Richly trimmed with terra-cotta decorations, the walls are constructed of what was described as old gold Pompeiian brick. Contrasting with the decorative surfaces of the station's front section, or headhouse, is the airy train shed projecting 530 feet from the rear. Built by the Pencoyd Iron Works of Pencoyd, Pa., the shed is one of the last gable-roof train sheds in the country. Its wrought-iron members employed riveted rather than pin-connected construction, a technique that became the standard truss construction method of modern buildings. The station was built to serve the Chesapeake and Ohio and the Seaboard Air Line railways. Closed to passenger service in the 1970s, the building has recently undergone a restoration for reuse as restaurants and a shopping mall. The roof of the headhouse was destroyed by fire in 1983 but has been accurately reproduced in the restoration. 127–172 (7/7/70); *National Historic Landmark.*

MANCHESTER COTTON AND WOOL MANUFAC-
TURING COMPANY BUILDING, *Hull Street at James
River.* Standing next to the south end of Mayo's Bridge, the
Manchester Cotton and Wool Manufacturing Company Building, built between 1837 and 1840, is one of the earliest surviving
industrial buildings in the Richmond area. Among the pioneers in the construction of textile factories closer to southern
cotton supplies, the Manchester firm became one of the most
successful of these enterprises in the state. The building, with
its distinctive stepped gable ends, is the foreground structure
in the Currier and Ives print of Richmond's 1865 Evacuation
Fire, in which most of the city's industrial buildings on the
north side of the James River were destroyed. 127–56 (4/19/83).

JOHN MARSHALL HOUSE, *East Marshall and Ninth
streets.* John Marshall, chief justice of the U.S. Supreme Court,
built this dignified but unpretentious late Georgian house in
1790 and made it his home for forty-five years. Marshall was
appointed to his high post in 1801 and held the position until
his death in 1835. Although his judicial duties took him away
from Richmond for months at a time, he was able to spend
long periods at home, writing many of his decisions establishing the fundamental principles for constitutional interpretation
in his Richmond residence. The house, one of the oldest brick
dwellings remaining in Richmond, was owned by Marshall descendants until 1907 when it was purchased by the city in order
to clear the site for a high school. Rescued from threatened
demolition in that year, the property in 1911 was handed over
to the perpetual care of the Association for the Preservation of
Virginia Antiquities. Maintained as a museum since that time,
the restored dwelling is furnished with many of Marshall's possessions. 127–73 (9/9/69); *National Historic Landmark.*

MASONIC TEMPLE, *101 West Broad Street.* Richmond's Masonic Temple, a brick-and-brownstone structure designed by
Baltimore architect Jackson T. Gott and erected in 1888–
93, is an impressive example of the American interpretation of the
Romanesque style. The weighty edifice, with its mass count-
ered by a large corner tower, delicate corner bartizans, and a
multiplicity of windows, was the largest building put up by
Virginia Masons to that time. In addition to the Masonic
meeting rooms, the building accommodated a department
store and cultural facilities, providing a grand setting for many
balls, concerts, and banquets, most notably a banquet held for
President Theodore Roosevelt in 1905. Abandoned by the Masons for a number of years, the building is currently unoccupied. 127–296 (12/14/82).

MASONS' HALL, *1807 East Franklin Street*. Standing aloof from the bustle of the surrounding wholesale food markets of Richmond's Shockoe Valley, the Masons' Hall is the oldest Masonic hall built as such in the country. The building has been in continuous use by Richmond Lodge No. 13 since its completion in 1787. Edmund Randolph and John Marshall belonged to the lodge, and the marquis de Lafayette was made an honorary member when he visited the hall in 1824. The late Georgian building, capped by a jaunty cupola, was remodeled in the mid-19th century when much of its exterior trim was replaced by Greek Revival work. However, the rather singular interior, decked out in Masonic paraphernalia on all three floors, retains much original fabric of interest. 127–19 (1/16/73).

MAUPIN-MAURY HOUSE, *1105 East Clay Street*. Dr. Socrates Maupin, one of the founders of the medical department of Hampden-Sydney College that later became the Medical College of Virginia, built this Greek Revival town house in 1846. Dr. Maupin sold the house in 1853 to Richmond stockbroker Robert H. Maury and moved to Charlottesville where he enjoyed a distinguished career on the University of Virginia faculty. In this house in 1861 Maury's cousin, Matthew Fontaine Maury, developed plans for his underwater torpedo for the Confederate navy. The house is representative of the scores of plain but commodious town houses that lined the streets of downtown Richmond until recent decades. Now surrounded by large hospital buildings, the house serves as the office of the Alumni Association of the Medical College of Virginia. 127–74 (11/5/68).

MAYMONT, *1700 Hampton Street*. The eclectic tastes of the late Victorian era in architecture, interior decoration, art collecting, and gardening are demonstrated at Maymont, the suburban estate created by Richmond railroad magnate and philanthropist Maj. James H. Dooley and his wife, Sallie May. The large stone mansion in a combination Romanesque and Châteauesque style was designed by Edgerton S. Rogers and completed in 1890. As a contrast to its somber exterior, each of the house's principal rooms has its own distinct, richly decorated character, from the Jacobean living hall, to the Turkish office, to the Louis XVI music room. The Dooleys filled the rooms with a singular collection of furnishings and works of art gathered on their world travels. They also developed the 100 acres of grounds into a series of different gardens, including an English-style rural park, formal Italian terraced gardens, a Japanese garden, a wilderness waterfall, and a grotto, all highlighted by pavilions, fountains, bridges, and other ornamental structures. At Mrs. Dooley's death in 1925, the house, grounds, and collections became a city museum and park. Custodianship for this unusually complete expression of upper-class late-19th-century American taste was given in 1975 to the Maymont Foundation, which has since undertaken a long-term restoration of its buildings and grounds. 127–182 (7/6/71).

MAYO HOUSE (MAYO MEMORIAL CHURCH HOUSE), *110 West Franklin Street*. As built for Samuel Taylor in 1845, this Greek Revival Franklin Street mansion was a three-part composition consisting of a two-story, temple-form center section with one-story wings. In 1883 the house was purchased by Richmond tobacconist Peter H. Mayo, who spared no expense in remodeling the interior to the current opulent taste and in adding a variety of modern conveniences. Mayo collected the finest cabinet woods and had them fashioned by artisans into door and window cases, stairs, mantels, and parquet floors, all intended to evoke a Renaissance flavor. He also added second stories to the flanking wings. The elaborate interior decorations were largely covered over during various modernizations after the Mayo family donated the house to the Episcopal Diocese of Virginia in 1923. An extensive effort was undertaken in 1982 to restore the interior's rich 1880s effect while keeping the house as a functioning diocesan office. 127–75 (5/16/72).

JAMES MONROE TOMB, *Hollywood Cemetery, 412 South Cherry Street*. The tomb of President James Monroe, the centerpiece of John Notman's romantically landscaped Hollywood Cemetery, is a tour de force of both Gothic Revival design and artistry in cast iron. The simple granite sarcophagus is enclosed by an iron screen surmounted by an ogee dome with open-work tracery. The scheme recalls that of Henry VII's tomb in Westminster Abbey, also enclosed by a metal screen but lacking a dome. The tomb was designed by Albert Lybrock, an Alsatian architect who settled in Richmond in 1852. The iron was cast by the Philadelphia firm of Wood and Perot and was assembled in 1858 by Asa Snyder, a Richmond ironworker. Monroe died and was buried in New York City in 1831. His body was moved to this final resting place upon the centennial of his birth in 1858, a cooperative effort by citizens of New York and Virginia. 127–382 (10/18/83); *National Historic Landmark*.

MONROE PARK HISTORIC DISTRICT, *bounded by Belvidere Street, West Main Street, and the properties on Laurel and West Franklin streets facing the park*. Defining the eastern boundary of Richmond's Fan District, Monroe Park occupies land acquired by the city in 1851 to serve as a park for what was developing into the stylish western suburbs. After serving as the location of an agricultural exposition and as a campsite for Confederate troops, the site was finally made into a park in the 1870s. The park layout currently combines plantings with a pattern of walks radiating from an elaborate triple-tier cast-iron fountain. Framing the park on its north and west sides is an assemblage of buildings ranging from Noland and Baskervill's Gothic Revival Grace and Holy Trinity Episcopal Church of 1895 to the 1906 Renaissance Revival Cathedral of the Sacred Heart by Joseph H. McGuire. The most conspicuous building is the Islamic-style Mosque Auditorium of 1927 by Marcellus Wright, Sr. Several late 19th-century town houses recall the earlier residential character of the park, and there are also two tall, 1920s Tudor-style apartment houses. The buildings, and especially their amazing skyline, demonstrate the eclecticism of the 1890s through the 1920s, while the park is a handsome example of late Victorian urban landscaping. 127–383 (11/15/83).

MONUMENTAL CHURCH, *1224 East Broad Street*. This inventive church was built in 1812–14 as a memorial to seventy-two people including the governor of the state who perished in a theater fire on the site in 1811. The committee that raised the funds for the church by public subscription was headed by John Marshall, who became a pewholder in the completed building. The church's architect, Robert Mills, had studied under Thomas Jefferson and Benjamin Henry Latrobe and combined design elements favored by both his mentors. The octagonal form and Delorme-type dome were features preferred by Jefferson, and the Greek Doric order and highly personalized, almost Soane-like classical details were frequently used by Latrobe. Mills's design also heralded a new approach in the state's ecclesiastical architecture. One of the first Episcopal churches built after the Revolution, it discarded the arrangement of the colonial Anglican church and treated the interior as an auditorium with the principal focus on the pulpit rather than the altar. Monumental Church served as an Episcopal parish church until 1965 when it became a chapel for the Medical College of Virginia. Later modifications were removed in the 1970s as part of a long-term restoration intended to restore Mills's design inside and out. The church is now owned by the Historic Richmond Foundation. 127–12 (11/5/68); *National Historic Landmark*.

MONUMENT AVENUE HISTORIC DISTRICT, *including Monument Avenue from one block east of Stuart Circle to Roseneath Road*. A splendid and well-preserved turn-of-the-century residential boulevard, Monument Avenue illustrates the best of Beaux Arts planning ideals as well as those of the City Beautiful movement, all rendered in a comfortable scale. The concept of a great street honoring the heroes of the Confederacy coincided with the 1888 planned extension of Franklin Street westward from Lombardy Street as a connector to the monument being erected to Robert E. Lee on the western edge of the city. The 1888 subdivision plat of the area called for a divided street, 130 feet wide, and identified it as Monument Avenue. Jean Antoine Mercie's equestrian statue of General Lee, intended as the focal point for a wholly new residential area of Richmond, was unveiled in 1890. In 1904 the United Daughters of the Confederacy selected a site to the west of the Lee monument for a memorial to Jefferson Davis. By 1907, both Edward Valentine's Davis monument and Fred Moynihan's equestrian statue of J. E. B. Stuart at the beginning of the avenue were completed. The avenue was extended farther westward, and in 1919 Frederick Sevier's equestrian statue of Stonewall Jackson at the Boulevard intersection was unveiled.

Sevier's monument to Matthew Fontaine Maury, several blocks to the west, was erected in 1929. The cohesive but individually distinctive architecture of the avenue went up primarily during a forty-year period from 1890 to 1930 and consists of mansions, town houses, churches, and apartment blocks. Among the architects were John Russell Pope, William Lawrence Bottomley, W. Duncan Lee, and the firm of Noland and Baskervill. The latter gave the avenue a visual terminus at its eastern end with the spire of St. James's Episcopal Church. United by its grassy median and rows of trees, the district is carefully protected by local historic zoning and a special city advisory commission. 127–174 (12/2/69).

MORSON'S ROW, *219–223 Governor Street.* The terrace of three bow-fronted Italianate town houses forming Morson's Row was erected as rental properties in 1853 by James Marion Morson and is the last vestige of the numerous handsome residences that once surrounded Capitol Square. The row is attributed to Richmond architect Albert Lybrock because Lybrock listed Morson as a client in 1854 and the houses are in the Italianate idiom Lybrock favored. The row closes the vista at the east end of the Capitol Street mall and forms a harmonious backdrop for the Executive Mansion. Inside, each house has an oval parlor with cherry and mahogany woodwork and heavily carved marble mantels. Beginning in 1920, 223 Governor Street was occupied for several decades by the Southern Planter Publishing Company. A. E. Peticolas, an anatomist, first rented 221 Governor Street; and it later was the home of Dr. Robert Gamble. The row is now the property of the Commonwealth, and no. 221 houses the offices of the Division of Historic Landmarks. 127–79 (11/5/68).

OLD CITY HALL, *1000 East Broad Street.* Richmond's Old City Hall, one of the nation's foremost examples of the High Victorian Gothic style, was designed by the Detroit architect Elijah E. Myers, architect of five state capitols. With its profusion of carved ornament and agitated skyline, the four-story building forms a vividly contrasting backdrop for Jefferson's Capitol. Built of Richmond granite, the massive yet graceful structure was begun in 1887 and completed in 1894 and was at once recognized as a symbol of the city's prosperity and growth after its defeat in the Civil War. Its construction was undertaken primarily by black day laborers under the supervision of City Engineer Col. Wilfred E. Cutshaw. The central interior court is an extraordinary composition of tiers of Gothic arcades and great flights of stairs all executed in cast iron, now richly polychromed. Given up by the city for a new city hall in the 1970s, the building was sold to the state in 1981 and has been leased to the Historic Richmond Foundation, which in turn has subleased it to private developers for conversion into commercial office space. 127–3 (11/5/68); *National Historic Landmark.*

OLD FIRST AFRICAN BAPTIST CHURCH, *College and East Broad streets*. Built in 1876, this church housed the mother congregation of Richmond's black Baptists until its members moved to a new location in 1955. The church stands on the site of the First Baptist Church of 1802 (where the Virginia Constitutional Convention of 1829–30 was held), which was sold to its black members in 1841 when the white Baptists erected their new church at Broad and Twelfth streets. The original congregation included slaves as well as free blacks. The 1802 building was taken down thirty-five years later and replaced with the present structure, which, with its Doric portico in antis, followed the model of Thomas U. Walter's stately First Baptist Church a block away. The choice of style illustrates the persistence of the Greek Revival in Richmond as well as the influence the Walter design had on a number of the city's Baptist churches. After its acquisition by the Medical College of Virginia in 1955, the interior was remodeled for office space. Although no longer used for worship, Old First African Baptist remains a symbol of the prosperity of Richmond's black citizens in the late 19th century. 127–167 (11/5/68).

OLD FIRST BAPTIST CHURCH, *East Broad and Twelfth streets*. Thomas U. Walter of Philadelphia provided the design for this restrained but distinguished Greek Revival church. Walter, architect of the dome of the U.S. Capitol, designed some ten buildings for Virginia, of which the First Baptist Church is his only commission surviving in Richmond. Construction of the church began in 1839, and the congregation moved here from its original building at College and East Broad streets in 1841. The design, dominated by a broad portico in antis, had a strong impact on ecclesiastical architecture in the city; at least four Baptist churches were modeled directly after it. During the Civil War, the church was used as an emergency hospital for Confederate soldiers. The Baptists occupied the building until 1938 when it was sold to the Medical College of Virginia for use as a student center. Threatened with demolition in the 1970s, the church is currently undergoing renovation for an upgraded student center. 127–168 (11/5/68).

OLD STONE HOUSE (POE MUSEUM), *1916 East Main Street*. This modest dormered house in the midst of the commercial and industrial bustle of Shockoe Valley is believed to be the capital's only remaining colonial dwelling. Its stone construction is unusual for its period and region. The obvious great age and enigmatic character of the house have inspired much legend and speculation. However, the earliest documented reference to the property appears in 1783 in the city land tax book, which records it as the property and residence of Samuel Ege, a flour inspector. The house may date two to three decades earlier than this reference, as the uneven spacing of the openings, original hall-parlor plan, and general proportions are features common to vernacular houses of the mid-18th century. The house was acquired by the Association for

the Preservation of Virginia Antiquities in 1911 and in 1921 became part of a museum complex commemorating Edgar Allan Poe, who spent his youth in Richmond. The building is leased and exhibited by the Poe Foundation, Inc. 127–100 (10/16/73).

PACE-KING HOUSE, *205 North Nineteenth Street*. Amid a cluster of old buildings in Shockoe Valley, the Pace-King house is one of the grand mansions erected in southern cities on the eve of the Civil War and represents a final expression of taste in domestic architecture before the dissolution of the Old South. The house was completed in 1860 for Charles Hill, an auctioneer and local politician. The Italianate dwelling is set off by its deep bracketed cornice and a cast-iron veranda, an outstanding example of the metalworker's art in a city famous for its ironwork. From 1865 to 1881 the house was owned by tobacconist and later bank president James B. Pace. The next owner was businesswoman Jane King, who operated an ice company in Shockoe Valley. The house was rescued from dereliction in 1976 by the Association for the Preservation of Virginia Antiquities and has been restored. 127–229 (4/20/76).

PLANTERS NATIONAL BANK BUILDING, *East Main and Twelfth streets*. Planters National Bank is a highly original interpretation of Richardsonian Romanesque architecture designed in 1893 by Charles H. Read, Jr. A native Virginia architect, Read contributed several other significant buildings to Richmond's cityscape, most notably the Union Theological Seminary quadrangle. Among the first of the grand banks to be built in Richmond, Planters exemplifies the Romanesque themes of solidity, permanence, and fortresslike protection. It survives as the last remaining specimen of the Romanesque idiom in Richmond's city center and has been carefully restored as the headquarters of the Virginia Supplemental Retirement System. The restoration project included the construction of an architecturally harmonious office wing on a vacant lot to the right of the bank. 127–150 (7/20/82).

PUTNEY HOUSES, *1010 and 1012 East Marshall Street*. Surrounded by the massive modern structures of the Medical College of Virginia, these two town houses were once part of a fashionable downtown neighborhood. Complementary in their use of the Italianate style with side-hall plans, the two houses were built in 1859 for Samuel Ayres. They were owned and lived in from 1862 until 1894 by Samuel and Stephen Putney, father and son, shoe manufacturers. The two-tier cast-iron veranda on the side of the Stephen Putney house was produced by the local Phoenix Iron Works and is the most ambitious example of domestic ironwork in a city noted for its cast iron. Both houses have recently undergone restoration by the Medical College for use as offices. Fragments of painted architectural panels were discovered on the walls of the large parlor of the Stephen Putney house during the restoration and were skillfully repainted. 127–85 (11/5/68).

REVEILLE, *4200 Cary Street Road*. This early 19th-century brick country residence was built for the Southalls on land purchased by the family in 1750. Its side-passage plan shows the influence of urban house types on the design of rural dwellings of the post-Revolutionary period. The house was enlarged with a wing and remodeled with Greek Revival woodwork ca. 1840 when it was owned by James M. Boyd. Reveille's farmland has since been incorporated into the city and has become part of a handsome residential area. The house was acquired by the Reveille Methodist Church in 1950 and was used first as the church rectory and later as administrative offices. Despite the loss of its rural setting, the dignified old house stands as a reminder of the once-agrarian character of Richmond's west end. 127–310 (10/17/78).

ST. ALBAN'S HALL, *300 East Main Street*. Construction of St. Alban's Hall began two years after central Richmond burned at the end of the Civil War and marked the beginning of the city's revival. The prototype for later Masonic buildings in Richmond, the hall contained shops and a concert hall as well as Masonic meeting rooms and was a center of postwar Richmond's social and political life. With its stuccoed walls, pedimented windows, and rusticated corners, the building shows the influence of the Renaissance Revival or Tuscan Palazzo mode widely used in the urban North in the 1850s and 1860s but rarely found in the war-torn South. 127–130 (7/20/82).

ST. ANDREW'S EPISCOPAL CHURCH COMPLEX, *Laurel and Idlewood streets*. The St. Andrew's Episcopal Church complex was built for the working-class Oregon Hill neighborhood by Grace Arents, a niece of tobacco magnate Maj. Lewis Ginter and heir to the Ginter fortune. With this philanthropic gesture, Arents was following the example of Andrew Carnegie, Jane Addams, and other nationally recognized exponents of social conscience during the Progressive era. Built between 1900 and 1908, the St. Andrew's group contains a church and school designed by A. H. Ellwood of Elkhart, Ind., and a parish hall, library, and faculty residence by Noland and Baskervill of Richmond. The richly embellished stone church is one of Richmond's purest examples of the High Victorian Gothic mode. The complex continues to serve the neighborhood. 127–314 (4/17/79).

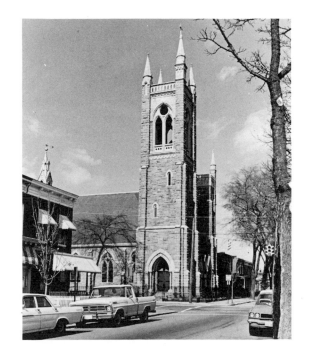

ST. JOHN'S CHURCH, *East Broad at Twenty-Fifth Street*. In St. John's Church on March 23, 1775, Patrick Henry delivered his "Liberty or Death" speech, sounding a clarion call for American independence before a convention of members of the Virginia General Assembly whose ranks included George Washington, Thomas Jefferson, George Mason, and Richard Henry Lee. The group met to debate the defense of the colony from ever-increasing British oppression. The assembly place for the convention , the wooden St. John's Church atop Richmond's Church Hill, was then the largest building in the fall-line village. Originally serving the venerable Henrico Parish, the oldest portion of St. John's, a simple rectangle, was built in 1739–41 by Richard Randolph on land donated by Richmond's founder, William Byrd II. Two years before Henry's speech, the church received an addition to its north side to accommodate additional seating. St. John's has been altered and enlarged several times since its great historic moment, but its simple dignity has been maintained. Buried in its churchyard are George Wythe and Elizabeth Arnold Poe, mother of Edgar Allan Poe. 127–13 (9/9/69); *National Historic Landmark*.

ST. JOHN'S CHURCH HISTORIC DISTRICT, *roughly bounded by Twenty-Second, East Marshall, Thirty-Second, East Main, and East Franklin streets and Williamsburg Avenue*. Popularly known as Church Hill, the neighborhood surrounding St. John's Church contains an assemblage of 19th-century domestic architecture that makes up the city's chief historic quarter. It was from the slopes of Church Hill that William Byrd II, upon seeing the view of the James River, was reminded of the Thames from Richmond Hill in England and thus named the Virginia city he founded in the mid-18th century. A scattering of houses was erected on Church Hill in the late 18th century, but all have disappeared. It was not until the early 19th century that building began in earnest. The filling in of the blocks came slowly, so that each street today presents a variety of domestic styles, including the Federal, Greek Revival, Italianate, and Queen Anne, all compatible in scale and materials. Throughout the 19th century the neighborhood was primarily a middle-class one, its houses modest compared to the mansions erected along the streets stretching west from Capitol Square. Because of the steep bluffs that frame three sides of the district, few of the streets are through ones; and a quiet residential air permeates the neighborhood despite its close proximity to both industrial and commercial areas. The deterioration and neglect suffered by Church Hill in the first half of the 20th century was checked in 1956 with the formation of the Historic Richmond Foundation, which over the past quarter century has acquired and restored many of the houses. The foundation was instrumental in having a historic zoning ordinance passed in 1957 to protect the district's some forty blocks. 127–192 (6/2/70).

ST. LUKE BUILDING, *900–904 St. James Street*. The St. Luke Building was erected as the national headquarters of the Independent Order of St. Luke, a black benevolent society founded after the Civil War to provide guidance and financial aid to struggling freed slaves. Under the leadership of Maggie L. Walker, the pioneering black businesswoman, philanthropist, and educator, the society prospered through services that helped bridge the gap between slavery and freedom. Its activities helped to ease the burdens of illness and death, encouraged savings and thrift, provided an outlet for inexpensive but well-made retail goods, and promoted Mrs. Walker's ideals for her race through a news weekly. The headquarters, the oldest black-affiliated office building in Richmond, was designed by John White and built in 1903. 127–352 (4/21/81).

ST. PAUL'S EPISCOPAL CHURCH, *Grace and Ninth streets*. This richly detailed Greek Revival church was designed by Philadelphia architect Thomas S. Stewart. Completed in 1845, the temple-form building is fronted by a portico in the Corinthian order of the Choragic Monument of Lysicrates, with capitals of cast iron. The belfry above the portico was originally topped by a needlelike spire which was removed in 1906. Inside, the nave is crowned by the largest and most highly ornamented Greek Revival plasterwork ceiling in the state. Except for the deepening of the apse and the installation of stained-glass windows, several from the studios of Louis Comfort Tiffany, the interior remains as it was designed. St. Paul's was established in the early 1840s when a part of the Monumental Church congregation split off to erect a new church more conveniently located to its ever-growing membership. Jefferson Davis, Robert E. Lee, and many of the state's governors have regularly attended services here. It was at St. Paul's, on April 2, 1865, that President Davis received word that General Lee no longer could hold the lines at Petersburg and thus defend the capital, a message that resulted in the immediate evacuation of the Confederate government from Richmond. St. Paul's remains one of the largest and most active Episcopal parishes in the state. 127–14 (11/5/68).

ST. PETER'S ROMAN CATHOLIC CHURCH, *Grace and Eighth streets*. This Classical Revival edifice in downtown Richmond was built in 1835 and survives as the city's oldest Roman Catholic church. Employing a Roman Doric order, the church has unusually tall proportions. Its facade is dominated by a portico of paired columns, above which is a stepped parapet gable and an octagonal cupola topped by a gilded cross. Many of St. Peter's first members were Irish and Germans who helped build the James River and Kanawha Canal. St. John Nepomucene Neuman, canonized in 1975, conducted a retreat for German immigrants in St. Peter's in 1843. With the establishment of the Diocese of Richmond in 1841, St. Peter's was elevated to cathedral status and served in that capacity until 1906 when the Cathedral of the Sacred Heart was opened.

James Gibbon, later Cardinal Gibbon of Baltimore, served as bishop of the diocese in the 1870s. The church continues to serve an active downtown parish and is a landmark in the heart of the city's shopping district. 127–14 (11/5/68).

ST. SOPHIA HOME OF THE LITTLE SISTERS OF THE POOR (THE WARSAW), *Floyd Avenue at Harvie Street.* The former charitable hospital of the Little Sisters of the Poor is a prodigious and rare example for Richmond of late Victorian institutional architecture. The building incorporates the walls of Warsaw, a brick farmhouse built in 1832 as the residence of William Anderson, on whose farm a large part of the surrounding neighborhood, the Fan District, was built. Warsaw was acquired by the mendicant order of nuns in 1877 and was transformed into the present Second Empire–style building over the next two decades. The nuns relocated in the late 1970s, and the building has been sold and remodeled into luxury condominiums now known as the Warsaw. 127–319 (2/19/80).

ST. STEPHEN'S EPISCOPAL CHURCH, *6004 Three Chopt Road.* Designed by Frank E. Watson of Philadelphia and initially completed in 1928, St. Stephen's well illustrates in its form, detailing, and materials the scholarship and loving care that was expended on America's Late Gothic Revival works. Built with rubble stone walls pierced by tall, pointed windows, the long, narrow building is an adaptation of an Early English–style parish church. The church was lengthened a bay and received a new facade in the Decorated style in 1950, under the direction of Philip H. Frohman, architect of the Washington Cathedral. St. Stephen's thus grew in size and with stylistic variation much as its medieval models did. Among its appointments are a collection of stained-glass windows by the Willet, D'Ascenzo, and J. & R. Lamb studios and a polychromed triptych reredos designed by Watson and executed by the woodcarvers of Oberammergau, Germany. 127–346 (1/20/81).

SECOND PRESBYTERIAN CHURCH, *9 North Fifth Street.* In its endeavor to build a new church that would be "the most symmetrical and pleasing to an educated eye," the congregation of Second Presbyterian Church authorized a committee to call on Brooklyn architect Minard Lafever to purchase a set of plans. The plans were duly transported back to Richmond, and the church was completed in 1848. The resulting work, Virginia's only Lafever building, is a demonstration of the strength and inspirational quality of the Gothic Revival mode. The restrained exterior, relieved chiefly by the pinnacled tower, contrasts with the lofty interior, culminated by a magnificent hammerbeam ceiling. Regarded from its beginning as the most beautiful specimen of Gothic architecture in the city, Second Presbyterian was long the pastorate of the Reverend Moses Drury Hoge, a leading evangelist in the 19th-century South. 127–16 (11/16/71).

SHOCKOE SLIP HISTORIC DISTRICT, *roughly bounded by East Main Street, South Twelfth Street, the Downtown Expressway, and the Seaboard System Railroad tracks.* Encompassing some nine city blocks on the southeastern edge of Richmond's financial quarter, the Shockoe Slip Historic District consists primarily of three- and four-story Italianate brick commercial structures, many with cast-iron architectural trim. The district has served as a neighborhood of warehouses, tobacco storage buildings, wholesale outlets, and mills since the 1780s. Leveled by the Evacuation Fire of 1865, it was quickly rebuilt. The heart of the district is a trapezoidal stone-paved piazza known as Shockoe Slip, part of an early passageway between Main Street and the James River and Kanawha Canal. In the center of the piazza is a ornamental fountain donated to serve as a watering spot for teams of horses. The well-preserved mid- and late 19th-century commercial and industrial buildings, while individually simple in design, achieve a lively texture, especially along East Cary Street, contrasting with the adjacent modern office towers. The area declined after World War II, but preservation activity since 1970 has transformed many of the buildings into restaurants, shops, offices, and apartments. Strictly protected by a locally established historic zoning ordinance, Shockoe Slip continues to have a strong identity in the business and social life of the city. 127–219 (11/16/71).

SHOCKOE VALLEY AND TOBACCO ROW HISTORIC DISTRICT, *roughly bounded by the Richmond-Petersburg Turnpike, Dock Street, Church Hill, Eighteenth Street, and Clay Street.* Named for the creek that served as the western boundary of Richmond's original town settlement and for the row of tobacco warehouses and factories that constitute its industrial quarter, this historic district encompasses the area of Richmond's earliest residential, commercial, and manufacturing activity. The roughly L-shaped district at the base of Church Hill includes approximately 129 acres containing over 500 buildings in architectural styles ranging from the colonial vernacular and Federal through the early 20th-century industrial idiom. The street pattern follows the original grid system laid out by William Mayo in 1737. The heart of the district is the Seventeenth Street Market, maintained as a farmer's market since the late 18th century and framed on its western edge by the Main Street Station and train shed. Many of the buildings around the market serve as the city's wholesale food outlets. Although the district was spared the destruction that the city's main financial area suffered in the Evacuation Fire of 1865, economic decline and neglect set in after World War II. In addition, the removal of much of Richmond's tobacco industry to the outskirts of the city in recent years has left the row of tobacco structures stretched along Dock Street standing idle. The scene of increasing rehabilitation activity, the district still presents a late 19th-century cityscape of houses, shops, factories, warehouses, and public buildings, providing a foil for neighboring modern office towers. 127–344 (7/21/81).

STEARNS BLOCK, *1011 East Main Street.* The cast-iron architecture of the Stearns Block illustrates the architectural exuberance that could be achieved with an otherwise pedestrian material. Constructed after the Civil War to replace commercial buildings destroyed in the Evacuation Fire, this and numerous other iron fronts gave downtown Richmond a rich, dignified architecture by the quickest and least expensive means. Inspired by the baroque palaces of Venice, most of America's iron fronts have several stories of openings topped by a deep ornamental cornice, with each opening framed by delicate classical elements. Giving special interest to this block are the comparatively large windows that leave little room for surrounding ornamentation, so that the effect is one of nearly all glass. The building was erected for Richmond businessman Franklin Stearns, at one time Virginia's largest landowner, and was completed in 1869. The ironwork was designed by George H. Johnson, an English architect who moved to America in 1851 and worked with the foundry of Hayward and Bartlett of Baltimore on this and other Richmond iron facades. The building is one of only three complete iron fronts remaining in the city. 127–23 (12/2/69).

STEWART-LEE HOUSE, *707 East Franklin Street.* This town house briefly served as the home of Robert E. Lee after his surrender at Appomattox. Almost the sole survivor of the scores of Greek Revival dwellings that lined the streets of downtown Richmond during the mid-19th century, 707 East Franklin Street was begun in 1844 for Norman Stewart, a tobacco merchant from Rothesay, Scotland. After the outbreak of the Civil War, Stewart's nephew, John Stewart, rented the house to Gen. Custis Lee and a group of fellow Confederate officers to serve as a bachelor officers' quarters. In 1864 the house was given over to Robert E. Lee's wife and daughters, who were left homeless after the federal government confiscated Arlington. Lee, seeking privacy after years of war, moved his family from here to Derwent in Powhatan County in June 1865. After it served a variety of tenants, the Stewart family presented the house to the Virginia Historical Society in 1893 for its headquarters. The building is now the property of the Historic Richmond Foundation. 127–64 (1/18/72).

THIRD STREET BETHEL AFRICAN METHODIST EPISCOPAL CHURCH, *616 North Third Street.* This landmark of the Jackson Ward Historic District was built ca. 1857 to house one of the first congregations in Virginia to join the African Methodist Episcopal denomination. The building is among the very small number of antebellum black churches remaining in the country. Richmond before the Civil War boasted a large free Negro population, thus an independent black congregation, while rare, was not extraordinary. In this simple building the Virginia Conference of the African Methodist Episcopal Church was organized in 1867. The congregation prospered, and in 1875 the church received a stylish new front with twin towers and traceried Gothic windows. 127–274 (2/18/75).

TREDEGAR IRON WORKS, *500 Tredegar Street*. This industrial complex was the leading ordnance foundry of the Confederacy. Tredegar maintained wartime production despite severe shortages of raw materials, skilled labor, and effective transportation and enabled the South to sustain itself as a viable war machine for four years. Chartered in 1837 and named for the ironworks at Tredegar in Wales, Tredegar's rise to preeminence began in 1841 when Joseph Reid Anderson took over the company. Known as the "Ironmaker to the Confederacy," Anderson guided the firm through the war and to prosperity in the decades following. Unable to make the transition from iron to steel in the late 19th century, Tredegar declined to a small local concern and eventually left its original site in 1958. The derelict complex was then acquired by the Ethyl Corporation, which has undertaken salvage and restoration of the complex's antebellum buildings. The principal structure of the group is the gable-roofed gun foundry where most of the Confederate armaments were produced. 127–186 (1/5/71); *National Historic Landmark.*

UNION THEOLOGICAL SEMINARY QUADRANGLE, *3401 Brook Road*. Begun in 1896, the quadrangle at Union Theological Seminary is framed by a collection of High Victorian Gothic, Late Gothic Revival, and Queen Anne buildings, all of dark red brick and all basically English in character. The ground plan of the complex and the majority of its buildings were designed by Richmond architect Charles H. Read, Jr. Later buildings were designed by the Richmond firms of Charles K. Bryant and Baskervill and Lambert, the latter firm completing the quadrangle in 1921 with Schauffler Hall, a delicately rich Late Gothic Revival Building. The whole forms a coherent expression of the dignity and style accorded academic buildings at the turn of the century. Founded in 1812 at Hampden-Sydney College as the Presbyterian Synod of Virginia's School of Theology, the seminary moved to Richmond in 1896 after receiving a gift of a twelve-acre site on the city's north side from Richmond industrialist and developer Maj. Lewis Ginter. Since its relocation, the seminary has played a leading role in religious education in the region. 127–316 (9/16/82).

U.S. POST OFFICE AND CUSTOMS HOUSE (U.S. COURTHOUSE BUILDING), *1000 East Main Street*. The two-story core of the U.S. Customs House in Richmond was designed by Boston architect Ammi B. Young, who as supervising architect of the U.S. Treasury Department supplied designs for numerous such buildings for cities throughout the country. Completed in 1858 under the direct supervision of local architect Albert Lybrock, the building was taken over by the Confederacy in 1861 to house both the treasury and the offices of President Jefferson Davis. The building remarkably escaped damage during the Evacuation Fire of 1865, and in 1867 Davis was brought here to face charges of treason against the Union. Although the building has been greatly enlarged over

the years, Young's distinctive Tuscan Palazzo style has been maintained. Forming a backdrop for the south side of Capitol Square, it now houses the U.S. District Court and U.S. Court of Appeals for the Fourth Circuit. 127–170 (11/5/68).

THE VIRGINIA, *East Main and Fifth streets.* The Virginia was erected in 1906 as the Richmond headquarters of the Virginia State Insurance Company and stands as an individualized example of early 20th-century commercial classicism. In addition to housing the city's second largest insurance company, the building accommodated other professional offices and prestige apartments, a combination of uses that was unique in Richmond at that time and was never again attempted in the city. Located on fashionable Fifth Street, the structure was carefully contrived to blend into the character of the neighborhood through a restrained and inventive treatment of the exterior. The architect has not been identified, but with his use of a curved facade, rusticated brickwork, and subtle spacing of bays, he exhibited an ability to give visual distinction to an otherwise straightforward building type. The building is now used exclusively for offices. 127–215 (12/14/82).

VIRGINIA MUTUAL BUILDING (VIRGINIA FIRST SAVINGS AND LOAN), *815 East Main Street.* Built as the headquarters of the Virginia Trust Company, this bank building is a salient example of the Neoclassical Revival, an architectural style of the early 20th century directly inspired by the grandiose works of the ancient world. The white granite facade is reminiscent of a Roman triumphal arch, and the banking room is dominated by a gilded coffered ceiling heavily encrusted with classical ornaments. Completed in 1921, the bank was designed by Alfred Charles Bossom, a native of England who maintained a New York practice from 1903 to 1926 and then returned to Britain for a political career which culminated in 1960 by his being made a life peer. The Virginia Mutual Building is the most elegant of the some half-dozen buildings Bossom designed for Richmond and is among the best-preserved bank buildings of its style and period in the state. 127–249 (2/15/77).

VIRGINIA STATE CAPITOL, *Capitol Square.* The Virginia State Capitol was designed by Thomas Jefferson with the assistance of the French architect Charles Louis Clérisseau. Inspired by the Maison Carrée, Roman temple in Nîmes, France, which Jefferson visited and greatly admired, the building marks the beginning of the Classical Revival in America. It is also the first instance in the world where the temple form was employed for a major modern public building. Begun in 1785 under the direction of contractor Samuel Dobie, the Capitol became the home of the General Assembly of Virginia after the

removal of the seat of state government from Williamsburg. The building served as the meeting place of the Confederate Congress during the Civil War but still continued to house the Virginia Assembly as well as the governor's office. Wings and hyphens designed by a team of architects headed by J. Kevan Peebles and William C. Noland were added in 1906 to provide larger chambers for the House of Delegates and the Senate. The front steps were also added at this time. Still in use, the Capitol is the home of the oldest legislative assembly in the Western Hemisphere. Jean Antoine Houdon's statue of George Washington, commissioned by Jefferson on behalf of the Commonwealth, stands in the Capitol rotunda. The grounds of the surrounding Capitol Square were laid out in the 1850s by Philadelphia landscape architect John Notman. 127–2 (11/5/68); *National Historic Landmark*.

VIRGINIA UNION UNIVERSITY, *North Lombardy Street and Brook Road*. The original complex of Virginia Union University is a late Victorian collegiate grouping in the Romanesque Revival style. The dormitories, classroom buildings, chapel, president's house, and power plant, each with its own massing and lively silhouette, were designed by Washington architect John H. Coxhead. The establishment of the university in 1896 through the merger of Richmond Theological Seminary and Wayland Seminary of Washington, D.C., was the culmination of efforts to provide higher education for freed blacks after the Civil War. Further mergers have transformed the school into a coeducational, four-year, predominantly black liberal arts college. 127–354 (6/16/81).

MAGGIE L. WALKER HOUSE, *110 East Leigh Street*. Maggie Lena Walker (1867–1934), née Maggie Mitchell, daughter of a former slave and a Northern abolitionist, rose from her work with a black fraternal order to become the first American woman to establish and head a bank. In addition to serving as president of the St. Luke Penny Savings Bank, later incorporated into the still-active Consolidated Bank and Trust Company, Mrs. Walker was active in many civic and charitable causes. She was founder and president of the Richmond Council of Colored Women and employed her fund-raising talents to aid improved health care for Negroes. She purchased a ca. 1883 Italianate town house in the heart of Jackson Ward in 1904 and enlarged and remodeled it with Colonial Revival elements. The house is preserved and furnished exactly as she left it and has been acquired by the Department of the Interior for exhibition as a National Historic Site. 127–275 (4/15/75); *National Historic Landmark*.

WHITE HOUSE OF THE CONFEDERACY, *1201 East Clay Street*. The house built for Dr. John Brockenborough in 1818 served as the South's executive mansion during the four years President Jefferson Davis resided in the Confederate capital. It was seized by the Union forces on April 3, 1865, and held by the U.S. government until 1870. Abraham Lincoln visited the house briefly on April 4, 1865, immediately after the evacuation of the Confederate government. In 1893 the house was acquired by the Confederate Memorial Literary Society and was made into a museum of Confederate memorabilia, now known as the Museum of the Confederacy. The design is attributed to Robert Mills, the Charleston architect who trained under Thomas Jefferson. Typical of Richmond houses, it was built with its portico on the garden side. The house was remodeled in the 1840s and received a third story in 1857. The interior was gutted in 1894 when the building was made fireproof, but great care was taken to preserve the cornices, woodwork, mantels, and other trim so that the rooms would appear as President Davis and his wife Varina knew them. A recent restoration and refurnishing has returned to the principal rooms the elegant mid-Victorian character that they had during the war years. 127–115 (9/9/69); *National Historic Landmark.*

WICKHAM-VALENTINE HOUSE (VALENTINE MUSEUM), *1015 East Clay Street*. This foremost example of Federal architecture recently has been documented to be the work of Alexander Parris with advice from Benjamin Henry Latrobe. Thus, it was a New England architect who produced this much-admired design, not Robert Mills as was long thought. Parris, a native of Portland, Maine, moved to Richmond ca. 1811 where he designed and supervised at least three houses including that of the Richmond lawyer John Wickham. He then settled in Boston, enjoying there a long and active career. Completed in 1812, Wickham's house has a restrained but carefully proportioned exterior. Parris followed the local idiom by placing a veranda across the garden front. Inside is an elegant suite of rooms arranged around a circular stair hall containing a curved stair ascending to a palette-shaped second-floor landing. Each of the rooms boasts neoclassical detailing and has been furnished to show a particular facet of 19th-century Richmond taste. Mann Valentine II purchased the house in 1882 and filled its rooms with his collection of prehistoric Indian artifacts, fine arts, and historic objects. At his death in 1892, he left the property and his collections to serve as a museum known today as the Valentine Museum. The museum has since been expanded into adjacent Italianate town houses as well as into the Bransford-Cecil house, an 1840 Greek Revival house moved from Fifth Street in 1854. With greatly expanded collections, the complex serves as the museum for the history and culture of Richmond. 127–20 (11/5/68); *National Historic Landmark.*

WILTON, *South Wilton Road.* This high-style Virginia Georgian plantation house was built in 1750–53 for William Randolph III on a site overlooking the James River in eastern Henrico County, some fifteen miles east of its present site. Randolph was a son of William Randolph II of Turkey Island and had married Ann Carter Harrison of Berkeley in 1735. The rectangular house has even-colored brick walls with regular five-bay facades designed with a carefully calculated proportional system. Its interior paneling, used on every wall of every room, even in the chimney closets on each floor, and its main stair with its spiral carved balusters show colonial artistry and craftsmanship at their best. Because of threatened industrial development of its surroundings, the National Society of Colonial Dames in America took title to the house in 1933 and had it dismantled and painstakingly reerected on a new site overlooking the James in the west end of Richmond. The accuracy of the rebuilding preserved the house as a landmark of the mid-Georgian style. Wilton's paneling is paralleled by that in few other American dwellings. The house is now exhibited by the Colonial Dames as a museum of colonial architecture and 18th-century furnishings. 127–141 (10/21/75).

JOSEPH P. WINSTON HOUSE, *103 East Grace Street.* The cheerfully decorous flavor that affluent late 19th century Americans required for their houses is exhibited in this narrow little Richmond town house, once part of the residential neighborhood that occupied the downtown blocks of Grace Street. Completed in 1874, the house was the home of Joseph P. Winston, a wholesale grocer. It was built at a time when elaborate architectural elements were becoming popularized in builders' catalogs; most of its details, such as the cornice, doors, moldings, mantels, and balusters, were stock materials available from local distributors or manufacturers. Although mass-produced, the quality of these various pieces was in keeping with the period's high standards of craftsmanship. Notable in this instance is the cast-iron front porch, which employs patterns found in no other of Richmond's many iron porches. Also giving the house special character is the ogee mansard roof sheathed in rounded slates. The building has been sympathetically preserved for office use by its present owner, the Richmond Art Company. 127–222 (2/21/78).

THE WOMAN'S CLUB (BOLLING HAXALL HOUSE), *211 East Franklin Street*. Bolling Haxall, member of a Richmond milling family, selected the Italian Villa style for his Franklin Street house in 1858. With its roof dominated by a square tower and its front accented by some of the best cast-iron railings of the period, the dwelling provided a rich foil for the more staid Greek Revival dwellings of the neighborhood. Other noteworthy features are the heavy bracketed cornice, the Doric porch, and the cast-iron hood moldings of the facade windows. The architect has not been identified, but he probably was Albert L. West of Richmond, who worked in the Italianate style. The house was acquired in 1900 by the Woman's Club, a group formed in 1894 for the cultural, intellectual, moral, and humanitarian development of its members, and has been in regular use by the club to the present. 127–33 (11/16/71).

WOODWARD HOUSE, *3017 Williamsburg Avenue*. John Woodward, captain of the sloop *Rachell* and other ships operating out of the nearby port of Rocketts, occupied this wood-frame house in the first two decades of the 19th century. Today, the house is the only remaining building of the dockside neighborhood where ship captains and sailors, harbormasters and tobacco inspectors, tavern keepers and draymen, and assorted craftsmen and laborers lived and worked through the decades following Richmond's designation as the state capital. Much evolved and enlarged over the years, the house began before 1780 as a modest one-room cottage. Its present appearance was achieved by 1829 when the front two-and-a-half-story portion was added. Captain Woodward's house was rescued from a proposed demolition in 1974 and has undergone exterior restoration since its acquisition by the Historic Richmond Foundation. 127–119 (5/21/74).

RICHMOND COUNTY

*Along the Rappahannock River side of the Northern Neck,
Richmond County was probably named for the borough of
Richmond in Surrey County, England. It was formed from the
extinct Rappahannock County in 1692.
Its county seat is Warsaw.*

BLADENSFIELD, *Lyells vicinity.* This weatherboarded old Northern Neck plantation house, on land that was once the property of Robert ("King") Carter, probably was built in the third quarter of the 18th century by Carter's grandson Robert ("Councillor") Carter. In its original form the house was a two-story, five-bay structure with a center passage. In 1790 the latter Carter gave Bladensfield to his son-in-law John C. Peck, who had succeeded Philip Fithian as tutor to the Carter children at Nomini Hall. The Reverend William N. Ward acquired Bladensfield in 1847, enlarged the house, and made it a female academy. Mid-19th-century life there was recorded in a memoir titled *The Children of Bladensfield* by Ward's daughter Evelyn. The place is still owned by Ward's descendants. 79–2 (2/19/80).

FARNHAM CHURCH, *Farnham*. Farnham Church has survived abandonment, wars, and fire. Dominating its tiny crossroads settlement, the church was built in 1737 to replace a mid-17th-century church. Its early parishioners included the Carters of Sabine Hall and the Tayloes of Mount Airy. It was left vacant after the disestablishment and was riddled with bullets in a skirmish during the War of 1812. Federal troops used it to stable horses during the Civil War; and although later restored to service, it was gutted by fire in 1887 and stood as a roofless ruin until it was again restored in 1921. The brick walls, the only original feature remaining, exhibit colonial masonry at its finest and hint at the early importance of the parish. 79–14 (9/19/72).

INDIAN BANKS, *Simonson vicinity*. The compactly proportioned colonial plantation house at Indian Banks, although traditionally dated 1699, more likely dates to 1728 when Capt. William Glasscock married Esther Ball and took up residence here. The place takes its name from a large Indian village that had been located nearby on the banks of the Rappahannock. The house, with its diminished scale, tall hipped roof, and comparatively large windows, has a distinctly English flavor, more Queen Anne than Georgian. The scrolled soffit of the jack arch above the main entrance was a common feature in England but is one of only two known in Virginia. Much of the interior woodwork has disappeared, but a fine stair, several doors, and window frames with paneled window seats remain. The house was built with an L-shaped plan; a one-story colonial-style wing was added in the 1970s. 79–9 (10/21/75).

LINDEN FARM, *Farnham*. The oldest portion of this colonial vernacular farmhouse was erected ca. 1700, making it perhaps the oldest dwelling on the Northern Neck. Surviving in a remarkably good state of preservation, the house has massive asymmetrical chimneys, a closed-string provincial Jacobean stair, and some original riven clapboard sheathing. Its tilted false-plate framing is a particularly early form of Virginia timber construction. Also surviving is evidence of a sliding casement window, a window type once common in early vernacular houses. The house was built for Charles Dew, who was established in the Farnham area by 1708. It was lengthened by an addition on the north (left) end ca. 1725. 79–10 (9/21/76).

MENOKIN, *Warsaw vicinity*. Now roofless, with two of its walls caved in and its woodwork removed, this house tenaciously defies complete obliteration. Menokin was the home of Francis Lightfoot Lee, colonial statesman and patriot and a signer of the Declaration of Independence. Small but unusually formal with its stuccoed walls and carved stone openings, the house was commissioned by Lee's father-in-law, John

Tayloe of Mount Airy, and was given upon its completion ca. 1770 to Lee and his bride Rebecca as a wedding present. The unsigned architectural drawings survive in the Tayloe papers at the Virginia Historical Society; Menokin's architectural kinship to Mount Airy suggests a common, but as yet unidentified, architect. The house was abandoned over thirty years ago. The woodwork was taken out in the 1960s, and is now in the custody of the Association for the Preservation of Virginia Antiquities. 79–11 (11/5/68); *National Historic Landmark.*

MOUNT AIRY, *Warsaw vicinity.* Sited in an impressively commanding position on a ridge above the broad bottomlands and marshes of the Rappahannock River, Mount Airy is the most architecturally sophisticated of all of Virginia's colonial seats. The elaborate house was built 1748–58 by the wealthy planter John Tayloe II to replace an earlier family house that burned. The designer of the five-part neo-Palladian mansion is unidentified, but the close adherence of the facades and plan to illustrations published in James Gibbs's *Book of Architecture* (1728) indicates that he could handle this refined architectural idiom with ease. A striking element of the composition is the curved hyphens linking the main block to the dependencies. The rusticated center pavilions of land and river fronts are both executed in Aquia Creek sandstone. In 1762 Tayloe employed designer and joiner William Buckland to finish Mount Airy's interior. Buckland's work here, believed to have been exceptionally rich, was destroyed when the house was gutted by fire in 1844. The interior was immediately rebuilt in a plain Greek Revival style by the builder brothers George H. and William P. Van Ness. A quantity of family furnishings and portraits survived the fire and are preserved in the house. The informal park on the land side and broad formal terrace on the river side are important remnants of colonial landscaping. The garden was composed of many beds and walks whose general pattern is discernible in the undulations of the terrace lawn. Mount Airy remains the home of the builder's descendants. 79–13 (9/9/69); *National Historic Landmark; Virginia Historic Landmarks Board and Virginia Outdoors Foundation joint preservation easement.*

RICHMOND COUNTY COURTHOUSE, *Warsaw.* Many of Virginia's colonial courthouses had arcaded fronts, but Richmond County's courthouse instead had arcades along two sides. The building dates from 1748 when Landon Carter was given the commission to have a new brick courthouse erected. The arcades were closed up with windows when the building was extensively remodeled in 1877 under the direction of Baltimore architect T. Buckler Chequiere. Chequiere apparently admired the structure, for he published a detailed description of its appearance before the changes. The courthouse remains in use and is the town of Warsaw's chief landmark. Next door is the colonial clerk's office. 321–4 (8/15/72).

SABINE HALL, *Warsaw vicinity.* The three sons of Robert ("King") Carter each built an early Georgian mansion on the plantations given to them by their father. Of the three houses, only Sabine Hall, the ca. 1735 home of Landon Carter, survives. The property has remained in the ownership of Carter's descendants to the present. The house was endowed with the requisite careful proportions and fine brickwork, plus the extra accent of handsomely trimmed and rusticated sandstone center bays on each front. When the house was remodeled ca. 1830–40, the hipped roof was lowered, the cornice and window sash were changed to their present form, and the north portico was added. The connecting wings are also the result of later alterations, although the end of the east wing was originally an early detached dependency. Inside is an accumulation of family furnishings and portraits in paneled rooms. The carved walnut stair, ascending in a lateral passage, is one of the finest of the period. Sabine Hall's terraced garden, with the top level retaining its original geometric pattern of beds and walks, is a rare surviving example of colonial landscape design. 79–15 (5/13/69); *National Historic Landmark; Virginia Historic Landmarks Board preservation easement.*

WOODFORD, *Simons Corner vicinity.* Woodford is an example of Virginia's transitional vernacular architecture, combining features of the simple cottage of early colonial times with more formal, symmetrical qualities of the Georgian style. Its traditional hall-parlor plan incorporates the central passage associated with Georgian plans. The otherwise formal exterior has irregularly spaced openings that reflect the unevenness of the room sizes. Built between 1756 and 1773 for Billington McCarty, Jr., whose family had owned the property since 1661, Woodford has an odd stair banister, at first appearing to have upside-down balusters but actually following sophisticated English precedents. A rare survival is the remnants of interior clapboarding, used here originally as a rude second-floor wall and ceiling finish. 79–20 (7/21/81).

CITY OF ROANOKE

*Originally known as Big Lick because of salt deposits in the
vicinity, this Roanoke Valley community was established in
1852 and was incorporated in 1874. Its name was changed to
Roanoke in 1882, and it became a city in 1884, having grown
rapidly after the headquarters of the Norfolk and Western
Railway were established here in 1881. The city was enlarged by
annexation from Roanoke County in 1976.*

BELLE AIRE, *1320 Belle Aire Circle, S.W.* This well-proportioned Greek Revival farmhouse illustrates the popularity of builders' guides in the mid-19th century and the uses to which an imaginative local craftsman could put them. Most of the detailing was adapted from plates published in the pattern books of architect Asher Benjamin and applied to the regional I-house form. The house was completed in 1849 for Madison Pitzer, a large landowner. The housebuilder Gustavus Sedon, who is known to have erected similar area houses, is recorded to have installed windows on Belle Aire and may have played a specific role in the design. An unusually stately air is achieved with the use of a two-level Doric portico. Like most of the Roanoke Valley Greek Revival houses, Belle Aire has wide corner pilasters and a low hipped roof. 128–52 (10/21/75).

BOXLEY BUILDING, *416 Jefferson Street, S.W.* Roanoke's Boxley Building was built in 1921–22, during the city's "Golden Age of Municipal Progress" in the decade after World War I. Eight stories high, with granite on the first story and beige-enameled brick with terra-cotta decoration above, and topped by a deep copper cornice, the building was designed by area architect Edward G. Frye in collaboration with Frank Stone. It was commissioned by W. W. Boxley, builder, developer, quarry owner, railroad contractor, and mayor of Roanoke at the time of its construction. Boxley ensured the use of the finest materials available for his building, creating a work which is still a dominant feature of the city's skyline. 128–47 (10/18/83).

BUENA VISTA, *Jackson Park, Penmar Avenue.* Buena Vista was built in 1850 for George Plater Tayloe (1804–1897) on property purchased in 1833 from his father-in-law, William Langhorne. Tayloe was born on his family's plantation, Mount Airy, in Richmond County and grew up in the Tayloes' Washington town house, the Octagon. He moved to the Roanoke Valley after his marriage in 1830 and managed two iron furnaces. He later became one of the founders of Hollins College, a member of the Virginia General Assembly, and a delegate to the Secession Convention of 1861. Atop a hill with panoramic views of the surrounding mountains, Tayloe's home is one of the bold though somewhat provincial Greek Revival works of the region, most of which employ plain, gleaming white architectural elements against red brick walls. The provinciality is emphasized here by the two-column portico. The house was regarded as one of the most impressive of the area; a visitor in 1862 described it as a "spacious peace-embowered house . . . with the summer breezes stealing around its white pillars and swaying its muslin curtains." Buena Vista remained in the Tayloe family until 1937 when the house and surrounding acres were sold to the city. It now is used by the city of Roanoke as a recreation center. 128–1 (1/15/74).

COLONIAL NATIONAL BANK (COLONIAL AMERICAN NATIONAL BANK BUILDING, COLONIAL ARMS BUILDING), *202–208 South Jefferson Street, S.W.* The Colonial National Bank was erected in 1926–27, part of Roanoke's growth as the banking hub of Southwest Virginia. Twelve stories high, with granite ashlar on the first three stories and gray-enamel brick and terra-cotta decoration above, the steel-frame building was designed by the local firm of Frye and Stone. With its lean ornamentation and functional aspect, it represents the transition from the neoclassical style to modernism in the area. Roanoke's tallest building for fifty years, the Colonial National was one of Virginia's first skyscrapers. The Colonial American National Bank was the successor to the Colonial National Bank. The bank sold the building in 1981 but continues to occupy the banking hall. The rest of the interior has since been remodeled for office rental, and the building has been renamed the Colonial Arms Building. 128–44 (9/16/82).

CRYSTAL SPRING STEAM PUMPING STATION, *Crystal Spring Park, 2016 Lake Street, S.E.* Manufactured in 1905 by the Snow Steam Pump Company of Buffalo, N.Y., the water pump at this station is believed to be the only one of its type to survive. The pump employs the Corliss method of valve control, a technical breakthrough for the period. It drew water from Roanoke's Crystal Spring until 1957, supplying the city with a reliable water source during its years of rapid growth. Recently restored, the pump, with its elaborate flywheel, pistons, and gears, is now exhibited as an artifact of industrial technology. The machine is housed in a plain industrial structure on the edge of Crystal Spring Park. 128–39 (12/28/79).

FIRE STATION NO. 1, *13 Church Avenue, S.E.* This Georgian Revival firehouse erected in the heart of downtown in 1907–8 is a product of the early civic pride of the rapidly urbanized city of Roanoke. With a facade recalling English town halls of the early 18th century, the building is a municipal ornament. It was designed by local architect H. H. Huggins, who gave the composition a pleasing accent with the fanciful cupola. Inside, the building remains as it was completed, although it is now equipped for motorized fire engines rather than horse-drawn ones. Over the first floor is an elaborate pressed-metal ceiling painted silver. On the second floor, most of the early woodwork and graining, including maple floor and pine trim, is intact. Still in use, the firehouse illustrates the continuity of fire-fighting facilities over the past eighty years. 128–33 (9/19/72).

FIRST NATIONAL BANK BUILDING, *101 South Jefferson Street, S.W.* Roanoke's former First National Bank building, built in 1910, is the work of J. Kevan Peebles of Norfolk. Planned according to the most modern concepts of bank and office design and fireproofing, the building with its French Renaissance influence exhibits Peebles's practical training as an engineer as well as his mastery of the repertoire of revivalist styles then in fashion throughout the United States. The First National Bank occupied the building until 1926 when it was sold to the Liberty Trust Company. In 1953 it was purchased by the People's Federal Savings and Loan Company, and in 1981 the building was bought by MFW Associates, who have renovated it for office use, preserving the columned banking hall. Although no longer serving its original function, the building remains one of the best-preserved and best-appointed Progressive-era bank buildings in the state and is a reminder of the establishment of Roanoke as a banking center in the early 20th century. 128–40 (2/16/82).

HARRISON SCHOOL, *523 Harrison Street, N.W.* Constructed in 1916, Roanoke's Harrison School was the result of the pioneering efforts of Lucy Addison and other black educators in Southwest Virginia to offer public academic secondary instruction to all children regardless of race. These efforts were all the more remarkable in view of the paucity of black public high schools in Virginia during this period and the prevailing educational theory of the Progressive era that blacks should receive industrial, rather than academic or collegiate, instruction. Serving throughout its history as a center of black educational, social, and cultural activities in Roanoke, the building is a typical example of public design of the period, employing a very modified Georgian format. No longer a school, the building is being renovated for housing. 128–43 (5/18/82).

LONE OAKS (BENJAMIN DEYERLE PLACE; also WINSMERE), *1402 Grandin Road Extension, S.W.* During the mid-19th century the now highly urbanized Roanoke Valley was dotted with farms with many of the more prominent farmhouses executed in a plain but imposing Greek Revival style. One of those that survive is the red brick, white-trimmed house currently known as Lone Oaks, built ca. 1853 by the industrious entrepreneur Benjamin Deyerle for his own house. Among his several business activities, Deyerle operated brick kilns, and tradition has it that he made and laid the bricks for Lone Oaks. Deyerle is also credited by local tradition with building a number of similar houses in the area, although his activities as a contractor or master builder are yet to be documented. Features that Lone Oaks shares with other Roanoke Valley Greek Revival houses are the plain Doric entablature with corner pilasters, a three-bay facade, a low hipped roof, and a portico sheltering the front entrance. Still a private residence, the tree-shaded old place retains several original outbuildings. 128–10 (1/16/73).

MONTEREY, *Tinker Creek Lane, N.E.* An architectural anomaly for the region, this low, verandaed Greek Revival dwelling is more akin to the spacious mid-19th-century cottages of the Gulf Coast than the more vertical houses of western Virginia. Despite its unusual form, the house, like many Greek Revival works throughout the state, has details derived from illustrations published in Asher Benjamin's pattern book *The Practical House Carpenter* (1830). Monterey was built in 1846 for Charles Oliver, a landowner. Family tradition holds that Oliver and his son Yelverton got the idea of the house's unusual form while on a trip to New Orleans to race horses. Monterey is an exceptionally well-crafted building, employing precise Flemish bond brickwork and boldly molded woodwork. A notable architectural feature is the exterior Doric cornice, which makes use of mutules on its soffit. The house retains a rural setting with views of the encircling mountains. 128–35 (4/16/74).

MOUNTAIN VIEW, *714 Thirteenth Street, S.W.* Built in 1907, Mountain View is one of the notable examples of the early Georgian Revival style in the Commonwealth. The house was designed by Roanoke architect H. H. Huggins for Junius Blair Fishburn, president of the National Exchange Bank of Roanoke. It served as his residence until his death in 1955 when it was given to the Roanoke Department of Parks and Recreation. Rather than to evoke a historical allusion, the Georgian Revival here is freely interpreted to make a grand effect suitable for the home of the city's leading newspaper owner, financier, and philanthropist at the beginning of the 20th century. Typical of many Georgian Revival houses of the period, Mountain View has a large central portico projecting over a long one-story porch. The entrance hall is dominated by a beamed ceiling and central stair. The house is well preserved with almost no alteration. 128–22 (6/17/80).

ROANOKE CITY MARKET HISTORIC DISTRICT, *roughly bounded by Church Avenue, Norfolk Avenue, South Jefferson Street, and Williamson Road.* Roanoke's Market District has served as the primary marketplace for the city and the surrounding six-county area for over a century. The district, which comprises more than sixty structures displaying the full range of late 19th- to early 20th-century commercial styles, has as its centerpiece the City Market building on Market Square, constructed in 1922 to replace the city's first market, erected on the same site in 1886. The district has a harmony of materials and an appealing human scale, with brick two- and three-story commercial buildings framing the open public space of the central market square. In recent years, the area has become the main target of the city's centennial revitalization efforts. Innovative design concepts and local historic district zoning have been combined with public and private backing for the planned adaptive reuse of the City Market building and for the renovation of the McGuire Building as a regional cultural and science center called Center in the Square. A number of commercial buildings have been rehabilitated through private effort. 128–45 (9/16/82).

ROANOKE WAREHOUSE HISTORIC DISTRICT, *109–133 Norfolk Avenue, S.W.* The Roanoke Warehouse Historic District, also known as Wholesale Row, consists of five warehouses, all erected between 1889 and 1902 for the storage of wholesale food in transit. Closely identified with Roanoke's emergence at the turn of the century as the wholesale capital of Southwest Virginia, the district's buildings exemplify the functional tradition of early industrial warehouse design. The brick structures have powerful rectangular lines, gabled ends, rows of deep-set segmental-arched windows, and iron door and window moldings. Their structural systems incorporate post-and-beam timber supports and cast tie-rods. Two of the warehouses have stepped gabled roofs with brick corbeling that make them look Dutch. 128–46 (9/16/82).

ST. ANDREW'S ROMAN CATHOLIC CHURCH, *631 Jefferson Street, N.E.* Overlooking downtown Roanoke, St. Andrew's Church is one of Virginia's foremost examples of the High Victorian Gothic, a style known for its solidity, color, and ornamentation. With twin spires, rounded apse, and tall gabled transepts, the composition follows basically French precedents. A departure from tradition is the use of the modern yellow pressed brick for the walls, which gives the building a striking golden hue. Its construction was due largely to the efforts of Father John Lynch, who organized Roanoke's Roman Catholic community, then composed primarily of recently arrived railroad workers. Lynch said his first mass in the Roanoke area in 1882 in a passenger coach. The number of communicants grew rapidly, and the church, designed by William P. Ginther of Akron, Ohio, was completed in 1902. Its interior, embellished with vaulting, carving, stenciling, and stained glass, is a dazzling expression of late Victorian Catholic art. 128–30 (10/17/72).

ROANOKE COUNTY

*Occupying the Roanoke Valley and named for the Roanoke River
that flows through it, Roanoke County is the gateway to
Southwest Virginia. It was formed from Botetourt County
in 1838, with part of Montgomery County added later.
The county seat is Salem.*

HOLLINS COLLEGE QUADRANGLE, *Hollins*. The Hollins College quadrangle is a harmonious complex of white-trimmed brick educational buildings grouped around a tree-shaded lawn. The school was founded in 1837 as the Roanoke Female Seminary at what was then the Botetourt Springs resort. Charles L. Cocke took charge in 1846 and made the seminary a leading woman's college. Its name was changed to Hollins in 1855 to honor Mr. and Mrs. John Hollins of Lynchburg, who granted money to erect East Dormitory (shown), the quadrangle's oldest building. Completed in 1858, this colonnaded structure was built by D. C. Yates, with its brickwork by O. W. Brown, and is one of the area's major Greek Revival works. Main Building, a long structure fronted by a veranda, was begun in 1861 with David Deyerle as mason and Gustavus Sedon as carpenter, and work on it continued as late as 1879. A modified Romanesque Revival building, Bradley Chapel, built by George Etter and Gustavus Sedon, was the school's first building erected after the Civil War. Sedon also worked on the octagonal dining room, Botetourt Hall, completed in 1890. West Dormitory, designed by H. H. Huggins of Roanoke, was built on the site of the original hotel building in 1900. Closing in the quadrangle is a neoclassical structure, the Charles L. Cocke Library, now the school's administrative offices, designed by the Lynchburg firm of Frye and Chesterman and completed in 1908. 80–55 (5/21/74).

OLD TOMBSTONE (DENTON MONUMENT), *Old Tombstone Cemetery, Hollins vicinity*. The Old Tombstone was carved sometime after 1805 by Laurence Krone, the most noted of the early 19th-century Valley German stone carvers. It was designed as a memorial to the young Robert Denton and as a register of his immediate family. The monument is in the form of a small coffin containing a folk image of the deceased child. It is decorated with Germanic folk motifs and is covered with a lengthy inscription in Latin, German, and English. The head and upper torso were originally covered by a removable stone lid which has since disappeared. 80–59 (7/19/77).

ROCKBRIDGE COUNTY

Rockbridge County was named for Natural Bridge, the natural formation much admired and once owned by Thomas Jefferson. The county was formed from Augusta and Botetourt counties in 1778. Its county seat is Lexington.

ANDERSON HOLLOW ARCHAEOLOGICAL DISTRICT, *Denmark vicinity.* The Anderson Hollow Archaeological District contains seven prehistoric and historic archaeological sites representing the full range of hollow settlement as it occurred within the ridge-and-valley province of western Virginia. In the 19th century, relatively poor but very independent families moved into the hollows once occupied by Indians. The historic sites within Anderson Hollow, dating from 1826 to 1960, are particularly significant because knowledge of the cultural adaptations that developed in this sort of environment is extremely limited. Several of the sites consist of stone foundations and chimney bases probably of log houses. Archaeological research in the area should yield new information about land use and its evolution over time, thus providing an opportunity to define with greater precision the various forms of agriculture and other subsistence practices within the uplands of western Virginia during successive periods. 81–407 (4/19/83).

BROWNSBURG HISTORIC DISTRICT, *including the entire village extending for approximately a half mile along Route 252.* Established in 1783, Brownsburg was laid out on the lands of Robert Wardlaw and Samuel McChesney along a main stage line. Brown was a common name among the area's early settlers, and it is not known for which particular family of Browns the town was named. By 1835 the Shenandoah Valley community was a hub of activity, containing about twenty dwellings, a mill, three stores, two shoe factories, three wheelwrights, two blacksmith shops, two tailors, a tanyard, a saddlery, a cabinetmaker, a carpenter, and a hatter. When the Valley Railroad was built several miles to the east in 1884, Brownsburg

began to lose its commercial importance and slid into a long decline. Now a well-preserved but somnolent residential community, Brownsburg contains buildings dating mostly from the first half of the 19th century and the period 1870–1910. The prevalent mode along the tree-shaded main thoroughfare is the unembellished Valley Federal style, in both frame and brick construction. Several of the earliest houses have log cores. 81–121 (2/20/73).

CHURCH HILL, *Timber Ridge*. At the south end of the settlement of Timber Ridge, Church Hill is a solid example of western Virginia Greek Revival. Built in 1848 for Horatio Thompson, a minister of the nearby Timber Ridge Associated Reformed Presbyterian Church, the house has the good craftsmanship and design of mid-19th-century rural American architecture. The exterior is set off by massive corner pilasters and by a carefully proportioned dwarf portico sheltering the entrance. The interior, though generally plain, has trompe l'oeil painted decoration on the main stair. The Houston family acquired title to the farm in 1742; in a log house probably demolished when the present house was built, Sam Houston, the Texas pioneer, was born in 1793 to Samuel and Elizabeth Houston. Tradition has it that some of the logs from the Sam Houston birthplace were incorporated in a later log structure here. 81–65 (6/21/77).

GOSHEN LAND COMPANY BRIDGE, *Route 746, Goshen.* This lacy metal truss bridge, with its thirty-degree skew, was built by the Groton Bridge Company for the Goshen Land and Improvement Company in 1890 when the Shenandoah Valley was undergoing a real estate and industrial boom. The developers of Goshen hoped that the community would grow into the "Birmingham of America"; but the boom ended quickly, and the bridge remains one of the company's few tangible accomplishments. Supported on limestone ashlar piers and abutments, the bridge is composed of a through Pratt truss consisting of two spans with an overall length of 258 feet. Above the portal is an ornate cresting sign listing the officers of the Goshen Company. 81–166 (11/15/77).

ZACHARIAH JOHNSTON HOUSE (STONE HOUSE), *Lexington vicinity.* On a tree-shaded knoll on the outskirts of Lexington, this solidly proportioned limestone house is a distinguished example of the early formal architecture of the region. As recorded on a date stone, the house was built for Zachariah Johnston in 1797 by John Spear, a little known but obviously skilled builder. Johnston served as a member of the Virginia ratification convention of 1788, a presidential elector, and a member of the House of Delegates, where he was chairman of the standing committee on religion and demonstrated his strong advocacy of religious freedom. The house is preserved with few changes. A modern passageway connects the main section to the original kitchen outbuilding. The front porch, with its massive chamfered posts, may be original. 81–168 (5/16/78).

KENNEDY-WADE MILL, *Wade's Mill*. Of the supportive industries required by the agrarian society of 19th- and early 20th-century western Virginia, the gristmill was the most essential. The Kennedy-Wade Mill, near Brownsburg, is the only operating example of such a mill in Rockbridge County. The collection of machinery is still powered by its metal Fitz overshot wheel. Andrew Kennedy, a large area landowner, acquired the tract on which the mill stands in 1799 and built the stone portion of the structure in the early years of the 19th century. The mill burned in 1873 and was rebuilt incorporating the original stone walls. The resulting mill, with its board-and-batten superstructure and updated machinery, was acquired in 1882 by James F. Waid (Wade), whose family has owned it ever since. The mill ceased operation for a number of years but recently has been reactivated by the Wades. 81–33 (5/16/78).

LIBERTY HALL ACADEMY RUINS, *Lexington vicinity*. Only the stone end walls remain of Liberty Hall Academy, the predecessor of Washington and Lee University. In 1749 Augusta Academy, the first school of consequence west of the Blue Ridge Mountains, was founded near Greenville. The academy was relocated twice before its move in 1792 to a ridge immediately west of Lexington where it was renamed Liberty Hall Academy. Constructed in 1793, the limestone building was three stories tall and covered with a wood-shingle roof. An unusual feature found mainly in Rockbridge County was the placement of a fireplace in the outside corner of each room, so that chimneys projected from the four corners of the building. The academy was housed here only a short while, for the building was gutted by fire in 1803. The school, by then known as Washington Academy, was moved to new buildings in Lexington where it evolved into the present university. 81–87 (12/21/76).

McCORMICK FARM AND WORKSHOP (WALNUT GROVE), *Steele's Tavern vicinity*. On this farm Cyrus Hall McCormick (1809–1884) developed an effective reaper shortly after he took over the project on which his father, Robert McCormick, had worked intermittently for twenty years. McCormick's reaper, successfully demonstrated in July 1831, revolutionized agricultural production, for it permitted the farmer to reap as much grain as he could sow. McCormick patented the machine in 1834 and made improvements to it in the 1840s. Commercial manufacture of the reaper began at Walnut Grove; however, in 1847, in partnership with his brother, Leander, Cyrus McCormick founded the McCormick Harvesting and Machine Company in Chicago and became one of the most successful manufacturers in America's industrial age. Owned by Virginia Polytechnic Institute and State University, the log workshop where the first reaper was built, the adjacent log mill, and the McCormick family home are preserved here. The farm currently functions as the VPI Shenandoah Valley Research Station. 81–73 (9/9/69); *National Historic Landmark*.

NEW PROVIDENCE PRESBYTERIAN CHURCH, *Brownsburg vicinity.* With its temple form, Doric portico in antis, and brick construction, this country Greek Revival church is patterned after designs by Robert Lewis Dabney, a Presbyterian minister and amateur architect. New Providence was completed in 1859. Its closest parallel is Dabney's 1850 Tinkling Spring Presbyterian Church not far away in Augusta County. Because New Providence's minister, James Morrison, was Dabney's father-in-law, it seems likely that Dabney may have had some direct influence on the design. Except for a large Sunday school addition, the building has been little altered. The main interior feature is the engaged tabernacle framing the pulpit, consisting of a Doric entablature with ornamented blocking course and paired Doric pilasters. Around three sides of the sanctuary is a gallery supported on Doric columns. The New Providence congregation was organized in 1746 by the pioneering Presbyterian pastor John Blair. The Female Benevolent Society, Virginia's earliest known missionary society, was founded at New Providence in 1819. 81–46 (2/21/78).

THORN HILL, *Lexington vicinity.* Thorn Hill, built ca. 1792, was the home of John Bowyer, who came to the area in 1753 as a schoolteacher. Bowyer helped organize Rockbridge County in 1778. In 1782 he became a colonel in the Rockbridge County militia and was made justice of the peace several years later. He was appointed one of the first trustees of Liberty Hall Academy in 1792. With fine views of the Rockbridge countryside and mountains, Bowyer's house has elaborate but eccentrically proportioned late Georgian woodwork with few parallels in the region. Its joiner was obviously untutored in architectural refinements but was highly skilled with an entertaining sense of design. The exterior is a Rockbridge brick I-house but with a modillion cornice and five bays rather than the molded-brick cornice and three bays of the standard I-houses. The south facade retains its delicate Federal porch; what was a two-level porch on the opposite front was replaced in the 19th century with four heavy Greek Doric columns. Several early outbuildings are placed to make a formal forecourt on the house's south side. 81–84 (2/18/75).

TIMBER RIDGE PRESBYTERIAN CHURCH, *Timber Ridge.* Though considerably altered and enlarged during its more than two centuries of service, this stone meetinghouse, built in 1755, is the second oldest Presbyterian church in the Shenandoah Valley. The congregation was organized in 1746 by the Reverend John Blair and worshiped in a log structure until this building was erected. For several years after 1776, Timber Ridge supported the newly opened Augusta Academy, the predecessor of Washington and Lee University. One of the congregation's early leaders was John Houston, great-grandfather of Sam Houston, the Texas pioneer. The present facade, with its arcaded porch, was added in 1871. 81–66 (9/9/69).

ROCKINGHAM COUNTY

Formed from Augusta County in 1778, this largely agricultural Shenandoah Valley county was named for Charles Watson-Wentworth, second marquess of Rockingham, who supported the colonists in their disputes with Great Britain. The county seat is Harrisonburg.

BAXTER HOUSE, *Edom vicinity.* The Baxter house, conspicuously located alongside the road between the towns of Broadway and Linville, preserves Virginia log construction at its finest. The western half of the double-pen structure has full dovetail corner notching; its precisely fitted logs, devoid of chinking, illustrate a building method associated with the Valley's German settlers. The eastern half, the earlier section, with its regular chinking and less uniformly dressed logs is typical of the log buildings of the Scotch-Irish settlers. This earlier part was built in the late 18th century for George Baxter, whose son served as one of the early presidents of Washington College in Lexington. 82–71 (7/17/73).

JOHN K. BEERY FARM, *Edom vicinity.* In a secluded vale in the Linville Creek area of Rockingham County, the John K. Beery complex is one of the most complete early rural homesteads in the region. The grouping, which boasts nearly a dozen farm structures, includes a stone dwelling house, springhouse, kitchen/wash house, and rare stone barn with slotted ends. Beery, a descendant of Swiss immigrants who settled in Pennsylvania, had the buildings put up in 1838–39. A strict Mennonite who opposed the use of churches, Beery for many years held services for the local congregation in the east wing of his house. The barn was burned in the Civil War but was rebuilt within the stone walls. Abandoned for over a decade, the complex has been carefully restored by its present owners. 82–2 (7/17/73).

BETHLEHEM CHURCH, *Tenth Legion*. Built in 1844–45 by the local stonemason Jeremiah Clemens, Bethlehem Church is the oldest stone church in Rockingham County and the second church of a Quaker meeting. With its rectangular form, gabled roof, lack of ornamentation, and limestone construction, the church reflects both the conservative character of mid-19th-century country churches in the Valley and the persistence of a strong local masonry tradition in the Linville and Smith Creek areas. During the Civil War the church stood in the line of battle in the Valley campaign and served as a hospital. The Quakers merged with the local Christian Church after the Civil War. Services ceased to be held in the building in 1952 when a new church was built next door. 82–3 (12/16/80).

BIG RUN QUARRY ARCHAEOLOGICAL SITE, *Big Run, Shenandoah National Park*. Covering about 1,400 square meters, this site has yielded huge amounts of stone debris typical of a quarry site. The site is the largest and most intensively used prehistoric quarry located within the Shenandoah National Park and contrasts with other quarry sites in the sheer amount of debris present. Projectile points found here date to the Middle and Late Archaic periods (ca. 5500–100 B.C.). 82–323 (9/16/82).

GEORGE EARMAN HOUSE, *Harrisonburg vicinity*. The George Earman house is an outstanding example of the creative carving, joinery, and painting used in Shenandoah Valley farmhouses in the early 19th century. Hidden within an exceptionally plain, ca. 1822 brick I-house, this decoration reveals the persistence of the German influence after the Continental house forms had been abandoned for the more popular English-influenced models. For the woodwork, the local craftsman freely interpreted Federal pattern-book motifs, carving them in the more robust German manner and integrating them with more traditional local designs to create very personal compositions. The parlor woodwork retains its original boldly colored painting scheme including marbleizing, wood-graining, and sponge-painted panels. 82–137 (9/15/81).

FORT HARRISON (DANIEL HARRISON HOUSE), *Dayton*. Built ca. 1749 for Daniel Harrison, one of the area's earliest settlers, this farmhouse was constructed of stone in the style favored by the region's early Germans for their more substantial dwellings. During the Indian raids associated with the French and Indian War, the strong, well-positioned house served as a defense point and was locally referred to as a fort. The property remained in the Harrison family until 1821. Later owners made alterations, especially in 1856 when the rear brick section was added. Recently restored, the house is now exhibited as a museum by Fort Harrison, Inc., a nonprofit organization. 206–1 (6/19/73).

JOSEPH FUNK HOUSE, *Singers Glen*. Joseph Funk (1777–1862) was the grandson of Henry Funk, the first Mennonite bishop in America, and the son of Henry Funk, Jr., founder of the "Funkite" branch of the Mennonite church. The Funks moved to the region from Berks County, Pa., when Joseph Funk was a child. In 1847 Funk established his own press at what became Singers Glen where he published his English translations of German Mennonite theological tracts and choral music. Funk also set up singing schools in the village and in other Shenandoah Valley towns and promoted the patent note system, which was employed in his own widely used hymnal, *Harmonia Sacra*. Funk's simple weatherboarded log house in Singers Glen was built ca. 1810. The press was located in the loom house nearby, which has since been destroyed. 82–69 (11/19/74).

STEPHEN HARNSBERGER HOUSE, *Grottoes*. Built in 1856 on the edge of what became the town of Grottoes, the Stephen Harnsberger house is a Shenandoah Valley example of the octagonal building fad that spread across the nation in the mid-19th century. While the facade and shape of the house clearly reflect an awareness of the new styles popularized in Orson Squire Fowler's *A Home for All, or The Gravel Wall and Octagon Mode of Building* (1848), the interior retains the traditional arrangement of spaces in a double-pile Georgian scheme. The house thus reflects the interpretation of pattern-book styles in a conservative agricultural area. 82–134 (1/20/81).

LINCOLN HOMESTEAD AND CEMETERY, *Broadway vicinity.* President Abraham Lincoln's great-grandfather John Lincoln moved from Pennsylvania and settled in the Linville Creek area of Rockingham County in 1768. Although John's eldest son, Abraham, grandfather of the president, migrated to Kentucky, a younger son, Jacob, remained to build the present Federal farmhouse ca. 1800 near the site of the original family home. With its refined details and academic proportions, the house is sophisticated for its time and place and contrasts with the neighboring German-style farmhouses. The property remained in the Lincoln family until 1874. The family cemetery, high on the hill behind the house, contains the graves of five generations of Lincolns, including John and Jacob Lincoln, and two of the Lincoln family slaves. 82–14 (8/15/72).

LINVILLE CREEK BRIDGE, *Broadway.* The Linville Creek Bridge is probably the state's only surviving example of the Whipple metal truss bridge. The Whipple truss is a hybrid system incorporating aspects of both the double-Pratt and Warren trusses, both popular structural systems for early metal bridges. The bridge was manufactured in 1898 by the Wrought Iron Bridge Company of Canton, Ohio, and remains in daily use. The span is unusually long. 82–127 (11/15/77).

MILLER-KITE HOUSE, *302 Rockingham Street, Elkton.* Henry Miller, Jr., descendant of one of the earliest settlers west of the Blue Ridge, had this substantial brick house erected for himself in 1827. As noted in the contract, the carpentry and joinery for the dwelling were executed by Samuel Gibbons of Rockingham, making this one of the few houses in the area with which a specific craftsman is associated. The woodwork, especially a mantel carved with tulip-and-vine motif, shows the influence of German style on the otherwise non-Germanic house. Stonewall Jackson is believed to have used the house as a headquarters in the Valley campaign. Although its roof has received minor alterations, the house is otherwise much as it was built, but the surrounding farmlands have been subdivided since the town of Elkton was laid out in 1890. 82–133 (10/17/78).

PETER PAUL HOUSE, *Dayton vicinity.* This plain dwelling near the town of Dayton is one of the few Continental farmhouses surviving from the heavy German settlement in the Shenandoah Valley. Built for Peter Paul between 1805 and 1815 on land purchased from the Harrison family, the central-chimney house is also one of the latest and most southern of these Germanic houses. The walls are of log construction but were stuccoed over at an early date. Nearly all of the original interior fittings, including beaded partitions, simple Federal mantels, a ladder stair, a paneled door, and a batten door, survive despite modern alterations. 82–31 (10/16/79).

PORT REPUBLIC HISTORIC DISTRICT, *bounded by town limits.* This small grid-plan town in eastern Rockingham County was founded in 1802 and became a booming river port. It served as the shipping point for the agricultural and industrial products of the upper Shenandoah River until the 1890s when the railroad was built to the east of the town. Through the town's collection of 19th-century vernacular buildings and its numerous archaeological sites can be traced the growth and decline of this 19th-century shipping and industrial community. Port Republic gave its name to a Civil War battle, the conclusion of Stonewall Jackson's Valley campaign, fought just to the north of the town. The town preserves an open, almost rural quality with houses and outbuildings sprinkled among large lots. Perhaps the most interesting structure is the Dundore house and office, an early 19th-century, two-part brick and log building with a squat Doric portico added later. It is one of several houses built facing the South River. 82–123 (7/18/78).

SINGERS GLEN HISTORIC DISTRICT, *encompassing the entire village complex stretching approximately a mile along Route 613.* This village began when Joseph Funk moved to the area in the first decade of the 19th century and established a publishing firm for Mennonite religious tracts and choral music. The settlement that grew up around his farm was called Mountain Valley but was renamed Singers Glen in 1860 in honor of its most conspicuous product. The publishing firm moved from Singers Glen in 1878, but the village continued to grow and prosper as other businesses, including a carriage works, located there. The late 19th-century prosperity resulted in the construction of a number of spacious wooden houses, many of them decked out with fanciful turned- and sawn-work front porches. Shown are houses built in the 1890s by members of the Funk family, who remained leading citizens of the community into the 20th century. Contrasting with these richly trimmed structures is Joseph Funk's plain little house in the center of the village. The halt of growth after World War I has preserved Singers Glen as a 19th-century Shenandoah Valley village. 82–125 (12/21/76).

SITES HOUSE, *Broadway vicinity.* The Linville Creek area of Rockingham County was first populated by settlers of German origin who incorporated Continental building forms into their New World homes. Although once common, only a handful of these German-style farmhouses remain; the Sites house is a notably pure and well-preserved one. Characteristic of these houses is the stone construction, the centered chimney stack, the three-room plan, and the sloping site location. Adding interest to the Sites house is the large amount of original woodwork, including the exposed, molded summer beam and joists and an unusual roof-framing system with molded purlins. Dating from ca. 1800, the house was the home of Christian Sites. It is currently unoccupied. 82–35 (10/17/78).

TUNKER HOUSE, *Broadway.* This plain Shenandoah Valley farmhouse was built by one of the German Baptist Brethren, or Dunkers, known originally in the area as the Society of Tunkers, who opposed the use of churches and held their religious services in selected homes. The owner, Benjamin Yount, outfitted the front portion of the house, erected between 1802 and 1806, with hinged partitions that could be raised to accommodate religious gatherings. Yount's daughter was the wife of Peter Nead, a leading member of the Tunkers and author of *Primitive Christianity,* which served as the Brethren's first theological work in English. Nead and his wife occupied her father's house until 1839. Although it is now a private residence, the hinged partitions of this combination church-home remain in place. 82–25 (3/2/71).

RUSSELL COUNTY

Formed from Washington County in 1786, this pastoral Southwest Virginia county was named for William Russell, a Clinch Valley pioneer and the member of the house of Delegates who introduced the legislation forming the county. The county seat is Lebanon.

DAUGHERTY'S CAVE AND BREEDING ARCHAEO-LOGICAL SITE, *Lebanon vicinity.* Along the banks of Big Cedar Creek near its junction with the Clinch River, these two sites contain prehistoric archaeological potential. Test excavations at Daugherty's Cave show 9,000 years of stratified cultural and natural deposits indicating occupation during the Cedar Creek Savannah River, and various Woodland period occupations. The adjacent Breeding site contains remains from the Early Archaic period that are not present in Daugherty's Cave. Future investigation of both sites should provide contrasting information on prehistoric Indian life-styles at various periods in both sheltered and open habitats. 83–22 (12/21/76).

OLD RUSSELL COUNTY COURTHOUSE, *Dickenson-ville vicinity.* The second courthouse of Russell County is one of the oldest public buildings in Southwest Virginia. The simple stone structure was built in 1799 to replace the first courthouse, a log building destroyed by fire, and served the county until the county seat was moved to Lebanon in 1818. The courthouse was then acquired by the Dickenson family, who made it the wing of a brick farmhouse. Despite its conversion to residential use, much of the building's original interior fabric was preserved. In recent years the property was again acquired by the county, and both the stone section and the brick addition have undergone a meticulous restoration for development into a museum. 83–1 (6/19/73).

CITY OF SALEM

The Roanoke county seat was laid out in 1802 and is said to have been named for Salem, N.J., home of one of the settling families. Still the county seat, it was incorporated as a town in 1836 and became an independent city in 1968.

ACADEMY STREET SCHOOL, *Academy Street*. Completed in 1890 on the site of a private female academy, the Academy Street School was one of the first modern public schools in Southwest Virginia, a result of the state's reforms in public education in the late 19th century. Taking advantage of its prominent location at the head of a street, the building has a fashionably Victorian silhouette emphasized by decorative brickwork, bracketed cornices, and an imposing entrance tower originally topped by a mansard roof. Its well-lighted, centrally heated, and spacious classrooms, arranged around an octagonal central hall, indicated an enlightened attitude toward public primary education, in contrast to the one-room, wooden schoolhouses that were serving most Virginians at the time. The school originally was in the Roanoke County school system but was later made part of the school system of the city of Salem. Closed in 1977, the school has since been sold by the city to a private developer for conversion into apartments. 129–2 (1/20/81).

EVANS HOUSE, *213 Broad Street*. John M. Evans, farmer, businessman, and investor in Salem's land boom, built this small-scale mansion on Broad Street in 1882. Although its architect is unknown, the house is a first-rate example of the American interpretation of the Second Empire style, employing both a mansard roof and a square domed tower. The bold outline and fine proportions skillfully disguise the building's relatively small size. Such exuberant late Victorian houses were never common in Virginia, and the majority of those that were built have since been demolished, leaving the Evans house a landmark both of its style and of the boom period in western Virginia. 129–17 (3/21/72).

ROANOKE COLLEGE MAIN CAMPUS COMPLEX, *College Avenue*. In a tree-shaded campus in the middle of Salem, this group of academic buildings displays the evolution of the area's architectural tastes from the mid-19th century through the early 20th century. First known as Virginia Collegiate Institute, Roanoke College was founded by two Lutheran pastors in Augusta County in 1842 and was moved to Salem in 1847. That same year a contract was given to James C. and Joseph Deyerle to erect the Main Building, now the Administration Building. Originally Greek Revival, the building was remodeled in the neoclassical taste in 1903 when it received its third floor and Corinthian portico. Flanking it are Miller and Trout halls, both begun in 1856. The Gothic-style Brittle Hall was completed in 1879 as a library, was converted to a chapel in 1894, and now serves other functions. 129–5,6,7 (5/16/72).

SALEM PRESBYTERIAN CHURCH, *East Main and Market streets*. The inventiveness and keen aesthetic sense of America's Greek Revival architects and master builders is displayed in Salem's Presbyterian church. Its designer has not been identified; however, much of the woodwork likely was executed by Gustavus Sedon, a skillful Roanoke Valley carver and master carpenter. Many of the classical details show a reliance on popular pattern books of the period such as those by Asher Benjamin and Owen Biddle. Organized in Salem in 1831, the Presbyterians outgrew their first church and began construction of the present building in 1851. The church tower was originally topped by a spire; the present octagonal lantern dates from 1928. 129–9 (6/18/74).

WILLIAMS-BROWN HOUSE-STORE, *East Main Street*. This combination commercial and residential building, conspicuously located on Main Street, is one of the few remaining examples of a type once prevalent in towns along the much-traveled Great Road west to Kentucky and Tennessee. Dating from ca. 1845–52, the building was constructed and occupied by William C. Williams, who was also one of the builders of Salem's first courthouse. It later passed to the Brown family, who owned it until 1963. Giving the house-store special relation to its street-front siting are the galleries incorporated into the main structure of the building and entered through arches in the side walls. 129–10 (7/6/71).

SCOTT COUNTY

This mountainous county near Virginia's southwestern tip was named for Gen. Winfield Scott, a native of Virginia, in recognition of his victories during the War of 1812. It was formed in 1814 from Lee, Russell, and Washington counties. Its county seat is Gate City.

A. P. CARTER HOMEPLACE, *Maces Spring vicinity.* This log structure tucked in Little Valley near Maces Spring is the birthplace of Alvin Pleasants Dulaney ("A. P.") Carter (1891–1960), who formed the Carter Family singing group with his wife, Sara, and his sister-in-law Maybelle. They performed a repertoire of songs traditional in the family as well as songs composed by Carter or collected from the mountain people. Their recordings popularized a folk art form of the southern highlands and helped start the country music industry. A one-room square, or English, cabin, with a single exterior chimney and an enclosed corner stair, the house, built in the late 19th century, is still owned by the family. 84–7 (12/16/75).

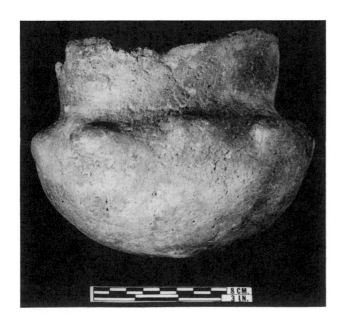

FLANARY ARCHAEOLOGICAL SITE, *Dungannon vicinity.* The Flanary archaeological site contains stratified deposits dating to the Archaic and Late Woodland periods of Indian settlement. Well-preserved Archaic period deposits (8000 to 1000 B.C.) occur rarely in the western portion of the state, and the site's Late Woodland period remains (A.D. 800–1600) overlying these deposits could provide crucial data for regional studies on Indian subsistence and settlement. Shown is a ca. 950 A.D. Late Woodland squash effigy vessel found there. The presence of artifacts at the site relating to the Indians of eastern Tennessee and western North Carolina is valuable in documenting the interactions of Virginia Indians with their neighbors to the south. 84–12 (9/16/82).

KILGORE FORT HOUSE, *Nicklesville vicinity*. Indians remained a threat to settlers in Southwest Virginia well into the last decades of the 18th century. Military blockhouses were no longer deemed essential, but strongly built log dwellings were considered prudent. Robert Kilgore's stout log house of ca. 1790 represents this stage in frontier development. Both its lower and upper stories are separated into two rooms by log partitions built as strongly as the outer walls, providing the possibility of several strategic retreats. Although threatened on several occasions, the Kilgore house survived the last Indian uprising. Kilgore, who lived here until his death in 1854 at the age of eighty-eight, was a Primitive Baptist preacher as well as a farmer. The house stood in deteriorated condition for many years but was restored in the 1970s by the Lenowisco Planning District Commission with the assistance of other area agencies to serve as a visitor attraction for a wayside park. 84–3 (1/18/72).

SHENANDOAH COUNTY

This Shenandoah Valley county originally was named in honor of Lord Dunmore, governor of Virginia at the time it was formed from Frederick County in 1772. The present name, honoring the river which passes through it was substituted in 1778 as an acommodation to anti royalist sentiment. The county seat is Woodstock.

EDINBURG MILL, *Edinburg.* The three-story gristmill on Stony Creek at the western end of the old Shenandoah Valley community of Edinburg is a relic of the region's early agricultural industry. The present structure was built ca. 1850 by George Grandstaff to support a mill complex developed by his father beginning in 1813. The mill was set afire during Sheridan's sweep of the Valley in 1865. Tradition has it, however, that the ladies of the town persuaded the Union officers to save the remaining flour supply. They and the Union soldiers then extinguished the flames, saving the mill and most of the contents. The machinery was modernized at the turn of the century, and milling operations continued until 1978. The mill has since been secured from a second threatened destruction through acquisition for adaptive use as a restaurant. 85–110 (6/19/79).

FORESTVILLE MILL (ZIRKLE MILL), *Forestville*. Probably dating from the late 18th century, this gristmill on Holmans Creek at the edge of the village of Forestville was erected by Andrew Zirkle, Sr., to accommodate the labor-saving machinery promoted by mill theorist Oliver Evans. The mill prospered in the antebellum period under the proprietorship of Jacob Bowers, who founded the adjoining village of Forestville on portions of the original mill property, in 1838. Unlike many of the region's mills the Forestville Mill survived the Civil War intact. The tall wooden building retains a collection of early milling machinery, illustrating the technological changes that transformed Zirkle's burr mill into a roller mill by the turn of the century. Although the mill ceased to function in the 1950s, it is being preserved through adaptive use as a furniture workshop. 85–122 (12/14/82).

FORT BOWMAN, *Strasburg vicinity*. Standing beside an undisturbed section of the old Valley Turnpike, this stone house is an example of the Pennsylvania German influence on the early architecture of the Shenandoah Valley. Notable German characteristics are the limestone construction, the use of exposed dressed ceiling joists in the principal rooms, and the heavy roof framing employing a principal purlin system. The house was built ca. 1753 for George Bowman, who with his wife, Mary, migrated to Virginia from Pennsylvania in 1731–32. Mary Bowman was the daughter of Jost Hite, regarded as the region's first white settler. Among those buried in the Bowman family graveyard behind the house are George Bowman's son Isaac Bowman, who aided George Rogers Clark in the conquest of the Northwest, and Samuel Kercheval, historian of the Shenandoah Valley. Except for the addition of the small Greek Revival portico and a kitchen wing, the house survives without significant change. 85–4 (11/5/68).

DR. CHRISTIAN HOCKMAN HOUSE, *Edinburg vicinity*. The Dr. Christian Hockman house is a rare example of the Italian Villa style in the lower Shenandoah Valley. Its mass-manufactured exterior and interior woodwork are illustrative of an important change in the building techniques in the region. Replacing ornaments made by hand, such components were sold through illustrated catalogs in major towns and cities and were distributed through rural areas by the ever-widening railroad network. The Hockman house was built in 1868–70 just as rail service was opened from Baltimore to nearby Edinburg. Dr. Hockman, who may have been related to the Hockman family of Harrisonburg, is listed in the 1885 atlas as a dentist living just north of Edinburg on the Valley Turnpike. The house stood unoccupied for several years but has recently been renovated as a private residence. 85–76 (1/17/84).

MEEMS BOTTOM COVERED BRIDGE, *Mount Jackson vicinity.* Constructed in 1893–94 under the supervision of F. W. Wisler, this 200-foot single-span structure is the longest of the Commonwealth's handful of remaining covered bridges. The bridge over the Shenandoah River is approached from the east by a tree-lined axial avenue across the bottomlands whence it derives its name. The structural system employed is a Burr truss or king-post arch system, which consists of two great wooden arches spanning the full distance between the abutments. The bridge was damaged by fire in 1976, but the structural timbers survived with only charring and were covered over with roofing and weatherboards by the Virginia Department of Highways and Transportation, allowing the bridge to be returned to limited use. 85–103 (4/15/75).

MILEY ARCHAEOLOGICAL SITE, *Maurertown vicinity.* In the Seven Bends area of the Shenandoah River, the Miley site consists of the remains of one of the few palisaded villages of the Late Woodland period yet discovered in the Shenandoah Valley. Approximately 15 percent of the site was excavated in 1964 under the direction of the Virginia State Library, revealing a village area over 250 feet in diameter with sites of circular structures within the palisade line. Also discovered were evidences of food storage pits and graves. The remaining unexcavated areas likely hold important information on the region's prehistoric Indian life. 85–101 (4/16/74).

NEW MARKET BATTLEFIELD, *New Market vicinity.* Gen. John C. Breckenridge's Confederate brigades, joined by the 247-man cadet corps of the Virginia Military Institute, repulsed the Union forces at New Market on May 15, 1964, thus preserving the supply and commmunication lines between the Army of Northern Virginia and the Shenandoah Valley. This victory permitted General Lee to concentrate his full efforts toward halting the Union advance on Richmond. In their only engagement of the war, the VMI cadets, the eldest of them under eighteen, distinguished themselves with a gallant charge and the capture of a battery and an enemy flag. The 160-acre battlefield, just west of the town of New Market, is owned by the Commonwealth and exhibited as a historical park and a memorial to the cadets who fought and died there. On the eastern edge of the battlefield is the restored Bushong house, used by both sides as a hospital. 85–27 (6/2/70).

NEW MARKET HISTORIC DISTRICT, *encompassing the town limits*. New Market, originally called Cross Roads because of its strategic location at the intersection of the Valley Turnpike with the east-west road through Massanutten Gap, is one of the best-preserved linear towns along the western roads. The town's site was selected by John Sevier, later governor of Tennessee, who established a trading post here in 1761. The village was laid out in lots of 1785 and was officially designated a town with its present name in 1796. Settled both by Germans and Scotch-Irish, New Market prospered by serving the many pioneers who either passed through or remained in the area. By 1830 it had become an active commercial and industrial center. Fierce fighting occurred around the town during the battle of New Market of 1864, and many of the citizens turned out to treat the wounded. Growth ceased in the middle of the 19th century when the town was bypassed by the railroad and travel on the Valley Turnpike dwindled. Lining the highway is a mixture of 19th-century brick, frame, and log structures. Many of the earlier houses employ German vernacular forms. 269–5 (5/16/72).

ORKNEY SPRINGS, *Orkney Springs*. In the shadow of the Allegheny Mountains, Orkney Springs presents the most complete picture of the spa complexes that sprang up in the 19th century around the mineral springs of western Virginia. Local farmers knew the springs as early as 1800, and a small community was established here in the 1830s. Resort development began in the 1850s. Surviving from Orkney Springs's period of greatest popularity is the 1876 Virginia House, a wooden hotel surrounded by tiers of galleries. The oldest building in the complex is the 1853 Maryland House, also highlighted by galleries. Other hotel structures and a range of cottages complete the picture of a 19th-century resort. Although many of its sister spas have succumbed to fire, abandonment, or demolition, Orkney Springs has managed to survive, as a summer music camp and a retreat for the Episcopal Diocese of Virginia. 85–39 (3/18/75).

QUICKSBURG ARCHAEOLOGICAL SITE, *Quicksburg vicinity*. Test excavations undertaken by the Virginia State Library at this site on the Shenandoah River have revealed evidence of one of the region's few palisaded Indian villages of the Late Woodland period. Within the village compound were indications of circular dwellings as well as food storage pits and graves. Further investigation of the site should provide important information on prehistoric communal life in the lower Shenandoah Valley. 85–102 (4/16/74).

SHENANDOAH COUNTY COURTHOUSE, *South Main and West Court streets, Woodstock.* The original two-story section of the Shenandoah County Courthouse was erected in the early 1790s and is considered to be the oldest court structure west of the Blue Ridge Mountains. The architecture of the limestone building reflects the dominance of the German settlers in the Woodstock area. The most distinctive feature, the hexagonal, ogee-roofed cupola, recalls the belfries of German baroque parish churches. Although its original form remains evident, the courthouse has undergone significant alterations and enlargements. A brick Greek Revival wing was added in 1840, and a handsomely ornamented Victorian clerk's office was attached in 1880. The Tuscan portico was placed on the facade in 1920. A new courthouse for Shenandoah County was built in the 1970s, and this one now houses county offices. 330–2 (6/19/73).

SNAPP HOUSE (WILDFLOWER FARM), *Fishers Hill vicinity.* This late 18th-century frame farmhouse is one of Shenandoah County's best representatives of the Continental central-chimney dwellings built by the area's German-speaking settlers. The Germanic tradition is evident in such features as the hillside setting, four-room or *Kreuzhaus* plan, and complex roof framing. An early 19th-century stone wing and the remains of a springhouse/kitchen add to the picture of early German-American life in the Shenandoah Valley. The exact construction date is unknown, although it is likely that the house was built for farmer Lawrence Snapp, Sr., before his death in 1782. 85–29 (11/21/78).

STRASBURG MUSEUM, *East King Street, Strasburg.* The Strasburg Stone and Earthenware Manufacturing Company built this two-story structure in 1891 as a factory intended to put the Shenandoah Valley's long tradition of pottery making on a high-volume industrial basis. The project was part of the brief economic boom experienced in the Valley in the 1890s. The company quickly failed because of competition from other regions and other wares. In 1913 the building was converted into a railroad depot by the Southern Railway. Although still owned by the railroad company, the building is leased to the Strasburg Museum, which maintains it as an example of industrial architecture, a relic of the Valley's short-lived venture into industrial development. The building further represents a failed attempt to convert a handicraft industry into one of mass production. 306–9 (4/17/79).

SMYTH COUNTY

In the heart of Southwest Virginia, Smyth County was named for Gen. Alexander Smyth, a congressman from western Virginia from 1817 to 1830. It was formed in 1832 from Washington and Wythe counties. The county seat is Marion.

ASPENVALE CEMETERY, *Seven Mile Ford.* Aspenvale Cemetery contains the grave of Gen. William Campbell, a Virginia-born hero of the American Revolution. It is the main tangible reminder in Virginia of Campbell and his victory over Loyalist forces at the battle of King's Mountain on October 7, 1780. The Campbell-Preston family plot in which he is buried also contains the gravestones of his mother, his widow, his daughter, his son, and several succeeding generations. Privately owned, the walled cemetery is above Seven Mile Ford, an early settlement on the Middle Fork of the Holston River. 86–13 (9/16/80).

FOX FARM ARCHAEOLOGICAL SITE, *McMullin vicinity.* In the horseshoe bend of the Middle Fork of the Holston River, opposite Wassum Valley, Fox Farm preserves a prehistoric Indian village site of the Late Woodland period. The site should provide invaluable information on the interaction and development of groups represented by two types of ceramics: the early Wythe (ca. A.D. 1300) and the later Radford (A.D. 1300–1600). The presence of marine-shell beads documents the participation of the site's inhabitants in the regional trade networks of the Late Woodland period. The site also should provide information on dwellings and burial practices; unlike other burials in the region, the heads of the burials here face south. Perhaps most important for a site of its type, Fox Farm remains relatively undisturbed with excellent chances for preservation. The site was documented in 1973 through test trenches excavated by the Holston Chapter of the Archeological Society of Virginia. 86–11 (4/19/77).

HERONDON (PRESTON HOUSE), *Seven Mile Ford*. On the Middle Fork of the Holston River at Seven Mile Ford, Herondon was built in 1842 for John Montgomery Preston on land that his wife, Maria Thornton Carter Preston, inherited from her mother. The property earlier had belonged to Maria Preston's grandfather Gen. William Campbell, Revolutionary War hero of the battle of King's Mountain. Preston had the house built to serve as a tavern, placing it on the site of an earlier log tavern. The first building had a dubious reputation, and tradition has it that Preston wanted to rid the region of its stigma by creating an establishment with superior service and architecture. The building, illustrating the transition from the Federal to the Greek Revival style, served travelers along the Wilderness Road until 1864 when it became a private residence for Preston's son and his bride. Union troops sacked the house that same year during a raid toward Saltville and Abingdon. Herondon formerly held the collection of Preston manuscripts now divided between the Library of Congress and the State Historical Society of Wisconsin. 86–3 (9/9/69).

OLD STONE TAVERN, *Atkins vicinity*. Old Stone Tavern on the Wilderness Road (now U.S. Route 11), was erected before 1815 by Frederick Cullop to accommodate travelers in the heavy migration through the Cumberland Gap to the west in the early 19th century. The oldest stone building in Smyth County, the tavern reflects the influence of the stone vernacular tradition of rural Pennsylvania on the settlement arteries into Kentucky and Tennessee. Typical of early taverns, the front is sheltered by a two-level gallery which here is given a festive quality by the use of scalloped eaves. The interior preserves its early, very plain woodwork. 86–2 (3/17/81).

ABIJAH THOMAS HOUSE, *Adwolf vicinity*. This brick structure is Virginia's most sophisticated representation of Orson Squire Fowler's advocacy of octagonal architecture that caught the imagination of Americans in the reform movement of the 1850s. In his book *A Home for All, or the Gravel Wall and Octagon Mode of Building* (1848), Fowler stated that an octagonal plan encloses one fifth more floor area than a square of the same total length of wall and allows for more compact internal planning. Built in 1856–57 for Abijah Thomas, a Smyth County landowner and developer of mines, mills, and foundries, the house retains a variety of graining, marbleizing, and stenciling. Sections of marbleizing on the plaster wall of one of the principal rooms may be a unique survivor in Virginia of this once popular decorative treatment. The house has stood empty and deteriorating for many years. 86–4 (9/16/80).

CITY OF SOUTH BOSTON

Surrounded by Halifax County, this Southside city was named for Boston, Mass. Established in 1796, it was originally located on the south side of the Dan River and was known as Boyd's Ferry. The village was destroyed by floods soon after and was reestablished on the north side of the river. It was incorporated as a town in 1884 and as a city in 1960.

REEDY CREEK ARCHAEOLOGICAL SITE, *Reedy Creek at Dan River.* The Reedy Creek site contains Late Archaic (2000–1000 B.C.) components and was the location of an Indian village between A.D. 900 and 1400. During the latter period the settlement apparently evolved from a hamlet to a concentrated, possibly palisaded village. The good state of preservation of the site's subsistence materials enhances the understanding of prehistoric cultural development in the Dan River drainage. In 1975 a limited salvage excavation of a portion of the site in the path of construction revealed post molds, house patterns, and substantial quantities of floral and faunal remains. Shown are two of the numerous late Archaic steatite bowl fragments found here. 130–3 (2/15/77).

SOUTHAMPTON COUNTY

Formed in 1749 from Isle of Wight and part of Nansemond counties, this rural southern Tidewater county was named for either the English borough of Southampton or the earl of Southampton. Its county seat is Courtland.

BEECHWOOD, *Beales vicinity.* Beechwood is the spacious but unpretentious sort of house favored by southeastern Virginia planters in the early 19th century. Like many of the region's rural dwellings, the house began in the late 18th century as a one-room, one-story house and evolved into its present form over several decades through a series of additions. The first owner of the property was Jordan Denson, and the property has remained in the ownership of his descendants to the present. Denson's son-in-law Thomas Pretlow made the last significant additions to the house by 1820. A more recent owner of Beechwood was Colgate W. Darden, Jr., governor of Virginia in 1942–46 and president of the University of Virginia for twelve years. 87–2 (9/19/78).

BELMONT, *Capron vicinity.* The Nat Turner Insurrection, the bloodiest and most notorious slave revolt in American history, was suppressed at Belmont on the morning of August 23, 1831. Turner, a black slave, believed he was divinely selected to lead his people out of bondage and drew about eighty followers to go on what became a journey of murder and pillage through Southampton County. The group was halted in an ambush at Belmont, home of Dr. Samuel Blunt. The insurrection formally ended with Turner's capture on October 30 and his hanging on November 11, 1831. The short but violent revolt so alarmed the South that any sentiment toward emancipation was seen as a dangerous threat to general security. A much stricter regimen against slaves and free blacks alike was soon instituted, leading to further hardening of attitudes between the North and South. Belmont's dwelling house, a typical homeplace of a Southside plantation, was built in the late 18th century for George Carey. Its one touch of elegance is a Chinese lattice railing framing the stairwell on the upper story. The Blunts acquired Belmont from the Careys in the early 19th century. The house was restored in 1984. 87–30 (7/17/73).

BROWN'S FERRY, *Drakes Corner vicinity.* Brown's Ferry is the birthplace of William Mahone (1826–1895), the colorful Confederate general who achieved fame during the siege of Petersburg. In July 1864 Union forces attempted to break through the Confederate lines by tunneling beneath them and setting off a huge charge of explosives. Immediately after the awesome blowup, Mahone rallied his men, closed the gaping hole, and became known as the "Hero of the Crater." After the war, Mahone was a railroad executive and leader of the Readjuster party. He failed in his bid for the governorship but played a significant role in improving the state's public schools. In the absence of certain evidence, family tradition maintains that Brown's Ferry is Mahone's birthplace. The house was completed by 1818 for William Hodges and is among the largest and finest Federal dwellings in Southampton County. Generous in scale, the two-story structure features fine brickwork and carefully detailed Federal woodwork, most of which is intact even though the house is unoccupied and deteriorated. William Mahone's father, Fielding Mahone, purchased the property from the Hodges heirs in 1826. 87–120 (3/20/79).

ELM GROVE, *Courtland vicinity.* Elm Grove is a vernacular domestic complex illustrating the rural lifestyle of Virginia's southern Tidewater region. The farm was probably organized by the Williams family in the late 18th century with additions made to the house by subsequent owners. Elm Grove's core is one room with a lean-to, an elementary house form popular among even the region's more prosperous planters well into the 19th century. The house was expanded to its present appearance by the 1820s. Its outbuildings include an early 19th-century office and an early dairy with ventilation slats. There is also a comparatively large saddle-notched log smokehouse which encloses four smokepits, the only known multipit smokehouse in the state; it is probably contemporary with the earliest portion of the main house. 87–103 (5/15/79).

ROSE HILL, *Capron vicinity.* The Rose Hill dwelling house is among the earliest and least-altered I-houses in Southampton County. Its two stories have a center passage separating two rooms on each floor. The house stands on land deeded to John T. Blow in 1792 by the Nottoway Indian tribe, and the property is referred to as Indian Land in some early 19th-century deeds. Contemporary records and modern archaeological research establish the continuous occupancy of the area by Indians during the colonial period. As recently as the early 20th century, Indians gathered on Rose Hill property for religious and cultural purposes. In 1804 Blow willed the land to his son Henry, who built the house between 1805 and 1815. The house's plain Federal woodwork retains its painting, graining, and marbleizing throughout. Its king-post roof trusses form a heavy framing system usually found only in 18th-century mansions. 87–52 (9/18/79).

SUNNYSIDE, *Newsoms vicinity.* This Southampton County plantation contains one of southeastern Virginia's most complete complexes of domestic and farm outbuildings, in addition to an architecturally evolved main residence. The earliest portion of the house, a one-room structure, was built ca. 1810–11 for Joseph Pope; it was remodeled and enlarged in 1847 and 1870 by his son Harrison who was among the county's most ambitious 19th-century planters. The porticoed front section, which combines Greek Revival and Italianate elements, is one of the few Reconstruction-period structures of any architectural pretension in the region. Around the house are a schoolmaster's house, dairy, tenant's house, smokehouse, kitchen, various sheds, and a peanut house. 87–98 (10/20/81).

SPOTSYLVANIA COUNTY

Straddling the fall line, Spotsylvania County was formed from
Essex, King William, and King and Queen counties in 1720.
It was named for Alexander Spotswood, lieutenant governor
of Virginia from 1710 to 1722. Its county seat
is Spotsylvania Court House.

ANDREWS TAVERN, *Glenora vicinity.* Andrews Tavern has served at various times as an ordinary, a school, a polling place, and a residence. The brick portion was built for Samuel Andrews soon after he reached his majority in 1815. Its even jointed masonry, simple but well-executed woodwork, and hall-parlor plan make it a model of the Federal provincial architecture of Piedmont Virginia. Andrews did not begin his tavern business here until he added the frame wing ca. 1848. The building housed a U. S. post office from 1842 until 1862, when it became a Confederate post office which functioned until 1865. Andrews served as postmaster for both governments. It became a U. S. post office again in 1885 during the ownership of Horace Cammack. Although now a private residence, the tavern, with its complex of outbuildings, is a tangible reminder of institutions important to 19th–century rural life. 88–136 (4/20/76).

PROSPECT HILL, *Belmont vicinity.* Built in 1806, Prospect Hill is one of Spotsylvania County's largest and best preserved early 19th-century plantation dwellings. The undisturbed condition of both the building's massive yet restrained exterior and its plain but sophisticated woodwork makes the house a good example of the spacious but unpretentious center-passage-plan dwellings favored by the more prosperous Virginia planters of the period. The plantation's first owner, Waller Holladay, experimented with crop rotation and fertilization here, an early effort at restoring Virginia's farmlands exhausted by years of tobacco planting. Holladay also held various local offices and served in the General Assembly. The property is still owned by the Holladay family. 88–56 (6/15/82).

RAPIDAN DAM CANAL OF THE RAPPAHANNOCK NAVIGATION, *extending from the mouth of the Rapidan River down the Rappahannock River for one and a half miles.* The Rappahannock Navigation, which consisted of twenty dams, each with its own system of locks, is ranked by canal experts as the country's best remaining example of a bateau lock-and-dam navigation system. The Rapidan Dam Canal with its associated locks is the system's best-preserved segment. The system was a compromise—typical in southern waterways—between an expensive continuous canal for horse-drawn boats and an inexpensive but unreliable riverbed sluice navigation for bateaux, which were poled and rowed and therefore required no towpath. The Rappahannock Navigation was a local project intended to draw trade from the Piedmont to Fredericksburg. Construction of the fifty-mile system began in 1829 and was not completed until twenty years later, just as railroad competition made it useless. The Rapidan Dam Canal parallels the right bank of the Rappahannock from the mouth of the Rapidan for one and a half miles along an unnavigable stretch and then reenters the river through three locks. Shown is lock no. 7. The Rapidan Dam, of which scattered sections remain, stretched across both the Rappahannock and the mouth of the Rapidan and guided bateaux into a guard lock designed to protect the canal from flooding. 88–137 (6/19/73).

ST. JULIEN, *New Post vicinity.* St. Julien was the home of Francis Taliaferro Brooke (1763–1851), who was appointed to the Virginia General Court the year he built this house and later served as president of Virginia's Supreme Court of Appeals. Brooke represented Essex County in the General Assembly in 1794 and 1795. In 1796 he transferred his law practice to Fredericksburg and purchased this farmland, which he named St. Julien. He described the dwelling that he constructed here in 1804 as a "small brick house with a shed to it." Although compact in scale, Brooke's house stands as one of the most sophisticated examples of rural Federal architecture in the region. Its two-level recessed entry capped by a pediment is an imaginative and effective facade treatment. The refinements of the building include its Flemish bond brickwork, carved stone lintels and keystones, and interior woodwork. Among St. Julien's several early outbuildings is a one-story office sheathed with board and batten. 88–61 (3/18/75).

SPOTSYLVANIA COURT HOUSE HISTORIC DISTRICT, *incorporating the historic buildings of the village, the Confederate cemetery, and the fields to the northeast of the village.* Spotsylvania Court House was the site of one of the most vicious and bloody struggles of the Civil War. In and around the tiny settlement in early May 1864 the Union army suffered 18,000 casualties and the Confederates under General Lee suffered an estimated 9,000 killed or wounded, with neither side claiming a clear victory. The Roman Revival courthouse, completed in 1840 by Malcolm F. Crawford, formerly employed by Thomas Jefferson at the University of Virginia, was largely rebuilt and faced with buff pressed brick after sustaining heavy damage during the conflict. Remaining in the village are four other buildings standing at the time of the battle: a ca. 1800 tavern, two antebellum churches, and a ca. 1840 farmhouse. Also within the district is a landscaped Confederate cemetery, located on the section of the battlefield through which the principal Confederate defense line ran. Spotsylvania Court House was established on what was once the main road from Richmond to Fredericksburg. 88–142 (1/18/83).

TUBAL FURNACE ARCHAEOLOGICAL SITE, *Chancellorsville vicinity.* The Tubal Furnace site contains the stone remains of the earliest archaeologically identified iron furnace in Virginia. Constructed ca. 1717 under the direction of Lieutenant Governor Alexander Spotswood, the furnace was operated by skilled black slaves, a pioneering use of slave labor for a technological industry. The industry continued under the direction of Spotswood's descendants for two generations. Archaeological excavation of this industrial complex could yield data on early 18th-century iron-manufacturing technology. 88–74 (5/18/82).

STAFFORD COUNTY

*On the Potomac River at the junction of Tidewater and
Northern Virginia, Stafford County was formed from
Westmoreland County in 1664 and named for the
English shire. Its county seat is Stafford.*

AQUIA CHURCH, *Garrisonville vicinity.* Aquia Church's elegant classicism contrasts with its isolated woodland setting, a good illustration of rural Virginia's use of ecclesiastical architecture endowed with urbanity and sophistication. The church's brick walls are highlighted by quoins and rusticated doorways in the fashion of Gibbs executed in stone quarried from nearby Aquia Creek. This church was begun early in 1751 but was seriously damaged by fire on February 17, 1754, just three days before its scheduled completion. It was rebuilt within the walls in 1754–57 under the direction of Mourning Richards, the original contractor, and William Copein, the mason. The interior preserves a unique three-tiered pulpit as well as the original Ionic reredos, west gallery, and pews, all excellent examples of colonial joinery. A church existed at this site as early as 1654. 89–8 (5/13/69).

BELMONT, *226 Washington Street, Falmouth*. Artist Gari Melchers made this old estate on a terraced ridge above Falmouth his home and studio from 1916 until his death in 1932. Born in Detroit in 1860 and trained in Europe, Melchers excelled in genre pictures, religious works, portraits, and mural decorations, drawing inspiration from many sources. His works are housed in many major American museums, and his murals of allegories on peace and war decorate the Library of Congress. The Belmont house and studio, along with their furnishings and many of his pictures, were left by Mrs. Melchers to the state and are exhibited as a museum by Mary Washington College. The residence was erected ca. 1761 by John Dixon of Williamsburg and enlarged after 1825, following its purchase by Joseph Ficklin, whose family owned it until Melchers bought it. The stone studio to the south of the main house was built by Melchers. 89–22,23,24 (9/9/69); *National Historic Landmark*.

CARLTON, *501 Melchers Drive, Falmouth*. This Georgian dwelling is one of several large old houses crowning the heights around Falmouth and Fredericksburg. The house follows a standard rectangular format, employing a five-bay facade and hipped roof. Most of its original exterior and interior fabric survives, including a large built-in glass-door cupboard in the dining room. At the edge of a steep promontory directly overlooking Falmouth, Carlton was the home of John Short, a merchant who had the house built ca. 1785 after his marriage to Judith Ball of Lancaster County. Enhancing the setting of the house are three original outbuildings: a kitchen/laundry, dairy, and smokehouse. 89–10 (7/17/73); *Virginia Historic Landmarks Board preservation easement*.

CLEARVIEW, *Telegraph Road, Falmouth*. On a hilltop overlooking Falmouth and Fredericksburg, Clearview is representative of the architecture of lesser plantation homes of the late 18th century. Using the rectangular form, hipped roof, and symmetrical five-bay facade, the composition varies little from that generally employed a half century earlier. Clearview probably was built shortly after the property was acquired in 1786 by Andrew Buchanan, a major in the Caroline County militia during the Revolution. The house has received a later wing and porches but retains most of its early interior woodwork. The farm was used for a Federal gun emplacement during the battle of Fredericksburg in 1862, and around the barn to the southeast of the house are some of the earthwork gun pits. 89–12 (11/19/74).

FALMOUTH HISTORIC DISTRICT, *corresponding approximately to the town limits.* Laid out in 1727 at the farthest navigable point of the Rappahannock, Falmouth was a prosperous port and regional trading center until 1850 when the dwindling river traffic and the construction of the railroad to the east of the town sapped its commercial life. Although modern intrusions have replaced much of Falmouth's early fabric, enough buildings remain from its period of ascendancy to illustrate Falmouth's early history. Along the waterfront are Basil Gordon's brick warehouse and an adjacent large commercial building of the early 19th century. Farther up, on Cambridge Street, is the tiny Federal-period customs house, one of the smallest in the nation. Scattered through the district is a variety of early residences, some of them rare examples of vernacular workers' housing. At the head of Carter Street is the facade of the Federal-period Union Church (shown). Its main body was destroyed by fire, but the front wall was preserved as an architectural focal point for the town. Also included in the district, on the heights overlooking the town, are the 18th-century houses Carlton, Clearview, and Belmont. 89–67 (12/2/69).

FERRY FARM, *712 Kings Highway, Fredericksburg vicinity.* George Washington moved to Ferry Farm, across the Rappahannock from Fredericksburg, with his parents from his birthplace at Wakefield in 1738, when he was six years old. Here he spent his boyhood, and here are set the legends of his cutting down the cherry tree and throwing the Spanish silver dollar across the river. Washington's widowed mother remained at Ferry Farm until the house burned in 1770. The several buildings now on the property are structures of the 19th century or later, but the archaeological sites of the original buildings are believed to remain intact. Although encroached upon by modern development, the central part of the original farm retains its agrarian atmosphere. 89–16 (11/16/71).

HUNTER'S IRON WORKS ARCHAEOLOGICAL SITE, *Falmouth vicinity.* Described as "one of the finest and most considerable iron works in North America" by the 18th-century traveler John David Schopf, Hunter's Iron Works played a vital role in supplying equipment for American forces in the Revolutionary War. James Hunter, a Falmouth merchant, started the works ca. 1750, and it quickly became the leading producer of hardware in the colony. With the outbreak of the Revolution, Hunter devoted his full energies to supplying the Continental army, so much so that Governor Thomas Jefferson ordered special military protection for the industry. Hunter was never adequately paid for the supplies, and the strain on his resources caused the decline of his operation. Although some of the buildings may have been in use during the Civil War, none remains today. A survey of the site undertaken by the Virginia Division of Historic Landmarks in 1974 located the foundations of at least five buildings, as well as many artifacts. A more detailed investigation would provide an opportunity to study American iron manufacture of the 18th century. 89–6 (10/16/73).

MARLBOROUGH POINT ARCHAEOLOGICAL SITE, *Indian Point vicinity.* Strategically sited at the tip of a peninsula jutting into the Potomac River at Potomac Creek, Marlborough Town was established under the Town Act of 1691 on the land of Giles Brent and served as the county seat of Stafford County. After its decline in the mid-18th century, it became the seat of John Mercer. A copy of the 1691 Theodoric Bland survey of the town preserved in John Mercer's letter book is shown. Archaeological investigation undertaken by the Smithsonian Institution in 1956 identified Marlborough Town's location. More extensive investigation of the townsite should provide much information on the commercial life of a Potomac River port town in the first half of the 18th century. 89–1 (12/2/69).

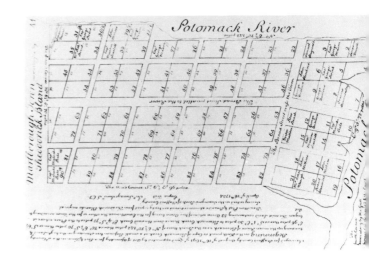

POTOMAC CREEK ARCHAEOLOGICAL SITE, *Indian Point vicinity.* On the peninsula formed by Accokeek and Potomac creeks was the site of the Potomeck Indian village known as Patawomeke, visited by Capt. John Smith in 1608 and repeatedly visited by traders until ca. 1630. Shown are samples of the decorative corded motifs that occur on the rims of Potomac Creek ware, dating to the Late Woodland period (A.D. 1300–1600). It was from this village that the Indian princess Pocahontas was taken hostage to Jamestown. The village had been abandoned by the Indians in 1635 when the property was patented by Giles Brent. The site was identified through an investigation undertaken in the 1930s. Further investigation should provide significant information on Indian life during the contact period. 89–2 (5/13/69).

CITY OF STAUNTON

The county seat of Augusta County most likely derives it name from Rebecca Staunton, wife of Sir William Gooch, lieutenant governor of Virginia from 1727 to 1749. Staunton was laid out in 1748 and was established as a town in 1761. It was incorporated in 1801 and became a city in 1871.

AUGUSTA COUNTY COURTHOUSE, *South Augusta and East Johnson streets.* Completed in 1901, the Augusta County Courthouse stands where all of the county's courthouses have stood since the first one was built in 1745. Its imposing architectural design is local architect T.J. Collins's interpretation of the florid classicism popular at the turn of the century. Dominated by a tall dome and Composite-order portico, the building is the local symbol of law and civil authority and the center of county political activity. 132–1 (6/15/82).

BEVERLEY HISTORIC DISTRICT, *roughly bounded by Lewis, Frederick, and Market streets and the Wharf Area Historic District.* The Beverley Historic District takes in approximately 150 buildings in some eleven blocks of Staunton's central business district. Although the area was part of the mid-18th-century settlement founded on the land of William Beverley, its main thoroughfare, Beverley Street (shown) is a classic example of a Victorian main street. This and the district's secondary streets are free of significant modern intrusions. The dome of the Augusta County Courthouse, the old YMCA clocktower, the observation tower of the Masonic building, and several church spires decorate its skyline. Nearly every phase of the region's 19th- and early 20th-century stylistic development is to be found on the district's narrow streets, from Federal commercial structures to a Beaux Arts bank. The buildings reflect the growth of Staunton from an early mill settlement to one of the Shenandoah Valley's mercantile centers. Many of the district's buildings have had their original character restored in recent years through a facade improvement program administered by the Historic Staunton Foundation. 132–24 (11/20/79).

BREEZY HILL, *1220 North Augusta Street.* The prosperity of Staunton's boom years at the turn of the century is well reflected in Breezy Hill, one of the most ambitious of the large houses of the period scattered through the city. This irregularly massed suburban villa of some thirty rooms is a knowing blend of the Queen Anne and Shingle styles, late Victorian modes favored by the nation's upper class. Begun ca. 1896 for Mrs. Thomas B. Grasty and completed in 1909 after many changes by the owner during construction, Breezy Hill is attributed to T. J. Collins, the city's leading architect for several decades. 132–30 (2/16/82).

CATLETT HOUSE, *303 Berkeley Place.* One of a collection of sophisticated turn-of-the-century dwellings dotting Staunton's downtown neighborhoods is the Catlett house, an American interpretation of the Queen Anne style. Completed in 1897 for Fannie Catlett, widow of local attorney R. H. Catlett, the house incorporates all the elements associated with the mode: a mixture of surface materials, asymmetrical floor plan, corner tower, gables, classical details, and a multiplicity of window types. Lending particular interest is the lavish use of wood shingle cladding, echoing the tile cladding of English vernacular buildings. 132–32 (5/18/82).

GOSPEL HILL HISTORIC DISTRICT, *roughly bounded by East Beverley, Kalorama, and Market streets and Mary Baldwin College campus*. Occupying most of the eastern section of the old portion of Staunton, the Gospel Hill Historic District is primarily a residential area. Within its boundaries are the site of the founding of Staunton by William Beverley in 1736, the birthplace of Woodrow Wilson, the home of military cartographer Jedediah Hotchkiss, and the home of Dr. J. C. M. Merrillat, a pioneer educator of the blind. The houses, mostly freestanding ones on relatively small lots, range from plain log structures dating from the early 19th century to mansions in the revivalist styles of the late 19th and early 20th centuries. Prominent among the styles represented are the Greek Revival, Italianate, Queen Anne, and Colonial Revival. Many of the more distinctive Colonial Revival residences were designed by the Staunton architectural firm of T. J. Collins. The district remains devoid of significant visual instrusions, and few of the streets are through ones, assuring an air of quiet dignity for most of the area. Two streets containing an interesting variety of dwellings are East Beverley Street and Kalorama Street (shown). The district is framed on the east by the Virginia School for the Deaf and the Blind and on the west by the campus of Mary Baldwin College. 132–35 (1/17/84).

HILLTOP, *Mary Baldwin College campus*. Built for Benjamin H. Brady, this ca. 1815 house is dominated by an original two-story portico with massive Tuscan columns and delicate Federal cornice. It was one of Staunton's most elegant residences during the half century after its construction and before its purchase in 1872 by the founders of the Augusta Female Seminary (now Mary Baldwin College). Circuit Judge Lucas P. Thompson lived here from 1842 until his death in 1866. A large wing designed by local architect T. J. Collins was added to the rear in 1904. Hilltop now serves as a dormitory for Mary Baldwin. 132–2 (12/19/78).

ARISTA HOGE HOUSE, *215 Kalorama Street*. The arresting facade of the Arista Hoge house survives as Staunton's only domestic example of the Richardsonian Romanesque style. Commissioned by local businessman and public servant Arista Hoge in 1891 as a new front for a house built ca. 1882 for G. G. Gooch, it is an early work of the firm of Collins and Hackett. The juxtaposition of the two styles illustrates the swing in taste during the 1880s from the delicacy of the Italianate to the solidity of the Romanesque. Formed in 1891, the Collins and Hackett architectural firm lasted only three years, but its partner T. J. Collins on his own embellished Staunton with some of its finest buildings over the next several decades. 132–15 (5/18/82).

KABLE HOUSE, *310 Prospect Street*. The Kable house was the first building of the Staunton Military Academy, a preparatory school which traced its origins to 1860 when Capt. William Hartman Kable founded the Charles Town Male Academy in Charles Town (now West Virginia). After the Civil War, Kable decided his school should be in Virginia proper, and in 1883 he purchased this Italianate bracketed villa in Staunton, which had been built in 1873–74 for John W. Alby. First known as the Staunton Male Academy, the school developed a military format in 1886. The house served as both a dormitory and the Kable family residence for many years. Its interior was remodeled in 1917 by the local firm of T. J. Collins & Son, but the exterior retains its Italianate flavor. The house was in use for classrooms and offices until the school's closing in 1976 and subsequent purchase by Mary Baldwin College. 132–22 (12/19/78).

MARY BALDWIN COLLEGE MAIN BUILDING, *Frederick and North New streets*. Mary Baldwin College was established in 1842 as the Augusta Female Seminary and is the nation's oldest women's college associated with the Presbyterian church. Construction of the main building was completed by 1844. With its stately Doric portico and cream-painted brickwork, the Greek Revival edifice established the architectural image of the school's modern campus. The college received its present name in 1895 in recognition of Mary Julia Baldwin, who served as the principal of the school in the difficult years following the Civil War. The building now houses administrative offices. 132–16 (6/19/73).

J. C. M. MERRILLAT HOUSE, *521 East Beverley Street*. The J. C. M. Merrillat house is a mid-19th-century Gothic Revival cottage complete with steep gables, scrolled bargeboards, board-and-batten siding, and diamond-pane windows. It is sited on a steep hillside in a large informally planted yard. Although the Gothic cottage was a very popular house form throughout the country, the Merrillat house is one of the few examples in the Staunton area and certainly the best. It was built in 1851 for Dr. Jean Charles Martin Merrillat, a native of Bordeaux, France, who in 1839 was appointed first head of the Department of the Blind at the nearby Virginia School for the Deaf and the Blind. In 1852 he became administrator for the entire school. During the Civil War he served as a surgeon when the school was used as a military hospital. 132–28 (9/15/81).

THOMAS J. MICHIE HOUSE, *324 East Beverley Street*. Built in 1847–48 for state delegate Thomas J. Michie, this Greek Revival dwelling, one of the earliest houses on Staunton's East Beverley Street, also has been the home of Claiborne Rice Mason, a civil engineer; John Echols, founder of the National Valley Bank; Alan Caperton Braxton, a leader in the establishment of the State Corporation Commission; and Henry Winston Holt, chief justice of the Virginia Supreme Court of Appeals. With its brick construction, deck-on-hip roof, and wide plain cornice, the house typifies the conservative, solidly proportioned structures favored by local builders working in the Greek Revival idiom. 132–33 (7/20/82).

C. W. MILLER HOUSE, *210 North New Street*. Staunton architect T. J. Collins's experimentation with a broad range of styles gave the city marvelous variety. Of his many surviving residential works, none is more elaborate than the big house he designed in the late 1890s for C. W. Miller, located across New Street from Mary Baldwin College. Drawing from the Châteauesque as well as Queen Anne style, Collins, with the use of buff brick, delicate ornamentation, and a variety of curves, gave the house a grace and lightness not seen in the average domestic work of the period. Just as delightful, the interior is highlighted by a spindle and scrollwork screen framing a paneled stair. The Mary Baldwin music department used the house for many years, but it is now privately owned. 132–18 (12/19/78).

NATIONAL VALLEY BANK, *12–14 West Beverley Street*. The influence of the Neoclassical Revival on America's Main Street is well demonstrated in the facade of the National Valley Bank. Inspired by ancient Rome's Arch of Titus, the bank was designed by local architect T. J. Collins and completed in 1903. The National Valley Bank was founded in 1865; its first president was former Confederate general John Echols. The present building was intended as a showcase for the bank's commercial success; craftsmen were brought from Baltimore to execute the impressive coffered ceiling, and furnishings and the fittings were brought from Cincinnati. Despite some later remodeling, much of the original character of the grand interior has been brought out in a recent restoration; the facade stands unaltered. 132–23 (12/19/78).

NEWTOWN HISTORIC DISTRICT, *roughly bounded by Lewis Street Middlebrook Avenue, the Chesapeake and Ohio Railroad, South Jefferson Street, and properties along the south side of West Beverley Street.* Begun in 1781 as a 25-acre annexation known as the Newtown Addition and since expanded, the Newtown Historic District is a large neighborhood whose development spans over a century and a half. On the east, where Newtown adjoins Staunton's two commercial historic districts, warehouses coexist with elegant brick houses on the border between the traditional downtown and the town's oldest continuously occupied residential area. On its steep hills Newtown has many 19th- and early-20th century houses as well as individual examples of late 18th-century architecture such as the Stuart house of 1791. Three girls' schools were located in the district, one of which survives today as Stuart Hall School. The religious buildings include Trinity Church (1855); the chapel of the city's first black church, organized in 1865; and the several late 19th-century churches of Staunton's early congregations. Also included in the district is the romantically landscaped Thornrose Cemetery. Shown, from the right, are the Robertson, Cochran, and Worthington houses on West Frederick Street, now owned by Stuart Hall School. 132–34 (6/21/83).

OAKDENE, *605 East Beverley Street*. This complex house shows the late 19th-century Queen Anne style at its most imaginative. Its skillful, though unidentified, architect borrowed forms and motifs from 16th- and 17th-century European precedents and combined them into a structure employing outstanding craftsmanship and fine materials. Characteristic of the style are the asymmetrical facade, the mixture of surface materials, and the many different window types. The conical tower is topped by an owl finial whose eyes are electrically lighted. Oakdene was built in 1893 for Edward Echols, lieutenant governor of Virginia from 1898 to 1902 and president of the local National Valley Bank. 132–27 (9/15/81).

THE OAKS, *437 East Beverley Street.* Set against a wooded hillside on Staunton's East Beverley Street is the home of Maj. Jedediah Hotchkiss, Confederate cartographer and aide to Gen. Stonewall Jackson. The campaign maps of central Virginia and the Shenandoah Valley produced by Hotchkiss, often under dangerous conditions, are now housed in the Library of Congress and are considered by Civil War historians to be among the finest of their type. After the war, Hotchkiss achieved financial success by speculating in land and minerals. He also wrote about Virginia's geology, geography, and Civil War history. The rear wing of Hotchkiss's house was begun in the 1870s as a wing of an earlier dwelling and features the deep bracketed eaves characteristic of the chalet style. The irregular Queen Anne-style front section, designed by the Boston firm of Winslow and Wetherall, was erected in 1888–90 to replace the oldest section of the house. The interior contains intricately detailed woodwork typical of the period. 132–21 (12/19/78).

OLD WESTERN STATE HOSPITAL ANTEBELLUM COMPLEX, *Greenville Avenue at U. S. Route 250.* First known as Western Lunatic Asylum of Virginia, this institution was founded in 1825 to serve the western portion of the state and to relieve pressure on the asylum in Williamsburg. Baltimore architect William Small was commissioned to design the main building. Completed in 1828, the five-part structure Small produced is one of the nation's best works of institutional architecture of the early 19th century. Handsomely crafted and detailed, the building remains remarkably unaltered, preserving most of its woodwork, hardware, and stairways, including a spiral stair winding from the third floor to the cupola. The building was given a more monumental aspect in 1847 when the tall Greek Ionic portico was added to the center section and the smaller pedimented porticoes were placed on the end pavilions. Included in the antebellum complex are two annex buildings flanking the main building, both designed by Robert Cary Long, Jr., of Baltimore and built by contractor William B. Phillips, who had worked for Thomas Jefferson at the University of Virginia. The northern building was completed in 1840 and the southern one in 1842. Both have engaged Doric porticoes and Chinese lattice roof railings. Behind the main building is the refectory and chapel building built in 1851 by Thomas Blackburn. A small ward building of 1842 to the east of the northern annex completes the antebellum complex. The whole grouping stands as an example of the tradition established by Thomas Jefferson of obtaining excellent architecture for the state's public institutions. The buildings are also a testament to Virginia's early effort to provide enlightened care to the mentally ill. The hospital was relocated west of town in the 1970s, and these buildings are currently used by the state as a prison. 132–9 (5/13/69).

ROSE TERRACE, *150 North Market Street*. Built ca. 1875 as a residence for Holmes Erwin, Rose Terrace's decorative brick-work, chimneys, and overall fine craftsmanship make the house an outstanding representative of Victorian-era taste in Staunton. Near the top of Staunton's highest hill, the L-shaped, two-and-one-half-story structure is in a freely interpreted Italianate style. It was purchased by Mary Baldwin Seminary (now College) in 1919 and served as the college president's home for a number of years. More recently, Rose Terrace has been used as a dormitory. High above the college's main complex, the dwelling is a lively architectural foil for Mary Baldwin's cream-colored classical academic structures. 132–17 (12/19/78).

SEARS HOUSE, *400 Marquis Street*. On a wooded hilltop overlooking Staunton's downtown, this board-and-batten cottage was once the home of the educator Barnas Sears, chosen in 1867 by philanthropist George Peabody to administer the Peabody Educational Fund for the promotion of free schooling in the war-devastated South. Sears selected Staunton as his base of operation because of its convenience to transportation lines. He purchased the house erected only a year earlier for Dr. Robert Madison, physician for the Virginia Military Institute cadets in the battle of New Market, and soon enlarged it with the addition of a polygonal, three-story tower to contain his library. The Sears house is a simple "bracketed cottage," promoted by Andrew Jackson Downing as the most pleasant, economical, and practical dwelling for middle-class Americans. The house was long owned by the city but was acquired and restored in the 1970s by the Historic Staunton Foundation and resold as a private residence. 132–12 (11/16/71); *Virginia Historic Landmarks Board preservation easement.*

STEEPHILL, *200 Park Boulevard*. Steephill was built in 1877–78 as a suburban villa for Col. John Lewis Peyton, who wrote *The History of Augusta County, Virginia* (1882) and other works of local and regional history. The house was remodeled in 1926–27 in the Georgian Revival style by Staunton architect Samuel Collins for Peyton's son, Lawrence Washington Peyton. The remodeling resulted in one of the city's best examples of this 20th-century mode. Adding interest to the place is its dramatic setting on a steep, terraced hill near the city's Gypsy Hill Park. During the remodeling, the extensive landscaping was redesigned to be more compatible with Steephill's new look. 132–31 (1/17/84).

STUART HALL SCHOOL, OLD MAIN, *235 West Frederick Street*. Founded in 1843 as the Virginia Female Institute, Stuart Hall is the oldest preparatory school for girls in the state. Its central building, "Old Main," was designed and built by Edwin Taylor and completed in 1846. The Greek Revival structure, dignified by its strong portico of Doric piers, is an early instance of a building erected specifically for the education of women and indicates the high esteem in which private education was held in Virginia in the period. The school became affiliated with the Episcopal church in 1856. From 1880 to 1898 it gained stature under the direction of its headmistress, Flora Stuart, widow of Gen. J. E. B. Stuart, and it was renamed in her honor in 1907. 132–11 (2/19/74).

STUART HOUSE, *120 Church Street*. This house built for Archibald Stuart in 1791 is one of Virginia's earliest expressions of the classical revival mode introduced to the state by Thomas Jefferson. Its temple form and two-story portico broke with the traditional house type and followed a format that was to be used for many houses and public buildings in subsequent decades. Stuart, a Virginia legislator and judge, was a close friend of Jefferson, and family tradition has it that Jefferson suggested the style of the house. That Jefferson was the architect is unlikely, for the provincial interpretation of the classical forms, especially evident in the portico, departs from the strict adherence to Roman precedent that characterizes Jefferson's documented works. Contrasting with the somewhat austere portico is rich interior woodwork. On the spacious grounds are an original Chinese-style gate and the small gambrel roof cottage Stuart used as an office. Stuart's son, Alexander H. H. Stuart, who was born in the house in 1807, was appointed secretary of the interior by Millard Fillmore. 132–6 (1/18/72.

TRINITY EPISCOPAL CHURCH, *West Beverley and South Lewis streets*. Though often associated with playful wooden cottages, the early Gothic Revival in America fostered solemn ecclesiastical works. In the heart of downtown, Trinity Church, with its ascetic medievalism, well demonstrates the Gothic Revival's more serious side. Built in 1855 as the third church of Augusta Parish, founded in 1746, the dark red brick building with its angle buttressed tower stands in a tree-shaded burying ground in use since the mid-18th century. Its architect is believed to have been J. W. Johns, who designed buildings for the Virginia Theological Seminary in Alexandria. The church was enlarged in 1870 under architect Edwin Taylor. The first church of the parish, which was located on the same lot, temporarily housed the Virginia Assembly when it was forced to flee Richmond during the Revolution. 132–7 (1/18/72).

VIRGINIA SCHOOL FOR THE DEAF AND THE BLIND, MAIN BUILDING, *East Beverley Street*. The high quality of the early architecture of many of Virginia's state-supported institutions is exemplified in the stately main building of the Virginia School for the Deaf and the Blind. Founded in 1838, the school did not see the final touches put on its huge central structure until 1846. Staunton was selected for the school's site because of its central location and because it was in the midst of "cheap and abundant country." Its designer was Robert Cary Long, Jr., a Baltimore architect whose mastery of the Greek Revival idiom is evident in the Greek Doric portico and the proportions and detailing of the rest of the building. The contractor for the ambitious undertaking was William Donoho of Albemarle County. The building still functions as the principal structure of this pioneering humanitarian institution. 132–8 (9/9/69).

WAVERLEY HILL *3001 North Augusta Street*. This elegant expression of the Georgian Revival style is the work of William Lawrence Bottomley, a New York architect who maintained an extensive clientele in Virginia for his richly detailed Georgian mansions. Drawing from Palladian, English, and colonial Virginia precedents, Bottomley fashioned imaginative and functional dwellings for affluent Virginians during the 1920s and 1930s and set a standard of excellence in domestic architecture that is still admired in the Commonwealth. The house was commissioned in 1929 by Mr. and Mrs. Herbert McKelden Smith. 132–29 (2/16/82).

WHARF AREA HISTORIC DISTRICT, *Middlebrook Avenue between South Lewis Street and Lewis Creek.* The completion of the Virginia Central Railroad to Staunton in 1854 made this Valley community a central point for the transfer of goods for the region. The area around the depot, on the south edge of the town's business district, became a busy commercial area, its importance signaled by the construction of the Greek Revival American Hotel in 1857. The colorful range of warehouses lining the tracks today date mostly from the last quarter of the 19th century and served commission merchants, wholesale grocers, saloon keepers, and liveries. The eastern end of the district is marked by the turn-of-the-century White Star Mill, now remodeled as a restaurant. The small but well-defined complex has been the scene of considerable preservation activity in recent years in an effort to preserve its character and to enhance the economy of downtown Staunton. The Wharf takes its name from the fact that it was a shipping point; there is no body of water nearby. 132–14 (12/21/71).

WOODROW WILSON BIRTHPLACE, *24 North Coalter Street.* Thomas Woodrow Wilson, twenty-eighth president of the United States, was born in this twelve-room Greek Revival manse in 1856. Built in 1846 to serve the ministers of Staunton's First Presbyterian Church, the manse's second occupants were Dr. and Mrs. Joseph Ruggles Wilson, Wilson's parents, who moved here in 1855. Although his family left Staunton to serve another congregation while he was still a baby, it was in this forthright dwelling that the seeds of Wilson's firm moral and intellectual training were planted. He carried these precepts into his adult life as professor, university president, governor of New Jersey, and finally president of the United States. Elected on a reform platform, he tried to keep the country out of war in Europe, but when it became necessary, he committed the nation to bringing about an Allied victory. To prevent future world wars, Wilson conceived the League of Nations, for which he was awarded the Nobel Peace Prize in 1919. He visited his birthplace in 1912 on his fifty-sixth birthday, just after his election as president. The manse was acquired by the Woodrow Wilson Birthplace Foundation in 1938 and was dedicated as a museum by President Franklin D. Roosevelt in 1942. 132–4 (9/9/69); *National Historic Landmark.*

CITY OF SUFFOLK

Probably named for the English shire, Suffolk was established in 1742 at the site of John Constant's warehouse on the banks of the Nansemond River. It was incorporated as a town in 1808 and as a city in 1910. Its size was greatly expanded in 1974 when it was merged with Nansemond County, which thereby became extinct.

GLEBE CHURCH, *Driver vicinity.* This simple colonial church takes its name from the fact that it was one of the few Virginia parishes that managed to retain its glebe lands—property owned by the parish used to produce income—after the Revolution and the disestablishment. The 300-acre glebe is still in the possession of the parish. The church, known in colonial times as Bennett's Creek Church, was constructed in 1737–38 and has suffered numerous vicissitudes during its long history, so that only its much-patched but well-crafted walls are original. It received its last extensive renovation in 1900. 133–61 (9/19/72).

RIDDICK HOUSE, *510 North Main Street*. Also known as Riddick's Folly, this Greek Revival town house is Suffolk's most distinguished early residence. The formality of its exterior is emphasized by its large scale and finely jointed brickwork, and its interior has large airy rooms with bold Greek Revival trim. Mills Riddick began construction of the house, next to the Nansemond County Courthouse, in 1837 after his former residence was destroyed in a fire that consumed much of the town. During the Civil War the house served as headquarters of Union general John J. Pick. In recent years the building housed county offices, but it has since been restored as a local cultural center and museum. 133–73 (11/20/73).

ST. JOHN'S CHURCH, *Chuckatuck vicinity*. Originally known as Chuckatuck Church after an Indian word meaning "crooked creek," St. John's was built in 1755 and is the third church at its location. Its rectangular form with gable roof was the most popular one for Virginia's smaller colonial churches. Like most of the state's early ecclesiastical buildings, it is constructed of Flemish bond brickwork highlighted by glazed headers and gauged-brick round arches. The church was abandoned for a half century after the Revolution but was reconsecrated with its present name in 1826. Union troops desecrated the building during the Civil War. The interior woodwork dates from a ca. 1900 renovation. 133–17 (10/17/71).

SURRY COUNTY

*On the south side of the James River, this rural Tidewater
county was formed from James City County ca. 1652 and was
named for Surrey County in England.
The county seat is Surry.*

BACON'S CASTLE, *Bacon's Castle*. The oldest documented
house in Virginia, Bacon's Castle was erected for Arthur Allen
in 1665 on land patented by him in 1649. It is the state's, if not
the nation's, outstanding example of 17th-century domestic architecture. It is, however, probably the least typical house of
its period. In contrast to the elementary timber-frame structures in which most 17th-century Virginians lived, Bacon's
Castle is a high-style Jacobean manor house, fully developed
with cruciform plan, baroque curvilinear gables, and clustered,
diagonally set chimney stacks. The handful of comparable early
Virginia mansions—Greenspring, Fairfield, and Corotoman—
have long since vanished, leaving only Bacon's Castle. The
house acquired the name by which it has been known for over
three hundred years in 1676, when, during Bacon's Rebellion,
it was fortified and held for three months by a group of Bacon's
followers. The house was somewhat modified in the 18th century when the first-floor paneling was installed and the windows were changed. Further alterations were made in the
1840s, and a Greek Revival wing was added; otherwise it has
come down through the years remarkably intact. The Association for the Preservation of Virginia Antiquities purchased Bacon's Castle in 1973 and has undertaken a long-term study and
stabilization of the building. It is now open to the public. 90–1
(9/9/69); *National Historic Landmark*.

CHIPPOKES (CHIPPOKES PLANTATION STATE
PARK), *Bacon's Castle vicinity*. Now a state park, this James
River plantation opposite Jamestown Island has been an iden-
tifiable entity since 1612 when it was first occupied by Capt.

William Powell. Powell was formally granted the plantation in 1616 and named it after Choupocke, a friendly Indian chief in whose domain the property was located. Governor William Berkeley claimed the plantation after Powell's death, and through Berkeley's widow Chippokes passed into the Ludwell family, in whose ownership it remained for five generations until 1837. Through its three-and-a-half-century history, Chippokes has remained a working farm, growing corn, grain, tobacco, and apples in the 17th and 18th centuries; mainly peanuts and tobacco in the 19th century; and a variety of crops, as well as livestock, in the present century. The plantation was never the principal residence of the Ludwells; the main dwelling here today is a plain Greek Revival house erected ca. 1854 for Albert C. Jones. Also on the property is an early 19th-century frame house in the Virginia vernacular probably built as a secondary dwelling during the Ludwell tenure (shown). Several early outbuildings and farm buildings stretched along Quarter Lane preserve the plantation atmosphere. The formal gardens were laid out by Mr. and Mrs. Victor Stewart after their purchase of Chippokes in 1917. In 1967 Mrs. Stewart gave Chippokes to the Commonwealth to serve as a learning center for the history of Virginia agriculture. 90–3 (11/5/68).

ENOS HOUSE, *Surry vicinity*. Erected before 1820 by the Warren family and last used as a private residence by the Enos family, this Surry County homestead is the sort of house occupied by middle-class farmers in rural Southside Virginia. A distinguishing aspect of the otherwise simple dwelling is its double-pile, hall-parlor plan, a regional peculiarity reflecting the infiltration of Georgian planning into the vernacular architecture of an area which clung tenaciously to traditional forms well into the 19th century. The steep gable roof and narrow dormers are features common to most small houses of the period. The building has stood abandoned for many years but has been acquired by Surry County, which plans its restoration as part of the facilities of an adjacent recreational center. 90–39 (5/17/77).

FOUR MILE TREE, *Surry vicinity*. Named for a tree marking its distance by water from Jamestown, this plantation has been an established unit since the early 17th century. It was first settled by the Browne family, who occupied it for over a century and a half. The present house, dating from the mid-18th century, shows the application of formal Georgian planning and detailing to a building of a more unassuming native quality. Its most dominant colonial form is the jerkinhead gambrel roof, pierced by five dormers on each front. The house was remodeled in the 19th century when its brick walls were stuccoed, its sashes were replaced, and the portico was added. However, much of the early paneled woodwork and a Georgian stair were left untouched. A family graveyard contains Virginia's oldest legible tombstone, dated 1650. 90–9 (10/6/70).

GLEBE OF SOUTHWARK PARISH, *Surry vicinity.* One of Virginia's collection of colonial glebe houses, this brick dwelling was first occupied by the Reverend John Cargill, a leader among Virginia's clergy of the early 18th century. Cargill was a delegate to the convention that met at the College of William and Mary in 1719 to consider Commissary James Blair's request that the clergy side with him in a political dispute with Governor Alexander Spotswood. Spotswood prevailed, but Cargill maintained his loyalty to Blair. Cargill began in Southwark Parish in 1708. In 1724 he complained to the bishop of London that "my glebe house is in very bad condition and the parish will not repair it." Architectural evidence suggests that the parish built Cargill the present house soon after he registered his complaint. As required by the legislature in 1802, the glebe house was sold into private ownership; and like most of these houses, it underwent extensive remodeling at the hands of its new owners. The exterior chimneys were added, the gable roof was rebuilt as a gambrel, and much of the present woodwork wa installed. Despite these changes, the simple straightforwardness that characterized the glebe houses is yet perceptible. 90–12 (10/21/75).

LOWER SOUTHWARK PARISH CHURCH RUINS, *Bacon's Castle.* These are the ruins of one of Virginia's group of colonial Anglican churches. The Southwark Parish vestry resolved to build a brick church to serve the lower part of the parish in 1751, and the building was completed by 1754. The church fell into a long period of disuse after the Revolution. In the early 19th century other denominations began to hold services here occasionally. The Episcopalians established a mission at the church in 1847 but were forced by the other denominations using the building to erect a church nearby. Before it was gutted by fire in 1868, Lower Church followed the format of the colonial rectangular church, with a single doorway on the west end and five bays on either side, including a side entrance. The surviving walls retain evidence of the location of many original fittings. They are owned and maintained by the Bacon's Castle Cemetery Association. 90–34 (9/16/82).

MELVILLE, *Alliance vicinity.* The refinement that colonial builders could impart to even the smallest plantation dwellings is demonstrated in Melville, an otherwise simple hall-parlor house in a fairly isolated location in Surry County. Setting the house apart from its more humble contemporaries are its detailing and brickwork; the clipped gable roof and the decorative chevron pattern with the glazed headers on the gable ends were treatments usually reserved for more pretentious houses of the period. Melville was the seat of Nicholas Faulcon, who likely built the house soon after he inherited the property from his brother in 1727. The Faulcons held the place into the 19th century; its designation as Melville first appeared in 1812. 90–13 (12/21/76).

MONTPELIER, *Cabin Point vicinity.* The closet windows in the wide exterior end chimneys of this late colonial farmhouse give singularity to a relatively standard domestic house of the period. Closets in colonial houses were not used strictly for storage but often served as pantries, dressing rooms, or toilet areas, uses requiring light. The pleasingly proportioned house, with its facades dominated by large windows preserving their original sash probably was built for John Cocke, whose family had been landowners in Surry County since the 17th century. The roof's clipped gables were covered over during an early 19th-century remodeling which included the installation of most of the present interior woodwork. The house stood in neglected condition for a number of years until it was restored in the late 1970s. 90–14 (2/21/78).

PLEASANT POINT, *Scotland vicinity.* Atop a bluff overlooking the James River opposite Jamestown Island, Pleasant Point exemplifies the formality of many of Virginia's lesser colonial seats. The complex consists of a compact story-and-a-half, brick-ended manor house flanked by the perpendicularly set laundry and reconstructed kitchen. A smokehouse and dairy at the corners of the yard on the riverfront define a symmetrical forecourt. The series of five terraces leading down to the James is a landscaping treatment common at river plantations but nevertheless impressive. These buildings and the terracing form a unified piece, probably accomplished ca. 1735–45 during the ownership of Benjamin Edwards, sheriff of Surry County. Pleasant Point was included in a 1624 grant to George Sandys, treasurer of the Virginia Company, who upon his return to England ca. 1628 gained famed as a poet and translator of classical literature. An archaeological investigation of the property may reveal the sites of Sandys's paled fort, two houses, two stores, and other buildings known to have existed there. 90–20 (9/17/74).

RICH NECK FARM, *Bacon's Castle vicinity.* This striking early 19th-century farmhouse was built as the core of a prosperous but unpretentious Southside plantation. The exterior of the house is dominated by the many window panes and a high gambrel roof framed by sloping parapets and paired chimneys. Flanking the axial avenue leading to it are two granaries nearly as old as the house. Behind the house are a 19th-century smokehouse and office, as well as a well house, privy, and chicken house dating from the present century. Rich Neck was acquired by the Ruffin family ca. 1675 and remained in its ownership until 1865. The present house was built for William E. B. Ruffin in the second or third decade of the 19th century. The use of parapets terminated by corbeled shoulders illustrates the reversion to pre-Georgian vernacular forms that occured in Virginia during the Federal period. 90–21 (6/17/75).

SECOND SOUTHWARK CHURCH ARCHAEOLOGI-CAL SITE, *Surry vicinity.* Although historical records suggest that more than eighty churches and chapels were constructed in Virginia during the 17th century, only St. Luke's Church in Isle of Wight County and the bell tower of the Jamestown church have survived. Accordingly, the archaeological remains at the Second Southwark Church could reveal information on the architecture of Virginia's 17th-century ecclesiastical structures and provide details about the utilization of the space around early colonial churches. This church was the second to serve Southwark Parish, which encompassed land on the south side of the James River between Upper Chippokes Creek and College Run. The second church was probably standing by 1673, replacing the earliest Southwark church, constructed before 1655. Abandoned shortly after the Revolution, the building stood in ruins until the time of the Civil War. The site is marked by a monument erected in 1927. 90–69 (1/17/84).

SMITH'S FORT, *Surry vicinity.* A barely discernible earthwork stretching across the tip of a steep finger of land above Gray's Creek is the remnant of what is likely the oldest extant construction of English origin in Virginia. The fort was begun in 1608 by order of Capt. John Smith as a refuge for the Jamestown settlers should the island be attacked. Destruction of supplies by rats forced the abandonment of the project, leaving only one line of earthwork completed. In 1614 the site was included in a parcel of land presented by the Indian chief Powhatan to his son-in-law John Rolfe, husband of Pocahontas. Three centuries later, in 1933, the site was acquired by the Association for the Preservation of Virginia Antiquities as part of the property of the nearby Smith's Fort plantation house. Positive identification of the fort came with archaeological investigations conducted by the Virginia Division of Historic Landmarks in 1968 and 1981. The surviving feature of this relic is an earthwork some two feet high extending for approximately 120 feet with an eight-foot-wide opening in the center, possibly the location of an extended entrance. 90–28 (12/2/69).

SMITH'S FORT PLANTATION, *Surry vicinity.* At once both refined and pleasingly straightforward, this compact Tidewater plantation house has provided the inspiration for countless 20th-century facsimiles. Long thought to have been the 17th-century home of either John Rolfe or Thomas Warren, it is now obvious from its architectural style that the house is of mid-18th-century origin, probably built between 1750 and 1775. Its first occupant was most likely Jacob Faulcon, who in this period was living on a plantation at this location owned by his father. Faulcon, who became the Surry County clerk in 1781, inherited the property in 1783. The place passed through many owners after leaving the Faulcon family in 1835 and finally was acquired in 1928 by the Williamsburg Holding Company,

predecessor of the Colonial Williamsburg Foundation. In 1934 Williamsburg gave the property to the Association for the Preservation of Virginia Antiquities, which has since restored and exhibited it as an outstanding example of colonial Virginia's sophisticated smaller-scale plantation houses. The property takes its name from Smith's Fort, an earthwork constructed under orders of Capt. John Smith which is in the woods behind the house. 90–22 (10/16/73).

SNOW HILL, *Gwaltney Corner vicinity.* This well-proportioned provincial farmhouse is an illustration of the persistence of Georgian forms well into the 19th century in rural Southside Virginia. Appearing earlier than its construction date of 1836, Snow Hill was first the home of Samuel Booth, a captain in the local militia. The symmetrical five-bay house is well preserved, retaining even its beaded weatherboarding. Adding a liveliness to its otherwise restrained interior woodwork is a decorative painting scheme of graining and marbleizing. Such fancy painting was a craft widely employed in the Virginia countryside in the 19th century but often disappeared under later coats of paint. 90–40 (9/18/79).

SWANN'S POINT ARCHAEOLOGICAL SITE, *Scotland vicinity.* Test excavations conducted by Virginia Division of Historic Landmarks archaeologists at Swann's Point in 1973 revealed two abutting brick domestic foundations measuring a total of sixty feet long and twenty feet wide. Related artifacts strongly suggest that the structure was built by either William Swann, who patented the land in 1635, or his son Thomas. Thomas Swann held numerous public offices including local justice and member of the governor's council. The fact that his house was used as a meeting place for royal commissioners in 1677 indicates that it was one of the colony's better residences. Swann had taken the side of Nathaniel Bacon during the latter's rebellion against Governor Berkeley but was spared punishment. His slab grave marker, ornamented with his coat of arms, remains on the site. Full archaeological investigation of the area should reveal much information on the architecture and objects associated with an individual of identifiable stature in the first century of settlement. 90–60 (12/17/74).

SUSSEX COUNTY

*Named for the English shire, this rural southern Tidewater
county was formed from Surry County in 1753.
Its county seat is Sussex Court House.*

CHESTER, *Homeville vicinity.* The massive chimney, complete
with windowed pent closets, lends architectural interest to this
late 18th-century plantation house. This type of chimney construction served a practical function by accommodating all the
fireplaces of the relatively large house in a single structure.
Chester was built for Capt. William Harrison in 1793, a date
found on an inscribed brick. Consistent with the quality of the
exterior is the Georgian interior woodwork, nearly all of which
is intact. The principal first-floor rooms are embellished with
paneled chimneypieces flanked by fluted pilasters. Except for
the addition of a two-story ca. 1820 wing, Chester remains
without significant alteration. The house stood in neglected
condition for many years but was purchased by a descendant
of the builder in 1969 and has been carefully restored. 91–21
(10/6/70).

FORTSVILLE, *Grizzard vicinity.* Fortsville was the home of
John Young Mason (1799–1859), who served in Congress and
held the offices of U.S. secretary of the navy, attorney general,
and minister to France. While holding the last position he
helped draw up the Ostend Manifesto of 1854, which stated the
necessity for the United States to take possession of Cuba. Mason had his Sussex County plantation dwelling built soon after
his marriage in 1821 to Mary Ann Fort, whose family had
owned the property. The three-part composition—a pedimented, two-story center section with one-story wings—is an
example of a local interpretation of the Palladian format used
by more educated Virginians in the early 19th century, following the precedent of the James Semple house in Williamsburg.
Fortsville has a larger scale and more finely detailed architec-

tural ornament than most of the houses of this type. The sophistication of the design is emphasized by the starkness of the setting in the flat fields along Sussex County's border with Southampton County. Although the house was built for Mason, the rear wing may be an earlier structure of the Fort family. After standing empty and deteriorating for many years, Fortsville has undergone a recent restoration, which included the building of the present porch, and is now occupied. 91–8 (6/2/70).

LITTLE TOWN, *Littleton vicinity*. A strikingly handsome specimen of eastern Virginia's rural architecture of the early national period, Little Town was built in 1811 for James C. Bailey, the county clerk. In the 1820 tax assessment Little Town received the highest value of any house in the county. The careful Flemish bond brickwork and fine joinery of the windows, cornice, and pedimented porch are marks of a building of quality. A folk painting of the national seal on the parlor chimneypiece has led to the claim that Bailey used the room for court sessions rather than the county courthouse, but such use would have been in conflict with normal practice of the time. More likely, the seal represented patriotic fervor on Bailey's part. Elsewhere in the interior are sections of original graining and marbleizing. The dining room mantel has a delicately molded frame with reliefs of exotic animals—two camels, a rhinoceros, and an elephant—in its bottom section. The house and surrounding farm remain in the ownership of the builder's family. 91–11 (9/21/76).

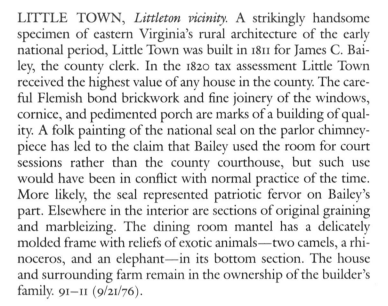

SUSSEX COURT HOUSE HISTORIC DISTRICT, *including entire crossroads settlement*. The tiny settlement of Sussex Court House typifies the early 19th-century eastern Virginia county seat, consisting of a small grouping of court structures with a few law offices and dwellings, all located in the geographic center of the county. Lending distinction to this complex is a Jeffersonian courthouse, completed in 1828 by the master builder Dabney Cosby, Sr., who built several court structures in the style he learned while he was in the employ of Thomas Jefferson at the University of Virginia. Here Cosby made use of a projecting pedimented pavilion with an arcaded ground floor instead of the more usual columned portico. The courthouse stands on the site of the first courthouse, erected in 1756. Across the court square is the mid-19th-century treasurer's office, a small one-story brick structure now used for another function. Immediately north of the courthouse is the ca. 1800 Dillard house, a two-story weatherboarded dwelling which likely served as the courthouse tavern. Flanking the courthouse are the 1924 clerk's office, a low building with a facade ornamented with four engaged Tuscan columns, and a similar building of the 1950s housing county offices. In a grove of trees to the northeast of the courthouse is the John Bannister house, a five-bay, two-story wood-frame house which at one time housed a girl's school. The district survives without significant modern intrusions. 91–6 (10/17/72).

TAZEWELL COUNTY

Tazewell County was formed from Wythe and Russell counties in 1799 and named for Henry Tazewell, U. S. Senator from Virginia from 1794 until his death in 1799. At the head of the Clinch River valley in Southwest Virginia, Tazewell County was later enlarged with parts of Russell, Wythe, Washington, and Logan (now in West Virginia) counties. Its county seat is Tazewell.

BIG CRAB ORCHARD HISTORIC AND ARCHAEO-
LOGICAL COMPLEX, *Pisgah vicinity.* The Crab Orchard
site was the location of one of the first settlements in Southwest Virginia. Patented ca. 1750, the tract was later owned by
William Ingles and was acquired by the frontier settler Thomas
Witten, Sr., who built his home here ca. 1760. In 1774 Witten's
log house was reinforced and became known as Witten's Crab
Orchard Fort, serving as a defense against the Indians until
1792. In 1793 the first Pisgah Church, also a simple log structure, was erected nearby, signaling the beginning of peaceful
occupation. The sites of both structures may hold data valuable
for the interpretation of frontier life as well as frontier military
and ecclesiastical architecture. In addition to its historic sites,
Big Crab Orchard contains considerable evidence of prehistoric occupation. Specifically identified prehistoric sites include a
large palisaded village, burial cave, campsite, and rock shelter
of the Late Woodland period (A.D. 800–1600). Part of the site
is now owned by the Historic Crab Orchard Museum and Pioneer Park Inc., which operates a museum of the area's history
and a reconstructed pioneer settlement. 92–13 (2/21/78).

BURKE'S GARDEN CENTRAL CHURCH AND CEMETERY, *Burke's Garden*. In the late 18th century settlers of German origin migrated from Pennsylvania to Southwest Virginia, settling in Burke's Garden, a bowl-shaped valley atop Garden Mountain. Here the Central Church and its cemetery were established in the 1820s. The cemetery is studded with German-style grave markers dating mostly from the 1830s. Decorated with stars, pinwheels, sunflowers, and hearts, the carved decorations are the same as those carved by an unidentified sculptor on stones for Sharon Lutheran Church in Bland County and for the Zion and Kimberling churches in Wythe County. Several other types of markers are scattered among the carved German ones, including a rare wooden marker and some uninscribed, uncarved fieldstone markers. The Central Church and its cemetery were long shared by several denominations, but in recent years they have been used exclusively by Lutherans. The present wood-frame church was built in 1875 and replaced the original building of the 1820s. 92–14 (11/21/78).

CHIMNEY ROCK FARM, *Witten Valley*. Chimney Rock Farm, also known as the Willows, is a notably sophisticated example of the three-part Palladian house in Southwest Virginia. Although this form was employed extensively in the Tidewater and Piedmont regions, Palladian houses are rarely found in the farther reaches of the state. On the west fork of Plum Creek in the shadow of a wooded mountain range, the house was built ca. 1843 for Maj. Hervey George, a lawyer and farmer who served as a delegate to the General Assembly during the Civil War. The house retains its delicate Federal interior woodwork, including some painted wood graining. Local tradition asserts that the house was constructed by a Bedford County builder who built four brick houses in the county. 92–3 (3/17/81).

INDIAN PAINTINGS PREHISTORIC SITE, *Cove vicinity*. These pictographs are on a rock face high on Paint Lick Mountain. Stretched in a horizontal line along the irregular exposure is a series of simple images representing thunderbirds, human figures, deer, trees, the sun, and a canoe painted in locally available ochers. Among the few prehistoric paintings extant in eastern North America, these images were executed by unknown Indians before European settlement. Although some weathering and vandalism have occurred, the paintings remain in relatively legible condition. The site is privately owned. 92–7 (5/13/69).

POCAHONTAS HISTORIC DISTRICT, *corresponding to the corporate limits of the town and including the Pocahontas cemetery.* This mountain community's mining structures, ornate commercial buildings, and rows of wooden workers' houses are those of a late 19th-century coal-mining company town. Pocahontas was founded in 1881 and developed by the Southwest Virginia Improvement Company during the opening of the region's rich coalfields. At first a bawdy boomtown, its hastily built shanties were soon replaced with orderly rows of company-built housing, and the downtown was embellished with richly decorated sheet-metal store fronts, a number of which remain. The Victorian town hall/opera house stands in contrast to the company store, the miners' bathhouse, and the tiny brick coal sheds in front of many of the dwellings. The town is nestled in the narrow Laurel Creek valley and is dominated by the huge spoil piles of the mines. Pocahontas mine no. 1 seam no. 3 was closed in 1955 after producing 44 million tons of coal in its working years. The original mine is now open as an exhibition mine. 92–11 (3/21/72).

ALEXANDER ST. CLAIR HOUSE, *St. Clair vicinity.* Built in 1879–80 for Alexander St. Clair, a county banker and farmer, this finely appointed dwelling is a documented work of local builder Thomas M. Hawkins, who was responsible for the construction of approximately twenty-five houses in the area. The modified Italianate dwelling, the only known brick house built by Hawkins, illustrates the introduction of stylish catalog-ordered wood trim into traditional house forms in the southwestern region of the state. The marbleized interior woodwork is signed by Frank T. Wall and O. T. Jones, skilled local artisans and painters. Surviving on the property are several early outbuildings erected to serve the main house. Across the road is an early log house which was the original farm residence. 92–16 (10/21/80).

GEORGE OSCAR THOMPSON HOUSE, *Thompson Valley vicinity.* Thomas M. Hawkins, Tazewell County's talented master builder, erected this robust house for George Oscar Thompson in 1886–87. The house blends traditional and more stylish late 19th-century ideals with unusual sophistication of detail and composition. Typical of Hawkins's work, the house is ornamented with Italianate detailing popularized by catalogs of woodworking companies of the period. Two earlier dwellings also survive on the property: a late 18th- to early 19th-century log house and a small frame farmhouse erected in three stages between 1831 and 1851. All built for the Thompson family, who pioneered in the settlement of the area in the 18th century, the three houses illustrate nearly two centuries of domestic habitation in Southwest Virginia. 91–18 (11/18/80).

WILLIAMS HOUSE, *102 Suffolk Street, Richlands*. The Williams house of 1890 was one of the first built in Richlands and served as the main office of the investment group that planned and founded the town. With high hopes of developing Richlands into the Pittsburgh of the South, the company made its headquarters a pretentious example of the popular Colonial Revival style as a demonstration that it intended to bring prosperous living to the area. Richlands did grow, but never to the extent its founders wished. The building was later used as the first hospital in Richlands and since has carried the name of Dr. W.R. Williams. The house was recently given by the Williams family to the town of Richlands and has since been restored to serve as the public library. 92–15 (9/16/82).

CITY OF VIRGINIA BEACH

Once just an oceanfront resort community, Virginia Beach was incorporated as a town in 1906 and as a city in 1952. Its area was greatly expanded in 1963 by consolildation with the rapidly urbanizing Princess Anne County, which thereby became extinct.

BAYVILLE FARM, *First Court Road and Shore Drive.* Bayville's broad, level fields, on a peninsula framed by Pleasure House Creek and Bayville Creek, remain one of the last major working farms in what used to be Princess Anne County. The Federal plantation house was begun in 1826 as a side-passage dwelling built for John Singleton by the contractor Jacob Hunter. Sold two years later to pay debts, the house was given its present five-bay form by its new owner, James Garrison. Its brick ends are an architectural feature characteristic of many houses in the Chesapeake region, especially the Eastern Shore. Preserved on the property is a series of undisturbed prehistoric and historic archaeological sites which may reveal significant information on the material culture of the area. 134–2 (6/17/75); *Virginia Historic Landmarks Board and Virginia Outdoors Foundation joint preservation easement.*

CAPE HENRY LIGHTHOUSE, *Fort Story.* This landmark commanding the entrance to Hampton Roads was the first lighthouse authorized, fully completed, and lighted by the newly organized federal government. Put into operation in October 1792, the tapered octagonal structure faced with hammerdressed sandstone ashlar was the first of three lighthouses built by John McComb, Jr. Its function was taken over by a new tower erected nearby in 1881. The old tower was deeded to the Association for the Preservation of Virginia Antiquities in 1930 and is now maintained as a museum. It stands near the spot where English colonists first set foot on Virginia soil in 1607. 134–7 (9/9/69); *National Historic Landmark.*

KEELING HOUSE, *3157 Adam Keeling Drive.* One of Virginia's early vernacular manor houses, the Keeling house preserves the decorative device of chevroning, a feature associated with pre-Georgian vernacular brick architecture. The chevrons are formed by parallel rows of glazed header bricks following the angle of the gables. The house probably was erected ca. 1700 for Thomas Keeling on property he inherited from his father in 1683. The closed-string stair and paneled parlor chimney wall appear to have been installed later in the 18th century. The house is at the head of a cove on the Lynnhaven River. 134–18 (4/17/73).

FRANCIS LAND HOUSE, *3133 Virginia Beach Boulevard.* Also known by its more recent name Rose Hall, the Land house is typical of the dwellings built by the more prosperous 18th-century planters of old Princess Anne County. Its gambrel roof was a form much favored in the area and imparts a picturesque quality to an otherwise formal and quite substantial house. Probably dating from the third quarter of the 18th century, the building's first owner, Francis Thoroughgood Land, who was a large landowner, served the on vestry of Lynnhaven Parish, and was a member of the county court. The city of Virginia Beach acquired the house in 1975 to assure its preservation and has completed its restoration. 134–64 (4/15/75).

LYNNHAVEN HOUSE, *near intersection of Wishart Road and North Witch Duck Road*. This compact brick dwelling is the sort of house built by many prosperous farmers immediately before colonial Virginia's Golden Age. With its irregularly spaced openings, exposed rafter ends, steep gable roof, and massive exterior end chimneys, the house is devoid of the classical influence of the Georgian period and maintains the character of English vernacular houses of the 17th century. The preservation of many of the interior features also makes Lynnhaven House an instructive example of its period. Especially notable is the closed-string Jacobean stair ascending in the hall of the two-room first floor. The ceilings of the two rooms are highlighted by exposed joists with molded edges. A large cooking fireplace is intact in the first-floor secondary room. Recent research has revealed that the house, long known as the Wishart house, was actually erected ca. 1724 by a member of the Thelabell family. The present name is a modern one, derived from the nearby Lynnhaven River. After standing derelict for many years, the house was donated in 1971 by the Oliver family to the Association for the Preservation of Virginia Antiquities. It has undergone a carefully researched restoration and is now exhibited as a relic of the state's oldest surviving housing. 134–37 (5/13/69).

OLD DONATION CHURCH, *4449 North Witch Duck Road*. Built in 1736 by Peter Malbone, Old Donation is the third building to serve the colonial Lynnhaven Parish, created soon after 1640. The church first was called Lynnhaven Parish Church but received its present name in the early 19th century in commemoration of a gift of land to the parish. Curiously placed windows on the side walls indicate that the church was outfitted during colonial times with private galleries, or "hanging pews," high on the side walls. As with most of Virginia's Anglican churches, Old Donation suffered neglect during the first half of the 19th century. The building burned in 1882 during a forest fire and stood as a roofless ruin until its restoration in 1916. It was granted parish church status again in 1943. Although only its walls are original, Old Donation, in its unspoiled wooded setting, is a reminder of the historic roots of the modern city of Virginia Beach. 134–25 (11/16/71).

PEMBROKE, *Constitution Drive*. This example of formal Georgian architecture was built in 1764 for Capt. Jonathan Saunders and his wife, Elizabeth Thoroughgood Saunders. During the Revolution the state confiscated the property from Saunders's son John because he remained an avowed British subject. The house is related architecturally to such mid-18th-century mansions as Carter's Grove, Wilton, Elsing Green, and especially the Wythe house, which Pembroke closely resembles. Long obscured by two-story galleries, Pembroke has been restored recently by the Princess Anne County Historical Society, but its rural setting has succumbed to intense suburban development. 134–26 (12/2/69).

PLEASANT HALL, *5184 Princess Anne Road, Kempsville.* Pleasant Hall, one of the last old houses in the all but totally redeveloped village of Kempsville, is an outstanding and little-altered example of Virginia's Georgian architecture. The formality of the exterior is emphasized by the symmetrical five-bay facade, Flemish bond brickwork, and gauged-brick jack arches. The interior has nearly all of its original woodwork including an open-well stair with a robust balustrade. The fully paneled parlor has a chimneypiece framed by full-height pilasters in the rarely used Corinthian order. In the attic is an unusual form of the king-post truss roofing system. Many of the original wide muntin sashes with original panes of glass are intact. Erected in 1779, Pleasant Hall was the home of Peter Singleton, a Princess Anne County landowner. Singleton later donated the land behind the house for a new courthouse which stood from the 1780s until its ruins were demolished in 1972. 134–27 (10/17/72); *Virginia Historic Landmarks Board preservation easement.*

SEATACK LIFESAVING STATION, *Atlantic Avenue and Twenty-fourth Street.* Stations of the U. S. Lifesaving Service, a predecessor of the Coast Guard, were constructed to rescue victims of shipwrecks and other maritime disasters. The Virginia Beach station was erected on the oceanfront at Twenty-fourth Street in 1903. Reequipped and renovated in 1933 for another generation of service, it was finally abandoned in 1969. The city of Virginia Beach has since acquired the building and had it moved a short distance and carefully restored for use as a museum and visitors' center. Its observation tower and shingled walls contrast strikingly with the dense modern development along the Virginia Beach boardwalk. 134–47 (3/20/79).

ADAM THOROUGHGOOD HOUSE, *Thoroughgood Lane.* This brick dwelling illustrates the transition from the temporary frontier structures erected by the Virginia colonists in the 17th century to the more permanent, albeit informal, brick dwellings that gained popularity in the early 18th century. The massive exterior end chimney, irregular spacing of the openings, and lack of classical architectural influences make the house a characteristic example of Virginia's pre-Georgian architecture. The house was altered ca. 1745 when the original woodwork was replaced with paneled woodwork and the casement windows were converted to sliding sash. The exterior and the part of the interior were returned to their original appearance after the Adam Thoroughgood House Foundation acquired the property. The house is on land obtained by Adam Thoroughgood in 1632. It was probably built later in the century by either his son or grandson. The house is now exhibited by the Chrysler Museum of Norfolk as a museum of Virginia's 17th-century life-style and architecture. 134–33 (9/9/69); *National Historic Landmark.*

UPPER WOLFSNARE, *Potters road, London Bridge vicinity.* Upper Wolfsnare, with its unusual floor plan and rich store of paneling, is a fortunate survival of a local house type once common in the Virginia Beach area. Maj. Thomas Walke wrote a will in 1759 that left to his son Thomas a plantation house he described as being under construction, presumed to be this brick dwelling. During the Revolution the younger Thomas Walke was one of the few Whigs in the predominantly Loyalist Princess Anne County. Features of Walke's house closely resemble those in several other colonial houses of the area. The double-pile plan with a corner staircase is similar to the floor plan in Pleasant Hall. The style of the paneling, bereft of molding, and other decorations seems to be a regional type. Known for many years as Brick House Farm, since 1939 it has been called by its present name, derived from Wolfsnare Creek, which ran by it until obliterated by the construction of the Virginia Beach Expressway. The house has been in the custodianship of the Princess Anne Historical Society since 1966. 134–34 (11/19/74).

WEBLIN HOUSE, *Moore's Pond Road.* Despite its rapid transformation into a highly developed metropolitan area, the city of Virginia Beach preserves several pre-Georgian vernacular houses documentating the taste of the more prosperous farmers toward the end of the first century of settlement. The only one of the group to retain any of its rural setting is the Weblin house, at the head of a creek amid broad, flat farmlands. With its hall-parlor plan and massive end chimney, the house is a representative of the "Virginia style," a vernacular house type evolved from the late medieval farmhouses of the western and upland regions of England and employed by the Virginia settlers who came from those areas. The exact construction date is uncertain, but the house probably was built ca. 1700 for John Weblin, Jr., who inherited the property from his father in 1686. The house's steep gable roof was changed to a gambrel roof in the mid-18th century. The interior has undergone modifications, but the original floor plan survives, as does a second-floor bolection fireplace surround. 134–35 (2/19/74).

WARREN COUNTY

*Formed from Shenandoah and Frederick counties in 1836,
this lower Shenandoah Valley county was named for Dr. Joseph
Warren, a Revolutionary patriot of Boston who was killed at the
battle of Bunker Hill. The county seat is Front Royal.*

COMPTON GAP ARCHAEOLOGICAL SITE, *Compton Gap, Shenandoah National Park.* Significant more for its strategic location than for the extent and richness of its artifactual data, the Compton Gap site played an important communications role in the Late Archaic period as a way station in north-south and east-west movement and exchange by prehistoric Indians. Located at the crest of the Blue Ridge, the site may be a valuable source of information about the relationship between cultural and environmental zones in the prehistory of the mid-Atlantic region. One of the northernmost prehistoric sites identified in the Shenandoah National Park, the Compton Gap site also should provide comparative data complementing the more familiar picture of prehistoric development in the Shenandoah Valley and Piedmont. 93–168 (9/16/82).

ERIN, *Nineveh vicinity.* Constructed in 1848 for David Funsten by a talented but unidentified master housewright, Erin is a sophisticated illustration of the influence of American architectural pattern books on the rural houses of the antebellum period. Although the three-part composition was developed in Virginia into a traditional regional form, Erin seems unrelated to Virginia prototypes and more likely was inspired by a design for a three-part house published in Minard Lafever's *Modern Builder's Guide* (1833). Moreover, its elegant Greek Revival detailing, particularly its richly ornamented entrance, is derived from illustrations in Asher Benjamin's *The Practice of Architecture* (1833). Erin's first owner was a farmer, lawyer, and politician. The house is set off by an interesting range of outbuildings, from a limestone kitchen to Funsten's law office, a miniature wood-frame temple fronted by a simple portico. 93–3 (10/16/79).

FLINT RUN ARCHAEOLOGICAL DISTRICT (includes THUNDERBIRD ARCHAEOLOGICAL DISTRICT), *Limeton vicinity.* The complex of sites within the approximately 2,300-acre tract spanning the South Fork of the Shenandoah River forms one of eastern North America's most significant archaeological zones. Integrated multidisciplinary research conducted in the area by the Department of Anthropology of the Catholic University of America and the Thunderbird Research Corporation since 1971 has resulted in the discovery of the only known sites on the continent exhibiting stratigraphy and cultural continuity between the beginning Paleo-Indian and terminal Early Archaic periods, as well as the discovery of the earliest reported evidences of structures in the New World. These and other discoveries have led to the development of paleoecological and chronological sequences for the middle Shenandoah Valley with ramifications for the Middle Atlantic and eastern North American regions in general. They have also led to the development of the only fully complete and documented Paleo-Indian settlement pattern in America. The Flint Run area is divided into three broad zones—the floodplain, uplands, and foothills—with important sites found in all three areas. A portion of the site has been developed as an archaeological park and museum exhibiting evidence of human occupancy spanning a 12,000-year period. Two sites within the district, the Thunderbird site and Site Fifty, have been named a National Historic Landmark with the designation Thunderbird Archaeological District. 93–165 (12/16/75); *National Historic Landmark.*

MOUNT ZION, *Milldale.* The architecture of the boxy mid-Georgian plantation houses of Virginia's Tidewater was given a regional interpretation in this massive farmhouse of the lower Shenandoah Valley. Built of native limestone with symmetrical facades and a hipped roof, Mount Zion's fortresslike exterior contrasts with the ambitious provincial woodwork of the lofty interior. The parlor chimneypiece, decorated with carved pendants, swags, animal heads, rope moldings and Greek fret, is an extraordinary example of the area's 18th-century craftsmanship. The house was built soon after 1771 on a farm bought by the Reverend Charles Mynn Thruston, an Anglican minister and native of Gloucester County who raised a company of troops during the Revolution. Wounded in the battle of Piscataway, he was known as the "Fighting Parson." Thruston is said to have held services in the spacious second-floor hall of Mount Zion, where there is an original stepped platform at the south end. Since 1842 the property has been the home of the Earle family. Alexander Earle of Mount Zion served as a quartermaster in the Confederate army and was elected a state senator from the region in 1881. 93–8 (12/2/69).

WASHINGTON COUNTY

At the southern end of Western Virginia's chain of valleys, Washington County was formed from the extinct Fincastle County in 1776, with part of Montgomery County added later. It is the first locality in the United States known to have been named for George Washington. Its county seat is Abingdon.

ABINGDON BANK, *225 East Main Street, Abingdon.* Early 19th-century bank buildings often were barely distinguishable from fine town houses because they incorporated the residence of the cashier. These banks usually had two entrances, one for the banking area and one leading to the private quarters, and most had three stories because the residential section had at least two levels. The Abingdon Bank, erected in the mid-1840s for Robert Preston, first resident cashier, is a fine illustration of this early commercial type. The banking area retains its large windows with iron bars and its vault. The plain interior trim of the residential section contrasts with the elaborate brick cornice and belt course of the exterior. No longer a bank, the building has been restored to serve as a private residence. 140–1 (5/13/69).

ABINGDON HISTORIC DISTRICT, *extending along Main Street between Cummings Street and Deadmore Street*. The historic district of Abingdon is the best-preserved example of the numerous linear commmunities that developed in the late 18th century along the Valley Turnpike. The town is unusual for its large quantity of Federal and antebellum buildings of brick, which serve to give the district an air of permanence and prosperity lacking in similar settlements containing mostly wooden buildings. Abingdon was founded in 1778 and flourished almost immediately. Secretary of the Treasury John Campbell, Confederate general Joseph E. Johnston, and three Virginia governors, Wyndham Robinson, David Campbell, and John Buchanan Floyd, all lived in Abingdon. Gen. Francis Preston built one of the largest houses in Virginia here in the 1830s; it later was converted to Martha Washington College and is now the Martha Washington Inn. Other early buildings are the Federal-period King house and Dr. Pitt's house, as well as the antebellum Washington County Courthouse (shown) and Abingdon Bank building. In recent times Abingdon has been the home of the Barter Theatre, a repertory theatre founded in 1933 by Robert Porterfield. 140–37 (12/2/69).

CRABTREE-BLACKWELL FARM, *Blackwell vicinity*. The log dwelling house, attendant outbuildings, and mountain setting of the Crabtree-Blackwell farm make a remarkably undisturbed picture of the folk culture of the Southwest Virginia uplands, a region settled by Tidewater English, Scotch-Irish, and Pennsylvania Germans. The resulting cultural amalgam is represented in the area's vernacular buildings, particularly the Crabtree-Blackwell house. The earliest section of the two-part dwelling is in the half-dovetail square-cabin form evolved from late medieval English prototypes. The later rectangular section, with its half story and V-notched corners, is more typical of the Scotch-Irish building traditions. The springhouse, with its cantilevered overhang, follows Central European vernacular building practices. The double-crib log barn is a common Appalachian form. The oldest portion of the house was probably built by the Crabtree family, who bought the land in 1818. The later section most likely came after 1824 when the farm was purchased by the Davenport family. 95–76 (12/17/74).

EMORY AND HENRY COLLEGE, *Emory.* Emory and Henry College, founded in 1838 by the Holston Conference of the Methodist Episcopal Church, is the oldest college in Southwest Virginia and one of the few colleges of its period in the South that has operated under the same name and with continued affiliation with its founding organization. The hilly, tree-shaded campus includes several structures from its early days. Among these are the Charles C. Collins house (1845), home of the first president; the Emily Williams house (1848), home of the second president; and the J. Stewart French house (1852), an early faculty residence and later the home of seven successive college presidents. In addition to these buildings, all of which survive with few alterations, the college possesses a fine collection of Georgian Revival buildings. Dominating the complex is Ephraim Emerson Wiley Hall (shown), the Georgian Revival administration building built in 1912 and rebuilt within its walls following a 1928 fire. With their uniform brick construction and light-painted classical trim, the buildings, both 19th and 20th century, form a cohesive architectural assemblage. 95–98 (1/18/83).

MONT CALM, *Cummings Street, S. W., Abingdon.* On a ridge overlooking the historic district of Abingdon, Mont Calm stands as one of the best examples of Federal domestic architecture in this Southwest Virginia community. The well-proportioned dwelling, with its formal facade, finely jointed brickwork, and Doric cornice, indicates the sophisticated lifestyle enjoyed in the early days of the region. Completed in 1827, Mont Calm has been the home of the Campbell, Cummings, and Mingea families. It was built for David Campbell, who served as Virginia's governor in 1837–40 and was an early champion of public education. The interior was significantly remodeled in the early 20th century when Mr. and Mrs. Wilton E. Mingea acquired the place. Mr. Mingea was in the lumber industry and developed the Virginia-Carolina Railroad. 140–18 (1/15/74).

WHITE'S MILL, *White's Mill.* A mill was established here in Toole Creek's narrow valley as early as 1796. The present mill probably dates from the mid-19th century and is one of the state's handful of gristmills still in operation and still powered by an overshot wheel. White's Mill was built in accordance with mill theorist Oliver Evans's concepts published in *The Young Millwright and Miller's Guide* (1795) and was expanded to include the late 19th-century innovations in roller mill machinery, so that it is a working example of the technological evolution of gristmilling. The original wooden wheel has been replaced by the currently used twenty-foot-diameter metal Fitz wheel. However, most of the original wooden gears and workings are intact. 95–27 (4/16/74).

CITY OF WAYNESBORO

Named for Anthony Wayne, a Revolutionary War general, and originally spelled Waynesborough, this Shenandoah Valley community was laid out in 1797 and established as a town in 1801. Incorporated in 1834, it was consolidated with Basic City, located immediately across the South River, in 1923. Waynesboro became a city in 1948.

COINER-QUESENBERY HOUSE, *332 West Main Street.* This Main Street town house is believed to be Waynesboro's first brick dwelling. The house was built in 1806 for Casper Coiner, who, like many of the area's first settlers, was of Pennsylvania-German origin. Coiner's residence is a simple but sophisticated representative of the houses found in the linear villages up and down the Shenandoah Valley. Following the precedent of densely settled communities, particularly Philadelphia, the settlers here located their houses on the front edges of their lots, giving their towns and villages an urban appearance. In its original form the house had a center entrance, but an alteration of 1832 gave it a more conventional side-passage plan, moving the entrance to an end bay. The original elaborate exterior cornice remains. After standing in deteriorated condition for many years, the house was restored to its mid-19th-century appearance in 1972 by the Quesenbery family. 136–1 (6/15/76).

FAIRFAX HALL, *Winchester Avenue*. Built in 1890 against the mountainside overlooking what was then Basic City, later joined to Waynesboro, Fairfax Hall is one of only two remaining of the late Victorian resort hotel buildings that once dotted the Shenandoah Valley. Most of these resorts were established in conjunction with the building of the Norfolk and Western Railway, which made them easily accessible to eastern and northern cities. The hotel, first known as the Brandon, was designed by Washington, D. C., architect William M. Poindexter, who provided a homey Queen Anne scheme in the shingled mode. In 1920 the building became Fairfax Hall, a preparatory school and junior college for girls. The building now serves as a staff training academy for the Virginia Department of Corrections. 136–10 (7/20/82).

WESTMORELAND COUNTY

Named for the English shire, this Northern Neck county was formed from Northumberland County in 1653, with part of King George County added later. Its county seat is Montross.

BLENHEIM, *Wakefield Corner vicinity.* Blenheim is the plantation next to Wakefield, birthplace of George Washington. The simple late Georgian house here was built in 1781 for William Augustine Washington, son of George Washington's half brother, as a successor to the house at Wakefield, which burned on Christmas Day, 1779. William Augustine Washington achieved the rank of brigadier general in the Revolution and served as sheriff of Westmoreland County. He vacated Blenheim ca. 1785, giving the place to his daughter Sarah Tayloe Washington, who was married to her cousin Lawrence Washington. Except for one break, Blenheim has remained in the ownership of Washington family descendants. The house, restored from near-ruinous condition in recent years, originally was covered by a hipped roof, making it an example of a dwelling type characteristic of the Potomac-Rappahannock region of the 18th century. 96–3 (2/18/75): *Virginia Historic Landmarks Board preservation easement.*

CHANTILLY ARCHAEOLOGICAL SITE, *Montross vicinity*. Chantilly, part of the John Hallowes patent of 1650, was acquired by Richard Henry Lee in 1763 and remained his home until his death in 1794. Born at nearby Stratford, the Lee family seat, Richard Henry Lee was a Revolutionary leader. He wrote the Westmoreland Resolves, and as a delegate to the Continental Congress in 1776, he moved the resolution for American independence from Great Britain. Lee was also one of Virginia's signers of the Declaration of Independence. His house at Chantilly, described by Thomas Lee Shippen as more commodious than elegant, was destroyed early in the 19th century, possibly during the War of 1812. The house site and its immediate environs remain a significant archaeological site. 96–5 (10/6/70).

INGLESIDE, *Oak Grove vicinity*. Ingleside was erected in 1834 as the Washington Academy, one of the numerous private preparatory schools founded in Virginia during the antebellum period. The porticoed structure, with its naive detailing, is a rare example of rural institutional architecture of the period. Tradition has it that the school's founders patterned the building along the lines of Thomas Jefferson's Capitol in Richmond. The academy operated for a decade before decreased enrollment forced it to close. After the sale of the property in 1847, the building was converted to a private residence and received its present name. After many changes of ownership, Ingleside was purchased in 1890 by Carl Henry Flemer of Washington, D.C., and has become the nucleus of a nursery and winery. 96–12 (12/21/76).

MORGAN JONES POTTERY KILN ARCHAEOLOGICAL SITE, *Glebe Harbor*. Archaeological evidence and historical documents combine to make the site of Morgan Jones's pottery kiln a unique relic of a 17th-century American craft industry. According to Westmoreland County records, on August 28, 1677, Morgan Jones entered into a partnership with Dennis White for the "making and selling of Earthen warre" from a kiln on the western side of Lower Machotick (Machodoc) Creek. Investigation of the site in 1973 by archaeologists of the Virginia Division of Historic Landmarks uncovered the kiln's remains and unearthed many fragmentary samples of pottery manufactured there. Sherds of wares similar to those found at the kiln site have been uncovered at numerous archaeological sites in Virginia's Tidewater region, making the kiln excavations a valuable tool for dating and identifying Virginia pottery of the period. 96–81 (6/18/74).

JAMES MONROE BIRTHPLACE ARCHAEOLOGICAL SITE, *Monroe Hall*. James Monroe, fifth president of the United States, was born in 1758 in a modest wood-frame house near the tiny settlement of Monroe Hall. Archaeological investigation of the site in recent years has revealed the foundation of a 57-by-18-foot structure which conforms to a print of the Monroe home in Robert Sears's *A Pictoral History of the American Revolution* (1845). Artifacts indicate a construction date of 1750, eight years before Monroe's birth. The artifacts, house plan, and a 1774 inventory made after the death of Monroe's father, Spence Monroe, who was a carpenter or joiner, indicate that the family was of modest means, holding most of their wealth in slaves, cattle, and land. James Monroe lived in the house from the time he was born until 1774 when he enrolled in the College of William and Mary. Monroe inherited the property at his father's death and sold it in 1781. The site is now preserved in a county-owned historical park. 96–46 (12/21/76).

ROXBURY, *Oak Grove vicinity*. Roxbury's Victorian villa of 1861 was the home of Dabney Carr Wirt, a son of the jurist, statesman, and author William Wirt. The Gothic-style house, with its asymmetrical plan and multigable roofline, conforms to the picturesque designs of the era popularized by Andrew Jackson Downing and Calvert Vaux. More typical of Vaux's designs, Roxbury is a highly original composition and avoids the strict historicism of the romantically inspired houses of the immediately preceding generation. Such houses are relatively common in the North but, because of agricultural depression and Civil War, rare in Virginia. No architect has been associated with Roxbury, suggesting that the design may have been adapted by a talented local builder from pattern-book designs by Vaux or one of his contemporaries. Around the turn of the century, Roxbury was the home of F.W. Alexander, who inaugurated a movement to acquire and restore Stratford as a memorial to the Lee family. 96–20 (12/21/76).

SPENCE'S POINT, *Sandy Point vicinity*. Writer John Dos Passos (1896–1970) made his home at this Westmoreland County farm from 1949 until his death. It was at this retreat on the banks of the Potomac that he wrote most of his later works. The property was purchased in the late 19th century by Dos Passos's father, John Randolph Dos Passos, a Portuguese shoemaker's son who became a successful New York lawyer. The young Dos Passos lived with his mother but made occasional visits to his father at Spence's Point. The plain, three-bay Federal farmhouse here was built in 1806 for Alexander Spence. Dos Passos added the brick wing when he restored the house as his residence. Among his more noted writings are *Three Soldiers* (1921) and his trilogy *U.S.A.*, which includes *The 42nd Parallel* (1930), *1919* (1932), and *Big Money* (1936). 96–22 (2/20/73); *National Historic Landmark*.

SPRING GROVE, *Mount Holly vicinity.* This architecturally conservative Federal farmhouse was erected in 1834 for Robert Murphy, an area landholder. The house is one of the small group of formal brick residences built on the Northern Neck in the early 19th century and reflects in its size and refinements the prosperity enjoyed by the region. The most distinctive exterior feature is the dwarf Ionic portico sheltering the main entrance. Inside, the principal rooms are set off by woodwork and decorative plasterwork derived from pattern books by Boston architect Asher Benjamin. William Rogers, a later owner, thoroughly recorded the house in the 1870s with a set of drawings which are preserved at the house by the present owners. The drawings are a rare instance of pictorial documentation of the period. The house survives with few alterations and has an unspoiled rural setting on the high, flat ground above Nomini Creek. 96–23 (6/21/83).

STRATFORD, *Lerty vicinity.* Few places in America can match Stratford in architectural interest or historical associations. The great colonial mansion, with its complex of outbuildings and dependencies, was begun in the second quarter of the 18th century under the direction of councillor and acting governor Col. Thomas Lee. Although Stratford is best known as the birthplace of Confederate general Robert E. Lee, it was also the birthplace of Richard Henry Lee and his brother Francis Lightfoot Lee, both signers of the Declaration of Independence. With its H-shaped plan, piano nobile, baroque clustered chimney stacks, and tray-ceilinged great hall, the house is unique among colonial plantation houses. Enhancing the architecture is the rural setting with long vistas created over the fields to focus on the house and on the Potomac River. Stratford passed out of the Lee family in 1828 and was acquired for preservation nearly a century later by the Robert E. Lee Memorial Association, Inc. Since restored, the house, its outbuildings, and grounds are exhibited as a museum honoring the Lee family and interpreting life on a great colonial plantation. 96–34 (9/9/69); *National Historic Landmark.*

GEORGE WASHINGTON BIRTHPLACE NATIONAL MONUMENT (WAKEFIELD), *Oak Grove vicinity.* The site of the birthplace of George Washington is on a 150-acre tract of land on Pope's Creek, just off the Potomac River, which was purchased by Washington's father, Augustine, in 1718. Born on February 22, 1732, the young Washington spent only his first three years here but returned at age eleven to study surveying with his half brother Augustine, Jr., who inherited the property. The dwelling in which Washington was born burned on Christmas Day, 1779, and the Washington family built a new house at Blenheim, an adjacent farm. The birthplace site was excavated in 1930 and 1936, revealing the brick foundations of a U-shaped timber-frame house, 58 feet by 30 feet, probably containing about nine rooms. The present dwelling, the Memorial House, erected in 1930–31, is not intended as a reconstruction of the birthplace but is meant to show a typical medium-size planter's house of the period. First known simply as the Pope's Creek plantation, it was renamed Wakefield several years before the original house burned. The property was acquired for preservation by the Wakefield National Memorial Association in 1923 and was transferred to the National Park Service in 1932. The place is maintained today as a living farm illustrating the peaceful agrarian environment in which Washington was born. 96–26 (10/18/83).

WIRTLAND, *Oak Grove vicinity.* Wirtland was erected in 1850 for Dr. William Wirt, Jr., one of the sons of the jurist, statesman, and author. With its romantically landscaped park and carefully articulated Gothic Revival mansion, the estate conforms to the mid-19th-century ideal of an American villa as defined by Andrew Jackson Downing. For Downing, a villa was "the most refined home of America," where "amid the serenity and peace of sylvan scenes . . . the artistic knowledge and feeling has full play." Downing recommmended various historic styles as appropriate for villas but maintained a preference for the Gothic. Although it would seem likely that such a sophisticated house was custom-designed, no architect has been identified with it; the design may have been based on published illustrations. After Dr. Wirt's death in 1898, Wirtland housed a female academy. The property is now part of the Ingleside Plantation Nurseries, with the house and its immediate grounds maintained as a private residence. 96–29 (12/21/76).

YEOCOMICO CHURCH, *Tucker Hill.* Its blending of medieval and classical elements make the only remaining colonial church in Westmoreland County, Yeocomico Church of Cople Parish, an illustration of the transition that occurred in colonial architecture at the beginning of the 18th century. The side entrance porch, possibly an early addition, with its wicket door (a smaller door cut into a larger door), is a common feature on medieval English churches but a unique survival here. The classically inspired modillion cornice is a harbinger of the Georgian style to come. Adding to its interest is its strangely inconsistent brickwork inscribed with no less than eleven sets of initials, suggesting the participation of many workmen. The inscription of 1706 may be a construction date, although the present form of the building is the result of the addition of the T-wing ca. 1730–40. Despite the fact that the building was used to house soldiers in three wars and was vacated after the disestablishment, it survives in a remarkably good state of preservation. 96–31 (9/9/69); *National Historic Landmark.*

CITY OF WILLIAMSBURG

*The Virginia colony's second capital was established by the
General Assembly as Middle Plantation in 1633. The seat of
government was moved here from Jamestown in 1698, and the
community was renamed Williamsburg in 1699 in honor of King
William III. It achieved borough status in 1722 and remained
the capital of Virginia until 1780. Williamsburg was
incorporated as a city in 1884.*

BRUTON PARISH CHURCH, *Duke of Gloucester Street.*
Bruton Parish Church, the official house of worship of Virginia's colonial capital, remains the state's principal representative of the era's ecclesiastical architecture. The church was constructed in 1712–15 to replace a former building that proved inadequate to accommodate the new capital's many visitors and growing population. The General Assembly voted to provide part of the construction costs because its members worshiped there while in session. The design of the oldest part is credited to Governor Alexander Spotswood, who called for a cruciform-plan church, the colony's first in that form. Responsibility for its construction was given to James Morris. The chancel was extended in 1752, and the tower, with its two-tiered steeple, was added in 1769. The removal of the capital from Williamsburg to Richmond ended Bruton Parish's role as Virginia's leading church and ushered in a long stagnant period. The interior was significantly rearranged in the 19th century but was restored in 1905. A more complete restoration was undertaken in 1931 under the guidance of Colonial Williamsburg architects. The church remains one of the main original buildings of its historic community. 137–7 (9/18/73); *National Historic Landmark.*

CAPITOL LANDING ARCHAEOLOGICAL SITE, *Williamsburg vicinity.* During the 18th century Williamsburg was served by two inland ports: College Landing on a tributary of the James River to the south and Capitol Landing, officially known as Queen Mary's Port, linking the city to the York River. Established in 1699, Capitol Landing was located on Queen's Creek at the end of what was then known as Queen's Road. Around its wharf grew a small settlement of shops, houses, and light industries. A succession of tobacco inspection warehouses stood at the wharf, regulating the colony's chief cash crop. A popular tavern, started by ferryman Giles Moody in 1717, served workers and travelers at the port for many years. All of the buildings vanished during the 19th century, leaving behind a series of archaeological sites. Although the area is bisected by a modern highway, many of Capitol Landing's sites remain undisturbed, holding a rich store of knowledge relating to colonial Virginia's commerce and transportation. 137–56 (6/21/77).

COLLEGE LANDING ARCHAEOLOGICAL SITE, *Williamsburg vicinity.* South of Williamsburg at the confluence of College and Paper Mill creeks, College Landing was a principal port for the colonial capital, connecting it with shipping traffic using the James River. Warehouses and wharves as well as a tavern and some light industrial structures, including a brewery, sprang up to complement the shipping trade. The landing also became an important military supply center during the Revolution. The small port remained a busy place throughout the 18th century, but after the removal of the seat of government to Richmond, its activity began to ebb. By this century the site was completely abandoned and grown over. What remains is a series of archaeological sites relating to colonial Virginia's transportation, commercial, and industrial life, as well as to the material culture of the lower- and middle-class transients who worked and lived near the landing. Several of the sites were the subject of salvage excavation when threatened by highway construction in 1976. 137–57 (12/21/76).

PEYTON RANDOLPH HOUSE, *Nicholson Street.* Peyton Randolph, Speaker of the House of Burgesses for nine years, made his home here from 1745 until his death in 1775. A principal champion of the cause of independence, Randolph served as president of nearly every important revolutionary assemblage of Virginia and was president of both the first and second Continental Congresses. The three-bay western section of his home, with its unusual square plan, was built ca. 1716 for William Robertson, clerk of the Council from 1701 to 1739. A story-and-a-half dependency to the east was built by 1724 and was later connected to the older part by a two-story, four-bay section probably built by Randolph's father, Sir John Randolph. A marble chimneypiece and paneled woodwork distinguish the Randolph section. The east wing had disappeared by 1783 but was reconstructed when the house was restored by Colonial Williamsburg in 1939–40. 137–32 (9/18/73); *National Historic Landmark.*

JAMES SEMPLE HOUSE, *Francis Street*. Among the most architecturally intriguing dwellings in Virginia's former capital is this three-part structure, which in 1809 St. George Tucker called "the handsomest house in town." Although its construction date has not been precisely documented, the house was probably built ca. 1778 as the home of William Pasteur. Its present name honors James Semple, a lawyer and judge who acquired the house ca. 1798. With its pedimented center section and one-story wings, the house follows the Palladian format as interpreted by English architects such as Robert Morris and William Halfpenny. Thomas Jefferson is known to have been an early advocate of the form and may have influenced the design of the house. Along with the first form of Monticello, the Semple house is a prototype of the many tripartite houses erected throughout Virginia and neighboring southern states in the early national era. The house was among the first to be acquired by Colonial Williamsburg and was restored in 1932. 137–33 (9/18/73); *National Historic Landmark.*

WILLIAMSBURG HISTORIC DISTRICT, *approximately bounded by Francis, Waller, Nicholson, North England, Lafayette, and Nassau streets*. Williamsburg served as the capital of the Virginia colony from 1699 until 1776 and as the capital of the Commonwealth of Virginia until the seat of government was moved to Richmond in 1780. Laid out by Governor Francis Nicholson, Williamsburg was one of North America's first formally planned towns, rich in open space and with a major building closing every principal axis. Over the subsequent decades the plan was executed; the first Capitol was finished in 1704, the Governor's Palace was begun in 1706, and houses, outbuildings, and shops were constructed. In its golden era Williamsburg was the colony's social and cultural center, and its institutions included not only the colonial government but the College of William and Mary and the Public Hospital, colonial America's first lunatic asylum. Here Virginia's political leaders, George Washington, Thomas Jefferson and Patrick Henry among them, began the discussions and debates that led the Old Dominion to revolution. Williamsburg fell dormant after the removal of the state government and remained a quiet village until the late 1920s when a complete restoration of its colonial appearance was undertaken with the support of John D. Rockefeller, Jr. Over eighty colonial buildings have been carefully restored, and numerous others, both prominent and humble, have been erected on their original sites. This monumental project, carried on over the course of a half century and still continuing, has set a standard for excellence in scholarship and historic preservation that has been emulated throughout the nation. 137–50 (9/9/69); *National Historic Landmark.*

WREN BUILDING, *College of William and Mary.* The main building of the nation's second oldest seat of higher learning was begun in 1695 and completed four years later. Hugh Jones in his *Present State of Virginia* (1724) stated that its architect was Sir Christopher Wren; the building's name has honored England's greatest architect ever since. Although Wren may or may not have had a hand in the design, Jones went on to state that the plans were altered by the Virginians to suit conditions there. The building was gutted by fire in 1705 and rebuilt in modified form within the original walls. It again burned in 1859 and 1862, but in each case the 17th-century walls survived and were retained in the rebuildings. The Wren Building's 1705 exterior appearance is well documented in both a ca. 1737 engraving plate found in Oxford's Bodleian Library and a pre-1859 photograph. It was to that form that it was returned during the restoration of 1928–31 directed by Colonial Williamsburg architects. Serving as dependencies for the Wren Building and forming a forecourt are the President's House (1732–33) and the nearly identical Brafferton, built in 1723 as an Indian school. The College of William and Mary was chartered in 1693 through the efforts of the Reverend James Blair. It is now a state-owned university. 137–13 (9/9/69); *National Historic Landmark.*

WYTHE HOUSE, *Palace Green.* Few colonial Virginia houses are so admired or have spawned so many imitations as this restrained Georgian dwelling in the heart of Williamsburg. The house was erected ca. 1750 as the town house of Richard Taliaferro, who most likely was its designer. Taliaferro received public acclaim as an architect when he directed the 1754 addition of the ballroom wing to the Governor's Palace. The house served for many years as the home of Taliaferro's son-in-law, George Wythe, a signer of the Declaration of Independence and first law professor at the College of William and Mary. The complex geometry of its proportions, combined with its subtle brickwork, demonstrate how Virginia's otherwise plain colonial architecture could transcend provinciality and achieve stateliness. The house survived in a remarkable state of preservation and required relatively minor repairs and replacements when restored by Colonial Williamsburg in 1939–40. 137–58 (9/18/73); *National Historic Landmark.*

CITY OF WINCHESTER

Located at the northern end of the Shenandoah Valley, the county seat of Frederick County was originally known as Opequon and then as Frederick's Town. Its name was changed to Winchester, for the English city, upon its establishment as a town in 1752. The town was incorporated in 1779 and became a city in 1874.

ABRAM'S DELIGHT, *Parkview Street and Rouss Spring Road.* Some of the oldest houses in the Shenandoah Valley are marked by the use of stone construction. One of these is the austere dwelling erected in 1754 for Isaac Hollingsworth on property settled in 1732 by his father, Abraham Hollingsworth, and named in his honor. The stonemason for Hollingsworth's home was Simon Taylor, who also is credited with Springdale, the home of John Hite several miles to the south in Frederick County. The house employs a two-over-two floor plan with center passage, a plan favored by the area's Scotch-Irish settlers. A two-story wing was added ca. 1801, and the original trim was replaced with Greek Revival trim in a mid-19th-century remodeling. Acquired by the city of Winchester in 1943, the house is now exhibited as a museum of early life in the area by the Winchester-Frederick County Historical Society, with the grounds maintained as a municipal park. 138–29 (11/9/72).

GLEN BURNIE, *801 Amherst Street.* This property was part of a 1735 grant to James Wood, who founded Winchester in 1752 and platted the town's lots. Wood's log-and-stone house was replaced by the earliest part of the present farmhouse, built ca.

1794 for his son Robert. As indicated by a break in the brick-work, the house was enlarged soon thereafter. Glen Burnie has continued in the ownership of Wood's descendants through the seventh generation. Although now within the city limits of Winchester, the property retains a rural atmosphere. Extensive gardens were laid out by the present owner after he inherited Glen Burnie in 1959. The first floor of the oldest section, containing the stair hall and dining room, is embellished with fine Federal woodwork including a paneled chimneypiece, an open-well stair with turned balusters, and a hall cornice decorated with gougework and stars. The grounds contain the Wood family cemetery. 138–8 (6/19/79).

HANDLEY LIBRARY, *Braddock and Piccadilly streets.* Judge John Handley of Scranton, Pa., who made a fortune in coal investments, late in life developed a warm affection for Winchester and its Scotch-Irish heritage. At his death in 1895, he left funds for the construction of a library "for the free use of the people of the city of Winchester." The result of this munificence is perhaps Virginia's purest expression of Beaux Arts classicism, a florid classicism promulgated in the late 19th century by the leading French architectural school. The designers of the library were the partners J. Stewart Barney and Henry Otis Chapman of New York. Begun in 1908 and completed in 1913, the Handley Library was a model for its time. The dome, colonnades, and esplanades encased the most modern facilities, including five levels of glass-floored stacks, an auditorium, and well-appointed reading rooms, all in fireproof construction. Still an efficient facility, the Handley Library is an illustration of the long-term benefits of good architecture. 138–28 (9/9/69).

STONEWALL JACKSON'S HEADQUARTERS, *415 North Braddock Street.* This Gothic Revival cottage in downtown Winchester's residential area served as the headquarters of Gen. Stonewall Jackson from November 1861 to March 1862. Jackson's firm stand during the battle of First Manassas had earned him his nickname and a promotion to the rank of major general with the task of defending the Shenandoah Valley. He established his winter headquarters in Winchester, and the following spring he began a series of diversions in the region to take the pressure off the Confederate forces in the east. The house chosen for him to occupy was built in 1854 for William McP. Fuller, who sold it two years later to Lewis T. Moore. With its diamond-pane windows and scrolled bargeboards in its several gables, the house follows the Gothic mode as popularized for domestic design in the writings of Andrew Jackson Downing. Mrs. Jackson came to stay with her husband during the winter of 1861–62 and described the dwelling as being in the cottage style and papered with elegant gilt paper. Jackson gave up the house when he evacuated Winchester on March 11, 1862. The property is now owned by the city and exhibited as a museum. 138–33 (9/9/69); *National Historic Landmark.*

OLD STONE CHURCH, *304 East Piccadilly Street*. Restored between 1941 and 1950 to its original appearance, Old Stone Church exemplifies the austere architecture favored by the 18th-century Scotch-Irish settlers of the Shenandoah Valley, who came to the region largely from the Cumberland Valley of Pennsylvania. The church was built in 1788 as a branch of the Opequon Church of Frederick County, organized in 1736. The Winchester Presbytery, covering parts of what is now West Virginia, southern Pennsylvania, western Maryland, and the lower Shenandoah Valley of Virginia, was organized in the church in 1794. The congregation merged with another congregation in 1834, and the building was sold to the Baptists. In 1875 the Baptists leased the building to the city of Winchester for use as a black school and it later was used as an armory by the local militia. The Presbyterians reacquired the church in 1932 and restored the building to its original appearance, carefully reconstructing its interior fittings. The church is now a museum and is used for special services by the First Presbyterian Church of Winchester. 138–19 (12/21/76).

WASHINGTON'S HEADQUARTERS (ADAM KURTZ HOUSE), *Braddock and Cork streets*. This building of frame, log, and stone construction, commonly known as Washington's Headquarters, is one of the oldest structures in Winchester. The center, or frame, portion most likely was standing in 1764 when Thomas Rutherford was recorded as occupying the lot. Persistent local tradition has it that this wooden section was occupied by George Washington as a surveyor in the years 1749–52 and that it later was his headquarters in 1756–57 while he was supervising the construction of Fort Loudoun, part of a chain of defense works guarding the frontier against the French and Indians. While Washington's associations with the building cannot be documented, the strong belief in its connection with him has made the structure a relic in its own right of the patriotic cultism that centered on Washington in the 19th century. One occupant who can be documented is Adam Kurtz, one of Daniel Morgan's riflemen, who bought the property from Rutherford in 1778. The stone section appears to be of 18th-century origin, while the log portion was probably an early 19th-century addition. 138–25 (12/16/75).

WINCHESTER HISTORIC DISTRICT, *roughly bounded by Hebron Cemetery, Fairfax Lane, Fairmount and Washington streets, Germain street, and Handley High School grounds.* Settled during the mid-18th century as a small farming community, Winchester became the county seat for Frederick County and a trade and mercantile center at the junction of several turnpikes. Its strategic location in the Shenandoah Valley contributed to the community's involvement in the French and Indian, Revolutionary, and Civil wars. From the 1870s to the 1920s, the community served as the commercial and industrial center of the Valley, with glove manufacturing the leading industry. During the present century, Winchester has become the center of the Virginia apple industry. The historic district is approximately forty-five city blocks and envelops both commercial and residential properties along its grid-plan streets. The area is particularly rich in early vernacular log buildings, stone houses, and Federal town houses, and it has a variety of Victorian commercial buildings and large residences. The center of the district is marked by the Greek Revival Frederick County Courthouse with its Doric portico. 138–42 (4/17/79).

WISE COUNTY

Formed in 1856 from Lee, Scott, and Russell counties, this coal-mining Southwest Virginia county was named for Alexander Wise, governor of Virginia from 1856 to 1860. Its county seat is Wise.

JOHN FOX, JR., HOUSE, *Big Stone Gap*. John Fox, Jr., novelist of the mountaineers' struggle to cope with the mining era and a more modern life-style, lived and wrote here, drawing inspiration from the people and culture of the region. He is best remembered for two works, *The Little Shepherd of Kingdom Come* and *The Trail of the Lonesome Pine*, both of which were best sellers. The shingled house was begun ca. 1890 for Fox's two eldest brothers, who came to Big Stone Gap from Kentucky as investors in mining options. Several additions were made to accommodate more of the family, including John Fox, Jr., and his wife, Viennese prima donna Fritzi Scheff. Throughout their ownership, which lasted until 1971, the Foxes made the homeplace a cultural and social center. The property is now maintained as a museum by the Lonesome Pine Arts and Crafts Association. 101–1 (11/20/73).

JUNE TOLLIVER HOUSE, *Big Stone Gap*. This modified Queen Anne-style house, typical of Southwest Virginia's late 19th-century boom architecture, was the residence of June Morris during the time of her schooling at Big Stone Gap. She was the local woman after whom the writer John Fox, Jr., patterned June Tolliver, heroine of his novel *The Trail of the Lonesome Pine*, published in 1908. In the book, this sheltered daughter of a local family falls in love with a mining engineer. Portraying the cultural clash that came with the region's mining boom, the book was one of the most popular of its time. The house is preserved as a literary landmark, with the novel that made it famous reenacted here seasonally as an outdoor drama. 101–3 (7/17/73).

U.S. POST OFFICE AND COURTHOUSE, *Main Street, Big Stone Gap*. Reflecting the prosperity brought by the coal industry to this mountain community at the turn of the century is this federal post office and courthouse, one of the more architecturally sophisticated federal buildings in the state. A refined example of the 20th-century Renaissance Revival, the stone-faced exterior, with its deep bracketed cornice, shallow hipped roof, and rusticated ground floor, recalls the architecture of Florentine palaces. Its architect, James Knox Taylor, was responsible for numerous government buildings across the nation. Taylor resigned his post in 1912, and the building was completed under the supervision of Oscar Wenderoth. It survives with no significant alterations and preserves a great quantity of early woodwork, metalwork, electrical fixtures, and custom-designed furniture. Noteworthy is the courtroom, decorated with a coffered ceiling, plasterwork, and mahogany woodwork. The building remains in use. 101–4 (10/21/75).

WISE COUNTY COURTHOUSE, *Wise*. The Wise County Courthouse reflects the wealth reaped by the county from the expansion of the railroads and the increased mining of coal in the region at the turn of the century. A rare use in Virginia of the Renaissance Revival style for a county courthouse, the building was completed in 1896 after plans by Washington, D.C., architect Frank P. Milburn and is the third courthouse to serve the county. With its paired towers, lively massing, and well-articulated masonry detailing, the building is perhaps the most successful of the several courthouses Milburn designed for Southwest Virginia counties. 329–1 (10/21/80).

WYTHE COUNTY

Named for George Wythe, a signer of the Declaration of Independence and, at the time of the formation of the county, chancellor of Virginia, this Southwest Virginia county was formed from Montgomery County in 1789, with part of Grayson County added later. Its county seat is Wytheville.

CORNETT ARCHAEOLOGICAL SITE, *Austinville vicinity.* Dating to the Late Woodland period, the Cornett archaeological site has proved to be significant in ceramic studies related to the prehistory of Southwest Virginia and neighboring regions. Further ceramic studies from data available at the site are likely to enable archaeologists to define better the nature of cultural interactions with societies farther to the south in North Carolina and adjacent areas. The site is also significant for regional studies on Late Woodland period demography, subsistence, community organization, and settlement patterns. Such studies are possible because of the presence of documented features such as burials and preserved organic materials within the sharply defined site boundaries representing a village with a possible palisade and central plaza. 98–54 (8/16/83).

FORT CHISWELL ARCHAEOLOGICAL COMPLEX, *Fort Chiswell vicinity.* The remains of a succession of settlements at this strategic location along Virginia's former frontier constitute one of Southwest Virginia's more significant archaeological complexes. Salvage excavations undertaken in 1976 under the direction of the Virginia Division of Historic Landmarks in the path of interstate highway construction revealed prehistoric remains dating from the Middle Archaic period and remnants of three successive periods of 18th-century occupation. Chimney bases from two log cabins erected ca. 1752 by Alexander Sayers, who lived here until 1757, were discovered, as well as evidence of the military outpost established by Col. William Byrd III in 1760 and occupied until early 1762. Also uncovered were remains of the fairly extensive settlement started here in the early 1770s by James McGavock, Sr. Although some of Fort Chiswell's sites were destroyed by highway construction, other areas remain untouched and hold information important to the study of the early history of Southwest Virginia. 98–49 (12/21/76).

FORT CHISWELL MANSION, *Fort Chiswell.* Fort Chiswell Mansion was built for two brothers, Stephen McGavock and Joseph Cloyd McGavock, overlooking the McGavocks' original homestead, since destroyed. The McGavocks were early settlers of the area and acquired large tracts of land. Their first home was at Fort Chiswell, a defense post on the Great Wilderness Road. Here they maintained a commercial establishment serving the many pioneers moving west. The two McGavock brothers contracted in 1839 with Lorain Thorn and James Johnson to build this brick house on a bluff above the Fort Chiswell settlement. The provincially interpreted Classical Revival structure has a two-column portico and paired semiexterior end chimneys, between which on either end is a large Palladian window at the attic level. A series of brick service buildings remains with the house. Except for the addition of the one-story front porch, the house has been little changed. It long served to signal the importance of the McGavocks to area newcomers. 98–5 (3/2/71).

HALLER-GIBBONEY ROCK HOUSE, *Monroe and Tazewell streets, Wytheville.* The Haller-Gibboney Rock House in the center of Wytheville is one of the simple but formally arranged stone vernacular houses that once were found in many of the Valley of Virginia's linear towns. The region's limestone proved to be a plentiful and easily worked material and gave texture and character to the otherwise plain architecture. This house is thought to have been started in 1822 by Adam Saftly but sold unfinished in 1823 to Dr. John Haller, a native of York, Pa., and Wytheville's first physician. Dr. Haller made the Rock House his home until his death in 1840. The house was riddled by bullets in a Union raid during the Civil War but survived in an otherwise good state of preservation. Purchased by the town of Wytheville in 1967, the dwelling is now a museum. 139–6 (4/18/72).

KIMBERLING LUTHERAN CEMETERY, *Rural Retreat vicinity*. On a steep hillside looking over the countryside and mountains of western Wythe County, this early burying ground has a large collection of traditional German gravestones. Approximately fifty monuments date from the period 1800–1850 and are embellished, in most instances, with a single, high-relief motif—a heart, cross, six-pointed star, or some vegetal form—nearly always framed by a double band. Most of the inscriptions are in English, illustrating the acculturation of the German settlers. The peculiar stylistic character of the German gravestones halts in the 1850s; those erected from that time onward are indistinguishable from those in non-German cemeteries. The present twin-towered church, dating from 1913, is the third on the site. 98–49 (12/20/77).

McGAVOCK FAMILY CEMETERY, *Fort Chiswell vicinity*. At the crown of a hill overlooking the Fort Chiswell mansion, a former McGavock home, with a backdrop of surrounding mountains, this family cemetery has a rich collection of 19th-century funerary art, including an important group of Germanic stones, the only ones of their type found in a family burying ground. The crisply carved markers dating from 1812 to the late 1830s are attributed to Laurence Krone, the county's most skillful stone carver. Like most German-style grave markers, those in the McGavock group are double-sided with differing designs on the obverse and reverse. Each stone is highlighted by a single central motif—a tulip, a fern, or a sunflower—and most have footstones. The first McGavock in the region was James McGavock, Sr., of Rockbridge County, who came to Fort Chiswell in 1771 and was buried in the cemetery in 1812 with a Germanic headstone marking his grave. 98–22 (3/20/79).

MARTIN ARCHAEOLOGICAL SITE, *Draper vicinity*. On the banks of the New River, the Martin site was a site of Indian occupation during the Late Woodland period. Test excavations on the site have established the presence of an Indian village, probably consisting of a cluster of domelike structures and perhaps enclosed by a palisade. Evidence of a succession of earlier occupations lies beneath the village remains. Artifacts found on the site include pottery sherds, lithic tools, ceramic and shell trade items, and floral and faunal remains. Shown is a shell gorget. A number of burials are also on the site. Some of the artifacts salvaged here are displayed by the site's owners in a small museum nearby. 98–46 (4/16/74).

ST. JOHN'S LUTHERAN CHURCH AND CEMETERY, *Wytheville vicinity*. During the early 19th century, German settlers were concentrated around the town of Wytheville under the leadership of George Daniel Flohr, a Lutheran pastor who organized the congregation of St. John's in 1800. Flohr's gravestone of 1826 in St. John's cemetery was executed by Laurence Krone, perhaps the most accomplished of the German stone carvers of the period and region. The marker is one of some thirty early 19th-century German-style stones remaining there. At the cemetery is the 1854 church, a plain, weatherboarded structure. Its heavy roof framing draws upon Continental framing systems practiced by German settlers in Pennsylvania, Maryland, and Virginia. The church, the mother church of the area's Lutherans, replaced the original building of ca. 1800. 98–18 (4/19/77).

SHOT TOWER, *Fosters Falls vicinity*. Thomas Jackson erected this tower on a bluff of the New River ca. 1807 to manufacture shot for the firearms of the frontier settlers. The enterprise was supplied with lead from the Austinville mines several miles away. Shot was produced by dripping the molten lead from the top of the tower through a hole in the floor at the bottom and then down a seventy-five-foot shaft sunk into the cliff, where it fell into a kettle of water. Upon hitting the water, the drops of lead developed into a round shape. The shaft was connected to the riverbank by a tunnel through which the shot was carried and loaded on boats. The shot tower, one of only three remaining in the United States, is now owned and exhibited by the Virginia Division of Parks and Recreation. 98–16 (11/5/68).

ZION EVANGELICAL LUTHERAN CHURCH CEMETERY, *Speedwell vicinity*. Forty-two well-preserved German-style gravestones, similar to those found in lesser numbers and in poorer condition in several other outlying Lutheran cemeteries around Wytheville, survive in the yard of Zion Church. Like the other markers of the region, the Zion group comprises thick sandstone slabs carved on both sides and often decorated on the edges. The fanciest have undulating tops and faces carved with petaled flowers or pinwheel motifs, often framed by spiral pilasters. The inscriptions are in English, most in a flowing script. The stones seem to have been produced by a single carver between 1835 and 1840, some to replace earlier markers. The simple Gothic-style church was built in 1940 and is the third church on the site. 98–28 (11/21/78).

YORK COUNTY

First named Charles River, York County was one of Virginia's eight original shires formed in 1634. The present name was given in 1643, probably in honor of James, duke of York, second son of King Charles I. The county seat is Yorktown.

BRUTON PARISH POORHOUSE ARCHAEOLOGI-CAL SITE, *Williamsburg vicinity.* This archaeological site consists of the remains of an 18th-century workhouse for the poor built by Bruton Parish Church of Williamsburg. A 1755 act of the General Assembly empowered all of the colony's parishes to erect poorhouses; the Bruton Parish poorhouse is one of the few known to have been built. A survey of the site, conducted by the Virginia Division of Historic Landmarks in 1978, located the foundations of one of the four buildings identified by the French cartographer Desandrouin in 1781–82 as the poorhouse complex. Shown is a sampling of the variety of 18th-century artifacts associated with daily life found in the surface investigation. A full-scale scientific investigation of the site could produce unique data about the architecture of the complex as well as the lives of a predominately inarticulate portion of the colonial population. Archaeological research also could provide new insights into the Virginia government's first attempt to provide institutional care for the colony's poor, who by the mid-18th century constituted a significant social problem. 99–70 (11/18/80).

BRYAN MANOR ARCHAEOLOGICAL SITE, *Williamsburg vicinity*. Frederick Bryan, deputy sheriff of York County, purchased a 500-acre plantation near Wiliamsburg in 1757 from John Fergason and Lewis Hansford and established his residence here. According to the Desandrouin map of 1781–82, the plantation complex then consisted of five buildings. Bryan had other landholdings and received considerable income from the sale of tobacco, pork, veal, and other products produced on his properties. Preserved in the York County records is a highly detailed househould inventory made at Bryan's death in 1771, documentation which would be interesting to compare with artifactual findings. A 1976 survey of the house site revealed an unusual footing made of sections of bog iron bonded together with shell mortar. Also at the site is a stone slab over the grave of Bryan's one-year-old son, John, who died in 1760. 99–65 (6/21/77).

GOOCH TOMB AND YORK VILLAGE ARCHAEOLOGICAL SITE, *U.S. Coast Guard Reserve Training Center, Yorktown vicinity*. The village of York, the first English settlement on the York River, was established on an elevated point near the west branch of Wormeley Creek before 1635 and remained the area's principal community until the 1690s when the present community of Yorktown was established two miles west. A church was built at York ca. 1638 and within its walls in 1655 was buried Maj. William Gooch, a burgess from York County and uncle of Sir William Gooch, acting governor of the colony from 1727 to 1749. Gooch's armorial slab is the second oldest legible tombstone in Virginia. The village and the church were abandoned in the 18th century, and the village buildings fell into ruin. The church site is marked by a small park maintained by the U.S. Coast Guard with the tombstone protected by a special cover. The village site remains undisturbed and no doubt holds artifacts and architectural remains of a village dating from the first period of Amcrica's European settlement. 99–60 (10/16/73).

GRACE CHURCH, *Yorktown*. Grace Church, originally known as York-Hampton Parish Church, was built ca. 1697. It seems to be the state's only remaining colonial structure built of marl, a soft material composed largely of shell matter which hardens almost to stone when exposed to air. The marl was taken directly from the Yorktown cliffs. The tenacity of these walls is remarkable given the church's history. The building was used as a magazine by Lord Cornwallis during the Revolution and lost its windows and pews. It was accidentally burned in 1814 and stood as a ruin until rebuilt in 1848. Further damage was done in the Civil War when Union troops put a signal tower on the roof and used the interior for a hospital. The church was returned to service in 1870 and received a thorough renovation in 1926 when the belfry, western door frame, and circular window were added. In its churchyard is the magnificent 1745 English table tomb of Thomas Nelson, as well as the grave of his grandson Thomas Nelson, Jr., a signer of the Declaration of Independence. 99–10 (6/2/70).

KISKIACK, *Yorktown Naval Weapons Station, Yorktown vicinity.* Named for a local Indian tribe, Kiskiack is an important example of Virginia's early vernacular architecture, one of the state's oldest illustrations of the regularity that was to become a hallmark of 18th-century colonial design. Although claims have been made for a 17th-century construction date, the house more likely was built in the early decades of the succeeding century as the home of William Lee, who owned the property from 1696 to 1728. Lee was the grandson of the immigrant Henry Lee who patented the land in 1641. Of the original fabric, only the Flemish bond brick walls and the T-shaped interior end chimneys remain. All wood members were destroyed by fire in 1915. Rebuilt within the walls, the house remained in the ownership of the Lees until 1918 when the property was acquired by the U.S. Navy for a high-security military installation, off-limits to the public. The house has been sealed up by the navy for long-term preservation. 99–12 (9/9/69).

PORTO BELLO, *Camp Peary, Williamsburg vicinity.* During his short term as Virginia's last royal governor, Lord Dunmore acquired a plantation called Porto Bello six miles from Williamsburg, between Queens Creek and the York River, where he maintained a country home. Here Dunmore sought refuge in 1775 when the hostility of the patriots forced him to leave the Governor's Palace. It is known through early descriptions that Dunmore maintained at Porto Bello two dwelling houses and some ten outbuildings and farm buildings. None of these remains. The one extant early structure, a much-altered small brick house, was probably built ca. 1800 when the property was owned by the Bright family. The site of Dunmore's complex apparently remains undisturbed and could be of significant archaeological interest. The property was acquired by the federal government at the beginning of World War II and is now maintained as a high-security facility for experimental training. 99–50 (11/9/72).

YORKTOWN HISTORIC DISTRICT, *including the village of Yorktown, the Yorktown Battlefield, and the Moore House.* Yorktown was established by the Virginia Port Act in 1691 and for much of the 18th century reigned as a busy commercial center, its excellent harbor used primarily by ships involved in the tobacco trade. Despite its prosperity, its population has never exceeded 3,000. Yorktown is chiefly remembered as the scene of the final battle of the Revolution and the surrender to George Washington of British forces under Lord Cornwallis. The terms of surrender were drafted on October 18, 1781, at the Moore house, on the edge of the battlefield, and were accepted the following day, bringing an end to America's colonial era. Yorktown declined after the victory, and much of the lower part of the town was destroyed in a fire in 1814. The community was the scene of a minor engagement during the Civil

War, and some of the fortifications remain from that period. In spite of wars and economic failing, some colonial buildings survive, including the two-story Nelson house with its pedimented gables, built between 1725 and 1740 either by Thomas Nelson or his son William. It was later the home of Thomas Nelson, Jr., a signer of the Declaration of Independence. Other early structures include Grace Church of ca. 1697, the early 18th-century Sessions-Shield house, and the Dudley Digges house of ca. 1744. At a street intersection, facing one another, are the tiny early 18th-century Pate house and the two-story brick store built in the first half of the 18th century by Richard Ambler, the customs collector. A focal point of the district is the Yorktown monument, a heroic column designed by Richard Morris Hunt and erected in 1881–84. The battlefield, the Moore house, the Nelson house, and several other properties in the district are owned and exhibited by the National Park Service as part of the Colonial National Historical Park. 99–57 (4/17/73).

YORKTOWN SHIPWRECKS MARITIME ARCHAEOLOGICAL SITE, *York River off Yorktown.* In October 1781 General Earl Cornwallis, his army blocked by the Americans under Washington and the French under Rochambeau, scuttled the majority of the British fleet, as many as twenty-six vessels, off Yorktown to prevent a landing by the French fleet. Cornwallis then attempted on the night of October 16 to transfer his troops across the York in small boats, but a violent squall prevented the evacuation. A British flag of truce was flown the next day; and on October 19, 1781, the articles of capitulation were signed, bringing the Revolutionary War to a close. The wrecks have remained undisturbed for the most part on the bottom of the York. Research conducted by the Virginia Division of Historic Landmarks has located nine ships believed to be part of the fleet, making them the largest fleet of associated shipwrecks yet discovered in the world. One of the ships has been positively identified as the 44-gun HMS *Charon,* Cornwallis's largest vessel. Because of the comparatively good state of preservation and documented date of demise, the wrecks are likely to yield much information on 18th-century British naval ships and their accoutrements. In 1982 a cofferdam was erected under the direction of the Virginia Division of Historic Landmarks around one of the best preserved wrecks, a yet unidentified supply ship. The dam, shown in the aerial photograph, provides filtered water for greater clarity in the salvage of the wreck. 99–58 (2/20/73).

APPENDIXES
ACKNOWLEDGMENTS
PICTURE CREDITS
INDEX

APPENDIX I
Destroyed Landmarks

These Virginia Historic Landmarks have been destroyed and subsequently removed from the Virginia Landmarks Register.

BENTFIELD, *Lawrenceville vicinity, Brunswick County.* This federal plantation house was built in 1810 by the Revolutionary War colonel John ("Hellcat") Jones, for his son, John Jones, Jr. First known as Melrose, and later as Bentfield, the property on the Meherrin River was acquired by the Flournoy family in 1859, who owned it into the middle of the present century. The house, with its finely jointed brickwork and delicately crafted Federal woodwork, was an example of how the Federal style was adapted to a Southside plantation house by skilled local craftsmen. It was undergoing restoration when it was gutted by fire in 1974. Only the end walls remain standing. 12–72 (11/20/73).

BOTETOURT COUNTY COURTHOUSE, *Fincastle, Botetourt County.* The Botetourt County Courthouse was built in 1845–48 by Schuyler W. Smith of Bedford on the site of an earlier building designed by Thomas Jefferson. The newly completed structure, an essay in the locally interpreted Greek Revival idiom, served the county until it was gutted by fire in 1970. The ruins were registered, but plans to rebuild the interior within the original shell were abandoned when the principal walls collapsed during site cleaning. The walls of the flanking wings were then demolished, leaving only the four Doric columns of the building. These columns were incorporated into the present courthouse, which is a copy of its predecessor. 218–25 (4/6/71).

WILLIAM H. BOWERS HOUSE, *254 North Sycamore Street, Petersburg.* The William H. Bowers house was long one of the state's best examples of urban Federal architecture. Marking the corner of a principal intersection, the three-and-a-half-story structure was articulated by ornamental panels, wrought-iron balconies, elaborate dormers, and beautiful brickwork. The house was erected in 1828–29 for William H. Bowers and, like many Federal urban structures, was designed to accommodate a shop on the first floor and well-appointed residential space on the upper floors. A Gothic Revival shop front was added to the facade in 1859 but was replaced after World War II by a less interesting modern one. The house was purchased by the Historic Petersburg Foundation in 1977 for restoration, but a serious structural movement developed, making the building too unsafe to repair. It was demolished in 1977, two months after its registration. 123–52 (7/19/77).

CASERTA, *Eastville vicinity, Northampton County.* An Eastern Shore plantation dwelling, this house had a curious side stair passage which towered well above the brick-ended main body of the structure. More typical of the region's early houses was the long, low wing, which may have incorporated a small 18th-century dwellilng. With the wing, Caserta thus had the "big house, little house, colonnade, and kitchen" arrangement indigenous to the Eastern Shore. The main part of the house was built ca. 1840 for George P. Upshur, a U. S naval commander and brother of Judge Abel Parker Upshur. Upshur named the place Caserta after the town near Naples, Italy, where he spent many pleasant days while on a naval tour. The house burned to the ground after it was struck by lightning in 1975. 65–51 (2/2/69).

CHRIST CHURCH, *West Freemason and Cumberland streets, Norfolk*. Christ Church on Norfolk's West Freemason Street was erected in 1828 to replace a church on the same site destroyed by fire. Although no connection has been found, the design was very similar to Thomas Jefferson's design for Christ Church in Charlottesville. Like Jefferson's church, the Norfolk building had a temple form with a Tuscan portico in antis topped by a belfry. The church was designed by Levi Swain, a local architect, with the assistance of a parishioner, Thomas Williamson, who was an amateur designer. The congregation traced its origins to the Elizabeth River Parish, which first built a church in the vicinity in 1637. Christ Church served the Episcopalians until 1910, after which it housed Norfolk's Greek Orthodox congregation. Between 1955 and 1960 it was one of the numerous "heavens" of black religious leader Sweet Daddy Grace. The building was purchased in 1960 by the Norfolk Redevelopment and Housing Authority, which had it demolished in 1973. 122–4 (4/6/71).

CRAWFORD HOUSE HOTEL, *450–454 Crawford Street, Portsmouth*. The Crawford House Hotel was erected in 1835 by J. W. Collins and was named in honor of William Crawford, founder of Portsmouth. The building was the city's first hotel and for a time was its tallest building. In its heyday it was noted as Portsmouth's "most fashionable place" and boasted such guests as presidents Martin Van Buren, John Tyler, James K. Polk, and Millard Fillmore. Differing from the more homespun 18th-century inns and taverns, this prototype hotel contained a row of shops on the first floor, public rooms on the second, and three upper floors of guest rooms. Despite its survival in essentially unaltered condition, the hotel was demolished in 1970 by the Portsmouth Redevelopment and Housing Authority for an urban renewal project. 124–26 (5/5/70).

DALTON THEATRE BUILDING, *Washington Avenue, Pulaski*. Designed in 1921 by James C. Lombard and Company of Washington, D.C., the Dalton Theatre followed the prototype theater design of Chicago's Auditorium by Louis Sullivan, in which the theater section is fronted by an office building. It was completed in 1922 for the local firm of Dalton and Richardson and was owned by Sexton Dalton from 1923 to 1939. The plain exterior contrasted with the plasterwork decorations of the theater interior, creating a dramatic transition from the outside to the entertainment section. A large portion of the rear section collapsed in 1982, and the rest of the structure was pulled down over a year later. 125–2 (11/15/77).

EXETER, *Leesburg vicinity.* The main house at Exeter in Loudoun County was the nucleus of one of the largest complexes of plantation buildings in the region. The buildings were erected in the 1790s for Dr. Wilson Cary Selden. The house successfully blended several roof types in a seven-part plan. It had a two-level Doric portico, pedimented dormers with intersecting tracery, and richly detailed mantels and other interior trim. This amalgam of Federal-style forms and motifs stood neglected for many years and was finally destroyed by fire in 1980. The surviving outbuildings are in ruinous condition. 53–77 (2/20/73).

MORRISON HOUSE *West Market and Liberty streets, Harrisonburg.* Erected between 1820 and 1824 for Joseph Thornton, this gracefully proportioned dwelling was among the few early houses remaining in downtown Harrisonburg. It stood practically without alteration, preserving all its original trim both inside and out. The glazed-header pattern in the brickwork of its south wall was one of the few examples of this kind of decorative brickwork remaining in the Shenandoah Valley. The relatively late use of glazed headers suggested that the mason was maintaining a tradition brought from Pennsylvania rather than eastern Virginia, where the tradition generally ceased in the mid-18th century. The Morrison family acquired the house in 1868 and owned it for a hundred years. Numerous efforts by public-spirited citizens to have it preserved failed, and the house was demolished in 1982 by the Wetsel Seed Company for a parking lot. 115–6 (11/3/70).

MOSS TOBACCO FACTORY, *Clarksville, Mecklenburg County.* The three-and-a-half-story Moss Tobacco Factory, erected in two stages during the 1850s, housed a complete manufacturing operation until 1862. A decade later, after Clarksville had lost the processing business to Richmond and Petersburg, the building was returned to service as a warehouse for the sale and exchange of tobacco. In time the Southside market became concentrated in Danville, and the building ceased connection with the tobacco industry. This rare survival of an antebellum industrial form was demolished in 1980. 192–13 (5/21/79).

PRESTON HOUSE, *Saltville, Smyth County.* On a knoll with a commanding view of Saltville and the surrounding country-side, the Preston house was a fine specimen of an early national plantation house. The house began ca. 1795 as a side-hall-plan dwelling and was soon expanded into a five-bay structure with finely detailed interior woodwork. It was the home of Francis Preston, who represented the area in Congress, controlled the salt-producing lands in the vicinity, and operated the salt-works. The Preston family retained ownership of the house and saltworks until 1862. The house received numerous additions after the Preston tenure, but the early fabric remained intact. The house was partially dismantled in 1976 and was completely demolished by 1978 to clear the site for a new dwelling. 86–6 (4/10/76).

ROSELAND MANOR, *Strawberry Banks, Hampton.* On landscaped grounds along the shore of Hampton Roads, Rose-land Manor was a salient example of a Queen Anne mansion. The house was built in 1886–87 for Harrison Phoebus, owner of the Hygeria Hotel at Old Point Comfort. Because of his many civic contributions, the adjacent community of Chesa-peake City was renamed Phoebus in his honor. The architect of the mansion was Arthur Crooks, a native of England who worked as a draftsman for Richard Upjohn and later set up his own practice, specializing in residential and ecclesiastical works. The house was originally ornamented with elaborate verandas and other exterior trimmings, most of which had been removed. The house was an architectural rarity for Vir-ginia since few houses of such scale and ostentation were built in the state in that period. It was completely destroyed by fire in 1985. 114–3 (7/18/78).

APPENDIX II
RECENTLY
REGISTERED
LANDMARKS

The following places have been added to the Virginia Landmarks Register after January 1984 when final preparation of this volume began.

Accokeek Furnace Archaeological Site, Stafford County. 89–66 (3/20/84)

Allied Arts Building, City of Lynchburg. 118–110 (4/16/85)

Balls Bluff, Loudoun County. 53–307 (10/16/84); *National Historic Landmark.*

Beaver Creek Plantation, Henry County. 44–1 (4/16/85).

Bedford Historic District, City of Bedford, 141–73 (8/21/84).

Bridgewater Historic District, Rockingham County. 176–3 (6/19/84).

Buckingham Female Collegiate Institute Historic District, Buckingham County. 14–127 (3/20/84).

Carter Family Thematic Nomination, Scott County. 84–20 (4/16/85).
    A. P. Carter Homeplace. 84–7
    A. P. and Sara Carter House. 84–14.
    Maybelle and Ezra Carter House. 84–15.
    Mount Vernon Methodist Church. 84–13.
    A. P. Carter Store. 84–6.

The Chamberlin Hotel, City of Hampton. 114–114 (10/16/84).

Christiansburg Depot, Montgomery County. 60–62 (4/16/85).

The Reuben Clark House, City of Hampton. 114–50 (5/15/84).

Clinch Valley Roller Mills, Tazewell County. 92–17 (8/21/84).

Crossroads Tavern, Albemarle County. 02–199 (5/15/84).

Elmwood, Culpeper County. 23–44 (6/18/85).

Faulkner House, Albemarle County. 02–146 (3/20/84).

Fishburne Military School, City of Waynesboro. 136–4 (8/21/84).

Fort Boykin Archaeological Site, Isle of Wight County. 46–95 (6/18/85).

Franklin Historic District, City of Franklin. 145–6 (4/16/85).

Maj. David Graham House, Wythe County. 98–8 (12/11/84).

Hampstead Farm Archaeological District, Orange County. 68–182 (5/15/84).

Home for Needy Confederate Women, City of Richmond. 127–380 (4/16/85).

Hotel Danville, City of Danville. 108–27 (10/16/84).

Dayton Historic District, Rockingham County. 206–2 (6/19/84).

Hotel Warwick, City of Newport News. 121–40 (8/21/84).

Intervale, Augusta County. 07–18 (12/11/84).

James River and Kanawha Canal Sites in Lynchburg, Virginia Thematic Nomination, City of Lynchburg. 118–209 (12/11/84).
  Upper Portion of Lower Basin and Ninth Street Bridge. 118–488.
  Blackwater Aqueduct. 118–206.
  Waterworks Dam, James River Dam and Guard Locks. 118–207.

Jerdone Castle, Louisa County. 54–45 (8/21/84).

Leesylvania Archaeological Site, Prince William County. 76–45 (6/19/84).

Madden's Tavern, Culpeper County. 23–29 (5/15/84).

Madison County Courthouse Historic District, Madison County. 256–4 (5/15/84).

Morea, City of Charlottesville. 104–44 (3/20/84).

Mount Hope, City of Falls Church. 110–15 (8/21/84).

Otter Creek Archaeological Site, Franklin County. 33–288 (4/16/85).

Park View Historic District, City of Portsmouth. 124–55 (8/21/84).

Piney Grove, Charles City County. 18–63 (6/18/85).

Public Schools of Augusta County, Virginia, 1870–1940 Thematic Nomination, Augusta County. 07–1175 (12/11/84).
  Glebe Schoolhouse. 07–706.
  Walker's Creek Schoolhouse. 07–539.
  Moffett's Creek Schoolhouse. 07–547.
  West View Schoolhouse. 07–426.
  Mount Meridian Schoolhouse. 07–1152.
  Estaline Schoolhouse. 07–524.
  Mount Zion Schoolhouse. 07–1165.
  Verona School. 07–1144.
  Mount Sidney School. 07–1155.
  Middlebrook Grade School. 07–686.
  Middlebrook High School. 07–686.
  Weyers Cave School. 07–1156.
  Craigsville School. 07–1146.
  New Hope High School. 07–1087.
  Crimora School. 07–964.
  North River High School. 07–1153.
  Deerfield School. 07–1154.
  Augusta County Training School. 07–755.

Randolph School, City of Richmond. 127–388 (8/21/84).

Reedville Historic District, Northumberland County. 66–83 (6/19/84).

Richmond Academy of Medicine, City of Richmond. 127–378 (5/15/84).

St. Paul's Episcopal Church, City of Alexandria. 100–104 (4/16/85).

Sayler's Creek Battlefield, Amelia and Prince Edward counties. 04–19 (10/16/84);
National Historic Landmark.

Southwest Historic District, City of Roanoke. 128–49 (4/16/85).

Stonewall Jackson School, City of Richmond, 127–376 (3/20/84).

Strasburg Historic District, Shenandoah County. 306–16 (5/15/84).

Stuart Addition Historic District, City of Staunton. 132–36 (3/20/84).

Victoria Boulevard Historic District, City of Hampton. 114–112 (8/21/84).

Virginia Intermont College, City of Bristol. 102–14 (8/21/84).

Virginia War Memorial Carillon, City of Richmond, 127–387 (8/21/84).

Walkerton, Henrico County. 43–19 (10/16/84).

Wertland Street Historic District, City of Charlottesville. 104–136 (12/11/84).

White Hall, Gloucester County. 36–51 (5/15/84).

Williamsville, Hanover County. 42–27 (4/16/85).

YWCA, City of Richmond. 127–300 (3/20/84).

APPENDIX III

NATIONAL HISTORIC LANDMARKS IN VIRGINIA

Alexandria Historic District, Alexandria
Bacon's Castle, Surry County
Balls Bluff, Loudoun County
Benjamin Banneker SW-9 Intermediate Boundary Stone, Arlington County
Barracks, Virginia Military Institute, Lexington
Belle Grove, Frederick County
Belmont, Stafford County
Berkeley, Charles City County
Berry Hill, Halifax County
Boxwood, Fauquier County
Brandon, Prince George County
Bremo Historic District, Fluvanna County
Bruton Parish Church, Williamsburg
Camden, Caroline County
Cape Henry Lighthouse, Virginia Beach
Carter's Grove, James City County
Christ Church, Alexandria
Christ Church, Lancaster County
Charles R. Drew House, Arlington County
Drydock Number One, Portsmouth
Egyptian Building, Richmond
Elsing Green, King William County
Exchange Building, Petersburg
Five Forks Battlefield, Dinwiddie County
Fort Monroe, Hampton
Fort Myer Historic District, Arlington County
Franklin and Armfield Office, Alexandria
Gadsby's Tavern, Alexandria

Ellen Glasgow House, Richmond
Carter Glass House, Lynchburg
Green Springs Historic District, Louisa County
Greenway Court, Clarke County
Gunston Hall, Fairfax County
Hampton Institute, Hampton
Hanover County Courthouse, Hanover County
Holly Knoll, Gloucester County
Jackson Ward Historic District, Richmond
Stonewall Jackson's Headquarters, Winchester
Kenmore, Fredericksburg
Lee Chapel, Lexington
McCormick Farm and Workshop, Rockbridge County
Main Street Station, Richmond
Marlbourne, Hanover County
John Marshall House, Richmond
Menokin, Richmond County
James Monroe Law Office, Fredericksburg
James Monroe Tomb, Richmond
Monticello, Albemarle County
Montpelier, Orange County
Monumental Church, Richmond
Mount Airy, Richmond County
Mount Vernon, Fairfax County
Oak Hill, Loudoun County
Oatlands, Loudoun County
Old City Hall, Richmond
Patowmack Canal at Great Falls Historic District, Fairfax County
Poplar Forest, Bedford County
Quarters 1, Fort Meyer Historic District, Arlington County
Peyton Randolph House, Williamsburg
Virginia Randolph Cottage, Henrico County
Reynolds Homestead, Patrick County
Ripshin, Grayson County
Rising Sun Tavern, Fredericksburg
The Rotunda, Charlottesville
Sabine Hall, Richmond County
St. John's Church, Richmond
St. Luke's Church, Isle of Wight County
Saratoga, Clarke County
Sayler's Creek Battlefield, Amelia and Prince Edward counties
Scotchtown, Hanover County
James Semple House, Williamsburg
Sherwood Forest, Charles City County
Shirley, Charles City County
Spence's Point, Westmoreland County
Stratford, Westmoreland County
Adam Thoroughgood House, Virginia Beach
Thunderbird Archaeological District (Flint Run Archaeological District), Warren
    County
Tredegar Iron Works, Richmond
Tuckahoe, Goochland County
University of Virginia Historic District, Charlottesville
Virginia Military Institute Historic District, Lexington

Virginia State Capitol, Richmond
Maggie L. Walker House (Maggie L. Walker National Historic Site), Richmond
Washington and Lee University Historic District, Lexington
Waterford Historic District, Loudoun County
Westover, Charles City County
White House of the Confederacy, Richmond
Wickham-Valentine House, Richmond
Williamsburg Historic District, Williamsburg
Woodrow Wilson Birthplace, Staunton
Wren Building, Williamsburg
Wythe House, Williamsburg
Yeocomico Church, Westmoreland County

APPENDIX IV

VIRGINIA HISTORIC LANDMARKS ADMINISTERED BY THE NATIONAL PARK SERVICE

National Park Service properties have National Historic Landmark status.

Appomattox Court House National Historical Park, Appomattox County

Arlington House, the Robert E. Lee Memorial, Arlington County

City Point Unit, (Appomattox Manor), Petersburg National Battlefield, Hopewell

Colonial National Historical Park (includes Jamestown Island and Yorktown Historic District), James City and York counties

Cumberland Gap National Historical Park, Lee County, Virginia, and Kentucky and Tennessee

Fredericksburg and Spotsylvania County Battlefields Memorial National Military Park, City of Fredericksburg and Spotsylvania and Stafford counties

Jamestown National Historic Site, James City County

Manassas National Battlefield Park, Prince William County

Mount Vernon Memorial Highway, Fairfax and Arlington counties and City of Alexandria

Patowmack Canal at Great Falls Historic District, Fairfax County

Petersburg National Battlefield, City of Petersburg, City of Hopewell, and Dinwiddie and Prince George counties

Richmond National Battlefield Park, City of Richmond and Henrico County

Maggie L. Walker National Historic Site, Richmond

Booker T. Washington National Monument, Franklin County

George Washington Birthplace National Monument (Wakefield), Westmoreland County

APPENDIX V
ARCHITECTS ASSOCIATED WITH VIRGINIA HISTORIC LANDMARKS

David Adler
  Waverley, Fauquier County
D. Wiley Anderson
  Miller School, Albemarle County
  Ednam, Albemarle County
John Ariss
  Lamb's Creek Church, King George County
  Little Fork Church, Culpeper County
Averill & Hall
  Blues Armory, Richmond
J. Stewart Barney
  Handley Library, Winchester
Baskervill & Lambert
  Union Theological Seminary, Richmond
Fred A. Bishop
  Byrd Theatre, Richmond
  Washington Street Methodist Church, Petersburg
Alfred C. Bossom
  First National Bank Building, Richmond
  Virginia Mutual Building, Richmond
William Lawrence Bottomley
  Monument Avenue Historic District, Richmond
  Rocklands, Orange County
  Waverley Hill, Staunton

Victor Bourgois
  Belgian Building, Richmond
Charles K. Bryant
  Union Theological Seminary, Richmond
William Buckland
  Gunston Hall, Fairfax County
  Mount Airy, Richmond County
Robert C. Burkholder
  Court Street Baptist Church, Lynchburg
  Daniel's Hill Historic District, Lynchburg
J. C. Cady
  Hampton Institute, Hampton
Carneal & Johnston
  Ellerslie, Colonial Heights
Carrère & Hastings
  Commonwealth Club Historic District, Richmond
  Hotel Jefferson, Richmond
  200 Block West Franklin Street Historic District, Richmond
Charles E. Cassell
  Protestant Episcopal Theological Seminary in Virginia, Alexandria
W. Chamberlin & Co.
  Pulaski County Courthouse, Pulaski County

Henry Otis Chapman
Handley Library, Winchester
T. Buckler Chequire
Richmond County Courthouse,
Richmond County
St. Stephen's Episcopal Church,
Northumberland County
Adolph Cluss
Alexandria City Hall, Alexandria
John Hartwell Cocke
Bremo Historic District, Fluvanna
County
Fluvanna County Courthouse Historic
District, Fluvanna County
Samuel Collins
Steephill, Staunton
T. J. Collins
Augusta County Courthouse, Staunton
Augusta Military Academy, Augusta
County
Breezy Hill, Staunton
Hilltop, Staunton
Arista Hoge House, Staunton
Kable House, Staunton
Lexington Historic District, Lexington
C. W. Miller House, Staunton
National Valley Bank, Staunton
Rockingham County Courthouse,
Harrisonburg
John H. Coxhead
Virginia Union University, Richmond
Preston Craighill
Elk Hill, Bedford County
Arthur Crooks
Roseland Manor, Hampton (*see* App. I)
Robert Lewis Dabney
Briery Church, Prince Edward County
Hampden-Sydney College Historic
District, Prince Edward County
Tinkling Spring Presbyterian Church,
Augusta County
J. B. Danforth
Waddell Memorial Presbyterian
Church, Orange County
Alexander Jackson Davis
Belmead, Powhatan County
Bremo Historic District, Fluvanna
County
Hawkwood, Louisa County
Powhatan Court House Historic
District, Powhatan County
Virginia Military Institute, Lexington
Frank Miles Day
Harvey House, Radford
St. Paul's Episcopal Church, Lynchburg

William Adams Delano
Mirador, Albemarle County
M. J. Dimmock
Brunswick County Court Square,
Brunswick County
Confederate Memorial Chapel,
Richmond
200 Block West Franklin Street Historic
District, Richmond
Hollywood Cemetery, Richmond
Henry C. Dudley
Carlheim, Loudoun County
John Eberson
Central Fidelity Bank, Richmond
Loew's Theatre, Richmond
William S. Ellison
Old Lynchburg Courthouse,
Lynchburg
A. H. Ellwood
St. Andrew's Episcopal Church
Complex, Richmond
Elzner & Anderson
The Homestead Hotel, Bath County
S. W. Foulke
Southern Seminary, Buena Vista
Philip H. Frohman
St. Stephen's Episcopal Church,
Richmond
Edward G. Frye
Boxley Building, Roanoke
Garland Hill Historic District,
Lynchburg
Frye & Chesterman
Academy of Music, Lynchburg
The Aviary, Lynchburg
Hollins College Quadrangle, Roanoke
County
Jones Memorial Library, Lynchburg
Frye & Stone
Colonial National Bank, Roanoke
Washington Gill
Almshouse, Richmond
William P. Ginther
St. Andrew's Roman Catholic Church,
Roanoke
Bertram Grosvenor Goodhue
Virginia Military Institute, Lexington
Jackson T. Gott
Masonic Temple, Richmond
George Hadfield
Arlington House, Arlington County
Haskins & Alexander
Orange County Courthouse, Orange
County

John Haviland
  Portsmouth Naval Hospital,
    Portsmouth
Vance Hebard
  Lafayette Grammar and High School,
    Norfolk
E. C. Horne & Sons
  Wells Theatre, Norfolk
H. H. Huggins
  Fire Station No. 1, Roanoke
  Hollins College Quadrangle, Roanoke
    County
  Mountain View, Roanoke
Reuben H. Hunt
  First Baptist Church, Norfolk
Richard Morris Hunt
  Hampton Institute, Hampton
  Yorktown Victory Monument,
    Yorktown Historic District, York
    County.
Thomas Jefferson
  Ampthill, Cumberland County
  Barboursville, Orange County
  Belle Grove, Frederick County
  Charlotte County Courthouse,
    Charlotte County
  Edgemont, Albemarle County
  Farmington, Albemarle County
  Monticello, Albemarle County
  Poplar Forest, Bedford County
  The Residence, Madison County
  The Rotunda, Charlottesville
  University of Virginia Historic District,
    Charlottesville
  Virginia State Capitol, Richmond
Francis Y. Joannes
  Hilton Village Historic District,
    Newport News
  Riverside Apartments, Newport News
J. W. Johns
  Trinity Episcopal Church, Staunton
George H. Johnson
  Donnan-Asher Iron-Front Building,
    Richmond
  Stearns Block, Richmond
Harvey N. Johnson
  Attucks Theatre, Norfolk
John E. Johnson
  Berry Hill, Halifax County
  Staunton Hill, Charlotte County
  Tarover, Halifax County
H. P. Kelsey
  Truxtun Historic District, Portsmouth
Sidney Fiske Kimball
  Shack Mountain, Albemarle County

Frances Koenig
  Colonial Village, Arlington County
Minard Lafever
  Second Presbyterian Church,
    Richmond
Benjamin H. Latrobe
  Long Branch, Clarke County
W. Duncan Lee
  Carter's Grove, James City County
  Monument Avenue Historic District,
    Richmond
John Minor Botts Lewis
  Avoca, Campbell County
  Garland Hill Historic District,
    Lynchburg
Lind & Murdock
  Morven Park, Loudoun County
H. T. Lindeberg
  Carter Hall, Clarke County
James C. Lombard & Co.
  Dalton Theatre, Pulaski County (*see*
    App. I)
Robert Cary Long, Jr.
  Virginia School for the Deaf and the
    Blind, Staunton
  Old Western State Hospital, Staunton
Albert Lybrock
  James Monroe Tomb, Richmond
  Miller School, Albemarle County
  Morson's Row, Richmond
  U. S. Post Office and Customs House,
    Richmond
Daniel Lynch
  Greensville County Courthouse,
    Emporia
Leland McBroom
  Stoneleigh, Henry County
William C. McDowell
  Mulberry Hill, Lexington
Joseph H. McGuire
  Cathedral of the Sacred Heart,
    Richmond
William H. Mesereau
  Westover, Charles City County
Frank P. Milburn
  Buchanan County Courthouse,
    Buchanan County
  Old Grayson County Courthouse,
    Grayson County
  Wise County Courthouse, Wise
    County
H. M. Miller
  Dickenson County Courthouse,
    Dickenson County

Robert Mills
  Howard's Neck, Goochland County
  Monumental Church, Richmond
  White House of the Confederacy,
    Richmond
Benjamin F. Mitchell
  U. S. Post Office and Court House,
    Norfolk
R. E. Mitchell
  Truxtun Historic District, Portsmouth
Homer G. Morse
  Agecroft, Richmond
Jeremiah Morton
  Greenville, Culpeper County
Elijah E. Myers
  Old City Hall, Richmond
Neff & Thompson
  Monticello Arcade, Norfolk
J. Crawford Neilson
  Lee Chapel, Lexington
Niernsee & Neilson
  Martin's Brandon Church, Prince
    George County
Noland & Baskervill
  Kent-Valentine House, Richmond
  Monroe Park Historic District,
    Richmond
  Monument Avenue Historic District,
    Richmond
  St. Andrew's Episcopal Church
    Complex, Richmond
  Swannanoa, Nelson County
  West Franklin Street Historic District,
    Richmond
Edward Overman
  Pythian Castle, Portsmouth
Alexander Parris
  Executive Mansion, Richmond
  Wickham-Valentine House, Richmond
J. Kevan Peebles
  First National Bank Building, Roanoke
  Hotel Jefferson, Richmond
William M. Poindexter
  Fairfax Hall, Waynesboro
  Randolph-Macon Woman's College
    Main Hall, Lynchburg
  Stevens Cottage, Page County
  West Franklin Street Historic District,
    Richmond
Calvin Pollard
  Petersburg Courthouse, Petersburg
John Russell Pope
  Branch House, Richmond
  Broad Street Station, Richmond

George B. Post & Sons
  Cradock Historic District, Portsmouth
B. F. Price
  Randolph-Macon College Complex,
    Hanover County
Charles H. Read, Jr.
  Planters National Bank, Richmond
  Union Theological Seminary,
    Richmond
Samuel McDowell Reid
  Lexington Historic District, Lexington
James Renwick
  Fredericksburg Historic District,
    Fredericksburg
Edgerton S. Rogers
  Maymont, Richmond
Isaiah Rogers
  Kent-Valentine House, Richmond
Bascom J. Rowlett
  English Village, Richmond
Ruben Sherriff
  Greensville County Courthouse,
    Emporia
B. Stanley Simmons
  Hume School, Arlington County
William B. Singleton
  General Douglas MacArthur Memorial,
    Norfolk
  Old Portsmouth Courthouse,
    Portsmouth
Samuel Sloan
  Leigh Street Baptist Church,
    Richmond
Wiliam Small
  Old Western State Hospital, Staunton
Alexander Spotswood
  Bruton Parish Church, Williamsburg
James Spratling
  Ripshin, Grayson County
Norris G. Starkweather
  Camden, Caroline County
  Mayhurst, Orange County
  Protestant Episcopal Theological
    Seminary in Virginia, Alexandria
Thomas S. Stewart
  Egyptian Building, Richmond
  St. Paul's Episcopal Church, Richmond
Frank Stone
  Boxley Building, Roanoke
William Strickland
  Grace Episcopal Church, Cismont,
    Albemarle County
Leo Stynen
  Belgian Building, Richmond

Richard Taliaferro
 Powhatan, James City County
 Wythe House, Williamsburg
Edwin M. Taylor
 Trinty Episcopal Church, Staunton
James Knox Taylor
 U. S. Post Office and Courthouse, Wise
 County
Robert E. L. Taylor
 Bremo Historic District, Fluvanna
 County
Taylor & Hepburn
 Auslew Gallery, Norfolk
John R. Thomas
 Brooks Hall, Charlottesville
 First Baptist Church, Lynchburg
Henri van de Velde
 Belgian Building, Richmond
Thomas U. Walter
 Freemason Street Baptist Church,
 Norfolk
 General Douglas MacArthur Memorial,
 Norfolk
 Lexington Presbyterian Church,
 Lexington
 Old First Baptist Church, Richmond
 Old Norfolk Academy Building,
 Norfolk
 Tabb Street Presbyterian Church,
 Petersburg
Warren & Wetmore
 The Homestead Hotel, Bath County
Harvey Warwick
 Colonial Village, Arlington County
Frank E. Watson
 St. Stephen's Episcopal Church,
 Richmond
Watson & Huckle
 Christ & St. Luke's Episcopal Church,
 Norfolk
Albert L. West
 Centenary Church, Richmond
 Woodside, Henrico County

William W. West
 Randolph-Macon College Complex,
 Hanover County
John White
 St. Luke Building, Richmond
Stanford White
 The Rotunda, Charlottesville
 University of Virginia Historic
 District, Charlottesville
Thomas Hoomes Williamson
 Lee Chapel, Lexington
John Wills
 Carter Glass House, Lynchburg
Wilson, Harris, & Richards
 Main Street Station, Richmond
Winslow & Wetherall
 The Oaks, Staunton
Waddy Wood
 Emmanuel Episcopal Church,
 Albemarle County
James Wren
 Christ Church, Alexandria
 Fairfax County Courthouse, Fairfax
 Falls Church, Falls Church
 Pohick Church, Fairfax County
Frank Lloyd Wright
 Pope-Leighey House, Fairfax County
Marcellus Wright, Sr.
 Monroe Park Historic District,
 Richmond
Wyatt & Nolting
 Auslew Gallery, Norfolk
 Old Norfolk City Hall, Norfolk
Yarnell & Goforth
 The Homestead Hotel, Bath County
Ammi B. Young
 Petersburg City Hall, Petersburg
 U. S. Customs House, Norfolk
 U. S. Post Office and Customs House,
 Richmond
Robert Young
 Ellerslie, Colonial Heights

ACKNOWLEDGMENTS

The Virginia Landmarks Register involves the participation of many people including property owners, public officials, Board members, and, especially, a dedicated staff. The Division of Historic Landmarks has truly benefited from many knowledgeable and capable employees. This volume does not adequately convey the amount of time the staff has spent in site visitation, research, and report preparation. The following list includes those members of the staff, past and present, who have played particularly active roles in the register program. This work is largely the result of their labor and expertise.

Susan Alexander
Martha McCartney Aschman
Steven M. Bedford
Florence Bland
William P. Boyer, Jr.
John Broadwater
Robert A. Carter
Edward A. Chappell
Richard C. Cote
David Edwards
Keith Egloff
Thea Ellesin
Jack L. Finglass
Eleanor Lane Fishburne
Junius R. Fishburne, Jr.
Herbert Fisher
Elizabeth Hagg
Douglas Harnsberger
Rebecca Harrison
David Hazzard
Marlene Heck
the late Grace Pierce Heffelfinger
Edward F. Heite
Julia T. Henley
Bernard Herman
Tucker Hill
Mary Ellen N. Hodges
Corrine Hudgins
Frances Jones
William M. Kelso
Mary S. Kilduff
Karen Kummer

Anne Carter Lee
John G. Lewis
Nicholas Luccketti
Ann McCleary
Leslie McFadden
Cynthia MacLeod
Verna M. McNamara
Carolyn Maness
Ann C. Miller
H. Bryan Mitchell
James W. Moody, Jr.
Elizabeth Cheek Morgan
Leslie Naranjo
Jeffrey M. O'Dell
Alain C. Outlaw
Merry A. Outlaw
Valerie Payne
Margaret T. Peters
Mary Warren Pinnell
H. Peter Pudner
Katherine T. Read
Vicenta Scarlett
Beverly Straube
Ruth Selden Sturgill
E. Randolph Turner
Dell T. Upton
Margaret P. Welsh
Gary Williams
J. Mark Wittkofski
Joseph F. Yates
Barry N. Zarakov

The editor wishes to extend special thanks to the following members of the staff who edited portions of the manuscript or provided other valuable assistance in the preparation of this work.

Martha McCartney Aschman
Lynn Bechdolt
Steven M. Bedford
John Broadwater
Robert A. Carter
Cathy Chatman
Richard C. Cote
David Edwards
Mary Ellen N. Hodges
Lisa Lahendro
Bruce Larson

Nicholas Luccketti
Ann McCleary
C. Vernon March III
Ann C. Miller
H. Bryan Mitchell
Jeffrey M. O'Dell
Margaret T. Peters
Dianne Pierce
Beverly Straube
E. Randolph Turner

The editor further wishes to extend special thanks to the following individuals who kindly read and edited pertinent portions of the manuscript and made helpful suggestions.

William L. Beiswanger, Thomas Jefferson Memorial Foundation
Richard C. Bierce, National Trust for Historic Preservation
Ben Brown, Gunston Hall
Nellie White Bundy, Historic Crab Orchard Museum
Martha Caldwell, James Madison University
Mary Calos, Historic Hopewell Foundation
Constance Chamberlin, Waterford Foundation
S. Allen Chambers, Historic American Buildings Survey
Edward A. Chappell, Colonial Williamsburg Foundation
Mary Tyler Cheek, Robert E. Lee Memorial Association
Elizabeth David, Fairfax County Office of Comprehensive Planning
Jean Federico, Historic Alexandria
William Gardner, Thunderbird Research Corporation
Jodie Gebhardt, Arlington County Department of Community Affairs, Planning Division
Michael Gold, Historic Richmond Foundation
Peter Hodson, Portsmouth Polytechnic, Portsmouth, England
Roy E. Johnson, Ethyl Corporation
Susan Ford Johnson, Historic Fredericksburg Foundation

Jon K. Kukla, Virginia State Library
Elizabeth McCue, Historic Staunton Foundation
R. Peter Mooz, Wilton House Museum
Angus Murdoch, Association for the Preservation of Virginia Antiquities
James Patton, Gay Mont
Constance Rameriz, Arlington County Historical Affairs and Landmark Review Board
Helen Scott Townsend Reed, Manakin-Sabot
John Rhodehamel, Mount Vernon Ladies' Association
Pamela Simpson, Washington and Lee University
the late Ransom True, Association of the Preservation of Virginia Antiquities
Dell T. Upton, University of California at Berkeley
Tyson Van Auken, the Virginia Outdoors Foundation
Catherine Von Briechinridge, Association for the Preservation of Virginia Antiquities
William L. Whitwell, Hollins College
Lee Winborne, Roanoke
David Wright, Lower Bremo
John G. Zehmer, Valentine Museum

The editor expresses particular gratitude to Stephen McMaster for donating his time to read aloud the galley proof. Lastly the editor extends special thanks to John Melville Jennings, director emeritus of the Virginia Historical Society and a founding member of the Virginia Historic Landmarks Board, whose broad knowledge and love of Virginia history and architecture have been an inspiration.

THE VIRGINIA LANDMARKS REGISTER is funded by a grant from the National Park Service, U. S. Department of the Interior. Under Title VI of the Civil Rights Act of 1964 and Section 504 of the Rehabilitation Act of 1973, the U. S. Department of the Interior prohibits discrimination on the basis of race, color, national origin, or handicap in its federally assisted programs. If you believe you have been discriminated against in any program activity, or facility described above, or if you desire further information, please write to the Office for Equal Opportunity, U. S. Department of the Interior, Washington, DC 20240. The contents and opinions of this publication do not necessarily reflect the views or policies of the Department of the Interior, nor does the mention of trade names or commercial products constitute endorsement or recommendation by the Department of the Interior.

PICTURE CREDITS

Unless noted in the following credits, all pictures in this volume are from the archives of the Division of Historic Landmarks, 221 Governor Street, Richmond.

INDEX

Asterisks indicate Virginia Historic Landmarks.